Employability via High
Sustainability as Schola

M000285635

Alice Diver
Editor

Employability via Higher Education: Sustainability as Scholarship

 Springer

Editor
Alice Diver ⓘ
School of Law
Liverpool John Moores University
Liverpool, UK

ISBN 978-3-030-26344-7   ISBN 978-3-030-26342-3   (eBook)
https://doi.org/10.1007/978-3-030-26342-3

This Springer imprint is published by the registered company Springer Nature Switzerland AG
The registered company address is: Gewerbestrasse 11, 6330 Cham, Switzerland

Foreword

I say that a cultivated intellect, because it is a good in itself, brings with it a power and a grace to every work and occupation which it undertakes, and enables us to be more useful, and to a greater number. There is a duty we owe to human society as such, to the state to which we belong, to the sphere in which we move, to the individuals towards whom we are variously related, and whom we successively encounter in life; and that philosophical or liberal education, as I have called it, which is the proper function of a University, if it refuses the foremost place to professional interests, does but postpone them to the formation of the citizen, and, while it subserves the larger interests of philanthropy, prepares also for the successful prosecution of those merely personal objects, which at first sight it seems to disparage.

Thus, John Henry Newman in *The Idea of a University*—a text which, for all its canonical status, might, when read in the context of twenty-first-century academia, appear rather old-fashioned in its defence of a generalist model of liberal education, 'aim[ed] at raising the intellectual tone of society, at cultivating the public mind, at purifying the national taste, at supplying true principles to popular enthusiasm and fixed aims to popular aspiration, at giving enlargement and sobriety to the ideas of the age, at facilitating the exercise of political power, and refining the intercourse of private life'. Some of us might indeed feel a sense of nostalgia for the kind of Newman-inspired academia, in which defiant Philosophy lecturers were prepared, when asked during a course validation exercise to state the aims and objectives of their course, to respond that they wanted to make their students better people. Noble as that ambition was, it would have been, however, rather difficult to translate into the language of key performance indicators as well as student satisfaction, retention, and employability statistics.

And yet, as the essays collected in *Employable Scholars: In Times of Austerity* demonstrate, there is perhaps rather more to the modern university and its profound concern with student employability than first meets the eye. The old distinction between vocational and non-vocational courses does, of course, continue to impact on our perception of the subjects we teach, not least in that it plays a decisive role in determining performance benchmarks for different specialist areas—but it is not as absolute as it used to be: these days, employability is as much of a factor in History and Classics as it is, albeit in a different way, in Computing or Nursing. Most importantly, it is not about training for a particular profession—it is about developing a mindset, about helping students to grow as flexible and independent individuals who would be able to embrace the challenges of a world in which the concepts of a single career and stable employment are increasingly seen as belonging in the past, and in which what counts is not so much the content of what they have studied—which in some areas is likely to become out of date almost by the time they leave university—but the skills they have acquired and their ability to continue to learn and develop as they move between different environments, different occupations, indeed different countries. In other words, it is what graduates are, rather than what they know and/or what they have trained as, that we need to focus on—and the diverse insights this volume offers, whether contextualising the issue, or outlining a range of innovative strategies to address it, or indeed analysing a selection of subject-specific approaches, share exactly that very objective. And that objective is not miles away from what Newman postulated …

Jan Jedrzejewski
Professor of English and Comparative Literature
School of Arts and Humanities, Ulster University
Northern Ireland, UK

Contents

Editor and Contributors

About the Editor

Alice Diver (Ph.D.) is Senior Lecturer in Law at Liverpool John Moores University, Liverpool, UK, having previously worked at Edge Hill University and Ulster University in Northern Ireland. She spent several years as a solicitor in private practice before joining academia in 1993. Her teaching experience includes property law, child and family law, and human rights law. Her research interests focus mainly on adoption, law in literature, and human rights. She is the author of a monograph on closed birth records in law and policy called '*A Law of Blood-ties: The "right" to access genetic ancestry*' (Springer, 2013) and co-editor of an essay collection entitled '*Justiciability of Human Rights Law in Domestic Jurisdictions*' (Springer, 2015). She has published in a wide variety of peer-reviewed academic journals. She is a long-serving board member of Apex Housing NI and a trustee of Kinship Care NI.

Contributors

Steven Altham Liverpool John Moores University, Liverpool, England, UK

Alana Barton Edge Hill University, Ormskirk, England, UK

Tina Bass Coventry, Coventry, England, UK

Kelli Bippert Texas A&M University-Corpus Christi, Corpus Christi, TX, USA

John Bostock Edge Hill, Ormskirk, England, UK

Stephanie Bridges University of Nottingham, Nottingham, England, UK

David M. Brown Northumbria, Newcastle, England, UK

Martha Caddell Heriot-Watt University, Edinburgh, Scotland, UK

Ian Charity Northumbria, Newcastle, England, UK

Andrew James Clements University of Bedfordshire, Bedfordshire, UK

Tania Crotti University of Adelaide, Adelaide, Australia

Dalton Tria Cusciano Fundacao Getulio Vargas, Sao Paolo, Brazil

Lorraine Dacre Pool University of Central Lancashire, Preston, UK

Robyn Davidson University of Adelaide, Adelaide, Australia

Howard Davis Edge Hill University, Ormskirk, England, UK

Janine Delahunty University of Wollongong, Wollongong, Australia

Lisa Dibben Southampton Solent, Southampton, England, UK

Doris Dippold University of Surrey, Guildford, England, UK

Alice Diver Liverpool John Moores University, Liverpool, England, UK

Gerard Diver Liverpool John Moores University, Liverpool, England, UK

Sue Eccles Bournemouth University, Bournemouth, England, UK

Susie Elliott Coventry University, Coventry, England, UK

Hilary Engward Anglia Ruskin University, Cambridge, UK

Ceryn Evans Swansea University, Swansea, Wales, UK

Clare Forder University of Brighton, Brighton, UK

Gillian Forster Northumbria, Newcastle, England, UK

Julie Fowlie University of Brighton, Brighton, UK

Stuart Fox Cardiff University, Cardiff, Wales, UK

Sally Goldspink Anglia Ruskin University, Cambridge, UK

Peter Gossman University of Worcester, Worcester, UK

Dawne Gurbutt University of Central Lancashire, Preston, UK

Kathryn Harden-Thew University of Wollongong, Wollongong, Australia

Peter Hartley Edge Hill University, Ormskirk, UK

Peter Hayes RMIT, Melbourne, Australia

Inge Hill Coventry, Coventry, England, UK

Kath Houston University of Central Lancashire, Preston, UK

Dawne Irving-Bell Edge Hill University, England, UK

Sandra Jones RMIT, Melbourne, Australia

Sophie Karanicolas University of Adelaide, Adelaide, Australia

Mauro Maia Laruccia Pontifical Catholic University, Sao Paolo, Brazil

Chris Lawton Edge Hill University, Ormskirk, UK

Deborah A. Lock University of Lincoln, Lincoln, England, UK

Harriet Lodge Coventry University, Coventry, England, UK

Rosemarie McIlwhan Open University, Milton Keynes, UK

Emmanuel Mogaji University of Greenwich, London, UK

Luis Fernando Salles Moraes Centro Universitario, FEI, Sao Paolo, Brazil

Dawn A. Morley Southampton Solent, Southampton, England, UK

Emma Mullen Northumbria University, Newcastle, England, UK

Vicki Louise O'Brien University of Central Lancashire, Preston, UK

Sarah O'Shea University of Wollongong, Wollongong, Australia

Braden Phillips University of Adelaide, Adelaide, Australia

Bethanie Pletcher Texas A&M University-Corpus Christi, Corpus Christi, TX, USA

Stephen Powell Manchester Metropolitan University, Manchester, UK

Ester Ragonese Liverpool John Moores University, Liverpool, England, UK

Andrew Robson Northumbria, Newcastle, England, UK

Jacinta Ryan RMIT, Melbourne, Australia

David Scott Open University, Milton Keynes, England, UK

Catherine Snelling University of Adelaide, Adelaide, Australia

Chris Taylor Cardiff University, Cardiff, Wales, UK

Theresa Thomson University of the West of England (UWE), Bristol, UK

Kellie Toole University of Adelaide, Adelaide, Australia

Michelle Turner RMIT, Melbourne, Australia

Corinne Valadez Texas A&M University-Corpus Christi, Corpus Christi, TX, USA

C. J. van Staden University of the Free State, Bloemfontein, South Africa

Francesca Dominique Walker-Martin University of Central Lancashire, Preston, UK

Janice Whatley Manchester Metropolitan University, Manchester, England, UK

Ruth Whitfield University of Bradford, Bradford, UK

Part I
Definitions

Chapter 1
Introduction

Alice Diver

Universities are an integral part of the skills and innovation supply chain to business. However, this supply chain is not a simple linear supplier purchaser transaction; it is not the acquisition of a single product or service. This supply chain is multi-dimensional, it has to be sustainable, and it has to have quality, strength and resilience. (Wilson, 2012: 2)

1.1 Introduction: Employability via Higher Education: A Sustainable Scholarship?

This edited collection is the result of a call for chapters made in early 2017,[1] which sought to collect, collate, and connect research across a wide variety of disciplines and jurisdictions, on the topic of graduate employability in times of austerity.[2] The contributing authors have all worked in Higher Education (HE) as, for example,

---

[1] I am very grateful to all of the authors for their time and efforts in contributing to this book: their deep commitment to their students, to their respective universities, and to the aims of Higher Education, is abundantly clear. Many thanks are also due to Astrid Noordemeer and Yoka Janssen of Springer, for their patience and support throughout the duration of this project. I am very indebted also to Professor Jan Jedrzejewski (English and Comparative Literature) of the School of Arts & Humanities, Ulster University, for his kindness in agreeing to pen the Foreword to this edited collection.

[2] On austerity measures within the UK generally see https://www.gov.uk/government/statistics/english-indices-of-deprivation-2015 (accessed 17.09.18); https://www.tuc.org.uk/sites/default/files/North%20West%20Final%20Report_2.pdf; https://www.theguardian.com/society/2015/jan/01/austerity-cuts-2015-12-billion-britain-protest; and http://www.independent.co.uk/news/uk/home-news/north-of-england-northern-powerhouse-george-osborne-cultural-wasteland-museums-are-hit-by-austerity-a6926321.html (accessed 18.10.18).

A. Diver (✉)
Liverpool John Moores University, Liverpool, England, UK
e-mail: a.r.diver@ljmu.ac.uk

© Springer Nature Switzerland AG 2019
A. Diver (ed.), *Employability via Higher Education: Sustainability as Scholarship*,
https://doi.org/10.1007/978-3-030-26342-3_1

academics, support staff and researchers, and all share a deep concern over the various issues discussed within the text, not least the changing role of the university. The need to promote economic and social development (McDonald & Van der Horst, 2007) whilst advancing knowledge via research and teaching (Brennan, Durazzi, & Sene, 2013) are key policy aspects of HE. The chapters collectively highlight how certain external factors have served to influence HE policy and practice locally and globally in recent years, namely via the following: increasing consumerisation, dwindling resources, occasionally hostile media scrutiny, rising levels of student anxiety, attrition rates, and the overarching need to convince employers of the 'work-readiness' (Allen, Quinn, Hollingworth, & Rose, 2013) of HE graduates. And yet, it is the positive contribution that HE can make to wider society generally that clearly underscores the arguments of these collected chapters.

The book is aimed at anyone with an interest in HE learning and teaching, or in graduate employability. It looks also at wider issues of social justice, and at the role and remit of the university. Rather than approaching the work chronologically, the reader may prefer to dip in and out of the various contributions, perhaps by theme (e.g. the challenges associated with defining or achieving learning gain, quality, student engagement, motivation, emotional resilience, learner identity, etc.), or by academic discipline. They may wish to start with the various practical suggestions aimed at HE practitioners or policy-makers e.g. on innovations to assessments, distance learning, CV-building, or the use of social media to foster connections across jurisdictions, professions and industries. The contributors share a common purpose: to pool our resources and ideas, in a bid to find practicable ways of better supporting our students in their achievement of employable 'graduate-ness,' and other 'learning gains.'[3]

Our students should also be or become 'critical thinkers' (Nussbaum, 1997) so that they might act as 'future generators of sustainable value for business and society at large ...to work for an inclusive and sustainable global economy...' (Gurpur & Rautdesai, 2014). There is a parallel need for HE managers and policymakers to similarly 'focus upon the notion of the greater, common good,' to try and engender a more socially conscious 'new breed of faculty' (Muff, Dyllick, Drewell, North, Shrivastava, & Haertle, 2013). As Muvingi (2009: 163) further observed, often, certain entrenched 'cycles of poverty can only be broken through structural reforms' especially during prolonged periods of economic austerity.[4] That there is therefore a need for greater 'sustainability' (*Agenda 2030*[5]) within HE is also evident throughout this collection, especially given the backdrop of increasing marketization (Molesworth, Scullion, & Nixon, 2010; Bunce, Baird, & Jones, 2017).

---

[3]On the notion of 'learning gain' see further http://www.hefce.ac.uk/lt/lg (accessed 12.09.18).

[4]See further Cooper and Whyte (2017) on austerity; and Wolf (2002) and Goddard (2009) on the notion of upward social mobility. See also however the argument and observations of McKenzie (2015) on how within disadvantaged communities 'strong, resourceful, ambitious people...are 'getting by' often with humour and despite facing brutal austerity.'

[5]Goal 4 (2016–2030) is to 'ensure inclusive and equitable quality education and promote lifelong learning opportunities for all.' See further, Palmer (2015) Introduction: The 2030 Agenda, *Journal of Global Ethics*, 11:3, 262–269.

The authors are fairly diverse in terms of geography (e.g. the UK, the U.S., Australia, South Africa, and South America) and disciplines but the various barriers to student success identified and discussed here (in addition to those caused or aggravated by ongoing austerity and political instabilities) are often generic and perennial in nature. Students increasingly indicate a number of issues, including low self-confidence, poor motivation, limited emotional resilience, and an inability or reluctance to engage fully with the HE curriculum or with the activities offered. A lack of opportunity to avail of work-relevant experiences is also frequently highlighted. The authors identify certain gaps in practice and policy, tentatively signposting some new (and perhaps at times more traditional) approaches to HE learning and teaching that might offer innovative pathways around or through some of the obstacles to academic success. Clearly, it is now no longer enough to produce graduates who might be described simply as 'ideal employees.' Universities are tasked with ensuring that students are fit to cope with a multitude of challenges. The embedding and enhancing of a wide range of practical key skills and intellectual competencies must be seen to be occurring right from the initial induction-level stages of the university 'journey' so that '…whole person models of experiential learning' might embed employability as an 'integrative, reflective and transitional' set of skills and attributes (Eden, 2014: 266).

That said, there is no simple answer to the questions surrounding the sometimes-nebulous notions of 'graduate-ness' and 'work-readiness.' The demands of differing professions and industries can vary profoundly, as do degree-pathways and curricula: students themselves represent a wider range of the population than ever before in terms of background, mind-set, expectations, and innate abilities. As Cable and Willets (2012) argued however:

> A degree remains a good investment in the long term and is one of the best pathways to achieving a good job and a rewarding career. Demand for more highly skilled employees continues to increase, with forecasts suggesting that half of the jobs that will become vacant this decade will be graduate ones. We must continue to encourage people to enter Higher Education, but we must also ensure that our students emerge from university with the right skills. (Cable & Willets, 2012, p. 18)

The duty to promote or enhance motivation and resilience (Pryce-Jones, 2014) amongst university learners and graduates is a further common feature. Put bluntly, to issue degree parchments (or 'guarantees' of career success) simply on the basis of fees paid, time spent, or the fear of litigation by aggrieved learners, is to devalue the achievements of those graduates who do engage successfully with the learning process, by attending classes, meeting deadlines, overcoming disappointments and setbacks, avoiding plagiarism, and managing anxieties.[6] Saying so does not diminish the seriousness of the often quite profound challenges that many of our students will face during (if not also before and after) their degree studies. Anyone working in

---

[6]See further Kamvounias and Varnham (2006), Cummings (2017), Swenson (1995), Palfreyman (2010). See also *Siddiqui v The Chancellor, Masters & Scholars of the University of Oxford* [2018] EWHC 184 (QB) for an interesting, if alarming, case on the 'contractual' nature of HE outcomes (examined in more detail in the Conclusion chapter).

HE will be aware of the fundamental importance, and clear value, of having in place robust student support systems, including comprehensive pastoral care, supervised peer assistance, disability/inclusion services, and welfare and wellbeing initiatives: we will also have seen how funding cuts have impacted adversely upon the student experience in recent years.[7] As tutors and employability facilitators we must remain mindful also of how people with similar levels of educational attainment can still possess significantly differing abilities, skills, and levels of knowledge (Allen & De Vries, 2004).[8]

The stresses of heavy workloads and tight deadlines have long been associated with university learning. The basic qualities of the highly employable worker can similarly include punctuality, reliability, diligence, politeness, common sense, respect for others, honesty, and the ability to think independently and behave ethically, whilst following instructions and completing set tasks: all of these can be framed as important components or aspects of a successful, fully engaged student journey. A generic notion of employability, if one exists, may perhaps then be most usefully defined in necessarily vague terms as the ability to 'perform the roles and tasks required by one's job to the expected standard'(Eraut & du Boulay, 2002). And yet, employers increasingly need more than traditional 'CV'-based displays of academic ability (Newcombe & Moutafi, 2009). Post-graduation, there is now an added expectation that graduates will quickly secure prestigious (or at least decently paid) jobs, and undertake an 'upwardly mobile' career pathway which will empower them and reflect their academic achievements. The evidencing of high levels of employability should, by implication, also showcase an underpinning 'teaching excellence' on the part of those who have supported students on their journey towards career success.

The difficulties of fitting essential employability skills into (or onto) HE curricula are therefore particularly relevant, in terms of designing and delivering workable learning and teaching activity templates, and addressing some thorny issues:

> While there is clearly a need to educate students on the theoretical aspects of their intended profession, classroom bound delivery limits the integration of theory and practice; a key element of developing work-readiness skills. (Ferns & Moore, 2012, p. 208)

Ascertaining what it is that employers expect or hope to see (or, perhaps more accurately, what they do *not* want to find) in graduate recruits is key, as is gauging how best to enable and/or enhance industrial or professional skills for these nascent employees. 'Bringing workplaces in' to a university setting is a common aim, often met via, for example, work-relevant simulations, peer/alumni networking or mentoring, short or longer-term work placements, formal or informal internships, and the (generally much-dreaded) group-working. Assessments are at the heart of this however (Fry, Ketteridge, & Marshall, 2009) not least in terms of having students face and survive the 'right level of challenge' (Eraut, 2007: 418). Tied to this also is the

---

[7]See further https://studentsunionucl.org/sites/uclu.org/files/u84290/documents/dsa_cuts_briefing1.pdf (accessed 10.02.19).

[8]Matching 'the supply of graduates with available jobs' is difficult (The Economist, 2015); in 2015 the proportion of unfilled vacancies for the average employer within the UK was however in the region of 5.4% (AGR, 2015).

ability to cope with disappointments, process and learn from tutor or peer feedback, and then engage in ongoing critical reflection e.g. upon why a particular career or learning pathway might have been chosen (Jones & Higson, 2012) or indeed altered, in favour of other options.

A dialogic, diagnostic approach to the notion of 'work-readiness' requires universities to acknowledge and address any skills deficits that might exist before, during or after 'the student journey.' The ability, for example, to cope with setbacks (which is seldom if ever set out as integral to surviving or thriving in HE) is perhaps one of the most significant attributes needed to attain the status of a successful, 'work-ready' graduate, who is able to crafting a professional or industrial identity. Self-sufficiency, gained via the tradition of *reading* for a university degree, places at least some of the onus for achievement squarely upon the shoulders of our students. Their 'investments' (i.e. material and emotional) in the processes of HE can be framed as symbiotic exchanges of effort, and ownership of one's results. This surely offers a fairer image of the 'consumer' student, who seeks to actively devour knowledge and opportunities rather than passively expecting guarantees of excellent results and 'refunds' when these are not obtained. In other words, if degree parchments were to be regarded perhaps as the 'title deeds' of learning (evidencing successfully negotiated learning landscapes, and the gaining of career-valuable core skills) then these would be more easily viewed as well deserved, hard-earned badges of honour. They are, and ought to be, indicative of substantial and significant personal growth, struggle, determination and exertion on the part of the mentally resilient, emotionally intelligent learner.

Clearly, no single blue-print or set template for achieving or evidencing enhanced employability exists, especially given the very differing demands of the various professions and industries that universities must cater for in attempting to predict workplace challenges and future job market trends. As academics, we are essentially united however in the need for fresh approaches to the issue of the perceived 'skills-deficit' of graduates and students. Together we should seek to spark further debate on the difficulties that tend to flow from the need to evidence enhanced graduate 'employability' during increasingly challenging times.[9] As such, the reader should be encouraged to question some of the current thinking within HE, and to find herein a useful selection of commentaries, research findings, and innovative practices, aimed at making our students' pathways a little bit easier.

The collection is divided into three sections of roughly equal size, based upon their content (with apologies for over-alliteration):

i. *Definitions—Key concepts and discourses within HE*

---

[9]Certain important aspects of HE learning and teaching (which can have a direct bearing on employability and academic success) have not been included in this collection e.g. issues arising from student plagiarism or malpractice, grade inflation, classroom or work placement behaviours, and online etiquette. The growing importance of strong and consistent pastoral care support (which, for example, can cover everything from studies advice and basic well-being tips, to acute issues of poverty, debt, unsafe housing, mental or physical ill-health, unmet disability needs, or sexual assault) should not be underestimated. The potential, indeed highly likely, impacts of such crises upon student engagement, exam success, and perhaps their eventual employability, will be obvious to anyone who has ever been tasked with attempting to improve things for their students.

ii. *Data, Designs and Difficulties*
iii. *Disciplines and Delivery*

Together, these set out and examine some of the fundamental core concepts and theories, to define and discuss those that have tended to increasingly underpin HE policy, practice, and decision-making, both within and beyond the United Kingdom. Throughout, the authors ask difficult questions about the nature and purpose of employability via HE, and examine the socio-cultural role(s) of university learning.

1.2   Section I: Definitions—Key Concepts and Discourses Within HE

Academics and support professionals tasked with enhancing—or perhaps simply engendering—often quite elusive 'employability skills,' will recognise the issues raised within these 10 critical essays. They look at such central concepts as Learning Gain, Academic Quality, Resilience, Learner Identity, Motivation, and Emotional Intelligence: at times there is a clear sense of near-exasperation on the part of some of the authors. Improving outcomes for students, nurturing their latent skills, reducing attrition rates, effecting meaningful pastoral care, encouraging contributions to civil society, and offering 'added value' within set degree programmes, is tiring work that often requires significant curricular change, and/or extra-mural effort from staff and students. And yet there is a shared, strong belief here in the social value of education, and our duty-led need to support those learners who are keen to engage with the challenges of academia and overcome barriers that might prevent them from doing so (i.e. economic disadvantage, disabilities, anxiety, or a lack of wider social supports). Common issues of concern amongst the authors in this first section are as follows: apparent student apathy (which may well mask other, more profound troubles) and fears over the political and economic uncertainties facing this—and indeed possibly also the next-generation of university graduates. This section contains however a positive note, highlighting the various positive changes and successes of recent years: significantly widened access and equity, increased academic willingness to innovate, more holistic forms of pastoral care, enhanced student (and staff) resilience, and greater public awareness of the wider benefits of engaging with HE.

It opens with (Chap. 2) the work of Evans (Swansea), Fox, and Taylor (Cardiff) which raises important questions about the very nature and purpose of HE, in terms of asking what contributions universities can or should make to civil society. HE may be harshly critiqued (e.g. as poor value for money or a waste of time) or framed as an essential aspect of national economic development (Universities UK, 2014). There are links clearly between what universities are 'good at' (e.g. research and teaching) and what they are 'good for,' in terms of making significant societal contributions on local, national or global scales (Goddard, 2009; Goddard & Kempton, 2016). Active participation in civil society by graduates (for example via membership of organisations, clubs and societies in later life) is often highly beneficial both for them and for the wider community, underpinning democratic frameworks (Putnam, 2000). The next chapter examines 'Learning Gain' in terms of accurately measuring it. Gossman and Powell (Manchester Metropolitan, Worcester) highlight how the UK's Quality Assurance Agency for Higher Education ('QAA') has noted an '…increasing tendency to see HE as a product with a price tag…' and the consequent 'growing interest in the extent to which academic programmes of study promote students' employability and earning power.' (QAA, 2013, para. 1) Defining learning gain requires more than a basic agreement on how best to measure it however (Boud, 2018): it is important to examine the motivations behind the need to both quantify and attribute credit (or causation) to the changes wrought in students as a result of having undergone university learning experiences. If we measure it in one particular way, this clearly also says something about the type(s) of learning that we most value and what sort of gain(s) might well exist within these. Chapter 4 looks to the notion of Quality and offers some critical reflections on its impacts upon academic practice (Chris Lawton, Edge Hill). The need to attain and maintain 'quality' standards (in respect of teaching, research, and the overall student experience) has been met with resistance by some academics. An alternative view, from both sides of the 'divide,' suggests that educators need not resign themselves to viewing the need for 'quality' as a bureaucratic exercise in fearful compliance (with perhaps unpalatable political and/or managerial agendas). Rather, well-designed quality processes used appropriately, as reflective tools for developing academic (best) practice frees staff and students to engage in effective ways of working.

The next three Chapters (5, 6 and 7, respectively) examine 'the student journey,' looking especially at what motivates learners, and at the psychological aspects of committing to HE (e.g. psychological resilience, emotional intelligence, learner identity). Clements (Bedfordshire) argues that some students simply seem to decide to avoid engagement with employability skills at an early stage in their studies and will not seek out our support. Gaps in the literature exist: clear job-searching strategies, and greater awareness of relevant environmental conditions within certain job markets, are essential, from an early stage of the student journey, to build and maintain motivation (Tansley et al., 2007). Dacre Pool, Gurbutt and Houston (UCLAN) similarly note how the 'consumerisation' of HE has altered the student-university relationship in many ways. Emotional intelligence has links to resilience: practical ideas presented here include the use of inter-disciplinary activities, aimed at developing emotional competencies (Pertegal-Felices, 2017). Irving-Bell (Edge Hill) similarly argues the significance of learner identity (especially as this might arise from or be affected by one's previous learning histories), noting how the influences of neoliberalism—and the vagaries of a harsh market economy—can at times challenge the very value, nature, and purposes of university education. A failure to effectively manage certain experience-related beliefs can lead to the imposition of barriers by students: these can significantly hinder their learning and personal development, not least in terms of identity-forming (Beauchamp & Thomas, 2009), academic success, and the cultivation of employability skills.

Some of these self-imposed barriers to success are examined in the next two chapters (8 and 9). O'Brien and Walker Martin (UCLAN) grasp a difficult nettle to some extent, highlighting how non-engagement by some students is an issue of serious concern for the academics and employability support staff seeking to improve learners' career outcomes post-graduation. Extra-curricular activities aimed at enhancing employability skills seem to be particularly problematic: low levels of student engagement may be down to an endemic apathy, innate non-resilience, or lack of emotional maturity. Addressing the notion that a troubled 'snowflake generation' (Kehoe, 2018) perhaps now exists, they argue that a robust system of peer-mentoring and clear linkage of assessments to essential learning elements offer possible strategies for combatting the twin problems of student non-attendance and high attrition rates. Exasperation on the part of HE staff is also evident within other jurisdictions. Cusciano, Laruccia, and Moraes (Fundação Getulio, Vargas) discuss student motivation and high drop-out rates in Brazil, analysing the often-complex relationship between labour markets, academic performance, student satisfaction, and learner disengagement. Expectations of upward social mobility (defined here as the gaining of better living conditions, and the accumulation of professional achievements) are held by most, if not all, students entering university in Brazil: this does not however guarantee that such initially high levels of motivation will be sustained throughout their course, or that students will complete their studies. As is the case elsewhere, fuller discussion and further debate is needed, both within and beyond Universities themselves, to better understand the nuanced relationships between academic success and subsequent professional performance, and to consider the fluctuating conditions within job markets, both global and local.

The section closes with two chapters (10 and 11) which look to the need to promote student resilience. Ryan, Jones, Hayes and Turner (RMIT, Australia) argue that although resilience theory has its roots in studies of individual mental dysfunction, it has since evolved to look beyond the individual, and to recognise the wider-ranging impacts of social and environmental influences. An increasingly diverse student cohort has seen universities transform from an elite-bound system to one of mass HE (Moir, 2010). Significantly, there are two pivotal transition points in a student's life: entry into university, and departure from it, to enter the workplace (Turner, Holdsworth, & Scott-Young, 2017a). The inter-relationships between leaving and entering university matter greatly in terms of promoting employability. As King, Newman, and Luthands (2016) argued, there have been four waves of development within resilience theory. The first focused on those factors and characteristics that might enable individuals to overcome adversity through increased self-esteem, self-efficacy, and optimism. A second wave framed certain factors as contributors to resilience, whilst the third argued for interventions aimed at building greater resilience. The final wave highlights genetic, neurological, and developmental factors. Although resilience is acknowledged generally as being a complex construct (and thus quite difficult to assess accurately) universities are becoming increasingly cognizant of its importance and are generally investing in research and services aimed at promoting it.

Adopting a strengths-based approach to the question of employable scholars, O'Shea and Delahunty (Wollongong, Australia) similarly argue that universities throughout the world are increasingly 'opening wide' their doors to highly diverse student cohorts. Students who are the first in their families to attend university have been viewed as requiring much institutional support so that they might be 'filled–up' with the particular skills needed to succeed. Such an approach suggests however that the knowledge derived from lived experiences is somehow at odds with the achievement of significant successes both at university and afterwards. An alternative, strengths-based perspective highlights the capabilities and social capital that such 'first generation' learners often bring with them, to counter such assumed deficit-framing. By exploring their strengths, skills, knowledge and work ethic, it is possible to look beyond the perception that some learners are automatically lacking in resilience or maturity. The underpinning support of family and friends is also highlighted here as an essential aspect of a successful student journey.

1.3   Section Two: Data, Design and Difficulties

The mid-section of the book comprises of 11 chapters (12–23), which include empirical studies and outlines of practical suggestions and innovations, aimed at enhancing 'employability' against a turbulent backdrop of austerity measures and political upheaval. Contributors offer glimpses of what has worked well within their own HE institutions to foster greater levels of 'work-readiness' and to raise student awareness of the need for enhanced professionalism. A common argument is that there is an urgent need for all involved to work together to create and maintain student-relevant academic and industrial/professional communities of practice, which engender meaningful ties to the wider 'world of work.' This may occur through work-based learning activities, internships, the involvement (e.g. curricular or extra mural) of employers and alumni, or via authentic, relevant simulations that seek to mirror the challenges of various workplaces to overcome social anxieties and gain relevant expertise. Assessments clearly matter too, not least in terms of their authenticity, and in their ability to appropriately challenge students to become (or remain) forward-looking and to take ownership of future plans and career opportunities. Perhaps the most significant message however is that there is a clear need (on the part of students and staff) to not only forge and maintain genuine connectedness with one's peers, but to also professionally network with persons yet-unknown, beyond their own circles. Technology has perhaps been to some extent neglected in this (Hargie, 2016). Helping students master the 'new' technologies is therefore important, in terms of improving online and distance learning skills, and gaining greater fluency in those internet resources which can enable the establishment of links across and beyond our own disciplines.

The first chapter in this section (Chap. 12) is multi-disciplinary (Business and Management, Media Studies, Pharmacy and Modern Foreign Languages) and multi-institutional (Northumbria, Bournemouth and Surrey, respectively). Mullen, Bridges, Eccles and Dippold focus on potential precursors to employability, by examining how first year undergraduate students plan and strategize to become employable graduates. They argue that although increasing emphasis has been paid to the university-workplace transition (as a means of evidencing the 'employability' of recent graduates), the first year at university is also a critical transition point (Murtagh, Ridley, Frings, & Kerr-Pertic, 2017; Coertjens, Brahm, Trautwein, and Lindblom-Ylanne 2017). Priorities for students during this time include making the necessary adjustments to life at university and developing positive friendships: it is important however for students to also find time to consider their future careers. The academic, social/personal and professional capital which students bring with them on entry to university clearly influences their subsequent, strategic decisions. The data from this study offers usefully detailed insights into the way in which 'freshers' typically plan (or fail to plan) for post-graduation employment. Holmes's (2001, 2015) graduate identity framework is utilised here to offer analysis of these case studies.

Chapter 13 (Bostock, Edge Hill) argues for a triadic approach to engagement, highlighting how students, staff and employers must be involved in the various processes, especially given the growing concerns over the UK's TEF (Teaching Excellence Framework) metrics and the revised NSS (National Student Survey). Even where students might already be vocationally or professionally focused upon achieving academic and career success (with resilience and fitness to train perhaps already evident) desirable graduate attributes and skills often differ profoundly across disciplines. Students must still locate and articulate these qualities within the specific context(s) of their own subject area. Again, any given 'student journey' will be tied to the needs and expectations of industries and professions: career nurturing at programme and subject level is therefore a necessary element. Staff development (e.g. CPD schemes and the gaining of PGCerts) serves to reinforce how discrete HE disciplines can both contain and further highly specialised knowledge, wisdom and skills. Academics and professionals are 'communities of practice' and as such must engage in developmental dialogues to both preserve and enhance HE students' learning and 'upskilling.' Tutor professionalism (here termed 'dual professionalism') requires academics to be subject specialists *and* expert teachers. Employer involvement (via curricular design, influencing individual modules or learning outcomes) offers a key means of identifying how transferable work skills might be successfully merged with academic and subject-specific, practical competencies, so that students are better supported in developing – and perceiving - their own employability levels.

The benefits of such connectivity (and the need to maintain and enhance connections made) are further argued by Gurbutt (UCLAN) in Chap. 14. Meaningful rapport and engagement with people who are not already part of our existing professional or industrial networks, is essential. The development of social confidence and collaborative skills are necessary for success within the workplace: this has traditionally been viewed as one of the consequences of HE, although whether this automatically arises via academic study, is less certain. The future is an interdisciplinary one: the HE sector needs to prepare graduates for a rapidly changing world where workplace problems are increasingly complex, and intersectional, in the sense that problem-solving, prioritization, and active networking are now crucial to career success. Social media can however serve to evidence the dissonances which exist between the need for active engagement with a large group of 'friends,' peers, or contacts, and the frequent reluctance to connect with persons or fields unknown.

An ability to collaborate and connect with others, using an appropriate degree of professionalism is such a desirable skill however that HEIs must find ways to afford students more opportunities to gain greater confidence in this, and to then evaluate their competencies—or otherwise—within this area.

As Thomson (University of the West of England) argues however (in Chap. 15), many students are fearful of what the future might hold for them. The uncertainty of the 2016 EU Referendum revealed a deeply divided society within the UK, with many people aged 18–24 years old voting overwhelmingly to 'Remain' with the European Union (Moore, 2016). For those students who had started their university education within the EU and now find themselves graduating within a country perceived as being increasingly isolationist, the question of what impacts 'Brexit' might have on their future careers is one that cannot be ignored. This small-scale qualitative research study, conducted one year after the EU Referendum result, reveals a strong desire on the part of HE students to 'create a more tolerant country' and a determination to find ways through an increasingly uncertain jobs market. The findings underscore how unforeseen political events can impact upon potential career choices, industries and professions. They confirm that a progressive shift in career guidance practice is urgently needed, to more fully acknowledge the importance of social, economic and political changes, especially where these serve as the backdrop for conversations about future career choices.

Chapter 16 offers a practical suggestion with Whitfield and Hartley (Bradford University) presenting a strategy for enhancing the student learning experience and achieving substantial learning gains (alongside other important benefits). Their call for a focus on programme-level rather than module-level assessment i.e. programme-focused assessment (PFA) draws upon related perspectives (such as recent work on the 'assessment environment') and successful alternative approaches which have been adopted elsewhere. Potential impacts and implications are also discussed here. Davidson, Snelling, Karanicolas, Crotti and Phillips (Adelaide University, Australia) similarly stress the importance of meaningful assessment, citing authenticity as the key feature, in Chap. 17. Work-integrated learning is now a fundamental aspect of many university courses: flexible, adaptable alumni are often seen as the most 'work ready' of graduates. The 'bridging' of gaps between workplace and learning environment (Yorke, 2016; Yorke, 2010) can also serve as an indicator of academic success given how HE is increasingly regulated in terms of monitoring and measuring its standards and outcomes (Bosco & Ferns, 2014). Generic skills may include meta-cognition, critical thinking, self-reflection and self-regulation, but, aligned with these skills, graduates also need discipline-specific abilities that can be transplanted to a wide range of contexts. Authentic assessment and learning therefore play a critical role: four cross-disciplinary exemplars of authentic learning and assessment approaches are analysed here (Accounting, Biology, Oral Health and Engineering), each one looking to theoretical aspects of authentic learning and assessment yet providing a practical approach to helping students transition from simulation to reality in workplace learning. Common themes and characteristics are also benchmarked against an authentic assessment framework, providing tutors with an operational approach to design, implement and evaluate their own authentic assessment tasks.

Delahunty and Harden-Thew (University of Wollongong, Australia) add a note of caution in Chap. 18 on how global trends in HE have seen increased research student enrolments but have also brought greater uncertainty over employment outcomes, encompassing both academia and industry (Jones, 2018). Related research has largely focused on the products of student work and the experience of supervision, with student voices often going unnoticed, overlooked or unobserved. Foregrounding student voices, this chapter explores the impacts of relationships on the student experience (in terms of negotiating academic culture and preparing for life, post-graduation). Findings are linked to the leitmotifs of Dr Seuss' '*Oh the places you'll go*' with its themes representing the highs, lows, uncertainties and unknowns inherent within academia and in those important relationships which sustain learners. Data was viewed through the lens of identity theory (Whannell & Whannell, 2015), using a narrative approach (Crotty, 1998) and gathered from an anonymous survey of research students and recent graduates across universities in 15 countries. The findings highlight students' rich experiences and perceptions across the postgraduate research process, especially the relationships that enabled or constrained their identity formation. Participants were diverse but there were many consistencies, particularly on how the quality of one's social interactions often impact upon a sense of belongingness.

The various interfaces between university and 'the work place' (via student internships) are the focus of the next chapter (Caddell and McIlwhan, Heriot Watt and Edinburgh Napier, Scotland, respectively). Despite offering useful opportunities for gaining work experience (and possibly securing routes to permanent jobs) internships have increased in notoriety. Where they are unpaid or vastly underpaid, a 'new elitism' arises, where often only those who can afford to work for free, or for very little, will be able to gain the experience necessary to access certain professions. As such, universities must be seen to be developing and supporting opportunities that are meaningful, fair and pedagogically informed. The Third Sector Internships Scotland programme, a national initiative, sought to offer students across all Scottish universities the opportunity to apply for paid internships, to experience working in the third sector, and receive appropriate feedback upon their applications. Multiple layers of impact should flow from effective employability initiatives, and the challenges associated with meeting the needs of diverse stakeholders.

The final three chapters (20, 21 and 22) of this section look at how innovations in technology have served in some measure to re-shape certain aspects of HE. Goldspink and Engward (Anglia Ruskin) highlight how distance-learning has blurred traditional geographic boundaries and widened remote access to universities, in addition to having a significant role in campus-based pedagogic practice. Technology provides a range of pedagogic advantages, but to maximise learning, the individual learners' experience must be considered, to steer our pedagogic assumptions, actions and aspirations. Relatively little is known about how people learn at a distance: the dynamic nature of the self is often unrecognised within course design and learning content. Learning itself can be misrepresented as linear and compartmentalised, through modular-designed courses and instrumental evaluations that mainly monitor superficial aspects of the modular experience. By better understanding what it means to be learning at a distance via the various interfaces of technology, we can design and deliver better learning, and use technologies more effectively, irrespective of where the learner is located. This interpretive, phenomenological research project on distance learning questions what it means to learn at a distance and offers practical suggestions about maximising outcomes.

In times of austerity and economic uncertainty, many students will focus particularly—and understandably—on the end goal of securing a job but may well overlook the importance of developing their employability more generally. One way of achieving this is by considering alumni networks as an invaluable community of practice within which students can connect and engage. Mogaji (Greenwich) discusses in Chap. 21 how student engagement with *LinkedIn* may serve to significantly enhance employability, given its overt focus on forging business connections between like-minded others, not least alumni, employers and professionals. Arguably, many students do not avail of the opportunity to network online as they consider the site and the process to be too 'profession-focussed.' The chapter offers suggestions to help students and tutors make the best use of *LinkedIn,* to improve student engagement and their subsequent employability. Fowlie and Forder (Brighton) similarly argue that students must consider their pre-professional identity: making connections with alumni is essential in this regard. Moving beyond a more traditional, skills-based approach to promoting work-readiness, undergraduates' pre-professional identity formation is presented here as a means of helping students navigate and understand the work-cultures of their intended profession or industry. Focusing on pre-professional identities also encourages them to take greater responsibility for their own levels of work-readiness. This chapter presents the results of a targeted project whereby participants were introduced to the concept of pre-professional identity and shown the value of connecting with alumni within their chosen field. *LinkedIn* is framed here as a valuable tool both for career exploration and for the gaining of a greater understanding of the graduate attributes sought by employers. Participants' attitudes towards using the platform changed as a result: for some this led to highly positive outcomes such as securing work and building new professional networks.

1.4   Section Three: Disciplines and Delivery

The third section of the book 'drills down' to the level of specific subject and discipline, to set out 12 examples of 'employability' activities, and further critiques of current frameworks and policies. The authors hail from throughout the UK, the U.S., South Africa and Australia. The subject areas covered include Law, Education, English, Criminology, Business, Computing, Media, Pharmacy, Modern Foreign Languages and Fashion. As Eden (2014) has argued, there seems to be a move away from the notion that self-contained 'employability skills' might somehow be encapsulated within one learner-generic blueprint or strategy: rather, the wider 'whole person models of experiential learning…[frame] employability as integrative, reflective and transitional' (Eden, 2014: 266) allowing students a glimpse of their 'future-fit…possible selves' (Plimmer & Schmidt, 2007). Despite the focus on largely discrete professional pathways, these chapters still serve to identify useful teaching and learning suggestions for practice that can be adapted by others to suit their own areas. These include for example the use of e-portfolios in distance learning, online activities, critical thinking, the importing of practice-based activities into under-graduate assessments, industry-relevant simulations, 'living CV' projects, and the use of charitable pop-up shops.

The first four chapters (23–26) focus on Business. Forster and Robson (Northumbria) discuss the current need to cultivate 'oven-ready' graduates, detailing how twin-track programmes can deliver specialist, discipline-based knowledge overlaid with 'employment preparedness.' Experiential learning aims here to 'squeeze a quart into a pint pot' by incorporating the academic rigour associated with subject expertise into the 'softer' practical skills and 'organisational deftness' so prized by employers and enriching for graduates. The various successes and challenges experienced (including the issue of student buy-in) are also analysed here. Lock (Lincoln) similarly sets out in Chap. 24 the challenges facing Business schools in ensuring that graduates can work well across boundaries, in terms of geography, functionality and academic disciplines. Complex skill-mixes are needed to operate within, and respond to, work place dynamics: instead of using extra-curricular activities to embed or enhance the competencies needed to get a job, employability has been centrally planted within the undergraduate curriculum. Graduates are prepared for profession-hopping and less-delineated working environments, as industries move towards more geographically dispersed teams and more varied working practices.

Brown, Charity and Robson (Northumbria) offer analysis of the 'Graduate Premium' (in Chap. 25) defining it as a balancing of the costs of any given programme against its expected benefits such as, for example, facilitated entry into, and progression within, fulfilling and well-remunerated business careers. Tutors must differentiate their own programmes from those of other institutions, not only to attract applicants, but to give their graduates a competitive advantage when out in the job market. Their literature review acknowledges the debates surrounding the use of technology, identifying pedagogical benefits and potential limitations, and makes suggestions as to how technology might be better harnessed to provide more transparent pathways towards professionalism. The benefits and challenges as experienced by modern, increasingly demanding students are also discussed here, in relation to how graduates might adapt to differing social and learning cultures after university. The next chapter describes in detail how the charitable pop-up shop can be used both to develop employability skills and contribute to civil society. Hill, Bass and Frost (Coventry, BCU) note firstly how UK austerity measures have led to an increased monitoring of university teaching and employability outcomes. Reduced public spending has also meant that fewer graduate-level jobs are available, even though employers are increasingly seeking high levels of 'work-readiness' from their graduate recruits. Here, an authentic business activity—the setting up and running of a pop-up shop—is used as a team-based, intra-curricular learning activity, linked to a modular assessment. Money is raised for a student-selected charity and learner resilience is developed through this challenging, practice-relevant scenario.

A not dissimilar approach is presented in Chap. 27, which looks to the promotion of professional development within second year computing degree programmes. Whatley (Manchester Metropolitan) outlines in detail how students (from a variety of disciplines including Computing, Computer Science, Software Engineering, Games, Forensics and Animation) undertake a unit of study called Professional Development (alongside careers-based advice and a Live Project) to prepare them for the demands of the workplace. In Chap. 28, Dibben and Morley (Southampton Solent) offer the exemplar of a 'Living CV' aimed at helping Fashion students take ownership of their own academic accomplishments, experience and learning gain(s). This mixed methods study was conducted across all three years of a fashion degree and involved students in 'before and after' questionnaires, with a presentation on their Living CV, which links to and highlights their academic learning outcomes. This offers a personalised and explicit form of coaching on 'work literacy' and provides useful preparation for job interviews, which can be integrated into different university programmes at all levels.

The next two chapters focus upon postgraduate programmes in other jurisdictions. Van Staden (University of the Free State, South Africa) presents a pilot study in Chap. 29 on the use of e-portfolios as a means of demonstrating 'graduateness'(Glover, Law, & Youngman, 2002) within distance education. The module in question relates to the curriculum for Instructional Technologies and Multimedia in Education (INTMAEU) and seeks to prepare postgraduate distance education students to take up lecturing positions in HE. Learning tasks were used, rather than assessment activities, and these provided for prompt tutor feedback to facilitate current and future learning, and to actively involve the students as self and peer assessors. Students were encouraged to use a variety of technologies and multimedia: the reflections of a top-achieving post-graduate student are particularly insightful and thus are analyzed here to demonstrate how e-portfolios may be used to evidence employability.

Bippert, Pletcher and Valadez (A&M University, Corpus Christi, Texas) similarly examine post-graduate online education and distance learning, via a socio-constructivist approach, in Chap. 30. They argue that even within an online learning environment, social interactions between students and tutors often require a blending of different teaching techniques given varying learning styles (Yoon, 2003). A socially constructed learning environment permits collaboration and opportunities for social interaction (Vygotsky, 1978). As online education becomes increasingly popular, tutors are challenged however by the shift from traditional face-to-face instruction to interactions mediated by computer technology. Knowledge comes from both biological and socio-cultural language-based interactions. For online instruction to be effective then, certain principles should apply: authenticity of learning experience, social interaction, students' contributions to their own individual experiences and perspectives, and instructors having a facilitative role (Doolittle, 1999). This chapter looks to one online Masters of Reading programme which initially provided relatively few flexible teaching techniques, and fairly limited opportunities for synchronous communication between students and instructors. To improve tutor presence, and provide students with authentic applications of new learning, some additional online tools were added: this made the learning more relevant, encouraged synchronous student interaction and collaboration, and facilitated discussions of multiple perspectives, grounded in students' individual experiences and contexts.

The final four substantive chapters of this section (31–34) are concerned with law, criminal justice and criminology. Toole (Adelaide) offers the exemplar of a compulsory criminal law course, which seeks to promote career readiness skills as part of the core curriculum. Simulated case files allow students to experience the fundamental processes of 'lawyering,' many of which will transcend jurisdictional differences, making the model used here highly relevant to other legal systems. Conversely, Lodge and Elliott (Coventry) argue in Chap. 32 that there is no such thing as an average law student, with the UK's national student body now more diverse than ever, and with the career aspirations of law students becoming increasingly broad. A declining legal employment market within the UK (together with the wide skill set gained by studying law) has meant that many LLB students will finish their undergraduate degree without having planned for a professional career in law. Change will likely be a constant feature of legal education and the legal sector for many years to come: the introduction of a new, exams-based pathway towards qualification as a Solicitor is a key example. Given this rapidly changing legal sector, HE providers can no longer limit legal employability provision to a traditional, straightforward 'barrister versus solicitor' debate. As service users, students demand visible value in return for their time and tuition fees: initial career aspirations can also change between the starting and completing of an undergraduate law degree. The results of this small-scale survey of graduates confirmed that the core aims of the Coventry scheme were in line with the needs and expectations of students and graduates. Further research is needed however to better gauge and understand law students' perspectives on the concept of legal employability and to determine how their unique needs and demands can best be met.

Ragonese and Altham (Liverpool John Moores) echo the view that the UK's HE sector has long recognised a changing landscape (QAA, 2013) in Chap. 33. Development of a broader understanding of the notion of employability is clearly needed. Here, a module specifically designed for and delivered to second year undergraduate Criminal Justice (CJ) students is presented. The teaching team worked in close partnership with careers staff, employers and students to ensure that its curricular design would embed those skills, knowledge, and experiences that students need to succeed after graduation, in terms of gaining graduate—level roles. A 'how to' framework with 'hints and tips' (which could be transplanted into any discipline and programme of study) aims to engage students in developing greater levels of self-efficacy and furthering their sense of professional development.

The final chapter in this section by Barton, Davis (Edge Hill) and Scott (Open University) looks to Mills' (1959) conceptualisation of the 'sociological imagination' to argue against the 'quiet silencing' of critical voices in academia, echoing the questions raised in Chap. 1 (Evans et al.) to bring this project to a sort of 'full circle' conclusion. Put briefly, they argue that an inability to recognise and understand how relations of power connect individual biographies to history contributes to a disaffecting social order. Often this is characterised by social alienation, moral insensibility, disproportionate power held by a small group of elites, new threats to liberty and freedom, and conflicts between bureaucratic rationality and human reason. Understanding social structures (and recognising the many intersections between individual lives and social and historical contexts) provides a means to make sense of the world and resist historical repetitions of alienation and systemic oppression. For criminology students, it is especially important to reject narrow, administrative notions of 'crime' which tend to focus too heavily on (often individualised) causes, and, in turn, marginalise the consideration of structural contexts (Reiner, 2012). In terms of ethical teaching, a sociological imagination generates much in the way of 'emancipatory knowledge' which can in turn contribute to transformative politics, the aim of which is to actively challenge injustices and inequalities, rather than simply accepting the status quo. Giving a voice to the otherwise voiceless, remains one of the core aims of Higher Education, as this edited collection has sought to argue.

1.5   Conclusion

> ...an unfair and unkind universe...divergent responses epitomize the North/South divide on development, income disparities, technology transfer, health, the environment, and related problems. (King, 2001: 485)

The underpinning aim of this book project has been to provide a collection of chapters grounded in relevant literature, and offering useful observations, shared findings, and practical suggestions on promoting our students' 'employability.' The contributing authors have done so, without losing sight of the other purposes of any HE system, namely, to empower and enlighten, offer meaningful opportunities, give a critical voice to the voiceless, and to remind those who hold power of the need to similarly 'aim higher,' in terms of crafting just societies, and preventing or remedying wrongs and inequalities. The role of the university is not simply to manufacture legions of 'identikit' proto-employees who will be quietly content to maintain potentially unfair systems, structures, policies and practices without engaging in critical discussion, debate or political enquiry. As Kushner has observed, 'human activities are not at all linear.'[10] Decision-makers should seek to 'reinforce the importance of adhering to professional, ethical principles and codes of behaviour' (Collinson, Diver, & McAvoy, 2018). One way of doing so is to ensure that we teach and train our graduates in accordance with high ideals (such as the UN's PRME principles and Sustainable Development Goals), to be the 'future generators of sustainable value for business and society at large and to work for an inclusive and sustainable global economy.'[11]

---

[10]S Kushner, 'A Return to Quality' *Evaluation* (2011) 17(3) pp 309–312 p 311.

[11]PRME Principle One, available at http://unprme.org/the-6-principles/index.php (accessed 12.11.18) See further http://www.unprme.org/about-prme/the-six-principles.php and https://www.unglobalcompact.org/library/319 (accessed 01.10.18). See further the *Principles for Responsible*

In sum, proposed changes in HE in relation to content, curriculum, and pedagogy should still aim to further 'the common good' (Muff et al., 2013). Often, quite small but significant reforms to thinking can allow for the gradual transformation of 'seemingly intractable issues of maldistribution of wealth (and) unequal influence' within wider society (Verbos & Humphries, 2015). Working in HE means therefore that the 'duty we owe to human society' (Newman, 2014) extends beyond the simple generation of economic advantages and the drafting of ever-expanding job descriptions. The human qualities associated with employability should be grounded in fundamental values that transcend and cut across the borders and limitations of academic disciplines. They should reflect higher virtues, such as empathy, honesty, diligence, and compassion for others, both within and beyond our own immediate circles, especially in times of economic austerity and political uncertainty, as the Conclusion (Chap. 35) will argue more fully.

References

Allen, K., Quinn, J., Hollingworth, S., & Rose, A. (2013). Becoming employable students and 'Ideal' creative workers: Exclusion and inequality in higher education work placements. *British Journal of Sociology of Education, 34*(3), 431–452.

Allen, J., & de Vries, R. (2004). *Determinants of skill mismatches: The role of learning environment, the match between education and job and working experience.* Research Centre for Education and the Labour Market (ROA).

Beauchamp, C., & Thomas, L. (2009). Understanding teacher identity. *Cambridge journal of education, 39*(2), 175–189.

Boud, D. (2018). Assessment could demonstrate learning gains but what is required for it to do so? *Higher Education Pedagogies, 3*(1), 54–56.

Brennan, J., Durazzi, N., & Sene, T. (2013). *Things we know and don't know about the wider benefits of higher education: A review of the recent literature.* London, UK: London School of Economics and Political Science.

Bosco, A. M., & Ferns, S. (2014). Embedding of authentic assessment in work-integrated learning curriculum. *Assessment and Evaluation in Higher Education, 39*(2), 205–222.

Bunce, L., Baird, A., & Jones, S. E. (2017). The student-as-consumer approach in Higher Education and its effects on academic performance. *Studies in Higher Education, 42*(11), 1958–1978.

Cable, V., & Willets, D. (2012). *Following up the Wilson Review of Business University Collaboration: Next steps for Universities, Business and Government.* BIS.

Coertjens, L., Brahm, T., Trautwein, C., & Lindblom-Ylanne, S. (2017). Students' transition into higher education from an international perspective. *Higher Education, 73,* 357–369.

Collinson, R., Diver, A., & McAvoy, S. (2018). Clients, clinics and social justice: Reducing inequality (and embedding legal ethics) via an LLB portfolio pathway. In *Higher Education, Skills and Work-Based Learning* (Vol. 8, pp. 323–336).

Cooper, V., & Whyte, D. (Eds.). (2017). *The violence of austerity.* Pluto Press.

Crotty, M. (1998). *The foundations of social research: Meaning and perspective in the research process.* St Leonards, NSW: Allen and Unwin.

Management in Education (PRME), a United Nations-led initiative, tied to the United Nations Global Compact (UNGC). PRME participants (e.g. universities) agree to uphold the Six Principles, not least 'to share and learn from each other, and to continuously move toward fulfilment of its purpose.' See further Waddock (2010); and King (2001).

Cummings, J. J. (2017). Where courts and academe converge: Findings of fact or academic judgment? *Australia & New Zealand Journal of Law & Education, 12*(1), 97–108.

Doolittle, P. (1999). *Constructivism and online education.* http://edpsychserver.ed.vt.edu/workshops/tohe1999/text/doo2s.doc.

Eden, S. (2014). Out of the comfort zone: Enhancing work-based learning about employability through student refection on work placements. *Journal of Geography in Higher Education, 38*(2), 266–276.

Eraut, M. (2007). Learning from other people in the workplace. *Oxford Review of Education, 33*(4), 403–422.

Eraut, M., & du Boulay, B. (2002). *Developing the attributes of medical professional judgement and competence.* Sussex: University of Sussex.

Ferns, S., & Moore, K. (2012). Assessing student outcomes in fieldwork placements: An overview of current practice. *Asia-Pacific Journal of Cooperative Education, 13*(4), 207–224.

Fry, H., Ketteridge, S., & Marshall, S. (Eds.). (2009). *A handbook for teaching and learning in higher education: Enhancing academic practice.* London: Routledge.

Glover, D., Law, S., & Youngman, A. (2002). Graduateness and employability: Student perceptions of the personal outcomes of university education. *Research in Post-Compulsory Education, 3*(7), 296–306.

Goddard, J. (2009). *Reinventing the Civic University.* London: Nesta.

Goddard, J., & Kempton, L. (2016). *The Civic University: Universities in Leadership and Management of Place.* Centre for Urban and Regional Development Studies, Newcastle University.

Gurpur, S., & Rautdesai, R. C. (2014). Revisiting legal education for human development: Best practices in South Asia. *Procedia - Social and Behavioral Sciences, 157,* 254–265.

Hargie, O. (2016). The importance of communication for organisational effectiveness. In F. Lobo (Ed.), *Psicologia do Trabalho e das Organizações* (pp. 15–32). Axioma: Braga, Portugal.

Holmes, L. (2001). Reconsidering graduate employability: The graduate identity approach. *Quality in Higher Education, 7*(2), 111–119.

Holmes, L. (2015). Becoming a graduate: The warranting of an emergent identity. *Education & Training, 57*(2), 219–238.

Jones, M. (2018). Contemporary trends in professional doctorates. *Studies in Higher Education.* https://doi.org/10.1080/03075079.2018.1438095.

Jones, C., & Higson, H. (2012). Work placements and degree performance: Do placements lead to better marks or do better students do placements? How can we incorporate findings into wider practice? In Green, & Higson. (Eds.), *Good practice guide in learning and teaching.* Aston University.

Kamvounias, P., & Varnham, S. (2006). In-house or in court? Legal challenges to university decisions. *Education & The Law, 18*(1), 1–17.

Kehoe, K. (2018). *Entitled snowflakes with student loans and side hustles: Media governmentality and the paradoxical construction of the millennial generation.* California State University, ProQuest 10752070.

King, D., Newman, A., & Luthands, F. (2016). Not if, but when we need resilience in the workplace. *Journal of Organizational Behaviour, 37,* 782–786.

King, B. (2001). The UN global compact: Responsibility for human rights, labor relations, and the environment in developing nations. *Cornell Int'l L.J., 34,* 481–486.

Kushner, S. (2011). A return to quality. *Evaluation, 17*(3), 309–312.

McDonald, Ria, & Van Der Horst, Helen. (2007). Curriculum alignment, globalization, and quality assurance in South African higher education. *Journal of Curriculum Studies, 39*(1), 1–9.

McKenzie, L. (2015). *Getting by: Estates, class and culture in Austerity Britain.* Policy Press.

Mills, C. W. (1959–2000). *The sociological imagination.* Oxford: Oxford University Press.

Molesworth, M., Scullion, R., & Nixon, E. (2010). *The marketisation of higher education and the student as consumer.* UK: Routledge.

Moir, J. (2010). *First things first: The first year in Scottish higher education.* http://www.enhancementthemes.ac.uk/docs/publications/first-things-first-the-first-year-in-scottish-higher-education.pdf.

Moore, P. (2016). *How Britain Voted.* you.gov.uk.

Muff, K., Dyllick, T., Drewell, M., North, J., Shrivastava, P., & Haertle, J. (2013). *Management education for the world: A vision for business schools serving people and planet.* UK: Edward Elgar Publishing.

Murtagh, S., Ridley, A., Frings, D., & Kerr-Pertic, S. (2017). First-year undergraduate induction: Who attends and how important is induction for first year attainment? *Journal of Further and Higher Education, 41*(5), 597–610.

Muvingi, I. (2009). Sitting on powder kegs: Socioeconomic rights in transitional societies. *The International Journal of Transitional Justice* (3), 163–182.

Newman, J. H. (2014). *The Idea of a University [1852].* Illinois: Assumption Press.

Newcombe, I., & Moutafi, J. (2009). *Perfect psychometric test results.* Random House.

Nussbaum, M. C. (1997). *Cultivating humanity: A classical defence of reform in liberal education.* Cambridge and London: Harvard University Press.

Palfreyman, D. (2010). HE's 'Get-out-of-jail-free card'. *Perspectives, 14*(4), 114–119.

Palmer, E. (2015). Introduction: The 2030 Agenda. *Journal of Global Ethics, 11*(3), 262–269.

Pertegal-Felices, M. L., et al. (2017). The development of emotional skills through interdisciplinary practices integrated into a university curriculum. *Education Research International* (2017) [article ID 6089859].

Plimmer, G., & Schmidt, A. (2007). Possible selves and career transition: It's who you want to be, not what you want to do. *New Directions for Adult and Continuing Education* (114), 61–74.

Putnam, R. D. (2000). *Bowling alone: The collapse and revival of American Community.* New York: Simon and Schuster.

Pryce-Jones, J. (2014). Motivation and resilience. *The Law Society Gazette.*

Quality Assurance Agency for Higher Education. (2013). *Skills for employability,* UK.

QAA, U. K. (2013–2018). Quality Code for. *Higher Education,* (https://www.qaa.ac.uk/quality-code/UK-Quality-Code-for-Higher-Education-2013-18).

Reiner, R. (2012). Political economy and criminology: The return of the repressed. In S. Hall & S. Winlow (Eds.), *New directions in criminological theory* (pp. 30–51). Abingdon: Routledge.

Swenson, E. (1995). Higher education law in the trenches. *Teaching of Psychology, 22*(3), 169–172.

Tansley, D. P., et al. (2007). The effects of message framing on college students' career decision-making. *Journal of Career Assessment, 15*(3), 301–316.

The Economist. (2015). Mismatch. Graduates and Employment. http://www.economist.com/blogs/freeexchange/2015/06/graduates-and-employment.

Turner, M., Holdsworth, S., & Scott-Young, C. M. (2017). Resilience at university: The development and testing of a new measure. *Higher Education Research & Development, 36*(2), 386–400.

Universities UK. (2014). *The economic impact of HEIs in England—Summary report.* London: Universities UK.

Verbos, A. K., & Humphries, M. T. (2015). Indigenous wisdom and the PRME: inclusion or illusion? *Journal of Management Development, 34*(1), 90–100.

Vygotsky, L. S. (1978). *Mind in society.* Cambridge, MA: Harvard University Press.

Waddock, S., et al. (2010). The principles for responsible management education—Where do we go from here? In: Fisher, et al. (Eds.), *Assessing business ethics education* (pp. 13–28). Charlotte, NC: Information Age Publishing.

Whannell, R., & Whannell, P. (2015). Identity theory as a theoretical framework to understand attrition for university students in transition. *Student Success, 6*(2), 43–52.

Wilson, D. L. (2012). *A review of Business–University Collaboration.* Department for Business, Innovation and Skills (Gov.UK).

Wolf, A. (2002). *Does education matter? Myths about education and economic growth.* Penguin Business.

Yoon, S. (2003). In search of meaningful online learning experiences. In S. R. Aragon (Ed.), *Facilitating learning in online environments. New directions for adult and continuing education* (Vol. 100). San Francisco: Jossey-Bass.

Yorke, M. (2010). Employability: Aligning the message, the medium and academic values. *Journal of Teaching and Learning for Graduate Employability, 1*(1), 2–12.

Yorke, M. (2016). The development and initial use of a survey of student 'belongingness', engagement and self-confidence in UK Higher Education. *Assessment and Evaluation in Higher Education, 41*(1), 154–166.

Alice Diver (Ph.D.) is a Senior Lecturer in Law at Liverpool John Moores University, Liverpool, UK having previously worked at Edge Hill University, and Ulster University (Northern Ireland). She spent several years as a solicitor in private practice before joining academia in 1993. Her teaching experience includes property law, child & family law, and human rights law. Her research interests focus mainly on adoption, law in literature, and human rights. She is the author of a monograph on closed birth records in law and policy called '*A Law of Blood-ties: The 'right' to access genetic ancestry*' (Springer, 2013) and co-editor of an essay collection entitled '*Justiciability of Human Rights Law in Domestic Jurisdictions*' (Springer, 2015). She has published in a wide variety of peer-reviewed academic journals. She is a long-serving board member of Apex Housing NI, and a trustee of Kinship Care NI.

Chapter 2
HE and Civil Society: What Contribution Can Universities Make to Civil Society?

Ceryn Evans, Stuart Fox and Chris Taylor

2.1 Introduction

Against a backdrop of escalating Higher Education (HE) fees in England and Wales, public debate has intensified regarding the contribution that universities make to society. Within this debate, HE is regarded as playing a central role in national economic development (Universities UK, 2014) and, as such, universities have come under increasing pressure to ensure the employability of their graduates. Whilst these concerns have featured significantly within policy discussions around the role of HE in society for decades, any serious discussion about HE's wider cultural and civic contribution has fallen from central stage over time and only recently begun to re-surface. The notion that universities should make contributions to a society's cultural and social life has a lengthy history which influenced the formation of some of Britain's civic universities (Annette, 2005; Nussbaum, 1997). Yet these questions have only recently re-emerged in the form of questions not only about what universities are 'good at' (research and teaching) but also what they are 'good for' in terms of their societal contribution on local, national and global scales (Goddard, 2009; Goddard & Kempton, 2016). Policy debate around this issue has accelerated in all parts of the UK, particularly in Wales, where Hazelkorn's (2016) review of post-compulsory education stated that civic engagement should be a core mission and an institution-wide commitment for all universities. Reflecting this, Kirsty Williams (the Education Secretary for Wales), made a clarion call to universities to 're-capture'

C. Evans (✉)
Swansea University, Swansea, Wales, UK
e-mail: ceryn.evans@swansea.ac.uk

S. Fox · C. Taylor
Cardiff University, Cardiff, Wales, UK
e-mail: FoxS8@cardiff.ac.uk

C. Taylor
e-mail: TaylorCM@cardiff.ac.uk

© Springer Nature Switzerland AG 2019
A. Diver (ed.), *Employability via Higher Education: Sustainability as Scholarship*,
https://doi.org/10.1007/978-3-030-26342-3_2

and 're-invent' their civic missions (Williams, 2016). She argued, with some urgency, the need for universities to bring to the fore their civic mission and to consider their responsibilities to their region and nation.

In light of these emerging policies, both in Wales and within the UK more generally, this chapter aims to further discussions on universities' civic contribution to society: consideration of this question is crucial given the rising financial cost of study, and increasingly pressing questions about what it is that students can expect to gain from a university education, and what universities can contribute to society beyond their economic input. Active participation in those organisations, clubs, and societies which make up civil society is beneficial to both individuals and communities through the way in which such participation helps foster trust, mutual respect, social networks, and subjective personal wellbeing. Given that these attributes are said to be essential for the formation of democratic and harmonious societies (Putnam, 2000), examination of the role that universities play in the development of such attributes is essential if we are to fully understand HE's wider contribution to society.

2.2   HE and Civil Society: A Paradoxical Relationship

As rates of civic participation across many Western democracies are said to be declining (Putnam, 2000), questions about HE's contribution to society have become particularly significant. Education is one of the most commonly cited drivers of greater civic engagement, with the most widely cited theories emphasising the benefits of HE: these include the values, skills and knowledge developed whilst studying in an institution, for engagement with community associations and politics in later life (Dalton, 2013; Putnam, 2000; Verba et al., 1995). Such theories present social researchers with something of a paradox however, as participation in HE has all but constantly increased in most Western societies for the past fifty years, while civic participation and engagement rates have declined. This paradox has prompted the development of various theories and re-examinations of the way in which education shapes civic engagement. One such explanation is that education has very little impact at all on our levels of civic engagement: instead, the appearance of a positive relationship between education and civic engagement reflects a 'selection effect,' in which the same people who attend university or college are also more likely to participate in their communities when they get older. Rather than reflecting the influence of education, this is said to reflect pre-adult experiences (such as upbringing in a civically active and highly educated household) that tend to predispose people towards both HE and civic participation, and which are extremely difficult to identify in survey research (Berinsky & Lenz, 2011; Kam & Palmer, 2008; Luskin, 1990; Persson, 2012).

Persson (2012), for example, argued that a process of self-selection may explain the relationship between higher levels of education and civic (and political) participation whereby people who are already politically orientated are more likely to select academic education over vocational education. Similarly, Kam and Palmer (2008) argue that, overall,[1] the positive relationship between HE and political participation is accounted for by the way in which pre-adult experiences propel individuals towards pursuing HE, which also encourage them towards political participation, and not into HE per se. According to this research, factors which operate prior to an individual embarking on a particular course of study (such as the political environment in the home, the amount of political discussion within the family, and familial socio-economic factors) may be more important to an individual's civic participation than the particular educational pathway that they pursue. Indeed, the role of extra-educational contexts (such as parental education and socio-economic status) in adulthood civic and political engagement has been well documented (Verba et al., 1995). This has prompted some researchers to conclude that after controlling for the effect of pre-adult experiences and influences, the effect of HE on political participation disappears (Kam & Palmer, 2008).

This theory explains the paradox of rising education levels alongside falling civic participation rates in terms of changes in the socialisation and pre-adult experiences of younger generations relative to their predecessors that are making them just as likely to enter HE, but less likely to be active within their communities. This may result from parents being less successful in (or concerned about) passing on their views regarding the importance of civic participation to their children, or it could reflect societal changes in which other influences (such as the media) have become more important in the socialisation of younger generations, promoting a more individualistic outlook that does not value civic participation. A further alternative explanation considers the effect of education on civic engagement in a different way, namely, by focusing on the influence of our educational experiences *relative to* others in our immediate environment. Such a perspective is widely employed in the fields of economics, where the role of education in, for example, obtaining favourable employment is conceptualised in terms of the 'sorting model.' This suggests that education acts perhaps as a 'sorting mechanism,' through which a limited number of jobs are distributed to those individuals who are competing for them (Hirsch, 1977).

Nie et al. (1996) argued that this same insight can be applied to civic and political participation: people compete for a limited number of meaningful opportunities to participate with others within their own community or social network, and that education is a mechanism by which these opportunities are distributed. This model hinges on the relationship between education and social status. People who acquire HE qualifications often come to occupy more prominent locations within social networks: this is partly the result of a superior income or economic position that they might well enjoy, and partly because educational qualifications can signal to others the possession of skills, knowledge, and economic status. Others will consequently be likely to view them more favourably and assign them a higher social status (Birdal & Ongen, 2016; Hirsch, 1977; Nie et al., 1996). People who occupy more central locations within social networks are also more likely to be able to access resources

---

[1]The one exception, Kam and Palmer (2008), argue that, as regards political protests, HE participation in America in the 1960s and 1970s was associated with a greater likelihood of civil society participation.

from that network, which in turn can facilitate greater civic participation, such as information or support to engage in collective action. Consequently, they become more likely to access limited opportunities for participation, or rather to 'win' the competition to access them, and so are more likely to be active (Helliwell & Putnam, 2007; Nie et al., 1996).

This theory explains the paradox of rising education levels and falling civic participation rates in the much the same way that the notion of 'credential inflation' has been used to describe the effect of the expansion of HE, and of student numbers, on graduate employment rates in recent decades (Brown, 2003; Campbell, 2009; Collins, 1979; Hirsch, 1977; Nie et al., 1996). Several researchers have argued also that the greatly increasing numbers of graduates has led to 'credential inflation' which has in turn undermined the value of HE qualifications for securing employment in the context of highly congested and competitive graduate labour markets (Brown, 2003; Collins, 1979; Hirsch, 1977). In much the same way that a commodity (such as gold) becomes less valuable the more common it is, HE qualifications arguably become less valuable in relative terms (i.e. in terms of assuring social network centrality) the more widespread they are. People who attend HE no longer occupy the same advantageous social network position that they used to, so they are no longer as successful in obtaining meaningful opportunities to participate. In the absence of an alternative sorting mechanism, it is increasingly difficult to distribute such opportunities to such a large population that seeks them. The result is a drop in overall participation rates, despite rising levels of absolute education in that population.

The notion that the relationship between HE and civic participation can be explained by the 'relative effects' of education on securing social status is appealing. It provides a framework for understanding the contribution that HE can make to society within the context of greatly expanded rates of participation in HE. Yet, despite the potential of both the 'proxy' explanation and the 'relative effects' model, their relevance within the British context has not been established. What's more, there has been a lack of any detailed examination of how, exactly, HE, including the experience of going to university, studying for a degree and participating in university life, might help explain this relationship between higher levels of education and civic participation which has been so well documented (Dalton, 2013; Dee, 2004; Egerton, 2002; Emler & Frazer, 1999; Nie et al., 1996; Sloam, 2014). These two concerns are at the centre of this chapter.

2.3 HE and Civic Participation: Exploring the Relationship

To gain a better understanding of the relationship between HE and civil society, research undertaken at the Wales Institute of Social and Economic Research, Data and Methods (WISERD) has brought to the fore questions about universities' civic contribution through analysis of large-scale survey data and qualitative interviews with graduates from a range of UK universities. Through exploration of large scale data-sets, including the British Household Panel study (BHPS), the UK Household

Longitudinal Survey (UKHLS) and the National Child Development (NCDS) study, this research has revealed some important relationships between HE and participation in those institutions, organisations and societies which together make up civil society. They also provided some insights regarding the way in which various university experiences, including the curriculum, pedagogical and social experiences might invariably encourage or amplify social and political attitudes and, in turn, civic participation. Analysis of the UKHLS data revealed that, overall, having a HE qualification makes someone more likely to engage in community associations (except for membership of trade unions and social clubs). Absolute levels of education are powerful determinants of a person's likelihood of participating in community associations.

That said, the effect of having a HE qualification varies with the type of association a person engages with. For example, having a degree is apparently a more important determinant of whether someone joins a sports club rather than a political party. We also find, however, that relative levels of education (i.e., their level of education in comparison with those around them) clearly matter in some cases, though the effect is variable across different associations and it is typically weaker than that of absolute education. Taking the example of participation in sports clubs, while people with degrees are more likely to join sports clubs than those without degrees, this effect is dampened somewhat if they happen to live in an area where people their age are considerably less well educated than they are. In other words, people with degrees are more likely to join sports clubs, but become less likely to do so if they are more highly educated than other people in the community who are also likely to join. Relative education is particularly important when it comes to a person's likelihood of joining a trade union. Absolute education has little impact: your level of education (and the skills, values and knowledge with which it provides you) has little to do with whether or not you join a trade union. What is more important is how your education compares with that of those around you: people who are considerably more educated than those around them are significantly more likely to join a union than those who have average levels of education.

This is the only instance, however, in which an individual's relative level of education was more important than their absolute level for determining whether they joined any given association. Since our findings suggest that, overall, higher levels of education are associated with a greater likelihood of civic participation, they leave unexplained the HE-civic participation paradox. Nor do they allow us to reject the possibility that HE might be masking other factors which impact on both HE participation and civic participation rates. They do, however, challenge assertions that rising numbers of graduates in British society might be in some way detrimental to the health of British civil society, as they suggest, overall, that higher levels of education should be positively associated with civic participation. Yet our findings also suggest that one's relative education matters in certain key ways.

Other research also suggests that relative education is more important than absolute levels of education for certain forms of political participation, such as voting, joining political parties, or taking part in political campaigns (Campbell, 2009; Nie et al., 1996; Tenn, 2007). These insights are significant in the context of debates about the effects of the massification of HE on society. As the UK has witnessed a shift from an elite to a mass HE system in recent decades (Trow, 2005), there are now important questions about the extent to which the contribution that HE makes to civil society has evolved, changed, or perhaps stayed the same over this period. This question is particularly pertinent given that our analyses suggest that relative education level matters to an individual's likelihood of participation in community associations, which prompts questions regarding the extent to which the massification of HE has led to changes in people's patterns of participation.

To explore this in detail we compared the civic participation of graduates from two distinct HE systems: 'elite' and 'mass'. In our analyses, we compared graduates who participated in an elite HE system (i.e. before the end of the 1980s when fewer than 15% of the population participated), with those who participated in a 'mass' HE system (in which more than 15% participated after the end of the 1980s). We found that graduates in our sample were more likely to be members of trade unions, environmental groups, residents' associations, religious organisations and sports clubs irrespective of whether they studied in an 'elite' or 'mass' HE systems. However, the 'effect' of being a graduate from an 'elite' or 'mass' HE system in terms of their likelihood of associational membership was hugely varied; 'elite' HE system graduates were more likely to participate in some types of associations whilst 'mass' system graduates were more likely to participate in other types, particularly, more traditional organisations. Our findings indicate that the type of HE system an individual participated in has important bearings on their likelihood of civic participation. These findings raised a variety of further questions regarding why and how participation in a particular HE system (elite or mass) should matter for civic participation and indeed what mechanisms are at play here. Whilst these questions exceeded the focus of our project we nonetheless sought to explore the precise nature of the relationship between HE and civic participation. This was addressed through our qualitative examination of graduates' civic participation and the role of their HE experiences in relation to this.

2.4   What Does HE 'Do' to Cultivate Civic Participation?

Having established a relationship between HE and civil society we wanted to explore the role of various HE experiences (including degree courses, types of university attended, social experiences) in graduates' civic participation rates. We sought to understand the precise nature of the relationship between HE and civic participation and the extent to which different kinds of HE experiences, including curricular, pedagogical and social experiences might matter to adulthood civic participation. To examine this, we interviewed 29 graduates, all of whom were aged 30–40 and who had participated in a 'mass' HE system in one of three different types of university. In total, we interviewed 11 Oxbridge graduates, 10 Russell Group university graduates and eight graduates from post-92 universities. Typically, they had graduated from university in the late 1990s to mid-2000s. The graduates had studied a range of degree disciplines and included nine social sciences graduates, eleven STEM graduates, seven arts and humanities graduates, and two business studies graduates. The interviews explored graduates' university experiences in detail including their experiences of their respective courses, the curriculum content of what they had studied at university and the nature of its delivery (i.e. the pedagogical experiences, including lectures, seminars, tutorials, and forms of assessment) and the kinds of social experiences they enjoyed whilst at university. We also asked graduates to reflect on their childhood experiences of education as well as participation in clubs, activities and societies. Lastly, we asked participants to tell us about their current participation in clubs and societies and the nature of their political participation, including their thoughts about the role of the university in cultivating their social and political views and attitudes, and the patterns of their current participation.

2.5   The 'Amplification' of Social and Political Values by HE

The interviews revealed some striking relationships between graduates' HE experiences and their civic participation: they revealed commonalities between graduates who had studied similar degree programmes in terms of their patterns of civic and political participation, as well as differences between those who had studied different degree courses and at different universities. Whilst Social Science graduates were most likely to be politically active, and Social Science and Arts and Humanities graduates were also highly active in terms of their adulthood civic participation, STEM graduates were not only the least active in terms of their political participation. They also tended to express less interest in politics or have any strong sense of loyalty towards or affiliation to any single party. Where they did participate in clubs or activities, these tended to be sports-related rather than aimed at cultural or political activities. These patterns could be at least partly explained by the way in which pre-university experiences (including childhood interests and patterns of participation, and social class background) cultivated both interest in subject discipline as well as social and political values and attitudes which in turn influenced civic participation. However, our data revealed an important, if subtle, role of the university in this relationship. For many of the Social Science and Arts and Humanities graduates, their degree appeared to have intensified or amplified their pre-existing social and political values which in turn had a knock-on effect in terms of their political and civic participation. The Social Science graduates tended to reflect on the way in which the social and political attitudes they'd held before starting their university course had been amplified or exacerbated by the degree they had studied for. For many of these graduates, acquiring new knowledge of social and political issues served to reinforce their pre-existing views. Amongst these graduates, learning about society including historical or contemporary social and political issues through studying politics, social science or humanities subjects appeared to develop and cultivate ideas, understandings and values which were conducive to participation. What's more, these graduates routinely reflected on the way in which their degree had helped them develop critical thinking, debating or discussion skills which had, in their view, been important in fostering their participation. By contrast, the STEM graduates were more likely to reflect on the more limited opportunities to develop debating, discussion and critical thinking skills during their under-graduate studies, placing greater emphasis on the way in which their degree had developed problem-solving skills.

We also sought to explore the extent to which studying at a particular kind of institution has any bearing on graduates' patterns of political and civic participation. A comparison of Social Science graduates who had studied at different kinds of institutions revealed that Oxbridge Social Science graduates made most reference to having opportunity to develop skills which were beneficial for civic participation such as debating and critical thinking skills. This suggested that the distinct peda-gogical practices present at Oxbridge, including the tutorial system in which students are expected to write essays and discuss them with a tutor, provides an important environment for fostering these skills. Moreover, such an intense pedagogical expe-rience in which the student is expected to discuss and debate their work with a tutor was, for some students, a mechanism for fostering greater levels of confidence and self-assuredness which for some appeared to have facilitated their adulthood partic-ipation.

These findings reveal important insights about the relationship between HE and participation in civil society. Whilst pre-university experiences (including childhood experiences) are likely to impact on both choice of degree course as well as levels of political and social participation, the degree course studied does appear to play an important role in amplifying these attitudes and values which underpin political and civic participation. They also indicate that the nature of the pedagogical expe-rience is important in mediating the relationship between the degree course studied and participation in civil society, with some pedagogical environments in HE being particularly effective in fostering the sorts of skills and attributes needed for civic participation.

2.6   Conclusion

The findings of our study have considerable implications for debates about univer-sities' contribution to society: they suggest that HE as an institution is valuable to society in a way that extends far beyond a mere economic contribution. This is sig-nificant given the emphasis in UK policy on widening participation in HE in recent years (BIS, 2011; Welsh Government, 2009). In recent decades, the governments of all four home nations of the UK have placed significant emphasis on widening access and participation, reflecting both economic and social justice imperatives. Improving rates of participation in HE amongst social groups under-represented within it has largely been justified in terms of the potential economic benefits for society and indi-viduals (BIS, 2016). In these terms, widening participation is also justified on social justice grounds, with HE seen as a key route for upwards social mobility (BIS, 2016; Welsh Government, 2009). However, if HE plays a role in fostering the skills and knowledge needed for civic participation, as our research indicates, there is strong justification for widening participation in HE which extends far beyond that of an economic rationale. Rather, justification on the grounds of enhanced social and cultural capital is also possible. Since collective participation in the sorts of societies, clubs and associations which make up civil society is both a source and product of social capital (Putnam, 2000), then widening participation in HE can be justified not just on the grounds of fostering greater economic equality, but also of promoting social equality.

What's more, our findings that HE matters to graduates' civic participation, (especially those degree subjects which cultivate critical thinking, debating and arguing skills) have substantial implications for debates about the future funding of UK HE. Our research revealed that some university subjects are especially important for developing those skills and knowledge that are beneficial for supporting graduates' civic participation. This evokes the arguments of several researchers (Freedman, 2003; Nussbaum, 1997) who have emphasised the value of liberal arts HE for fostering critical thinking, reasoning, debate and discussion skills, and a sense of collective social responsibility. Our findings suggest that the kinds of HE Nussbaum (1997) and others celebrate (including arts, humanities, and social science subjects) may be important spaces for developing these skills. And yet in recent years, many schools and departments for art, humanities and social sciences within parts of the UK (and indeed internationally) have faced considerable funding cuts at the hands of Government policy agendas which have prioritised STEM subjects (Gov.Uk 2013; UK Parliament 2018). Whilst STEM subjects have been celebrated for the direct contribution they make to the 'knowledge economy,' the drastic oversight on the part of HE policy makers regarding the valuable offerings of social science subjects (in terms of their cultivation of skills, knowledge and values highly beneficial for individuals and society) may have significant implications. Failure to recognise the positive contributions that the social sciences, arts and humanities degrees offer society has, potentially significant consequences for the health of a democratic society.

Whilst our research contributes to the arguments made in favour of the kind of HE programmes that cultivate skills, attributes and knowledge that is beneficial to society, we do not deny HE roles in the reproduction of social and economic inequalities. As discussed above, HE's 'effect' on graduates' civic participation rates is not equal. In our research, the graduates were not equally placed in terms of their capacity for civic participation, reflecting key divergences in the degree discipline that they had studied for, and the universities that they had studied at. Some universities, degree programmes, and university 'experiences' appear to play a more or less important role in equipping graduates with the skills and credentials needed to take part actively in civic life. The graduates in our study varied in the extent to which they were likely to engage in civic participation, or in their patterns of political participation in adulthood. It seems that some university experiences (and some degrees subjects studied) were more significant than others in terms of amplifying pre-existing social and political attitudes. This suggests that within a massified HE system, students are not homogenous, whether in terms of their experiences of HE, or in terms of what they will gain from it. These differences are not limited to those that are associated with employment opportunities (Chevalier & Conlon, 2003).

Elite HE experiences continue to exist, and these elite experiences are particularly effective in cultivating the sorts of skills and attributes needed for meaningful civic participation. Thus, whilst widening participation might be justified on the grounds of addressing social inequality, our findings also urge us to consider the role of HE in reproducing inequalities in society, many of which are not simply economic but are related directly to inequality of access to social and cultural capital. These findings therefore bring to the fore questions which have remained at the periphery of policy debates about the contribution of HE to civil society: such questions should urge policy makers to consider just how universities can be made more equitable in terms of their capacity to encourage and foster active citizenship, and indeed social capital amongst graduates. More generally, our findings also contribute to debates about the implications of massification in HE as they clearly challenge any notion that such massification will lead to reduced patterns of participation. Whilst our findings do not allow us to solve the education-civil society participation paradox, they do suggest that stifling rates of participation in HE is not the answer. Notwithstanding, they urge us to consider more fully the implications of massification, around which debate so far has tended to focus exclusively on questions over the consequences of increasing rates of HE participation for graduate employability. There has been little equivalent discussion around the extent to which relative education levels might matter in terms of an individual's participation in civil society. Whilst absolute education matters most, in some cases, relative education level also matters which indicates that massification might have implications not only for graduates' employability, but also participation in civic life and thus for the accruement of social capital. If congested labour markets encourage graduates to pursue ever-increasing levels of education to 'get ahead' in the labour market (Brown, 2003), we might also speculate that graduates will likely also pursue increasing levels of post-graduate education in a bid to secure advantageous social positions and higher levels of social capital. If such a situation arises, this might potentially fuel greater social inequalities along the lines of economic and social capital, between those who can invest in ever increasing levels of education and those who cannot.

References

Annette, J. (2005). *Character, civil renewal and service learning for democratic citizenship in HE.* Paper 15. [Online] Available at: https://digitalcommons.unomaha.edu/slceciviceng/15/?utm_source=digitalcommons.unomaha.edu%2Fslceciviceng%2F15&utm_medium=PDF&utm_campaign=PDFCoverPages. Accessed 21/0/18.

Berinsky, A. J., & Lenz, G. S. (2011). Education and political participation: Exploring the causal link. *Political Behavior, 33*(3), 357–373.

Birdal, M., & Ongan, T. H. (2016). Why do we care about having more than others? Socioeconomic determinants of positional concerns in different domains. *Social Indicators Research, 126,* 727–738.

Brown, P. (2003). The Opportunity trap: Education and employment in a global economy. *European Educational Research Journal, 2*(1), 141–179.

Campbell, D. E. (2009). Civic engagement and education: An empirical test of the sorting model. *American Journal of Political Science, 53*(4), 771–786.

Chevalier, A. N., & Conlon, G. (2003). *Does it pay to attend a Prestigious University?*. London: Centre for the Economics of Education, LSE.

Collins, R. (1979). *The credential society: An historical sociology of education and stratification.* New York, NY: Academic Press.

Dalton, R. J. (2013). *The Apartisan American*. Thousand Oaks: CQ Press.

Dee, T. S. (2004). Are there civic returns to education? *Journal of Public Economics, 88*(9), 1697–1720.

Department for Buisness, Innovation and Skills. (2011). *Higher education: Students at the heart of the system*. London: Department for Business, Innovation and Skills.

Department for Business, Innovation and Skills. (2016). *Success as a knowledge economy: Teaching excellence, social mobility and student choice*. London: Department for Business, Innovation and Skills.

Egerton, M. (2002). HE and civic engagement. *The British Journal of Sociology, 53*(4), 603–620.

Emler, N., & Frazer, E. (1999). Politics: The education effect. *Oxford Review of Education, 25*(1–2), 251–273.

Freedman, J. O. (2003). *Liberal education and the public interest*. Iowa City: University of Iowa Press.

Goddard, J. (2009). *Reinventing the Civic University*. London: NESTA.

Goddard, J., & Kempton, L. (2016). *The Civic University. Universities in leadership and management of place.* Centre for Urban and Regional Development Studies, Newcastle university.

Hazelkorn, K. (2016). *Towards 2030: A framework for building a world-class post-compulsory education system for Wales.*

Helliwell, J. F., & Putnam, R. D. (2007). Education and social capital. *Eastern Economic Journal, 33*(1), 1–19.

Hirsch, F. (1977). *Social limits to growth*. London: Routledge and Kegan Paul.

Kam, C. D., & Palmer, C. L. (2008). Reconsidering the effects of education on political participation. *Journal of Politics, 70*(3), 612–631.

Luskin, R. C. (1990). Explaining political sophistication. *Political Behaviour, 12*(4), 331–361.

Nie, N. H., et al. (1996). *Education and democratic citizenship in America*. London: University of Chicago Press.

Nussbaum, M. (1997). *Cultivating humanity*. London: Harvard University Press.

Persson, M. (2012). Does type of education affect political participation? Results from a panel survey of Swedish adolescents. *Scandinavian Political Studies, 35*(3), 198–221.

Putnam, R. D. (2000). *Bowling alone: The collapse and revival of American Community*. New York: Simon and Schuster.

Sloam, J. (2014). New voice, less equal the civic and political engagement of young people in the United States and Europe. *Comparative Political Studies, 47*(5), 663–688.

Tenn, S. (2007). The effect of education on voter turnout. *Political Analysis, 15*(4), 446–464.

Trow, M. A. (2005). Reflections on the transition from elite to mass to universal access: Forms and phases of HE in modern societies since WWII. In: J. J. F. Forest & P. G. Altbach (Eds.), *International handbook of HE* (pp. 243–280). Heidelberg: Springer.

Universities, U. K. (2014). *The economic impact of HE Institutions in England. Summary report.* London: Universities UK.

Verba, S., et al. (1995). *Voice and equality: Civic voluntarism in American politics*. Cambridge University Press.

Welsh Government. (2009). *For our future. The 21st Century HE Strategy and Plan for Wales.* Cardiff: Welsh Assembly Government: Department for Children, Education, Lifelong learning and Skills.

Williams, K. (2016). *In full: Kirst Williams challenge to Welsh Universities over Brexit* (Online). Available at: https://www.libdemvoice.org/in-full-kirsty-williams-challenge-to-welsh-universities-over-brexit-51806.html. Accessed August 14, 2018.

Ceryn Evans (Ph.D.) is a lecturer in the School of Education, Swansea University, Wales. Her research interests fall broadly within the sociology of education and she has carried out research in areas including post-16 transitions, widening participation in HE, and civil society. She completed her Ph.D. in the School of Social Sciences at Cardiff University in 2014.

Stuart Fox (Ph.D.) is a quantitative research associate at the Wales Institute for Social and Economic Research, Date and Methods (WISERD), Cardiff, Wales. Stuart provides quantitative research expertise to ongoing projects in WISERD's Civil Society Research Centre and develops new research projects that build on the overlap between his ongoing research and the interests of the Centre.

Chris Taylor (B.A.) is a Professor of Education at Cardiff University and Co-Director of Wales Institute for Social and Economic Research, Date and Methods (WISERD). Chris led the Welsh Government funded independent three-year evaluation of the Foundation Phase. He also helped lead the recent evaluation of the Pupil Development Grant (PDG). Chris has published extensively on a range of educational issues, from early years education to widening access to Higher Education.

Chapter 3
Learning Gain: Can It Be Measured?

Peter Gossman and Stephen Powell

3.1 Introduction: Measuring 'Learning Gain'

With an increasing tendency to see higher education as a product with a price tag, there is understandably growing interest in the extent to which academic programmes of study promote students' employability and earning power. (The Quality Assurance Agency for Higher Education (QAA), 2013, para. 1)

This chapter addresses the 'basics' underpinning the notion of learning gain including its measurement and the motivations behind the recent interest in quantifying (and attributing) changes in students, as brought about by their learning experiences at university. However, it is firstly worth considering a rather larger question: if we wish to quantify some gain in learning then arguably we first need to define *what* we are really seeking to measure, rather than starting from a position of what *might* actually be measured, in the hope that *something* can be found. This is a criticism that could perhaps be laid against the Higher Education Funding Council for England (HEFCE) learning gain programme (which will be addressed later). Put simply, learning gain becomes a different thing according to the instrument of measurement applied to it. Further, if we measure learning gain in one particular way, this says something about the kind of learning, and any gains within it, that we most value.

There are many stakeholders within the UK's higher education (HE) system, and when considering what to measure, it is important to recognise that there are different views about what the purpose of higher education is and, by extension, what we should measure to assess the effectiveness of particular approaches. For example, physicists may put great store in assessing key concepts that are core to becoming

P. Gossman (✉)
University of Worcester, Worcester, UK
e-mail: p.gossman@worc.ac.uk

S. Powell
Manchester Metropolitan University, Manchester, UK
e-mail: stephen.powell@mmu.ac.uk

© Springer Nature Switzerland AG 2019   37
A. Diver (ed.), *Employability via Higher Education: Sustainability as Scholarship*,
https://doi.org/10.1007/978-3-030-26342-3_3

a physicist (Sands, Parker, Hedgeland, Jordan, & Galloway, 2018: 610): this might be done using inventory tools, but this is very different from assessing progress against broader curricular aims. For many students and employers, a state of work-readiness may be considered a core outcome of any university experience, although this is also a contested viewpoint (Cameron, Wharton, & Scally, 2018, p. 41). From a national funding perspective, one of the key purposes of measuring learning gain is to allow comparisons of the effectiveness of learning processes between different institutions, and to better understand what works and why. This is possibly motivated by a political desire to promote greater market competition (Blackmore & Kandiko, 2012). Professional associations, employers, parents, and students all have views on the purpose of a university education and, by inference, what learning gain should be measured. What are the implications of this for selecting the means of measurement? In an era of increasing institutional competition, could the sector come to agreement or will competing values result in a mixed economy of measurement determined by local needs and values?

It can be argued that the need to measure gain in HE is in fact due to the problem of not knowing what HE produces in terms of graduate outcomes, although many institutions have codified their expectations of what it means to be a graduate. Of course, this is not easy to answer simply, and HEFCE, in running a range of projects, notes that any valued gain exists in relation to a specific context, defining it as: 'The improvement in knowledge, skills, work-readiness and personal development made by students during higher education' (HEFCE, 2015). This broad definition does not discriminate between learning gain and the 'value added' aspects of education however (again, an issue that will be unpacked later in this chapter.) In contrast to a contextual approach, learning gain can instead be framed as a measure of account-ability. However, this is perhaps a circular argument, since if students are prepared to pay (albeit in many contexts through soft loans) and commit to a significant amount of effort, then they must in some way value the product on offer. Nonetheless, as Shavelson and Huang (2003) stressed, calls for assessment-based accountability are unlikely to go away. Similarly, the Organisation for Economic Cooperation and Development (OECD) has noted that:

> In a complex, ever changing and growing higher education context, where a variety of rankings are often being used as the yardstick of academic excellence, there is a clear need for a way to effectively measure the actual outcomes of teaching and learning. (OECD, 2013, p. 2)

Shavelson and Huang (2003) also note that the diversity of HE institutions in the US (in terms of inputs, processes, outputs and valued outcomes) is vast, and that there are obvious parallels with the UK. The following section explores learning gain using Biesta's (2015) functions of education to propose a contextual framework that takes account of the plurality of valued outcomes and outputs of HEIs. We suggest that consideration must be given to the question of what institutions should measure in terms of learning, before jumping straight to the measurement of what can be easily measured: the latter approach has great potential both for distortion of results and is quite open to the effects of unintended consequences.

3.2 A Contextual Framework for Learning Gain?

Gossman, Powell and Neame (2018) use Biesta's (2015) three functions of education to consider learning gain in relation to institutions' mission statements around learning. These functions are: qualification, socialisation and subjectification. Some measures of learning gain will fit neatly into the 'qualification' category. 'Qualification,' is about an ability to do something:

> a 'doing' that can range from the very specific (such as in the case of training for a particular job or profession, or the training of a particular skill or technique) to the much more general (such as an introduction to modern culture, or the teaching of life skills, etcetera). (Biesta, 2015, p. 19)

Immediately within this 'doing,' a wide range of learning gain measurements could be undertaken. HEFCE argue that an appropriate measure of gain is therefore one that is suited to the context of the institution as perhaps outlined in a mission statement. If we take a simple example, we could test a student on their ability to describe the role of 'x' and 'y' in the function of 'z'. The test could then be applied at the start of a course of study and then repeated at the end. The difference between the results is the quantified learning gain in that aspect of 'qualification,' i.e. the one that we value. Biesta (2015) notes further that 'qualification' has a range of purposes that are not just economic insofar as this can also contribute to 'citizenship or cultural literacy more generally' (2015, p. 11). This serves as a further illustration of the debate surrounding educational purpose. Biesta's second function of education is socialisation: 'Through its socializing function education inserts individuals into existing ways of doing and being' (2015, p. 19). This function is perhaps most apparent when an institution adopts a particular ethos, or the course a student enrols upon relates to a set of professional values and practices that a student is then acculturated into (e.g. nursing or accountancy).

It is worth emphasising that whatever is identified as the key aspect of education to measure for learning gain also has a political context (aside from being valued, in itself). Clarke (2017) further notes that the 'pressure to provide evidence of the value and effectiveness of tertiary education has come from two main sources—governments and employer groups' (2017, p. 1). This statement has a bearing on both the skills within a given 'qualification,' and on the need for demonstrable learning gain in the first place. Put broadly, the assessment of HE learning outcomes (if we assume that learning gain *can* be defined and is measurable) can provide a comparison between individuals, and, when aggregated and benchmarked, between the courses studied, and the institutions where studying occurs. It is then a short step to league tables of learning gain and an overly simplified notion of greater gain equating to a better education and possibly better value for money.

The pressure, as noted above, from employer groups relates to graduate employability and the development of skills and attributes by students during their course: communication, teamworking, and problem solving (Sin & Neave, 2014). The range of titles for these skills, includes such terms as "transferable skills, generic skills, generic attributes, generic competences, generic capabilities or key skills" (Jääskelä,

Nykänen, & Tynjälä, 2016, p. 132) and is indicative of the scope of the field. As Jääskelä et al. note 'these terms refer to competencies that education should provide regardless of the specific field and that can be used in a variety of tasks' (2016, p. 132). This is a key point, which raises the question of whether there is a set of competences that HE should provide? Operationalising concepts to enable these to be measured is a rich field for learning gain. See for example, the Wabash longitudinal study in the United States which examined the graduate outcomes of a liberal arts education (2006–2012).[1] The selected outcomes are presented as follows:

• Critical thinking	• Positive attitude toward literacy
• Moral reasoning	• Interest in contributing to the arts
• Socially responsible leadership	• Interest in contributing to the sciences
• Interest in engaging intellectually challenging work	• Openness to engaging new ideas and diverse people
• Interest in political and social involvement	• Orientation toward interacting with diverse people
• Well-being	• Academic motivation

As Biesta observed, aside from 'qualification' and 'socialisation,' the act of 'subjectification' is also an educational function. This process should 'allow those educated [to] become more autonomous and independent in their thinking and acting' (2015, p. 20). This has immediate appeal and it is hard to argue against this function being a key HE aim and/or outcome, with graduates gaining enhanced autonomy and the ability to engage in moral reasoning.

3.3   The Mechanics of Learning Gain

Implicit in learning gain and any measurement of it (especially if it is to be applied to individual students) is that it must involve two measurements, one at the start of a time-period—perhaps a course of study—and one at the end of it. Learning gain as such, for a student, is a simple idea and can be outlined as a pre/post test score difference (T_1 to T_2 position P_1 to P_4, as per Fig. 3.1). This appears to be straightforward and can be referred to as the 'distance travelled' by a student. However, in practice, in an HE context, it is rather more complex, especially if linked to benchmarked comparisons, where for example, any given student's gain is then compared to gains made by 'similar' students. Boud (2018) describes what would be required for assessment approaches to measure learning gain at a programme (or course) level, which essentially comes down to the application of a consistent set

---

[1] Ernest T. Pascarella & Charles Blaich (2013) Lessons from the Wabash National Study of Liberal Arts Education, *Change: The Magazine of Higher Learning*, 45:2, 6–15, DOI: https://doi.org/10.1080/00091383.2013.764257.

Learning Gain

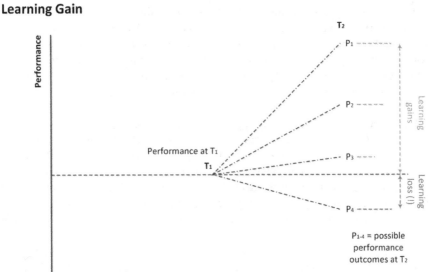

Fig. 3.1 Visualisation of individual learning gain

of learning outcomes and graduated set of assessment criteria across the levels of a given programme. Although this approach could work at a programme level, it does nothing to address the desire for comparisons between institutions. A clear illustration of where the above approach works is in the compulsory education sector in England. There, a national curriculum framework sets out the programme of study and attainment targets for children from early years (age 3) to the end of Key Stage 4 (age 16). Initially the focus is on reading, writing and maths, before broadening out in Key stage 3 and 4 to a wider range of subjects. Because children are studying the same curriculum and have standardised assessments at the end of Key stage 1 and 2 (culminating for most in GCSE examinations at year 11), it is possible to measure the gain of individuals and groups of students and compare them against each other.[2] In HE, there is no structured national curriculum nor are there national assessment standards beyond the QAA subject benchmark statements and standards set by professional regulatory bodies.

In Fig. 3.1 the performance of a student is measured by a test/assessment at the start of a programme or module (T_1). There are many factors to be considered here. For example, how long will the assessment be, when will it be administered, could/should all students take it at the same time (if they do not, what variations in results might occur due to some unknown effect modifier?) and how many assessments will a student take? Following T_1, the student undertakes their programme of study and

---

[2] See further https://www.compare-school-performance.service.gov.uk (accessed 10.11.18).

is re-tested at T_2 on, for example, their teamwork skills. Again, there are issued to be considered: should the test be the same one, administered twice? Should it be a different one with the validity of the test assured in some way? At very least the test must reliably address the same outcomes using consistent assessment criteria calibrated for the level of study. In Fig. 3.1 three gain results are shown: P_1, P_2 and P_3 alongside one learning loss position (perhaps an unlikely outcome), P_4. When the results of P_1–P_4 are aggregated across a programme of study and averaged (Pmean), the mean course/programme learning gain can be represented.

Further questions arise: to whom can the learning again be attributed? In the case of an individual, we might ask if the gain is solely that of the student? This would seem a logical answer, but gains might also be attributed to the teacher(s) of the programme, or perhaps to the student's parents or guardians, or to their friends and the encouragement they give. The average gain across a group of students might seem to be better attributed to the teachers, programme and institution, but is this really the case?

Taking this reasoning further, programme learning gains could in turn be aggregated together as a measure of institutional learning gain, as shown in Fig. 3.2. However, the challenge of comparing learning gain between institutions rests upon the adoption of a common set of standards across the sector: everyone needs to be measuring the same set of things for this to work in a sensible way. Of course, this is not the case, and this is in part the reason why university league tables depend

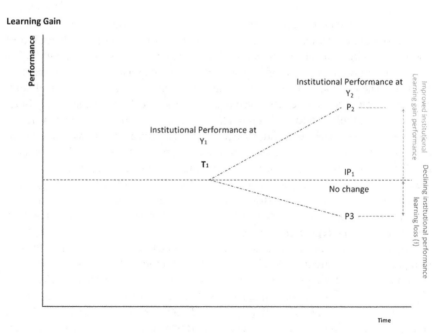

Fig. 3.2 Visualisation of institutional learning gain

upon proxies for learning gain, such as employability that measure (arguably) the work-readiness aspects of learning gain (Cameron et al., 2018).

The next section highlights possible debates around what might be used as measures of learning gain and some of the challenges to be faced. For example, can learning gain for an institution simply be the aggregated and averaged difference between the two scores (at T_1 and T_2) for all that institution's students? At what point should pre and post-testing take place? Might different times for these tests mean different results for a student, or a particular group of students, or for different types of institutions? Can these mean scores for institutions be compared between different parts of an institution and across the sector? If this is not the case then pre/post score differences make less sense and a more benchmarked approach (with all the complexity that it brings in terms of predicting student progress on entry to an institution and tracking their progression at exit from the institution) becomes more meaningful. This in turn moves learning gain closer to a 'value-added' notion. Whatever choices are made, there are significant resource implications. It is possible that an institution's mean learning gain score could be good when compared against the whole sector mean, but worse than the comparable benchmark intuitions' mean. It is also possible to hypothesise that high UCAS tariff institutions may not be able to demonstrate a greater distance travelled as compared with institutions with a lower entry tariff.

Before discussing the possible measure of learning gain however, it is worth exploring the distinction between measures of learning gain and value added. Learning gain, as illustrated above, involves an ipsative comparison. In other words, for an individual student, the T_2 result is referenced back to a T_1 result. In the case of value-added (see for example the A-Level Information System [Alis[3]]), the learning of the student is compared with a statistically predicted result. In the case of A-Level examinations, the grade of the A-level is assigned a numeric score and a student's actual result is compared with the statistically predicted result, extrapolated from GCSE results, and considering attitudinal data from the Alis questionnaire, which can in turn help understand a student's attitude to their learning environment. A range of other factors (such as postcode, socio-economic background or ethnicity) can be used in a context value added approach (CVA), to consider a wider range of variables that might impact upon learning. When the difference between actual and predicted results is positive then there is value-added and vice versa. Like learning gain, these individual scores can be aggregated and averaged, again for courses and institutions. And yet, there is a note of caution to be sounded here: the student population at universities can be highly selective, depending largely upon the filters of previous academic results. This means that not only will learners have different starting points but also that there will be concentrations of different ability levels within different institutions. In effect, this is like a setting in selective schools and

---

[3] 'Alis' is a value-added measurement, described by Durham University's Centre for Evaluation and Monitoring (CEM) as 'providing detailed value-added progress information for each student and subject at the end of the course.' (CEM, 2017, para. 1). Alis was originally a straightforward value-added system: currently, more sophisticated versions are available whereby a test adapted according to student responses can be used to provide a learner benchmark.

it would be expected that those student (who have proven already to have the most ability) would outperform their peers, having both higher levels of learning gain and apparently higher value added. However (as the Sutton Trust found), such

> ...so-called 'grammar school effect' disappeared once they took into account the fact that pupils who entered grammar school were progressing faster than their peers before they entered the grammar schools... Theirs is a self-selected sample predisposed to prepare for and take entry tests and perform well, so they do much better than those of a similar general ability, (Wheadon, 2013, p. 1).

Arguably, to make more secure judgements about value-added, a sophisticated CVA approach is required.

3.4 What May Be Measured (HEFCE Learning Gain Projects)

At the time of writing, HEFCE (now The Office for Students)[4] notes five potential ways of measuring learning gain. These measures stem from a RAND European report (McGrath, Guerin, Harte, Frearson, & Manville, 2015) in which 14 potential methods for measuring learning gain were reviewed and allocated to one of five ways. They are: grades, surveys, standardised tests, mixed methods, and other qualitative methods. Some of these are inspired by the potential for technical developments within the realm of learning analytics and linked data. Grades are a self-explanatory measure, but the lack of granularity in outcomes-based assessment as used in many HE systems causes significant issues (Boud, 2018). The five grade bands (1st class, 2:1 and so on) are too broad to illustrate gain between entry and exit for a student on any given course. In addition to this, there are serious challenges in attempting comparison across disciplines and institutions. In part, it is this lack of precision with grades that prompts some of the debate in relation to the requirements of illustrating learning gain. Self-reporting surveys by students report on gain extent in relation to what is asked, again, via an ipsative approach. For example, the National Student Survey (NSS) asks students about communication skills (Q.20).

As McGrath et al. (2015) note, this is only one of three potential learning gain questions from the NSS: The United Kingdom Engagement Survey, (UKES) contains 12 skills development questions (see Table 3.1, for an example that relates directly to Biesta's (2015) educational purpose of socialisation).

Currently, the NSS and UKES are only undertaken once during a student's course of study. This would need to be addressed to allow T_1 and T_2 comparisons of gain. Other possible surveys include: student skills audits, surveys of workplace skills and surveys of career readiness. In all cases the problems of self-reporting are apparent, as is the potential for such surveys to be 'gamed,' perhaps via the artificial depression of pre-test scores or some degree of 'coaching' of students by academic staff towards

---

[4]See The Office for Students (OfS) website https://www.officeforstudents.org.uk/advice-and-guidance/teaching/learning-gain/ (accessed 09.11.18).

Table 3.1 UKES learning gain sample question

How much has your experience at this institution contributed to your knowledge, skills and personal development in (Q9) Being an informed and active citizen: (Response categories)
very much / quite a bit / some / very little

desired responses that are mutually beneficial. Standardised tests can be generic (e.g. the Collegiate Learning Assessment test) or discipline-specific, and seek to measure gain in identified, stated skills. Discipline tests, as McGrath et al. (2015) note, can be more readily compared and thus have greater validity than generic ones. They give the example of repeatedly testing medical students during their studies using an exam of 125 items. Clearly testing like this is demanding of resources, even just in terms of generating questions, but it can provide longitudinal data for each student as well as school comparisons, so long as there is consistent use of the test instruments.

These first three of HEFCE's five categories for measuring learning gain (i.e. grades, standardised tests, and self-reporting surveys) can all be administered to follow the simple 'distance travelled' model (T_1 to T_2 position P_1 to P_4, as per Fig. 3.1). Existing data collection instruments within institutions could be modified to make them suitable to this approach but in all cases there are significant administration costs. The least costly option might be via grades using a system similar to Alis. However, this still fails to take account of context value added, an approach strongly recommended by the Fisher Family Trust for Schools (Thompson, 2018). Mixed methods (as the name suggests) is the use of combined tools to track student performance changes. This draws on a range of tools and indicators to track improvements in performance (for example through a combination of grades, student learning data and student surveys). In terms of truly representing learning gain, such approaches arguably have the most to offer as they recognise the complexity of the challenge being faced. Balancing out the relative contributions of the different measures, and the resources required to administer such an approach, remain significant, however. It may be that in the medium and longer-term developments in the sophistication of learning analytics and the ability to more readily stitch together different data sets will make such approaches increasingly possible.

The fifth category, other qualitative methods, is rather more grounded in mastery of learning and is markedly different from pre/post difference. These encourage students to reflect upon their own learning, acquired skills, and any skills gaps. They can also stimulate productive discussions between students and their tutors. Arguably, these methods offer much value insofar as they not only assess learning but serve to promote it through reflective and evaluative processes.

In terms of research done in the U.S., Benjamin and Clum (2003, para 2) outline the significant genesis of 'a new assessment approach for higher education … the Collegiate Learning Assessment (CLA) project.' (para., 2). They note that the CLA is 'an assessment that focuses on "general education skills" … [which] measures students' demonstrated ability to use information.' (para., 10). They suggest that such general education skills include, but are not limited to, critical thinking, analytical reasoning, and written communication. (para., 5). The CLA uses a pre/post testing model that also allows for 'value-added' comparisons within and between institutions (although these are produced differently to the UK version as outlined above). The method of pre/post testing is not a simple individual student T_1 to T_2 comparison and it is therefore not simply a basic measure of an individual's travelled journey. Rogers (2016) stresses however that over 200 institutions will be using CLA+ (para. 2). What is also interesting is that the CLA is voluntary but cost \$35 in 2016. Students, it is argued, will likely take the assessment to demonstrate their learning during their time at college ('to justify the price tag.)' (2016, para 1). This may be framed as the higher education 'market' spawning another 'market' to demonstrate that the HE 'product' is worth the cost. This development of a market for testing individual university learning (i.e. the CLA+) is also a change from original institution level data.[5] Apparently, a degree result offers insufficient evidence of learning gain, with the CLA+ providing a defining measure of 'learning:'

> students can no longer rely on the collection and mastery of discipline-based information…they need to be able to analyse and evaluate information, solve problems, and communicate effectively to a variety of audiences.[6]

In an Association of American Colleges and Universities (AAC&U) commissioned study (Hart Research, 2015) of 613 students and 400 employers, the students (as a percentage of the number responding) consistently reported themselves as being 'well prepared' for the workplace. For example, for the skill of 'written communication,' 65% of students responded that they were 'well prepared' as compared with 27% of employers. For critical/analytical thinking, the percentages were 66% of students and 26% of students. The smallest gap was 46% of students and 36% of employers when considering the issue of being 'well prepared' for 'staying current on technologies.' The report also asked employers about 'specific skills for a job' as compared with having gained a 'range of knowledge.' Unsurprisingly, 'both' was the preferred option. However, Arum and Roksa (2010) reported that many students (45%+) do not show any gain in the CLA, in their first two years of HE study and that the figure for the four years of study was 36%. The following section looks to the implications for higher education providers.

---

[5]Indeed, one student guide to the CLA + suggests that (for \$89) students 'will be able to demonstrate to employers how your 21st century skills attainment compares to students nationwide.' Council for Aid to Education (CAE) (2012). *Student Guide to CLA +*. (https://s3.amazonaws.com/StraighterLine/Docs/studentguide_straighterline.pdf (accessed 10.10.18).

[6]Ibid, p. 1.

3.5 Conclusion

Adopting any measurement of learning gain raises questions about the very nature and purpose of higher education. If learning gain is defined as positive change in (for example) decision-making skills how might this alter the way in which a degree is taught and/or the actual curricular content of that degree? What pedagogies might be adopted and promoted to facilitate such learning gain(s)? As Biesta (2015) noted, educational purpose must provide a starting point for institutions thinking about measuring learning gain. Figure 3.3 represents the proportion of a university's mission that could be attributed to each of Biesta's categories: qualification (the ability to do something); socialisation (professional values and practices that a student is acculturated to); and subjectification (developing autonomy in thinking and doing). These functions overlap. However, as a trigger for further discussion about the potential influence of learning gain on university mission, we present them here as discrete concepts. Thus, 'Triangle' University sees its mission as 20% subjectification, 50% qualification and 30% socialisation. It is perhaps a liberal arts focused institution and its neighbour, 'Circle University' has a mission of 10% subjectification, 80% qualification and 10% socialisation and is a much more employability/employment focused institution.

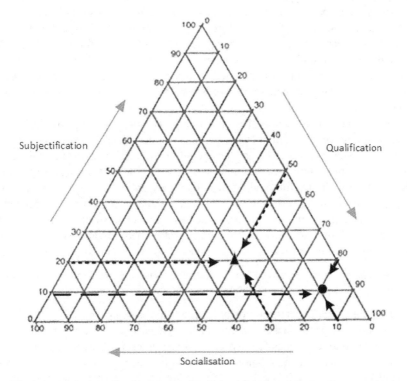

Fig. 3.3 A representation of how a university's mission might be proportionally represented

Table 3.2 Analysis of mission statements

Biesta category of purpose	Number of statements
Qualification	4
Subjectification	6
Socialisation	1
Qualification + subjectification	1
Qualification + socialisation	0
Subjectification + socialisation	2
Qualification + subjectification + socialisation	4
No evident educational purpose	2

Earlier analysis (Gossman, Powell, & Neame, 2018), based on an opportunity sample of 21 UK HEIs, found that it was possible to allocate HE mission statements to the different categories or combinations of Biesta's categories (see Table 3.2). However, the extent to which institutions take seriously the operationalisation of their mission statements in relation to learning of the student experience is debateable. Are institutions intentionally seeking to address multiple purposes here or are these examples, perhaps, of poor institutional focus? Might it be that a learning gain-focused agenda, a purpose reinforced by league tables, pushes universities, and indeed their 'customers,' further towards a qualification-focus? Arguably, for many students, the market is already primarily about qualifications for employment. We invite the reader to find and analyse their own institution's mission statement and to firstly identify it in terms of the Table 3.2 in relation to statements around learning and teaching and then (where there appear to be differing purposes), to try and locate it on Fig. 3.3.

Institutional policies and processes (from marketing for prospective students, to investment choices, for example in relation to student support services) reflect an institution's view of its mission and the overall experience that a student will receive. Arguably, the most important decisions as far as teaching and learning are concerned are not taken at the institutional level. Rather, they are made at programme levels, in respect of the unit of learning. The relationships between learner and teacher are clearly at the heart of the student experience and are where Biesta (2015) categories of purpose will be found, and where the connection between an institution's stated values and purpose are to be given real meaning. As Gibbs (2010, p. 2) concludes:

> …what best predicts educational gain is measures of educational process: in other words, what institutions do with their resources to make the most of the students they have.

This points squarely at the notion of learning gain as being something that the best run institutions can make a difference with, through the quality of teacher interactions, resulting in better outcomes for students, not just in terms of learning gain but also in relation to value added. When conversations between teaching academics touch on student motivations, it is common for the view to be expressed however that all that students care about is their grades: pedagogies that attempt to engage them via more creative teaching approaches are sometimes met with less than full enthusiasm. It could be argued that approaches such as these would do the best promote the characteristics of Biesta's subjectification category. Teachers' efforts to promote workplace visits and engagement with the subject or discipline outside of the assessed curriculum may not be welcomed by all students, but they may be very effective in the subjectification purpose of the curriculum. There is a tension here between what the purpose of higher education is, the institutional imperative to perform well in league tables, the values and motivations of teachers, and the diversity of learners with different motivations and personal desires. These forces interact in complex ways and will often be pulling in competing directions.

Once beyond a superficial consideration of learning gain and value-added, it becomes apparent that identifying appropriate metrics is more challenging than might be first anticipated. The attraction of objective, empirical measures of performance is clear to see, from the point of view of some stakeholder groups. Whatever the precise funding mechanism for higher education, whether it includes loans systems or not, the stakes are high for national governments, not least in ensuring that money is being well spent and that the system is performing in the national interests. However, when we dig beneath the surface numerous problems can be identified, starting with the heterogeneous nature of higher education institutions and their declared educational missions or purposes, not to mention the desired changes that institutions are seeking to bring about in their students and what they would logically be seeking to measure. This is a criticism that can be made of the HEFCE learning gain projects in that they started from a position of *what* could be measured without first establishing an adequate understanding of the different *purposes* of higher education within a wider educational context. Moreover, when we drill down to a more granular level the potential for diversion from an institution's stated purpose is great: discipline and subject characteristics come to bear, as do the values and priorities of teaching academics. In other words, context is important.

An obvious note of caution over learning gain needs to be sounded. If measures of learning gain are based upon what it is practical to measure, then the possibility of unintended consequences becomes very real. For example, there will be pressure on institutions to 'game' the measurements in a similar way as they perhaps do now with other league tables. The impact of linking learning gain to the student taught experience is hard to predict: so too are the potentially detrimental constraints that might be applied in any quest to improve the measuring of learning gain. A quote generally attributed to Peter Drucker, is apposite here: '[w]hat gets measured gets managed—even when it's pointless to measure and manage it, and even if it harms the purpose of the organisation to do so.'[7] It is not difficult to apply such an analysis to the measuring of learning gain. However, in opening up the debate about how best to define the concept of learning gain, we aim to provoke further discussion and exploration of what is meant by the notion of the benefits flowing from higher education, both in terms of our learners, and indeed in respect of wider society.

---

[7]See further https://athinkingperson.com/2012/12/02/who-said-what-gets-measured-gets-managed/ (accessed 30.11.18).

References

Arum, R., & Roska, J. (2010). *Academically adrift: Limited learning on college campuses*. Chicago, Ill: University of Chicago Press.

Benjamin, R., & Clum, M. (2003). A new field of dreams: The collegiate learning assessment project. *Peer review, 5*(4), 26–29.

Biesta, G. (2015). What is education for? On good education, teacher judgement, and educational professionalism. *European Journal of Education, 50*(1), 75–87.

Blackmore, P., & Kandiko, C. (2012). Change: processes and resources. In P. Blackmore & C. Kandiko (Eds.), *Strategic Curriculum Change, Global Trends in Universities*. Abingdon: Routledge.

Boud, D. (2018). Assessment could demonstrate learning gains, but what is required for it to do so? *Higher Education Pedagogies, 3*(1), 54–56.

Cameron, A., Wharton, Y., & Scally, J. B. (2018). An investigation into the comparative learning gain and 'value added' for students from widening participation and non-widening participation groups: A case study from sports degrees. *Higher Education Pedagogies, 3*(1), 83–102.

CEM. (2017). *Alis*. Retrieved from https://www.cem.org/alis.

Council for Aid to Education (CAE). (2012). *Student guide to CLA+*. Retrieved from https://s3.amazonaws.com/StraighterLine/Docs/studentguide_straighterline.pdf.

Clarke, M. (2017). Rethinking graduate employability: The role of capital, individual attributes and context. *Studies in Higher Education*.

Gibbs, G. (2010). Dimensions of quality. *International Journal*. Retrieved from http://www.heacademy.ac.uk/assets/York/documents/ourwork/evidence_informed_practice/Dimensions_of_Quality.pdf.

Gossman, P., Powell, S., & Neame, C. (2018). Pain, gain—Mission. *Higher Education Pedagogies, 3*(1), 7–9.

Hart Research Associates. (2015). *Falling short: College learning and career success*. Washington, D.C.: Hart Research Associates.

Hefce. (2015). *Higher Education Funding Council for England*. Retrieved from: http://www.hefce.ac.uk/news/newsarchive/2015/Name,105306,en.html.

Jääskelä, P., Nykänen, S., & Tynjälä, P. (2016). Models for the development of generic skills in Finnish higher education. *Journal of Further and Higher Education, 1*(13), 1–13.

McGrath, C. H., Guerin, B., Harte, E., Frearson, M., & Manville, C. (2015). *Learning gain in higher education*. Cambridge, UK: RAND Corporation. Retrieved from: https://www.rand.org/pubs/research_reports/RR996.html.

OECD. (2013). *Assessment of higher education learning outcomes, feasibility study report*. Volume 1 – Design and implementation, Executive Summary. Retrieved from: http://www.oecd.org/education/skills-beyond-school/AHELO%20FS%20Report%20Volume%201%20Executive%20Summary.pdf.

Rogers, K. (2016). A new final exam for college seniors. *Fox Business*. Retrieved from: http://www.foxbusiness.com/features/a-new-final-exam-for-college-seniors.

Sands, D., Parker, M., Hedgeland, H., Jordan, S., & Galloway, R. (2018). Using concept inventories to measure understanding. *Higher Education Pedagogies, 3*(1), 173–182. https://doi.org/10.1080/23752696.2018.1433546.

Shavelson, R. J., & Huang, L. (2003). Responding responsibly to the frenzy to assess learning in higher education. *Change, 35*(1), 11–18.

Sin, C., & Neave, G. (2014). Employability deconstructed: Perceptions of Bologna Stakeholders. *Studies in Higher Education, 41*(8), 1–16.

The Quality Assurance Agency for Higher Education. (2013). *Skills for employability*. Retrieved from: http://www.qaa.ac.uk/assuring-standards-and-quality/skills-for-employability.

Thompson, D. (2018). *Value added measures in performance tables: A recap of the main issues for primary schools—FFT Education Datalab*. Retrieved from: https://ffteducationdatalab.org.uk/

2018/05/value-added-measures-in-performance-tables-a-recap-of-the-main-issues-for-primary-schools/.

Wheadon, C. (2013). *Where's the value in 'value-added'?* Retrieved from: https://cerp.aqa.org.uk/blog/bloggers/christopher-wheadon.

Peter Gossman (Ed.D.) is a Principal Lecturer in Education at the University of Worcester, England, within The School of Education and The Department of Education and Inclusion where he is the programme leader for the post-graduate certificate in learning and teaching in Higher Education. Peter has published on a range of subjects in HE including the scholarship of teaching and learning.

Stephen Powell (Ph.D.) is a Principal Lecturer at Manchester Metropolitan University, England, having worked in education for over 20 years, initially as a teacher in the compulsory school sector, and then in HE as a developer of innovative online programmes. He has particular experience in curriculum design and development to meet the needs of learners in the workplace and the use of inquiry-based approaches to learning, and patchwork text as a form of assessment. He has developed and managed numerous projects in HE working with colleagues to develop new taught provision and improve institutions educational systems and processes using action research and systems thinking. He leads the PGCert in Learning and Teaching in HE as well as running externally funded projects.

Chapter 4
Conceptions of Quality: Some Critical Reflections on the Impact of 'Quality' on Academic Practice

Chris Lawton

4.1 Introduction

One way of navigating national and institutional Higher Education (HE) policy changes, (not least for the purpose of enhancing students' learning and improving our own practice) is to undertake a critical exploration of the challenges we face (Ashwin et al., 2015: 355). Even if we do not agree with the way in which the concept of quality in HE has been presented, this need not require us to be resistant in terms of the extent to which we engage with quality (i.e. enhancement and assurance) processes. As Ashwin et al. (2015: 366) rightly point out, as reflective practitioners and the creators of knowledge, we are citizens with a duty to use this wisdom to influence and inform HE policy at institutional and national levels. The creation of the OfS and the implementation of the TEF will indeed force us to confront essential questions about our identity and our values as educators. However, the answers that we might arrive at need not commit us to the concept of quality as simply a value-for-money notion, as has perhaps been quite implicit in successive UK government policies.

Over the past 20 years, the UK Higher Education (HE) sector has experienced a significant amount of change in response to the ideologies and policies of its successive governments (Ashwin et al., 2015; Brennan, 2012; Entwistle, 2009; Howie, 2009; Pokorny & Warren, 2016; Staddon & Standish, 2012). Given the scale and scope of these changes, there have inevitably been knock-on effects for the learning environments in which HE takes place, as well as for the individuals working within them (Cranfield, 2016: 62; Entwistle, 2009: 82). The concept of 'quality' in relation to teaching, research, and the wider student experience has become a clear priority for HE institutions and successive governments alike. However, despite being one of the "most dominating and influential 'meta ideas' globally over the last 20 years" (Stensaker, 2007: 99), 'quality' is typically acknowledged as being a highly contested

C. Lawton (✉)
Edge Hill University, Ormskirk, UK
e-mail: lawtonc@edgehill.ac.uk

© Springer Nature Switzerland AG 2019
A. Diver (ed.), *Employability via Higher Education: Sustainability as Scholarship*,
https://doi.org/10.1007/978-3-030-26342-3_4

concept (Newton, 2002: 47) with multiple meanings which shape our perceptions and understanding of HE (Tam, 2001). Consequently, there has also been significant debate over the ways in which organisations have sought to measure the quality of UK HE (Ashwin et al., 2015).

For instance, although there have been numerous attempts to rank universities in league tables based on student surveys and university outcomes data (Pokorny & Warren, 2016:1), the validity of this type of exercise has often been called into question. According to McLean, Abbas, and Ashwin (2013), the problem with measuring the quality of higher education in this way is that the criteria used in compiling university league tables often typically reflects the financial status and historical reputation of an institution as opposed to students' actual engagement with, and academic knowledge of, their subject. Moreover, against the current backdrop of global austerity and political uncertainty, government rhetoric typically presents the quality of UK HE as being inextricably linked to the financial success of graduates, and subject to measurement through such proxy mechanisms as the Teaching Excellence and Student Outcomes Framework (TEF) and the National Student Survey (BIS, 2016). Given the way in which the political narrative around the purpose and value of HE has been framed, one of the key challenges facing academic practitioners currently is reconciling this conception of quality with how we think about ourselves and our academic disciplines. This chapter offers a brief overview of the evolution of the concept of quality in UK HE followed by a critical reflection on how this has had an impact on the academic practice of an early career researcher working within this context. In contrast to the existing literature's focus on academics' resistance to quality processes,[1] the purpose of this paper is to argue an alternative picture whereby we need not resign ourselves to a conception of quality as bureaucratic compliance, with unpalatable political and/or managerial agendas. Rather, well-designed quality processes, used appropriately and understood to be reflective tools for developing our academic practice (as well as that of our students) can allow us to get on with the real university business of teaching, learning, and researching in more effective ways.

4.2   The UK Higher Education Quality Revolution

To understand the impact of 'quality' on academic practice in the age of austerity, it is important to firstly acknowledge the political context which has shaped recent HE policy changes. This section outlines briefly the way in which quality assurance in UK HE has been transformed in response to government ideologies over the past three decades. According to Howie (2009), at the heart of UK government policy sits a neoliberal ideology which has prioritised the marketisation of the HE sector through the introduction of two inter-related mechanisms, namely, 'tuition fees' and

---

[1] For indicative examples see further Anderson (2006); Cheng (2009, 2010); Lucas (2014); and Newton (2000, 2002).

'quality assurance'. For Staddon and Standish (2012: 631) and Pokorny and Warren (2016: 2), the main political strategy for introducing market conditions into the sector has been the transfer of financial responsibility for university tuition from the public purse to the private individual via the introduction of student loans. The other way in which successive UK governments have sought to marketize HE is through what Harvey (2005: 271) has described as 'the British Quality Juggernaut,' whose sole political purpose is to implement the uniformity necessary to commercialise HE (Brown, 2010; Howie, 2009: 6; O'Byrne & Bond, 2014: 576).

Arguably, what has concerned many academics most about the future of UK HE is the fact that the vision found in HE policy, as well as the language in which it is expressed, has not altered despite changes in government (Staddon & Standish, 2012: 634). Rather, as Brennan (2012: 8) and Howie (2009: 1) point out, UK governments since 1997 have consistently behaved as if the best way to ensure the quality of our HE system is through an appeal to market forces, as opposed to the professional judgement of academics, which has since been 'relegated to a voice of self-interest' (O'Byrne & Bond, 2014: 574). For example, between 1997 and 2011 a range of independent reports and government White Papers have led to the introduction, and subsequent increases, of university tuition fees under the auspices that doing so would 'put students at the centre of the process of learning and teaching' (Dearing, 1997, para 35).[2]

More recently, the government White Paper *'Success as a Knowledge Economy: Teaching Excellence, Social Mobility and Student Choice'* (2016) deliberately frames students as purchasers of HE services, and champions their rights as consumers through the creation of a new government regulator, the Office for Students (OfS) and the introduction of the Teaching Excellence and Student Outcomes Framework (TEF). However, despite the name of this new government regulator, the prevailing narrative around its role has been primarily concerned with more 'value for money' as opposed to increasing students' academic success. For example, rather than basing its judgement of a university's teaching quality upon what goes on in the classroom, or even any perceived academic development demonstrated by students, the current iteration of the TEF prioritises graduate employment and salary data as key proxy metrics for gauging 'quality'.

And yet, historically, the quality and standards of a University, and by extension its reputation, were maintained through a combination of external peer review and professional body accreditations, as well as internal processes such as course validations and the activities of learning, teaching and research committees (Brennan & Shah, 2000). Universities would typically invite respected academic peers from other institutions, and/or academic/professional societies, to periodically review their teaching and research activities to reassure themselves that their academic provision was comparable to that found elsewhere. However, the early 1990s marked the beginning of what Newton (2002: 40) describes as the 'UK Quality Revolution'. This period saw the beginning of a trend for HE institutions to adopt increasingly managerial approaches to, and conceptions of, quality assurance. One example can be seen in

---

[2]See also DFES (2003, 54), Browne (2010), and BIS (2011, p. 32).

the way in which models of quality management, such as Total Quality Management (TQM), were migrated from industry into the university campus (Harvey & Williams, 2010a; Houston, 2007; Luizzi, 2000; McGettrick, Dunnett & Harvey, 1997). This radical departure from the traditional, trust-based conception of quality assurance, in favour of a more regulatory approach, was said to be driven by a goal of making the UK HE sector more transparent (Turnbull, Burton, & Mullins, 2008) as well as increasing accountability within Universities (Pratasavitskaya & Stensaker, 2010).

Following this initial wave of attempting to migrate industrial quality management strategies into higher education, a second phase of the UK Quality Revolution began to take shape in the mid-1990s. Based on recommendations made by a Joint Planning Group of representatives from Universities and the funding councils, the Quality Assurance Agency (QAA) was established in 1997 to oversee a new unified system of quality assurance (McClaran, 2010: 108). Previous attempts to implement industry-model quality assurance processes such as TQM were gradually phased out in favour of developing an alternative approach more cognisant of the nature of UK universities (Harvey, 1995).[3] This emphasised an improvement agenda owned by academics (Moon & Geall, 1996); known, as 'Subject-level Review', and ran in England from 1995 until 2001 (Harvey & Williams, 2010a: 14). To cut a long story short, by the end of the 1990s, all UK providers of HE had become subject to various quality assurance frameworks overseen by the QAA on behalf of the funding bodies, and latterly the OfS. But what has any of this meant for academic practitioners in the classroom? In the next section I consider how the conception of quality has impacted on different areas of academic practice. Critical reflections follow, on both the existing literature and my own experience/dual identity as a higher education quality professional and early career researcher.

4.3   The Impact of 'Quality' on Academic Practice

One key way in which the conception of 'quality' has impacted upon academic practice recently concerns the changes in the relationships between students, academics, and universities. Within the existing literature it is widely accepted that the political use of tuition fees and quality assurance mechanisms to position students as *purchasers* of higher education has created a consumer culture which has had a direct impact on how academics go about 'the business' of teaching.[4] For example, the use of the National Student Survey (NSS) as a performance metric in compiling university league tables (and more latterly the TEF) has influenced the way in which institutions have typically moved towards a student-centred approach to teaching and learning activities (Ashwin et al., 2015: 81), placing heightened emphasis on the importance

---

[3] See Houston (2007); Pratasavitskaya and Stensaker (2010); and Harvey and Williams (2010a).

[4] See further Jones (2006, 2010), Biggs and Tang (2011), Staddon and Standish (2012), Williams (2013), Kandiko and Mawer (2013), Collini (2012) and Ashwin et al. (2015).

of individual academics managing students' increasingly high expectations (Bates & Kaye, 2014: 659).

In principle this is to be welcomed (in terms of putting students at the centre of HE) but concerns remain in relation to the conception of quality as a driving factor, given how this can have a potentially negative impact on an individual tutor's academic practice.[5] Students enter HE with a wide range of personal, cultural, social, sexual, and economic identities all of which play a significant role in how they approach (and engage with) teaching, learning, and assessment activities.[6] Although it is often relatively straightforward to address such characteristics when providing advice or guidance to an individual student (Entwistle, 2009: 117), this presents a significant challenge for how we go about our teaching practice for an entire cohort who may have competing views as to what counts as a 'quality' student experience, as well as entirely different motivations for studying (Ashwin, et al., 2015: 185). Indeed, it is worth pointing out here that there is something ironic in the fact that the conception of quality and the mechanisms through which successive governments have attempted to measure it, may unintentionally lead to a reduction in the actual quality of teaching. For instance, as Bright, Eliahoo and Pokorny (2016: 212) claim (and in keeping with my own experience), the first few years of one's teaching career are often the most stressful as one makes the transition from a subject specialist in a particular academic discipline to a teacher of HE. In particular, given that the kinds of creative and innovative practices that can often best challenge and develop students' learning are also the ones that involve the biggest risks (in the sense that they can produce new and unexpected/unfamiliar teaching and learning experiences) the pressures associated with achieving good NSS scores and first-time pass rates can often result in individual academics restraining their teaching style: tried and tested activities may be opted for instead, which will typically produce "the kinds of predetermined, quantifiable educational outcomes that managers and fee-paying, employment-focused students (it is often assumed) expect" (Harrington, Sinfield & Burns, 2016: 109).

Another key area of academic practice which has been affected by the way in which austerity has re-framed the narratives around 'quality' in HE, is the issue of how we go about the process of designing and developing academic curricula. A particularly good example of this can be seen in how the recent trend for the value of HE to be quantified in terms of how it benefits the economy and/or enhances the career earnings of individual graduates.[7] This has increased expectations on individual academics to visibly embed 'employability' skills within their curriculum. This emphasis on the economic value of HE has received significant criticism within the existing literature prior to the age of austerity.[8] The emphasis on 'employability'

---

[5] See further Staddon and Standish (2012: 635), Ashwin et al. (2015: 81), Hutchinson and Loughlin (2009); and McGhee (2009).

[6] See further Pokorny and Warren (2016: 5), Entwistle (2009: 28), and Ashwin et al. (2015: 88).

[7] For indicative examples see Howie (2009, p. 6), Ashwin et al. (2015, p. 353) and BIS (2016, p. 43).

[8] See McClean (2006).

in government HE policy,[9] as well as recent studies linking student perceptions of tuition fees to their prospects of employment,[10] has presented an inescapable narrative whereby it is the responsibility of individual academics to ensure that their students develop the requisite graduate employability skills required by industry and the professions.[11] Consequently, when presenting new modules and programmes for approval through university quality processes such as validation, academics are typically required to demonstrate how employability considerations have been taken into account during the curriculum design process. Whilst the task of ensuring that students are well equipped to enter graduate employment may come naturally to some colleagues teaching on vocationally-facing programmes that bestow professional accreditation (i.e. Qualified Teacher Status) or admittance to a professional register of practice (such as that maintained by the Nursing & Midwifery Council), this is arguably more challenging for someone whose academic discipline does not have a natural and immediate link to a graduate-level job. Similarly, whilst Pegg, Waldock, Hendey-Issac, and Lawton (2012) claim that academic subjects and the employability agenda need not necessarily be seen as competing influences within teaching practice, this line of reasoning often sits uncomfortably with academics.[12] An institutional approach could however see an embedding of employability within the curriculum (Barrie, 2006), as well as making explicit the links between what goes on in class and how it benefits a student's employability, for example via development and evidencing of particular graduate skills and attributes.

That said, such conceptions of 'quality' have had a negative impact on academic practice, as seen through the apparent paradoxes between individual academics' fierce commitment to quality in their teaching and learning activities on the one hand, and their resistance to quality assurance processes in their own institutions on the other hand (Harvey & Williams, 2010b: 84). Although there is relatively little disagreement over the extent to which we should draw on evidence when reflecting upon the effectiveness of our own academic practices (Ashwin et al., 2015: 282), there are persistent criticisms still being made about the authenticity and legitimacy of the processes used for assuring quality within higher education.[13] Broadly speaking, the majority of the existing literature on academics' perceptions of quality processes falls into one of two categories. Quality processes are seen either as burdensome and bureaucratic exercises in compliance which have little impact on academic practice (Cheng, 2010: 259), or they are depicted as managerial tools for disciplining and/or restricting the freedom of academics (Blackmore, 2009; Jarvis, 2014; Newton, 2002). Although much of this criticism precedes the age of austerity, the recent creation of the

---

[9] For examples, see DFES (2003), BIS (2011) and BIS (2016).

[10] See Bates and Kaye (2014), Moore, McNeill and Halliday (2011), and Gedye, Fender and Chalkley (2004).

[11] See Yorke (2004), Pegg, Waldock, Hendey-Issac, and Lawton (2012), and Walsh and Kotzee (2010).

[12] For example see McGhee (2009, p. 28).

[13] See Newton (2000, 2002, 2010), Anderson (2006), Cheng (2009, 2010), Teelken and Lomas (2009), Lucas (2014), Cardoso, Rosa, and Stensaker (2016), Akalu (2016).

OfS and the introduction of the TEF are arguably paradigmatic cases of an approach to quality assurance which sees concepts of 'standards' and 'quality' as poorly defined: our attempts to measure them therefore make little sense. Consequently, it is easy to empathise with the suggestion that (despite their commitment to quality teaching and research) academics often struggle to see a meaningful relationship between their own academic practices and the processes used to measure and assure the quality of that practice (Harvey & Williams, 2010b: 84).

4.4   How Has This 'Quality Engagement Paradox' Arisen?

Reflecting on the existing academic literature (as well as drawing upon my own experience), it seems that one possible reason for this could be the fact that the topic of 'quality' in higher education generally remains the territory of quality professionals, sector agencies, and policy makers (Cardoso, Rosa, & Stensaker, 2016), while a lack of empirical research into academics' perceptions of quality in higher education may have contributed to a marginalising of the voice of the academic community in relation to engagement with quality processes (Saarinen, 2010). Even the most well-designed quality assurance processes and frameworks can create unintended changes to the power dynamics between academics and administrators. On the one hand, as Harrington et al. (2016: 110) point out, even the most respected and distinguished professors in a particular academic or professional discipline can often be highly inexperienced when it comes to curriculum design and/or teaching development. On the other hand, my experience as a quality professional unfortunately suggests that it is highly unlikely that many working in such a role possess the academic capital required to persuade some of the more 'traditional/hierarchical' academics that there is significant value in quality assurance processes beyond that of fulfilling our compliance requirements.

Other reasons which may explain the quality engagement paradox in HE are typically concerned with the notion of 'quality burden' (Anderson, 2006; Lucas, 2014; Newton, 2000, 2002; Watty, 2003). This is the claim that the capacity and ability of individual academics to develop their academic practice and support students' learning is becoming undermined by the time and workload pressures associated with the demands of quality assurance processes (Morgan, 2010). Poorly defined conceptions of quality (and ill-conceived approaches to measuring it) can result in inauthentic academic practice, as well as workload pressures and stress amongst academic staff (McClean, 2006). However, this line of criticism is only valid against those kinds of compliance-based approaches to quality, rather than quality assurance processes *per se*. Well-designed quality processes should reduce any perceived burden by pre-emptively addressing perennial student support issues, and by making smart use of existing data/evidence to meet external compliance requirements. In both cases, the 'burden' should be that of the quality professional. Despite the concerns raised about the extent to which UK HE policy has attempted to impose a conception of 'quality as value-for-money' (and reinforce existing hierarchies on the basis of historical reputation and financial power) the following offers indicative reasons as to why we should remain open to the possibility that quality assurance processes are not simply a matter of bureaucratic compliance that have little positive impact on teaching and learning activities.

4.5   Quality as a Space to Reflect Upon Academic Practice

Despite the repeated emphasis in government rhetoric on how the creation of the TEF and the OfS will put students at the centre of UK HE, quality assurance has, for many academics, become 'a 'beast-like' presence, requiring to be 'fed' with ritualistic practices by academics seeking to meet accountability requirements' (Harvey & Williams, 2010b: 84). As Entwistle (2009: 185) points out, our conception of quality and how it is measured is concerned with productivity as opposed to teaching and learning activities in the classroom: as long as this is so there will be a fundamental schism between the rhetoric of HE policy and the view of academic practice as espoused by academics. Although this picture of what 'quality' means currently may look pretty depressing, this need not be the case. As Smith (2010: 727) rightly points out, 'whilst the language and rhetoric of contemporary higher education may feel inhospitable, the gaps in which to exercise autonomy still remain'. This does not mean academics ought to just comply with quality processes and be grateful for whatever tokenistic opportunity they get for expressing autonomy. Rather, as Smith (2010) seems to be arguing here, while we must always remain cognisant of the need to accommodate the various demands of regulatory frameworks and the marketplace, HE retains a rich, critical and empowering potential that can be harnessed to develop approaches to educating students and practicing research that addresses the complexities of today's world (Fanghanel, 2012: 14).

In response to the existing literature on the various criticisms of 'quality' in higher education, arguably, the best approach is not to resist quality processes per se, but to subvert the neoliberal ideologies of successive UK government policies. This can be done by using the regulatory strictures and bureaucracies that are emerging from the OfS and the TEF as levers for institutional activities that can generate genuine and meaningful enhancement within teaching and learning, with as little 'burden' as possible being placed upon academic staff. In persuading colleagues to remain open to this possibility, it might be helpful here to note that one of the key features of national and institutional quality frameworks is that they are concerned with both ensuring that institutions are aligned with appropriate academic standards and accountable for their funding (i.e. quality *assurance*), as well as systematically enhancing the quality of the teaching and learning experience and improving the academic practice of their staff (i.e. quality *enhancement*) (Teelken & Lomas, 2009: 260). Although the explicit notion of enhancement is unfortunately absent from the core practices of the latest iteration of the UK Code for Quality Assurance (2018), the distinction between what constitutes an example of quality assurance process as opposed to a quality enhancement process is problematic in practice (Harvey & Newton, 2007).

Although a quality assurance process, such as the periodic review of a department's academic portfolio, may be primarily concerned with ensuring that the programmes and modules under review are set at the right academic level (as well as appropriately benchmarked against key national and institutional reference points) there is an implicit enhancement opportunity going on insofar as this process may then identify examples of good academic practice that can be shared elsewhere within (or beyond) the institution. On the other hand, the possibility of quality enhancement activities is also usually dependent upon the existence of quality assurance processes insofar as the latter assesses existing practice with which the former is then contrasted. This reminder of the relationship between quality assurance processes and the possibility of quality enhancement offers a useful illustration of how reflective academic practitioners can develop their own agency when confronted with systems and policies that 'serve to frame, as well as delimit and constrain, what counts as good academic work in teaching and research' (Tennant, McMullen & Kaczynski, 2010: 1).[14]

Going forward, one way in which we could potentially go about actively subverting the conception of 'quality' is to reframe how we think about the concept of quality in terms of providing a structure which can help create a space where we can meaningfully reflect on our academic practice, especially in relation to areas such as curriculum design and development, by fostering engagement between academic developers, quality professionals, and academics. This does not mean that we should all 'drink the neoliberal-quality-Kool-Aid' and pretend that 'everything is awesome' in relation to the conception of 'quality' recently espoused by government. Rather, within our own institutions, academics and quality professionals can come together to use even such uncomfortable instruments as the TEF as a tool to leverage opportunities for genuine and meaningful pedagogic enhancement activities, as opposed to merely effecting bureaucratic compliance. Whereas, two decades ago, Gosling and D'Andrea (2001) expressed disappointment that it would be unlikely to happen, clearly with the right institutional leadership, we can use the concept of 'quality' as a catalyst for developing a more holistic educational development approach to enhancing the student experience through the combined efforts of educational developers, academics and quality assurance professionals.

4.6 Conclusion

In reflecting on what the concept of 'quality' now means (in terms of academic practice, and HE professionalism) the observations of Hutchinson and Loughlin (2009: 41) on teaching philosophy seem particularly apposite:

---

[14]Or as a colleague, Professor Mark Schofield once put it to me, 'for the reflective academic, the art of creativity in relation to quality and educational development is to never let a structure become a stricture.'

As practitioners/teachers of philosophy we are like the makers of the most effective wooden stakes in an environment dominated by vampires, and we also do an excellent line in therapies for those victims of the blood-suckers.

In other words, one way of navigating national and institutional HE policy changes, (not least for the purpose of enhancing students' learning and improving our own practice) is to undertake a critical exploration of the challenges we face (Ashwin et al., 2015: 355). Even if we do not agree with the way in which the concept of quality in HE has been presented, this need not require us to be resistant in terms of the extent to which we engage with quality processes. As Ashwin et al. (2015: 366) rightly point out, as reflective practitioners and the creators of knowledge, we are citizens with a duty to use this wisdom to influence and inform HE policy at institutional and national levels. The creation of the OfS and the implementation of the TEF will indeed force us to confront essential questions about our identity and values as educators. However, the answers that we might arrive at need not commit us to the concept of quality as simply a value-for-money notion, as has been implicit in successive UK government policies.

References

Akalu, G. A. (2016). Higher education 'massification' and challenges to the professoriate: Do academics' conceptions of quality matter? *Quality in Higher Education, 22*(3), 260–276.

Anderson, G. (2006). Assuring quality/resisting quality assurance: Academics' responses to 'quality' in some Australian universities. *Quality in Higher Education, 12*(2), 161–173.

Ashwin, P., Boud, D., Coate, K., Hallett, F., Keane, E., Krause, K., et al. (2015). *Reflective teaching in higher education*. London: Bloomsbury.

Barrie, S. C. (2006). Understanding what we mean by the generic attributes of graduates. *Higher Education, 51*(2), 215–241.

Bates, E. A., & Kaye, L. K. (2014). "I'd be expecting caviar in lectures": The impact of the new fee regime on undergraduate students' expectations of higher education. *Higher Education, 67*(5), 655–673.

Biggs, J., & Tang, C. (2011). *Teaching for quality learning at university* (4th ed.). Maidenhead: Open University Press.

Blackmore, J. (2009). Academic pedagogies, quality logics and performative universities: Evaluating teaching and what students want. *Studies in Higher Education, 34*(8), 857–872.

Brennan, J. (2012). *Talking about quality: The changing uses and impact of quality assurance*. Gloucester: The Quality Assurance Agency for Higher Education. Retrieved from http://eprints. lse.ac.uk/55677/.

Brennan, J., & Shah, T. (2000). *Managing quality in higher education: An international perspective on institutional assessment and change* (1st ed.). Buckingham: Organisation for Economic Co-operation and Development & Open University Press.

Bright, J., Eliahoo, R., & Pokorny, H. (2016). Professional development. In H. Pokorny & D. Warren (Eds.), *Enhancing teaching practice in higher education* (pp. 206–226). London: Sage.

Brown, R. (2010). The current brouhaha about standards in England. *Quality in Higher Education, 16*(2), 129–137.

Browne, J. (2010). *Securing a sustainable future for higher education: An independent review of higher education funding and student finance (The Browne Review)*. Retrieved from https://www.gov.uk/government/uploads/system/uploads/attachment_data/file/422565/bis-10-1208-securing-sustainable-higher-education-browne-report.pdf.

Cardoso, S., Rosa, M. J., & Stensaker, B. (2016). Why is quality in higher education not achieved? The view of academics. *Assessment & Evaluation in Higher Education, 41*(6), 950–965.

Cheng, M. (2009). Academics' professionalism and quality mechanisms: Challenges and tensions. *Quality in Higher Education, 15*(3), 193–205.

Cheng, M. (2010). Audit cultures and quality assurance mechanisms in England: A study of their perceived impact on the work of academics. *Teaching in Higher Education, 15*(3), 259–271.

Collini, S. (2012). *What are universities for?*. London: Penguin Books.

Cranfield, S. (2016). Teaching by leading and managing learning environments. In S. Pokorny & D. Warren (Eds.), *Enhancing teaching practice in higher education* (pp. 47–68). London: Sage.

Dearing, R. (1997). *Higher education in the learning society*. London: HMSO.

Department for Business Innovation and Skills, [BIS]. (2011). *Higher education: Students at the heart of the system*. London: HMSO.

Department for Business Innovation and Skills, [BIS]. (2016). *Success as a knowledge economy: Teaching excellence, social mobility and student choice*. London: HMSO. Retrieved from https://www.gov.uk/government/uploads/system/uploads/attachment_data/file/523546/bis-16-265-success-as-a-knowledge-economy-web.pdf.

Department for Education and Skills. (2003). *The future of higher education*. Retrieved from http://www.educationengland.org.uk/documents/pdfs/2003-white-paper-higher-ed.pdf.

Entwistle, N. (2009). *Teaching for understanding at university: Deep approaches and distinctive ways of thinking*. Palgrave MacMillan.

Fanghanel, J. (2012). *Being an academic* (1st ed.). Milton Park, Abingdon, Oxon: Routledge.

Gedye, S., Fender, E., & Chalkley, B. (2004). Students' undergraduate expectations and post-graduation experiences of the value of a degree. *Journal of Geography in Higher Education, 28*(3), 381–396.

Gosling, D., & D'Andrea, V. (2001). Quality development: A new concept for higher education. *Quality in Higher Education, 7*(1), 7–17.

Harrington, K., Sinfield, S., & Burns, T. (2016). Student engagement. In H. Pokorny & D. Warren (Eds.), *Enhancing teaching practice in higher education* (pp. 106–124). London: Sage.

Harvey, L. (1995). Beyond TQM. *Quality in Higher Education, 1*(2), 123–146.

Harvey, L. (2005). A history and critique of quality evaluation in the UK. *Quality Assurance in Education, 13*(4), 263–276.

Harvey, L., & Newton, J. (2007). Transforming quality evaluation: Moving on. In D. Westerheijden, B. Stensaker, & M. Rosa (Eds.), *Quality assurance in higher education* (pp. 225–245). Dordrecht: Springer.

Harvey, L., & Williams, J. (2010a). Fifteen years of quality in higher education. *Quality in Higher Education, 16*(1), 3–36.

Harvey, L., & Williams, J. (2010b). Fifteen years of quality in higher education (part two). *Quality in Higher Education, 16*(2), 81–113.

Houston, D. (2007). TQM and higher education: A critical systems perspective on fitness for purpose. *Quality in Higher Education, 13*(1), 3–17.

Howie, G. (2009). Teaching philosophy in context: Or knowledge does not keep any better than fish. In A. Kenkmann (Ed.), *Teaching philosophy* (pp. 5–22). London: Continuum.

Hutchinson, P., & Loughlin, M. (2009). Why teach philosophy? In A. Kenkmann (Ed.), *Teaching philosophy* (pp. 38–54). London: Continuum.

Jarvis, D. S. L. (2014). Regulating higher education: Quality assurance and neo-liberal managerialism in higher education—A critical introduction. *Policy and Society, 33*(3), 155–166.

Jones, G. (2006). 'I wish to register a complaint': The growing complaints culture in higher education. *Perspectives: Policy and Practice in Higher Education, 10*(3), 69–73.

Jones, G. (2010). Managing student expectations: The impact of top-up tuition fees. *Perspectives: Policy and Practice in Higher Education, 14*(2), 44–48.

Kandiko, C. B., & Mawer, M. (2013). *Student expectations and perceptions of higher education: Final report*. London: King's Learning Institute. Retrieved from https://www.kcl.ac.uk/study/learningteaching/kli/People/Research/DL/QAAReport.pdf.

Lucas, L. (2014). Academic resistance to quality assurance processes in higher education in the UK. *Policy and Society, 33*(3), 215–224.

Luizzi, V. (2000). Some dissatisfaction with satisfaction: Universities, values, and quality. *Journal of Business Ethics, 25*(4), 359–364.

McClaran, A. (2010). The renewal of quality assurance in UK higher education. *Perspectives: Policy and Practice in Higher Education, 14*(4), 108–113.

McGettrick, A., Dunnett, A., & Harvey, B. (1997). Continuous quality improvement in higher education. *Quality in Higher Education, 3*(3), 235–247.

McGhee, M. (2009). Wisdom and virtue: Or what do philosophers teach? In A. Kenkmann (Ed.), *Teaching philosophy* (pp. 23–37). London: Continuum.

McLean, M. (2006). *Pedagogy and the university*. London: Continuum.

McLean, M., Abbas, A., & Ashwin, P. (2013). The use and value of Bernstein's work in studying (in)equalities in undergraduate social science education. *British Journal of Sociology of Education, 34*(2), 262–280.

Moon, S., & Geall, V. (1996). Total quality management: Disciples and detractors. *Quality in Higher Education, 2*(3), 271–273.

Moore, J., McNeill, J., & Halliday, S. (2011). Worth the price? Some findings from young people on attitudes to increases in university tuition fees. *Widening Participation and Lifelong Learning, 13*(1), 57–70.

Morgan, J. (2010). *Audit overload*. Retrieved from https://www.timeshighereducation.com/features/audit-overload/410612.article.

Newton, J. (2000). Feeding the beast or improving quality?: Academics' perceptions of quality assurance and quality monitoring. *Quality in Higher Education, 6*(2), 153–163.

Newton, J. (2002). Views from below: Academics coping with quality. *Quality in Higher Education, 8*(1), 39–61.

Newton, J. (2010). A tale of two 'qualitys': Reflections on the quality revolution in higher education. *Quality in Higher Education, 16*(1), 51–53.

O'Byrne, D., & Bond, C. (2014). Back to the future: The idea of a university revisited. *Journal of Higher Education Policy and Management, 36*(6), 571–584.

Pegg, A., Waldock, J., Hendey-Issac, S., & Lawton, R. (2012). *Pedagogy for employability*. York: Higher Education Academy. Retrieved from https://www.heacademy.ac.uk/system/files/pedagogy_for_employability_update_2012.pdf.

Pokorny, H., & Warren, D. (2016). Introduction: Teaching in the changing landscape of higher education. In H. Pokorny & D. Warren (Eds.), *Enhancing teaching practice in higher education* (pp. 1–10). London: Sage.

Pratasavitskaya, H., & Stensaker, B. (2010). Quality management in higher education: Towards a better understanding of an emerging field. *Quality in Higher Education, 16*(1), 37–50.

Saarinen, T. (2010). What I talk about when I talk about quality. *Quality in Higher Education, 16*(1), 55–57.

Smith, J. (2010). Academic identities for the twenty-first century. *Teaching in Higher Education, 15*(6), 721–727.

Staddon, E., & Standish, P. (2012). Improving the student experience. *Journal of Philosophy of Education, 46*(4), 631–648.

Stensaker, B. (2007). Quality as fashion: Exploring the translation of a management idea into higher education. In D. Westerheijdin, B. Stensaker, & M. Rosa (Eds.), *Quality assurance in higher education* (pp. 99–118). Dordrecht: Springer.

Tam, M. (2001). Measuring quality and performance in higher education. *Quality in Higher Education, 7*(1), 47–54.

Teelken, C., & Lomas, L. (2009). "How to strike the right balance between quality assurance and quality control in the perceptions of individual lecturers": A comparison of UK and Dutch higher education institutions. *Tertiary Education and Management, 15*(3), 259.

Tennant, M., McMullen, C., & Kaczynski, D. (2010). *Teaching, learning and research in higher education.* Abingdon: Routledge.

Turnbull, W., Burton, D., & Mullins, P. (2008). 'Strategic repositioning of institutional frameworks': Balancing competing demands within the modular UK higher education environment. *Quality in Higher Education, 14*(1), 15–28.

Walsh, A., & Kotzee, B. (2010). Reconciling "graduateness" and work-based learning. *Learning and Teaching in Higher Education, 4*(1), 36–50.

Watty, K. (2003). When will academics learn about quality? *Quality in Higher Education, 9*(3), 213–221.

Williams, J. (2013). *Consuming higher education: Why learning can't be bought.* London: Bloomsbury.

Yorke, M. (2004). Employability in the undergraduate curriculum: Some student perspectives. *European Journal of Education, 39*(4), 409–427.

Chris Lawton (Ph.D.) is Academic Quality Officer and a University Learning & Teaching Fellow at Edge Hill University, in the North West of England, UK. He holds a Ph.D. in Philosophy as well as a Postgraduate Certificate in Teaching in Higher Education, and is a Fellow of both the Higher Education Academy (FHEA) and the Association of University Administrators (FAUA). He was one of the authors of the UK Quality Code for Higher Education Advice and Guidance on External Expertise published by the QAA in 2018.

Chapter 5
What Motivational Processes Underpin Student Engagement with Employability? A Critical Review

Andrew James Clements

5.1 Introduction

Across the globe, participation in Higher Education (HE) is expanding for several reasons, not least competition for desired career outcomes, with non-attendance of HE often incurring opportunity costs (Marginson, 2016). Higher Education Institutions (HEIs) are therefore positioned as having responsibility to the wider economy (Hunter, 2013), e.g. via providing "work-ready" graduates (Tomlinson, 2012). In Britain, HEIs are expected to justify their high tuition fees through enhanced graduate employability levels (Tholen, 2014). Employability has variously been described as the ability to gain and maintain desired forms of employment (Rothwell & Arnold, 2007) and as a collection of achievements and understandings that will promote future career success (Knight & Yorke, 2004). More recently, Clarke has proposed an integrative model of employability, in which perceived employability is informed by human capital, e.g. skills, social capital such as networks, individual behaviours such as career management skills, and individual attributes such as adaptability (Clarke, 2018). Significantly, Clarke's model also acknowledges the role of labour market factors, i.e. supply and demand, on both perceived employability and actual career outcomes.

In modern labour markets, individuals are responsible for managing their own career progress and outcomes (Smith, 2010) and need to be adaptable (Clarke, 2013). There have been calls for HEIs to improve graduate employability, as UK governments (Browne, 2010) and some portions of British industry (CBI, 2015) have claimed that graduates are not prepared for the world of work—although other reports have claimed that employers are generally satisfied with the quality of graduates (UK Commission for Employment and Skills, 2015). Employers report large numbers of "hard-to-fill" vacancies (CIPD, 2018), but there are signs of an "over-

A. J. Clements (✉)
University of Bedfordshire, Bedfordshire, UK
e-mail: andrew.clements@beds.ac.uk

© Springer Nature Switzerland AG 2019
A. Diver (ed.), *Employability via Higher Education: Sustainability as Scholarship*,
https://doi.org/10.1007/978-3-030-26342-3_5

supply" of graduates (Humburg, de Grip, & van der Velden, 2017) which is seen as resulting from mass participation in HE that has not been matched by increased demand for highly skilled workers (Verhaest & Van Der Velden, 2013). This has consequences for graduates, in that there is increased competition for a finite supply of desired occupations (Helyer & Lee, 2014). Brown and Hesketh (2004) characterise this as "positional conflict", whereby graduates are now required to find a means beyond that of their degree to make themselves distinctive to employers. Logically, while it is possible to help individual students become more employable, employability interventions are unlikely to enhance the career outcomes of graduates as a whole (Greenbank, 2017) as the number of graduate positions remains finite. The focus in this chapter therefore is on how career outcomes might be improved for individuals, although structural issues (e.g. inequality) must also be considered. Individuals have largely been given the task of managing their own careers. Inevitably people vary in how well they perform this task, for a variety of reasons.

The role that motivation plays in the pursuit of career goals is key. Some scholars have expressed concern that students do not engage with employability early enough during their time in HE (Tansley, Jome, Haase, & Martens, 2007). Early in their studies, students may be less likely to place a high value on work experience as compared to how they view it in their final year of study (Tymon, 2013). There is evidence too that some students fail to seek advice from careers services, in part perhaps because students prefer to speak to people whom they know and who know them as individuals (Greenbank, 2011). Greenbank (2011) noted that students thus preferred to speak with lecturers or family rather than the careers service, even though this preferred source may lack the career-specific knowledge needed by the enquiring student. For example, the parents of first-generation HE students are less likely to have labour market knowledge relevant to their children's goals (Tate, Caperton, Kaiser, Pruitt, White, & Hall, 2015). There are also several reasons that students may put off engaging with employability, including a preference for focusing on immediate concerns (e.g. assignments), a tendency to base career decisions on intuition rather than research, and passive reliance on the provision of information (Greenbank, 2017). However, some students clearly engage better than others with the development of employability skills, despite these competing demands. To discuss why this may be, motivation theory will be looked at, given how motivation reflects the direction, intensity and duration of action (Locke & Latham, 2004).

5.2   Social Cognitive Career Theory

Social cognitive career theory (SCCT) was formulated to account for the processes by which people form career interests, make academic and career choices, and pursue career goals (Lent, Brown, & Hackett, 1994). A key concept in SCCT is self-efficacy, a construct representing an individual's perception of their capability (Bandura & Cervone, 1983). In SCCT it is expected that career interests are influenced by self-efficacy, i.e. one's perceived ability in a career field, perceived outcomes (e.g.

rewards) and perceived barriers (Brown & Lent, 1996). For example, a graduate may intend to have a career in management. They believe themselves capable of managing others, find the work interesting, and the pay appealing—yet the question of whether they do apply for a job in management may be influenced by their self-perceptions e.g. that they are able to get the job. Influences on self-efficacy might include previous performance, direct and indirect learning, and others' persuasion of the individual (Brown, Lent, Telander, & Tramayne, 2011; Lent & Brown, 1996). The hypothetical graduate seeking management work may well have a sense of their own ability that is informed by their experience of a work placement, feedback from supervisors and tutors, and advice from their HEI's careers service. More recently, Lent et al. proposed an SCCT model of career self-management (CSM) to explain developmental processes in careers (Ireland & Lent, 2018; Lent & Brown, 2013; Lent, Ezeofor, Morrison, Penn, & Ireland, 2016). The CSM is intended to extend SCCT, which focuses more on career interests and choices—career content—by examining career processes, such as career planning, career exploration and decision-making (Lent & Brown, 2013). CSM draws also upon Savickas' concept of career adaptability, which relates to individuals' ability to adapt to changing circumstances (Savickas, 1997). CSM distinguishes between developmental tasks, such as career decision-making and seeking employment, and the coping skills that enable an individual to manage key transitions such as school-to-work or job loss (Lent & Brown, 2013). The model draws upon the earlier work of Super (1975) in distinguishing between a series of life stages, each of which are associated with particular adaptive tasks (Lent & Brown, 2013):

- Growth, an early stage in which the emphasis is upon skill development
- Exploration, in which skills are further developed, but additional tasks include career exploration and career decision-making
- Establishment, which includes the tasks of obtaining work and adjustment to work environments
- Maintenance, which includes the task of career self-renewal, but may also lead to recycling of earlier stages (e.g. due to voluntary or involuntary departure from a job)
- Disengagement/reengagement, which can include adjustment to changing responsibilities, or adjustment from work to leisure (i.e. retirement).

This chapter looks at the stages of exploration and establishment. In line with CSM, it is important to recognise that these stages may apply not only to young HE students, but also to mature students who have decided to attend HE as part of a strategy for making career changes, i.e. recycling exploration and establishment as part of the maintenance stage. As in SCCT, CSM proposed that learning experiences influenced self-efficacy and outcome expectations, which in turn inform career goals. Contextual factors (such as the presence of support and barriers) are expected to influence goals, the actions implemented to pursue goals, and goal outcomes e.g. by contributing to self-efficacy. As predicted, self-efficacy and outcome expectations have been found to influence career exploration goals (Lent, Ezeofor, Morrison, Penn, & Ireland, 2016). Learning experiences associated with success, operationalised as mastery experiences, have also been associated with self-efficacy (Bandura, 1977; Ireland & Lent, 2018; Warner et al., 2018). A meta-analytic review demonstrated further that cognitive ability and conscientiousness—a personality trait reflecting discipline and persistence—also influence self-efficacy (Brown et al., 2011). While SCCT and CSM identify a key role for self-efficacy, these models do not address the characteristics of career goals. As such, Goal-Setting Theory requires discussion here.

5.3   Goal-Setting Theory

Goal-Setting Theory (GST) proposes that goal characteristics influence the level of effort and persistence individuals devote to their goals, and thus shapes the likelihood of success (Latham & Locke, 2007; Locke & Latham, 2004, 2013). Specifically, GST states that people perform better when they have "high goals," i.e. goals that are specific, achievable, and challenging (Locke & Latham, 1990). A challenging target requires new behaviours, encouraging the formation of strategy, while the specific nature of the high goal enables an individual to monitor goal progress (Locke & Latham, 2013). As in SCCT and CSM, self-efficacy is an important feature of the goal-setting process. Individuals with higher self-efficacy set themselves more challenging goals (Bandura & Locke, 2003; Donovan, 2009) and persist longer when striving for these goals (Locke & Latham, 2002). Feedback is an important part of the goal-striving process, as it enables individuals to see how much progress has been made, and how much is perhaps still needed (Bandura & Cervone, 1983). Individuals with higher levels of self-efficacy combined with goal commitment are more likely to recover from failures during goal attainment, while those individuals with higher self-efficacy levels may respond by setting new, more challenging goals (Bandura & Locke, 2003).

5.4   Career Goal Pursuit

The creation of discrepancy is a crucial feature of Goal-Setting Theory (Bandura & Locke, 2003). In other words, people are motivated to achieve, and this therefore leads them to setting challenging goals. After all, if one merely wished to experience no discrepancy between current and desired states, it would be simpler not to set goals at all. On the other hand, discrepancies between what we want to achieve and what we have actually achieved can also create distress (Creed, Wamelink, & Hu, 2015). This may be weakened by engagement in career exploration and planning however, as Creed et al. (2015) noted (albeit in relation to young people in general rather than those specifically enrolled in HE). Creed, Hood, and Hu (2017) surveyed 564 young people in their first year of HE. They reported that students with proactive orientations experienced less career goal-performance discrepancy, and therefore had less career-related distress and more employability confidence: those with higher interpersonal rejection sensitivity experienced greater career-goal discrepancy and thus saw higher distress and lowered confidence. Through moderated mediation models, Creed et al. (2017) also demonstrated that goal commitment (which they treated as a measure of goal importance) buffered the impact of rejection sensitivity and strengthened the impact of proactive orientations. In other words, when students were more committed to their career goals, those who were proactive experienced even less discrepancy, and those who were worried about disappointing others experienced less discrepancy than they otherwise would.

In another study examining aspects of self-regulation in the career goal pursuit, Hu, Hood, and Creed (2017) explored the impact of negative career feedback in a sample of 184 HE students. As might be expected, negative career feedback was associated with a greater inclination amongst students to abandon their career goals. However, this effect was weakened for those who had a higher career-related growth mind-set (i.e. who see struggle as a normal part of career pursuit) and strengthened for those with a higher career-related destiny mind-set (i.e. who see adversity as a sign that the career path is not 'meant to be'). In a study exploring engagement with employability amongst a sample of 432 UK undergraduates, mastery approach—a tendency towards seeking challenges in order to personally develop—was associated with greater engagement in three out of four proactive career behaviours: career consultation, network building, and skill development—but not career planning (Clements & Kamau, 2018). They reported that career goal commitment was positively associated with all four proactive career behaviours. Goal commitment is a key concept in Goal-Setting Theory (Hollenbeck, Williams, & Klein, 1989). A meta-analytic review has demonstrated that goal commitment moderates the relationship between goal difficulty and performance, with goal commitment becoming more important at higher levels of difficulty (Klein, Wesson, Hollenbeck, & Alge, 1999). Clements and Kamau (2018) predicted that goal commitment would moderate the relationship between mastery approach (used as a proxy for the setting of challenging goals) and proactive career behaviours. Instead, they found that goal commitment acted as a full mediator between mastery approach and career planning, and as a partial mediator between mastery approach and the other three proactive career behaviours (career consultation, network building, and skill development). Taken together, key attributes for students to engage with employability would appear to include self-efficacy, commitment to career goals, proactive approaches and a tendency towards seeking challenge. However, drawing on the CSM, it is possible to further explore the specific stages of career goal pursuit for students.

5.5 Career Exploration

Career exploration is an important activity within the exploration stage of the CSM (Lent & Brown, 2013). Career exploration can include both self-exploration (to identify relevant personal qualities) and environmental exploration (to identify career opportunities and barriers) (Guan et al., 2017), and may take place across the life-span as a developmental process (Cheung & Arnold, 2010). This developmental task is expected to have benefits in terms of enhancing the ability to make career decisions, including reduced indecision or decision-related anxiety (Lent et al., 2016). In other words, career exploration should result in more confidence for students as they come to realise what their own preferences are, and what options are available that align with those preferences. To the extent that career exploration identifies potential career barriers, we might also expect career exploration to inform adaptation of career strategies.

Betz and Voyten (1997) conducted a study of career decision-making self-efficacy, career indecision, and career exploration in a sample of 350 students. As might be expected, career decision-making self-efficacy was negatively related to career indecision. Interestingly, they reported that career indecision was in turn related to intentions to engage in career exploration for women, but not for men. More recently a three-wave longitudinal test of the CSM in 420 students found that exploratory intentions were positively predicted by outcome expectancies and career decision-making self-efficacy, and these intentions (alongside self-efficacy) then predicted exploratory behaviours (Lent et al., 2019). In contrast to the study by Betz and Voyten (1997), Lent et al. (2018) did not find that career indecision predicted exploration intentions. Instead, decisional anxiety was consistently negatively predicted by self-efficacy, while career decidedness was positively predicted at T2 by exploratory actions at T1, and at T3 by self-efficacy and social support measured at T2. Given the longitudinal design of the study by Lent et al. (2019), we may have greater confidence in their findings, which enabled the testing of reverse and reciprocal relationships. For example, the study was able to show that T2 self-efficacy was influenced by T1 decidedness—positively—and by T1 decisional anxiety—negatively. Lent and colleagues interpreted this as support for the existence of a feedback loop, with prior experiences informing self-efficacy, and thus shaping future behaviour.

Social support is a further, contextual factor expected to influence career exploration via enhanced self-efficacy (Lent et al., 2016). While some correlational studies have found a relationship between social support and students' career exploration (e.g. Lent et al., 2016; Zhang & Huang, 2018), other longitudinal studies have failed to support this (Cheung & Arnold, 2010; Lent et al., 2019). Combined with the findings of Lent et al. (2019), we may perhaps expect support to influence confidence in making the right choices, rather than encouraging students to simply explore what choices are available. However, an important consideration may be the use that students make of support. Help-seeking behaviours often receive more attention in the context of career decisions.

5.6 Career Decision Making

It has been previously suggested that many students struggle to make career decisions (Tokar, Withrow, Hall, & Moradi, 2003) and thus universities are seen as playing a key role in providing students opportunities to improve in this career task (Esters & Retallick, 2013). One of the challenges is that people do vary in their tendency towards decisiveness; Jaensch, Hirschi, and Freund (2015) reported two three-wave longitudinal surveys that demonstrated a strong stable component of career indecision, which was associated with lower core self-evaluations (i.e. a generally negative view of self) and perceived career barriers. However, it should be noted that Jaensch et al. did not use a full-panel design, with only career indecision measured across all three time points. Individual differences in self-awareness may also play an important role in decision-making; in a study of 189 Chinese students, both goal commitment and occupational commitment were reported to mediate the relationship between emotional intelligence and career decision-making self-efficacy (Jiang, 2016). This was thought to reflect the role of self-awareness in helping students to form goals in which they are interested, leading to greater commitment.

Work-based or work-integrated learning is expected to have benefits for students' skill development (Jackson, 2015). Esters and Retallick (2013) reported that students doing placements increased in both career decision self-efficacy and vocational identity. A similar effect was reported by Jackson and Wilton (2016) who compared career management competencies in those participating in placement with those who did not – although this effect was only found once the impact of current employment was controlled. Support has also been examined as a potential influence on career decision-making. Garcia, Restubog, Bordia, Bordia, and Roxas (2015) reported that parental and teacher support was positively associated with career decision-making self-efficacy, and that the latter was positively associated with career optimism. While this was a longitudinal study, only career optimism and demographic variables were measured at T2, which limits the rigour of the analysis. De Lange, Taris, Kompier, Houtman, and Bongers (2003) recommend the use of complete panel designs, in which the full range of measures are used at each point of data collection, to permit the identification of reverse or reciprocal causations.

As well as the provision of support, support-seeking has attracted attention in career research. In a study of 1176 Israeli students, perceptions of difficulty in making career decisions was associated with greater procrastination, slower speed and more effort in making decisions, and less interest in finding an ideal occupation (Vertsberger & Gati, 2015). Similarly, those who were more inclined to seek help from others tended to procrastinate, made slower decisions, and with greater effort. As has been reported elsewhere (e.g. Greenbank, 2011), Vertsberger and Gati found that their participants were most likely to approach friends and family for advice, despite identifying expertise as the most important consideration when seeking assistance. In another longitudinal study, differences in career indecision coping styles were associated with career decision difficulties and decision status (Lipshits-Braziler, Gati, & Tatar, 2015). Specifically, non-productive coping (e.g. helplessness and isolation) was associated with greater decision difficulties; those scoring more highly in this coping were more likely to remain undecided in their career choices. Support-seeking was also higher in those who remained undecided, whilst productive coping (e.g. problem-solving and information-seeking) was unrelated to career difficulty or to the final career decision status (i.e. decided vs. undecided).

5.7 Job Search

The job search process marks a key stage in the transition from HE to work, following career decisions, but also incorporating further decisions (e.g. identification of targets and strategies). Graduates may begin with high expectations, but these are often lowered as a result of repeated rejections (McKeown & Lindorff, 2011). Job search self-efficacy, i.e. confidence in one's ability to effectively seek work, is an important predictor of job search behaviour in students and graduates (Lim, Lent, & Penn, 2016; Liu & Wang, 2014), likely via the mediator of job search intentions (Lim et al., 2016). Job search self-efficacy has been predicted by conscientiousness and social support (Lim et al., 2016), career adaptability (Guan et al., 2013), and perceived job search progress (Liu & Wang, 2014). Guan et al. (2013) reported that job search self-efficacy is associated with subsequent employment status; we may expect that this is because job search self-efficacy predicts job search behaviour, which is also associated with the number of job offers received (Liu & Wang, 2014). However, evidence from a longitudinal study suggests that higher job search self-efficacy is associated with increased job search effort in those students motivated to avoid failure but lower effort in those motivated by success (Sun, Song, & Lim, 2013). Thus, job search self-efficacy may not be a universal panacea for motivational interventions. Given that there is far more evidence in favour of the beneficial impact of self-efficacy, it may be helpful for replication studies to take place.

Da Motta Veiga and Gabriel (2016) reported a study of the dynamics of job searching in business students over the course of five weeks. They found that autonomous (i.e. intrinsic) motivation for job search declined during the search period before plateauing at the mid-point, whilst controlled motivation (i.e. a sense of necessity) remained stable. While autonomous motivation was positively associated with strategizing about job search (and thereby influenced job search effort), controlled motivation was initially negatively associated with strategizing and effort but became positively associated with strategizing later in the job search process. Although there has been research exploring student and graduate engagement with the job search process, there seems to be a lack of research on the broad strategies that they use. Previous research in the broader job search literature has distinguished between focused, exploratory, and haphazard job search strategies (Bonaccio, Gauvin, & Reeve, 2014; Crossley & Highhouse, 2005).

A focused job search sees the individual only seeking work in which they are interested and for which they are qualified (Crossley & Highhouse, 2005) and choices are planned and driven by criterion rather than emotions (Bonaccio et al., 2014). This search strategy is associated positively with job offers (Koen, Klehe, Vianen, Zikic, & Nauta, 2010), re-employment amongst the unemployed (De Battisti, Gilardi, Guglielmetti, & Siletti, 2016) and job satisfaction in obtained employment (Crossley & Highhouse, 2005). Those higher in perceived employability are more likely to report using a focused job search strategy (De Battisti et al., 2016), which suggests that outcome expectancies may prompt beneficial strategies. By contrast, haphazard job search is characterised by passive information gathering (e.g. relying on others to supply information), the setting of ill-defined goals, a tendency to react to external events and changing tactics without rationale (Crossley & Highhouse, 2005). In this approach, decisions are much more likely to be grounded in emotions (Bonaccio et al., 2014). Those adopting this approach are less likely to experience job satisfaction, because they may not realise what jobs would suit them, and because they might accept the first job offer made to them (Crossley & Highhouse, 2005). The exploratory job search strategy is one in which individuals are open to a number of job options, and is characterised by information search across a number of sources, including friends and colleagues (Crossley & Highhouse, 2005). This search strategy is positively associated with the receipt of job offers, although one longitudinal study suggested that an exploratory approach was negatively associated with subsequent reemployment quality (Koen et al., 2010).

5.8 Implications and Future Directions

Considerable attention has been directed toward student engagement with employability. There are some limitations to the literature, attention to which might help enhance our understanding of the motivational processes underpinning employability. Much of the published research is based upon correlational survey designs. This limits the kind of causal claims that can be supported (de Lange et al., 2003). There have been some longitudinal studies, but more are needed. It would also be useful for researchers to publish evaluations of interventions, for example using randomised controlled trials to provide greater confidence in causal claims. There is a rich tradition of experimental research in the goal-setting literature (Locke & Latham, 2013) which could be applied to the challenge of promoting student employability.

One possible intervention is to provide training (Kamau & Spong, 2015), which could involve the setting of high goals (Clements & Kamau, 2018). The impact of self-efficacy on various stages of career planning (exploration, decision-making, and job search) is one of the most consistently supported findings within the literature. There is some evidence that career management training can help enhance such self-efficacy (Jackson & Wilton, 2016) and reduce negative thoughts about career choice (Belser, Prescod, Daire, Dagley, & Young, 2018). As noted above, feedback is an important contributor to self-efficacy (Bandura, 1977; Ireland & Lent, 2018), as well as leading to the setting of more challenging goals (Donovan, 2009). However, we might also consider what kind of goals should be set. So far, the employability literature does not seem to have addressed this question. The broader goal-setting literature suggests that when tasks are new and complex, a specific, challenging performance goal may be detrimental to achievement as compared to a learning goal (Locke & Latham, 2004). In other words, when acquiring a new skill, concern over end results is less helpful than learning more about how to perform that skill. Given that many HE students will be new to career self-management, we should direct their attention initially to learning how to evaluate self, search for career options, and so on. Providing feedback on specific skill attainment should enhance confidence and promote career exploration and career decision-making. Encouraging students to see struggle as normal and to see failure as a learning opportunity should aid them in remaining engaged during a process that can be discouraging (Hu, Hood, & Creed, 2017).

As students gain greater competence in career self-management, they can be encouraged to set more concrete goals, e.g. for meeting a specified number of recruiters to discuss employment opportunities. Meta-analysis suggests that job search interventions that address both job skills (e.g. search, self-presentation) and motivation (e.g. goal-setting) are more effective than those interventions that address only one of these factors (Liu, Huang, & Wang, 2014). Other interventions might include mentoring. Career mentoring has been associated with increased career planning and job search intentions, and reductions in negative job search behaviours such as procrastination, failing to network, and impulsively accepting the first job offer that is received (Renn, Steinbauer, Taylor, & Detwiler, 2014). Further, the provision of mentoring may help supply students and graduates with relevant feedback for skill acquisition. Although research has shown links between some stages of the career planning process, e.g. career exploration's association with decision-making self-efficacy, it would be useful to examine the career planning process from career exploration to job search.

There has been a lack of research exploring job search strategies in student and graduate samples. It seems reasonable to expect that students who have appropriately engaged in career exploration, because of increased career decision-making self-efficacy, would be more likely to engage in a focused job-search strategy. Given the criterion-based nature of a focused job search strategy, we might also expect those adopting this strategy to be more inclined to set high goals, i.e. challenging, specific, and achievable (Locke & Latham, 1990), which should result in greater motivation and thus job search intensity, which has been shown to influence the number of job offers received. By contrast, inadequate engagement in career exploration, e.g. in terms of the time spent on this process or low effort, might be associated with later adoption of a haphazard job search strategy.

As well as further exploring motivational processes in employability for students and graduates as a larger group, it will also be helpful to examine variations in the journey from exploration to job attainment. For example, SCCT points to the role of perceived barriers in shaping career choices (Brown & Lent, 1996). Research has demonstrated the existence of barriers for marginalised groups such as women and people of ethnic minority background in part due to consciousness of negative stereotypes (Owuamalam & Zagefka, 2014). Further, the lack of transparency in job selection processes may contribute to perceptions that discrimination plays a role in hiring decisions (Clements, 2018). More attention is needed to address these barriers, including identifying the most appropriate interventions. As noted early in this chapter, motivation-based interventions may address behaviour in individuals, but these are not able to address environmental challenges. There is therefore also a need for examining structural inequality in the environment, which may contribute to self-efficacy via feedback processes. In examining motivation in disadvantaged students and graduates, I therefore suggest it is important to also examine the behaviour of employers who make hiring decisions—an important source of feedback.

5.9 Conclusion

While it is not the aim of this chapter to claim that motivating students is a "magic bullet" that will address the employability agenda in full, it can be argued that motivation theory and research offers useful insights into ways to make progress. The strongest findings in the literature identify the role of self-efficacy, which should direct our attention towards interventions that best enable students to experience mastery of challenging tasks. We need to consider too the role of failure, given that this is a potential outcome of challenging activities, and in the case of job search, likely to be frequent. Some research on learning goals and growth mind-set suggest that these are qualities we should encourage, for example by identifying failure as a normal part of career pursuit. To encourage engagement with employability, we therefore should consider how students may be given opportunities for mastering career management skills and gaining feedback, e.g. via training or mentorship. We should also consider the psychological role that perceived barriers play in helping to perpetuate disadvantage for particular groups of students. Motivation theory and research often direct our attention to internal processes, but we should consider motivation as an interaction between the individual and their environment. Further attention is therefore needed to identify productive ways of helping students overcome barriers and challenging those with the influence to address such structural inequality.

References

Bandura, A. (1977). Self-efficacy: Toward a unifying theory of behavioral change. *Psychological Review, 84*(2), 191–215.

Bandura, A., & Cervone, D. (1983). Self-evaluation and self-efficacy mechanisms governing the motivational effects of goal systems. *Journal of Personality and Social Psychology, 45*(5), 1017–1028.

Bandura, A., & Locke, E. A. (2003). Negative self-efficacy and goal effects revisited. *Journal of Applied Psychology, 88*(1), 87–99. https://doi.org/10.1037/0021-9010.88.1.87.

Belser, C. T., Prescod, D. J., Daire, A. P., Dagley, M. A., & Young, C. Y. (2018). The influence of career planning on career thoughts in STEM-interested undergraduates. *Career Development Quarterly, 66*(2), 176–181. https://doi.org/10.1002/cdq.12131.

Betz, N. E., & Voyten, K. K. (1997). Efficacy and outcome expectations influence career exploration and decidedness. *The Career Development Quarterly, 46,* 179–189.

Bonaccio, S., Gauvin, N., & Reeve, C. L. (2014). The experience of emotions during the job search and choice process among novice job seekers. *Journal of Career Development, 41*(3), 237–257. https://doi.org/10.1177/0894845313486354.

Brown, P., & Hesketh, A. (2004). *The mismanagement of talent.* Oxford: Oxford University Press.

Brown, S. D., & Lent, R. W. (1996). A social cognitive framework for career choice counselling. *Career Development Quarterly, 44,* 354–366. https://doi.org/10.1002/j.2161-0045.1996.tb00451. x.

Brown, S. D., Lent, R. W., Telander, K., & Tramayne, S. (2011). Social cognitive career theory, conscientiousness, and work performance: A meta-analytic path analysis. *Journal of Vocational Behavior, 79*(1), 81–90. https://doi.org/10.1016/j.jvb.2010.11.009.

Browne, J. (2010). Securing a sustainable future for higher education. Retrieved from http://www. educationengland.org.uk/documents/pdfs/2010-browne-report.pdf. Accessed 9 Jul 2019.

Confederation of British Industry [CBI]. (2015). *Inspiring growth: CBI/Pearson education and skills survey 2015.* Retrieved from https://www.pearson.com/content/dam/corporate/global/pearson-dot-com/files/press-releases/2015/CBI-Pearson-Skills-survey-FINAL.pdf. Accessed 9 Jul 2019.

Cheung, R., & Arnold, J. (2010). Antecedents of career exploration among Hong Kong Chinese university students: Testing contextual and developmental variables. *Journal of Vocational Behavior, 76*(1), 25–36. https://doi.org/10.1016/j.jvb.2009.05.006.

Chartered Institute of Personnel and Development [CIPD]. (2018). *Labour market outlook.* Spring 2018, 23. Retrieved from https://www.cipd.co.uk/Images/labour-market-outlook_2018-spring-1_tcm18-42044.pdf. Accessed 9 Jul 2019.

Clarke, M. (2013). The organizational career: Not dead but in need of redefinition. *The International Journal of Human Resource Management, 24*(4), 684–703.

Clarke, M. (2018). Rethinking graduate employability: The role of capital, individual attributes and context. *Studies in Higher Education, 43*(11), 1923–1937. https://doi.org/10.1080/03075079. 2017.1294152.

Clements, A. J. (2018). Exploring diversity and employability within Higher Education students and graduates. In *Division of Occupational Psychology Annual Conference abstracts* (pp. 59–61). Stratford-upon-Avon.

Clements, A. J., & Kamau, C. (2018). Understanding students' motivation towards proactive career behaviours through goal-setting theory and the job demands–resources model. *Studies in Higher Education, 43*(12), 2279–2293. https://doi.org/10.1080/03075079.2017.1326022.

Creed, P. A., Hood, M., & Hu, S. (2017). Personal orientation as an antecedent to career stress and employability confidence: The intervening roles of career goal-performance discrepancy and career goal importance. *Journal of Vocational Behavior, 99,* 79–92. https://doi.org/10.1016/j.jvb. 2016.12.007.

Creed, P. A., Wamelink, T., & Hu, S. (2015). Antecedents and consequences to perceived career goal-progress discrepancies. *Journal of Vocational Behavior, 87,* 43–53. https://doi.org/10.1016/ j.jvb.2014.12.001.

Crossley, C. D., & Highhouse, S. (2005). Relation of job search and choice process with subsequent satisfaction. *Journal of Economic Psychology, 26,* 255–268. https://doi.org/10.1016/j.joep.2004. 04.001.

da Motta Veiga, S. P., & Gabriel, A. S. (2016). The role of self-determined motivation in job search: A dynamic approach. *Journal of Applied Psychology, 101*(3), 350–361.

De Battisti, F., Gilardi, S., Guglielmetti, C., & Siletti, E. (2016). Perceived employability and reemployment: Do job search strategies and psychological distress matter? *Journal of Occupational and Organizational Psychology, 89*(4), 813–833. https://doi.org/10.1111/joop.12156.

de Lange, A. H., Taris, T. W., Kompier, M. A. J., Houtman, I. L. D., & Bongers, P. M. (2003). "The very best of the millennium": Longitudinal research and the demand-control-(support) model. *Journal of Occupational Health Psychology, 8*(4), 282–305. https://doi.org/10.1037/1076-8998. 8.4.282.

Donovan, J. J. (2009). Antecedents of discrepancy production in an achievement setting. *Journal of Managerial Issues, 21*(3), 402–420.

Esters, L. T., & Retallick, M. S. (2013). Effect of an experiential and work-based learning program on vocational identity, career decision self-efficacy, and career maturity. *Career and Technical Education Research, 38*(1), 69–83. https://doi.org/10.5328/cter38.1.69.

Garcia, P. R. J. M., Restubog, S. L. D., Bordia, P., Bordia, S., & Roxas, R. E. O. (2015). Career optimism: The roles of contextual support and career decision-making self-efficacy. *Journal of Vocational Behavior, 88,* 10–18. https://doi.org/10.1016/j.jvb.2015.02.004.

Greenbank, P. (2011). "I'd rather talk to someone i know than somebody who knows"—The role of networks in undergraduate career decision-making. *Research in Post-Compulsory Education, 16*(1), 31–45. https://doi.org/10.1080/13596748.2011.549726.

Greenbank, P. (2017). Encouraging students to develop their employability: "Locally rational" but morally questionable? In M. Tomlinson & L. Holmes (Eds.), *Graduate employability in context: Theory, research and debate* (pp. 273–293). London: Palgrave Macmillan.

Guan, Y., Deng, H., Sun, J., Wang, Y., Cai, Z., Ye, L., et al. (2013). Career adaptability, job search self-efficacy and outcomes: A three-wave investigation among Chinese university graduates. *Journal of Vocational Behavior, 83*(3), 561–570. https://doi.org/10.1016/j.jvb.2013.09.003.

Guan, Y., Zhuang, M., Cai, Z., Ding, Y., Wang, Y., Huang, Z., et al. (2017). Modeling dynamics in career construction: Reciprocal relationship between future work self and career exploration. *Journal of Vocational Behavior, 101*, 21–31. https://doi.org/10.1016/j.jvb.2017.04.003.

Helyer, R., & Lee, D. (2014). The role of work experience in the future employability of higher education graduates. *Higher Education Quarterly, 68*(3), 348–372. https://doi.org/10.1111/hequ.12055.

Hollenbeck, J. R., Williams, C. R., & Klein, H. J. (1989). An empirical examination of the antecedents of commitment to difficult goals. *Journal of Applied Psychology, 74*(1), 18–23.

Hu, S., Hood, M., & Creed, P. A. (2017). Negative career feedback and career goal disengagement in young adults: The moderating role of mind-set about work. *Journal of Vocational Behavior, 102*, 63–71. https://doi.org/10.1016/j.jvb.2017.07.006.

Humburg, M., de Grip, A., & van der Velden, R. (2017). Which skills protect graduates against a slack labour market? *International Labour Review, 156*(1), 25–43. https://doi.org/10.1111/j.1564-913X.2015.00046.x.

Hunter, C. P. (2013). Shifting themes in OECD country reviews of higher education. *Higher Education, 66*(6), 707–723. https://doi.org/10.1007/s10734-013-9630-z.

Ireland, G. W., & Lent, R. W. (2018). Career exploration and decision-making learning experiences: A test of the career self-management model. *Journal of Vocational Behavior, 106*, 37–47. https://doi.org/10.1016/j.jvb.2017.11.004.

Jackson, D. (2015). Employability skill development in work integrated learning: Barriers and best practice. *Studies in Higher Education, 40*(2), 350–367.

Jackson, D., & Wilton, N. (2016). Developing career management competencies among undergraduates and the role of work-integrated learning. *Teaching in Higher Education, 21*(3), 266–286. https://doi.org/10.1080/13562517.2015.1136281.

Jaensch, V. K., Hirschi, A., & Freund, P. A. (2015). Persistent career indecision over time: Links with personality, barriers, self-efficacy, and life satisfaction. *Journal of Vocational Behavior, 91*, 122–133. https://doi.org/10.1016/j.jvb.2015.09.010.

Jiang, Z. (2016). Emotional intelligence and career decision-making self-efficacy: Mediating roles of goal commitment and professional commitment. *Journal of Employment Counseling, 53*(1), 30–47. https://doi.org/10.1002/joec.12026.

Kamau, C., & Spong, A. (2015). A student teamwork induction protocol. *Studies in Higher Education, 40*(7), 1273–1290. https://doi.org/10.1080/03075079.2013.879468.

Klein, H. J., Wesson, M. J., Hollenbeck, J. R., & Alge, B. J. (1999). Goal commitment and the goal-setting process: Conceptual clarification and empirical synthesis. *Journal of Applied Psychology, 84*(6), 885–896.

Knight, P., & Yorke, M. (2004). *Learning, curriculum and employability in higher education.* Oxon: Routledge.

Koen, J., Klehe, U., Van Vianen, A. E. M., Zikic, J., & Nauta, A. (2010). Job-search strategies and reemployment quality: The impact of career adaptability. *Journal of Vocational Behavior, 77*(1), 126–139. https://doi.org/10.1016/j.jvb.2010.02.004.

Latham, G. P., & Locke, E. A. (2007). New developments in and directions for goal-setting research. *European Psychologist, 12*(4), 290–300. https://doi.org/10.1027/1016-9040.12.4.290.

Lent, R. W., & Brown, S. D. (1996). Social cognitive approach to career development: An overview. *Career Development Quarterly, 44*, 310–321.

Lent, R. W., & Brown, S. D. (2013). Social cognitive model of career self-management: Toward a unifying view of adaptive career behavior across the life span. *Journal of Counseling Psychology, 60*(4), 557–568. https://doi.org/10.1037/a0033446.

Lent, R. W., Brown, S. D., & Hackett, G. (1994). Toward a unifying social cognitive theory of career and academic interest, choice, and performance. *Journal of Vocational Behavior, 45*(1), 79–122. https://doi.org/10.1006/jvbe.1994.1027.

Lent, R. W., Ezeofor, I., Morrison, M. A., Penn, L. T., & Ireland, G. W. (2016). Applying the social cognitive model of career self-management to career exploration and decision-making. *Journal of Vocational Behavior, 93*, 47–57. https://doi.org/10.1016/j.jvb.2015.12.007.

Lent, R. W., Morris, T. R., Penn, L. T., & Ireland, G. W. (2019). Social—Cognitive predictors of career exploration and management model social—Cognitive predictors of career exploration and decision-making : Longitudinal test of the career self-management model. *Journal of Counselling Psychology, 66*(2), 184–194. https://doi.org/10.1037/cou0000307.

Lim, R. H., Lent, R. W., & Penn, L. T. (2016). Prediction of job search intentions and behaviors: Testing the social cognitive model of career self-management. *Journal of Counseling Psychology, 63*(5), 594–603.

Lipshits-Braziler, Y., Gati, I., & Tatar, M. (2015). Strategies for coping with career indecision: Concurrent and predictive validity. *Journal of Vocational Behavior, 91*(380), 170–179. https://doi.org/10.1016/j.jvb.2015.10.004.

Liu, S., Huang, J. L., & Wang, M. (2014). *Effectiveness of job search interventions: A meta-analytic review, 140*(4), 1009–1041. https://doi.org/10.1037/a0035923.

Liu, S., & Wang, M. (2014). Self-regulation during job search: The opposing effects of employment self-efficacy and job search behavior self-efficacy. *Journal of Applied Psychology, 99*(6), 1159–1172.

Locke, E. A., & Latham, G. P. (1990). Work motivation and satisfaction: Light at the end of the tunnel. *Psychological Science, 1*(4), 240–246. https://doi.org/10.1111/j.1467-9280.1990.tb00207.x.

Locke, E. A., & Latham, G. P. (2002). Building a practically useful theory of goal setting and task motivation: A 35-year odyssey. *American Psychologist, 57*(9), 705–717. https://doi.org/10.1037/0003-066X.57.9.705.

Locke, E. A., & Latham, G. P. (2004). What should we do about motivation theory? Six recommendations for the twenty-first century. *Academy of Management Review, 29*(3), 388–403. https://doi.org/10.5465/AMR.2004.13670974.

Locke, E. A., & Latham, G. P. (2013). Goal setting theory, 1990. In E. A. Locke & G. P. Latham (Eds.), *New developments in goal setting and task performance* (pp. 3–15). Hove: Routledge.

Marginson, S. (2016). High participation systems of higher education. *The Journal of Higher Education, 87*(2), 243–271. https://doi.org/10.1353/jhe.2016.0007.

McKeown, T., & Lindorff, M. (2011). The graduate job search process—A lesson in persistence rather than good career management? *Education and Training, 53*(4), 310–320. https://doi.org/10.1108/00400911111138479.

Owuamalam, C. K., & Zagefka, H. (2014). On the psychological barriers to the workplace: When and why metastereotyping undermines employability beliefs of women and ethnic minorities. *Cultural Diversity and Ethnic Minority Psychology, 20*(4), 521–528.

Renn, R. W., Steinbauer, R., Taylor, R., & Detwiler, D. (2014). School-to-work transition: Mentor career support and student career planning, job search intentions, and self-defeating job search behavior. *Journal of Vocational Behavior, 85*(3), 422–432. https://doi.org/10.1016/j.jvb.2014.09.004.

Rothwell, A., & Arnold, J. (2007). Self-perceived employability: Development and validation of a scale. *Personnel Review, 36*(1), 23–41. https://doi.org/10.1108/00483480710716704.

Savickas, M. L. (1997). Career adaptability: An integrative construct for life-span, life-space theory. *The Career Development Quarterly, 45*, 247–259. https://doi.org/10.1002/j.2161-0045.1997. tb00469.x.

Smith, V. (2010). Review article: Enhancing employability: Human, cultural, and social capital in an era of turbulent unpredictability. *Human Relations, 63*(2), 279–300. https://doi.org/10.1177/ 0018726709353639.

Sun, S., Song, Z., & Lim, V. K. G. (2013). Dynamics of the job search process: Developing and testing a mediated moderation model. *Journal of Applied Psychology, 98*(5), 771–784. https:// doi.org/10.1037/a0033606.

Super, D. E. (1975). Career education and career guidance for the life span and for life roles. *Journal of Career Education, 2*(2), 27–43. https://doi.org/10.1177/089484537500200204.

Tansley, D. P., Jome, L. M., Haase, R. F., & Martens, M. P. (2007). The effects of message framing on college students' career decision making. *Journal of Career Assessment, 15*(3), 301–316. https://doi.org/10.1177/1069072707301204.

Tate, K. A., Caperton, W., Kaiser, D., Pruitt, N. T., White, H., & Hall, E. (2015). An exploration of first-generation college students' career development beliefs and experiences. *Journal of Career Development, 42*(4), 294–310. https://doi.org/10.1177/0894845314565025.

Tholen, G. (2014). Graduate employability and educational context: A comparison between Great Britain and the Netherlands. *British Educational Research Journal, 40*(1), 1–17. https://doi.org/ 10.1002/berj.3023.

Tokar, D. M., Withrow, J. R., Hall, R. J., & Moradi, B. (2003). Psychological separation, attachment security, vocational self-concept crystallization, and career indecision: A structural equation analysis. *Journal of Counseling Psychology, 50*(1), 3–19. https://doi.org/10.1037/0022-0167.50. 1.3.

Tomlinson, M. (2012). Graduate employability: A review of conceptual and empirical themes. *Higher Education Policy, 25*(4), 407–431. https://doi.org/10.1057/hep.2011.26.

Tymon, A. (2013). The student perspective on employability.pdf. *Studies in Higher Education, 38*(6), 841–856. https://doi.org/10.1080/03075079.2011.604408.

UK Commission for Employment and Skills. (2015). *Catch 16–24*. Retrieved from https://assets. publishing.service.gov.uk/government/uploads/system/uploads/attachment_data/file/404997/ 15.02.18._Youth_report_V17.pdf. Accessed 10 Jul 2019.

Verhaest, D., & Van Der Velden, R. (2013). Cross-country differences in graduate overeducation. *European Sociological Review, 29*(3), 642–653. https://doi.org/10.1093/esr/jcs044.

Vertsberger, D., & Gati, I. (2015). The effectiveness of sources of support in career decision-making: A two-year follow-up. *Journal of Vocational Behavior, 89*, 151–161. https://doi.org/10.1016/j. jvb.2015.06.004.

Warner, L. M., Stadler, G., Janina, L., Knoll, N., Ochsner, S., Hornung, R., et al. (2018). Day-to-day mastery and self-efficacy changes during a smoking quit attempt: Two studies. *British Journal of Health Psychology, 23*, 371–386. https://doi.org/10.1111/bjhp.12293.

Zhang, H., & Huang, H. (2018). Decision-making self-efficacy mediates the peer support-career exploration relationship. *Social Behavior and Personality, 46*(3), 485–498. https://doi.org/10. 2224/sbp.6410.

Andrew Clements (Ph.D.) is a Lecturer in Organisational Psychology at University of Bedfordshire, England, UK. His research interests focus on the processes by which people become members of professions, and make their early career moves. He is involved in applied research and consultancy projects (e.g. wellbeing at work, employee engagement) and has worked for organisations across a range of sectors. He leads on Employability within psychology, having been twice shortlisted for Commitment to Employability awards. He has contributed to organisational development in relation to wellbeing challenges through delivery of *World Cafe* sessions, and has upskilled workers through the design and delivery of bespoke training.

Chapter 6
Developing Employable, Emotionally Intelligent, and Resilient Graduate Citizens of the Future

Lorraine Dacre Pool, Dawne Gurbutt and Kath Houston

6.1 Introduction

The context of Higher Education (HE) has been changing rapidly in recent years, from the escalation of student fees in 2012 (which positioned students as customers as well as consumers of education), to the emphasis placed upon the wider 'student experience.' This reconfiguration of the student relationship has altered the ways in which students see universities and the ways in which universities view students: an increasingly consumerist approach to education has also led to innovations in the HE sector which are focused upon trying to determine, and subsequently measure, what constitutes a 'good' student experience. This included the introduction of the National Student Survey in 2005 which follows an annual cycle (HEFCE, 2017) and research into such specific areas as student contact hours (NUS, 2012). These are attempts to identify those sometimes quite elusive elements which can coalesce into a good student experience and often also indicate preparedness for graduate life beyond university. As such, a 'good' student experience is increasingly perceived to be an interconnected and collaborative education, which mirrors the challenges of the real world and includes opportunities for students to develop their employability, including their emotional intelligence (EI) and resilience.

The increasing inclusion of employability and enterprise curricula, in preparing students for the workplace upon graduation, also confirms the importance of 'real world' experience (Butcher et al., 2011). For at least a decade, the importance of including opportunities for students to develop emotional intelligence (EI) as part

L. Dacre Pool (✉) · D. Gurbutt · K. Houston
University of Central Lancashire, Preston, UK
e-mail: LDacre-pool@uclan.ac.uk

D. Gurbutt
e-mail: DGurbutt@uclan.ac.uk

K. Houston
e-mail: khouston@uclan.ac.uk

© Springer Nature Switzerland AG 2019
A. Diver (ed.), *Employability via Higher Education: Sustainability as Scholarship*,
https://doi.org/10.1007/978-3-030-26342-3_6

of their university experience has been asserted (Dacre Pool & Sewell, 2007; Dacre Pool & Qualter, 2012). More recently, the HE community and employers have both confirmed the need to assist students in developing the resilience required for the rapidly changing, and challenging futures that they are likely to face when entering the world of work (e.g. Burns & Sinfield, 2004). Additionally, the influence of social media and the resultant change in relationships, networks and connectivity, make both EI and resilience even more relevant.

The concepts of EI and resilience are closely related. This chapter argues therefore that developing EI also supports the growth of resilience, resulting in students who are better equipped to deal with, and bounce back from, life's unavoidable setbacks. The chapter firstly defines EI and examines the research evidence that supports its inclusion as an essential aspect of graduate employability development. It then explores the concept of resilience and explains why it is of vital importance to our students and graduates, both for their success within HE and in the years that follow. The chapter incorporates practical ideas that academic staff can utilise to support the development of these essential concepts in their students. This includes the use of interdisciplinary activities, which research has demonstrated can help students to develop their emotional competencies (Pertegal-Felices, Marcos-Jorquera, Gilar-Corbi, & Jimeno-Rorenilla, 2017). Finally, the chapter looks ahead and argues that, in a world that includes large-scale automation, artificial intelligence, and other significant changes within both workplaces and society in general, EI and resilience will assume even greater importance for the global, graduate citizens of the future.

6.2 Defining Graduate Employability

Although there is no globally accepted definition of the term graduate employability, most people now recognise that it is much more than 'just teaching students how to write a CV', nor is simply about graduates 'getting a job,' or engaging in basic skills development. A distinction needs to be made between 'employment' as a graduate outcome, and the notion of 'employability,' which is a much broader concept as it relates to HE pedagogy, and to personal and career development activities. Employability is not something that a person obtains and gains for life, as they do for example with a degree qualification. Rather, it is a lifelong process:

> Employability is having a set of skills, knowledge, understanding and personal attributes that make a person more likely to choose, secure and retain occupations in which they can be satisfied and successful. (Dacre Pool & Sewell, 2012).

More recent debates further support the notion of employability as a process rather than as an outcome (Smith, Bell, Bennett, & McAlpine, 2018). The importance of meaningful work is stressed: 'Employability is the ability to find, create and sustain meaningful work across the career lifespan.' (Bennett, 2018).

6.3 The *CareerEDGE* Model of Graduate Employability

There are several employability models and frameworks; a full discussion of these goes beyond the scope of this chapter.[1] The CareerEDGE model (Dacre Pool, & Sewell, 2007) however, emphasises the importance of students being given the opportunity to develop their EI whilst in HE. CareerEDGE is a mnemonic device to aid recall of the five components on the lower tier of the model (see Fig. 6.1): **Career** Development Learning; **E**xperience (work and life); **D**egree Subject Knowledge, Skills and Understanding; **G**eneric Skills; and **E**motional Intelligence. For students to stand the best chance of developing employability and reaching their potential, they should be able to access activities in relation to all the areas on this lower tier and, essentially, gain opportunities to reflect upon and evaluate these experiences. This should result in higher levels of self-efficacy, self-confidence and self-esteem, which together with resilience (Forsythe, 2017) provide crucial links to life-long employability development. The model serves as a helpful tool for auditing employability-related activities which are embedded in the curriculum and for identifying areas where further development would be helpful.

Prior to the introduction of CareerEDGE, previous models and theories (e.g. Fugate, Kinicki, & Ashforth, 2004; Knight & Yorke, 2004) had alluded to EI as an aspect of employability. However, CareerEDGE was the first to give it such prominence, arguing that EI was an essential element for inclusion in any model or framework looking to provide employability development opportunities for students within HE.

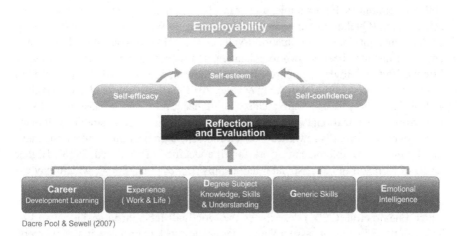

Dacre Pool & Sewell (2007)

Fig. 6.1 The CareerEDGE model of graduate employability

---

[1]On this, see further Cole and Tibby (2013), Small, Shacklock, and Marchant (2018).

6.4   Emotional Intelligence ('EI')

EI has been a topic of much discussion and debate in the academic literature (Dacre Pool & Qualter, 2018). Some researchers prefer to conceptualize it as a personality trait (e.g. Petrides & Furnham, 2001), with others arguing that it is an ability (Mayer & Salovey, 1997). Clearly, it is something that can be developed and improved upon through learning activities. As Mayer, Salovey, and Caruso (2004: 197) argue, EI is an ability, which involves:

> ...the capacity to reason about emotions, and of emotions to enhance thinking. It includes the abilities to accurately **perceive** emotions, to **access and generate** emotions so as to assist thought, to **understand** emotions and emotional knowledge, and to reflectively **regulate** emotions so as to promote emotional and intellectual growth.

This ability model, often referred to as the four-branch model of EI, has been extensively, empirically researched over the last two decades. Rather than framing it as a relatively stable personality trait, EI may be viewed as an ability: if so then it is something that we can teach, and a skill that our students can develop (Dacre Pool & Qualter, 2012).

6.4.1   Why EI is Essential for Graduate Employability

EI has been found to influence several outcomes that may contribute to the employability of graduates. For example, higher levels of EI tend to predict better academic achievement (Qualter, Gardner, Pope, Hutchinson, & Whiteley, 2012) and can help students in a job interview situation (Nelis et al., 2011). Beyond their HE experiences, EI has also been shown to enhance performance in the workplace (Côté & Miners, 2006; O'Boyle, Humphrey, Pollack, Hawver, & Story, 2010), and to lead to more effective decision-making (Yip & Côté, 2013) and effective leadership (Walter, Cole & Humphrey, 2011). Individuals with higher levels of EI are also more likely to perform Organizational Citizenship Behaviours, which are desirable, voluntary behaviours, not formally rewarded, but helpful to the organization in potentially making it a more desirable place to work for all concerned (Turnipseed, 2018). Higher levels of EI result in better social relationships (Lopes et al., 2004), which may aid the development of more harmonious relationships with managers and peers. It is these enhanced relationships that will also help graduates build their 'social capital' which Fugate et al. (2004) describe as the 'goodwill inherent in social networks.' This can be an invaluable asset to graduates as they seek to progress in their careers. Indeed, research has also shown that EI does foster the development of social capital, leading to longer term success, including higher salary levels when examined ten to twelve years after entry to the workplace (Rode, Arthaud-Day, Ramaswami, & Howes, 2017).

6.5 Resilience

Graduate citizens face a future of unparalleled change, including a Fourth Industrial Revolution (World Economic Forum, 2016), 'destabilising political events' and 'economic uncertainty' (HECSU, 2017). If we allow that the pace and rate of change can in itself be perplexing, bewildering, or stressful, it is reasonable to assume that a degree of resilience will be a necessity. Global workforce changes, technological advances, uncertainty about the predicted reach of automation and the demise of certain job roles demand reserves of resourcefulness for the domino game of 'happenstance' (Krumboltz, 2008) that constitutes graduate career planning. The term 'planned happenstance' (Krumboltz, 2008; Mitchell, 2004), a career planning theory, seems particularly appropriate for the career haze facing graduates. This oxymoronic pairing of 'planned' and 'happenstance' seems more than contradictory. However, the proposition that effective career planning for graduates constitutes a degree of strategic future-scoping (and yet does not preclude grasping at serendipitous opportunities) recognises the reality of how graduates need to function with resilience in a changing and challenging job market. Planning for a career necessitates proactivity and opportunistic stratagems. Making multiple decisions in a super-complexity (Barnett, 2014) career universe requires graduates to expand their thinking, be curious, and grasp opportunities as they emerge, whilst holding onto a sense of personal control during regular disturbance.

The study of resilience, grit (Duckworth, 2016), or hardiness[2] is relevant in terms of employability in HE. As a starting point, the definition offered by Edinburgh University for their student resilience model identifies the student experience as being one that requires specific levels of resilience:

> Resilience is both a key graduate attribute and an integral part of any transitions framework as it enables students to better cope with the challenges that they will encounter on their own unique learning journey. The term 'resilience' can be applied to both academic and social/personal aspects of the student journey and is often equated with wellbeing. (Edinburgh University, 2016)

Whilst this definition pre-supposes challenge and even difficulties, it is worth noting that this negative view of life is balanced by the Centre for Confidence's claim that 'bouncing back from adversity' can be 'positively good for us'. (Centre for Confidence, 2018). Resilience is clearly a key graduate attribute and rite of passage for students, which extends into the graduate career start process. 'Grit,' as Duckworth (2016) defines it, means 'sticking with things over the very long term until you master them:' together with hardiness (with its 'adversity to advantage' mantra[3]) these feature as key components of resilience. As such, resilience can be viewed as both an extension of EI and a valuable attribute in its own right. Reivich and Schatter (2003) argue that 'Everyone needs resilience' and view it as a 'basic ingredient

---

[2]See further Maddi, S.R., *The Hardiness Institute* (available http://www.hardinessinstitute.com/ accessed 14.11.18).

[3]*ibid*

to happiness and success'. Maddi and Khoshaba (2005) regard it as an attitudinal characteristic and while there may be some disagreement about the matter of whether it is to any degree innate, most agree that it is a learned ability (e.g. Costa, 2016). As Costa (2016) argues, 'we are wired for resilience' and this capacity relates to Dweck's (2006) notion of a mastery focus and the development of self-efficacy. In addition, Kwek, Bui, Rynne, and So (2013) argue that resilience is a major predictor of academic performance. If we can support students to develop resilience during their undergraduate study, they will become 'future fit' (UUK/CBI 2009), primed and equipped for the possible disequilibrium of a fast-changing work environment. The ability to bounce back from adversity is a valuable aspect of resilience, based on the experience of tough times or difficulties, and evidencing the process of becoming resilient, resulting in the outcome of being successfully resilient.

However, it is apparent that resilience is also an intentional activity, and a way of thinking. Reivich and Schatter (2003) maintain that thinking style affects emotions and behaviour and that 'accurate thinking, not positive thinking' is the best means of cultivating resilience. Self-reflective practices may be included in the curriculum alongside or within their subject discipline, to develop the capacity of students to recall past experiences of resourcefulness, which can be the source of present resilience. Whilst university teachers may resist the inclusion of personal development activities (Grant & Hooley, 2017), there are ways of aligning these to particular subject areas or as preparation for placement experience which will ensure that students become aware of their own resilience, whether innate or learned. These types of learning activities allow students to develop awareness of their thinking style with the added benefit of possibly adapting or changing a less than effective thinking style. Reivich and Schatter (2003) suggest three main thinking patterns that need to be challenged. An 'achievement-oriented thinking style' is apparent from statements such as: 'I have to be the best.' An 'acceptance thinking style' may be expressed through statements such as: 'I want to be loved,' whilst a 'control thinking style' may be articulated through a statement such as: 'I need to feel in control.' Awareness of these mindsets as examples of restricted thinking (at best), serves to support the need to effect changes in thinking, resulting in adaptability and resilience.

Discussion in relation to student resilience is also becoming ubiquitous throughout HE. As is the case with employability and EI, there is no single, agreed-upon definition. Like EI, there is growing evidence to suggest that resilience is not an innate, fixed trait, but rather something that people can learn and develop (Grant & Kinman, 2013). Additionally, it is linked to other psychological factors including self-efficacy, self-confidence and self-esteem (Robbins, Kaye, & Catling, 2018), all of which feature in the CareerEDGE model of graduate employability. It could be argued also that it is essential to develop resilience alongside these concepts for students to gain - and retain - occupations that will bring them satisfaction and success, thereby achieving their full potential.

6.6 Developing Employability, EI and Resilience within HE

There are numerous ways for us to help our students develop their employability and EI through the curriculum. Providing opportunities for students to improve their EI is also likely to help them develop resilience. EI positively impacts upon resilience-related constructs such as life satisfaction and happiness (Sanchez-Alvarez, Extremera, & Fernandez-Berrocal, 2015). A further resilience-related construct, Psychological Well Being, is closely affected by the ability to understand and manage emotions (Altaras Dimitrijevic, Jolic Marjanovic, & Dimitrijevic, 2018). Therefore, developing EI, the ability to identify, understand and manage emotions, will also support the development of resilience. For example, where a student who receives an unexpectedly poor grade for an assignment has a low level of EI, they could feel overwhelmed with disappointment which could in turn result in feelings of helplessness ('I can't do this') and/or anger at the assignment marker/tutor. Neither of these emotions are going to be helpful in the long term. However, a student with a good level of EI will be able to recognise that they feel disappointed and go through the process of understanding that disappointment (they may have put a lot of work into the assignment and the emotion is a perfectly appropriate one in the circumstances). They can then engage in deciding how they will use and manage their emotions. Reframing the disappointing situation as one from which there is much to learn could be a helpful strategy and provide motivation to use this learning (and the feedback provided) to aim for better results next time. As such students are also developing resilience, learning that disappointing results are, in many domains, a part of life: we can deal with and bounce back from such experiences, often stronger and wiser than we were before. Teaching our students such basic reframing techniques can be helpful in developing their EI and their resilience.

On developing an 'emotional curriculum for the helping professions,' Grant and Kinman (2013) suggest several evidence-based strategies that have the potential to enhance EI and resilience in students from any discipline. These include: mindfulness approaches, reflective practices (e.g. narrative writing, logs, journals), peer mentoring/coaching and experiential learning (e.g. case studies, role-plays, simulations). The next section includes some practical examples of resilience-building activities.

6.7 Practical Examples of EI and Resilience Building Activities

6.7.1 Reflection and Reflexivity

The opportunity to reflect and challenge thinking using models such as the 'ABCDE' (Adversity, Behaviour, Consequences, Disputation, Energising) technique (Seligman, 2012) could be the best route to resilience. For example, students might be encouraged to undertake carefully controlled peer conversations using the ABCDE framework to talk through a low-level challenging situation that they have encountered. This would allow them to recognise the consequences of misinterpreting a difficult life event, offering the opportunity for a re-think and realisation of their own capacity to be resilient. Additionally, reflecting on experiences where things have not gone quite to plan (often the best opportunities for a learning experience) can be quite valuable, especially if poor emotional management was involved. Encouraging students to consider what they might have said or done differently to bring about a more positive outcome, provides them with alternative strategies to use in future similar situations and helps them to develop their EI ability.

6.7.2 Timeline Exercise

It can be useful to remind students of transition points throughout their lives (changing schools, minor setbacks, exam re-sits, obstacles encountered and surmounted) through a simple timeline activity. Students plot a timeline of their life from birth to present (horizontally or vertically) and are encouraged to note down key moments of dealing with changes in their life experience. This is undertaken on an individual basis to begin with. For most students, this activity will pinpoint normal life changes such as starting school, a first Saturday job or a bad school report. Instructions for this activity should recommend care and sensitivity in relation to more troubling memories. Students then reflect on what helped them through such key transition points. They uncover their own approach to overcoming these obstacles and then share with a peer their own resilience strategy. As a result, they become more fully aware of their own resilience quotient and can be encouraged to see future changes in a more positive light. This exercise affirms and commends their own personal resourcefulness and raises valuable self-awareness, a key aspect in the development of EI.

6.7.3 Gratitude Practices

Gratitude practices are characterised by purposeful activities that requires someone to recall on a regular basis what they are grateful for. This encourages a high positivity to negativity ratio in the mind (Fredrikson, 2009) or a 'brightening' of the mind (Wilson, 2016). This 'gratitude attitude' (Action for Happiness, 2018) or 'grateful recounting' (Watkins, Udher, & Pichinevskiy, 2014) encourages a resourcefulness habit, building resilience for learning: 'College students who practice gratitude on a consistent basis…experience increased ability to focus while learning and remain resilient when learning felt challenging.' (Wilson, 2016). The 'Three Blessings Technique' (Centre for Confidence, 2018) or the 'Find Three Good Things Each Day' practice (Action for Happiness, 2018) can also be included within a personal development segment of a university teaching session. Students may also be encouraged to test out a gratitude journal entry, write a gratitude letter or engage in a gratitude conversation with a peer.[4]

Any activities that involve students working collaboratively provide opportunities for the development of EI and resilience. Recent empirical research provides further evidence for the notion that Interdisciplinary Education (IDE) activities are particularly helpful in relation to students' development of emotional competence (Pertegal-Felices et al., 2017).

6.8 Interdisciplinary Education (IDE) and the Development of EI and Resilience

Other drivers that have accompanied the cultural shifts in HE include the introduction of the Research Excellence Framework (HEFCE, 2017) and the Teaching Excellence Framework (GovUK, 2017) both of which encourage interdisciplinary working. Collaborative working and working alongside stakeholders is increasingly viewed as one of the measures of effective education, mirroring broader cultural shifts.

6.8.1 IDE and Connectivity

A tension exists between what constitutes preparedness for work, from the standpoints of students and employers. Clearly, discipline knowledge is important, but increasingly students (and those who pay their fees) want to be reassured that they will be able to secure graduate employment, function effectively in the workplace and manage the transition to work: this includes being able to make connections, work collectively in teams and manage relationships with colleagues and stakeholders. Interprofessional education is a requirement of professional statutory bodies in Health and Social care and is defined as 'occasions when two or more professionals learn with, from and about each other to improve collaboration and the quality of care' (Centre for Advancement of Interprofessional Education, CAIPE, 2017). For collaborative learning to be inclusive of all students and not only those in specific contexts, it is necessary for the parameters to be extended to include disciplines as well as professions, thereby ensuring that the benefits are experienced across the student body. Learning about others enables students to also learn about themselves, which is one of the components of resilience and an essential aspect of developing EI.

Within specific disciplines, IDE is increasingly part of educational and practice landscapes, (e.g. Police Foundation, 2016; NHS 2014). The NHS focus on inte-

---

[4]Having tested out these resilience-building and EI development activities with students, the authors have found that students valued the opportunity to develop self-awareness and recognise that these practical strategies benefit them in the present and for the future.

grated care is a key driver in increasing collaboration across services. This is however restricted to the public sector. Increasingly, businesses require connected, integrated, adaptable, culturally aware graduates whatever their primary field: 'Interdisciplinarity looks at the same phenomena from different viewpoints but tries to integrate the explanations producing connected stories.' (Adunmo, Bitterberg & Schindler-Daniels, 2013). For many HEIs this is supported by a 'solution focused approach' to interdisciplinary learning, where examples are drawn from the workplace to simulate real-world problem solving. IDE is driven also by the belief that students benefit from learning together. IDE thus includes the 'ability to change perspectives, to synthesize knowledge of different disciplines and to cope with complexity.' (Spelt et al., 2009). This is important in a context where HEIs must prepare students for roles which may not yet exist, and in working closely with people they may never meet face-to-face. Increasingly, portfolio careers will be characterized by adaptability and agility between disciplines, contexts and sometimes identities, with the 'constant' being the individual's own ability to evolve, connect and reframe their skills.

6.8.2   IDE and Emotional Resilience

Interdisciplinary work with students indicates that opportunities to work together enables not only learners, but also their lecturers, to understand the roles and perspectives of other disciplines and professions (Gurbutt & Williams, 2018). This is a relatively unexplored facet of IDE, namely the learning about collaboration which occurs between staff, leading to increased interconnectedness across faculty (and providing a site for co-creation). It also provides an opportunity for students to learn from the ways in which academic staff model collaborations, in addition to teaching the theory of collective working. One of the challenges experienced by students is the requirement to work in teams, and not just familiar teams, but the shifting teams that mirror the practice inherent in some workplaces. Developing a rapport with others, building confidence and trust, and being confident within their own professional identity are areas in which carefully constructed IDE can help to build resilience and EI. IDE facilitates a raised awareness of different perspectives and insights, helps develop empathy, and the cross fertilisation of knowledge and skills. Students are enabled to consider alternative perspectives, priorities and practices. In short, IDE provides a safe space to practice skills for employability, including EI and resilience, and to develop and express an emerging professional identity (Gurbutt and Milne, 2018).

6.8.3   IDE and Employability

Quantifying the 'good' student experience remains elusive. The benefits of IDE are difficult to measure via the traditional modes of assessment, but there is a growing awareness within industry and the public sector that the prevalence of so-called 'wicked problems' requires an innovative approach to employment and employability. The emphasis is increasingly on collaboration, problem-solving and disruption of traditional boundaries. The HE sector increasingly is enabling students to develop these skills in collaboration with others within and across disciplines:

> Many of the major challenges that society faces today will require solutions developed through interdisciplinary research and cross disciplinary collaboration. Improving support for and addressing the barriers to this work could contribute to major scientific breakthroughs at the interface of disciplines, develop new technologies and ultimately support the economy and develop novel solutions to societal challenges. (The Royal Society, 2015)

6.9   Conclusion

Our students and graduates face a rapidly changing landscape in relation to the world of work, but this is not necessarily a negative thing. Change can bring increased opportunity, but to take advantage of this, graduates need to be equipped with the knowledge, skills, abilities and personal attributes that will allow them to adapt, effectively communicate and collaborate globally. As the use of large-scale automation and artificial intelligence increases throughout the labour market, some current job roles will no longer exist. In many areas, such as consulting, project management, and in fields like medicine, dentistry, legal, and customer service occupations, there will always be a need for resilient, adaptable people with effective interpersonal skills and a willingness and capacity to work in interprofessional and interdisciplinary ways. Nearly all job growth since 1980 has been in occupations that are relatively social-skill intensive: this is because people are generally much better than computers at human interaction (Deming, 2017). By providing our students with opportunities to develop their employability, including EI and resilience, we should ensure that they stand a much better chance of achieving their goals, gaining and retaining the occupations that will bring them satisfaction and success, and making their unique contribution to the world based on an education model that favours self-direction and personal development.

References

Action for Happiness. (2018, 1 August). Retrieved from http://www.actionforhappiness.org/take-action/find-three-good-things-each-day.

Adunmo, K., Bitterberg, C., & Schindler-Daniels, A. (2013). *Pulling it together*. European Union Policy Brief, NET4SOCIETY. Retrieved from http://www.net4society.eu/_media/PB_N4S_FINAL.pdf..

Altaras Dimitrijevic, A., Jolic Marjanovic, Z., & Dimitrivijevic, A. (2018). Whichever intelligence makes you happy: The role of academic, emotional, and practical abilities in predicting psychological well-being. *Personality and Individual Differences, 132,* 6–13. https://doi.org/10.1016/j. paid.2018.05.010.

Barnett, R. (2014). Imagining the humanities – Amid the inhuman. *Arts and Humanities in Higher Education, 13*(1–2), 42–53. https://doi.org/10.1177/1474022213511338

Bennett, D. (2018). *Embedding employABILITY thinking across Australian higher education.* Canberra: Australian Government Department of Education and Training.

Burns, T., & Sinfield, S. (2004). *Teaching and learning and study skills: A guide for tutors.* London: Sage.

Butcher, V., Smith, J., Kettle, J., et al. (2011). *Review of good practice in employability and enterprise development by centres of excellence in teaching and learning.* York: Higher Education Academy.

CAIPE. (2017). Centre for Advancement of Interprofessional Education. Retrieved from https:// www.caipe.org/.

Centre for Confidence. (2018, 1 August). Retrieved from www.centreforconfidence.co.uk/ flourishing-lives.

Cole, D., & Tibby, M. (2013). *Defining and developing your approach to employability.* York: Higher Education Academy.

Costa, K. (2016, January 15). When your kid emotionally throws up on you [Blog post]. Retrieved from https://www.psychologytoday.com/intl/blog/reset-247/201601/when-your-kid-emotionally-throws-you.

Côté, S., & Miners, C. T. H. (2006). Emotional intelligence, cognitive intelligence and job performance. *Administrative Science Quarterly, 51,* 1–28.

Dacre Pool, L., & Qualter, P. (2012). Improving emotional intelligence and emotional self-efficacy through a teaching intervention for university students. *Learning and Individual Differences, 22,* 306–312.

Dacre Pool, L., & Qualter, P. (Eds.). (2018). *An introduction to emotional intelligence.* Chichester: Wiley.

Dacre Pool, L., & Sewell, P. (2007). The key to employability: developing a practical model of graduate employability. *Education + Training, 49*(4), 277–289.

Dacre Pool, L., & Sewell, P. (2012). 'The CareerEDGE model of graduate employability'. *Pedagogy for employability 2012, implications for practice, 12 June 2012* (L. Dacre Pool, Presentation). Birmingham City University.

Deming, D. J. (2017). The growing importance of social skills in the labor market. *Quarterly Journal of Economics, 132*(4), 1593–1640. https://doi.org/10.1093/qje/qjx022.

Duckworth, A. (2016). *Grit: The power of passion and perseverance.* New York: Scribner.

Dweck, C. (2006). *Mindset: The new psychology of success.* New York: Random House.

Edinburgh University Student Resilience Model. (2016, 2 August). *Building student resilience model.* Retrieved from https://www.ed.ac.uk/institute-academic-development/learning-teaching/ staff/levels/academic-transitions-toolkit/building-student-resilience-model.

Forsythe, A. (2017). I doubt very seriously whether anyone will hire me; factors predicting employability perceptions in higher education. *Cogent Psychology, 4,* 1385131. https://doi.org/10.1080/ 23311908.2017.1385131.

Fredrikson, B. (2009). *Positivity.* New York: Crown Publishing/Random House.

Fugate, M., Kinicki, A. J., & Ashforth, B. E. (2004). Employability: A psychosocial construct, its dimensions, and applications. *Journal of Vocational Behavior, 65,* 14–38. https://doi.org/10. 1016/j.jvb.2003.10.005.

GovUK. (2017). *Teaching excellence framework.* London: Department of Education, GovUK. Retrieved from https://www.gov.uk/government/news/universities-rated-in-teaching-excellence-framework.

Grant, K., & Hooley, T. (2017). *Graduate career handbook.* Bath: Crimson Publishing.

Grant, L., & Kinman, G. (2013). *The importance of emotional resilience for staff and students in the 'helping' professions. Developing an emotional curriculum.* York: Higher Education Academy.

Gurbutt, D. J., & Williams, K. (2018). Performing good teaching: the frontstage and backstage work of interdisciplinary working. In *INTED Conference,* Valencia, Spain: Published Proceedings.

Gurbutt, D. J., & Milne, P. (2018). The path to transformation: navigating the barriers to forming transient and transitional learning groups in interprofessional education. In *INTED Conference*, Spain: Published Proceedings.

HECSU. (2017). Retrieved from https://www.hecsu.ac.uk/assets/assets/documents/Graduate_Market_Trends_Autumn_2017(1).pdf.

HEFCE. (2017). National Student Survey. Retrieved from http://www.hefce.ac.uk/lt/nss/.

HEFCE Research Excellence Framework. (2017). London: HEFCE. Retrieved from http://www.ref.ac.uk/.

Knight, P., & Yorke, M. (2004). *Learning, curriculum and employability in higher education*. London: Routledge Falmer.

Krumboltz, J. (2008). The happenstance learning theory. *Journal of Career Assessment, 17, 2*. https://doi.org/10.1177/1069072708328861.

Kwek, A., Bui, T., Rynne, J., & So, K. (2013). The impacts of self-esteem and resilience on academic performance: An investigation of domestic and international hospitality and tourism undergraduate students. *Journal of Hospitality & Tourism Education, 25*(3), 110–122.

Lopes, P. N., Brackett, M. A., Nezlek, J. B., Schutz, A., Sellin, I., & Salovey, P. (2004). Emotional intelligence and social interaction. *Personality and Social Psychological Bulletin, 30,* 1018–1034. https://doi.org/10.1177/0146167204264762.

Maddi, S. R. (n.d.). The Hardiness Institute. Retrieved from http://www.hardinessinstitute.com/.

Maddi, S. R., & Khoshaba, D. M. (2005). *Resilience at work*. New York: Amacom Books.

Mayer, J. D., & Salovey, P. (1997). What is emotional intelligence? In P. Salovey & D. Sluyter (Eds.), *Emotional development and emotional intelligence: Implications for educators* (pp. 3–31). New York: Basic Books.

Mayer, J. D., Salovey, P., & Caruso, D. R. (2004). Emotional intelligence: Theory, findings and implications. *Psychol. Inq., 15,* 197–215. https://doi.org/10.1207/s15327965pli1503_02.

Mitchell, K. (2004) *The unplanned career—how to turn curiosity into opportunity*. Vancouver: Chronicle Books.

Nelis, D., Kotsou, I., Quoidbach, J., Hansenne, M., Weyens, F., Dupuis, P., et al. (2011). Increasing emotional competence improves psychological and physical well-being. *Social Relationships and Employability. Emotion, 11*(2), 354–366. https://doi.org/10.1037/a0021554.

NHS Five Year Forward View 2014. Gov.UK. Retrieved from https://www.england.nhs.uk/five-year-forward-view/.

NUS/QAA. (2012). *Student experience research 2012*. Retrieved from https://www.nus.org.uk/PageFiles/12238/2012_NUS_QAA_Independent_Learning_and_Contact_Hours.pdf.

O'Boyle, E. H., Jr., Humphrey, R. H., Pollack, J. M., Hawver, T. H., & Story, P. A. (2010). The relation between emotional intelligence and job performance: A meta-analysis. *Journal of Organizational Behavior, 32*(5), 788–818. https://doi.org/10.1002/job.714.

Pertegal-Felices, M.L., Marcos-Jorquera, D., Gilar-Corbi, R., & Jimeno-Rorenilla, A. (2017). Development of emotional skills through interdisciplinary practices integrated into a university curriculum. *Education Research International, 2017*, Article ID 6089859.

Petrides, K. V., & Furnham, A. (2001). Trait emotional intelligence: Psychometric investigation with reference to established trait taxonomies. *European Journal of Personality, 15,* 425–448. https://doi.org/10.1002/per.416.

Police Foundation. (2016). *Improving policing for the benefit of the public*. Retrieved from http://www.police-foundation.org.uk/uploads/catalogerfiles/working-together-building-effective-multi-agency-partnerships/multi_agency_partnerships.pdf.

Qualter, P., Gardner, K. J., Pope, D. J., Hutchinson, J. M., & Whiteley, H. E. (2012). Ability emotional intelligence, trait emotional intelligence, and academic success in British secondary schools: A 5-year longitudinal study. *Learning and Individual Differences, 22,* 83–91. https://doi.org/10.1016/j.lindif.2011.11.007.

Reivich, K., & Schatter, A. (2003). *The resilience factor: 7 keys to finding your inner strength and overcoming life's hurdles*. New York: Broadway Books/Random House.

Robbins, A., Kaye, E., & Catling, J. C. (2018). Predictors of student resilience in higher education. *Psychology Teaching Review, 24*(1), 44–52.

Rode, J. C., Arthaud-Day, M., Ramaswami, A., & Howes, S. (2017). A time-lagged study of emotional intelligence and salary. *Journal of Vocational Behavior, 101*, 77–89. https://doi.org/10.1016/j.vb.2017.05.001.

Sanchez-Alvarez, N., Extremera, N., & Fernandez-Berrocal, P. (2015). Maintaining life satisfaction in adolescence: Affective mediators of the influence of perceived emotional intelligence on overall life satisfaction judgements in a two-year longitudinal study. *Frontiers in Psychology, 6*, 1892.

Seligman, M. (2012). *Flourish: a visionary new understanding of happiness and well-being.* New York: Simon and Schuster.

Small, L., Shacklock, K., & Marchant, T. (2018). Employability: a contemporary review for higher/education stakeholders. *Journal of Vocational Education & Training, 70*(1), 148–166. https://doi.org/10.1080/13636820.2017.1394355.

Smith, M., Bell, K., Bennett, D., & McAlpine, A. (2018). *Employability in a global context: Evolving policy and practice in employability, work integrated learning, and career development learning.* Retrieved from https://www.researchgate.net/publication/326264677_Employability_in_a_Global_Context_Evolving_Policy_and_Practice_in_Employability_Work_Integrated_Learning_and_Career_Development_Learning.

Spelt, E. J. H., Biemans, H. J. A., Tobi, H., et al. (2009). Teaching and learning in interdisciplinary higher education: A systematic review. *Educational Psychology Review, 21*, 365. https://doi.org/10.1007/s10648-009-9113-z.

The Royal Society. (2015). Response to the British Academy's call for evidence on 'Interdisciplinarity'. Retrieved from https://royalsociety.org/~/media/policy/Publications/2015/29-06-15-rs-response-to-ba-inquiry-interdisciplinarity.pdf.

Turnipseed, D. L. (2018). Emotional intelligence and OCB: The moderating role of work locus of control. *The Journal of Social Psychology, 158*(3), 322–336. https://doi.org/10.1080/00224545.2017.1346582.

Universities UK/CBI. (2009). *Future fit: Preparing graduates for the world of work.* Retrieved from https://www.universitiesuk.ac.uk/policy-and-analysis/reports/Pages/future-fit-preparing-graduates-for-the-world-of-work.aspx.

Walter, F., Cole, M. S., & Humphrey, R. H. (2011). Emotional intelligence: Sine Qua Non of leadership or folderol? *Academy of Management Perspectives, 25*(1), 45–59.

Watkins, P. C., Udher, J., & Pichinevskiy, S. (2014). Grateful recounting enhances subjective well-being: The importance of grateful processing. *The Journal of Positive Psychology*, 1–8.

Wilson, J. T. (2016). Brightening the mind: The impact of practicing gratitude on focus and resilience in learning *Journal of the Scholarship of Teaching and Learning, 16*(4), 1–13.

World Economic Forum. (2016). *The future of jobs. Employment Trends.* Retrieved from http://reports.weforum.org/future-of-jobs-2016/employment-trends/.

Yip, J. A., & Côté, S. (2013). The emotionally intelligent decision maker: Emotion-understanding ability reduces the effect of incidental anxiety on risk taking. *Psychological Sciences, 24*(1), 48–55. https://doi.org/10.1177/0956797612450031.

Lorraine Dacre Pool (Ph.D.) is a Chartered Psychologist and Principal Lecturer, Student & Staff Development, at the University of Central Lancashire, (UCLAN), England, UK. She designed and published the *CareerEDGE* model of graduate employability and later developed the Employability Development Profile, both of which are in use in many universities nationally and internationally. She has particular expertise in the subject of Emotional Intelligence (EI) which was the topic of her Ph.D. research: this also involved the successful design, delivery and evaluation of a taught module, details of which were published in the journal of *Learning and Individual Differences*. She has published a number of articles on graduate employability and EI, and has recently co-edited a textbook for the British Psychological Society '*An Introduction to Emotional Intelligence*'. She is a Principal Fellow of the Higher Education Academy.

Dawne Gurbutt (Ph.D.) is a Professor and Head of Collaborative Education at the University of Central Lancashire (UCLAN), England. An experienced person-centred practitioner and academic, her background is in health, having had extensive experience of working in areas of social deprivation prior to moving into HE. She has managed a wide range of HE provision across different settings and has held strategic roles including working for the HEA, UK, where she led on initiatives to increase collaboration across disciplines and explore innovative ways of achieving interdisciplinary working. Through mentoring and coaching for many years, she is committed to widening participation, community engagement, collaborative education and service-user engagement. She is an Honorary Fellow of the Centre for the Advancement of Inter-professional Education (CAIPE) and a member of the CAIPE Board where she co-leads the Learning and Teaching group.

Kath Houston (M.Ed) is a Senior Lecturer of Employability and Enterprise at the University of Central Lancashire (UCLAN), England, a career guidance practitioner, and a career management author of books for schools, college and university students. Her current role includes responsibility for undergraduate and postgraduate employability education and the innovative use of all modes of learning to engage students and enhance the learning experience and the future career destinations of graduates. Her Masters level study was on the psychology of attention. She holds postgraduate diplomas in career guidance and in university teaching and learning.

Chapter 7
The Role of 'Learner Identity' and Experience-Related Beliefs in Developing Desirable Graduate Attributes

Dawne Irving-Bell

7.1 Introduction

Negotiating Higher Education can be a difficult and daunting experience for many students: in addition to helping them gain a qualification, Universities must also ensure that their students develop professional, work-related competencies, skills and attributes during their course of study. Against a backdrop of neoliberalism (where the forces of the market economy have led to much debate around the value, purpose and role of a university education), this chapter explores the expectations upon those working in Higher Education to deliver 'work-ready' graduates with skills and attributes beyond those linked immediately to their degree. Based upon findings from research undertaken to explore the formation of learner identity, the chapter begins by discussing the significance that entrenched personal learning histories may play in the construction of an individual's identity as a learner. Specifically, it asks how an individual's perceptions of learning are shaped by their previous learning experiences, and how the meanings assigned to those experiences might influence and shape their current and future learning attitudes and approaches to study. In other words, failure to effectively manage one's own experience-related beliefs may lead some students to impose unintentional barriers upon themselves that may limit their own learning. Emotion and self-efficacy matter: the impact that anxiety, and feelings of inadequacy or vulnerability may have upon a student's ability to effectively access learning cannot be overlooked.

The chapter discusses issues around student development and introduces the concept of self-sabotage, where the influence of unintentional, closed-learning behaviours impacts adversely upon an individual, restricting their opportunities for learning and personal growth. Potential strategies are suggested: these are aimed at those working in Higher Education to create purposeful learning environments,

D. Irving-Bell (✉)
Edge Hill University, England, UK
e-mail: belld@edgehill.ac.uk

© Springer Nature Switzerland AG 2019
A. Diver (ed.), *Employability via Higher Education: Sustainability as Scholarship*,
https://doi.org/10.1007/978-3-030-26342-3_7

designed to support students, by helping them develop the skills and competencies needed to cope with setbacks. Via the development of emotional and academic resilience, students should emerge from Higher Education not merely as 'work-ready' personnel, but as well-rounded, confident individuals possessing both the agency and the capital to sustain their own self-development as they move from University into the workplace and beyond.

7.2   Defining 'Work-Readiness'

Arguably, many students will already hold some form of employment experience, at the time of entry to Higher Education. As such, they may have experience of completing online application forms, or engaging with some form of psychometric testing, and will likely have experienced both telephone and face-to-face interview procedures. Taking the likelihood of this prior experience into account, it is important to define what exactly is meant by the term 'work-readiness,' and to highlight how this concept relates to those work-related skills and competencies that are desired by employers and identify which attributes Universities are being tasked with developing. Here, the term 'work-related attributes' refers to the skills and competencies students must acquire in addition to their degree i.e. attributes developed in addition to subject knowledge, relating to its application in practice. Preparation for employment is defined here as the gaining of such personal characteristics as self-efficacy, alongside the development of transferable skills (namely, critical thinking, problem-solving, communication and teamworking). As such, 'work-readiness' refers here to the development of individual agency and autonomy, personal resilience, not necessarily with the sole purpose of becoming a graduate, but to become a 'whole person' with a life-long curiosity for learning.

7.3   Defining Learner Identity

Identity may be said to arise from the collection of stories that people tell themselves about their lives. As Sfard and Prusak (2005) argue, identity is the meaning we assign to those stories. According to Bukor (2015: 323), an individual's identity emerges from an 'intricate and tangled web of influences... rooted in personal and professional life experiences.' Exploring identity within the context of students as learners, Beauchamp and Thomas (2009) note the link between identity and agency, and the key role emotions play in shaping identity, stressing the power of stories and discourse in respect of supporting our understanding. Clearly, emotions are deeply entwined within an individual's identity (Hong, 2012; Yuan & Lee, 2016; Zembylas, 2005). Identity is not something that is fixed or unchangeable. As Nghia (2017) states, the shaping and reshaping of identity may be viewed through the lens of self-determination theory: Deci and Ryan (2017) similarly suggest that individuals do have control over their own destinies, including the ability to exercise agency over the construction of their own identities. Identity is a fluid, socially constructed, ever-changing concept: new meanings are made as a result of an individual's interpretation of their (new and past) experiences. How individuals' approach learning and respond to (and subsequently assign meaning to) new experiences, is inextricably bound to whatever meanings they might have assigned to experiences that they have experienced in the past. In sum, the potential impact of negative learning experiences is quite clear and may in some instances lead inadvertently toward unhelpful attitudes toward present and future learning, and to harmful patterns of learning behaviour.

7.4 Understanding Students' Approaches to Learning

Studies by Entwistle and Ramsden (1983) and Marton and Säljö (1976) have identified two qualitatively different ways in which students approach the task of learning.

7.4.1 Surface Approaches to Learning

According to Marton and Säljö (1984), the cognitive activities of those learners who adopt surface approaches tend to involve the memorisation of facts for the basic purpose of recalling knowledge. From a learner's perspective, learning is conceived as the act of 'increasing one's knowledge' (Virtanen & Lindblom-Ylänne, 2010). As Savin-Baden (2000) and Gibbs (1992) explain, the characteristics of surface learning include:

- The adoption of 'rote' approaches to learning
- Concentration on the memorisation of facts, giving the impression that understanding has occurred
- The recall of knowledge
- Remembering, or finding the 'right' answers.

And yet, in some instances the surface approach is not as superficial as it may first appear. At times, 'superficial' learners may be employing a sophisticated strategy, using this approach as a strategic learning tool to increase achievement, to pre-select and prioritise only what they need or want to learn with the specific intention of achieving only a minimal pass (Biggs & Tang, 2007). Setting the strategic surface approach aside, as Biggs and Tang (2007) outline, factors associated with surface learning (from the student's perspective) may well include the following:

- A cynical view of education
- Non-academic priorities exceeding academic ones (insufficient time combined with a high workload)

- Misunderstanding of the necessary depth of understanding required (for example thinking that factual recall is adequate)
- A genuine inability to understand the topic or subject (at a deep level).

7.4.2   Deep Approaches to Learning

While it is acknowledged that there is a general lack of research to explore students' conceptions of teaching (Virtanen & Lindblom-Ylänne, 2010), deep approaches to learning seem to be associated with students who can see real value in learning and who aim to understand more fully the concepts taught (Marton & Säljö, 1984). Many studies (Marton & Säljö, 1997; Trigwell, Prosser, & Waterhouse, 1999; Van Rossum & Schenk, 1984) have shown that deeper approaches to learning can be related to higher quality learning outcomes: these may be attributed to higher levels of motivation, enjoyment, or independent learning (Prosser & Trigwell, 1999; Ramsden, 1992). Where a student adopts a deep approach to their own learning they are clearly seeking to understand ideas and concepts, and underpinning theory to find meaning within the learning materials under consideration (Fry, Ketteridge, & Marshall, 2009; Gibbs, 1992; Savin-Baden, 2000). Findings from our recent research (Irving-Bell, 2018) showed that those students who adopt '*deep*' approaches to their own development are often better able to manage their own internal beliefs and to challenge their own vulnerabilities. They have the agency to work autonomously and believe they have control in shaping their own identity which leads to increased confidence, higher levels of motivation, and feelings of self-satisfaction.

Subsequently they are more open to working collaboratively within new and unfamiliar cultures (Van Veen, Sleegers, & van de Ven, 2005) and more likely to develop and demonstrate positive attitudes towards their own learning, with benefits including autonomy (Lea, Stephenson, & Troy, 2003). Deep approaches were also likely to result in students' engagement with learning, including discourse, debate, questioning, explanation, and feedback (Ramsden, 1997). As Trigwell and Prosser (2004) noted, irrespective of the quality of teaching, students who adopt deeper approaches to learning (i.e. where participants immersed themselves '*deeply*' in their chosen programme) show an ability to challenge themselves, take ownership, and be reflective of their own learning. Conversely, where participants exhibited traits of having adopted surface approaches to their personal learning development, they were less likely to challenge their own existing attitudes and beliefs. They were more likely to adopt behaviours that could limit their development (Irving-Bell, 2018; Trigwell and Prosser, 2004).

7.5   The Impact of Personal Histories on Learner Identity and Learning Approaches

This section discusses the potential impacts of prior learning experiences on an individual's development. It argues that the failure to manage experience-related beliefs may lead some students to self-impose barriers that can limit their own learning and prevent them from developing essential and professional 'work-related' attributes such as self-efficacy, self-regulation and confidence.

7.5.1   Self-efficacy

The theoretical foundations of self-efficacy are grounded in social cognitive theory (Bandura,1993) and characterised as a belief or judgement about one's own capabilities, not least the extent to which a person believes in their own ability to accomplish a given task and reach their set goals. Self-efficacy is comprised of two components: efficacy expectations (defined as a belief in personal capacity to affect behaviour) and outcome expectations (the belief that one's behaviour will result in a desired outcome). (Bandura, 1997) Where an individual shows elevated levels of self-efficacy they may exhibit increased confidence and motivation, and be more likely to be goals and achievement orientated (Khorrami-Arani, 2001) and more likely to invest greater time and effort into their personal development. Guskey (1998) similarly explored efficacy in terms of 'receptivity to change' and found that those with self-efficacy were more likely to be more open to new practices. Conversely, where learners exhibited low self-efficacy levels, they tended to be less self-reflective and less receptive to new styles of teaching.

7.5.2   Self-regulation

Closely linked to efficacy, self-regulation (or self-regulated learning) describes an individual's ability to consciously control their own learning (Zimmerman, 2000). Here, self-regulation is categorised either as High Self-Regulation (HSR) or Low Self-Regulation (LSR). According to Zimmerman (2002, 2008, 2011) those who possess HSR tend to be more active in their own learning, more able to challenge themselves and work vigorously to address their own professional vulnerabilities. Where HSR is evident, participation in learning is autonomous, often born out of pure self-interest, stemming from desire or self-identified need. Zimmerman (2001, 2011) also identifies a link between HSR and those who adopt deep approaches to their learning, possess increased motivation, and have a fairly powerful 'sense of self.' Therefore, they tended to adopt a deeper approach to their own learning, and as autonomous learners were more likely to be more confident, resilient and emotionally stronger, and exhibit increased agency. Littlejohn (2016) and Milligan, Littlejohn, and Margaryan (2014) further argue that where self-regulation is high, learning tends to be driven by the individual, with both satisfaction and learning being increased. In contrast, those who exhibit LSR often have limited belief in their own agency, or ability to initiate change (Milligan et al., 2014). Linking self-efficacy to learner achievement, suggests that those with higher self-efficacy levels tend to enjoy better learning outcomes (Bandura, 1997) and enhanced autonomy, confidence and self-motivation (Midgley, Feldlaufer, & Eccles, 1989), which are of course all extremely desirable characteristics in terms of what prospective employers are likely to seek.

7.6   Navigating Personal Learning Histories

Very few studies consider the role that personal learning histories play in determining how students approach learning and the accessing of new knowledge. In relation to developing work-related graduate attributes (and based upon the outcomes of research which observed the meanings that learners in Higher Education assigned to their previous experiences of learning) Irving-Bell (2018) explores how the experiences that students bring with them might influence not only their approaches to learning but might also affect self-efficacy and confidence levels. Grounded firmly in student narratives, analysis of the data found that experience-related beliefs have a significant impact upon Higher Education students' attitudes toward, and their engagement with, academic life whilst at university. The meaning they assign to their prior experiences as learners is an important factor in determining how they approach current learning, and hence plays a crucial role in the formation of their identity as learners within Higher Education. Irving-Bell (2018) found that where the meanings assigned to prior experiences were negative, students tended to exhibit limited agency, believing they will have little or no control over their personal development. This influenced their ability to navigate learning effectively, and, as a result, self-efficacy was also restricted. Because the process of remembering causes them to act, think and feel as they do, research also found that where meaning is assigned in this way students were more likely to adopt surface approaches to learning: there was a strong correlation between the students' limited efficacy and lowered self-confidence levels.

Students were then more likely to be passive consumers of knowledge and have low levels of self-efficacy. They were less likely to be confident, nor would they easily develop strong graduate, work-related attributes which employers and market forces tend to demand. In practice this means that a student may have limited confidence in their abilities as learners and possess low social capital. Consequently, they may be hesitant or unable to engage fully with learning activities presented to them, not least self-assessment, critical thinking and problem-solving activities. As such, they were less likely to be able to take full advantage of the opportunities open to them, including engagement with key employability-enhancing activities and experiences.

7.7   The Notion of Self-sabotage

Irving-Bell (2018) argues that, for some students, meanings self-assigned (to their personal learning experiences, philosophies, ideological beliefs, views and opinions) have the potential to lead to the unintentional sabotage of their own still-emergent identities. Unintentional self-sabotage, if unchallenged, may lead the learner to engage in behaviours which have the potential to impede their development as learners. The result is that they unintentionally incapacitate themselves, halting or impeding the evolution of their identity as a leaner and ultimately slowing down their own development. At a fundamental level, self-sabotage occurs where the individual is unaware of (or unable to challenge) their own experience-related beliefs, personal narratives and stories that individuals tend to tell themselves. Research suggests that behaviours are influenced by underlying beliefs, values and attitudes (Reynolds, Sammons, De Fraine, Townsend, & Van Damme, 2011). Unless an individual is convinced of the need to alter their approach, they will avoid adapting their behaviours. The process of challenging, let alone changing, one's own personal beliefs is problematic: as Bell and Gilbert (1994), Day and Sachs (2004), Pekrun and Linnenbrink-Garcia (2014), and Stoll et al. (2006) observe, it is likely to lead to an emotional response. With respect to one's emotional state, self-sabotaging behaviours are likely to manifest in negative feelings, which will likely include uncertainty and powerlessness, which can in turn lead to the lowering of self-esteem. Self-sabotage leaves learners unable to move beyond their internally imposed boundaries and damages their own development, as they unintentionally incapacitate themselves and halt the formation of their own identity. Deep-rooted personal philosophies and naïve expectations are likely to be a significant contributory factor in self-sabotaging student behaviours. In some instances, students may be aware of the potential need to '*modify*' their fixed ideas (beliefs), and only then may new (different) professional practices emerge. With regards to the emotional impact, self-sabotage manifests as unpleasant feelings of uncertainty and of being powerless. This in turn leads to the lowering of self-esteem and conditions that will serve to limit the individual's ability to acquire the highly sought-after attributes that enable them to fully develop or acquire their identity. Self-sabotaging behaviours may be classified as per Fig. 7.1.

7.8   Strategies to Help to Overcome Self-sabotaging Behaviours

There can be no doubt that high-quality teaching has a significant impact on maximising a student's learning. If, however a student isn't receptive to or able to access new knowledge, teaching will have little impact, irrespective of its quality. The process of learning is a complex phenomenon, and learners need to be supported to understand how prior experiences might influence and inform their current behaviours. For those new to Higher Education it is important to ensure effective access to learning early

A classification of self-sabotaging behaviours	
1	*Unaware* There is no conscious awareness on behalf of the individual that their actions, attitudes, or behaviours are potentially contributing to the sabotage of their own development. Consequently, there is no awareness by the individual of any negative impact upon the development or formation of their identity.
2	*Difficulty* The individual may have limited belief in their own agency, believe that they have limited ability to make independent choices and decisions and as such may experience significant difficulty engaging with authentic self-reflection, which may serve to impede identity development.
3	*Reluctance* The individual is reluctant, or there is a disinclination, to embrace anything new or unfamiliar. They may have a limited belief in their own abilities and be closed to new concepts.
4	*Inflexible* The individual is inflexible in their approach, which manifests internally and externally as a resistance to change. In practice, this creates barriers to embracing anything perceived by the individual as different or new, irrespective of the origin of the idea or innovation being considered.
5	*Rigid* The individual is rigid in their approach, unable, or unwilling to move from their established views and beliefs. There is an inability to change, or to challenge personal philosophies around learning.

Fig. 7.1 A classification of self-sabotaging behaviours (Irving-Bell, 2018)

in their studies, particularly for those students with limited or limiting self-beliefs. Obviously the earlier the adoption of strategies to encourage deep approaches to learning, the better, in terms of avoiding self-sabotaging behaviours. Such strategies should help students avoid surface and shallow approaches and aim to scaffold the development of deep, reflective learning and development. They should aid students in becoming more emotionally resilient, to overcome difficulties and gain the attributes needed to motivate themselves to overcome obstacles and hurdles and persevere even when the work is challenging.

This chapter is divided into two parts. The first part focuses upon the implementation of extrinsic strategies, i.e. those systems and processes which institutions can utilise to help tutors support their students. The second part presents strategies designed specifically for tutors, which scaffold reflective learning, and can help move students into a suitable frame of mind where they are open to unfamiliar ideas, and able to take ownership of (and develop) their own intrinsic motivations.

7.8.1 Personalised Approaches to Attribute Development in Higher Education

One strategy that is effective in supporting students' transition into Higher Education is the adoption of personalised approaches to support and learning, not least in terms of providing a strong personal tutor programme, and a peer mentoring network.

7.8.2 Personal Tutoring

Irrespective of the label assigned (i.e. academic tutor, learning coach, or mentor) the role of the personal tutor is a well-established one within Higher Education. However, in practice it is often likely that the organisation of pastoral care at University will be very different from the systems a student may have experienced previously at school or college. It is therefore important, in addition to firstly having a strong system in place, to establish mutual expectations from the outset. Depending upon the subject discipline, degree, or programme of study the personal-tutor role will likely differ between departments: tutors should be mindful however of programmes where students may be working across two or more departments. Personal tutor meetings should focus upon learner development, progress and wellbeing: where the influence of prior personal learning experiences is working against a students' ability to engage fully, personal tutoring offers an ideal opportunity to introduce bespoke scaffolding strategies that are designed to encourage the learner to challenging their existing experience-related beliefs in a safe and supported environment. Peer Mentoring can similarly be beneficial to students, both as mentors and mentees, with both roles presenting students with opportunities for personal development and growth.

7.8.3 Effective Curriculum Design

It is essential that students follow a strong, well thought out curriculum. In practice this entails programmes designed by academics, often in conjunction with employers, practitioners, and students, and delivered by a range of appropriate professional services. When developing programmes, it is essential to reflect aspects of potential workplaces, presenting students with opportunities to engage in the practical application of their chosen degree of study. These should be integral to the programme of study, and not necessarily require skill development through the completion of added on, extra-curricular activities. Students with insufficient social or academic capital may lack the confidence needed to engage successfully with such extramural tasks.

7.8.4 Obtaining and Using Student Feedback

Given fees, the need to show 'value for money,' and the sense that Higher Education is now traded on the open market (available to purchase like an 'off the shelf' product), delivering a high-quality outcome for the 'consumer' is essential. It is increasingly necessary to try and understand, from the student-customer's perspective, what exactly they expect, want, and need. In addition to internal HEI student surveys and the UK's National Student Survey (NSS), many HEIs undertake a new student survey at the start of each academic year. In addition to a central survey, such department-level, early local surveys are often beneficial,[1] in terms of helping tutors respond to what students need to tell them, having curricular and planned activities meet expectations, and ensuring that student expectations align with those of academic staff, and their intended course content. This approach enables tutors to quickly identify areas where issues might arise, and act to ensure students can be supported, and (if appropriate) that aspects of the planned curriculum can be changed. In gauging a student's disposition towards learning, tutors may also find value in short surveys which capture significant student preconceptions and perceptions (e.g. on wellbeing, interests and expectations).

7.8.5 Self-reflection

There is much power in the use of self-reflective stories in shaping one's identity, combining parts of the past with the present (Feiman-Nemser, 2001: 1029). Engagement in genuine self-reflection helps students begin to understand how experience-related beliefs can, and do, shape the formation of their identity. Learners can actively help themselves become aware of (and avoid) potentially damaging, perhaps unintentional, self-sabotaging behaviours.

7.9   Conclusion

While still highly valued, an academic degree alone is not enough in today's competitive field, where employers adopt stringent recruitment and selection screening processes. As workforce demand for graduates continues to increase, so have employer expectations: graduates too expect to emerge from University with commercial awareness and to be in possession of a wide range of transferable key skills and competencies to secure the 'best' jobs. However, before students can begin to develop these highly sought-after qualities, often it is firstly necessary to strip away harmful experience-related learning beliefs. Only then, with firm foundations in place, might students have the agency and self-confidence to access learning, and acquire 'graduate, work-ready' attributes. There are many potential dangers in ignoring the complexities of a student's previous experiences. The influence and impact that these may have on an individual's interpretation of different pedagogical approaches cannot be discounted. How they are likely to respond to examinations and testing, or how they interpret and engage with differing styles of questioning and go onto demonstrate knowledge acquisition, can all be affected by earlier experiences and lingering perceptions. Learning is a complex phenomenon and supporting

---

[1] This should be carefully monitored so as not to overwhelm students with evaluations and surveys in their first weeks on campus and might best occur through the adoption of subtle mechanisms to gauge student views and opinions on their given subject.

students to overcome potentially self-sabotaging behaviours that hinder not only the individuals access to learning, but their wider ability to develop graduate attributes, is key in enabling them to enhance their academic resilience. As they grow in confidence, they should more easily develop a range of transferable skills which should in turn enable them to acquire the buoyancy required to successfully overcome a range of everyday challenges. Universities must consider the development of the individual holistically, and embed within their provision clear, compassionate strategies that will cultivate within students a genuine passion for life-long learning, ensuring that students have the necessary tools, agency and capital to sustain them well beyond University and into their future careers.

References

Bandura, A. (1993). Perceived self-efficacy in cognitive development and functioning. *Educational psychologist, 28*(2), 117–148.

Bandura, A. (1997). *Self-efficacy: The exercise of control*. New York: W. H. Freeman.

Beauchamp, C., & Thomas, L.. (2009). Understanding teacher identity: an overview of issues in the literature and implications for teacher education. *Cambridge Journal of Education, 39*(2), 175–189. Research Papers in Education 489.

Bell, B., & Gilbert, J. (1994). Teacher development as professional, personal and social development. *Teaching and Teacher Education, 10*(5), 483–497.

Biggs, J., & Tang, C. (2007). *Teaching for quality in learning at university* (3rd ed.). England: Society for Research into Higher Education and Open University Press.

Bukor, E. (2015). Exploring teacher identity from a holistic perspective: reconstructing and reconnecting personal and professional selves. *Teachers and Teaching, 21*(3), 305–327. https://doi.org/10.1080/13540602.2014.953818.

Day, C., & Sachs, J. (2004). Professionalism, performativity and empowerment: Discourses in the politics, policies and purposes of continuing professional development. C. Day & J. Sachs (Eds.), *International handbook on the continuing professional development of teachers* (pp. 3–32). Maidenhead: Open University Press.

Deci, R. M., & Ryan, E. L. (2017). Self-determination theory; basic psychological needs in motivation, development, and wellness. Guilford Press. ISBN 9781462528769. http://selfdeterminationtheory.org/authors/edward-deci/. Accessed 2 Oct 2018.

Entwistle, N., & Ramsden, P. (1983). *Understanding student learning (Routledge revivals)*. London: Routledge.

Feiman-Nemser, S. (2001). From preparation to practice: designing a continuum to strengthen and sustain teaching. *Teachers College Record, 103*(2001), 1013–1055.

Fry, H., Ketteridge, S., & Marshall, S. (2009). Understanding student learning. *A handbook for teaching and learning in higher education: Enhancing academic practice, 2*, 9–25.

Gibbs, G. (1992). *Improving the quality of student learning: Based on the Improving Student Learning Project funded by the Council for National Academic Awards*. Technical and Education Services.

Guskey, T. R. (1998). The age of our accountability. *Journal of Staff Development, 19*(4), 36–44.

Hong, J. Y. (2012). Why do some beginning teachers leave the school and others stay? Understanding teacher resilience through psychological lenses. *Teachers and Teaching: Theory and Practice, 18*, 417–440.

Irving-Bell, D. (2018). The formation of science, technology, engineering and mathematics teacher identities: pre-service teacher's perceptions. Lancaster University. https://doi.org/10.17635/lancaster/thesis/404.

Khorrami-Arani, O. (2001). Researching computer self-efficacy. *International Education Journal,* *2*(4), 17–25.

Lea, S. J., Stephenson, D., & Troy, J. (2003). Higher education students' attitudes to student-centred learning: Beyond 'educational bulimia'. *Studies in Higher Education, 28,* 321–334. https://doi. org/10.1080/03075070309293.

Littlejohn, A. (2016). Nine things autonomous learners do differently. In *SOLSTICE eLearning and Centre for Learning and Teaching Conference: A celebration of Learning and Teaching.* Edge Hill University, 9th and 10th June.

Marton, F., & Säaljö, R. (1976). On qualitative differences in learning—ii Outcome as a function of the learner's conception of the task. *British Journal of Educational Psychology, 46*(2), 115–127.

Marton, F., & Säljö, R. (1984). Approaches to learning. In F. Marton, F. Hounslow, & N. Entwistle (Eds.), *The experience of learning* (pp. 36–55). Scottish Academic Press.

Marton, F., & Säljö, R. (1997). Approaches to learning. In F. Marton, D. J. Hounsell, & N. J. Entwistle (Eds.), *The experience of learning* (2nd ed.). Edinburgh: Scottish Academic Press.

Midgley, C., Feldlaufer, H., & Eccles, J. S. (1989). Change in teacher efficacy and student self- and task-related beliefs in mathematics during the transition to junior high school. *Journal of Educational Psychology, 81*(2), 247.

Milligan, C., Littlejohn, A., & Margaryan, A. (2014). Workplace learning in informal networks. *Journal of Interactive Media in Education, 1*(6).

Nghia, T. L. H. (2017). What hinders teachers from translating their beliefs into teaching behaviours: The case of teaching generic skills in Vietnamese universities. *Teaching and Teacher Education, 64,* 105–114.

Pekrun, R., & Linnenbrink-Garcia, L. (Eds.). (2014). *International handbook of emotions in education.* New York: Routledge.

Prosser, M., & Trigwell, K. (1999). *Understanding learning and teaching. The experience in higher education.* Buckingham: Open University Press.

Ramsden, P. (1992). *Learning to teach in higher education.* London: Routledge.

Ramsden, P. (1997). The context of learning in academic departments. In F. Marton, D. J. Hounsell, & Entwistle, N. J. (Eds.), *The experience of learning* (2nd ed., pp. 198–216). Edinburgh: Scottish Academic Press.

Reynolds, D., Sammons, P., De Fraine, B., Townsend, T., & Van Damme, J. (2011). *Educational effectiveness research (EER): a state of the art review.* Paper presented at the 24th Annual Meeting of the International Congress for School Effectiveness and Improvement, 4–7 January 2011, Limassol, Cyprus.

Savin-Baden, M. (2000). *Problem-based learning in higher education: Untold stories.* Buckingham, UK: Open University Press/SRHE.

Sfard, A., & Prusak, A. (2005). Telling identities: In search of an analytic tool for investigating learning as a culturally shaped activity. *Educational Researcher, 34*(4), 14–22.

Stoll, L., Bolam, R., McMahon, A., Wallace, M., & Thomas, S. (2006). Professional learning communities: A review of the literature. *Journal of Educational Change, 7*(4), 221–258.

Trigwell, K., & Prosser, M. (2004). Development and use of the approaches to teaching inventory. *Educational Psychology Review, 16,* 409–425.

Trigwell, K., Prosser, M., & Waterhouse, F. (1999). Relations between teachers' approaches to teaching and students' approaches to learning. *Higher Education, 37,* 57–70.

Van Rossum, E. J., & Schenk, S. M. (1984). The relationship between learning conception, study strategy and learning outcome. *British Journal of Educational Psychology, 54,* 73–83. https:// doi.org/10.1111/j.2044-8279.1984.tb00846.x.

Van Veen, K., Sleegers, P., & van de Ven, P. (2005). One teacher's identity, emotions, and commitment to change: A case study into the cognitive-affective processes of a secondary school teacher in the context of reforms. *Teaching and Teacher Education, 21,* 917e934.

Virtanen, V., & Lindblom-Ylänne, S. (2010). University students' and teachers' conceptions of teaching and learning in the biosciences. *Instructional Science, 38*(4), 355–370. http://www. jstor.org/stable/23372854. Accessed 2 Oct 2018.

Yuan, R., & Lee, I. (2016). 'I need to be strong and competent': a narrative inquiry of a student-teacher's emotions and identities in teaching practicum. *Teachers and Teaching, 22*, 1–23. https://doi.org/10.1080/13540602.2016.1185819.

Zembylas, M. (2005). *Teaching with emotions: A postmodern enactment*. Greenwich: Information Age Publishing.

Zimmerman, B. J. (2000). Attainment of self-regulation: A social cognitive perspective. In M. Boekaerts, P. R. Pintrich, & M. Zeidner (Eds.), *Handbook of self-regulation* (pp. 13–39). San Diego, CA: Academic Press.

Zimmerman, B. J. (2001). Theories of self-regulated learning and academic achievement: An overview and analysis. In B. J. Zimmerman & D. H. Schunk (Eds.), *Self-regulated learning and academic achievement: Theoretical perspectives* (2nd ed., pp. 1–37). Mahwah, NJ: Erlbaum.

Zimmerman, B. J. (2002). *Becoming a self-regulated learner: An overview: Theory into practice, 41*(2), 64–70.

Zimmerman, B. J. (2008). Investigating self-regulation and motivation: Historical background, methodological developments, and future prospects. *American Educational Research Journal, 45*(1), 166–183.

Zimmerman, B. J., & Schunk, D. H. (Eds.). (2011). *Handbook of self-regulation of learning and performance*. New York, NY: Routledge.

Dawne Irving-Bell (Ph.D.) is a Senior Lecturer in Teaching and Learning Development within the Centre for Learning and Teaching at Edge Hill University, England. She has extensive experience of working in secondary, further and Higher Education settings and is a member of The Centre for Higher Education Research and Evaluation at Lancaster University. Her research interests include the influence personal narratives have on the formation of learner identity. Pedagogical approaches to STEM Education, and the Scholarship of Teaching and Learning, particularly the use of technology (and social media) to engage learners and enhance learning. She is a Principal Fellow of the Higher Education Academy (PFHEA), leads on her university's Graduate Teaching Assistant (Ph.D.) Teaching in Higher Education Programme and the Postgraduate Certificate in Teaching in Higher Education Developing Practice through Pedagogic Research Module. She chairs institutional enquiries and leads on university-wide strategies to enhance the student learning experience, including Personal Tutoring, Induction, and Transitions.

Chapter 8
Pushing Water Uphill? The Challenges of Non-engagement

Vicki Louise O'Brien and Francesca Dominique Walker-Martin

8.1 Introduction

The creation of 'gold-plated horse troughs' (from which some students will fail to drink) has been an abiding mystery for many involved in academia. This chapter suggests several likely reasons as to why certain students simply seem to prefer not to engage with the wealth of extracurricular activities that have been designed to enhance their employability. It considers also the pivotal role of the peer mentor, and the value of clearly linking assessments to those essential learning elements that students will need to succeed in terms of work placements and finding graduate employment. It sets out the various challenges that may be faced and evaluates suggestions for workable solutions that may make the student route towards employability a little less painful. In particular, the chapter seeks to address the issues (e.g. poor resilience, non-resilience, disengagement, attrition rates) that seem to be associated with a 'snowflake generation' (Collins, 2018).

The term 'gold-plated horse trough' was coined by a colleague who had worked tirelessly to develop students' employability skills over a period of some 20 years. It reflects the wealth of information and services that students can access across the university, from careers help, to one-to-one support with employability professionals. Although additional services were provided to enhance the student experience and develop skills which would be attractive to employers, student engagement often just didn't happen. This did not stop employability professionals from offering their services (and some students did indeed engage with them) but it did see a significant decline in funding for such areas and a gradual deterioration in the contents of the horse-trough. Because of declining resources, a robust, School-level review into

V. L. O'Brien · F. D. Walker-Martin (✉)
University of Central Lancashire, Preston, UK
e-mail: fdwalker@uclan.ac.uk

V. L. O'Brien
e-mail: Vlo-brien@uclan.ac.uk

© Springer Nature Switzerland AG 2019   113
A. Diver (ed.), *Employability via Higher Education: Sustainability as Scholarship*,
https://doi.org/10.1007/978-3-030-26342-3_8

how activities were offered to students was undertaken. One thing became abundantly clear: unless there was an obvious academic reason for engaging in any activities outside of the classroom, students would simply not take part, viewing such opportunities as unneeded, unnecessary effort. Nixon, Scullion, and Hearn (2016, p. 934) provide an example:

> ...and he said [the lecturer], "Oh you'll have to redo it" and I was like "Oh what? I've been here for two hours ... is this marked?" and he was like "No" and I was like "Oh well I'm not doing it then ...". To me if it's not marked and I hate it, I'm just not going to do it, I might as well turn my attention to something where it's credited ... So I was just like, whatever, I don't need to do it, it isn't important to me.

Another consideration was time. Within a very short period, the world had changed, students had changed, and a different approach to engagement was required. The troughs would always be there in various guises, but the methods of engaging with the students clearly needed to change.

8.2   A Threshold Too Far?

Within the Lancashire School of Business and Enterprise (LSBE), it was found that many students would put off the search for graduate roles until completion of their degree courses. Students initially saw little value in the need for professional development modules, only attending and submitting work that was credited as part of their taught degree programme. For some students, it was only following graduation that the realisation hit that professional development sessions and work-based learning opportunities lay the foundations for graduate life and equip them with the tools needed to be successful.[1] Research into these 'lightbulb moments' illustrates the similarities to the idea of 'threshold concepts' and 'troublesome knowledge.'[2] The rationales of threshold concepts and troublesome knowledge suggest that students often struggle to master or indeed understand certain areas of knowledge: students are often only able to skim over this at surface level (Davies & Mangan, 2005), not exploring the bigger picture, or doing the deeper level of learning required. As Meyer and Land (2006) also note, there are clearly 'barriers to understanding' here. To support students effectively, a review of the employability curriculum (and the way it was developed within LSBE) was needed to aid students over and past this threshold, moving from a superficial level of learning (and the mentality of 'I will only complete this to pass the module') towards activities that encourage lifelong learning. The first step in reviewing the student offer was to look at student expectations.

---

[1] The authors frequently received comments such as: "I understand what you mean now," or "I wish I had understood this at the beginning of second year." These tend to come from final year students who have completed year-long placements in industry, or from had graduates.

[2] See further Kumar, A. *Threshold Concepts in Employability Curricula* (available at https://www.heacademy.ac.uk/knowledge-hub/threshold-concepts-employability-curricula, accessed 20.06.18) who applied threshold concepts within the context of the employability curriculum, identifying 'Self Concept' as a threshold.

8.3   '31 Miles and a Company Director Within 3 (Ideally 2) Years, Please!'

Walker and Bowerman (2010) found that the distance that an average student would be willing to travel for work experience or employment in general was thirty-one miles.[3] Puri (2018) further notes that employers are expecting more from their graduates, namely, more work-based experience and the ability to apply their skills on entering the workforce. This repeats the warnings heard nationally that students with no previous work experience are unlikely to be successful during selection processes (High Fliers, 2018). Despite these repeated messages to students however, some still hold unrealistic expectations regarding the level of role they can enter on placement or graduation, or in terms of salary. All too frequently, students seem to have dreams of working for a specific company, or in a particular role (e.g. as a company director) without much (or indeed any) relevant work experience or understanding of what it would take to secure such a position. Employers increasingly expect a great deal from graduates, not least work experience or experience from a real-world perspective which can then be applied to their business in order to make a difference.

The authors worked closely with students to help them understand the opportunities on their doorstep. These were often to be found within the less "Instagrammable" industries which offered students the career pathways that they sought, without the commute or competitiveness of the global graduate schemes. They worked also with local employers to raise awareness on campus, for example via field trips to factories, 'audience with' events in company showrooms, and seeing business professionals in assessment centres and at speed-networking events. For those students whose aspirations included the 'Top 100' companies, a significant amount of time was spent creating an effective alumni network, focusing on those students who had graduated from LSBE within the last eight years. Case studies of alumni were created, together with booklets and videos detailing the steps these students had taken whilst at university (and beyond) to secure the role that they held at that time. Alumni were also invited onto campus, providing crucial support to students seeking placements and graduate roles, providing support to students researching companies and working through recruitment processes. Such activities, have started to have an impact, not least on the unrealistic expectations of some students.

---

[3]UCLan is based in the North West of England, has a strong commitment to widening participation, and, as with all universities, seeks to develop students to degree level and beyond. Many students come from families where they were the first family member to enter degree level education. In an area dominated by Small, Medium and Micro Enterprises (SMEs), some students sought job roles that would provide them with a lifestyle apparently showcased by their online idols, or roles that would require them to 'move from the area without moving:' in other words, Big four, Big city but wanting to be back home in a small Lancashire town within 35 min of finishing work.

8.3.1 Removing the Blinkers

It was clear that students needed to understand the challenges facing them when entering the graduate labour market: a First Class degree does not arrive through the post with a job contract attached. However, the 'reality bite' had to ensure that class-room messages did not dull students' aspirations. The authors still wanted students to 'dream big,' but needed to break the steps down into achievable pathways, working towards destinations. For some students, their understanding of their current skills is out of line with reality. O'Brien (2018, p. 54) explains how students often felt at the start of their journey towards finding a sandwich placement:

> The students spoke about how they had applied, the rejections that they got, and how they got over the rejections. Very honestly, one had over 36 rejections and I remember thinking that's you, that won't be me… your applications can't be very good, or you have applied for the wrong place, you're stood there telling me you're great and going to get a first, surely the first person will snap you up. I can't believe how naïve I was.

To tackle the expectations of students (and to aid them towards a fuller understanding of the challenges ahead), time was spent in classrooms and in one-to-one support sessions, to help them understand and recognise their own strengths, and identify areas for development. Strengths and areas for development were mapped against career pathways, to outline the skills needed for the 'dream role,' and identify any skills gaps in need of closure between starting and leaving university. The focus was on understanding and aligning the values of organisations with those of the individual to allow for a greater degree of 'fit' and enhanced job satisfaction (Cameron & Green, 2015). Arguably, prior to university many students have not yet considered what their own values are. Helping students to recognise what their values are helps them to make better decisions in terms of their future career pathways. 'Values exercises' often play a pivotal role in students' personal development, breaking through their dreams to concentrate on what matters deep down. It is through such awareness-raising that students often gain a deeper understanding of what will or will not work for them in their future careers. Feedback from such values-focussed sessions were extremely positive, with students commenting on how challenging they found the activities and, on occasion, how eye-opening. One international student commented for example that despite having a graduate career offer already in place, the exercise had led him to question the role he would be taking on, and the company which he would work for.

Values exercises allowed for a greater focus on which companies to make applications to, as O'Brien (2018, p. 65) found, when researching students' journeys towards placement: as one participant stated, 'I was already fairly attached to the company with supporting certain views and beliefs that I already had …'

8.4   Experience? What Experience?

Traditionally, UCLan LSBE students gained a significant amount of experience through part-time roles, both to gain essential work experience and earn some money. Whilst a high number of students (particularly the more mature students) still worked part time, increasingly the authors were seeing a significant decline in this approach to gaining skills from the younger, fresh-from-college students. It was unclear whether this was due to a lack of opportunities in the area, or because employers were reluctant to apply for working permits (You Gov, 2018). Another reason for the decline in work experience was a focus on studies i.e. gaining the grades needed to enter Higher Education, rather than gaining a breadth of skills. However, this compromises the long-term view: a focus only on their studies may continue into their degree, so that students might leave with a good honours degree, but no real understanding of the working world. High but unrealistic expectations may see highly qualified graduates taking on entry-level roles, which in turn creates frustration and drops in the DLHE tables for the University. Of those students who did work part time, some lacked a clear understanding of how this equipped them with valuable skills that employers sought, with others undervaluing their experiences. When asked what work experience students had, 'none' was often the reply. When probed further ('so you've never worked?'), responses were likely to include 'well, in the local supermarket for three years.' And yet these students struggled to fully articulate the skills gained or developed within these roles. A further challenge for those who worked part time was that they were often reluctant or unable to give up their part-time jobs to gain experience in the career area to which they aspired (O'Brien, 2018). Upon graduation, these students lacked the experience to enter into new career pathways and would sometimes simply increase their hours in their part-time job roles.

8.5   Now—I'm Worth It!

It was clear that the world that the students were living in was a world wherein everything is 'now' and achieved at the push of a button, and where gratification is instant through the method of a 'Like.' Sinek (2017, p. 53) highlights the effects of the 'dopamine reward system' on the younger generation, who seek and gain instant gratification on a regular basis:

> Texting, e-mail, the number of likes we collect, the ding, the buzz or the flash of our phones that tells us "You've got mail," feels amazing. As it should. We have associated the dopamine-releasing feeling of "ooh, something for me" with getting a text e-mail or the like.

It was indeed challenging to offer something to students that would show them the value of developing skills via work-based learning, projects or placements, which are considered to be the gold-standard in terms of preparing students for the working world. All of these approaches take time and may be slow to achieve results: they can often result in rejection (the equivalent of 'no likes at all'), which would significantly reduce the students' inclination to take part in the activity. The past decade has been a time of austerity and dwindling resources, from staffing to resources. The authors had to be clever in their approach to engaging with students, developing methods that might provide instant results, and exploring and unpacking student assumptions in a safe yet challenging environment. The methods used were small, but powerful.

8.6   Gamification

Student engagement has been the thorn in the side of many an academic for a very long time. How do we engage with our students and show them the value of what we deliver in the classroom/workshop/lecture theatre? The authors chose to think outside the box as resources were in short supply: a relatively new approach was undertaken in some areas, namely, 'Gamification' (Buckley & Doyle, 2014; Dicheva, Dichev, Agre, & Angelova, 2014; Kingsley & Grabner-Hagen, 2015). A very simple Red Amber Green approach to employability skills development and a range of interventions (e.g. games) allowed students to demonstrate a wide range of employability skills, such as team-working, problem-solving, leadership, creativity, effective communication, and analysis and synthesis of information to reach logical conclusions. The students were set a range of tasks such as CV building, cover letter writing, application completion, interview experience, improving communication skills, and developing Excel skills. Each task had an agreed completion date (outside of the normal assignment completion date), which was linked then to a Check Point. The Check Point was brought into the curriculum due to a high number of failure rates: the system was simply a regular meeting with the student to check progress against agreed deadlines. The Check Point session was built into second and final year employability modules to check the students' progress towards attaining their agreed employability skills. At each check point the student was given instant feedback on their progress: Red (not started yet), Amber (on track) and green (good to go). By having clear goals and getting near-instant results (moving from red to green), the students started to engage more fully. There was a clear purpose to engaging in activities, in that they could *see* their progress and were motivated by the desire to turn all their sections from red to green. It was pleasing that such a small and inexpensive intervention could produce such positive results, in the absence of real-world experience. The ongoing challenge was keeping the students motivated throughout regular interventions.

8.7   We're Paying £9,000 for This!⁴

The concept of the 'student as consumer' has been highlighted as creating considerable challenges since the introduction of higher student fees. Bunce, Baird, and Jones (2016) highlighted the issue of the increasing feeling of entitlement amongst the student body, in which, because they are paying a significant amount of money, they should do well simply from having made such payment. Using Gibbs' model of structured de-brief (Dye, 2011), the authors worked with students to generate insights into their own learning, understand their behaviours and those of others and to unpack the range of skills relevant to employability that they had demonstrated during short exercises. Students quickly identified the following skills as being both key and transferable: communication, problem solving, team working and leadership. This was then unpacked further to explore the transferability of such skills as would be useful within the working environment. By using the approach of a 'challenge and support' environment they were able to safely explore the range of emotions that they might encounter in the workplace (challenge), to recognise, understand and manage feelings and their responses to a range of situations (support). By using short games (no more than 20 min) the authors were able to demonstrate that such experiences may transfer beyond the classroom, and students were left with lasting impressions which resonated across other areas of their studies and indeed their daily lives. Such evidence was seen through their reflective writing. The games developed for these purposes were created inexpensively and based on games available from companies such as Metalog (2018) incorporating the deep level learning involved in Lego Serious Play (2018).

8.8   Making Links

Communication with the students was also reviewed. The authors spent time working with the students to gain an understanding of the best ways in which to influence opinions and validate the claims made by the ('really old') academics. It became clear that peer opinion was one of the keys to effective communication of vital messages, but the core question was how to get experienced students (i.e. those in their final year) to talk to their younger, less-experienced peers. The answer came in the form of linked modules. Final year students who had been on a placement year in industry were linked to second year students who were either looking for additional work experience (summer internships, or part-time work) or a full 48-week placement. Both groups were assessed on their levels of interaction with the final year students

---

⁴The phrase 'we're paying £9,000 for this!' was a direct quote from a rather irate student as he tried to (as a team member) put a 2-m stick onto the floor, without success. The students struggled for what seemed to be an endless amount of time, completely failing to lower a simple stick to the ground ('why is it going up???') as their other classmates looked on laughing, only to fail themselves when their turn came.

choosing how they would engage with the second years. This was based simply on what *they* would have liked when they were second year students. Initially, the idea was to simply express key messages through peer influence, but the outcomes were found to be beneficial for both groups not least the final year groups who noted the following:

- Gained the ability to pass on help and learned the importance of being approachable. The interaction helped my leadership and people management skills - it also helped me to work with others.
- Working with the second years helped to be objective about my own placement experience and to reflect on a rather negative experience and move on from it.
- Made me realise how much I have changed and developed. Looking back, I am more confident now and have developed so many skills. Recognising how much I had changed - made me want to keep developing.
- Due to shyness I am often unwilling to talk to strangers; I used the sessions with the 2nd years to help me with this, which was especially useful as I am attending assessment centres. Overall, the experience enhanced my communication skills with unfamiliar people.

(O'Brien, 2014 p. 34)

The exercise encouraged second year students to seek additional work experience and to see the benefits in real time from the people who had already 'been there, seen it and done it'. Peer support in a University setting is not a new concept however (Anderson & Boud, 1996; Collier, 1966; Rudduck, 1978), linking students via module assessment was a bold move, which worked well and indeed continues to work effectively.

8.9 The World—It Is Real!

A wide range of issues attaches to the provision of employability initiatives: engaging students is a challenge. The literature clearly supports the value of work-based learning however, whether as Government recommendations (Dearing, 1997; The Department of Education, 2017; Wilson, 2012), business reports (Confederation of British Industries, 2016) or scholarly research (Brooks and Youngson, 2016; Bullock Gould, Hejmadi, Lock, 2009; Little & Harvey, 2006). The benefits of undertaking a 48-week paid placement within industry are well known (Aggett & Busby, 2011; Bourner & Ellerker, 1998; Bullock et al., 2009; Hejmadi, Bullock, Gould, & Lock, 2012; Little & Harvey, 2006; Morgan, 2006; Walker & Ferguson, 2009). Evidence of the value of work-based learning has been further championed by organisations such as ASET (2018) and WACE (2018) for over two decades, with impacts evidenced most recently by Poisson (2018, p. 24) in a 7-year, longitudinal, empirical study:

> This study demonstrates that placement students achieve better academic performance than full-time students. When the two groups of students are compared, it is clear that placement

students outperform full-time students. Thus, a placement year has a real impact on the degree classification…

Through the support of peer mentors and a strong focus on gaining skills (either in the classroom or through other work or voluntary experience) students are encouraged to enter a 48-week placement to gain essential knowledge, skills and abilities in a live environment. Such an experience provided a useful focus for their future careers and often led to graduate roles (where, for example, companies retained them on a part-time basis, pending graduation). The authors found that, following a 48-week placement, students' worlds often grew beyond the self-imposed 31-mile perimeter for work-travel. They generally learn that the world is bigger, yet more accessible than they had first believed and that they can achieve their heart's desire with hard work and dedication. They experience the reality of entering the work force and learn that they need to apply their hard-earned knowledge, earn their place, and strive to make a real difference, not just to the businesses that employ them, but perhaps also to their own lives. A First-Class honours degree *plus* work experience is likely to open many doors that are often closed to the graduate with only their degree to showcase their abilities. In summary, students with a completed placement have enhanced credibility.

From a pedagogical perspective, the impact on the teaching workforce can also be seen. Academics comment on the distance travelled between the end of the second year of the degree and the students' return from placement a year later. The students are more focussed, confident and engaged. They are able synthesise their knowledge and experiences with new concepts and understand how these could be applied in the workplace environment.

8.10 Motivation—Working Together

The world of employability can occasionally be a lonely one. Sometimes those who work in this area are not considered to be credible, with the subject itself seen as 'not real.' It is not clear whether such attitudes may have impacted resource allocation. The authors found that dwindling resources did not necessarily mean that 'the offer' for students would or indeed should be any less than it was previously. They embraced team and cross-functional working, gaining a greater understanding of their own work environment (universities are large…) which ensured that they could still deliver a quality product. They reached out to the careers team, business development team, ERASMUS+, Unite+ and local businesses to provide a range of opportunities (linked to assessments) which would give a breadth of offer to appeal to students from a wide range of subject areas. The authors also worked on establishing a strong bond with their students, building in one-to-one time to get to know their students, beyond the personal tutor role, through the medium of Check Points. This allowed them to gain deeper insights into their students' motivations, hopes and fears, to be able to tailor interventions to meet those individual needs. Knowing a student's passion ensured that their needs were met and that they knew how to achieve their goals: often, beneath the blasé exterior lay a sea of doubt, a lack of confidence, self-awareness and self-worth. Students want to be understood, but do not yet have the skills to express themselves or to ask for help. By working with the students on an individual basis the authors gained profound insights into their motivations and were able to guide them in the way that they wanted—and needed—to be guided.

8.10.1 Snowflake Melting

With deeper insights into student motivations (and the employability message delivered in a way that would be heard and responded to) the authors have begun to see changes in results, student motivation and engagement: all are on the increase. But such interventions come at a price. Austerity means that finite resources are stretched—it could be argued that they are stretched too far and are now the responsibility of too few.

8.10.2 Pushing Water Uphill

Anyone who has ever tried to push water uphill will know that you can get some of the water over the summit, but that the majority will flow back down to join the river. Achievements in the field of employability are often few when measured against figures such as those seen in the DLHE. And yet, 'light-bulb' moments may come weeks, months, or years later, via email, a Facebook message, a card or personal visit. Recently, following a final year practical assessment, a student who had completed all their studies including a placement year (and knew that they were walking out of the university with an excellent degree classification and a graduate job) stated quite simply: '*You changed my life*' *(Anon).*[5]

8.11 Conclusion

A few small changes, such as the introduction of gamification into the curriculum, can make very big differences and provide students with something that *they* recognise as clearly worthwhile. Difficulties exist where students are loath to travel far enough to achieve their goals: working in the field of employability in times of austerity, (when resources are re-directed but targets still need to be met) is also particularly

---

[5]To hear that, may be all you will ever need in a role which is always challenging. The rewards can often be few, but when they do come, they are solid gold.

challenging. And yet staff dedication in this area of academia, remains a small but very powerful factor.

References

Aggett, M., & Busby, G. (2011). Opting out of internship: Perceptions of hospitality, tourism and events management undergraduates at a British University. *The Journal of Hospitality Leisure Sport and Tourism, 10*(1), 106–113.

Anderson, G., & Boud, D. (1996). Extending the role of peer learning in university courses. *Research and Development in Higher Education, 19,* 15–19.

ASET—The work based and placement learning association http://www.asetonline.org/aset/. Accessed 17 Oct 18.

Bourner, T., & Ellerker, M. (1998). Sandwich placements: improving the learning experience—part 1. *Education + Training, 40*(6), 283–287.

Buckley, P., & Doyle, E. (2014). *Interactive Learning Environments*, 2016, *24*(6), 1162–1175.

Bullock, K., Gould, V., Hejmadi, M., & Lock, G. (2009). Work placement experience: should I stay or should I go? *Higher Education Research & Development, 28*(5), 481–494.

Bunce, L., Baird, A., & Jones, S. E. (2016). The student-as-consumer approach in higher education and its effects on academic performance. *Studies in Higher Education*, 1–20.

Brooks, R., & Youngson, P. L. (2016). Undergraduate work placements: An analysis of the effects on career progression. *Studies in Higher Education, 41*(9), 1563–1578.

Cameron, W., & Green, M. (2015). *Making sense of change management a complete guide to the models, tools and techniques of organizational change.* London, UK: Kogan Page.

Collier, K. (1966). An experiment in university teaching. *Higher Education Quarterly, 20*(3), 336–348.

Collins Online Dictionary. (2018). *Snowflake generation definition.* https://www.collinsdictionary.com/dictionary/english/snowflake-generation. Accessed 17 Oct 18.

Confederation of British Industries' CBI and Pearson. (2016). The right combination. http://www.cbi.org.uk/cbi-prod/assets/File/pdf/cbi-education-and-skills-survey2016.pdf Accessed 2 June 2018

Davies, P., & Mangan, J. (2005). Recognising Threshold Concepts: an exploration of different approaches.

Dearing, R. (1997). *Higher education in the learning society: The dearing report.* London, UK: National Committee of Inquiry into Higher Education.

Department for Business, Innovation & Skills. (2012). *A review of business-university collaboration: the Wilson review* (BIS/12/610). https://assets.publishing.service.gov.uk/government/uploads/system/uploads/attachment_data/file/32383/12-610-wilson-review-business-university-collaboration.pdf. Accessed 5 April 2018.

Department for Education. (2017). *Planning for success: Graduates' career planning and its effect on graduate outcomes.* https://assets.publishing.service.gov.uk/government/uploads/system/uploads/attachment_data/file/604170/Graduates_career_planning_and_its_effect_on_their_outcomes.pdf. Accessed 20 June 2018.

Dicheva, D., Dichev, C., Agre, G., & Angelova, G. (2015). Gamification in education: A systematic mapping study. *Educational Technology & Society, 18*(3), 75–88.

Dye, V. (2011) Reflection, Reflection, Reflection. I'm thinking all the time, why do I need a theory or model of reflection? In D. McGregor & L. Cartwright (Eds.), *Developing reflective practice: A guide for beginning teachers.* Open University Press.

Hejmadi, M. V., Bullock, K., Gould, V., & Lock, G. D. (2012). Is choosing to go on placement a gamble? Perspectives from bioscience undergraduate. *Assessment and Evaluation in Higher Education, 37*(5), 605–618.

High Fliers Research Limited. (2018). *The graduate market in 2018.* https://www.highfliers.co.uk/download/2018/graduate_market/GMReport18.pdf. Accessed 28 March 2018.

Kingsley, T. L., & Grabner-Hagen, M. M. (2015). Gamification questing to integrate content knowledge, literacy, and 21st-century learning. *Journal of Adolescent and Adult Literacy, 59*(1), 51–61.

Kumar, A. (No date). *Threshold concepts in employability curricula.* https://www.heacademy.ac.uk/knowledge-hub/threshold-concepts-employability-curricula. Accessed 20 June 2018

Little, B., & Harvey, L. (2006). *Learning through work placements and beyond.* A report for the Higher Education Careers Service Unit and the Higher Education Academy's Work Placements Organisation Forum. England: Centre for Research and Evaluation, Sheffield Hallam University.

Lego Serious Play. https://www.lego.com/en-us/seriousplay. Accessed 23 Oct 2018

Meyer, J. H. F., & Land, R. (2006). *Overcoming barriers to student understanding: Threshold concepts and troublesome knowledge* (p. 2006). London, UK and New York: Routledge—Taylor & Francis Group.

Meta Log Training Tools. https://www.metalogtools.co.uk/. Accessed 23 Oct 2018

Morgan, H. (2006). *Why do students avoid sandwich placements?* http://www.ece.salford.ac.uk/proceedings/papers/hm_06.rtf. 13 April 2018.

Nixon, E., Scullion, H., & Hearn, R. (2016). Her majesty the student: marketized higher education and the narcissistic (dis)satisfactions of the student-consumer. *Studies in Higher Education, 43*(6), 2018—Issue, 927–943.

O'Brien, V. L. (2014) *To what extent does peer to peer support encourage second year students to actively seek placements?* ASET Research Bursary Paper. Accessed 17 Oct 2018.

O'Brien, V. L. (2018) *A case study investigation into the decline in uptake of sandwich degree placements within the Lancashire School of Business and Enterprise* (A thesis submitted in partial fulfilment for the Degree of Master of Education in Professional Practice in Education).

Poisson, R. (2018). *Does a 48-week placement increase the chances of a higher degree classification?* (pp. 107–131). http://www.asetonline.org/events/conference-proceedings/. Accessed 23 Oct 2018.

Puri, I. K. (2018). *Why learning from experience is the educational wave of the future.* https://theconversation.com/why-learning-from-experience-is-the-educational-wave-of-the-future-92399. Accessed 29 Oct 18.

Rudduck, J. (1978). Interaction in small group work. *Studies in Higher Education, 3*(1), 37–43.

Sinek, S. (2017). *Leaders eat last—why some teams pull together and others don't.* London, UK: Penguin Random House.

WACE—World Association of Co-operative Education. http://www.waceinc.org/. Accessed 17 Oct 2018.

Walker, F., & Ferguson, M. (2009). *Approaching placement extinction? Exploring the reasons why placement students are becoming a rare breed at the University of Central Lancashire: Work in progress.*

Walker-Martin, F. D., & Bowerman, M. (2010) *Beyond placement extinction*, HECSU Article. Accessed 26 Mar 2018.

Wilson. (2012). A review of business–university collaboration. GOV.UK. https://assets.publishing.service.gov.uk/government/uploads/system/uploads/attachment_data/file/32383/12-610-wilson-review-business-university-collaboration.pdf. Accesssed 02 Aug 2019.

You Gov—Child Employment. https://www.gov.uk/child-employment/local-council-rules-for-child-employment-permits. Accessed 16 Oct 2018.

Vicki Louise O'Brien (M.Ed) joined UCLAN in 2014 as a Lecturer in Employability, and as Placements Officer for the Lancashire School of Business and Enterprise. She supports students in understanding the needs of graduate employers, and assists them in seeking out and undertaking placements and internships at undergraduate and postgraduate levels.

Francesca Dominique Walker Martin (MBA) is a Principal Lecturer and Reader in Work Based Learning in the Lancashire School of Business and Enterprise at the University of Central Lancashire (UCLAN), England, CMDA Course Leader and CMI Approved Centre Director. She has the great pleasure of being able to share experiences from her portfolio career, which includes project management, operations management, change management, recruitment and training.

Chapter 9
Student Motivation and 'Dropout' Rates in Brazil

Dalton Tria Cusciano, Mauro Maia Laruccia
and Luis Fernando Salles Moraes

9.1 Introduction

Student motivation is an important issue in Higher Education (HE). Choosing a career is often quite difficult, irrespective of jurisdiction: the consequences of choosing the wrong degree or of dropping out of university altogether can be both emotionally and economically devastating for students and their families. And yet, in 2014, the National Institute of Educational Studies and Research Anísio Teixeira (INEP) found that 49% of Brazilian college students had withdrawn from their course.[1] Over the last decade, the dropout rate for HE has averaged out at a rate of 21%, which means that approximately 900,000 students have dropped out of college during that time. This chapter examines the issue of motivation in respect of students in Brazil, for example in relation to choosing an undergraduate degree course, and in deciding to complete or withdraw from their degree programme. It asks also what factors are likely to make college students drop out of their university course. In terms of student attrition, public funds are being invested with little to no return on that investment, which has further implications in terms of finite, scarce university resources, including for example misuse or wastage of staff time, equipment usage, and wasted space. Much of the literature in Brazil highlights that students may interrupt their studies because

---

[1]INEP/MEC (2016). Censo de Educação Superior 2015. Brasília. (http://portal.mec.gov.br/component/tags/tag/32044-censo-da-educacao-superior date accessed 01.11.18).

D. T. Cusciano (✉)
Fundacao Getulio Vargas, Sao Paolo, Brazil
e-mail: dalton.cusciano@gmail.com

M. M. Laruccia
Pontifical Catholic University, Sao Paolo, Brazil
e-mail: mauro.laruccia@gmail.com

L. F. S. Moraes
Centro Universitario, FEI, Sao Paolo, Brazil
e-mail: luissalles@hotmail.com

© Springer Nature Switzerland AG 2019
A. Diver (ed.), *Employability via Higher Education: Sustainability as Scholarship*,
https://doi.org/10.1007/978-3-030-26342-3_9

of financial issues.[2] The causes of non-attendance and attrition may be much more complex however: a broader analysis of the processes underpinning student attrition and motivation is clearly needed. This chapter argues that student attrition has many, quite diverse causes e.g. social, political or cultural, and that much more research (together with key policy changes) is needed to tackle this difficult issue.

9.2   Factors Associated with Attrition Rates

Generally, factors such as career-choice, a sense of identity, determined personality, work orientations, good socio-economic status, strong academic performance and intellectual activities, supportive interpersonal relationships, course or university teaching quality, and favourable perceptions of the current or future labour market, are all associated with raised student satisfaction levels (Bardagi, Bizarro, de Andrade, Audibert, & Lassance, 2008; Chow, 2005; Lounsbury, Tatum, Chambers, Owens, & Gibson, 1999). Issues associated with high levels of attrition tend to focus on such issues as less than satisfactory teaching quality, poor pedagogies, or inadequate course structure, specific subject problems, having to work long hours to fund one's degree studies, the teacher-student relationship, or the lack of social integration within the chosen university (Lehman, 2014; Ribeiro, 2005; Veloso & de Almeida, 1994). As Lehman (2014) has recently stated, in Brazil there is a growing number of university students deemed to be in crisis within the field of study that they have chosen, a factor that often leads to the student in question dropping out. Student satisfaction (i.e. the quality of the student-university relationship) clearly matters. Ribeiro (2005) has similarly argued that incompatibility between a student and their chosen institution, and a lack of meaningful preparation for HE study, together with financial hardship are all highly significant reasons for withdrawing from a university. Class size is another key factor, especially given the increasingly high numbers of students coming to higher education from culturally or socio-economically disadvantaged backgrounds.

Course drop out may be framed as a process of exclusion, in the sense that is often an institutional phenomenon, and especially where it is perhaps very reflective of the absence of any clear retention or attendance policies (Veloso & de Almeida, 1994). Labour market reviews and academic performance are also particularly relevant to the issue however in terms of trying to define and explain high rates of attrition. Academic success is essential for HE students' sense of self-confidence, career competence, for developing academic projects, forming professional networks, promoting successful university-to-work transitions, post-graduation. The labour market will vary according to prevailing wider economic conditions and geographical area; not all job opportunities in Brazil will correspond precisely either with the regulated professions or to the undergraduate courses chosen. Performance evaluations, may

---

[2]MBCM Lobo (2012). *Panorama da evasão no ensino superior brasileiro: aspectos gerais das causas e soluções*. Associação Brasileira de Mantenedoras de Ensino Superior. Cadernos, (25).

vary and depend on how scholarly outputs are being assessed at each institution, and per course, or discipline: in addition to the grades obtained, student successes may well be defined in terms of gaining entry onto certain professional pathways, the various barriers and obstacles to employment notwithstanding (Bardagi et al., 2008; de Püschel, Inácio, & Pucci, 2009). In terms of such barriers however, the literature suggests that several clear gaps in training exist. There have been several calls for curricular reforms and for much more support for mapping out the destinations of those 'professional' graduates who are leaving HE with a good qualification.

de Püschel et al. (2009) for example argue that we must consider the ease or otherwise with which university graduates can enter the job market, and the extent to which employment difficulties relate to their education, inherent disposition, or limited social networks. The ever-changing demands of the workplace may well allow for only the most highly qualified professional graduates to be hired, in terms of their possessing relevant experience, and a 'good quality' university education. Again, there is a need for much more research into just how students' perceptions of modern, highly competitive job markets might relate to, and adversely affect, attrition rates (Rainie & Anderson, 2017). The psychological effects of seeing very high unemployment levels simply cannot be ignored (Neiva, 1996). As Neiva (1996) has further suggested, most HE students can fully and accurately anticipate the various difficulties that they will likely encounter (not least the very real possibility of unemployment) after graduation. They must be able to plan useful strategies and picture realistic alternatives, although, perversely, the carrying out of such plans may well lead directly or indirectly to non-attendance or reduced attendance whilst at university (Pyhältö, Toom, Stubb, & Lonka, 2012).

Teixeira and Gomes (2005) interviewed university students from a range of HE courses: one cohort had a favourable job market to look forward to, while the other group's outlook was quite unfavourable. Optimistic expectations were found in both groups, although the learners' levels of knowledge about the job market was, oddly, largely dependent upon their interpersonal and familial relationships. Those students who had family members currently or previously working within the same professional discipline tended to relate to and describe their job market in a much more detailed way and, significantly, they were often more aware of potential difficulties and opportunities. Those who were distanced from the profession (with no links to information via friends or family) admitted that they did not know much about the realities of their market situation. It is clearly often quite difficult to assess the harsh realities of labour markets within various professions: much of the research does aim to gauge HE students' perceptions of the market, however. These held perceptions do seem to deeply influence both student satisfaction rates and the levels of commitment needed to successfully complete their chosen course of study.

As Bardagi et al. (2008) point out, where students were dissatisfied with their chosen pathway, they tended to cite such factors as a poor job market and then perhaps a weak course structure. Amongst those who were very satisfied or satisfied with their degree programmes, the job market was generally largely perceived as being favourable. Teixeira and Gomes (2005) found also that favourable market perceptions were often associated with an increased optimism for the future, in terms of their now enhanced job prospects. de Melo and de Borges (2007) emphasize the need for institutional interventions that would introduce young people and HE students to those contexts in which they will be eventually working as professionals, not least the psycho-social aspects of the workplace (such as professional identity, personal image, and organizational socialization) that can so often interfere with employability skills. Others have argued that a university education does not always prepare students fully for the job market, nor does it necessarily always provide realistic information or advice about all job markets or indeed the 'real' experience that is so often needed for the development of work-related skills (de Melo & de Borges, 2007; de Püschel et al., 2009; Gondim, 2002; Teixeira & Gomes, 2005).

That said, as Gondim (2002) observes, students themselves do not always have a very clear idea as to what professional profiles or skills they will be required to demonstrate when they enter those labour markets relevant to for their own discipline, which clearly hampers their ability to engage in articulation of consistent plans for a future career. Many students seem to have only a general idea of what characteristics might be most highly valued by their potential employers, and they do not always seem to know how to integrate these into a work profile or CV that is relevant to their specialisms. Ignorance of the realities of the job markets may also cause students to have idealized or distorted images of their chosen profession: this can then lead to demotivation and dropping out from classes or courses. Self-perceptions of their anticipated grades, and harsh comparisons with their peers can also have this effect. As Brown et al. (2008) argue, academic or career successes may be determined by a complex set of variables that were perhaps present long before the student entered HE e.g. organisational abilities and personal characteristics. However, early academic performance perhaps remains the best predictor of whether or not any given student will retain their initial motivation and either complete or withdraw from their university course (Allen, Robbins, Casillas, & Oh, 2008; Brown et al., 2008). Brazilian studies on academic performance do show correlations between performance in college and inherent cognitive abilities (Primi, dos Santos, & Vendramini, 2002), entrance exam performance (Silva & Padoin, 2008), gender, and the type of high school attended (Maia, Pinheiro, & de Pinheiro, 2009).

9.3   Dropping Out of Higher Education

There has been an increased interest in attrition rates in Brazil in recent years (da Cunha, Nascimento, & Durso, 2014). High HE dropout rates are one of the main problems currently afflicting universities in Brazil and several other Latin American countries. Completion rates per course do tend to be linked to the quality of the higher education institution (Hanushek, Lavy, & Hitomi, 2008; Schnepf, 2014). As da Cunha et al. (2014) argue, some students' lack of motivation could however well be the main factor that makes them drop out before graduating. And yet, initial commitment to a chosen vocation and deep enthusiasm for academic study does not necessarily always guarantee that any individual student will show the attitudes and core skills needed to realise their professional aspirations and overcome any obstacles or setbacks. A government report produced by the National Institute of Educational Studies and Anísio Teixeira (INEP) in 2017 (based on a longitudinal study of students throughout their education) confirmed that dropout rates remain very high in Brazil: 12.9% and that 12.7% of students enrolled in the first and second years of high school, respectively, evaded school (according to the School Census) between the years 2014 and 2015. The 9th year of elementary school had the third highest dropout rate at 7.7%, followed by the 3rd year of high school, with 6.8%. This report concluded that dropout rates reached a level of 11.2% of the total number of students who were at this stage of their education (INEP/MEC, 2017). The data for higher education (INEP/MEC, 2017) is worrying too, with 49% of students who enrolled in 2010 dropping out of courses over a five-year period.[3]

Although the economic crisis is clearly a macro-factor influencing student attitudes, psychological and personal circumstances also matter, as social or emotional causes may well be contributing to dropout rates, especially in the crucial early months following admission. Onboarding Programs and student mentoring are therefore very important tools to decrease the dropout rate and improve retention. One means of improving retention rates is to perhaps seek some increase to curricular flexibility for students during their initial induction period, post-admission, with more opportunities to choose the right subject discipline for them based on their interests and abilities. The quality of the students' interactions with each other and with their teachers, together with mentoring, is also key to their successful integration into academic life and very useful for overcoming any difficulties. Careful yet innovative course and induction planning is needed, especially if intake numbers are very high or where the costs of attrition rates might well have inhibited managers from making pedagogical changes previously.

There is still a lack of clear policies, projects, and strategies aimed at addressing the issue of high HE attrition rates (beyond those looking mainly at financial issues). And yet the consequences of high drop-out rates are profound and many, especially given the high public and private costs of higher education in Brazil. In sum, high HE drop-out rates make the cost per graduate much higher than the cost per student enrolled. In the case of private colleges, the time spent in the classrooms, and the money spent by the families on tuition costs could have been better spent elsewhere. Colleges too may end up having to charge higher tuition fees because of high attrition rates. Again, to address or reduce high dropout rates in HE, more students should be perhaps encouraged to postpone their specialization choices until *after* they have had meaningful contact with several different disciplines, and potential career environments. Entrance Exams should also be revisited, including more tests involving socio-emotional attributes and skills. The quality or otherwise of students' primary

---

[3] In private institutions, attrition rates reached 53% of the total numbers enrolled in public institutions, reaching 47% in municipal institutions. 30% of the students in private institutions left their courses in the first term, while in the public network this figure stood at 19%. In subsequent terms the rate decreased but still occurred until the last term.

education cannot also not be overlooked, in terms of accommodating students' often very diverse backgrounds and skills.

9.4 Conclusion

In Brazil, school dropout, as an interruption to the study cycle, clearly causes significant economic, social and human damage, regardless of the level of education involved. The environment of HE is increasingly competitive and university or course economic viability is often strongly linked to successful student retention programs. Societal rewards for students are also related to the obtaining of degrees or diplomas: institutions, particularly private ones, do suffer loss of prestige and risk losing the conditions needed for their financial survival, where attrition rates are high. Wider society loses out too because of such poorly-utilized investments: students occupy a place on the course but then do not finish their degree. It is similarly not uncommon for a student to decide to change their major, leaving his or her former course place empty. This place will only rarely be filled in public universities: in private institutions, such 'idle spaces' are only filled again in relation to the most popular courses (and careers), and even then, only at those institutions with a high reputational credibility.

Simply entering higher education does not guarantee educational or employment successes for any given student: this level of education clearly differs very greatly from primary and secondary education. Disconnects concerning what the student has experienced up until entering HE can also cause grave uncertainties over their future career plans and may require significant changes in terms of altering their personal learning habits, and the use of new learning strategies. Acquiring for example the ability to work or live with one's peers, who may have profoundly differing backgrounds, family situations, intellectual abilities, and career aspirations (that might not match their own very closely at all), is key. Less than adequate physical resources, over-crowded classrooms, an unfriendly or indifferent atmosphere, and weak teaching methodologies can all serve to severely disappoint HE students in terms of their long-held expectations of university life. The absence of clear public policies aimed at actively preventing or at least reducing college drop-out rates in public universities compounds the difficulties associated with a perhaps less than stellar early education received in childhood or adolescence. Familial interference, such as inducing teenagers to select a course of study that they are not suited to, or which has content which is totally different to what they might have been expecting, is also a contributory factor.

These issues, together with the lack of financial resources available, are urgent situations that clearly need to be resolved to reduce the high college dropout rates in Brazil at the moment. Remedial actions could include more consistent approaches to student support via more intensive coaching and mentoring, to help students form and reach clearer goals and relevant, career-related study strategies. As noted above, entrance exams could be amended to include a useful level of socio-emotional skills testing as a key parameter. Crucially, the quality of primary and secondary education must be revisited, studied and enhanced. However, in the search for long term answers, it is perhaps ultimately necessary to analyse what *is* being effectively implemented at present, to create more favourable academic conditions, maintain the levels of motivation that are present at enrolment, and ultimately improve retention rates within Brazil's national education system.

References

Allen, J., Robbins, S. B., Casillas, A., & Oh, I.-S. (2008). Third-year college retention and transfer: Effects of academic performance, motivation, and social connectedness. *Research in Higher Education, 49*(7), 647–664. https://doi.org/10.1007/s11162-008-9098-3.

Bardagi, M. P., Bizarro, L., de Andrade, A. M. J., Audibert, A., & Lassance, M. C. P. (2008). Avaliação da formação e trajetória profissional na perspectiva de egressos de um curso de psicologia. *Psicologia: Ciência E Profissão, 28*(2), 304–315.

Brown, S. D., Tramayne, S., Hoxha, D., Telander, K., Fan, X., & Lent, R. W. (2008). Social cognitive predictors of college students' academic performance and persistence: A meta-analytic path analysis. *Journal of Vocational Behavior, 72*(3), 298–308. https://doi.org/10.1016/j.jvb.2007.09.003.

Chow, H. P. H. (2005). Life satisfaction among university students in a Canadian Prairie City: A multivariate analysis. *Social Indicators Research, 70*(2), 139–150. https://doi.org/10.1007/s11205-004-7526-0.

da Cunha, J. V. A., Nascimento, E. M., & Durso, S. O. (2014). Razões e influências para a evasão universitária: um estudo com estudantes ingressantes nos cursos de Ciências Contábeis de instituições públicas federais da Região Sudeste. In FEA-USP (Ed.), Anais do XIV Congresso USP Controladoria e Contabilidade (p. 17). São Paulo: FEA-USP.

da Silva, M. & Padoin, M. J. (2008). Relação entre o desempenho no vestibular e o desempenho durante o curso de graduação. *Ensaio: Avaliação E Políticas Públicas Em Educação, 16*(58), 77–94. http://doi.org/10.1590/S0104-40362008000100006.

de Melo, S. L., & de Borges, L. O. (2007). A transição da universidade ao mercado de trabalho na ótica do jovem. *Psicologia: Ciência E Profissão, 27*(3), 376–395. http://doi.org/10.1590/S1414-98932007000300002.

de Püschel, V. A. A., Inácio, M. P., & Pucci, P. P. A. (2009). Inserção dos egressos da Escola de Enfermagem da USP no mercado de trabalho: Facilidades e dificuldades. *Revista Escola de Enfermagem USP, 43*(3), 535–542.

Gondim, S. M. G. (2002). Perfil profissional e mercado de trabalho: relação com formação acadêmica pela perspectiva de estudantes universitários. *Estudos de Psicologia (Natal), 7*(2), 299–309. https://doi.org/10.1590/S1413-294X2002000200011.

Hanushek, E. A., Lavy, V., & Hitomi, K. (2008). Do students care about school quality? Determinants of dropout behavior in developing countries. *Journal of Human Capital, 2*(1), 69–105. https://doi.org/10.1086/529446.

INEP/MEC. (2016). Censo de Educação Superior 2015. Brasília. Retrieved from http://portal.mec.gov.br/component/tags/tag/32044-censo-da-educacao-superior.

INEP/MEC. (2017). INEP divulga dados inéditos sobre fluxo escolar na educação básica. Brasília.

Lehman, Y. P. (2014). University students in crisis: University dropout and professional re-selection. *Estudos de Psicologia, 31*(1), 45–53. https://doi.org/10.1590/0103-166X2014000100005.

Lobo, M. B. C. M. (2012). Panorama da evasão no ensino superior brasileiro: aspectos gerais das causas e soluções. Associação Brasileira de Mantenedoras de Ensino Superior. Cadernos, (25).

Lounsbury, J. W., Tatum, H. E., Chambers, W., Owens, K. S., & Gibson, L. W. (1999). An investigation of career decidedness in relation to "big five" personality constructs and life satisfaction. *College Student Journal, 33*(4), 646–652.

Maia, R. P., Pinheiro, H. P., & de Pinheiro, A. S. (2009). Heterogeneidade do desempenho de alunos da Unicamp, do ingresso à conclusão. *Cadernos de Pesquisa, 39*(137), 645–660. https://doi.org/10.1590/S0100-15742009000200015.

Neiva, K. M. C. (1996). Fim dos estudos universitários: efeitos das dificuldades do mercado de trabalho na representação do futuro profissional e no estabelecimento de projetos pós-universitários dos estudantes. *Psicologia USP, 7*(1–2), 203–224. https://doi.org/10.1590/S1678-51771996000100010.

Primi, R., dos Santos, A. A. A., & Vendramini, C. M. (2002). Habilidades básicas e desempenho acadêmico em universitários ingressantes. *Estudos de Psicologia (Natal), 7*(1), 47–55. https://doi.org/10.1590/S1413-294X2002000100006.

Pyhältö, K., Toom, A., Stubb, J., & Lonka, K. (2012). Challenges of becoming a scholar: A study of doctoral students' problems and well-being. *ISRN Education, 2012,* 1–12. https://doi.org/10.5402/2012/934941.

Rainie, L., & Anderson, J. (2017). *The future of jobs and jobs training.* Washington: Pew Research Center.

Ribeiro, M. A. (2005). O projeto profissional familiar como determinante da evasão universitária - um estudo preliminar. *Revista Brasileira de Orientação Profissional, 6*(2).

Schnepf, V. S. (2014). *Do tertiary dropout students really not succeed in European labour markets?* IZA Discussion Papers. Institute for the Study of Labor (IZA).

Teixeira, M. A. P., & Gomes, W. B. (2005). Decisão de carreira entre estudantes em fim de curso universitário. *Psicologia: Teoria E Pesquisa, 21*(3), 327–334. http://doi.org/10.1590/S0102-37722005000300009.

Veloso, T. C. M. A., & de Almeida, E. P. (1994). Evasão nos cursos de graduação da Universidade Federal de Mato Grosso, campus universitário de Cuiabá: um processo de exclusão. *Série-Estudos - Periódico Do Programa de Pós-Graduação Em Educação Da UCDB, 0*(13), 1–16.

Dalton Tria Cusciano is a Ph.D. candidate in Public Administration and Government at Fundação Getulio Vargas, Brazil (FGV/SP) which is a Higher Education Institution and think tank founded on December 20, 1944, with the aim of stimulating Brazil's socioeconomic development and preparing qualified people for work in public and private administration in Brazil. Dalton is also a Federal Public Servant at Fundacentro, and a University Professor.

Mauro Maia Laruccia (Ph.D.) holds a Ph.D. in Communication and Semiotics from the Pontifical Catholic University of São Paulo, Brazil (PUC/SP). He is a Federal Public Servant at Fundacentro, and a University Professor at PUC/SP, Brazil.

Luis Fernando Salles Moraes holds a Ph.D. in Business Administration at Centro Universitário FEI (FEI/SP) Brazil, and is a Federal Public Servant at Fundacentro, and a University Professor.

Chapter 10
Building Student Resilience for Graduate Work Readiness

Jacinta Ryan, Sandra Jones, Peter Hayes and Michelle Turner

10.1 Introduction

In the complex, constantly changing environment that characterises business in the twenty-first century, organisations are increasingly recognising the importance of developing organisational resilience. Globalisation, technological change, communication openness and transparency affect all types of organisations, whilst policies governing business are continually changing in response to emergent issues. It is thus no wonder that organisational resilience is attracting increased attention. To effectively navigate this complex world there is a need for organisations to not only develop robust systems and processes, but also to recruit, develop, and support a resilient workforce that can operate successfully within this demanding environment (Cooper, Flint-Taylor, & Pearn, 2013). Whilst resilience theory has its roots in studies of individual mental dysfunction, it has evolved to look beyond the individual, to recognise the impact of social and environmental influences.

King, Newman, and Luthands (2016) described how there have been four waves of development in resilience theory. The first wave focused on the factors and characteristics that enable individuals to overcome adversity through self-esteem, self-efficacy and optimism. This evolved into a second wave whereby the investigation turned to how certain factors contribute to resilience. The third wave focused on the development of interventions to build resilience, with the final wave looking at the role

J. Ryan (✉) · S. Jones · P. Hayes · M. Turner
RMIT, Melbourne, Australia
e-mail: Jacinta.ryan@rmit.edu.au

S. Jones
e-mail: sandra.jones@rmit.edu.au

P. Hayes
e-mail: peter.hayes2@rmit.edu.au

M. Turner
e-mail: michelle.turner@rmit.edu.au

© Springer Nature Switzerland AG 2019
A. Diver (ed.), *Employability via Higher Education: Sustainability as Scholarship*,
https://doi.org/10.1007/978-3-030-26342-3_10

that genetic, neurological, and developmental factors may play in resilience capability. Studies to date have focused on at-risk youth, management of athletes and military personnel, with limited focus on resilience in the workplace, or on how to develop resilience in new graduates to function effectively within a complex workplace. Where resilience has been explored in the workplace, the focus has been on how to promote individual resilience for teamwork to produce a positive outcome, with little research undertaken into how resilience may affect individual behaviours at work. This has resulted in little research into how management and leadership actions may affect individual resilience.

While resilience is acknowledged as a complex construct that is difficult to assess, universities are recognising its importance and are beginning to invest in research and services aimed at building student resilience. However, to date, there has been little research into the levels of, and contributors to, student resilience. This is an important issue that needs further research. At the same time universities are facing greater austerity as government funding continues to be reduced. This is compounded by the impact of an increasingly diverse student cohort as universities are being transformed from an elite to a mass, higher education system (Moir, 2010). Some of the students attracted to universities would previously have been prevented from participating in Higher Education (HE) for a range of reasons, both academic and non-academic, with many of these students requiring additional support (AEI, 2010; Trotter & Roberts, 2006). In other words, despite the economic austerity facing universities, the increased diversity of students requires universities to provide students with additional assistance. This support is especially evident with regards to student resilience. In focusing on the question of developing student resilience as an employability capability, this chapter takes a systems approach to explore the various layers that contribute towards student resilience. The research provided identifies two pivotal transition points in a student's life: entering university life and leaving university for the workplace (Turner, Holdsworth, & Scott-Young, 2017a). While these pivotal points relate to two distinct time periods within the student experience, the interrelationship between the two requires attention by universities, to graduate students as employable scholars. Before identifying detailed examples of this, the next section will provide a definition of resilience and will outline some of the current literature on resilience in the workplace.

10.2 Resilience in the Workplace

Resilience is traditionally understood as "a trajectory of coping that defies the expectation of negative outcomes" (Liu, Reed, & Girard, 2017, p. 111). It is considered a protective factor that interacts with stressors to reduce the likelihood of negative outcomes (Seery & Quinton, 2016). Resilience is associated with positive social and personal wellbeing together with enhanced mental health and adjustment to (and through) life (McGillivray & Pidgeon, 2015). As the theory of resilience has advanced, two main conceptualisations as to its meaning and focus have emerged.

Firstly, resilience may be a trait or capacity that helps individuals deal with, and positively adjust to, adversity (Jackson, Firtko, & Edenborough, 2007). This psychology-based approach has led to the development of scales that capture an individual's capacity to deal with adversity (e.g., Block & Kremen, 1996). The second approach perceives resilience as a phenomenon, which can be developed as a "dynamic process encompassing positive adaptation within the context of significant adversity" (Luthar, Cicchetti, & Becker, 2000, p. 543). To reconcile the differences and help explore the impact of this on the workplace, the authors will argue that the term *resiliency* should be used to refer to a trait, with *resilience* referring to the process or phenomenon of positive adjustment despite adversity. This is particularly important for workplace resilience as it enables a focus on how organisations may develop both resilience and resiliency to adjust to, and thrive within, challenging situations and environments. In turn, organisational resilience has been seen from two different perspectives. On the one hand there is a focus on the ability of an organisation to 'bounce back' from unexpected, stressful and adverse situations, with attention given to how quickly the organisation can avoid dysfunction and develop strong fit with the new reality (e.g., Balu, 2001). On the other hand, there is the perspective on the ability of the organisation to not simply restore what was, but to progress to new capabilities and expand their ability to create new opportunities (e.g., Coutu, 2002; Hamel & Valikangas, 2003).

Such recognition of the importance of workplace and organisational resilience has seen increased research into how to develop and create capacity for resilience in organisations that goes beyond the initial field of psychology towards the field of human resource management (HRM) (Lengnick-Hall, Beck, & Lengnick-Hall, 2011). Referring to the work on collective constructs (Morgeson & Hofman, 1999), Lengnick-Hall et al. (2011) argue that an understanding of resilient individuals provides a useful starting place for defining resilient organisations since actions and interactions among individual organisational members underpins the emergence of a firm's collective capacity for resilience.

In so doing Lengnick-Hall et al. (2011) provide the example of the experience of Navy SEAL graduates who possess the ability "not only to survive brutal conditions but actually thrive because of the multiple conditions confronted…to develop new capabilities and transform themselves into exceptional warriors" (p. 245). Based on this example, they argue that certain organisational capabilities and routines (cognitive, behavioural and contextual) can indeed be "derived from a combination of individual level knowledge, skills, abilities and attributes that are systematically developed and integrated through a firm's human resource system" (p. 245). Their research identifies that a targeted human resource development strategy can enhance resilience through developing behaviours, skills and traits of learned resourcefulness, ingenuity and bricolage. Bardoel, Pettit, De Cieri, and McMillan (2014) take this further and, using a combination of research from positive psychology and resource theory, argue a link between psychology (positive) and human resource management. They claim that, psychological capital (an extension of the concept of human capital) implies "a sequencing of efforts to promote resilience and the results of those efforts: the initial efforts can be viewed as investments, with returns accruing in the future, akin to investment in and returns to human capital" (p. 281). They use the Luthans, Youssef, and Avolio (2007) identification of an individual's psychological capital as including having confidence (self-efficacy) to take on and put in the necessary effort to succeed at challenging tasks; making a positive attribution (optimism) about succeeding now and in the future; persevering toward goals and, when necessary, redirecting paths to goals (hope) in order to succeed; and when beset by problems and adversity, sustaining and bouncing back even beyond (resilience) to attain success. On the other hand, resource theory (Shin et al., 2012), argues this can be extended to view resilience "as an individual resource *[that]* can be enhanced… to both reduce the strains and stresses associated with organisational change and to support employees commitment to change" (Bardoel et al., 2014, p. 282). Based on this combination the authors claim that "HRM practices could provide examples of workplace interventions that 'inoculate' employees" (Bardoel et al., 2014, p. 282) against stresses and strains in the workplace through their capacity to develop resilience.

Given the recent research into the importance of organisational resilience in times of rapid change and uncertainty, the contribution that individual resilience can collectively contribute to organisational resilience, and recognition of strategies that can be identified to build individual and organisational resilience, it is not surprising that organisations are starting to look to universities to graduate students with this psychological capital.

10.3   Resilience as a Work-Ready Capability

Work-ready graduates have the required skills to meaningfully contribute to their profession. Students, while at university, participate in learning opportunities to develop the confidence to approach employment with enthusiasm, appropriate knowledge and commitment, and to possess the skills needed to contribute to their professional community (Hager, 2006). However, the transition from university to work is often characterised as being highly stressful for students. The challenges experienced by students include: time demands and constraints, feelings of isolation and bewilderment, and general stress (Maute, 2007). This transitional challenge is not new. Kramer (1974) first introduced the term 'reality shock' in relation to the experience of new workers transitioning into a work environment. Reality shock may be described as

> "…the specific shock-like reactions of new workers when they find themselves in a work situation which they have spent several years preparing for and for which they thought they were going to be prepared, and then suddenly find they are not" (Kramer, 1974, p. viii).

Arguably, one of the key roles of university is the preparation of students to be able to cope with the general pressures felt by those new to the workplace (McNamara et al., 2011). Besides learning the requisite skills and knowledge aligned with a given profession, universities can actively prepare students for success by facilitating the skills required to manage this challenging time of transition. Together with suffering from 'reality shock' as they transition into the work place, young professionals

(18–25 and 26–35-year age groups) report the highest levels of stress and distress in the workplace (APA, 2017; Casey & Liang, 2014). Helping young professionals to overcome transitional challenges and proactively manage their stress is a critical work-ready capability.

Resilience, the ability to bounce back and adapt, has been recognised as an important capability which enables individuals to manage stress. Accordingly, resilience is increasingly being identified as a key competency for new graduate appointments (Edgar et al., 2013). Educators are similarly recognising that resilience is a critical skill that can assist students in their transitions to professional life (Grant & Kinman, 2012). Nurturing resilience during university will increase the likelihood of positive employment outcomes particularly in professions where stress, burnout and job insecurity is high. Importantly, resilience is conceptualised as a capability which can be learned (Windle, 2011; Winwood, Colon, & McEwen, 2013) and that improves with life experience (APA, 2010). It is further understood that resilience developed in one system (such as university) can be transferred across systems (such as work) (APA, 2010; Turner, Scott-Young, & Holdsworth, 2017b). Accordingly, the development of resilience at university can be considered as nurturing a life skill which can be applied both at university and beyond, enabling graduates to survive and thrive (Holdsworth, Turner, & Scott-Young, 2017).

10.4   Resilience and Wellbeing

The relationship between resilience and wellbeing reiterates the importance of resilience development for university students. Resilience is a critical life skill which assists students to thrive at university and in other parts of their life. This is especially significant, as many students have been found to suffer from poor mental health. For example, research in 2016 into Australian university students found that 67% of students rated their mental health as fair or poor, while 65% reported high or very high psychological distress (Rickwood, Telford, O'Sullivan, Crisp, & Magyar, 2016). Given these concerning findings, there has been a call to action. In developmental psychology and psychiatry, the causal relationship of resilience-to-wellbeing has been well-established (see Rutten et al., 2013). Recent research undertaken by Turner et al. (2017b) has explored the relationship between mental wellbeing and resilience for university students. The authors used the Resilience at University (RAU) scale based on six dimensions to measure resilience. Resilience was found to have a positive relationship with subjective happiness (Lyubomirsky & Lepper, 1999), and a negative relationship with depression, anxiety, and stress (Lovibond & Lovibond, 1995). Five of the six dimensions of resilience identified in the RAU (apart from managing stress) had a negative relationship with depression, anxiety or stress. The dimensions of building networks, maintaining perspective, and staying healthy were negatively associated with depression. Maintaining perspective and staying healthy had a negative relationship with anxiety, while interacting cooperatively, living authentically and maintaining perspective had a negative relationship with stress. Staying healthy had a positive relationship with subjective happiness.

10.4.1 Resilience at University

As stated earlier, common to definitions of resilience is the ability to bounce back in the face of stress and adversity (Gerson & Fernandez, 2013). While resilience is acknowledged as a complex construct and one that is difficult to assess, universities are recognising its importance and are beginning to invest in research and services aimed at building student resilience. However, there is limited research into the levels of, and contributors to, student resilience. This is an important issue that needs further research. At the same time, universities are facing greater austerity as government funding continues to be reduced. This is compounded by an increasingly diverse student cohort as universities transformed from an elite to a mass higher education system (Moir, 2010). This increasing diversity demands that universities increase their level of student support, which limits their capacity to focus on key research into issues such as student resilience.

In a university setting, resilience moves beyond merely bouncing back and is inclusive of student progress, growth, and learning (Holdsworth et al., 2017). Pooley and Cohen (2010) argue that the degree to which an individual is resilient can be influenced and determined by the presence of protective factors, defined as moderators of adversity, that enable successful adaption (Werner, 1990). Two types of protective factor are associated with resilience—internal and external (Dias & Cadime, 2017). Internal protective factors focus on individual qualities or characteristics specific to the individual such as self-efficacy and optimism (Dias & Cadime, 2017), a flexible coping style (APA, 2010; Grant & Kinman, 2012), the ability to maintain perspective (APA, 2010; Winwood et al., 2013), moving towards goals (APA, 2010; Winwood et al., 2013), and well-developed reflective skills (Grant & Kinman, 2012). External protective factors focus on positive aspects within the individual's environment and life, such as social support (APA, 2010) and family cohesion (Friborg, Hjemdal, Rosenvinge, & Martinussen, 2003). The combination of internal and external factors emphasises the multi-dimensional nature of resilience. For educators, this is particularly important as it moves the focus away from students being solely responsible for their own resilience, to instead recognise that resilience is contextual, driven by internal protective factors as well as having access to external protective factors, available from within and outside of the university (Turner et al., 2017b).

Recognition of the complex interplay of internal and external factors that universities need to consider to assist students in building resilience capability requires universities to recognise the need for a multi-layered system in which students are provided with opportunities to build resilience at various levels. At the internal protective level there is innate resilience at course (subject) level, nested within a program (degree) in which students engage in learning. At the external level there is support provided at the organisational-nested faculty (discipline) level and at university level.

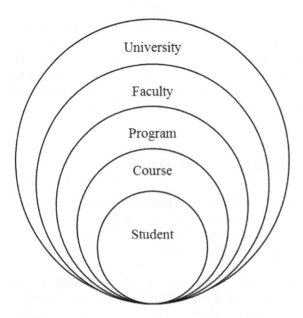

Fig. 10.1 The university as a multi-layered system in which students participate

This multi-layered system is shown in Fig. 10.1. Systems theory can be used to identify interconnections between each layer, including how the practices in one layer can impact other layers (Bronfenbrenner, 1979). For instance, in a recent Australian study, the lack of mandatory class attendance was found to reduce the ability of first-year students to transition from high school into university as it directly affected their ability to develop and maintain support networks. In other words, university policy related to class attendance was found to affect the ability of these students to develop support networks that are an integral component of resilience capability (Turner et al., 2017b).

In another Australian study, undergraduate students were asked what they considered to be important in the development of their own resilience while at university (Holdsworth et al., 2017). A range of internal and external protective factors were identified, including: staying healthy, maintaining perspective, social support from friends within and outside of university, high quality feedback from educators, and extra-curricular activities. Using a systems framework, the study highlighted that students call on various layers of the system to develop their resilience while at university.

The implication of these findings for universities is the need to apply an integrated system approach that links external protective factors for students within various layers of the system with education to build internal protective factors. This can be achieved through university-led policies such as mandatory class attendance which can lead to social support, and program-led services such as mentoring and access to extra-curricular activities. Together with this, universities can facilitate learning opportunities which help students develop the internal protective factors considered important for resilience, such as reflection, and the ability to re-frame problems. This may be facilitated at course-level and be integrated into curriculum design, assessment, and feedback. These have cost implications for universities which means that before they can develop such an integrated systems approach, there is need to develop a means to measure levels of student resilience.

10.5   Measuring Student Resilience

Various measures of resilience have been applied in university settings, however progress has been hindered by a lack of consistent measurement. Based on the Resilience-at-Work (RAW) scale (Winwood et al., 2013), a Resilience at University (RAU) scale has been developed (Turner et al., 2017a). The RAU adopts three critical principles of the RAW, namely that: resilience is a skill which can be developed through carefully targeted interventions; resilience is a multi-dimensional construct comprised of internal and external protective factors; each resilience dimension can be translated into specific initiatives which can be implemented in an applied setting. The RAU is underpinned by six dimensions, which closely replicated the seven dimensions of RAW (Winwood et al., 2013). The major difference is the grouping of the items from the interacting cooperatively and living authentically subscales onto one factor.

1. **Living authentically**: Knowing and holding onto personal values, deploying personal strengths, and having a good level of emotional awareness and regulation, and **Interacting cooperatively**: Seeking feedback, advice, and support as well as providing support to other students..
2. **Finding your calling**: Undertaking studies which link with career goals, fit with core values and beliefs, and enable a sense of belonging at university.
3. **Maintaining perspective**: Having the capacity to reframe setbacks, maintain a solution focus, and manage negativity.
4. **Managing stress**: Using routines that help manage everyday stressors, maintain study-life balance, and ensure time for relaxation.
5. **Staying healthy**: Maintaining a good level of physical fitness and a healthy diet.
6. **Building networks**: Developing and maintaining personal support networks, both within and outside the university.

The RAU scale's instructions provided to students specify that the questions refer to their experience at university, including the time spent at university, as well as the time spent on studies outside of university. Students are asked to indicate their agreement with the items across a seven-point Likert scale ranging from "strongly disagree"(0) to "strongly agree" (6). The scale has demonstrated good internal reliability ($\alpha = 0.81$). Examples of scale items include: 1) "The university work that I do fits well with my personal values" and 2) "Beliefs I have a strong and reliable network of supportive students at university" (Turner et al., 2017a).

The RAU was used to assess the resilience of students enrolled in an introductory management course at an Australian university. Students who had participated in a resilience-related survey and activity as part of their learning about management, were invited to also submit their survey as part of a research activity studying the resilience levels among university students. Of the 1412 students studying the course 900 completed the survey, 808 (90%) agreed to participate in the research. Of the research participants, 85% ($n = 685$) were in their first-year of study in higher education, 12% ($n = 95$) were undertaking their second year, and 3% ($n = 28$) were undertaking their third, fourth or fifth year (subsequently referred to as third plus) of study. Most participants were Australian residents (82.2%), with a smaller proportion of international residents studying in Australia (17.8%). The gender split between participants was 57% male and 42.4% female. The mean age of participants was 19.3 years ($SD = 4.1$).

Analysis of the findings calculated a mean (M) and standard deviation (SD) for each factor of the RAU. Means ranged from "neither agree nor disagree" (3) to "slightly agree" (4) (Table 10.1). This suggests that these participants self-identified as having modest levels of resilience. An independent-samples t-test was applied to the data to enable further analysis of resilience according to the gender, home country, year of study, and whether participants were working (e.g., part time/full-time) or not working.

The means and standard deviations for comparisons where significant differences were found between groups (i.e., male/female and working/not working) are outlined in Tables 10.2 and 10.3. These tests found that there was a significant difference between males and females for dimension 2 ($t(807) = -2.11, p = 0.038$), dimension 3 ($t(807) = 5.67, p = 0.000$), dimension 4 ($t(807) = 2.94, p = 0.004$) and dimension 5 ($t(807) = 2.03, p = 0.035$). There was a significant difference between working and not working students for dimension 3 ($t(807) = 2.23, p = 0.026$) and dimension 5 ($t(807) = 3.28, p = 0.001$). There was no significant difference between first and third plus-year students and no significant difference for international and local students.

Of the six dimensions of resilience identified in the RAU, students in this study scored highest on 'living authentically' and 'interacting cooperatively'. As noted earlier, this refers to knowing and holding onto personal values, deploying personal strengths, and having a good level of emotional awareness and regulation. It also encompasses seeking feedback, advice, and support as well as providing support to

Table 10.1 Mean responses for each dimension (subscale)

Dimension (subscale)	Mean	SD
1: Living authentically and interacting cooperatively	4.55	0.77
2: Finding your calling	4.41	0.84
3: Maintaining perspective	3.73	1.22
4: Managing stress	4.39	1.01
5: Staying healthy	4.12	1.01
6: Building networks	4.00	1.41

Table 10.2 Mean scores and standard deviations of student resilience dimensions for male and female participants found to be significantly different from independent-sample t-tests

Dimension (subscale)	Male		Female	
	Mean	SD	Mean	SD
1: Living authentically and interacting cooperatively				
2: Finding your calling	4.35	0.87	4.48	0.78
3: Maintaining perspective	3.93	1.16	3.45	1.26
4: Managing stress	4.48	1.00	4.27	1.02
5: Staying healthy	4.18	.99	4.03	1.05
6: Building networks				

Note Non-significant results are not reported (i.e., $p > 0.05$)

Table 10.3 Mean scores and standard deviations of student resilience dimensions for working and non-working student participants found to be significantly different from independent-sample t-tests

Dimension (subscale)	Working		Not working	
	Mean	SD	Mean	SD
1: Living authentically and interacting cooperatively				
2: Finding your calling				
3: Maintaining perspective	3.81	1.20	3.73	1.22
4: Managing stress				
5: Staying healthy	4.21	0.96	4.12	1.02
6: Building networks				

Note Non-significant results are not reported (i.e., $p > 0.05$)

other students. This high score may reflect a generational pattern as it is consistent with research into millennials, who see themselves as individuals who are strongly values and purpose driven. This could be resulting in a student population wanting to know 'why they are doing' rather than simply 'what they are doing' (Jacobowitz, Lachter, & Morello, 2016), and wanting their work to contribute high order value to their lives (Vecchione, Alessandri, Barbaranelli, & Caprara, 2011). They are also strongly relationship-based, reliant on networks and support from each other (Jokisaari & Nurmi, 2009).

The students' lowest score was in 'maintaining perspective'. As noted earlier, this refers to having the capacity to reframe setbacks, maintain a solution focus, and manage negativity (Winwood et al., 2013). Perspective-taking is reliant on social and emotional learning or SEL (Zin, Weissberg, Wang, & Walberg, 2004) requiring self-awareness and social awareness. It is considered an important individual asset related to resilience (APA, 2010). Within the university experience, maintaining perspective allows for translation from student experience to student learning. Poulos and Mahony (2008) claim that "maintaining perspective is critical for receiving and learning from constructive feedback from peers and educators" (p. 144). An inability to reframe challenging experiences as learning opportunities may inhibit students' learning capacity. Interestingly, at an item level, the survey results indicate students are not strong on asking for feedback on their work ($M = 3.52$ $SD = 1.52$). This data suggests students may be reluctant to engage in the education process in a way that could challenge their existing perspectives, thus limiting the capacity for the university experience to contribute to resilience development.

Findings also indicated a significant difference in resilience between males and females (see Table 10.2). This relates particularly to the dimensions of 'maintaining perspective', 'finding your calling', 'managing stress' and 'staying healthy'. As it relates to 'finding your calling', females scored higher than males. For the other three factors, males scored higher. This data may reflect broader patterns of variation in resilience between genders that is highlighted in the literature (Bezek, 2010). This variation has been shown to relate to the way individuals attain resilience (Blatt-Eisengart, Drabick, Monahan, & Steinberg, 2009; Bonnano 2008), as males and females use different resources as coping mechanisms. Males are prone to more individualistic means, whereas females rely more on social support and communal means (Sneed et al., 2006). As it relates to the case study data, the higher level for 'finding your calling' for females could link to a strong sense of self and purpose (Winstone, 2017), so may support resilience in females students, whereas higher levels of self-efficacy, as reflected in 'managing stress' and 'staying healthy' may contribute to higher levels of resilience in the males in the study (Schwarzer & Warner, 2013).

While it is recognised that one cannot generalise a cause-effect relationship from one study, these research findings do suggest that universities need to become cognisant of a range of factors before establishing an effective systems approach to building students' resilience. For example, there appears to be a gender disparity that affects different developmental needs. In addition, whether students live at home or not can have an impact on their resilience, with studies finding that women experience better adjustment when they are more independent (Blatt-Eisengart et al., 2009).

The analysis did not identify any significant differences between first and third plus-year students for any of the six dimensions. Indeed, the dimensions that might be expected to strengthen across the university trajectory (e.g., 'finding your calling' and 'building networks') were no higher for third plus-year students than first year students. This might be explained by either the students developing a more realistic perspective of their own resilience over their years of study or, alternatively, it may reflect a lack of capacity of HE institutions to develop students' resilience as a component of helping them become workplace-ready. This latter alternative is in keeping with the argument by Bonnano (2008) that people with a college degree are less likely to be resilient in comparison with those who did not attend college, a finding contrary to the assumption that more education leads to better psychological wellbeing.

A significant relationship was found between resilience, work and the dimension of 'maintaining perspective'. This suggests that there may be an important link between students undertaking employment and an increase in perspective-taking.

Furthermore, a meaningful relationship was found between resilience, work (i.e., part or full-time employment) and 'staying healthy'. These results may indicate self-selection in which more resilient students may have advantages in seeking and maintaining workforce participation. It may also suggest that ongoing experience in the workplace might support and encourage the development of resilience through workplace mechanisms such as feedback, an extended social network, social learning, and greater responsibilities.

In summary, the findings from this study provide insights into the current levels of (internal perspective) resilience in university students. As resilience is associated with positive social and personal wellbeing, together with enhanced mental health and adjustment to university life (McGillivray & Pidgeon, 2015), understanding the factors that promote and hinder resilience development is important to enhancing the student learning experience. In addition, resilience should be a graduate capability intentionally acquired or deliberately strengthened during the student experience (Cranney & Andrews, 2016), to graduate students capable of adjustment to life in the workplace.

10.6   Building Student Resilience Across the Internal and External Protective Layers

Given that research to date does identify that building student capability for resilience has both internal and external dimensions, the challenge for universities is how to develop the internal dimension while also providing the external supportive factors: environment, life and social support. The first challenge for universities is to design curricula able to cope with this variation. At the same time, universities need to design systems, support mechanisms, and processes external to the actual learning process, that contribute to the development of student resilience. This is a significant challenge for universities also facing financial austerity. The next section outlines some of the resilience programs that have been developed in Australian HE.

10.6.1   Building Student Resilience—An Australian Experience

Recently, Australian HE institutes have increasingly attempted to address the issue of student resilience. The interest in developing programs focused on resilience development has stemmed not only from the desire to enhance the student learning experience and develop work-ready graduates, but also as an effective way of responding to the ongoing reductions in HE budgets. These budget pressures mean that resilience interventions (by enhancing the retention and likely graduation of students) offer important cost savings to institutes. In 2008 the cost of failing to retain one full fee-paying student at the end of their first-year was estimated to be between \$20,000 and \$30,000 in lost fee income for their second and third years of study (Scott, Shah, Grebennikov, & Singh, 2008). Of the almost quarter of a million students commencing an undergraduate degree in Australia during 2018, more than 50,000 of these students will leave university without completing their degree (Norton, Cherastidtham, & Mackey, 2018). Improving the resilience of students is one of the approaches universities can take to help address retention and reduce the costs associated with student attrition.

The research and various interventions developed to tackle resilience have varied in their approach to providing academic and social support, student engagement, and social climate (Pidgeon & Pickett, 2017). A range of closely related research projects on student stress, wellbeing, and mental health has also been undertaken (e.g., Larcombe et al., 2016; Pidgeon & Pickett, 2017; Stallman, 2010). Some universities have focused on programs designed to help build specific skills whilst others have sought to ensure the campus services and facilities they offer foster support for greater resilience. Using the framework of internal and external factors that help support the development of resilience, this section briefly discusses a small sample of programs that exemplify what is happening in this area in Australia. This overview is in no way comprehensive, but it does provide a flavour of how the sector is addressing this issue.

a. *Approaches addressing internal factors*

These programs have used course curriculum, workshop-based, and online materials to help students become more knowledgeable about resilience and have provided strategies that students can use to improve their self-management. These materials have largely been developed by academic and counselling services staff. For example, Stallman (2011) developed a 90-min seminar called *Staying on Track*, which has been used with law and health science students in two Queensland universities. The seminar is based on six building blocks for resilience. The first three help students buffer against stress (i.e., realistic expectations, balance, and connectedness), and the second three assist student to manage stressful situations (i.e., positive self-talk, stress management, and taking action). Stallman reported high scores for student satisfaction for the seminar and that 90% of students noted that at least one of the blocks was useful to them.

A slightly different approach has been taken by the University of Tasmania. In 2016 the university introduced an undergraduate-breadth subject titled *Resilience in the face of emergencies (XBR206)*. This subject aims to help students develop "a better understanding of resilience as broader concept that can be applied to many aspects of their student, personal and professional life" (Brooks, Carnes, & Owens, 2016, p. 3). The core content for this subject includes material on: resilience and emergencies, the physiology of resilience, the psychology of resilience, resilience across the lifespan, community resilience, organisational resilience, analysis of resilient behaviour, and translating resilience.

Rather than create a dedicated subject on resilience, RMIT University introduced resilience-related content into several courses (subjects) in late 2016 and early 2017.

These courses are taught within the School of Building, Construction and Project Management and the School of Management. The resilience materials focus on concepts central to RAU scale and are discussed during tutorials in the middle part of the semester. These materials are supplemented by other activities during the semester designed to encourage the development of self-management skills such as time management, planning for assessments, and navigating group projects.

Based on growing concerns that trainee teachers could be better supported to build the necessary resilience to succeed in the profession, a consortium of six Australian universities have developed the BRiTE (Building Resilience in Teacher Education) program (Staying BRiTE, 2018). This online program uses five core modules to helps pre-service teachers develop greater resilience for their teaching practice and covers:

- building resilience (e.g., what is it and why it matters),
- relationships (e.g., maintaining support networks and building new relationships),
- wellbeing (e.g., personal wellbeing and work-life balance),
- taking initiative (e.g., problem solving and professional development), and
- emotions (e.g., developing optimism and managing emotions) (Mansfield, Beltman, Weatherby-Fell, & Broadley, 2016).

Beta versions of the modules were live-tested to refine the content delivery and evaluated using online Likert scale items and open-ended questions. Overall the feedback was very positive with the mean score for content 4.2 out of 5 and the mean score for online design 4.3 out of 5. The qualitative comments were largely very favourable with some helpful suggestions provided to further refine the modules.

Mansfield et al. (2016) highlighted two notable features of the BRiTE program. Firstly, it noted that the importance of pre-service teachers' learning was not only to bounce back, but also to bounce forward (Walsh, 2002). Bouncing forward not only has a restorative aspect to it but it also enables individuals to grow and develop, an important aspect of professional development. The second point was that the program challenges the trait-based view of resilience and helps pre-service teachers recognise the importance that broader social ecologies play in the profession by enabling resilience.

b. *Approaches addressing internal and external factors*

Some of the programs undertaken by universities have sought to address both internal and external factors to support resilience. Higher education institutes can provide external resources in the form of services or opportunities that provide positive support to students. An example of a university that has followed this approach is the University of the Sunshine Coast (USC). This university adopted a Healthy University Initiative based on WHO Health Promoting Universities framework. This program includes some elements that are internally focused (e.g., resilience, mindfulness, and self-awareness knowledge and skills) but also a focus on creating a supportive university environment that promotes healthy food choices, smoke-free campus, a cultural centre, quiet reflection rooms, and healthy learning and natural spaces (USC, n.d.).

Student peer mentoring programs are a further example of an approach tackling internal and external resilience factors. The Queensland University of Technology and RMIT University have introduced these types of programs to support students (Heirdsfield et al., 2008; Ryan & Kemlo, 2012). Although these programs are more focused on students who may be at greater risk of dropping out of study, some of these programs do engage a wider cross section of students, including the mentors who are typically very capable students. These programs are coordinated by the university but work at a peer-level and offer the opportunity for students to obtain support and advice from a fellow student. The mentors can play a vital role in helping support students' social integration into the university setting. This may be as simple as helping students recognise that they are not alone in their challenges and that they are part of wider student network. Hearing mentors discuss their own challenges can often help students (mentees) gain perspective that the issues confronting them are usually quite common. The mentors can help direct students to appropriate university services such as the study and learning centre, student services, and health and counselling services. Mentors also share their own insights on successfully navigating various aspects of university life include etiquette, seeking advice from teaching staff, joining university clubs and societies, and tips on planning assessments and exam technique. A further important aspect of these programs has been the careful design and incorporation of data collection and evaluation processes to understand the student experience and assess the program's effectiveness.

10.7 Conclusion

To become resilient, organisations require robust systems and processes, and a suitably skilled and resilient workforce. The increasing requirement for more resilient graduates creates some interesting challenges and opportunities for universities. In describing and contextualising resilience, it was observed that it is not just the capacity to bounce back from adversity, but also the capacity to bounce forward and grow in response to difficulties and challenges. The close relationship between resilience and wellbeing underlines the importance of developing university students' resilience. In the university setting, the fostering of resilience needs to embrace student progress, growth and learning. The literature shows that there are two types of factors central to resilience, namely internal and external. The combination of these factors highlights the multi-dimensional nature of resilience and some challenges for universities to meet students' needs within organisational structures, service delivery arrangements, and traditions that do not readily map to this requirement. Careful analysis is required given that less obvious arrangements such as compulsory class attendance may influence the opportunity to enhance student resilience. There is a clear need for universities to develop an integrated systems approach to tackle student resilience. However, for some universities, assessing levels of student resilience is perhaps the most immediate need.

Research undertaken with Australian university students suggests that their resilience levels are probably best described as modest. There were some differences in various aspects of resilience between male and female students and higher levels of some aspects of resilience found in students working compared to those not working. These patterns of student resilience suggest that Australian students are largely still a 'work in progress' but that there are some very good opportunities for universities to help students grow their resilience. Given the ongoing budgetary pressures on Australian universities, interventions that enhance student resilience and ongoing successful study are becoming increasingly valuable.

Australian universities have invested in several initiatives to support the development of more resilient students. The sample of programs discussed highlighted the range of initiatives that have been trialled or are currently underway. So far Australian universities have developed programs that address selected internal and external factors, although not in the strongly integrated and systematic manner required to really enhance opportunities to develop student resilience. Given that Australian universities are still learning to build, deliver, and integrate these initiatives, well-designed programs that incorporate sound data collection and evaluation will be important in helping the sector to grow its understanding of how to better support the development of student resilience.

References

AEI. (2010). *International student survey*. Canberra: Department of Education, Employment and Workplace Relations. http://www.aei.gov.au/research/Publications/Documents/2010_International_Student_Report.pdf. Accessed October 20, 2018.

APA. (2010). *The road to resilience*. American Psychological Association. http://www.apa.org/helpcenter/road-resilience.aspx. Accessed September 15, 2018.

APA. (2017). *Stress by generation*. Washington: American Psychological Association.

Balu, R. (2001). How to bounce back from setbacks. *Fast Company, 45,* 148–156.

Bardoel, E. A., Pettit, T. M., De Cieri, H., & McMillan, L. (2014). Employee resilience: An emerging challenge for HRM. *Asia Pacific Journal of Human Resources, 52,* 279–297.

Bezek, E. (2010). *Gender differences in resilience in the emerging adulthood population*. Rochester: RIT Scholar Works.

Blatt-Eisengart, I., Drabick, D. A. G., Monahan, K. C., & Steinberg, L. (2009). Sex differences in the longitudinal relations among family risk factors and childhood externalizing symptoms. *Developmental Psychology, 45*(2), 491–502.

Block, J., & Kremen, A. M. (1996). IQ and ego-resiliency: Conceptual and empirical connections and separateness. *Journal of Personality and Social Psychology, 70,* 349–361.

Bonnano, G. A. (2008). Loss, trauma, and human resilience: Have we underestimated the human capacity to thrive after extremely aversive events. *Psychological Trauma: Theory, Research, Practice, and Policy, S*(1), 101–113.

Bronfenbrenner, U. (1979). *The ecology of human development*. Cambridge, MA: Harvard University Press.

Brooks, B., Carnes, D., & Owens, C. (2016). Resilience in the face of emergencies (XBR 206). In *Semester 2, 2016 unit outline*. University of Tasmania: Launceston.

Casey, L., & Liang, R. (2014). *Stress and wellbeing in Australia Survey 2014*. Melbourne: Australian Psychological Society.

Cooper, C. L., Flint-Taylor, J., & Pearn, M. (2013). *Building resilience for success: A resource for managers and organisations*. Basingstoke: Palgrave-MacMillan.

Coutu, D. L. (2002). How resilience works. *Harvard Business Review, 80*(5), 46–55.

Cranney, J., & Andrews, A. (2016). *Curriculum renewal to build student resilience and success: Phase 1 Final report 2016*. UNSW Australia.

Dias, P. C., & Cadime, I. (2017). Protective factors and resilience in adolescents: The mediating role of self-regulation. *Psicología Educativa, 23*(1), 37–43.

Edgar, F., Cathro, V., Harrison, S., Hoek, J., McKenzie, K., Malcolm, N., et al. (2013). Employing graduates: Selection criteria and practice in New Zealand. *Journal of Management & Organization, 19*(3), 338–351.

Friborg, O., Hjemdal, O., Rosenvinge, J., & Martinussen, M. (2003). A new rating scale for adult resilience: What are the central protective resources behind healthy adjustment? *International Journal of Methods in Psychiatric Research, 12*, 65–76.

Gerson, M. W., & Fernandez, N. (2013). PATH: A program to build resilience and thriving in undergraduates. *Journal of Applied Social Psychology, 43*(11), 2169–2184.

Grant, L., & Kinman, G. (2012). Enhancing wellbeing in social work students: Building resilience in the next generation. *Social Work Education, 31*(5), 605–621.

Hager, P. (2006). Nature and development of generic attributes. In P. Hager & S. Holland (Eds.), *Graduate attributes, learning and employability*. The Netherlands: Springer.

Hamel, G., & Valikangas, L. (2003). The quest for resilience. *Harvard Business Review, 81*(9), 52–63.

Heirdsfield, A. M., Nelson, K. J., Tills, B., Cheeseman, T., Derrington, K., Walker, S., & Walsh, K. (2008). Peer mentoring: Models and outcomes at QUT. In *AARE 2008 International Education Conference: Changing Climates: Education for Sustainable Futures*, November 30–December 4, 2008. Brisbane: Queensland University of Technology.

Holdsworth, S., Turner, M., & Scott-Young, C. M. (2017). … Not drowning, waving. Resilience and university: A student perspective. *Studies in Higher Education, 43*, 1837–1853.

Jackson, D., Firtko, A., & Edenborough, M. (2007). Personal resilience as a strategy for surviving and thriving in the face of workplace adversity: A literature review. *Journal of Advanced Nursing, 60*, 1–9.

Jacobowitz, J., Lachter, K., & Morello, G. (2016). Cultural evolution or revolution? The Millennial's growing impact on professionalism and the practice of law. *The Professional Lawyer, 23*, 20–34.

Jokisaari, M., & Nurmi, J. (2009). Change in newcomers' supervisor support and socialization outcomes after organizational entry. *Academy of Management Journal, 52*, 527–544.

King, D., Newman, A., & Luthands, F. (2016). Not if, but when we need resilience in the workplace. *Journal of Organizational Behaviour, 37*, 782–786.

Kramer, M. (1974). *Reality shock: Why nurses leave nursing*. Saint Louis: The C.V. Mosby Company.

Larcombe, W. Finch, S., Sore, R., Murray, C. M., Kentish, S. … Williams, D. A. (2016). Prevalence and socio-demographic correlates of psychological distress among students at an Australian university. *Studies in Higher Education, 41*(6), 1074–1091.

Lengnick-Hall, C., Beck, T., & Lengnick-Hall, M. (2011). Developing a capacity for organizational resilience through strategic human resource management. *Human Resource Management Review, 21*, 243–255.

Liu, J. W., Reed, M., & Girard, T. A. (2017). Advancing resilience: An integrative, multi-system model of resilience. *Personality and Individual Differences, 111*, 111–118.

Lovibond, S. H., & Lovibond, P. F. (1995). *Manual for the depression anxiety and stress scales* (2nd ed.). Sydney: Psychology Foundation.

Luthans, F., Youssef, C., & Avolio, B. (2007). *Psychological capital: Developing the human competitive edge*. Oxford, UK: Oxford University Press.

Luthar, S., Cicchetti, D., & Becker, B. (2000). The construct of resilience: A critical evaluation and guidelines for future work. *Childhood Development, 71*, 543–562.

Lyubomirsky, S., & Lepper, H. (1999). A measure of subjective happiness: Preliminary reliability and construct validation. *Social Indicators Research, 46*(2), 137–155.

Mansfield, C. F., Beltman, S., Weatherby-Fell, N., & Broadley, T. (2016). Classroom ready? Building resilience in teacher education. In R. Brandenberg, S. McDonough, J. Burke, & S. White (Eds.), *Teacher education: Innovation, intervention and impact* (pp. 211–229). Singapore: Springer.

Maute, J. L. (2007). Lawyering in the 21st century: A capstone course on the law and ethics of lawyering. *Saint Louis University Law Journal, 51*(4), 1291–1316.

McGillivray, C. J., & Pidgeon, A. M. (2015). Resilience attributes among university students: A comparative study of psychological distress, sleep disturbances and mindfulness. *European Scientific Journal, 11*(5), 33–48.

McNamara, J., Brown, C., Field, R. M., Kift, S. M., Butler, D. A., & Treloar, C. (2011). Capstones: Transitions and professional identity. In *2011 WACE World Conference—Conference Proceedings, Philadelphia*.

Moir, J. (2010). *First things first: The first year in Scottish higher education*. http://www.enhancementthemes.ac.uk/docs/publications/first-things-first-the-first-year-in-scottish-higher-education.pdf. Accessed September 16, 2018.

Morgeson, F. P., & Hofmann, D. A. (1999). The structure and function of collective constructs: Implications for multilevel research and theory development. *Academy of Management Review, 24*(2), 249–265.

Norton, A., Cherastidtham, I., & Mackey, W. (2018). *Dropping out: The benefits and costs of trying university*. Grattan Institute: Melbourne.

Pidgeon, A. M., & Pickett, L. (2017). *Examining the differences between university students' levels of resilience on mindfulness, psychological distress and coping strategies*. http://epublications.bond.edu.au/fsd_papers/506. Accessed October 27, 2018.

Pooley, J., & Cohen, L. (2010). Resilience: A definition in context. *Australian Community Psychologist, 22*(1), 30–37.

Poulos, A., & Mahony, M. J. (2008). Effectiveness of feedback: The students' perspective. *Assessment & Evaluation in Higher Education, 33*(2), 143–154.

Rickwood, D., Telford, N., O'Sullivan, S., Crisp, D. & Magyar, R. (2016). National tertiary student wellbeing survey 2016. In *Headspace and National Union of Students*. https://headspace.org.au/assets/Uploads/headspace-NUS-Publication-Digital.pdf. Accessed September 15, 2018.

Rutten, B. P., Hammels, C., Geschwind, N., Menne-Lothmann, C., Pishva, E., Schruers, K., et al. (2013). Resilience in mental health: Linking psychological and neurobiological perspectives. *Acta Psychiatrica Scandinavica, 128*(1), 3–20.

Ryan, J., & Kemlo, L. (2012). Student transition: Changes in higher education demand innovative designs for early intervention strategies. In *First Year Higher Education Conference 26–29 June 2012, Brisbane*.

Schwarzer, R., & Warner, L. M. (2013). Perceived self-efficacy and its relationship to resilience. In S. Prince-Embury & D. H. Saklofske (Eds.), *Resilience in children, adolescents, and adults: Translating research into practice* (pp. 139–150). New York: Springer.

Scott, G., Shah, M., Grebennikov, L., & Singh, H. (2008). Improving student retention: A University of Western Sydney case study. *Journal of Institutional Research, 14*(1), 9–23.

Seery, M. D., & Quinton, W. J. (2016). Understanding resilience: From negative life events to everyday stressors. *Advances in Experimental Social Psychology, 54*, 181–245.

Shin, J., Taylor, M., & Seo, M. (2012). Resources for change: The relationships of organizational inducements and psychological resilience to employees' attitudes and behaviors toward organizational change. *Academy of Management Journal, 55*, 727–748.

Sneed, J. R., Johnson, J. G., Cohen, P., Gilligan, C., Chen, H., Crawford, T. N., et al. (2006). Gender differences in the age-changing relationship between instrumentality and family contact in emerging adulthood. *Developmental Psychology, 42*(5), 787–797.

Stallman, H. M. (2010). Psychological distress in university students: A comparison with general population data. *Australian Psychologist, 45*(4), 286–294.

Stallman, H. M. (2011). Embedding resilience within the tertiary curriculum: A feasibility study. *Higher Education Research & Development, 30*(2), 121–133.

Staying BRiTE. (2018). *Promoting resilience in higher education.* https://www.stayingbrite.edu.au/. Accessed October 27, 2018.

Trotter, E., & Roberts, C. A. (2006). Enhancing the early student experience. *Higher Education Research and Development, 25*(4), 371–386.

Turner, M., Holdsworth, S., & Scott-Young, C. M. (2017a). Resilience at university: The development and testing of a new measure. *Higher Education Research & Development, 36*(2), 386–400.

Turner, M., Holdsworth, S., & Scott-Young, C. M. (in press). Developing the resilient project professional: Examining the student experience. *International Journal of Managing Projects in Business.*

Turner, M., Scott-Young, C. M., & Holdsworth, S. (2017b). Promoting wellbeing at university: The role of resilience for students of the built environment. *Construction Management and Economics, 35*(11–12), 707–718.

USC. (n.d.). *Healthy university initiative.* https://www.usc.edu.au/learn/student-support/health-and-wellbeing/healthy-usc/healthy-university-initiative. Accessed October 27, 2018.

Vecchione, M., Alessandri, G., Barbaranelli, C., & Caprara, G. (2011). Higher-order factors of the big five and basic values: Empirical and theoretical relations. *British Journal Psychology, 102*(3), 478–498.

Walsh, F. (2002). Bouncing forward: Resilience in the aftermath of September 11. *Family Process, 41,* 34–36.

Werner, E. E. (1990). *Protective factors and individual resilience: Handbook of early childhood intervention* (pp. 97–116). New York, NY: Cambridge University Press.

Windle, G. (2011). What is resilience? A review and concept analysis. *Reviews in Clinical Gerontology, 21*(02), 152–169.

Winstone, N. E. (2017). The '3Rs' of pedagogic frailty: Risk, reward and resilience. In I. M. Kinchin & N. E. Winstone (Eds.), *Pedagogic frailty and resilience in the university.* Rotterdam: Sense Publishers.

Winwood, P. C., Colon, R., & McEwen, K. (2013). A practical measure of workplace resilience: Developing the resilience at work scale. *Journal of Occupational and Environmental Medicine, 55*(10), 1205–1212.

Zin, J. E., Weissberg, R. P., Wang, M. C., & Walberg, H. J. (2004). *Building academic success on social and emotional learning. What does the research say?.* New York: Teachers College Press.

Jacinta Ryan (Ph.D.) has predominantly worked in health care management, in both the public and private health sectors. In addition to focusing on developing best practice in service delivery, she has built and implemented a range of programs and services aimed at capitalising on leadership management potential, building strong team dynamics and maximising individual performance. She has a strong interest in helping organisations develop pathways that bring spiritual influences into organisational systems. Her doctoral research has provided applied approaches that help organisations in practical ways to build health and well-being in the workplace and maximise their growth potential. To support this work she is a university lecturer at RMIT, Melbourne, Australia, and a researcher in education and management. Her strong commitment to student wellbeing has been a key driver behind her work on student success and retention.

Sandra Jones (Ph.D.) is Professor of Employment Relations at RMIT University, Melbourne, Australia, and a Principal Fellow of the Higher Education Academy. She has been recognised in national and institutional teaching awards for her design, use of, and scholarship on Virtual Situated Learning Environments. She combines her professional practice and research on employment relations with her innovations in teaching practice to engage and support students to graduate with the skills needed by industry. To achieve this, she consults extensively with external stakeholders

to model the university as a Living Learning Laboratory through which industry partners can identify their emergent skill needs.

Peter Hayes (Ph.D.) lectures at RMIT, Melbourne, Australia, having initially worked in forest
management in both New Zealand and the UK. A developing interest in people and behaviour
in the workplace led him to complete an M.Sc. in industrial and organisational psychology. His
doctorate used simulations to investigate decision-making and teamwork in emergency incident
management teams. Since completing it, he has continued to teach university business students
and undertake research within the emergency management and higher education sectors. He has
authored and co-authored various publications on coaching and mentoring, capability development, decision-making, and human factors in emergency management.

Michelle Turner (Ph.D.) holds postgraduate qualifications in psychology and project management and is an Associate Professor at RMIT University in Melbourne, Australia where she teaches
in the project management program. Her research focuses on psychological resilience, mental
health and well-being, and work readiness. Her work on resilience has been published in leading
education, project management, and construction management journals. She leads the translation
of her research into university curriculum to support resilience-development of undergraduate and
postgraduate students.

Chapter 11
"That Working-Class Ethic … Where There's a Will There's a Way:" A Strengths-Based Approach to Developing Employable Scholars

Sarah O'Shea and Janine Delahunty

11.1 Introduction

Globally, the numbers of students accessing Higher Education (HE) are increasing; Marginson (2016) reports between 2007 and 2013, worldwide the number of tertiary students multiplied by 6.12. Since the 1990s, this participation has grown at a much more rapid rate, at approximately 1% per year meaning that most high and mid-income countries are either approaching or exceeding 50% participation across their populations (Marginson, 2016). The drive to access university is largely defined in terms of obtaining better employment opportunities and a more secure financial future (Marginson, 2016; Norton & Cherastidtham, 2014; O'Shea, Stone, May, & Delahunty, 2018). However, how obtaining a degree actually translates into employability within an increasingly competitive labour markets needs further consideration. These markets are largely stratified and success can be defined by existing social status and also, economic power (Reay, 2013). For many students, particularly those from diverse backgrounds, the 'relations between HE and work are fragmented' (Marginson, 2016, p. 418). Increasing costs of attaining a degree, coupled with limited guarantee of employment post-graduation, suggest that we need to carefully consider what being an 'employable scholar' means to those from less advantaged backgrounds. Both the UK and Australian HE systems adhere to an understanding of 'individualized life choices' within educational discourses, essentially positioning learners as unencumbered free agents responsible for their own educational choices and activities (Opengart & Short, 2002). In this way, failure or non-attainment of expected post-graduation goals is also individualised, often blamed upon lack of

S. O'Shea (✉) · J. Delahunty
University of Wollongong, Wollongong, Australia
e-mail: saraho@uow.edu.au

J. Delahunty
e-mail: janined@uow.edu.au

© Springer Nature Switzerland AG 2019   155
A. Diver (ed.), *Employability via Higher Education: Sustainability as Scholarship*,
https://doi.org/10.1007/978-3-030-26342-3_11

abilities, planning or understanding, rather than on external constraints (McKay & Devlin, 2016).

Moving away from the discourse of the individual, this chapter explores how students are social entities who arrive at university with existing capitals and capabilities that can be underutilised and unrecognised within the HE landscape. We propose a strengths-based approach as the point of departure, drawing upon findings from an Australia-wide study which explored persistence strategies of first-in-family students in the final stages of their undergraduate degree (O'Shea, 2017–2019). Utilising richly descriptive interviews and surveys, this chapter focuses on how the stories of these students provides a counter-narrative to perceptions of lack and instead, foregrounds the existing capabilities and capitals utilised to enact success and progress. We hope that this offers alternative perspectives to persuasive deficit discourses by providing insight into how individuals maximised such resources to achieve educational goals and objectives.

11.2 Literature Review: Exploring Capitals and Capabilities to Persist and Succeed at University

There is a diversity of literature on university participation of learners from diverse backgrounds, much of which is framed within widening participation discourses and educational equity agendas. The focus of this literature review is on three related areas to provide context to the data and discussion that follow:

- Considering 'employability' for diverse learners
- Degree attainment and the idyll of social mobility
- Defining success beyond neoliberal discourses.

11.2.1 Considering Employability for Diverse Learners

Emerging research indicates that employment outcomes for graduates from more diverse or disadvantaged backgrounds are poorer than for their more advantaged counterparts (Burke, Hayton, & Stevenson, 2018). This difference may be attributed to a number of factors including lacking the necessary social or cultural capitals that enable individuals to move seamlessly into preferred professional fields. Using Pierre Bourdieu's work (1986) we define social capital as a type of networking that serves to legitimise the positioning of the powerful and dominant classes. As Bourdieu explains:

> Social capital is the sum of the resources, actual or virtual, that accrue to an individual or a group by virtue of possessing a durable network of more or less institutionalized relationships of mutual acquaintance and recognition. (Bourdieu & Wacquant, 1992, p. 119)

Bourdieu (1986) perceives social capital as a means to produce or reproduce inequality, a mechanism that ensures the reproduction of existing social structures. Having the accepted forms of social capital is particularly important in high-status professions such as law and medicine, which often continue to operate under the auspices of an 'old boy's network' (Reeves, Friedman, Rahal, & Flemmen, 2017). This type of invisible barrier is defined in Southgate et al.'s (2017) work with first-in-family students studying medical degrees. They evocatively describe how these learners have a low sense of belonging in their degrees despite being the high academic achievers of their community, highlighting the significant 'social, economic and symbolic distance' (p. 251) that existed between them and those from wealthier backgrounds. This situation is echoed in Lehmann's study (2007) with Canadian working-class youth who were also first in their family to attend university. Lehmann (2007) explains how this cohort 'choose, enter and experience university in unique ways' (p. 91) which can often situate them as 'cultural outsiders' forced to 'mimic' behaviours and manners designed to obscure their working-class backgrounds (pp. 91–92). For Lehmann's participants, it was the lack of appropriate or valued 'cultural capital' that foreclosed success, leading Lehmann to conclude that: 'Inequality is explained by personal qualities and abilities rather than...unequal life chances rooted in social class differences' (2009, p. 632).

Applying these understandings to employability, it becomes clear that the 'purchasing power' (Bathmaker, 2015, p. 66) available to individuals within the employment market varies according to the range and type of capitals held. The capitals favoured within the market are those generally associated with the middle classes, creating an invisible but persistent social inequality. Despite this inequity, the desire to enter and participate in HE has not abated and so the next section explores this through what we have termed the 'idyll' of social mobility.

11.2.2 Degree Attainment and the Idyll of Social Mobility

The term social mobility is largely understood in terms of movement or change in social status that occurs when individuals shift 'from social origins to a new social destination' (Southgate et al., 2017, p. 243). The idyll of social mobility is thus defined within a 'celebratory discourse' (Friedman, 2014) that characterizes such movements as unquestioningly positive. This assumption of the positive fails to consider deeply how such actions actually play out in the lives of the individuals concerned.

Parental expectations and family or community obligations are often the drivers of social mobility which is perceived as a means to a better or more financially secure life. This can be motivated by missed opportunities in the past or a desire for children to have a better life than parents or caregivers had, positioning university as a 'ticket to a successful life' (O'Shea et al., 2018, p. 1028). Similarly, a study of first-in-family students in Malaysia found family influence was a significant factor in choosing to study (Kutty, 2014). While students' objectives focused on '[the] desire for self-improvement: educationally, financially, and professionally' (p. 51), influential parental expectations and encouragement to study were for financial security or family financial support. Yet achievement at university does not always move students towards greater fiscal security. Within Australia, Daly, Lewis, Corliss and Heaslip (2015) report that the investment benefits for degrees are not guaranteed and in fact in some cases, acquiring a degree may increase the cycle of poverty. Students leave university with no guaranteed employment but substantial debt which then impacts on future economic security and purchasing power. In some degrees, these authors argue that learners would have been 'better off' if they had simply entered full-time employment after completing their high school education, if this employment was available. Similarly, Milburn (2012) reports that in the UK those from professional families have a greater chance of obtaining relevant full-time work upon graduation.

Reay (2013) refers to social mobility as an 'inadequate sticking plaster over the gaping wound social inequalities have become' (p. 663); this 'mythic concept' performs a lot of work for sustaining and feeding neoliberal discourses. In many ways, the idyll of social mobility underpins capitalist society, as with the promise of reward for hard work, comes the utopian ideal that anyone can make it, and everyone has the power to succeed regardless of birthright or background. However, as the previous section indicated, there are other forms of capital that often work invisibly to limit success and determine post-graduation outcomes. In social mobility discourse, achieving success relies on the 'mirage' (Reay, 2013, p. 662) of individual capacities or skills rather than systemic advantage; this implies an assumption of universal freedom to achieve desires without any consideration for the forms of capital that individuals have genuine access to.

Given the limiting nature of social mobility and the restricted access to preferred forms of capitals available to dominant classes, an important perspective to consider is how students from more diverse backgrounds perceive their own success within the HE environment. The following section explores the concept of academic success in much broader terms to provide alternative understandings of HE participation.

11.3   Defining Success Beyond Neoliberal Discourses

Understanding how success is constructed at both a collective and subjective level is key to unpacking how HE both defines, and is defined by, students. At an institutional level, academic success is generally understood in meritocratic terms, the acquisition of an expected volume of knowledge, which in turn leads to the conferring of a qualification that 'presumably bestows on its possessor increased power (in the form of social and cultural capital, and in the form of credentials)' (Beilin, 2016, p. 16). However, Nyström, Jackson and Salminen Karlsson (2018) argue that success is variously defined by students, examining those in high status degrees they describe a 'valorisation of high achievement' (p. 6) that is both gendered and also, requires an elevated level of performativity. Similarly, O'Shea and Delahunty (2018) point to how understandings of success are differentiated for students who are the first in their families to attend university. These authors explore how succeeding at university was understood in an emotional and transformative sense; this embodied nature sitting alongside, sometimes uncomfortably, neoliberal discourses of future job prospects and the attainment of high grades. Overall, the literature points to the concept of student success as a complex one, differing across educational environments and student populations. Sullivan (2008) argues that institutions identify different definitions of 'success' that reflect the realities of various student cohorts, specifically a 'definition of success that acknowledges the unique complexities, challenges and material conditions' (p. 629) of these students.

In terms of employability, the skills and transformations that occur such as attitudes, open-mindedness, personal transformation and disrupting the status quo, are essential for future employment but not necessarily reflected in the neoliberal discourse of what constitutes 'success'. If focus remains on the meritocratic achievement model students from diverse backgrounds may not consider the capitals and capabilities they already possess as being useful or applicable to their HE experiences. Our position is that, rather than expecting learners to adopt institutional discourses of the successful student, the HE sector should value and build upon what learners arrive with to provide better preparation for life post-graduation. The following section highlights a study that focussed on how students used their existing capitals and capabilities to persist and succeed in the HE environment, providing an alternative lens to consider the contours of employability and post-graduation achievement.

11.4   Research Design and Theoretical Framing

The study occurred in Australia in 2017, funded by the Australian Research Council (DP170100705), exploring how students understood their persistence at university. All participants were in the latter stages of their degree and were asked to deeply reflect upon the capabilities and capitals that enabled them to manage their studies. Participants from nine Australian universities were invited to complete an online survey (N = 306) or participate in an in-depth biographical interview (N = 72). This study foregrounds the lived university experience by adopting a narrative biographical approach (Clandinin & Connelly, 2000), which provides insight into how individuals maximised cultural and social resources to achieve their educational goals and objectives, and the various qualities or experiences the students themselves considered as being impactful to their university experience.

Participants were also invited to provide demographic information, which gave some insight into the diversity of students' lives and indicated a high level of intersectionality amongst this cohort. Table 11.1 summarises this information.

After interviews were transcribed and deidentified (pseudonyms for interviews, codes for surveys) the two researchers independently engaged in line-by-line inductive coding process on a selection of interviews and surveys. The emerging themes formed the basis for collective discussion and reflection. The data was then imported into QSR NVivo11 and coded across these themes, at this stage some of the themes

Table 11.1 Demographic summary

Demographic categories	Surveys #	Interviews #
Female	239	53
Male	50	18
Other or skipped	17	1
Note: More than one of the categories below could be selected		
Aboriginal or Torres Strait Islander	13	1
Disability	15	15
Low socio-economic status (LSES)	83	29
Rural/isolated	93	23
Non-English speaking background (NESB)	20	7
Refugee	4	2
Other[a]	125	30
Participants with children	69	33
Partnered	143	37
Single	146	19

[a]Comments in '*Other' often included more information about the category/ies selected or indicated uncertainty about a category, such as being from Aboriginal or Torres Strait Islander backgrounds but not identifying as such. Categorizing one's situation as LSES was sometimes difficult such as "I wouldn't say low socio-economic background, but we are definitely by no means rich" (Survey), or "My parents were [LSES] but I'm not now" (interview)

became redundant and others were redefined and clarified. Data analysis was aided by the theoretical framing which drew on Sen's Capabilities (1992) approach and understandings of capital theory (Bourdieu, 1986; Yosso, 2005). In this process, we chose to walk with these theorists to assist us to more deeply consider, and in some cases, interpret, what students told us in a much broader political and social sense.

The Capabilities approach emphasizes how true equality and freedom relies on what each person is 'able to be' and 'able to do' (p. 3) or as Sen (1992) terms 'the freedoms [people] actually enjoy to choose the lives that they have reason to value' (p. 81). By employing the work of Sen, we consider how access to university is not sufficient unless it is accompanied by the necessary 'process freedoms' that support and enable everyone to achieve their preferred 'flourishings.' Combining this approach with capital theory enabled deep consideration of the role of culture in the enactment of life choices (Bowman, 2010). We build upon Bourdieu's understanding of cultural and social capital to employ Yosso's Community Cultural Wealth Framework which recognizes a range of capitals that are not traditionally recognized within Bourdieuian analysis; these include 'aspirational, navigational, social, linguistic, familial and resistance' capitals (Yosso, 2005). This theoretical framing enabled us to consider the data in a multifaceted way and encouraged a critical interpretation of the student narratives.

11.5 Presentation of Findings

In both interviews and surveys, participants revealed how they were intersected by a range of equity categorisations including being from LSES or working-class backgrounds and many referred to qualities derived from these diverse life experiences as underpinning their HE participation. Rather than construing such varied backgrounds as a disadvantage, these learners acknowledged that the lessons learnt through their life actually set them in good stead for persevering through their studies.

As these participants were all towards the end of their degrees, the ways in which they conceived of themselves as persisting learners provided insights into how success was considered within the HE sector and beyond. These findings will be presented under three broad themes:

- Getting to university: Dreams and aspirations
- The art of perseverance and resistance
- Utilising existing life experiences to succeed.

Each of the themes will be explored separately in the sections that follow but importantly, these co-existed across student narratives and should be considered holistically. The closing section of this chapter will then explore how these findings relate to wider literature and also highlight implications for HE practices.

11.5.1 Getting to University: Dreams and Aspirations

Many participants in this study were mature-age and attending university was the realisation of a long-held ambition or dream. This was described as a deeply held desire, sometimes hidden from those around, but tightly and quietly grasped. One survey respondent explained that she had always wanted to go to university to '*do something with my final years on this planet*' but dismissed it in her youth because she came '*from a low socio-economic background* [where] *food was scarce and rife with domestic violence.*' Instead, she waited until '*an age that I felt safe and secure* [then] *I decided to embark on the journey of study*' (Survey H02, Female, 41–50, 3rd year, LSES).

In these stories we note a theme of exceptionality, demonstrated through the determination to secure personal educational futures. Such actions are characterised by an ability to keep going despite setbacks or obstacles. Attending university is daunting for most students regardless of background, but for those who are the first in their families, often with fragmented educational biographies, just getting through the university 'gate' is an achievement worth acknowledging. Students like Jennifer and Hannah indicate the profound impact of realising ambitions:

> I didn't actually graduate high school so for me, it's kind of that opportunity to have that piece of paper and that celebration that I achieved something big, or bigger than what I have already achieved. (Jennifer, 28, 3rd year, online, LSES upbringing, partnered, 1 child)

> It had always been there in the back of my mind; I always wanted to be a teacher. I never thought I'd be able to achieve it, so I never pursued it and then when I found I could, that's when I went for it. (Hannah, 26, 3rd year, Aboriginal or Torres Strait Islander, LSES, Rural/Isolated, partnered, 2 children)

Such sentiments reflect what Yosso (2005) terms as 'aspirational capital', a cultural strength which acknowledges the inner strength required to sustain hopes and dreams despite the presence of obstacles or restrictions. This form of resilience allows an individual to 'dream of possibilities beyond their present circumstances, often without the objective means to attain those goals' (Yosso, 2005, p. 78). The next section explores how persistence was enacted throughout the degree and how this informed participants' world views and post-graduation goals.

11.5.2   The Art of Perseverance and Resistance

Given the diversity, it is not surprising that many students spoke of a range of life circumstances that impacted negatively on their HE experiences and also, the life they conceived after graduation. A number of students reflected upon the need to push past perceived 'limitations', informed by others' perceptions of what was possible to achieve, as well as self-imposed restrictions. Students described how barriers to entering HE ranged from poor exam results, coming from poorer or disadvantaged backgrounds or highly dysfunctional family units, chronic health issues, parental and familial attitudes to further education as well as resistance from others concerning their desire to attend university, as both Molly and Eleanor explained:

> It was basically mum was always about us working but her advice was like, 'Molly, you're not going to uni'…uni was always not even a possibility for our family – why would any of us ever go to uni? That's for people that had a lot of money. (Molly, 38, 3rd year, LSES, single mother, 2 children)

> We were low socioeconomic kind of…dad was on a parenting payment…and we didn't have much money…I was just kind of floating around…I enrolled in a diploma of Liberal Arts and I started that but then I dropped out because of the anxiety and instability of my life. (Eleanor, 29, 3rd year, Disability, LSES, Rural/Isolated)

However importantly, alongside these reflections on difficulties, were also references to both resilience and determination, often existing in tandem, one informing the other. We argue that without the particular set of life experiences these students arrived with, their ability to persevere and carve out their HE trajectory could have been curtailed. Such interplay was similarly reflected upon by learners themselves—both Isabel and Michelle evocatively describe the strengths that helped them through their university degrees:

my resilience...I'm very proud of that...I've had to be resilient – I dropped out of high school, I was homeless for a while, the father of my first born child passed away, then I got married, my husband and I had a child that passed away – I've had a whole huge massive difficult life and...I'm a survivor. (Isabel, 28, 4th year, LSES, single mother of high needs child)

the really kick-ass exciting thing about this is I feel that I've been able to put a lot of the experiences that I've had in a toolbox, you know, it's really exciting because I thought the worst thing that could ever happen in my life is if I ever ended up just being a victim of it and I'm not. (Michelle, 61, final year, Disability, Rural/Isolated)

For Mahalia, a 43 year old single mother of three children, in her 3rd year of Social Work, success at university was attributed directly to her ability to survive poverty as this required her to develop skills in *'creativity'*. This experience and the associated skills were integral to her ability to persevere in her studies: *'Anyone that can survive poverty, definitely. Definitely, because you really do have to be creative...when I talk about survival, you know, it's being creative.'* Similarly, Hayley reflected upon her resiliency at university as being derived from her lived experience, reflecting what Yosso (2005) terms as 'resistance capital':

I've got my resilience because I've spent pretty much most of my life people telling me that I won't amount to much, I won't get to university, I'm not smart enough. (Hayley, 26, Final year, LSES)

In Hayley's case, she refused to accept limiting perspectives and instead actively resisted those who wished to curtail her aspirations and desires. The final section explores more deeply how life experiences, like Hayley's, translated into a source of advantage within the university landscape and ambitions post-graduation.

11.5.3 Utilising Existing Life Experiences to Succeed

Experiences that were regarded as assisting students in their educational endeavours were largely attributed to personal or family biographies. For example, Donna described how her *'very strong work ethic'* had been derived from her parents. In Donna's case this provided both a sense of pride in her background and also represented a quality she was deliberately passing on through the generations via her academic pursuits: *'I'll always be wanting to do and do and do and to the best of my ability. That's the thing we instil in our kids now'* (Donna, 39, 3rd year, LSES, Rural/Isolated, partnered, 2 children).

In a comparable way, Erin recognised that the drawbacks and difficulties she had encountered in life provided a resource for her university studies:

that persistence – you just keep on going because that's what you want; you don't give up...but when you've been surrounded by your whole life in the face of sadness, grief, you know, the unknown – after seeing all those things play out, you just keep on going. (Erin, 32, Final year, single mother, 1 child)

In Bradley's case, his experience of mental illness provided the resilience that supported him in his studies and the realization of his ambitions post university:

> the resilience that you need to acquire to overcome a mental health condition is life-changing and while it's a horrible experience to go through, I think that capacity for resilience is something that a lot of people coming to uni often lack and so having that was a really useful mentality. (Bradley, 20, 3rd year, Rural/Isolated)

Repeatedly, participants in this study referenced extreme hardships or difficulties as providing them with the necessary skills to move forward in their educational and vocational pursuits, such as Patrick (quoted below) who was in his final year of Community Youth Work. Crucial to the realisation of educational and vocational ambitions were qualities such as motivation, determination, inner strength and also, passion, often realised through prior life experiences:

> I became healthy, I work out, I run, I do yoga, meditate, eating healthy. I changed my perception of things, but I still have no house...like I'm practically homeless my whole way through...Our neighbour lets me and my son live there so I still have no house, I still have no electronics, I still have poverty but it's *how* I look at it. (Patrick, 35, LSES, single father, 1 child)

> the experience of growing up in low socioeconomic circumstances, and seeing the struggles my mother faced made me want to get out of the cycle. (A08, Female, 21–25, 5th year, LSES)

The narratives of these students in both interviews and surveys, provided insights into how these first-in-family students engaged in university. It was an emotive activity and clearly defined by their life experiences and understandings of self. These implications will be discussed with particular reference to how students drew on their cultural baggage to move through and ultimately succeed within these educational spaces.

11.6   Conclusion

The data we have presented undoubtedly indicates that the diverse backgrounds of these first-in-family learners was not necessarily a burden or a disadvantage. Rather, for a number of students this was a source of wealth with accompanying capabilities. Our findings reflect those of Lehmann (2007) who reported that working-class students drew upon their backgrounds to 'construct uniquely working-class moral advantages' (p. 631), including 'a strong work ethic, maturity, responsibility and real-life experiences' (p. 631). Lehmann (2007) contends that students from diverse backgrounds such as working class or first-in-family, experience university in 'different' and 'unique' ways. We argue that anyone who does not have an educational biography of university attendance arrives at the institution with different sets of expectations and knowledges than those who have a generational biography of HE attendance. However, similar to Lehmann, we recognise that if these contexts are considered largely in deficit terms or as a form of 'lack', this limits understanding of how such learners actually enact success within the HE sector and beyond.

Goldingay et al. (2014) propose the need to consider learners in a deeply contextualised sense arguing that the acquisition of academic skills and abilities should not be separated from other aspects of students' lives such as outside pressures and distractions (p. 47). In their study, students themselves recognised how they had applied their existing abilities in order to develop 'work/life balance, self-control, confidence, and...discerning in their choices around study' (p. 49). Yet this is not necessarily explicitly recognised or supported within the HE sector, instead the learners in our study had to complete additional and often invisible work to apply their existing capitals to their university activities. Arguably, it was only on reflection and because they were at the end of their degrees that connections were made between their existing cultural strengths and capabilities, and those skills and knowledges required within academia and the workplace.

Poorer outcomes then are not always a reflection of a student's capabilities. Collier and Morgan (2008) found very little variation between traditional students and first-generation students in terms of academic ability. However, in terms of understanding implicit expectations and requirements of faculty, first-generation students may need more explicit instruction (O'Shea, May, Stone, & Delahunty, 2017). Cultural capital is accumulated over time and through experience, so poorer outcomes can be attributed to difficulty deciphering what is required especially if students are unable initially to 'apply their existing skills to meet those expectations successfully' (Collier & Morgan, 2008, p. 425).

As these students' stories have indicated, their biographies and cultural settings are not necessarily conceived as something to be changed or adapted to the university or work environment. Instead, our data indicates how these contexts and qualities can be capitalised upon in order to manage and succeed within academic settings and no doubt, also applied to future employability. By foregrounding students' perceptions on persistence behaviours and the achievement of success within university settings, this chapter has identified how institutional policy and practice needs to better acknowledge the unique capabilities held by diverse student populations and thereby carefully leverage what students bring to learning environments instead of adopting a deficit view that positions such learners solely in terms of lack.

References

Bathmaker, A. (2015). Thinking with Bourdieu: Thinking after Bourdieu. Using 'field' to consider in/equalities in the changing field of English higher education. *Cambridge Journal of Education, 45*(1), 61–80.

Beilin, I. (2016). Student success and the neoliberal academic library. *Canadian Journal of Academic Librarianship, 1*(1), 10–23.

Bourdieu, P. (1986). The forms of capital. In J. Richardson (Ed.), *Handbook of theory and research for the sociology of education* (pp. 241–257). New York: Greenwood Press.

Bourdieu, P., & Wacquant, L. (1992). *An invitation to reflexive sociology.* Chicago: University of Chicago Press.

Bowman, D. (2010). Sen and bourdieu: Understanding inequality. Retrieved from http://library.bsl. org.au/jspui/bitstream/1/2131/1/Bowman_Sen_and_Bourdieu_understanding_inequality_2010. pdf.

Burke, P. J., Hayton, A., & Stevenson, J. (2018). *Evaluating equity and widening participation in higher education.* UK: Trentham Books.

Clandinin, D. W., & Connelly, M. F. (2000). *Narrative inquiry: Experience and story in qualitative research.* California: Jossey-Bass.

Collier, P. J., & Morgan, D. L. (2008). "Is that paper really due today?": Differences in first-generation and traditional college students' understandings of faculty expectations. *Higher Education, 55,* 425–446. https://doi.org/10.1007/s10734-007-9065-5.

Daly, A., Lewis, P., Corliss, M., & Heaslip, T. (2015). The private rate of return to a university degree in Australia. *Australian Journal of Education, 59,* 97–112.

Friedman, S. (2014). The price of the ticket: Rethinking the experience of social mobility. *Sociology, 48*(2), 352–368.

Goldingay, S., Hitch, D., Ryan, J., Farrugia, D., Hosken, N., Lamaro, G., et al. (2014). "The university didn't actually tell us this is what you have to do": Social inclusion through embedding of academic skills in first year professional courses. *The International Journal of the First Year in Higher Education, 5,* 43–53.

Kutty, F. M. (2014). Mapping their road to university: First-generation students' choice and decision of university. *International Education Studies, 7,* 49–60.

Lehmann, W. (2007). "I just didn't feel like I fit in": The role of habitus in university drop-out decisions. *Canadian Journal of Higher Education, 37*(2), 89–110.

Lehmann, W. (2009). Becoming middle class: How working-class university students draw and transgress moral class boundaries. *Sociology, 43*(4), 631–647.

Marginson, S. (2016). The worldwide trend to high participation in higher education: Dynamics of social stratification in inclusive systems. *Higher Education, 72,* 413–434.

McKay, J., & Devlin, M. (2016). "Low income doesn't mean stupid and destined for failure": Challenging the deficit discourse around students from low SES backgrounds in higher education. *International Journal of Inclusive Education, 20,* 347–363. https://doi.org/10.1080/13603116. 2015.1079273.

Milburn, A. (2012). *University challenge: How higher education can advance social mobility: A progress report by the independent reviewer on social mobility and child poverty.* London: Cabinet Office.

Norton, A., & Cherastidtham, I. (2014). *Mapping Australian higher education, 2014–15.* Carlton: Grattan Institute.

Nyström, A., Jackson, C., & Salminen Karlsson, M. (2018). What counts as success? Constructions of achievement in prestigious higher education programmes. In *Research Papers in Education, Online First.* Available from https://www.tandfonline.com/doi/full/10.1080/02671522. 2018.1452964.

Opengart, R., & Short, D. C. (2002). Free agent learners: The new career model and its impact on human resource development. *International Journal of Lifelong Education, 21,* 220–233. https:// doi.org/10.1080/02601370210127837.

O'Shea, S. (2017–2019). Capitals and capabilities: Rethinking higher education persistence. In *Australian Research Council Discovery Project (DP170100705).*

O'Shea, S., & Delahunty, J. (2018). Getting through the day and still having a smile on my face! How do students define success in the university learning environment? *Higher Education Research and Development, 37*(5), 1062–1075. https://doi.org/10.1080/07294360.2018.1463973.

O'Shea, S., May, J., Stone, C., & Delahunty, J. (2017). *First-in-family students, university experience and family life: Motivations, transitions and participation.* London: Palgrave Macmillan.

O'Shea, S., Stone, C., Delahunty, J., & May, J. (2018). Discourses of betterment and opportunity: Exploring the privileging of university attendance for first-in-family learners. *Studies in Higher Education, 43*(6), 1020–1033. https://doi.org/10.1080/03075079.2016.1212325.

Reay, D. (2013). Social mobility, a panacea for austere times: Tales of emperors, frogs, and tadpoles. *British Journal of Sociology of Education, 34*(5–6), 660–677.

Reeves, A., Friedman, S., Rahal, C., & Flemmen, M. (2017). The decline and persistence of the old boy: Private schools and elite recruitment 1897 to 2016. *American Sociological Review., 82*, 1139–1166. https://doi.org/10.1177/0003122417735742.

Sen, A. (1992). *In equality re-examined.* Oxford: Oxford University Press.

Southgate, E., Brosnan, C., Lempp, H., Kelly, B., Wright, S., Outram, S., et al. (2017). Travels in extreme social mobility: How first in family students find their way into and through medical education. *Critical Studies in Education, 58*(2), 242–260.

Sullivan, P. (2008). 0PINIoN: Measuring "success" at open admissions institutions: Thinking carefully about this complex question. *College English, 70*(6), 618–630.

Yosso, T. (2005). Whose culture has capital? A critical race theory discussion of community cultural wealth. *Race Ethnicity and Education, 8*(1), 69–91.

Sarah O'Shea (Ph.D.) is Professor in the School of Education, University of Wollongong, Australia. She has spent over twenty-five years working to effect change within the HE sector through research that focuses on access and participation of students from identified equity groups. Her institutional and nationally funded research studies advance understanding of how underrepresented student cohorts enact success within university, navigate transition into this environment, manage competing identities and negotiate aspirations for self and others. This work is highly regarded for applying diverse conceptual and theoretical lenses to tertiary participation, which incorporate theories of social class, identity work, gender studies and poverty. She has published extensively been awarded over $3 million AUD in grant funding since 2009. She is an Australian Learning and Teaching Fellow (ALTF), and Principal Fellow of the Higher Education Academy and was awarded a Research Fellowship with the Australian National Centre for Student Equity in HE in 2018.

Janine Delahunty (Ph.D.) is a Lecturer in Learning, Teaching and Curriculum, at the University of Wollongong, Australia. She works in the Academic Professional Development and Recognition team and is involved in various research projects. Her core interest is how the learning-teaching experience can be enhanced in HE, and how the student experience can be improved through the professional development of staff to foster their teaching and reflective practices. Her research has involved people from diverse backgrounds including first-in-family, regional, and Indigenous students, research degree students, and online educators and learners. Her motivations stem from her own venture into university study as a mature-age student, studying part-time for many years and doing the family-study-work balancing act. She has published across linguistic, HE and academic development journals.

Part II
Designs and Difficulties

Chapter 12
Precursors to Employability—How First Year Undergraduate Students Plan and Strategize to Become Employable Graduates

Emma Mullen, Stephanie Bridges, Sue Eccles and Doris Dippold

12.1 Introduction

Debates surrounding the ability of Higher Education Institutions (HEIs) to produce work-ready graduates have dominated Higher Education (HE) debates at both academic and policy levels for many decades. Whilst increasing emphasis is placed upon university-workplace transitions and evidencing 'employability' as a new graduate, Murtagh, Ridley, Frings, and Kerr-Pertic (2017) remind us that a student's first year at university is also a critical transition period. Whilst students will have several priorities during this time, including adjusting to university life and developing friendships, it is important to also consider their early thoughts and plans concerning their future careers. It is not surprising, for this reason, that Coertjens, Brahm, Trautwein, and Lindblom-Ylanne (2017) highlight how research into the transition into HE has received increasing attention in recent years. This chapter offers an account of how the academic, social/personal and professional capital students bring with them influences their strategic decisions regarding their future employability. First year students' stories and experiences from a multi-disciplinary study across four UK universities offer insights into the way they plan for post-graduation employment.

E. Mullen (✉)
Northumbria University, Newcastle, England, UK
e-mail: emma.mullen@northumbria.ac.uk

S. Bridges
University of Nottingham, Nottingham, England, UK
e-mail: Stephanie.bridges@nottingham.ac.uk

S. Eccles
Bournemouth University, Bournemouth, England, UK
e-mail: seccles@bournemouth.ac.uk

D. Dippold
University of Surrey, Guildford, England, UK
e-mail: d.dippold@surrey.ac.uk

© Springer Nature Switzerland AG 2019
A. Diver (ed.), *Employability via Higher Education: Sustainability as Scholarship*,
https://doi.org/10.1007/978-3-030-26342-3_12

Holmes's graduate identity framework (Holmes, 2001, 2015) is utilised to explore these case studies: what aspirations, expectations and experiences they bring with them and how they believe their degree and broader student experiences contribute to developing who they become as employable graduates.

12.2 Graduate Employability

12.2.1 HE Expansion and Graduate Job Market Shifts

In the context of graduate-level employment, the Robbins (1963) and Dearing (1997) reports were two of the earliest and most cited publications based on governmental inquiry aimed at addressing the role and impact of HEIs in the UK, emphasising the significant contribution which HE would make to the (then) modern UK economy. Using human capital theory (HCT) as a means of analysis (Becker, 1993; Schultz, 1971), UK HEIs are seemingly entrusted with the task of preparing graduates with appropriate knowledge, skills and attributes to enter the graduate labour market (GLM), gain suitable employment (Harvey, 2001; Little, 2011; Smith, McKnight, & Naylor, 2000), and secure a desirable standard of living. In this sense, participation in HE can be considered as added human capital, placing graduates more favourably within the job market with greater earning potential (Tomlinson, 2015) and increased likelihood of securing "*good jobs*" (Kalfa & Taksa, 2013, p. 583) associated with their skill and productivity potential, as compared with non-graduates. Since the 1990s in particular however, the UK HE system has undergone expansion, or 'massification' (Daniel, 1993; Storen & Aamodt, 2010; Wilton, 2011). An increase in the number of HEIs which have attained university status during this time, namely polytechnics formed through the merging of local authority colleges (Sutherland, 2008), combined with a policy-level drive to improve previously lower levels of participation (Eriksen, 1995) has resulted in a surge in the supply of graduates entering the UK employment market (Rae, 2007). Between July and September 2017 alone, there were 14 million graduates in the UK (Office for National Statistics, 2017). Therefore, it can be suggested that, firstly, the increase in graduate 'supply' has overtaken the level of employer 'demand' in the GLM and, secondly, graduate recruits are no longer drawn from a narrow section of the population characteristic of the earlier, elite HE system (Hinchliffe & Jolly, 2011). Instead, HE expansion has given rise to an increasingly heterogeneous blend of graduates (Tomlinson, 2012).

12.2.2 Graduate Skills and Employer Expectations

Due to the increased number of graduates, job competitiveness has increased correspondingly, and the value of degree credentials has declined (Tomlinson, 2015), leading to questions being raised over the human capital potential of graduates. Dissatisfaction amongst employers has increased also, an issue which appeared less prevalent during the previous 'elite' HE system (BIS, 2015), but also surprising given the expanded 'pool' of graduates available. HEIs are often on the receiving end of such criticism; via increased student recruitment, graduates are of 'lower quality' and do not possess the skills and attributes required by employers. In response to these pressures, there has been increased emphasis on 'sandwich degrees' (McMurray, Dutton, McQuaid, & Richard, 2016; Silva et al., 2018; Weiss, Klein, & Grauenhorst, 2014) and the embedding of skill development into programme curricula (Helyer & Lee, 2014; O'Leary, 2016). Despite the efforts of HEIs to more closely align with the requirements of graduate employers, 'gaps' still exist between employer expectations and the extent to which graduates will meet these (Brown & Hesketh, 2004; Cranmer, 2006; Hesketh, 2000; Jackson, 2014). Collet, Hine, and Plessis (2015) offer several explanations, such as the structure of HE making it difficult to implement change and employers being unclear on their skill requirements, and not communicating their desires to HEIs. Jackson (2014) adds that generic skill development provision in HE may also contribute to these 'gaps', as this often does not account for industry-specific expectations.

12.2.3 Alternative Perspectives on Graduate Employability

One of Holmes's (2001, 2013, 2015) primary observations is that traditional skills-led approaches, which he characterises as the 'possession' approach (possession of skills, credentials, human capital), dominate graduate employability (GE) discourses. These tend to limit the focus of GE to the point at which a student graduates and secures employment. Current metrics tend to focus on employment outcomes (e.g., Destinations of Leavers from HE (DLHE) annual survey). However, with an increasing emphasis on the student 'journey' and challenges in transitioning into (as well as out of) HE, it is essential also to consider how understandings of employability and professionalism are formulating, even in the initial stages of a student's university experience, which formal, objective indicators of 'employability' typically fail to capture. Whilst DLHE outcomes provide objective measures in relation to graduates, similar ones exist for first year students through attrition and withdrawal rates (Palmer, O'Kane, & Owens, 2009). Traditional metrics do not acknowledge that graduation is just the first of many significant stages which make up an employment trajectory. Graduates experience different, individual trajectories, and survey-led research may not appropriately reflect or document these complexities. It is perhaps not surprising therefore that Holmes (2013, p. 539) frames employment outcomes as "crude measures" of GE. Similarly, first year 'drop-out' rates may seemingly not encompass accountability for individual student transition experiences.

Overall, GE research has progressed away from HCT assumptions, to consider GE via alternative theoretical approaches, indicating possible directions for further research. The extent to which Holmes's approach is utilised within extant research however, is still quite limited, presenting opportunities to provide a different means of theoretical framing and analysis. According to Holmes (2001, 2013, 2015) a 'processual', rather than 'possessive', approach sees GE as not fixed, but formed over time, an ongoing process. Tomlinson (2012, p. 413) supports this perspective, claiming that in an increasingly challenging job market graduates must adapt to this dynamic environment and "continually maintain their employability". These views contrast with the characteristically static interpretations of graduate employability within the literature, pertaining mainly to evidence, or lack of evidence, of skills.

12.3   First Year Undergraduate Students, Transition into HE, and Employability

Amidst this prevalent focus on skills for employability, an increasing number of studies remind us of the personal and emotional challenges graduates may experience as they transition out of HE into their first post-graduation role. Through their longitudinal, qualitative study consisting of interviews with 56 graduates new to the workplace, Fournier and Payne (1994) found that graduates may experience vulnerability when entering employment, as did Dyess and Sherman (2009) in relation to the workplace transitions of new graduate nurses. 'Professional isolation', saw participants report feelings of loneliness in their first graduate role. Similar concerns about entering the workplace may even be experienced as students approach the end of their university studies (Kasler, Zysberg, & Harel, 2017). More recently, Finn (2016) noted the emotional and relational experiences of recent graduates in the workplace: the 24 graduates in her longitudinal, qualitative study needed to 'feel valued,' in terms of receiving support but also in supporting those in their workplace networks. Gallagher (2015) highlighted the challenges of university-workplace transitions, with significant mismatch between employer and graduate expectations. Like Finn's study, his findings draw attention to the role of workplace mentoring, interactions and communication, and the need for supervisors and support mechanisms (formal and informal).

Whilst the above research emphasises personal and emotional struggles of new graduates transitioning *into the workplace*, other studies note similar challenges for new undergraduates transitioning *into HE*. Research on transitioning into university life looks at student engagement and wellbeing, the sense of belonging, student identity, intercultural and global outlook and skills development during year one (Dippold, Bridges, Eccles, & Mullen, 2018). Some experiences are positive, with others characterised by feelings of insecurity and upset (Tett, Cree, & Christie, 2017). Attention is drawn to the potential impact of HE transitions on first year students' mental health, for example, due to financial burdens, academic pressures and limited social support structures (Gibson et al., 2018; Kara, Eisenberg, Gollust, & Golberstein, 2009). Harding (2011) comments further on financial concerns, specifically student debt. Perhaps exacerbated by the increase in undergraduate (UG) tuition fees from £3375 to £9000 per annum in 2012 (Tomlinson, 2015; Wilkins, Shams, & Huisman, 2013), being in debt can create significant levels of stress, as the need to be in paid employment alongside studying increases (Harding, 2011). Arguably this workplace exposure and consequent skill development could be perceived as a positive outcome in terms of boosting student employability: respondents to Harding's study claim that this pressure made it increasingly difficult to balance study with work commitments, however, and to meet living costs, potentially impacting negatively upon their psychological wellbeing. More recently, Coertjens et al. (2017) noted the vast changes first year students face when transitioning into HE, not just in terms of academic level and change of programme, but through more personal challenges around becoming more independent in their domestic, social and academic spheres. Consequently, this calls into question how students cope with such changes, and the support available to them. Despite attempts to support and guide new students, (for example, through induction sessions providing crucial information about programmes of study and academic and social aspects of university life) the majority of course withdrawals unfortunately still occur during first year (Coertjens et al., 2017), with almost one third of students not completing their degree In sum, it is clear that transition into university life is not a static event, rather it is a process occurring over time, subject to a range of factors including the individual students' own background and previous experiences, and contextual factors relating to the specific HEI. 'Becoming' a student extends beyond mere acquisition of skills which would prove advantageous as a future graduate. It is also about constructing a new identity and a sense of belonging (Wilcox, Winn, & Fyvie-Gauld, 2005). As such, it is important to consider alternative methods in which this 'processual' journey into HE can be explored and understood, particularly considering assertions (Palmer et al., 2009; Tett et al., 2017) that little research to date has considered the personal views and experiences of first year students undergoing this journey, following their experiences and transitions over time.

12.4 Theoretical Framing: Holmes's Modalities of Graduate Identity

Holmes's framework supports exploration of emergent 'graduate identities', in terms of the interaction between identity claims by the graduate and identities ascribed by 'significant others' (Holmes, 2001, 2015). The model presents five 'modalities' of such emergent identity; a graduate may pass through these in varied post-graduation trajectories (Fig. 12.1). In this sense, graduate identity is negotiated and constructed as graduates experience, make sense of, and engage with, their particular personal, social and professional settings. Application of the model allows for discussion of the purported warranting of identity claims and ascriptions. For recent graduates, it provides useful insights into the processes by which an individual 'becomes' a graduate. Implicitly, the model also challenges dominant approaches to understanding

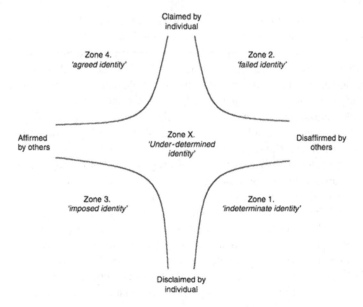

Fig. 12.1 Holmes's modalities of emergent graduate identity (Holmes, 2015)

graduate 'employability' which tend to focus on acquisition of knowledge and skills, which Holmes asserts may not be conceptually or theoretically robust in providing an understanding of the complexity of post-graduation life.

In terms of how Holmes's model may be employed to explore the experiences of first year students, there is an opportunity to use the five 'modalities' to capture and understand early emergent identities. Through application of the framework, early 'claims', affirmations, rejections and ascriptions can be mapped and tracked during the initial stages of a student's university experience, and their contribution to future 'graduate identity' explored. Whilst a graduate may present themselves as a prospective employee to a prospective employer on the premise of 'being' a graduate worthy of such employment, such identity 'claims' for first year students may take the form of 'being' a student with the potential to take on an undergraduate internship/placement and be a successful future graduate. For exploring graduate identity, the model focuses on interactions and 'critical moments' such as graduation, securing graduate employment, losing graduate employment, etc., with 'significant others' being primarily prospective employers and line managers. For first year students, these critical moments may emerge from factors including pre-university study, work experience acquired prior to and alongside university, course content and pedagogy, travel, volunteering, or extracurricular activities. Significant others involved in affirming/rejecting/ascribing identity claims include family, university tutors, careers advisors, college/sixth form mentors or fellow students.

Intertwined with the above is the opportunity to explore choices first year students make both prior to and during university regarding career aspirations and building employability, and challenges faced during this 'journey' to becoming employable scholars. As each student's university 'journey' is personal the model allows for different accounts to be considered across various institutions and degree disciplines, capturing themes whilst also retaining the 'richness' of each account. There may be multiple identity 'claims', affirmations and rejections during a student's first year experience, or even reversion back to earlier 'modalities:' and, if so, how may a previous 'claim' impact on a subsequent claim? As a result, several 'trajectories' may appear through the model. Such findings pose interesting questions for HEIs: are we taking account of the employability capital first year students bring with them, and how may first year students' early experiences at university impact on their future graduate aspirations? These trajectories are contextually and socially bound, and complexity can occur where multiple identity claims are present. To address this complexity, identified trajectories can be organised according to the corresponding identity 'claims', allowing analysis of trajectories which intersect or impact on one another, and those which may contribute to future graduate aspirations. A student's early identity 'claims' may be mapped according to three core themes: academic, social/personal and professional, enabling us to 'make sense' of this complexity and highlight 'agreed/achieved' identities which may impact on priorities and choices later on, addressing the following research aim, namely, to explore how Holmes's modalities of graduate identity can be applied to the experiences and lives of first year undergraduates, in order to support their development and aspirations as employable scholars—both through and beyond HE.

12.5 Methodology

This multidisciplinary, cross-institutional project is a longitudinal, qualitative study which captures first year student perceptions and experiences of employability, illustrated through a series of case study vignettes. Data from student interviews at two points during their first year (once in each semester) provide insights into their early views on employability and professionalism, what influences these views, and the impact of their early HE experiences on becoming 'employable'. The study sought to understand, rather than explain (Hennekam & Herrbach, 2015; King & Horrocks, 2010) first year students' experiences through qualitative inquiry aligning with Holmes's methodology. The research was conducted across four UK universities and consisted of semi-structured interviews with first year students at the start of the academic year 2016–17 (a total of 70 interviews; 45 Phase 1, 25 Phase 2). Different degree disciplines are represented across the four institutions: Business and Management, Media Studies, Pharmacy and Modern Foreign Languages. Here, we present four selected case studies (one from each institution with all four participants having participated in both Phase 1 and 2 interviews), explored through the lens of Holmes' framework in order to better understand first year students' transitions according to their academic, social/personal and professional trajectories.

12.6   Case Study 1—'Mary' (University W)

12.6.1   "The Butterfly"

Mary is in her first year of a Business Management degree. Prior to university, she studied A-Levels and completed a retail management apprenticeship in North West England. She speaks positively about her experience as a retail apprentice, recalling how well she fitted in with her colleagues and the support received from her manager (*"we were like a family"*). She describes this experience as a *"completely different kettle of fish"* in comparison with grammar school, where she felt she'd struggled academically and socially (*"nobody wants to be friends with the one who doesn't really understand what's going on"*). Post-apprenticeship, she travelled alone around Europe for a year before starting university: *"I'd reached twenty and thought, I haven't done anything except for work and school...I feel like I should've actually done something by now."* As per her apprenticeship, she speaks positively about her travelling experiences particularly in terms of learning to be more independent and adaptable.

Mary's choice to study Business Management was influenced by her apprenticeship: she aspired to learn more about the 'management side' of business and wanted a hands-on, practical course. She experienced some hesitation during her first few weeks at university—for example, feeling unprepared for her first classes and low confidence in her academic writing skills or ability to achieve high marks. However, she set herself development goals for semester 2, such as improving her time management and was keen to achieve the best degree classification possible to secure a good graduate job in the future—an attitude which she attributes to having worked and travelled prior to university. She seems reluctant to be characterised as the 'typical' student who she describes as only being at university *"for fun"* and prefers to socialise with students who are also *"quite sensible,"* taking their studies seriously and rarely drinking. She even goes as far as saying she has a *"mild dislike of students."* Regarding her interactions with others during the early stages of university life, Mary feels she has fallen into a *"trap"* of remaining with one small group of new friends, which she had not originally intended to do. Moving forward, she hopes to revert back to her *"travelling mindset"* and expand her friendship groups/networks. However, by the end of the second semester she still has one friendship group. She claims this is due to a higher workload in semester 2, meaning there is less time to spend with different people. At this point, Mary feels it is better to have one group of people upon whom she can rely. By this stage she has also become friendly with students in other year groups whom she finds more understanding of her commitments to study: their larger workloads help keep her own in perspective.

In terms of employability, Mary has secured a study-abroad semester in Germany for Year 2, and hopes to stay there for third year, to gain a dual degree from the partner institution. She believes this will boost her employability, develop her language skills and enhance her CV. By second semester, Mary feels she has become more ambitious. Her initial plans for graduate employment were centred on working abroad and perhaps pursuing a graduate role in retail however now she aspires to higher level/business to business roles. These aspirations were influenced by some of her lecture topics, her experience working as a Christmas temp and also by being surrounded by ambitious people at university: one friend wants to be an entrepreneur.

12.7 'Mary': Analysis in Terms of Modalities of Emergent Identity

12.7.1 Trajectory 1: Academic

Mary initially experiences disaffirmation of her student identity whilst studying for A-Levels at grammar school (*Zone 2*), exemplified through references to struggling to fit in, make friends or perform well in her studies. The impact of this 'failed' identity claim can also be seen during Mary's initial stages at university, where she experiences similar apprehensions regarding her preparedness for university study and meeting tutor expectations. She describes her first workshop as *"two hours of being made to feel guilty that I didn't know what was going on."* These concerns continue into semester 2. However, at this point Mary also talks positively about a mathematics module she initially struggled with which she is now performing well in:

> I was sat in one of the seminars trying to follow what they were doing and then at the end it just clicked…Oh My God, I've got this…literally I ran to my mates like guys, I get it…

Mary is pleased with her achievement, as she feels she has overcome something she does not usually excel in, indicating a move away from an initial 'failed' identity towards *Zone X* ('tentative' identity).

12.7.2 Trajectory 2: Social/Personal

Mary's close relationships with her colleagues during her apprenticeship, and friendships developed whilst travelling, indicate 'agreed' pre-university identity claims (*Zone 4*). Further 'agreed' claims can be identified during the early stages of her university experience, for example, her appointment as Social Secretary for a society she'd joined in semester 1. She talks about feeling part of the group and believes that everyone, like her, is committed to their position and the purpose of the society. In comparison, certain other elements of her trajectory appear rather complex. During her first year, Mary is reluctant to be associated with the 'typical' student stereotype, suggesting disclaimed identity on her part (*Zone 3*—imposed identity). This is emphasised through comments on feeling obligated to be a *"carer figure"* for her friends, for example, taking care of them on nights out and checking they have done their washing and prepared for room inspection. *"I don't know how I've ended up like that"* she says. She seems to prefer spending time with other friends who are open to different activities such as playing football and board games, with whom she feels she can be more relaxed, and not expected to 'take care of them.' A further example of 'imposed' identity can be highlighted in Mary's discussion around working with other students on groups at university. Mary disclaims the identity ascribed to her by her team mates as 'Project Manager' as she often ends up completing work by herself which she finds frustrating.

This in turn impacts her approach to group work in semester 2, where she describes making a conscious effort to delegate more tasks to others. Looking forward to second year, Mary plans to move into different halls which are self-catered rather than the catered accommodation of her first year. She explains that she has purposely made this choice as part of her hope to become more independent, representing a tentative move towards *Zone X*.

12.7.3   Trajectory 3: Professional

Mary's pre-university work experience is centred on her retail apprenticeship. She feels that she performed well in her role and talks about her colleagues being accepting of her views and ideas, representing 'agreed identity' (*Zone 4*). It is interesting to note how Mary refers back to this experience in considering what she would contribute to the success of a team as a future graduate; she states that she is the one who *"gets the ball rolling"* and stimulates new ideas. This demonstrates the impact of this pre-university experience on Mary's early perceptions of what makes a graduate employable. Regarding her initial plans for graduate employment, one could also highlight the impact of Mary's earlier 'achieved' identity claims. As a result of her retail apprenticeship and her positive experiences travelling abroad (see 'social/personal' trajectory), she hopes to work initially in Europe as a tour guide when she graduates, before moving into working in retail as at this point it is *"really the only business experience"* she has obtained. However, these initial plans appear to broaden as Mary begins to consider alternative options such as business to business roles or self-employment, indicating a move towards *Zone X* (tentative identity) (see Fig. 12.2).

12.8   Case Study 2: 'Martin' (University X)

12.8.1   "The Juggler"

Martin studied at a private school in Vietnam, before moving to the UK for his A-Levels. After this, he commenced his university degree in Pharmacy. His parents,

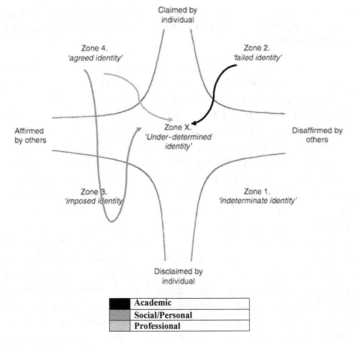

Fig. 12.2 Mary's Trajectories

both pharmacists, played a key role in his choice of degree subject. This provided him with direction, and perhaps also contacts for work experience. Martin enjoys the practical aspects of pharmacy, and how it is continuously changing, although he does not necessarily feel that he was *"born to learn pharmacy."*

He admits that his move from Vietnam to the UK for college was *"quite a big jump"* due to lack of cultural awareness, leaving him feeling quite lonely. Once in the UK, Martin's strategy was firstly to form friendships with Asian students, before making friends with home students. Martin believes that his experience of studying for his A-Levels prepared him well for university, in that he was expected to study independently; academically, he found this to be a useful prerequisite when transitioning into university. By semester 2 however, possibly in part due to actively adjusting and adapting to his new environment and prioritising making new friends, he is disappointed with his semester 1 marks: *"I know I can get high marks, but I didn't study, and I got average. That's how bad it is."* Despite initially claiming that he had developed his independence through having already studied in the UK for A-Levels, Martin still struggles with finding the motivation to proactively organise his workload; *"I'm by myself so it is hard to hold back the urges and not study because now there's no one to tell you, to just remind you..."*

During his early interactions at university, Martin found people much friendlier than he'd expected:

We just said hello in the first few days…it's kind of click together. Yeah? So, we just seek each other out in lectures and sit with each other. And then eat lunch with each other. And naturally, we've become closer…

By the end of semester 2, Martin has secured three different friendship circles; friends from classes, his Vietnamese friends, and a group of friends from the Christian society (although Martin emphasises that he is not himself Christian). He describes his closest friendship group as being supportive and respectful, saying these new friendships enrich his life and *"make your life colourful."* Admitting he is typically shy and has struggled to make friends previously, he really values the new friendships he has created and could elaborate on how, over time, he became better at starting conversations with new people. On reflection, he feels that he could have socialised more during his first few days at university, perhaps developing friendships at an earlier stage. However, he discloses; *"I was not prepared to go out mentally".*

During the first semester, Martin joins a variety of different clubs and societies including science club and the negotiation society and, at this point, would usually go to the events/meetings with the same group of friends he tended to stick with. He plans to try out more societies, moving forward. Interestingly, we see a shift in intentions by semester 2. He claims that, unlike the early weeks of university when he was 'forcing' himself to attend clubs/societies to seek out new friends, he no longer feels the need to do this as he has established sufficient connections: *"I think in those kinds of events, you just meet people once and you never meet them again. So, it's the same as not meeting anyone…"*

As a result, he feels as his social life has now 'stabilised' and should be able to improve his semester 2 results through focusing more on his studies. Martin has experience of group work from both A-Levels and his university classes to date, stating that *"interacting with other people makes me feel alive."* He talks about an experience during A-Levels where he was leading a team of five students on a task; he felt he expected too much of the other students due to his lack of experience of group work and also the group members' unfamiliarity with each other. From this experience, he has learnt the importance of balancing completion of the task with ensuring the group are happy and working well together. His experiences of group work during his first year at university have been quite frustrating. He notices that often there would be a couple of enthusiastic group members, however the rest of the group would be *"disconnected"* or too shy to offer their thoughts: *"people just want to get out the room."* He suggests that smaller groups would be more effective, to encourage discussion and contribution, as compared with larger groups. Martin is not living in student halls, but in a rented flat half an hour away from campus, with two friends he knew before starting university (their parents are friends), who are also studying pharmacy. Despite this, he still advises that new students should focus on making friends and learning to do the basics, such as cooking: although students might be academically capable they may still be lacking in more basic 'life' areas which can affect transition into university.

In terms of employability, Martin describes his main priorities from semester 1 as acquiring a high level of pharmacy knowledge but also to take opportunities to develop his 'soft skills' and research abilities, as he is hoping to work in community pharmacy as a graduate. He has also had some exposure to different elements of the pharmacy process through his parents' contacts. In semester 2, Martin is clear that he still has no doubts about his career choice, however his plans have refined as he is no longer interested in community pharmacy. He now feels this would be *"boring"* and wishes to pursue a different type of pharmacy career which he would find more interesting. He is hoping to find summer work experience in a pharmacy through the university careers service, claiming he would prefer to get experience in the UK rather than at his parents' pharmaceutical company in his home country. He appreciates the value of being exposed to different cultures at university, as he understands that he would need to work with different customers and patients in his profession:

> I think I'm one of the lucky guys who don't really judge people from the start. For example, the closest guy in the class with me, he swears in almost every single sentence of his speech, but I never swear, but we get along fine and I'm open…different personalities, it interests me, so I'm fascinated by them if they're different rather than I'm weirded out by them…

He has found it easy to interact with students of a similar culture both in and out of university as he finds they have similar interests and 'click' easily, whereas he finds it more difficult to start a conversation with a student from a different culture, due to unfamiliarity with each other's background. In semester 2, he is still enjoying interacting with others of different backgrounds, cultures and personalities although he admits that most of his friends are still Asian. He would like to make more English friends but struggles to find common topics of conversation as he is not interested in such topics as drinking or sports.

12.9   Martin: Analysis in Terms of Modalities of Emergent Identity

12.9.1   Trajectory 1: Academic

Martin's confidence in his academic abilities, from studying A-Levels in the UK and parental reinforcement over degree choice, initially positions him in *Zone 4—agreed identity*. Unfortunately, this initial identity claim is disaffirmed when he receives disappointing semester 1 marks, and further evidenced through his reduced confidence in his knowledge/understanding of his subject area *(Zone 2): "I understand more, so it's actually quite good, but get the hang of it? No, we're just first year, how on earth can we know?…"* There is an indicative transition towards *Zone X,* as Martin attempts to more effectively balance his studies and social activities with the aim of improving his grades.

12.9.2 Trajectory 2: Social/Personal

Martin has apprehensions around interacting with others and making new friends, stemming from his experiences at college and his own self-perception of being shy (*Zone X*). Things improved a little during his second year at college, as he hosted a chess club where he found it progressively easier to make friends as they shared a common hobby, meaning he could build on these initial friendships and expand his friendship circles. A few weeks into semester 1 Martin is in a much more positive frame of mind, having used his previous experiences to adapt and create friendships more easily: *"...way better than I expected. At first I thought that I would have no friends and I would be sad and that I'd have to wait until people come to me and the- the thing would be really intense..."*

This is illustrated in various contexts, including his involvement with a number of societies and friendship groups by the end of first year, representing a move towards *Zone 4—agreed identity*. Combined with this transition, however, Martin also appears to detach himself from certain affirmed identifies in favour of new priorities (*Zone 3*). For example, whilst he initially craves new friendships, by semester 2 he no longer feels the need to 'force' this, going as far as saying that although these friendships are important, he sees them as 'temporary' as he doesn't think they would stay in contact after graduation, although these are needed now to avoid loneliness. This contradicts his earlier comments in semester 1, where he claims that he does not wish to focus on one hobby as he did previously at college, but instead plans to test out different potential hobbies to see what develops, including new friendships. Conversely, other identities appear to hold value to Martin, seen through his decision to live in a private flat with two friends from his own country rather than moving into halls, contributing to his progressive move towards *Zone 4*. Consequently, a rather complex trajectory emerges.

12.9.3 Trajectory 3: Professional

Martin enters HE with an already-strong sense of purpose, in terms of chosen degree and intended graduate career path (*Zone 4*). Key influences are his previous exposure to pharmacy environments and his understanding of the value of his cultural exposures for working in this profession. However, the primary influence on his choices to date is his parents' professional background (arguably relating to the 'social/personal' trajectory too). Even when his career intentions appear to refine in semester 2, partly due to exposure to different topics through his studies, Martin still refers this back to his understanding of his parents' jobs:

> ...when I see my parents work, it's really interesting. They don't just sit on a chair and do the same work every day. They do different work every day and then sometimes people come in with a problem and they talk with them about it, they go and see problem, they solve it...so they're exposed to a lot of things, a lot to care about and they had the opportunity to dream.

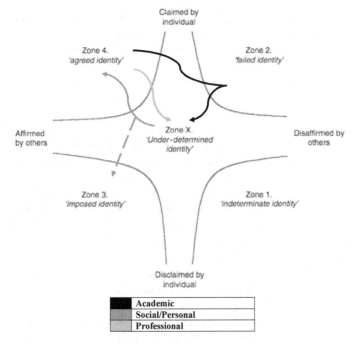

Fig. 12.3 Martin's Trajectories

> What I mean is, they have future plans. So, it's amazing. Being a worker is just so boring. You do the same thing every day. You have no plans…

Although he is still very clear on the type of graduate career he aspires to, his decision to move away from community pharmacy and to pursue work experience in the UK rather than in his home country with his parents, suggest a potential shift to *Zone X-tentative* (see Fig. 12.3).

12.10   Case Study 3: 'Dimitris' (University Y)

12.10.1   *"The Dreamer"*

After studying an International Baccalaureate (IB) diploma in his home country, Greece, Dimitris decided to pursue a Liberal Arts degree in the UK. His decision to study Liberal Arts appears to have been influenced by his combined study of English Literature and Psychology at college. He wanted to undertake a course where different subjects could be studied in combination, rather than focusing on only one topic—although he admits that his decision was also partly influenced by the fact he was undecided on what degree subject to study at the time.

Interestingly, Dimitris claims that he did not find his transition into university life particularly challenging: *"I didn't find it as...a big transition, I just felt like...it flowed really well from what I'd already been doing, it wasn't something so different...".*

He says that he enjoyed being exposed to more in-depth academic material during the early stages of university, such as more *"sophisticated"* textbooks, and learning to incorporate literature into his work. He speaks positively about his early interactions with others on his university course. As first year Liberal Arts students are mixed with students on other programmes for lectures, he felt well integrated with other courses and departments; *"I felt like I was part of more than one group of people, not that I was left behind or anything like that."* He describes his experiences of working with others on group projects prior to university as being imbalanced, in terms of co-operation and motivation. In comparison, his early experiences of working in groups at university are encouraging, with only some initial awkwardness/discomfort. He attributes this awkwardness to being unfamiliar with each other at this stage, and seemingly having little in common aside from the module assessment. This appears to flow into semester 2, where he perceives group work as *"fruitful"* when students are genuinely interested in the subject matter and connect in discussion, although he finds that in cases where students are disinterested in the class, this can have significant effects upon his own experience.

Dimitris also attended two summer preparatory programmes prior to university, where he interacted with students from a variety of different cultures and backgrounds. He never had the opportunity to experience these interactions previously in his home country, and found it exciting to learn about other students' experiences first-hand. He highlights that from such interactions he feels they often have more similarities than differences, for example, sharing similar concerns about university. His views are similar in semester 2; if he notices any differences he feels these are often due to a range of factors which *"go beyond culture"* (e.g., individual personalities). Through participating in these summer programmes, Dimitris was already familiar with student accommodation, although he does feel that he now needs to *"be more organised to survive."* By semester 2, he feels he is progressing in this goal as he is managing his workload more effectively, balancing academic and social priorities. Due to his experiences on the summer programmes, Dimitris feels well equipped to handle new challenges which emerge as he moves through his degree course, in the sense that he is familiar with busy periods with lots of coursework, as well as calmer periods.

His first social experience at university was a society event, where he enjoyed meeting new people with similar interests and felt supported in integrating with others at the event: *"...even though I felt like I didn't know anyone, everyone who was in charge there wanted to make me feel, you know, part of the group..."* Overall, his best experiences so far have been at society events. In semester 1 he joined a variety of societies including writers, radio and band societies. Despite there being a Greek student society, he *"rejected"* this opportunity in favour of opening up his prospects to different people and cultures, saying that to join the Greek society would be almost like a *"false defence mechanism."* On reflection he feels he could have made more of an effort to speak to people and make friends at these society meetings. In semester 1, he believes he has more 'acquaintances' than friends, often only knowing another student's name and course of study. In fact, he says that when back at his accommodation, he prefers to spend his time alone claiming that it is part of his personality that he does not wish to force friendships. He hopes to get involved in future in more societies and find closer friendships as in college. However, by the end of semester 2 he admits that he has in fact stuck with the same group of friends claiming that he thinks it is easier to make friends at the start of the year compared with later on as by then it is *"just your comfort zone…so, you're just comfortable with what you have"*.

In terms of work experience, Dimitris has never had a part-time job, but did complete a voluntary internship at a school during the summer. In the semester 2 interview he talks of pursuing another internship opportunity as he believes it will help him grow on a more personal level aside from merely obtaining work experience. He feels this is important as, although he covers topics of interest in his course of study, he has other interests such as music, which he hopes also to pursue through work experience, both during and after university. He appears to have mixed ideas on his career plans after graduation, being interested in a few different routes, for example, teaching, publishing or journalism. Though still undecided at the end of semester 2, he offers music journalism as a potential career route. In terms of graduate skills, he believes that the key skills he brings to a team are his in-depth research and organisation skills, and hopes to develop his confidence whilst at university to stand him in good stead as a graduate.

12.11 Dimitris: Analysis in Terms of Modalities of Emergent Identity

12.11.1 Trajectory 1: Academic

Dimitris appears to bring an established student identity with him to his university studies, previously affirmed through his college and summer programme experiences (*Zone 4*), which he feels have enabled him to handle some of the typical transition difficulties relating to academic study more effectively (e.g., being ready to handle more 'sophisticated' academic material). The effects of this can also be seen in semester 2, where Dimitris states he is proactively taking on additional opportunities to speak with tutors about his work and coping well with busy assessment periods, representing continued positioning in *Zone 4—agreed identity*.

12.11.2 Trajectory 2: Social/Personal

In comparison with his 'academic' trajectory, Dimitris's social/personal experiences appear to be a little more complex. Whilst he speaks positively about his experiences of group work throughout the academic year, his efforts to establish and build friendships during semester 1 suggest a move towards *'tentative' identity (Zone X)*, away from *Zone 4 ('agreed' identity)* based on his pre-university friendships created in his home country and also at college. His comments on his tendency to avoid forcing friendships, preference for being alone, and desire to form closer friendships, highlight the significance of this identity shift, emphasised further by his conscious decision to avoid the Greek society (potentially a shift towards *Zone 3—imposed identity*, also.). By semester 2, there appears to be movement back towards *Zone 4*. Although Dimitris initially states that he would like to join more societies and continue trying to make new friends, by semester 2 this goal seems to have been replaced by new priorities: to work on balancing study and social activities, and to focus on the small group of friends he has become closer to since semester 1 rather than broadening out his social network. To some extent, Dimitris attributes this to the size of the university, which can be *"overwhelming"* and as a result it is easier to seek connections with a smaller group of people. He now spends less time on society activities, and no longer attends one of them as he could not find someone else to go with him.

12.11.3 Trajectory 3: Professional

Having only previously undertaken a short internship, and not having had a part-time job, Dimitris begins his 'professional' trajectory in *Zone X*, as his initial professional identity is 'under-determined'. This is supported further by his indecision about his chosen career path; in semester 1 he is considering a few different career options, and admits he chose his degree course partially because he is unsure what he would like to do in the future. Moving into semester 2, his plans appear a little more refined though his interest in music journalism specifically indicates a potential transition towards *Zone 4*. However, this would be dependent on affirmation from others later on (for example, an internship/graduate recruiter). It is also possible to discern the influence of Dimitris's interactions with individuals of different backgrounds/cultures during his first year. He believes these experiences will contribute significantly to his employability as a graduate, perceiving that it will allow him to cooperate with others in a professional manner which could also prove advantageous in setting him apart from others in the application process. He adds that he feels open-mindedness is also essential for interacting with individuals of different backgrounds/cultures. Both contribute to a gradual transition towards *Zone 4*, as Dimitris continues to shape his plans and intentions for graduate employment and the skills/attributes required in his target career (see Fig. 12.4).

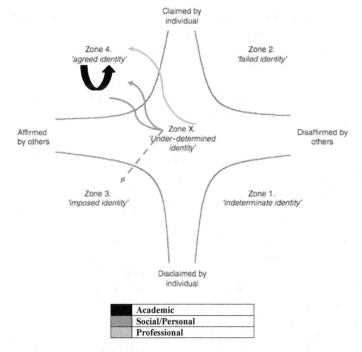

Fig. 12.4 Dimitris's Trajectories

12.12 Case Study 4: 'Vanessa' (University Z)

12.12.1 "The Wallflower"

Vanessa is studying Media Production and living in private student accommodation with her partner, who is also studying a similar degree discipline. In semester 1, she describes how she chose the university following guidance primarily from her college tutor. She is an only child, and her parents did not attend university, therefore they were not necessarily able to provide in-depth guidance on her options. Regarding her early transition into HE, Vanessa initially found this *"intimidating"* mostly because she found herself surrounded by individuals from different parts of the UK who sometimes had more work experience than her. She also admits she faced some difficulties when speaking with new people who already knew each other (e.g., if they lived in halls together or came from the same part of the UK) as she struggled to find common interests to talk about:

> It's been difficult...I don't socialise well. I'm quite a bit of an awkward person when it comes people in my own age group. So, it's been- has been difficult getting to know people. There hasn't been a lot of...[pause] time to get to know people. Like you're in lessons and stuff...you're here to do work...and in my apartment share...they're sort of congregating on their own...

Living with her partner has helped to alleviate these struggles to some extent; *"I'm comfortable not getting to know that many people, because I've already got someone."* Despite these challenges, Vanessa feels in semester 1 that she has eased into university life and is now confident she made the right choice. She attributes the ease of her transition to supportive staff and appropriate pacing in introducing certain topics on her course, which have made her transition a little more manageable. She also found her first lecture experience to be quite reassuring; *"a lot of people were late. So it made me feel more like not everyone here's gonna be perfect...everyone's human, everyone's late, everyone's lost...".* By semester 2 though, Vanessa decided to withdraw from her course, opting to study costume design at another institution. She sought advice from her college tutor on her predicament, and subsequently decided to change courses, concluding that she was more interested in the creative side of the role. She is excited about learning new topics and perspectives.

Regarding her experiences of group work in semester 1, Vanessa found that there were many strong, confident personalities. Rather than finding this intimidating however, she enjoyed this experience as she found her group mates would encourage her to work hard and develop her own confidence. She hopes that her main group would continue to build their relationship and become closer, more like other groups she has observed, because she believed her group to be a little 'split'. Her eagerness to form this closeness could perhaps be attributed to a further setback she faced in semester 1, after a good friend she made during her early stages left the university. She struggled with this, particularly as she does not find it easy to establish new friendships. She goes so far as disclosing that she has felt somewhat *"outcasted"* at times. Speaking more generally about group work, Vanessa asserts that her experiences of working in groups at college were quite frustrating, as some individuals would not pull their weight, leaving her to complete work on their behalf. She prefers that everyone in the group share responsibility for a task, finding this a useful way of getting to know others and make friends. Consequently, she found herself consciously stepping back from taking on a leadership role for her first group task at university, to allow her the opportunity to observe who would pull their weight and who would not.

Vanessa does not speak optimistically about her first 'freshers' event, saying that she and her boyfriend left after an hour as they are *"not really going out drinking people."* Instead, Vanessa prefers to spend her free time on her hobbies: professional make up (in which she was trained in previous employment), playing computer games and reading. She found socialising with other students difficult at times, not being interested in student nightlife—which seemed to be the main topic of conversation amongst her peers. She admits that her experiences with students of different cultures/backgrounds at university has been limited, although she does perceive differences in social class between herself and other students, which she finds difficult at times in terms of varying perceptions and necessities such as acquiring part-time work, budgeting, and other financial priorities. In terms of work experience, Vanessa previously had a part-time job in retail whilst at college, where she studied a BTEC in television and film. She claims that she purposely chose to attend college over sixth form so as to pursue one specific subject rather than selecting a few different A-Level subjects. She also enjoyed the practical aspects of the course in which she was able to complete relevant work experience and shadowing as part of the programme. As a result, she felt she left college with a good understanding of this type of career.

Considering graduate employment, in semester 1 Vanessa aspires to work as a producer's assistant in a TV studio. Her interest in this role stems from previous shadowing experience, where she was drawn to the creative and organisational aspects of the job, and her experience of working in a studio as part of her BTEC. At this point, she says that her best experience at university so far was an occasion where she took part in a production/audition simulation in the studio, as she had the opportunity to put her experience from college into practice:

> ...it was very fast paced...it was surreal, like this is what I'm getting myself into, which was really exciting.... really thought I could be a professional...this is what I'm gonna do when I leave here...this is what I want...

This contrasts significantly with Vanessa's comments in semester 2, where she claims that if she continued with her course, she ultimately would *not* want to end up working in a production role. Rather, she would prefer to focus on the creative aspects of costume design. Vanessa also had exposure to the professional expectations of this role during her college course where, despite witnessing potential conflicts between various staff in the department (directors, actors, wardrobe staff, etc.), she noted how they remained professional at all times.

12.13   Vanessa: Analysis in Terms of Modalities of Emergent Identity

12.13.1   Trajectory 1: Academic

Having studied a relevant qualification in college, which included work experience, it could be argued that Vanessa enters HE with a strong sense of academic identity (*Zone 4*). However, her departure in semester 2 takes her to *Zone 1-indeterminate identity*. To some extent, this may also coincide with her 'social/personal' trajectory, as she experiences a number of challenges in integrating with other students both in the classroom and socially, which may also have contributed to her first-year experience and decision to leave. However, Vanessa does offer other reasons for her decision to transfer, related specifically to academic aspects:

> I felt like the course wasn't really challenging enough, with things that I did there previously like the same sort of thing at the college, and I felt like it wasn't moving on much compared to what I'd already learnt...

Through changing her course to one where she believes she will might focus on the creative aspects she most enjoys, there is a suggestion of a progressive move towards *Zone X*.

12.13.2   Trajectory 2: Social/Personal

Vanessa faces difficulties interacting with others (both on her course and in halls) and making friends particularly during semester 1, indicating a starting point within *Zone 2-failed identity* as she continuously attempts to establish connections with her peers. To some extent her living arrangement could be partly attributed to her social struggles. Living with her partner can be partially disadvantageous as she feels that other students may be reluctant to speak and socialise with her, as they may think or assume she would prefer to be with her partner. On a more individual level, Vanessa also highlights her difficulties integrating with groups during her university transition, potentially contributing further to her negative experience. Unfortunately, in semester 2 before her course transfer she has an *"intense"* negative group work experience, as her group mates already knew each other, and she felt *"invisible"* to them. On reflection she wishes she had voiced her opinion more assertively.

12.13.3   Trajectory 3: Professional

Akin to her 'academic' trajectory, Vanessa exhibits clear focus on her target graduate career in semester 1, strengthened by her previous work experience, relevant BTEC qualification, and explicit enthusiasm for the role (*Zone 4—agreed identity*). However, her decision to withdraw appears tied to her plans for graduate employment; she acknowledges that she no longer aspires to this type of role, with an apparently logical rationale for her alternative target role in costume design. Rejection of her initial claim positions her in *Zone 3—imposed identity,* with a tentative move towards *Zone X* as she commences her new course of study. It is interesting to note that, aside from her college tutor's guidance on her future career and choice of degree programme, Vanessa also has work experience in professional makeup, which perhaps raises a query about the additional impacts of this experience on her decision to swap to a more creative programme/her desire for a more creative role (Fig. 12.5).

12.14   Discussion: From First Year Student to Employable Graduate

12.14.1   Acknowledging and Harnessing First Year Employability Capital

It is important to note the identification of various employability precursors across the four students. There is an (entirely understandable) tendency for empirical studies and HE/Government policy to focus on final year students and graduates. This

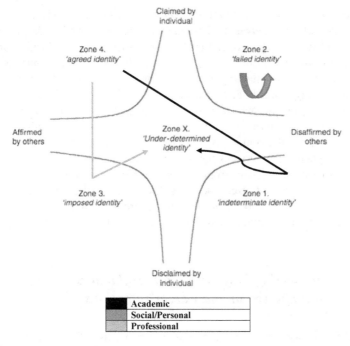

Fig. 12.5 Vanessa's Trajectories

is often an attempt to better understand experiences and perceptions relating to their employability at the point in time where they are actively undergoing this transition. The findings of this study contribute to this discussion and encourage further consideration of the employability capital that first year students bring with them to HE. Across the four case studies, and aside from their shared college qualifications (A-Levels, BTEC, apprenticeship, IB diploma), these students bring a host of additional capital which they'd acquired prior to university, such as exposure to other cultures via travel and resultant language skills. Dippold et al. (2018) draw attention to the value of such qualities for first year students, in terms of their progress towards being 'global graduates,' and in developing the confidence to challenge stereotypes and think flexibly. The students also have work experience, e.g., interacting within a team/leading a team and, in Martin's case, prior awareness and understanding of this target profession via his family. All are valuable examples of post-graduation employability capital already manifesting prior to commencing first year. In recognition of these employability 'precursors,' further attention must be paid to their impact upon student perceptions of 'employability' more generally, as well as their understanding of their initial target graduate careers: HEIs must actively acknowledge such capital and utilise it for the benefit of the wider first-year student experience.

In relation to the case studies, first-year students have useful perceptions of their indicative employability skills as future graduates, and the skills they hope to develop over time. Lizzio and Wilson (2004) argue too that students often reflect on workplace skill demands whilst at university. For example, Mary felt she had developed independence and adaptability through travelling across Europe alone, in addition to creativity skills developed during her apprenticeship, but hoped to continue developing language skills through studying abroad in Germany in year 2. Dimitris acknowledged his existing research and organisational skills, but also hoped to continue working on his confidence whilst at university. Each of the four students refined their graduate career plans during their first year. Several influences on this shift can be identified, for example, course peers (Mary), college tutor (Vanessa), course content and placements (Martin) and personal hobbies/interests (Dimitris). It is unclear whether this necessarily results from support offered by the university, such as skills development sessions and careers services. We could question the extent to which students utilise such support, or indeed, how aware they (and course staff) may be of the range of support initiatives available to them.

12.14.2 Intersecting Trajectories and Influences on Employment and Career Intentions

Across the four cases, instances can be identified where different first year trajectories overlap and influence students' priorities and choices, including those relating to employability, indicating that such trajectories do not necessarily reside in isolation. For instance, there is evidence of intersection between 'academic' and 'social/personal' trajectories across their HE transitions. Deighton et al. (2017) highlight that with a more heterogenous student community, due to increased student numbers, HEIs must also acknowledge diverse student support requirements, such as the different challenges they face and the consequent levels of emotional intelligence they may therefore benefit from. Earlier acknowledgment of this requirement is offered by Wilcox et al. (2005), following interviews with 34 first year students. The authors advocate the impact of early social integration and stable, compatible friendships to ease first year transitions, particularly with regards to emotional support. Their findings draw specific attention to living arrangements (e.g., student accommodation, private flat, living with parents, etc.) as having a greater influence on student support as compared with tutor support or connections with classmates. This certainly comes through in the four case studies, where there is relatively little reference to reliance upon tutor support. Instead, as Wilcox et al. (2005) found, social relationships both in and out of university hold considerably more value to students. Just as new graduates may expect and rely upon such support mechanisms when transitioning out of university and into the workplace (Gallagher, 2015), we see similar effects for first year students moving into HE.

The intersection between social/personal and academic trajectories can be located where socialisation and forming new friendships are seemingly high priorities at the start of the academic year, yet sometimes rejected in semester 2, in favour of academic priorities. Mary does not identify with the typical student stereotype, whilst Martin and Dimitris withdraw from society engagement having established 'enough' friendships. These early friendships and interactions are almost treated as 'safety nets,' essential during the initial stages in HE, but eventually discarded. Martin signifies this shift in perception via his comment on university friendships only being 'temporary.' The timing of these friendships, and perhaps other support provision, is key, in terms of their value—or otherwise—for first year students' transitions into HE, perhaps raising questions about awareness within HEIs in this regard.

Interaction between academic and professional trajectories is also significant. Primarily, we see the influence of previously acquired qualifications and current degree studies on graduate career intentions. Mary specifically chooses a business management degree because of her retail apprenticeship, explaining that she wanted to know more about the management side of business, and aspiring to a business-to-business role in the future. Similarly, Dimitris was initially unsure about his choice of degree subject and his future graduate career: he eventually makes his decision based on his having studied combined subjects in college, claiming he would prefer a graduate role which provides flexibility and breadth of interest.

One can decipher interaction between all three trajectories in the case of Vanessa. Here, the potential impact of social/personal experiences during first year, led her to change both her degree course (academic) and her plans for graduate employment (professional), although she claims this was purely due to her original degree programme not being the right 'fit.' On the contrary, both Deighton et al. (2017) and Wilcox et al. (2005) highlight the importance of support and relationships for ease of first year transition. Vanessa experiences several challenges (e.g., struggling to make friends on her course and in halls, her reluctance to take part in typical student social activities, etc.). Likewise, overlap across all three trajectories can be identified in the case of Martin, where his choice to study pharmacy (academic) and pursue it as a career in pharmacy was influenced by his parents' professional background (social/personal). Whilst students may actively plan and strategize graduate employment goals, some influences may be outside of their control.

12.14.3   Differences According to Degree Discipline

From the interviews, choice of university and degree course (and where they may lead in terms of graduate careers) were important considerations for the students, particularly for those choosing vocational or professional degrees (e.g., Martin and Vanessa). Those on broader, generalist degree programmes often had less specific graduate career goals, favouring aspirations in terms of opportunities such as travel, and future earning potential (e.g., Mary and Dimitris). Prior work experience influences perceptions and aspirations in differing ways. Vanessa's prior work experience (at least initially) appears to affirm her plans to pursue a role as a production assistant, whereas by semester 2 Martin refers back to his pre-university exposure to pharmacy environments in asserting that he no longer aspires to that type of role.

Whereas several empirical studies highlight the value of work experience for new graduates, the present study raises queries over the value of additional work experience in first year, for shaping future career intentions. It is interesting to note that Dimitris has the least work experience out of the four and appears the least focused in terms of his career intentions or employment post-graduation. As High Fliers (2018) note, the Times Top 100 Graduate Employers reduced their graduate recruitment by 4.9% in 2017, the first drop in graduate recruitment for five years. A quarter of the companies involved in the study however offered paid internships for first years, and over a third offered open days and other taster experiences for first years. There are opportunities available to students having a similar mindset to Dimitris.

12.15   Conclusion

Early UG experiences inform and form future identities, including graduate identities, which may still shift over the three or four years at university. Holmes' (2015) model of 'emergent identities' has been adapted here to explore the negotiation and construction of academic, self/social and professional identities. Our study notes the *transitions* of identity and how this is important in supporting students throughout university, so that they become employable, not just in terms of having certain skills but also a claimed and ascribed self and social identity, as required for successful transitions into graduate employment. As summarised by Tett et al. (2017), and evidenced by these case studies, students may need to 'undo' previously affirmed identities and understandings in preparation for entering the new HE environment. Becoming employable is an iterative process which can and often does start in first year. This contributes to current debates at policy and practice level around students' acquisition of skills and attributes (as articulated, for example, in the UK Teaching Excellence Framework) versus the process of 'becoming a graduate' and modalities of emergent identity (Holmes, 2015) in order to meet the needs of both employers and graduates within the labour market.

Students are focused on how they might enhance their employability in the early stages of their university journey. The case studies illustrate students' understanding of the skills they need, early plans concerning their graduate careers, and how these might influence their early days at university. As part of their 'settling in' some are strategic in joining clubs and societies, engaging in group work, and pursuing work experience to boost their employability. Curricular design, consistency across disciplines, engagement with extra-curricular activities and reflection upon work experience, are all important 'learning gains' that acknowledge and build on their existing experiences and aspirations, developing and embedding work-readiness and professionalism at an early stage. Universities must find ways to harness the aspirations of 'career-committed' students who have arrive with clear sign-posting, support and advice from an early stage (e.g., from their family). Those who are less career-focused must also be supported however in making the connections between their wider learning, university experiences and opportunities, and their employability potential.

References

Becker, G. S. (1993). *Human capital: A theoretical and empirical analysis with special reference to education* (3rd ed.). Chicago: University of Chicago Press.

Brown, P., & Hesketh, A. (2004). *The mismanagement of talent: Employability and jobs in the knowledge economy*. Oxford: Oxford University Press.

Coertjens, L., Brahm, T., Trautwein, C., & Lindblom-Ylanne, S. (2017). Students' transition into higher education from an international perspective. *Higher Education, 73,* 357–369.

Collet, C., Hine, D., & Plessis, K. (2015). Employability skills: Perspectives from a knowledge-intensive industry. *Education + Training, 57*(5), 532–559.

Cranmer, S. (2006). Enhancing graduate employability: Best intentions and mixed outcomes. *Studies in Higher Education, 31*(2), 169–184.

Daniel, J. (1993). The challenge of mass higher education. *Studies in Higher Education, 18*(2), 197–203.

Dearing, R. (1997). *Higher education in the learning society*. England: National Committee of Inquiry into Higher Education (NCIHE).

Deighton, K., Hudson, J., Manley, A. J., Kaiseler, M., Patterson, L. B., Rutherford, Z. H., et al. (2017). Effects of emotional intelligence and supportive text messages on academic outcomes in first-year undergraduates. *Journal of Further and Higher Education, 49*(4), 464–507. https://doi.org/10.1080/0309877x.2017.1377161.

Department for Business Innovation and Skills. (2015). *Understanding employers' recruitment and selection practices: Main report (research paper)*. https://www.gov.uk/government/uploads/system/uploads/attachment_data/file/474251/BIS-15-464-employer-graduate-recruitment.pdf.

Dippold, D., Bridges, S., Eccles, S., & Mullen, E. (2018). Developing the global graduate: How first year university students narrate their experiences of culture. In *Language and Intercultural Communication,* https://doi.org/10.1080/14708477.2018.1526939.

Dyess, S. M., & Sherman, R. O. (2009). The first year of practice: New graduate nurses' transition and learning needs. *The Journal of Continuing Education in Nursing, 40*(9), 403–410.

Eriksen, S. D. (1995). TQM and the transformation from an élite to a mass system of higher education in the UK. *Quality Assurance in Education, 3*(1), 14–29.

Finn, K. (2016). Relational transitions, emotional decisions: New directions for theorising graduate employment. *Journal of Education and Work, 30*(4), 419–431. https://doi.org/10.1080/13639080.2016.1239348.

Fournier, V., & Payne, R. (1994). Change in self construction during the transition from university to employment: A personal construct psychology approach. *Journal of Occupational and Organizational Psychology, 67,* 297–314.

Gallagher, P. (2015). Graduate transition into work: The bridging role of graduate placement programmes in the small- and medium-sized enterprise workplace. *Journal of Education and Work, 28*(5), 461–480.

Gibson, A., Shaw, J., Hewitt, A., Easton, C., Robertson, S., & Gibson, N. (2018). A longitudinal examination of students' health behaviours during their first year at university. *Journal of Further and Higher Education, 42*(1), 36–45. https://doi.org/10.1080/0309877X.2016.1188902.

Harding, J. (2011). Financial circumstances, financial difficulties and academic achievement among first-year undergraduates. *Journal of Further and Higher Education, 35*(4), 483–499. https://doi.org/10.1080/0309877X.2011.584969.

Harvey, L. (2001). Defining and Measuring Employability. *Quality in Higher Education, 7*(2), 97–109.

Helyer, R., & Lee, D. (2014). The role of work experience in the future employability of higher education graduates. *Higher Education Quarterly, 68*(3), 348–372.

Hennekam, S., & Herrbach, O. (2015). The influence of age awareness versus general HRM practices on the retirement decision of older workers. *Personnel Review, 44*(1), 3–21.

Hesketh, A. (2000). Recruiting an elite? Employers' perceptions of graduate education and training. *Journal of Education and Work, 13*(3), 245–271.

High Fliers. (2018). The graduate market in 2018. https://www.highfliers.co.uk/download/2018/graduate_market/GMReport18.pdf.

Hinchliffe, G. W., & Jolly, A. (2011). Graduate identity and employability. *British Educational Research Journal, 37*(4), 563–584.

Holmes, L. (2001). Reconsidering graduate employability: The graduate identity approach. *Quality in Higher Education, 7*(2), 111–119.

Holmes, L. (2013). Competing perspectives on graduate employability: Possession, position or process? *Studies in Higher Education, 38*(4), 538–554.

Holmes, L. (2015). Becoming a graduate: The warranting of an emergent identity. *Education + Training, 57*(2), 219–238.

Jackson, D. (2014). Testing a model of undergraduate competence in employability skills and its implications for stakeholders. *Journal of Education and Work, 27*(2), 220–242.

Kalfa, S., & Taksa, L. (2013). Cultural capital in business higher education: Reconsidering the graduate attributes movement and the focus on employability. *Studies in Higher Education, 40*(4), 580–595.

Kara, Z., Eisenberg, D., Gollust, S. E., & Golberstein, E. (2009). Persistence of mental health problems and needs in a college student population. *Journal of Affective Disorders, 117*(3), 180–185. https://doi.org/10.1016/j.jad.2009.01.001.

Kasler, J., Zysberg, L., & Harel, N. (2017). Hopes for the future: Demographic and personal resources associated with self-perceived employability and actual employment among senior year students. *Journal of Education and Work, 30*(8), 881–892. https://doi.org/10.1080/13639080.2017.1352083.

King, N., & Horrocks, C. (2010). *Interviews in qualitative research.* Thousand Oaks: Sage Publications Ltd.

Little, B. (2011). Employability for the workers-what does this mean? *Education + Training, 53*(1), 57–66.

Lizzio, A., & Wilson, K. (2004). First-year students' perceptions of capability. *Studies in Higher Education, 29*(1), 109–128. https://doi.org/10.1080/1234567032000164903.

McMurray, S., Dutton, M., McQuaid, R., & Richard, A. (2016). Employer demands from business graduates. *Education + Training, 58*(1), 112–132.

Murtagh, S., Ridley, A., Frings, D., & Kerr-Pertic, S. (2017). First-year undergraduate induction: Who attends and how important is induction for first year attainment? *Journal of Further and Higher Education, 41*(5), 597–610. https://doi.org/10.1080/0309877X.2016.1159288.

Office for National Statistics. (2017). Graduates in the UK labour market: 2017. https://www.ons.gov.uk/releases/graduatesintheuklabourmarket2017.

O'Leary, S. (2016). Graduates' experiences of, and attitudes towards, the inclusion of employability-related support in undergraduate degree programmes; trends and variations by subject discipline and gender. *Journal of Education and Work, 30*(1), 84–105. https://doi.org/10.1080/13639080.2015.1122181.

Palmer, M., O'Kane, P., & Owens, M. (2009). Betwixt spaces: Student accounts of turning point experiences in the first-year transition. *Studies in Higher Education, 34*(1), 37–54. https://doi.org/10.1080/03075070802601929.

Rae, D. (2007). Connecting enterprise and graduate employability: Challenges to the higher education culture and curriculum? *Education + Training, 49*(8/9), 605–619.

Robbins, L. (1963). *Higher education: Report of the committee appointed by the Prime Minister under the chairmanship of Lord Robbins 1961–63.* Retrieved from http://www.educationengland.org.uk/documents/robbins/robbins00.html.

Schultz, T. (1971). *Investment in human capital*. New York: Free Press.

Silva, P., Lopes, B., Costa, M., Melo, A. I., Dias, G. P., Brito, E., et al. (2018). The million-dollar question: Can internships boost employment? *Studies in Higher Education, 43*(1), 2–21. https://doi.org/10.1080/03075079.2016.1144181.

Smith, J., McKnight, A., & Naylor, R. (2000). Graduate employability: Policy and performance in higher education in the UK. *The Economic Journal, 110*, 382–411.

Storen, L. A., & Aamodt, P. O. (2010). The quality of higher education and employability of graduates. *Quality in Higher Education, 16*(3), 297–313.

Sutherland, J. (2008). Higher education, the graduate and the labour market: From Robbins to Dearing. *Education + Training, 50*(1), 47–51.

Tett, L., Cree, V. E., & Christie, H. (2017). From further to higher education: Transition as an ongoing process. *Higher Education, 73*, 389–406.

Tomlinson, M. (2012). Graduate employability: A review of conceptual and empirical themes. *Higher Education Policy, 25*(4), 407–431.

Tomlinson, M. (2015). Between instrumental and developmental learning: Ambivalence in student values and identity positions in marketized UK higher education. *International Journal of Lifelong Education, 34*(5), 569–588.

Weiss, F., Klein, M., & Grauenhorst, T. (2014). The effects of work experience during higher education on labour market entry: Learning by doing or an entry ticket? *Work, Employment and Society, 18*(2), 287–293. https://doi.org/10.1177/0950017013506772.

Wilcox, P., Winn, S., & Fyvie-Gauld, M. (2005). 'It was nothing to do with the university, it was just the people': The role of social support in the first-year experience of higher education. *Studies in Higher Education, 30*(6), 707–722. https://doi.org/10.1080/03075070500340036.

Wilkins, S., Shams, F., & Huisman, J. (2013). The decision making and changing behavioural dynamics of potential higher education students: The impacts of increasing tuition fees in England. *Educational Studies, 39*(2), 125–141.

Wilton, N. (2011). Do employability skills really matter in the UK graduate labour market? The case of business and management graduates. *Work, Employment & Society, 25*(1), 85–100.

Emma Mullen (Ph.D.) is a Senior Lecturer in Human Resource Management at Newcastle Business School, Northumbria University, England. She is Programme Leader for the Leadership and HRM department's CIPD accredited B.A. (Hons.) HRM programme, and leads on the employability curriculum at both undergraduate and postgraduate levels. Her research interests primarily lie with graduate employability and careers, recruitment and selection, and multigenerational working. She currently has four doctoral students, is a Fellow of the HEA and an Academic Associate of the CIPD.

Stephanie Bridges (Ph.D.) is an Associate Professor in the School of Pharmacy at the University of Nottingham, England, UK. She is a registered pharmacist, member of the Royal Pharmaceutical Society and a Fellow of the Higher Education Academy. She teaches across a range of undergraduate modules about professional, legal and clinical pharmacy practice. Her research interests focus on teaching and learning in HE, aspects of professional and intercultural education, including global pharmacy education, and the potential for HE to act as a space for students to explore and develop more cosmopolitan-aware selves. She is looking at the Capability Approach as a means of conceptualizing, evaluating and informing thinking about pedagogical environments within HE which promote intercultural capability development.

Sue Eccles (Ph.D.) is an Associate Professor in the Centre for Excellence in Learning at Bournemouth University, England. Her research interests focus around inclusive teaching and learning and her research portfolio includes the transition of (international) students into HE, widening participation, and the experiences of young people as they make choices and decisions prior to HE. Her recent studies on leadership within HE have enabled her to explore staff experiences and perceptions of developing and maintaining inclusive education practice. She has six doctoral students, and has seen four others to completion. She is a regular reviewer for several journals, an Editor for the *Journal for Learning Development in HE* and on the Editorial Board of the *International Journal of Management Education.*

Doris Dippold (Ph.D.) is a Senior Lecturer in Intercultural Communication at the University of Surrey, England, UK. Her research interests focus on the internationalisation of HE, in particular internationalisation at home, but she looks also at classroom interactions and at digitally enhanced learning and teaching methods. Doris is the author of a MOOC on *"Communicating with Diverse Audiences"* to be launched on *Futurelearn* in Spring, 2019. She is also interested in the concept of "Global Citizenship" and has recently been the main author of a paper on the development of graduate citizenship attributes, published in *Language and Intercultural Communication* (2018).

Chapter 13
Engaging Students, Staff, and Employers in Developing Student Employability

John Bostock

13.1 Introduction

Graduates who leave university almost invariably enter the world of work, ideally, at graduate-level, and therefore must be equipped to survive and prosper in increasingly-competitive regional, national and global jobs markets. Curricular design that combines academic, subject-related practical and transferable skills to meet the needs and expectations of employers, industries, and professional bodies is therefore of tremendous importance. This has wide implications for teaching staff: it is essential to also identify and explore their developmental needs. It is vital that academics be afforded opportunities to develop their conceptual and procedural knowledge around the developing of student employability skills, to build repertoires of varied techniques and activities within teaching, assessing, and subsequent evaluating, and to amass knowledge of a variety of resources, grounded within their own discipline and at various levels.

Similarly, it is important to show how employers are actively involved in the design of curricula. Scrutiny of the Teaching Excellence Framework (TEF) metrics[1] and revised National Student Survey (NSS) questions[2] must cause some consternation even amongst those staff who deliver HE programmes to students already vocationally/professionally focused (and for whom notions of resilience and fitness to train are perhaps already 'embedded'). The TEF draws on nationally collected data to measure the performance of Higher Education (HE) providers within the following areas:

---

[1]http://webarchive.nationalarchives.gov.uk/20180319114451/http://www.hefce.ac.uk/lt/tef/ (date accessed 31.10.18).

[2]https://www.thestudentsurvey.com/content/NSS2017_Core_Questionnaire.pdf (date accessed 01.11.18).

J. Bostock (✉)
Edge Hill, Ormskirk, England, UK
e-mail: bostojo@edgehill.ac.uk

© Springer Nature Switzerland AG 2019
A. Diver (ed.), *Employability via Higher Education: Sustainability as Scholarship*,
https://doi.org/10.1007/978-3-030-26342-3_13

- Student satisfaction—How satisfied students are with their course, as measured by responses to the National Student Survey (NSS).
- Continuation—The proportion of students that continue their studies from year to year, as measured by data collected by the Higher Education Statistics Agency (HESA).
- Employment outcomes—What students do after they graduate, as measured by responses to the Destination of Leavers from Higher Education survey (DLHE).

It is to this latter point that most attention is given especially for students whose programmes are not directly focused on any particular vocation or profession, and who, it is anticipated, will leave HE with appropriate competencies, skillsets, behaviours (i.e. motivations and attitudes) and professional practices. This chapter contains nine sections: the first six together explore how graduate attributes and skills may be fairly common across different disciplines but, significantly, they examine how students locate and articulate these qualities within the specific contexts of their own subjects. Drawing upon degree characteristics statements and subject benchmarks (QAA, 2018), generic and key transferable skills are identified here alongside those skills that are purely academic, subject-specific, or practical in nature. The student journey and their skills development along the way will be presented here as a triadic concept, firstly in terms of student induction and transition through programme-levels, secondly, in respect of the needs and expectations of employers, industries and professions and thirdly, in relation to employer engagement. Employer engagement is examined in terms of how it is developed and nurtured at programme or subject level, to encompass work-related and placement learning models, and the various activities designed to enable students to understand the real-world workplace-relevance of their academic studies. There are numerous quotations from students throughout and each were obtained through module evaluations and student consultative for a conducted as an expected part of the QA and QI processes.

Section 13.7 of the chapter identifies and explores staff development needs. With reference to Continuing Professional Development (CPD) schemes and Postgraduate Certificates (in Teaching and Learning) it argues that HE disciplines or subjects represent and serve as seats of highly specialised knowledge: professionals (as communities of practice) can and must engage in developmental dialogues which will both preserve and enhance such knowledge. The notion of teacher professionalism (referred to here as 'dual professionalism') which requires staff to become expert subject specialists as well as being expert teachers, will also be analysed. The concluding sections look to employer involvement in the design of curricula, modules, and learning outcomes, asking how key transferable skills may be merged with academic and subject-specific practical ones, whilst students are being supported to better articulate their own employability.

13.2   Locating and Articulating Graduate Attributes and Skills

Higher Education is currently undergoing some of the most profound changes in its history. Against a backdrop of increasing marketization, rising levels of student debt, and greater numbers of fully online offerings, HE tutors are contending with new ways of working and with increasingly high expectations around teaching quality. Graduate attributes and skills tend to be articulated similarly across certain disciplines. Generic skills typically demonstrated by students on completion of an undergraduate degree (FHEQ level 6) usually include the ability to:

i.   Deploy accurately established techniques of analysis and enquiry.
ii.   Devise and sustain arguments and/or solve problems, framing appropriate questions to identify solutions.
iii.   Critically evaluate arguments, assumptions, abstract concepts and data to make judgements.
iv.   Communicate information, ideas, problems and solutions to both specialist and non-specialist audiences.
v.   Initiate and carry out projects.
vi.   Manage own learning.
vii.   Make decisions in complex and unpredictable contexts.
viii. Exercise initiative and personal responsibility.

A student's decision to continue on in education instead of joining the world of work means not only foregoing potential income that could be earned for the duration of their course, but also incurring additional costs. This is a rational decision given the expectation of graduate employment and enhanced earnings later on in life. Thus, the success of a university's graduates in finding appropriate, 'graduate level' work (a requirement of the TEF metrics) translates into better destination table results. This can mean attracting the more able prospective students, who, with everything else being equal, should be more employable owing to their greater innate abilities. A university could initiate a virtuous circle, to the benefit of three interested parties: themselves, students and prospective employers. Employers also expect students to possess transferable skills. So, learning at university based as closely as possible on real work situations (e.g. case studies, projects, study visits and simulated work environments) provides a variety of methods to embed and enhance employability. Generally, this touches on meaningful and practical approaches to teaching and learning such as modelling, scaffolding and motivation as well as authenticity and reliability in assessment methods. In the next section there are examples of how this and students' employability skills should be carefully explored and nurtured in certain disciplines.

13.3 Embracing Employability

Developing and promoting student employability by definition entails the preparation of graduates to enter the world of work and survive and prosper in an increasingly-competitive regional, national and global jobs market. This can be achieved through curricula which integrate academic, subject-related practical and transferable skills with the needs and expectations of employers, industries and professions. As such they enable graduates to enter the global job market as:

- Subject specialists
- Independent critical analysts who are inquisitive, intuitive and reliable
- Positive communicators
- Self-starters and self-managers
- Innovative and creative decision-makers
- Ethical and responsible employers and employees
- Lifelong learners.

These attributes should also include numeracy and literacy skills (Bostock & Wood, 2014, p. 23). Existing programmes in the HE sector continue to undergo significant revision to try and provide distinctive alternatives to the current provision and practices, especially in terms of supporting students' employability. HE tutors attempt to make sense of those practices to identify with successive curriculum models with a particular focus on the way in which these identifications frame learning. Looking at how certain disciplines identify and support the development of graduate attributes is of pivotal importance and enables an appreciation of their transferability across most, if not all, other disciplines. The following examples are taken from current provision in one HEI and demonstrate the breadth and depth of provision required to meet the employability needs of students.

13.4 Non-vocational Degrees

The majority of non-vocationally oriented disciplines increasingly stress a dedication to providing meaningful student experiences by integrating a number of key employability strategies both within the core curriculum as well as via extra-curricular provision.

13.4.1 Educational Placements

Students on one Educational Psychology course are required to undertake educational work placements to aid their critical reflections of psychological theory in educational practice. Partnerships with Educational Psychologists in the North West enable students to undertake shadowing work during the second year of their course. Students have observed the following on the value of their respective extra-curricular provision: *I was given the opportunity to work in a Primary School and an Educational Psychology Company. It was invaluable in helping me see how the theories are realised in practice.'* Another noted: *'I could shadow an Educational Psychologist and see how in a hands-on way the job is carried out with the chance to ask questions, observe and learn.' (Psychology Year 2 student).*

13.4.2 Sandwich Years

Students may apply to complete a sandwich year placement as part of their programme (between Years 2 and 3) to gain highly relevant work experience: *'Working alongside future colleagues and employers has helped me tremendously and more importantly has made the studies I undertake totally relevant.' (Psychology Year 3 student).*

13.4.3 Mock Assessment Centre

Students actively engage in the process of writing job application forms, psychometric testing, and being interviewed:

> This is just a fantastic opportunity to articulate my academic skills into transferable workplace skills. For example, I write a lot essays and I have to condense and critique a wide range of literary sources into a coherent account. This is precisely the skill many bosses want when they require a report for example. (Psychology Year 1 student)

13.4.4 Reflections and Future Directions Module

This is a final year compulsory module in which students are encouraged to consider the broader nature of psychology in practice. The programme module is typically structured around a 'Dragon's Den' event which requires groups of students to develop an initiative in any area of Applied Psychology, but with particular emphasis on how it can be applied to the commercial world: *'Taking part in such events not only gives me a feel of what interviews might be like, but also raises my confidence and perhaps even a competitive spirit.' (Final Year Psychology student).*

13.4.5   Study Abroad and Language Learning

Within one Business Studies Department there is an opportunity to study abroad and learn a new language: students may apply to spend an additional year studying or working abroad. By diversifying, enriching and complementing their studies, learning a language provides an ideal opportunity to develop new skills or consolidate and enhance existing language skills. Studying a language improves communication skills, provides insight into other cultures, and enables students to experience the rewards (and enhanced employability skills) that fluency in a second language can bring: *'Learning Mandarin has opened up so many potential opportunities for me to really show my cultural awareness and communication skills' (Year 1 Business Student).*

The employability strategies of academic degree programmes in Humanities subjects have been traditionally based on the acquisition of transferable skills. However, since 2011, there has been a move towards optional placement modules that allow students to develop employability skills in a way that is relevant to their degree but also respects the fact that work-placement modules have often been considered inappropriate for students who made an active decision to study on a non-vocational course. Nevertheless, it is evident that compulsory work placement modules are likely to become commonplace across HE within the next few years, to reflect the changing academic climate.

13.4.6   Independent Project

This module is an option for Level 5 (second year) English Language students who want to make a direct connection between the subject matter of their degrees in non-vocational humanities and social science subjects and their plans for a graduate career. Students research and initiate a work-related project with an external agency, supported by the University Careers Centre and a specially appointed Work Placement Officer. Academic supervision and assessment is provided by the relevant department. The project entails gaining detailed familiarity with a cultural, public sector or voluntary organisation; making a meaningful contribution to the work of this organisation; the use of skills developed on the degree programme; and a final reflection and self-evaluation, which looks ahead to immediate and longer-term career plans: *'This was a fantastic opportunity to help me understand mid-way through my studies how immensely valuable it is to engage in project work and develop my project management skills.' (Year 3 English student).*

13.5   Humanities

13.5.1   History in Practice: Community Project

The History in Practice 'Community Project' is an optional module which enables students to make a direct connection between the subject matter of their degree and the working world. Students negotiate a project with an external agency/professional body: the finished product, in the form of a publication, web-page, YouTube, or other platform, must enhance the work of the partnership body, and be outward-facing to the general public in its character: *'I now have many hits on YouTube as a result of this option and so many potential employers have taken an interest in my work.' (Year 3 History student).*

13.5.2   Inside the Publishing Industry

This optional module develops awareness of publishing across literary genres with a focus on poetry, fiction, scripts and digital publishing. Students explore what modern writers and publishers are looking for and receive talks by guest speakers from leading publishing presses and industry professionals. A study of all genres is designed to explore the differences between writing and production via print, digital media and performance. Self-directed placements in publishing or group projects help develop new skills and experience of cultural industries. Additionally, this module involves a visit to a major literary event (e.g. festival or book fair) where students can learn more about current trends and predicted futures within a fast-moving publishing climate. This module makes use also of existing publishing outputs, such as Black-Market Re-View and The Wolf. Following group work and/or placements (and as part of the assessment strategy) students submit an essay on a specific aspect of the publishing industry that they have researched throughout the module: *'I met one of my favourite authors, researched digital media and prepared an outline of my own proposal for publication.' (Year 3 English student).*

13.5.3   Hosting a Literary Festival

Hosting a Literary Festival is another option module which enables students to engage with workplace practice via a group project. Students work collaboratively to research, plan and initiate an in-house literary festival whilst reflecting on and evaluating their ability to do so. Academic supervision and assessment is provided by the Department of English, History and Creative Writing with support from the University's Careers Centre: *I was so excited to be able to host such an event and demonstrate my presentation and communication skills in this way.'(Year 3 Creative Writing student).*

13.6 Embedding Employability

In addition to the above activities, aspects of employability are also embedded within modules as and when appropriate, for example, having visiting speakers who are industry professionals or including activities that use work-based scenarios. For instance, in Forensic Linguistics the students have an educational field trip to a court during which they meet barristers and other legal professionals and participate in a mock trial in which they play almost all parts: clerk, Judge, witnesses, and defendant. Such activities demonstrate for students the diverse graduate career opportunities available within the Arts and Humanities. To further promote employability, increased dialogic contact between experienced professional mentors and students provides effective support. Those mentors who have high quality experience, knowledge and skills across the sector are encouraged to nurture the metacognitive and metalinguistic skills of their respective students i.e. the language used to talk about their subject, the employability skills contained therein, and reflection on their application to other contexts. In other words, encouragement to discuss and debate how to best articulate skills to maximise employability. Students explicitly respect and welcomed the support of experienced mentors who have had first-hand knowledge of professional practices and processes. Increased triadic engagement (tutor, mentor and student) to explore concerns and issues is an effective opportunity to discuss and enhance practice throughout the discipline.

Students have also involved themselves in cycles of appraisal and observation within their chosen professional settings. This assures the institution of high quality education which would not only help students maintain their employability skills, but also support dialogic engagement over the optimum ways to apply that knowledge. Lave & Wenger (1991) offer a conceptualisation known as Communities of Practice (CoP), proposing a socio-cultural theory of learning to explain how context generates meaning and identity. Professional identity is neither, in this theoretical perspective, a stable nor a static notion. In other words, practices, which serve to define a community, are constituted by the participants. The community is dynamic, and the members are developing continually as practices evolve. Communities do not have a set of practices set in stone, which new members acquire and perform. Rather, in performance, the practices are reconstituted and developed. A CoP is, therefore, conceived as a set of relations amongst persons, activity, and world, over time and in relation to other tangential and overlapping CoPs (Lave & Wenger, 1991).

An alternative construct to Wenger's CoP proposed by Gee (2005) and known as 'affinity spaces,' helps to understand more deeply the supports afforded to students. In other words, spaces, whether virtual or face to face, built to resource those who share a particular endeavour (an affinity) governed by a theoretical framework which drives context and relationship to the fore i.e. mutually constitutive relationships. Thus, the community or affinity is made coherent by practices which focus on up-to-date employability skills and discussions which promote appropriate engagement with the connection between HE curricula, employability, content and its application in the professions. It is these affinities which help support and develop meaningful dialogue between students and employers. Such dialogic opportunities can be scheduled within modules or provided as group tutorial sessions but the emphasis on face to face debate and discussion is at the fore.

Employability workshops provide material for students to further develop and reflect upon their specialist subject knowledge, their employability skills and the processes underpinning their own learning. The university and related professional experiences continue to provide the central learning activities and context in which the complex and inter-related skills of teaching are developed, namely: independent critical analysts who are inquisitive, intuitive and reliable; positive communicators; self-starters and self-managers; innovative and creative decision-makers; and ethical and responsible employers and employees. This goes some way towards improving what is currently an issue within some of these programmes, by providing dialogic opportunities to improve understanding and engagement with employability skills and their distinct professional or specialism application.

Minimising issues of communication involves detailed knowledge and research of the respective subject/professional settings. Students are more likely to benefit from opportunities to engage with specialist input alongside professional mentor support: greater results will be achieved if students are encouraged to network and view expertise in their respective professions and are given access to subject specialist advice both in terms of resources and taught sessions. HE attempts to reflect the reality of vocational application, yet the professional needs of students can also be met if dialogue is increased between vocational professionals and students, to cement positive and cohesive relations. Subject teaching that is rich in real world examples, research projects and opportunities to see how the subject and its methods are applied, is vital.

13.7 Staff Development

Dual Professionalism i.e. being both an expert subject-specialist or professional and an expert teacher, ties to a variety of discourses on professional practice that in turn lead to conceptualisations which stress the salience of disciplinary knowledge over pedagogic practice (or at the very least the need to bring parity of importance to each). Dual professional identities amongst academic staff are often problematic since each brings with them considerable but diverse experiential, professional knowledge of practice and professionally related, specific concepts of teaching and learning within their own disciplines. However, certain professional standards for lecturers (HEA, 2011) do enable dialogue that produces and reproduces useful concepts around teaching disciplines. Dialogue is premised on using academic knowledge to interpret and translate that knowledge into discipline-focused pedagogical practice. In other words, content knowledge (CK) becomes pedagogical content knowledge (PCK) (Bostock, 2018). Therefore, pedagogical discussion processes require critical refection on how subject matter becomes taught matter, and, crucially in this context, how the taught matter embraces employability skills.

There are two significant opportunities within HE for this to happen: Post Graduate Certificate in Teaching and Higher Education (PGCTHE[3]) and the Continuing Professional Development (CPD[4]) Schemes (UKPSF). Both offer flexible and creative opportunities for staff to engage in professional development that is meaningful to them and supports them in enhancing their practice, with a clear focus on continuous enhancement of the student experience. Certainly, in terms of such accredited provision, one of the standards (V4) encourages staff to 'acknowledge the wider context in which Higher Education operates recognising the implications for professional practice' (HEA, 2011). Cohorts of staff on such programmes are typically diverse, often composed of senior university academics, teacher educators from other sectors, and even Ph.D. students with varied research backgrounds. Debates are often about the differences and commonalties of academic practice, yet researching and articulating events in these contexts raises many questions about the significance of embedding generic employability skills into staff development programmes.

Adopting a holistic, practice-based approach to preparing staff is key as is ensuring that essential skills and knowledge are premised on the use of academic expertise to interpret and translate such knowledge into pedagogical practices. There are three concepts for understanding pedagogies of practice namely: representation, decomposition and approximation. The second is quite salient and is often described as the essential skill of breaking down practice into its constituent parts for the purposes of teaching and learning. Employability requires critical reflection on how content becomes taught matter, so the perspective of decomposition must be understood in terms of a combination of content and pedagogy.

Focusing on the academic development of teaching across disciplines suggests that teaching that is generic reduces the activity to the technical matter of performance as, perhaps, something that you 'lay on top of your real work,' unconnected to the disciplinary community and this is a real problem to be addressed. The significance of curriculum design is rendered stronger however in terms of identifying disciplinary contexts and subject decomposition as being pivotal to the process of providing more meaningful experiences in developing employability. In one HEI, the Advance-HE accredited provision (i.e. CPD Scheme and PGCTHE) enable distinct opportunities to demonstrate how curricula are developed, to maximise optimum student success. Through modules and fellowship applications there are distinct requirements to design curricula within HE (i.e. UKPSF A1-5). In one module for example participants are encouraged to critically analyse a range of definitions of curriculum and to consider these from the perspective of their particular role or dis-

---

[3] Accredited provision typically used to award HEA Fellowships to experienced staff i.e. with more than three years' experience of teaching.

[4] Accredited provision typically offered to all staff new to teaching in HEIs i.e. with less than three years' experience.

Skill	Definition
Self-management	Using initiative without supervision
Communication	Presenting information clearly and appropriately
Teamwork	Participating fully in any group work
Problem solving	Analysing facts and situations and coming up with appropriate solutions
Project management	Planning, organising and supporting a project through its various development stages
Creativity and innovation	Identifying and taking opportunities
Commercial awareness	Understanding the key drivers behind a successful business or organisation
Social, cultural and global awareness	Relating with people from a range of different backgrounds
Application of numeracy	Carrying out arithmetic operations and understand data
Application of IT	Demonstrating confidence in the use of information technologies
Resilience	Being flexible and willing to rethink and adjust plans accordingly to ensure success
Employer Engagement	Showing willingness to talk to employers e.g. at presentations, skills sessions

Fig. 13.1 Employability skills and possible definitions

cipline. Staff interrogate the ways in which curriculum design can inhibit or extend opportunities for students from a range of social and cultural backgrounds. It also centres on staff reflections upon their own role within the planning, delivery and evaluation of curricula. Particular attention is paid here to the distinctive nature of their subject/discipline, which includes its relation to supporting employability. Therefore, in the construction of Learning Outcomes, Content and Assessments, staff are encouraged to not only identify the relevant skill but to *define* clearly what this means to students (See Fig. 13.1).

13.8   Involving Employers in Curricular Design?

Employability is clearly an issue of direct concern to students. Arguably, a prime motivation in attending university is, for many students, not to necessarily study a particular subject in depth, but to enhance their own employment prospects. Supplementing a student's education in a subject-specific discipline with a wide range of key skills (such as communication and teamworking), is beneficial to a student's future placement in the world of work. However, the individual subject skills may still not fully meet employer requirements, as often there is a tension between formal education and vocational training. Employability is typically embedded into the curriculum through work based exercises and learning: these are often achieved by employers visiting as a guest speaker or with students having a placement with an employer. Notwithstanding the activities outlined above (which clearly attempt to reflect the demands and meet the needs of employers), a particular, indeed essential approach to curriculum design is to engage employers as industry experts (i.e. consultants) and abide by professional bodies' guidance and regulations when developing module content, learning outcomes and assessments. As a result, teaching strategies do make use of real-world case-studies or simulations within learning activities and assessments, especially when these are based upon practical scenarios and problems, or on highly topical issues. Where possible, employers are invited to deliver sessions and participate in assessment, alongside academic staff, e.g. contributing to assessment of student presentations, performances or projects.

Work-Based Learning (WBL) further enriches the student experience through placements whereby students apply theoretical concepts in workplace settings and reflect critically on their experiences. Programme teams describe how employer engagement is fostered, developed and nurtured at programme or subject level, for example, via breakfast clubs or twilight 'employers fora.' Employers may provide mentoring and deliver developmental feedback to students. It is also advantageous that validation and review panels can explore how placement settings, including those initiated or arranged by students themselves, are both quality-assured and risk-assessed to ensure appropriate and consistent quality in terms of the learner experience.

Another approach is to adopt a holistic perspective in relation to curriculum design with all stakeholders being involved in every aspect of programme development thus delivering high levels of programme ownership across the whole programme development team (including those stakeholders who are not part of the teaching team). A broad range of stakeholders is crucial to good curriculum design. An example of this, taken from a Business Degree, is the aptly-entitled 'Employability Module' which runs typically over two semesters and involves considerable work experience i.e. direct involvement with potential employers. Culminating in an Assessment Centre Day, students and their work are judged by external employers from a variety of business settings. However, prior to this, numerous employer-led opportunities are provided in the style of projects, presentations, business simulation games and even study abroad as outlined above. As one Business School Director stated:

> Programmes which provide a solid academic foundation for employment in a wide-ranging and advancing graduate employment market are of vital importance to students. Employers from the fields of accountancy, administration, banking, education, finance, human resource management, marketing, product development, public sector management, retailing, small and medium sized enterprise management and general management enhance the potential for students to develop their own business ideas and operate in a global business environment. There is increasing evidence of a growing, healthy involvement with employers.

The range and scope of potential employer engagement can be illustrated further by a comprehensive list of activities in which students might engage:

- Visitors from business and the community at the university, including former alumni.
- Industry days and challenges.

- Careers fairs and information.
- Work experience.
- Mentoring by a professional in the specific field or business.
- Enterprise projects supported by business.
- Mock interviews and assessment centres.
- 'Live' projects set by external organisations.

However, even more research is needed to understand how meaningful employer input can be integrated into individual degree programmes and to gauge how employers can best be involved in work-related assessment or other professionally focused activities in supporting student learning.

13.9 Conclusion

Employability is a lifelong concern and no one student is ever perfectly employable. There will always be aspects of student employability training that would benefit from improvement especially with regards to the importance of identifying students' abilities on entry to university as well as being clearer about desired graduate attributes and developmental goals. This chapter does not argue for a process that a student might embark upon during their time in HE which then graduates them with a sort of 'employability for life.' The concerns and debates within HE are likely to be revisited many times in the future to ensure adaptability to the demands of a rapidly changing world and to provide graduates with a better chance of occupational satisfaction and success.

References

Bostock J. (2018). Exploring in-service trainee teacher expertise and practice: Developing pedagogical content knowledge in innovations. In *Education and Teaching International*.

Bostock, J., & Wood, J. (2014). *Supporting student transitions 14–19: Approaches to teaching and learning*. London: Routledge.

Gee, J. P. (2005). *An introduction to discourse analysis: Theory and method*. Oxon: Routledge.

HEA. (2011). The UK Professional Standards Framework for Teaching and Supporting Learning in Higher Education.

Lave, J., & Wenger, E. (1991). *Situated learning: Legitimate peripheral participation*. Cambridge: Cambridge University Press.

QAA. (2018). *Expectations and practices*. The revised UK Quality Code for Higher Education. Available online https://www.qaa.ac.uk/quality-code#

John Bostock (Ph.D.) is a Senior Lecturer in Teaching and Learning Development (2012–present) and formerly Post-Compulsory Education and Training (2007–2012) at Edge Hill University, England, UK. He is a National Teaching Fellow, Principal Fellow of the Higher Education Academy, Senior Fellow of the Staff and Educational Development Association. He has over thirty-two years' experience of teaching, twenty years teaching and managing in the PCET/FE sector (1987–2007) as Lecturer and Head of Department of Modern Foreign Languages/Linguistics and Teacher Education, and twelve years' experience in HE. He leads a university-wide learning and teaching fellowship programme that promotes and maintains a high quality, transformative student experience. His research interests include the significance of social interaction in on-line learning, transitions in 14–19 education, conceptualisations of teacher education in professional training, and the use of technology to enhance the quality and impacts of teaching, learning and assessment.

Chapter 14
Learning from and About Each Other: Developing Skills for a Connected Interdisciplinary World

Dawne Gurbutt

14.1 Introduction

Reviewing the strategic directions taken by diverse professional regulatory bodies, business leaders and employers, it is apparent that the future is interdisciplinary. Therefore, the Higher Education (HE) sector needs to prepare graduates for a dynamic, changing world where problems are complex, inter-sectoral and 'wicked' by nature, and where problem solving, prioritization and networking are crucial to the success of groups and individuals, who will be working in interconnected ways, globally and using transferrable skills. That said, although employees and HE students inhabit a world of connectivity and constant contact via social media, there is still a need to establish rapport, form connections and maintain contacts with people beyond our existing networks. This is one of the challenges which is becoming apparent with the rise of social media, namely, the dissonance which exists between active engagement with a large group of friends, and the frequent reluctance to engage with unfamiliar colleagues. The development of social confidence and collaboration skills necessary for full participation in the workplace has traditionally been viewed as one of the consequences or impacts of HE; it was not however considered a core focus for many programmes, given the belief that this upskilling would readily occur alongside academic study.

However, it is becoming increasingly apparent that the ability to collaborate and connect is such a desirable skill that HE Institutions need to find ways to actively ensure that students are exposed to opportunities to gain confidence in working together and to evaluate and improve their competencies in this area. One of the challenges is to identify and uncover the spaces in which students will have the opportunity to learn about each other. Learning together is an opportunity to also learn about themselves. Traditionally, students have learned within sharply defined

D. Gurbutt (✉)
University of Central Lancashire, Preston, UK
e-mail: DGurbutt@uclan.ac.uk

© Springer Nature Switzerland AG 2019
A. Diver (ed.), *Employability via Higher Education: Sustainability as Scholarship*,
https://doi.org/10.1007/978-3-030-26342-3_14

subject areas amidst the structures of the University: departments, schools and faculties, provide organisational boundaries which assist learners in acquiring discipline-specific identities. But these same structures serve also to separate learners from each other and have a tendency to increase the probability that learners will only have the opportunity to learn from people with very similar aspirations, experiences and skills to themselves. Society needs connected and interconnected learners, who will challenge, innovate and explore, and who can transplant skills and practices from one area to another, thinking creatively about problem-solving and considering where other problem solvers might be located. Employers need to be able to identify those who think across set boundaries and are able to see the bigger picture from a wide range of perspectives. In short, the HE sector needs to ensure that its old boundaries are made more permeable, flexible and fluid. As Lyall et al. (2015: 5) state: 'The employability agenda accentuates the desire for agile learners who can utilise their graduate skills rather than simply accrue knowledge.'

Inter-professional education (IPE) has been established for a long time in Health and Social Care professions. Inter-professional Education is defined by the Centre for Advancement of Interprofessional Education (CAIPE, 2002) as: 'Occasions when two or more professions learn with, from, and about each other to improve collaboration and the quality of care.' As a requirement of the professional bodies, HE providers must demonstrate that students have an opportunity to learn together as preparation for practice contexts, which are increasingly integrated in terms of care provision and service delivery and where traditional boundaries can flex around the needs of the patient and also accommodate the economic constraints of the sector. IPE is challenging both in terms of resources and systems. Cohort sizes in the Health and Social Care professions are generally large and a substantial proportion of learning takes place in work-based placements. Timetabling, synchronising curricula and identifying learning areas which are mutually beneficial, can pose problematic issues for HEIs and curriculum developers. Yet, learners and employers alike agree that embedding IPE within the curriculum is good preparation for working within those team structures that pervade many areas of practice.

Hean et al. (2018) assert that failures in service delivery from the Bristol Inquiry (DoH, 2001) to the Climbie Inquiry (DoH, 2003) indicate that health and social care professionals do not always demonstrate effective, collaborative team working, and that IPE has thus been 'proposed as a way of optimizing the delivery of safe, high quality care.' IPE has had a higher profile however since the publication of the Francis Report into the failings of the Mid Staffordshire Hospital Trust (2013). The report considered various aspects of work culture, including values. Inherent in the report (and in the debates which followed it) was the need to create an environment where staff are enabled to work effectively together, to be accountable and challenge unsatisfactory practices, and prioritize patient safety. The emphasis on collaborative practice requires educators to embed inter-professional education and prepare learners for team-working (WHO, 2010). This has led to an emphasis on professionalism, by considering what it means to be 'professional,' and the importance of focusing upon the service user and teamwork. In sum, this means aiming for collaborative practice which involves key stakeholders. Pellegrino (1984: 254) argued also that

> …medicine connects technical and moral questions….it sits between the sciences and the humanities being exclusively neither one nor the other, but having some of the qualities of both.

This is true of many areas of education and leads to conceptualising education differently. Hedy et al. (2018: 1) (citing Mann, 2017; Wald et al., 2015) argue for the inclusion of humanities within medical education to 'support learners developing essential qualities such as, professionalism, self-awareness, communication skills and reflective practice.' This example demonstrates how the boundary between IPE and Interdisciplinary education (IDE) is becoming less impermeable within Health and Social Care. There are increasing examples of collaborative education which includes Health and Social Care professions working alongside other disciplines (such as Law and Policing) which could be identified as an element of 'Public Service' in addition to areas such as Creative Arts, Engineering, Business. The identified benefits of Interprofessional education in Health and Social Care are consistent with the positive effects of inter-disciplinary working across other subject areas. The issues and cross-cutting themes which are common to IPE are also relevant across many curricular areas. These range from such transferrable skills as problem-solving, team work, communication, prioritisation, decision-making, time management, networking and project management, to increased learner confidence in articulating identity when working across varied disciplines. The challenge is in being able to evaluate IDE effectively: Hean et al. (2018) argue that inter-professional education (and the same could be said for interdisciplinary education) need to have a curriculum which is carefully designed in relation to underpinning theoretical perspectives that follow through on delivery and evaluation, with a logical progression through these elements.

14.2 Defining IDE

It is sometimes difficult to reach agreement on definitions of 'interdisciplinarity' but it is generally recognized that inter-disciplinary activity attempts to combine knowledge, methodologies and theoretical perspectives from more than one disciplinary area (Ellis, 2009; Klein, 2009; Miller, 1982). This endeavour includes combining and integrating approaches. Interdisciplinary working can be viewed as an attempt to solve complex real world problems by working with external stakeholders, or it can be viewed as an attempt to synthesise ideas from different disciplines. Interdisciplinarity can also be framed as the processes of combining existing approaches in a new manner. This is distinct from pedagogical interdisciplinary working where learning and teaching are aligned. Similarly, there are various iterations of collaborative working across disciplines: multi-disciplinary approaches see each discipline providing an explanation from its located viewpoint, whilst interdisciplinary approaches have explanations considered from different viewpoints, but are then integrated.

Transdisciplinary approaches see differing viewpoints drawn together into a new framework, creating a new disciplinary perspective.

14.2.1   Why IDE Matters for Employability

The last decade has seen an increase in the identification of problems which cross traditional boundaries. Often referred to as 'wicked problems,' the focus is on non-linear issues which will not be easily solved by a single discipline or approach. Some universities have focused on working across traditional boundaries with initiatives such as 'Grand Challenges,' which enable a cross disciplinary approach to problem-solving and innovation. Initiatives such as this reinforce the importance of recognising interdisciplinary work in problem-solving alongside the acknowledgment that some issues can *only* be resolved through interdisciplinary approaches, collaborative action and collective solution-focus. This is a key element of the interconnected, non-linear challenges which are inherent in a global workplace, where dynamic factors interact constantly with one another. It is also the fundamental underpinning of innovation where collectives view problematic issues from a broad perspective.

It is not just the curriculum which matters in IDE. Traditionally, College-based universities have emphasized the importance not only of HE study, but also the networking and connection elements of study. When interdisciplinary experiences work well they enable students to form connections and relationships which extend beyond the classroom. Gurbutt and Milne (2016) for example conducted evaluations of groups of Medical and Pharmacy students who had participated in IPE. The students began to form Communities of Practice which met to support each other outside of the formal curriculum quite early in the programme of study. This manifested itself in individual students providing support to each other, which focused on discipline knowledge, but also in groups of students supporting each other by participating in a course validation event involving co-design.

One of the elements which students learn (in addition to learning about different skills and perspectives) is an awareness of where particular skills may reside, enabling learners to have much better understanding of what they know, but also where to seek out expertise they do not have themselves. For widening participation students this is particularly important as working together can help to blur established social boundaries. Often the HE sector focuses on widening access, giving learners from non-traditional backgrounds the opportunity to engage with HE. But it could be argued that widening participation is also about being enabled to fully participate in a graduate setting: the opportunity to extend networks and mix with other professional and disciplinary groups is a positive aspect of working in collaboration which can contribute to confidence in this area. Learning design needs to focus not only on the acquisition of knowledge, but also on competence and confidence in applying knowledge in a graduate context. Confidence can include feeling enabled to not only function in the workplace, but also to seek help and guidance when required.

14.3 Meaningful Learning Experiences

One of the important factors in interdisciplinary or interprofessional education is ensuring that the learning experience is meaningful. Each participant, individual or group, should feel that the learning is appropriate and beneficial to them and not designed to promote the learning of the other cohorts or disciplines engaged in the learning session. This is crucial, not only because the curriculum should always link to learning outcomes and be focused on the needs of the learner, but also because learners are being encouraged to understand the complexities of the context. That is not to say that learning for the different cohorts will be the same within any given session. One example involves creating a learning episode for design students working with medical students to create an anatomical model which could be used to explain a procedure to patients. The learning for the medical students centers on the ability to present complex discipline information in a clear format and to clarify its accuracy in order to provide a workable brief. For the design students the focus may be on negotiating an achievable brief and managing expectations and resources. For both groups there will be mutual learning around teamwork, decision-making, problem-solving, time management and communication. Therefore, the learning shares some specific elements and yet is still quite discipline-specific in respect of others. This mirrors the workplace where joint common outcomes may incorporate very different activities on the part of the team. This adds an additional layer to the learning experience: understanding shared accountability, commitment and tenacity in relation to developing a shared project. It could be argued that meaningful learning incorporates the visible curriculum, and subject-specific learning, but also rests upon the 'hidden curriculum' (Giroux & Penna, 1983) which encompasses things which are learned, but might not have been actively taught. It therefore encompasses the learning which may occur through exposure to culture, expectations, practices and values. This is particularly important when contemplating such concepts as 'professionalism.'

Barr, Low, and Howkins (2012) highlight that where there are changes in practice, it is necessary to manage the 'unintended consequences' of working in new ways. In considering the teaching of medicine, Adhikari (2007: 443) highlights how including humanities in the curriculum can influence the development of culturally aware 'global physicians' and argues that the without humanities the curriculum can be 'found lacking to achieve the goal of producing a compassionate, caring, ethical doctor who can reflect on what s/he reads or sees.' Collaborative education can provide a space in which to expose learners to the views and values of others, and expose them to the tensions between perspectives and disciplines, thereby offering a safe space in which to explore and reflect. This offers a response to areas of concern identified by employers relating to teamwork and professionalism, e.g. the Francis Report (2013).

Initial development of IPE at UCLan involved 3 faculties and 9 schools centred on the newly configured medical school, but quickly expanding to incorporate more IDE. Creating a curriculum which was collaborative included working with stakeholders and service users to ensure that there was a strong 'real world' element to learning.

This led to close liaison with local employers to ensure that learning reflected the workplace environment. IDE and IPE offer the opportunity to design a curriculum which is co-created or created in consultation with employers. The stakeholder and service user involvement also rendered aspects of the curriculum visible within the locality and region. This in turn led to other requests for involvement in employer-led collaborative working projects, for example, a Dementia Awareness project in a local NHS Trust involving students from different disciplines. This is an indication of one of the ways in which collaborative learning not only prepared students for the workplace, but enabled them to engage in work experience of different kinds during their programme of study. Designing IPE and IDE curricula can enable a closer relationship with employers and a greater understanding of transferrable skills.

14.4   Intended and Unintended Consequences of Collaborative Learning

The perceived benefits of collaborative curriculum and interdisciplinary learning were centred on the experience of students and learners working together. This was further enhanced by the involvement of stakeholders and service users in co-designing the curriculum. However, one of the unintended benefits of the collaborative education programme was the impact of academic staff working together more closely. Students commented on the positive experience of witnessing staff working in collaboration together and gaining a better understanding of individual and professional skill sets and they ways in which academics from different disciplines approached shared tasks and navigated differences (Gurbutt & Milne, 2018). Students also reflected on the ways in which staff role-modelled different approaches to decision-making, drawing on situated knowledge from within their own disciplines and professional experience. In small group discussions, students reflected that the learning was enhanced when they were led in their deliberations by academics from contrasting disciplines. This was also evident in different approaches to planning, administration and enabling feedback. The staff also reported that they had learned from each other, some citing the benefit of an opportunity to update their knowledge of the changes in the health and community sectors by being in contact with staff from different disciplines. They also mentioned sharing teaching techniques, resources and networks. The latter included widening opportunities for students from other programmes to engage with extra-curricular activities provided by schools and faculties. There was a direct opportunity to enhance the student experience by enabling access to a wider range of already existing opportunities. This reflected one of the benefits of staff being more connected with colleagues across the campus: a move towards a more collaborative campus, in which student connections are facilitated.

Staff connections and networks in the locality led directly to students being offered the opportunity to participate more in community engagement initiatives and extra-curricular projects. Some of these were formal and offered to all students within a cohort, others were available for students to 'opt into.' Hence there was a combination of formal and non-formal learning opportunities, compulsory and non-compulsory activities and also the stimuli for students to connect with each other socially having met via shared-learning. Such collaborations require a degree of tenacity to overcome such barriers as timetabling, scheduling and aligning curricula. Often, collaborative initiatives attract those academics already committed to team working, or from discipline backgrounds which require close connection and co-operation. These synergies and the subsequent collaboration in IDE led to the right conditions for a Community of Practice to form around interdisciplinary practice. This resulted in a connected group of academic staff, working together, sharing developments and with strong links to employers and stakeholders. One of the identified difficulties was in finding times to schedule meetings, to more foster collaborative working: the group became more actively involved in using technology and digital tools to liaise with each other. Using on-line tools to collaborate has facilitated IDE, and further enhanced student experience. Academic staff also have reported an increased confidence in the consistent use of technology to enhance collaboration (Gurbutt & Williams, 2018).

14.5 Learning from Collaboration and Interdisciplinary Learning

Working collaboratively within a HEI enables a unique insight into shared experiences. Feedback on learning and teaching always includes multiple variables, but these are greatly expanded when considering feedback from Interdisciplinary groups, where the participants have differing backgrounds and multiple perspectives. The initial programme of IPE comprised over 2000 learning episodes based around simulation, case-based students and problem-solving scenarios. The initial aim of the curriculum design was to enable transformational learning, underpinned by Activity Theory (Engestrom, 1987). All of the sessions were evaluated by questionnaire and specific focus groups (Gurbutt & Milne, 2018). This resulted in more than 1800 evaluations. The student feedback contained some patterns which are generally common in learning and teaching in groups. This included comments on the content and how this aligned with the module and assessment, the teaching accommodation and administration of the sessions. These are feedback patterns which could be anticipated when compared with other types of module feedback. However, some feedback was quite distinctive in that students commented on their own values, perspectives and attitudes alongside their reflections on learning.

They particularly identified other groups of students who they felt had helped them to understand something more clearly, through changes in perception, identity, role or values. They also identified the benefits of learning alongside students who had already had some element of work experience; their learning about work and how to prepare for the workplace was emphasised. There were also expressions of appreciation for the skills and knowledge of the other participants, and reflections on how it felt to be perceived as 'knowledgeable' in their own area within a group. Of particular interest was a pair of students had who found themselves in the IDE session by mistake, having attended the wrong venue for their own timetabled session. These students came to a Mental Health session, which on the face of it bore little relationship to their own course. In spite of this, they rated the session very highly, felt that they had 'learned a lot' and 'had a better understanding of Mental Health.' They also found the collaborative elements of the learning process 'compelling' and 'not something they were used to.' These responses indicate the benefits of thinking 'outside of the box' when considering learning elements within courses, in relation to content and delivery. In sum, the best learning occurs when the conditions are right: one of the key messages from evaluations was that students had found that IDE had uncovered new spaces for them to learn within and on occasion engendered different types of learning.

The evaluations from the early sessions were used to further develop the programme. One of the key areas to emerge was the benefit of co-creation, the identification of cross-cutting themes and the opportunity to work with students from other cohorts. Students commented that 'networking' was an area in which they had felt under-confident and IPE had given them an opportunity to practice. 85% of respondents felt that IDE had been beneficial. Interestingly, some participants also stated that one of the challenges was the lack of direct assessment. These learners felt that they wanted to spend time on elements of the programme which were assessed. There is potentially a correlation here with perceptions of the workplace, with students valuing knowledge acquisition (particularly knowledge which is going to be assessed) but overlooking, or failing to value as highly, those other skills and attributes which are so important to employers, such as the ability to build rapport, work in teams and communicate with people from different backgrounds. Not all students reported that they 'enjoyed' the collaborative learning: only 58% felt this to be the case, with typical observations including the following: [it] 'took them firmly out of their comfort zone, particularly in early sessions', and they 'prefer to work with friends.' This contrasted sharply with their evaluation of 'usefulness': 'This has already helped me in placement, I feel more confident—but also more able to say that I don't know something'; 'it is good to know that other students feel the same as you'; 'I feel I think more broadly about what other people do, than I did at first' and 'I have gained real confidence in working with strangers and working in teams.' The early evaluations shaped the ongoing development of IPE and IDE, including a stronger focus on the 'real world' elements of the programme, specifically those aspects co-created with key stakeholders. Co-production enables a stronger connection with employers and professionals working in the field, ensuring that content is contemporary, contextual and reflective of the complexities of the workplace. Engaging students and staff in design of the IPE portfolio also ensures that learning and teaching approaches are contemporary, but that students are encouraged to reflect on how—and where—learning takes place.

14.6   Communities of Practice

Learning occurs within multiple places. It is often assumed in education that learning generally takes place in formal settings such as classrooms and within prescribed sessions. In reality, learning is not confined to location, time or context. Learning may occur in places which are not readily identified as offering a learning context (Milne, 2007). This is an important factor for learners to understand as they move into the workplace: learning happens when the conditions exist in which learners can learn. Interdisciplinary learning is by nature based on connections, networks and collaboration. This is down to academic staff and other facilitators supporting the programmes of learning. The development of beneficial long-term networks provides an environment in which Communities of Practice are enabled to form and thrive on campus (Lave & Wenger, 1991) and these groups can also include stakeholders. These communities have multiple settings, from Interdisicplinary task and finish groups, to cross-university committees and themed networks. The establishment of communities has led to the development of successful collaborative writing groups, curriculum design groups and the creation of databases to link those staff who have a shared interest in IDE, enabling them to work together. Hence, the IDE initiative has been a stimulus for developing, extending and creating collaborations, sharing good practice and developing accessible learning opportunities for students across faculties and campus.

The focus on working across disciplines encourages development of core skills for employability and innovation. These commonly involve elements of collaboration, but also can encompass sharing at a more personal developmental level. Enhanced personal resilience is one of the areas that students and staff identified as resulting from Interdisciplinary education.

Health students, for example, whose course incorporated work-based learning, commented on the benefits of discussing with each other various ways of coping with difficult issues arising on placement during the IPE sessions, and this resulted in a greater focus on preparing students for the psychological and social elements of such early immersion in the workplace. This has also identified the opportunities afforded by placements where collaborative education can help students from different backgrounds to support each other and share information on the wider support available.

14.7   Conclusion

The workplace is becoming increasingly interconnected, focused on 'insoluble' problems that require innovation, insight and collaboration. Students will graduate into a workplace which is constantly evolving, where they may have multiple careers during their working lives and may well work in roles that have yet to be created and working across the globe with individuals they may never meet face to face. They must become agile thinkers, adaptable, and able to evolve into new roles, forming networks which enable them to co-operate and work in teams. Interdisciplinary and interprofessional education enables students to develop the skills, competencies and professional networks that will help prepare them for this new landscape.

Students who have participated in IDE and IPE have commented that they feel more prepared for placements and practice having worked across disciplines. They have become more confident about expressing their own perspective and gained communication skills. IPE and IDE enabled them to gain confidence in asking questions. Students also highlighted how gaining recognition for subject specific knowledge when working with others builds their confidence and that they are better able to engage with decision-making, listening, problem solving and prioritising with more diverse groups than those found amongst their own disciplines and usual colleagues. In sum, working in collaborations enables learners to actively acquire the cross-cutting skills that are most valued by employers.

References

Adhikari, R. K. (2007). Humanities in education of doctors. *Kathmandu University Medical Journal.* (*KUMU 5*, 443–444).

Barr, H., Low, H., & Howkins, E. (2012). *Interprofessional education in pre-registration courses.* London: CAIPE.

CAIPE. (2002). *Centre for advancement of interprofessional education.* London. www.caipe.org.

Department of Health. (2001). *Learning from Bristol: The report of the public inquiry into children's heart surgery at the Bristol Royal Infirmary.* London: Department of Health.

Department of Health. (2003). *Victoria climbie: Report of an inquiry by lord laming.* London: Department of Health.

Ellis, R. J. (2009). Problems may cut right across the borders. In B Chandramohan & S. Fallows (Eds.), *Interdisciplinary learning and teaching in higher education. Theory and practice* (pp. 3–17). New York: Routledge.

Engeström, Y. (1987). *Learning by expanding: An activity-theoretical approach to developmental research.* Helsinki: Orienta-Konsultit.

Francis, R. (2013). *Report of the mid-staffordshire NHS foundation trust public inquiry.* London: Stationary Office.

Giroux, H. & Penna, A. (1983). Social education in the classroom: The dynamics of the hidden curriculum. In H. Giroux & D. Henry and Purpel (Eds.), *Berkeley the hidden curriculum and moral education* (pp. 100–121). California: McCutchan Publishing Corporation.

Gurbutt, D. J. & Milne, P. (2016). *Surveying the Landscape in the development of a new medical programme: The challenges of creating a learning space for Interprofessional Education and Collaborative Working.* EDULEARN16 Conference. Barcelona, Spain: Published Proceedings.

Gurbutt, D. J. & Milne, P. (2018). *The path to transformation: Navigating the barriers to forming transient and transitional learning groups in interprofessional education.* INTED Conference. Spain: Published Proceedings.

Gurbutt, D. J. & Williams, K. (2018). *Performing good teaching: The frontstage and backstage work of interdisciplinary working.* INTED Conference. Valencia, Spain: Published proceedings.

Hean, S., Green, C., Anderson, E., Morris, D., John, C., Pitt, R. & O'Halloran, C. (2018). The contribution of theory to the design, delivery and evaluation of interprofessional curricula. BEME Guide no 49. *Medical Teacher, 40*(6), 543–558.

Hedy, S., McFarland, J. M., & Markovina, I. (2018). Medical Humanities in medical Education and Practice. *Medical Teacher* 1497–151. https://doi.org/10.1080/0142159x.

Klein, J. T. (2009). A conceptual vocabulary of interdisciplinary science. In P. Weingart & N. Stehr (Eds.), *Practising interdisciplinarity*. Toronto: University of Toronto Press. https://www.theguardian.com/higher-education-network/2018/jan/24/the-university-of-the-future-will-be-interdisciplinary.

Lave, J., & Wenger, E. (1991). *Situated learning: Legitimate peripheral participation*. Cambridge: Cambridge University Press.

Lyall, C., Meacher, L., Bandola, J., & Kettle, A. (2015). *Interdisciplinary provision in higher education current and future challenges*. HEA/University of Edinburgh.

Mann, S. (2017). *Focusing on arts and humanities to develop well-rounded physicians*. Washington, DC: AAMC News.

Miller, R. (1982). Varieties of interdisciplinary approaches in the social sciences. *Issues in Integrative Studies, 1*, 1–37.

Milne, P. (2007). *Contesting the freedom to learn: Culture and learning in a british general practice*. (Ph.D. thesis). UCLan.

Pellegrino, E. (1984). The humanities in medical education: Entering a post-evangelical era. *Theory Medical, 5*, 253–266.

Wald, H., Anthony, D., Hutchinson, T., Liben, S., Smilovitch, S., & Donato, A. (2015). Professional identity formation in medical education for humanistic, resilient physicians, strategies for bridging theory to practice. *Academic Medicine, 90*, 753–760.

World Health Organisation. (2010). *Framework for action on interprofessional education and collaborative practice*. Geneva: WHO.

Dawne Gurbutt (Ph.D.) is a Professor and Head of Collaborative Education at the University of Central Lancashire (UCLAN), England. An experienced person-centred practitioner and academic, her background is in health, having had extensive experience of working in areas of social deprivation prior to moving into HE. She has managed a wide range of HE provision across different settings and has held strategic roles including working for the HEA, UK, where she led on initiatives to increase collaboration across disciplines and explore innovative ways of achieving interdisciplinary working. Through mentoring and coaching for many years, she is committed to widening participation, community engagement, collaborative education and service-user engagement. She is an Honorary Fellow of the Centre for the Advancement of Inter-professional Education (CAIPE) and a member of the CAIPE Board where she co-leads the Learning and Teaching group.

Chapter 15
What Happens When Politics and Career Dreams Collide? Considering the Impact of Brexit on Graduate Career Aspirations

Theresa Thomson

15.1 Introduction

The EU Referendum revealed a deeply divided society, with many 18–24-year olds voting overwhelmingly for Remain (Moore, 2016). For those students who started their university education within the EU and now find themselves graduating in a country that is perceived as increasingly isolationist and politically divided, what impact is Brexit having as they consider their futures in a post-Brexit world? Findings from a small-scale qualitative research study, conducted one year after the EU Referendum result, reveal a strong desire to create a more tolerant country and a determination to find a way through an uncertain jobs market. Although ultimately there is little firmly conclusive that can be drawn from this study, the findings do show the impact of the wider context of the world that we live in, including the impact of political events, on potential career choices. Furthermore, the study provides a deeper understanding of the concerns and barriers facing a group of final-year students in one post-1992 university. A progressive shift in career guidance practice is clearly needed, which acknowledges the importance of social, economic and political context as the meaningful background for any conversations about career choice.

15.2 Why Study the Impact of Brexit on Graduate Career Choice?

In an era of global economic austerity and the rise of right-wing populism across Europe, the UK is attempting to negotiate a Brexit deal that is both economically and politically favourable. This task is far from easy. The EU does not wish Brexit to be

T. Thomson (✉)
University of the West of England (UWE), Bristol, UK
e-mail: theresa2.thomson@uwe.ac.uk

© Springer Nature Switzerland AG 2019
A. Diver (ed.), *Employability via Higher Education: Sustainability as Scholarship*,
https://doi.org/10.1007/978-3-030-26342-3_15

advantageous to the UK, for fear of triggering further exits across its membership. Meanwhile, political opinion in the UK is divided over 'soft' versus 'hard' Brexit proposals, fuelling cross-party calls for a new Referendum. At the time of writing, the very real prospect of a 'no-deal Brexit' looms ever closer. It is this lingering uncertainty that faces the next generation of UK graduates, as they contemplate their futures.

In terms of employment, graduate level or otherwise, the simple truth is that no-one knows what exactly the impact will be. Reports agree that the impact of Brexit on the UK labour market is far from clear (BBC News 2018; Institute for Employment Studies, 2017). However, large scale quantitative surveys of UK undergraduates, from predominantly Russell Group universities, suggest that up to three quarters of graduates believe it will be harder to find graduate level employment because of the Brexit vote (e.g. The UK Graduate Careers Survey 2017, conducted by Higher Fliers Research, 2017). According to Trendence UK, 77% of domestic students believe that there will be fewer opportunities to work or study overseas (as cited in Recruitment International, 2017). Meanwhile, UK universities need to demonstrate that their graduates can quickly secure professional employment, thereby evidencing both 'teaching excellence' and an ability to secure graduate 'career success' in this uncertain economic climate.

This study comprised in-depth individual interviews with 15 final year (domestic) undergraduates at the University of the West of England in Bristol, from a cross-section of degree programmes. Research interviews were conducted from July until December 2017, i.e. 12–18 months after the Referendum result. This was sufficiently recent for Brexit to potentially still stir up strong feelings and opinions. However, arguably enough time had passed for participants to digest the potential impacts of Brexit on their lives, particularly as they entered their final year of undergraduate study. Therefore, one can posit with reasonable confidence that the thoughts and opinions expressed during the research interviews were not simply 'knee jerk' emotional reactions in the immediate Brexit aftermath, but were thoughtful reflections given after a period of time. In brief, a thematic analysis of the interviews identified three broad, yet interrelated themes: a stronger emphasis being placed on personal values when considering career choice; anxiety about the future in an uncertain economy; and deep sadness and frustration with the Brexit result and its impact upon society.

15.3   Brexit: A Wake-up Call for Personal Values?

Amongst the participants, Brexit kindled a strong sense of social purpose: 'It's definitely made me more motivated to try and create a better society' (participant 9), and personal responsibility 'It does like, really solidify your morals' (participant 4). Rather belatedly for some participants who did not vote, the Referendum result showed that 'if nothing else, it does prove that the democratic system works, even if it's not the way a lot of people wanted.' (participant 2) Nearly all the participants were shocked by the result: 'Brexit really woke me up!' (participant 3) and many were prompted to want to 'do something:' 'it's definitely encouraged me to try and get into politics, and try, and I don't know, at least do something. As much as I can.' (participant 9). Brexit has also been a reminder that graduates can be role models for showing tolerance and openness. 'I want to be a teacher, this kind of teacher, because of Brexit,' said participant 1, when referring to how, as a potential future teacher, they could have a strong influence on younger minds, adding—'I'd try and work where maybe there are signs of this kind of division. I'd seek out the problem. I'm not sure if I'd succeed, but I'd at least try.' Another interviewee stated clearly:

> I don't want to be seen as that English person who has these beliefs and values, working in a place where this is all we are, this is England, this is how we'll stay. I'd want to work with people and try and open up the social boundaries. (participant 10)

When considering future plans, participants were determined to do something purposeful: "Maybe before I was just… I want some job. But now it's what can I do? What can I contribute? So, it's probably made me a lot more passionate, but also more serious about it." (participant 7). Career decisions and a general sense of purpose were directly attributed to Brexit;' "I would say there's a massive line, a direct comparison, between the EU Referendum and what I want to study now at postgraduate level." (participant 9) Considering their future in the light of social purpose and meaning, these next generation graduates are realizing that they are essentially part of a collective: "You see people working really hard to make this country better, which makes you think that you should do your bit to somehow help." (participant 12) There is an understanding too that meaningful careers require commitment and time: "It's made me realize that you can't just go and do a job, 9-5, earn your money, go home, because that's not how society changes for the better." (participant 4)

15.4 The Emotional Impact of Brexit

All the participants agreed that the Brexit campaign and Referendum result had been a negative experience that revealed a divided country that now risked being regarded as unwelcoming by other nations. "I thought we were doing so well, and then people mass supported something I thought we'd overcome. With Trump, and with Brexit…it's just lowered the bar," said participant 4. "I thought we were better. I thought we were a progressive country" added participant 15. "There's a growing intolerance towards diversity and different people, and less compassion than perhaps there used to be." This sentiment, noted by participant 13, typifies the sentiment expressed by many in the study. There was strong concern that the UK is now viewed as regressive and isolated:

Not that I would argue that everyone's a racist, or that everyone's intolerant, but it definitely does feel like a sort of cultural isolationism going on in the UK. There's some sort of regression going on, an intolerance towards migrants. And I think maybe Brexit didn't create that, but it definitely revealed it. Or maybe legitimized it. (participant 9)

Another observed: "The way we view other people. It's quite closed, I think. Socially, slowly, once you start taking out these people and controlling these people, it gets smaller and smaller and smaller, until you're kind of mediaeval Britain again." (participant 10) For some of the participants, this negative impact on what they consider to be 'their country, their society' means that they no longer wish to live and work in the UK: "The impact it will have on me specifically is that I won't look for work in the UK and I won't continue my studies in the UK." (participant 6). Another confirmed,

I don't want to live in a place where those values aren't existing or they're going backwards. So that's definitely pushed me away. So, I don't think I'll live in England. I would live in England if we stayed in the EU. (participant 9)

Anger and frustration were palpable in the interviews:

Brexit, and then the Trump vote, and then the last General Election, it just seems to be cascading massive amounts of civil unrest, where it's 'do I really want to be in a state where I can see things potentially collapsing?' It begs the question, is this a state that I want to reside in? Or pay taxes into anymore, when it can't do its main purpose of keeping civil unrest as low as possible. It's certainly a consequence of the political climate we're in. (participant 7)

There was contempt for politicians: "they're all greedy, horrible people" (participant 4), and some expressed a lack of respect for the Government: "They don't strike me as the most competent of people. It feels like I'm watching some sort of mockumentary." (participant 14) The interviews revealed a lack of trust in politicians, also: "Both sides lie. They just make it up and try to say the right thing" (participant 5), with one participant asking: "I wonder what it might mean for society, if we don't trust the people who are running our country?" (participant 1). It was clear from these research interviews that Brexit has had a negative emotional impact for some: "It makes me upset because I feel excluded a little bit from society." (participant 6) "It's just a world I don't want to have to live in because it seems to be going back, you know, five steps." (participant 3). When referring to the day of the Referendum result, the emotional impact was vivid: "It's almost like in a kid's cartoon where they live in a happy colorful world and then it's suddenly all gone black and white and cold and scary." (participant 11).

Undoubtedly, some people cope better with uncertainty than others, but what has become evident in recent times is the increasing numbers of students and young people reporting mental health issues (Universities UK, 2018). It is clear from this research study that Brexit is potentially having an impact on the emotional wellbeing of some of these individuals.

15.5   The Importance of Career Adaptability and Emotional Resilience

There were mixed emotions amongst the participants when they talked about their futures and about the impact of Brexit. Some were pessimistic—"It's all like 'is everything going to go wrong now?' That sort of sensation." (participant 4). Some were anxious:

> This world that I'm going to be an adult in, that I'm going to be working in, that I'm going to be bringing my own children into, is it going to be a very secure one? I was nervous, I must say. (participant 11)

Higher levels of anxiety were expressed when talking specifically about job prospects:

> I think it's made people a bit more stressed out. There's more confusion and people are getting panicked. I think it's because of the uncertainty. People at university keep going on about it - because it's brought up in the news so often, it's always at the forefront of the discussion of things. (participant 14)

Although it was acknowledged that Brexit "might make finding a job harder" (participant 2), the concern expressed by a few participants was not so much about lack of job opportunities in the UK, but more about restricted opportunities to live and work in Europe:

> I never really thought about it, but then as soon as the door was closed off, it was almost noticeable that I had that opportunity, I had some bridge into Europe. Now a lot of those doors have been closed off. (participant 1)

"Nobody really knows what's going to happen" (participant 12). This was the feeling of all of the participants. Many believed that there was no point in worrying about it just yet: "I don't worry about things that I don't know about." (participant 3). However, there was an underlying sense of anxiety caused by not knowing: "You don't know what they're doing, so you can't really be worried about the implications of what they are doing. They don't seem to know. That's more unnerving than worrying about something concrete, isn't it?" (participant 15). Perhaps out of self-preservation, some preferred not to think about it just yet—"I feel that if I worry about it now, I'll be completely stressed out." (participant 14)

A few recognized that adaptability and a positive mind-set will be needed: It's about being adaptable and, to use an environmental word, *resilient* to the change." (participant 8). One related this to their future teaching aspirations:

> It does worry me that I will be trying to prepare children for an uncertain world, but then I suppose on the flip side you just have to teach them to cope with unexpected challenges and not see these as massive obstacles. I think you've just got to teach them to be resilient. (participant 11)

This sentiment was echoed more simply by participant 10—"Things change, people change. The world is ever changing." Surprisingly perhaps, there was some optimism: "Jobs are out there, and they are jobs where an impact can be made." (participant 8). This was coupled with a belief that it will all work out somehow: "There will be impacts that are positive. We may not know what they are yet." (participant 7). "It's all too easy to see the negative side of things, but there are positive outcomes somewhere." (participant 13). Perhaps more matter-of-factly, one added that: "The world is still going to need teachers and childcare workers. That's not going to go away because we've left the EU." (participant 11) Towards the end of the interviews, a few of the participants were even sounding quite hopeful about the personal impact of Brexit—"Martin Lewis, the money-saving expert guy, he predicts that in the long term, we might be better off" (participant 13). "Maybe it's time for a change?" asked participant 5.

15.6 All Graduates Are Equal, but Perhaps Some Are More Equal Than Others

Although one cannot predict the impact of Brexit, equality of opportunity and social mobility do help individuals make favourable career decisions in times of uncertainty. However, serious challenges in respect of inequality and social mobility do exist within the UK and will continue to do so after the UK leaves the EU. Furthermore, it is feared that inequality and social mobility may deepen further, as Brexit will likely "skew spending priorities" and those public services already hit by austerity measures will find themselves competing with powerful lobbies from other sectors looking to replace lost European Union resources (Helm, 2017). If the next generation of graduates are hoping to successfully find their way in the world, then they will need to navigate and challenge inequalities.

And yet the playing field of graduate employment is a far from level one. Some graduates will have the social capital and financial means to still access their preferred career options. Others will need to be more independent. Unless access to opportunities is fair and open to all, then those more independent graduates may well fall behind from the very start. And what does this mean for graduates from post-1992 universities, where there is a higher proportion of students from 'widening participation' backgrounds? Will these graduates be less well placed to succeed in an uncertain, more competitive post-Brexit world, where inequality already exists, and social mobility has perhaps become a "postcode lottery?" (Social Mobility Commission, 2017).

15.7 How Can Careers Guidance Support Our Next Generation of Graduates?

If the findings from this study can be considered as potentially reflective of other students from other UK universities, particularly the post-1992 universities, then arguably there could be interesting times ahead for the careers guidance practitioner. If we know that some of our students are looking more critically at the (post-Brexit) world around them and are wanting to have a career, indeed, a future, that 'has meaning' (and is part of a momentum to help create a more tolerant society) then this opens up the opportunity for practitioners to revisit their practice and engage in much more challenging 'careers conversations.' We could spend much more time exploring personal values and how these relate to potential career choices, including the issue of how to best manage the emotional impacts of trying to plan and make career decisions in a world that seems to be constantly changing. As wider access to graduate opportunities remains variable at best, then practitioners could engage with a more socio-political ideological basis of careers guidance, to find out and discuss how our students would like the world of work to be.

Although practitioners "may feel unsure about adopting a political position and concerned about the ethics of passing on their own beliefs to clients" (Hooley, 2015, p. 14), the current climate means that the time feels right to transition towards a model of guidance that actively recognises the importance of context in career decision-making processes, in a world that regularly experiences economic and political uncertainty. To date, career guidance theory and practice has tended to promote an individualistic approach to career decision-making. In higher education, the drive to achieve 'positive graduate outcomes' has, arguably, resulted in an approach that is largely about "recruitability" (Grey, 2018), and favours those who are emotionally tough enough to 'win' in the arena of graduate competition for scarce jobs. Despite widening participation initiatives by many universities to facilitate greater access (to opportunities that boost the chances of attaining a 'positive graduate outcome'), inequalities in the labour market remain largely unchallenged and careers guidance practice has largely shied away from engaging directly with this socio-political context.

15.8 Conclusion

There is an inter-relationship to be explored further here. Practitioners could locate their work within a context that encourages their clients to view their career aspirations as part of a wider drive i.e. to create the type of society that they wish to live and work in. Therefore, a more progressive approach to careers guidance is needed, if we wish to have more challenging 'career conversations.' Such an approach remains partly psychological and individual (e.g. *who am I? what motivates me? what do I want to achieve in life?*) but also includes a sociological dimension (e.g. *what sort of society do I want to live in? what do I want to change? can I be a part of that change?).* Admittedly, not every student will want to 'change the world.' However, many graduates will be seeking the sort of life that fits with their values and aspirations. To do this, they will need to be adaptable and emotionally resilient in a potentially quite tough post-Brexit economy. They will perhaps have to be less worried by changes and unforeseen events, and more able to accommodate, even embrace, new and shifting realities. As careers practitioners, we should consider leading by example, so that we adapt and shift our practice to accommodate the changing needs of our clients, and so that we can embrace these more challenging, yet interesting, 'career conversations.'

As one student observed, "Brexit really woke me up!" Perhaps Brexit is also the wake-up call for career guidance practice. If it is down to the next generation of graduates to take up the challenge of helping to create a more tolerant and just society, then as practitioners we too need to be prepared to play our part.

References

BBC News. (2018, February 8). *Brexit: Official forecasts suggests economies throughout the UK will be hit.* [News release]. Retrieved from http://www.bbc.co.uk/news/uk-politics-42977967.

Grey, M. (2018, January 16). *Has employability become a toxic brand?* [Blog post]. Retrieved from https://wonkhe.com/blogs/has-employability-become-a-toxic-brand/.

Helm, T. (2017, April 9). Crisis looms for social policy agenda as Brexit preoccupies Whitehall. *The Guardian.* Retrieved from https://www.theguardian.com/global/2017/apr/09/focus-brexit-obliterates-social-policy-agenda.

High Fliers Research Limited. (2017, July 12). *New research shows fewer graduates from the 'Class of 2017' want to work for the City's top investment banks because of Brexit job fears.* [Press release]. Retrieved from https://www.highfliers.co.uk/download/2017/uk_graduate_careers_survey/Release2017.pdf.

Hooley, T. (2015, September 17). *Emancipate yourselves from mental slavery: Self-actualisation, social justice and the politics of career guidance.* Retrieved from http://derby.openrepository.com/derby/bitstream/10545/579895/1/Hooley+-+Emancipate+Yourselves+from+Mental+Slavery.pdf.

Institute for Employment Studies. (2017). *Brexit observatory: Labour market.* Retrieved from http://www.employment-studies.co.uk/brexit-impact-workforce/brexit-observatory-labour-market.

Moore, P. (2016, June 27). *How Britain voted.* Retrieved from https://yougov.co.uk/news/2016/06/27/how-britain-voted/.

Recruitment International. (2017, February 16). *Graduate talent pool to get shallower as a third of UK international students reconsider staying and working in the UK.* Retrieved from https://www.recruitment-international.co.uk/blog/2017/02/graduate-talent-pool-to-get-shallower-as-a-third-of-uk-international-students-reconsider-staying-and-working-in-uk.amp.

Social Mobility Commission. (2017, November). *State of the nation 2017.* Retrieved from https://assets.publishing.service.gov.uk/government/uploads/system/uploads/attachment_data/file/662744/State_of_the_Nation_2017_-_Social_Mobility_in_Great_Britain.pdf.

Universities UK. (2018). *Minding our future.* Retrieved from https://www.universitiesuk.ac.uk/policy-and-analysis/reports/Documents/2018/minding-our-future-starting-conversation-student-mental-health.pdf.

Theresa Thomson is a Careers Consultant and Associate Fellow of the Higher Education Academy. She is involved in Employability and Enterprise, and Student Success Services at the University of the West of England, Bristol, England. She is a qualified, experienced careers guidance practitioner and researcher, a full member of the Career Development Institute, and a registered Career Development Professional. She is currently researching the impacts of Brexit upon the career aspirations of undergraduate students.

Chapter 16
Assessment Strategy: Enhancement of Student Learning Through a Programme Focus

Ruth Whitfield and Peter Hartley

16.1 Introduction

This chapter argues that the most effective strategy to enhance the student learning experience and achieve substantial learning gain (alongside other benefits) is to focus on programme-level rather than module level assessment, i.e. programme-focused assessment (PFA). After identifying significant issues affecting assessment in Higher Education (HE), it looks to the main principles of PFA from the PASS project,[1] offering discussion of key, related perspectives, such as work on the 'assessment environment' (which emerged from the Transforming the Experience of Students Through Assessment (TESTA) project),[2] before reviewing differing approaches which have been adopted, identifying their impact, and discussing major implications for any programme or institution considering possible implementation.

---

[1]Our definition of programme-focussed assessment (PFA) is drawn from our work on the PASS project, at Bradford University: See further http://www.bradford.ac.uk/pass/ (date accessed 18.7.19).

[2]See further https://www.testa.ac.uk/ (date accessed 18.7.19). The TESTA project was funded by the UK's Higher Education Academy (HEA) as a National Teaching Fellowship Group Project in parallel with the PASS (Programme Assessment Strategies) project (https://www.bradford.ac.uk/pass/ accessed 18.7.19).

R. Whitfield (✉)
University of Bradford, Bradford, UK
e-mail: r.whitfield@bradford.ac.uk

P. Hartley
Edge Hill University, Ormskirk, UK
e-mail: profpeter@btinternet.com

© Springer Nature Switzerland AG 2019
A. Diver (ed.), *Employability via Higher Education: Sustainability as Scholarship*,
https://doi.org/10.1007/978-3-030-26342-3_16

16.2   Why Worry About Assessment?

The central argument of this chapter is that assessment processes are often key to the realisation of important outcomes for students, including learning gain. This is so, whether one interprets such gain as the acquisition of very specific subject or discipline-based skills and understanding, or whether it is taken to mean broader, more generic, capabilities. General questions and complexities on the concept of learning gain have recently seen considerable debate after the round of projects sponsored by the UK's HE funding council.[3] Reviewing and revising assessment practices is a fundamental step however in improving students' learning, whatever the focus or scope of that learning might be. And yet, despite their importance, assessment processes continue to present major challenges for most if not all HE institutions. In the UK, this can be illustrated by the prominence of assessment as a critical issue within successive generations of the National Student Survey (NSS). In 2017, the summary of results suggested that student satisfaction with assessment had 'increased markedly.' However, the level of student satisfaction was still clearly below the levels that attached to most of the other main factors.[4] In the 2018 results, the level of overall student satisfaction with assessment had decreased slightly, although it did increase in relation to part-time HE students.[5] As the number of part-time students enrolled in HE within the UK has decreased significantly over the last few years, it can be safely concluded that assessment is still a major issue for many students. And there is no sign of an immediate or easy resolution.

Assessment has also re-emerged as a regular focus for public concern and debate, as illustrated by current media and press reports of apparent 'grade inflation.'[6] There has certainly been a significant increase in the number of 'good' degrees awarded by universities across the UK, and this is true across all subject areas. The contentious question is how we might best explain this change. The predominant explanation (which has been repeated regularly in the media) is that universities are simply responding to market pressures by lowering their standards. These reports almost invariably ignore more positive factors such as the increased resources now available to students both through their institution and more generally (e.g. via the internet and

---

[3]For a useful review of outcomes from the UK's Learning Gain projects see further: https://wonkhe.com/blogs/something-ventured-something-gained (date accessed 31.01.18). The evaluation report on the learning gain projects has now been published by OfS: https://www.officeforstudents.org.uk/publications/lg-pilot-projects-evaluation/ (date accessed 18.7.19).

[4]See further http://www.hefce.ac.uk/lt/nss/ (date accessed 18.7.19).

[5]See further https://www.officeforstudents.org.uk/advice-and-guidance/student-information-and-data/national-student-survey-nss/ (date accessed 18.7.19).

[6]There have been media reports on apparent 'grade inflation' issue every year, for at least the past 5 years. These reports can be found in all sectors of the UK press (and the negative language of 'falling standards' is often very similar) as the following tabloid and broadsheet headlines illustrate: http://www.dailymail.co.uk/news/article-2456254/Dozens-British-degree-courses-single-student-getting-grades.html;   http://www.telegraph.co.uk/education/2017/01/12/one-four-students-now-obtain-first-class-degrees-employers-voice/ (date accessed 18.7.19).

academic databases) or the increasing professionalisation of lecturers via formal certification, such as the Fellowship awards from the Higher Education Academy—now AdvanceHE—which are themselves based upon the UK's Professional Standards Framework (UKPSF)[7] or the Staff Educational Development Association (SEDA) Professional Development Framework (SEDA-PDF) scheme.[8]

Whatever the full explanation of the improvement in grades, UK HEIs will have to produce more detailed explanations of future improvements in student performance in order to comply with new rules introduced by the OfS in 2018.[9] In terms of specific issues which seem to be affecting the quality of assessment in HE, useful starting points are to be found in the 'issues paper' produced by the PASS project (2010) and the subsequent findings of Rust (2017). Table 16.1, compares the issues identified in these two studies.

These two lists suggest that the issues identified in 2010 are still current, e.g. on the coherence of HE programmes (or rather, the lack of coherence, at times) as perceived by both students and staff. They also share the rather pessimistic view that although programme outcomes may be fully described in programme documents, this might not translate fully into the wide range of assessments which students must actually confront. The original PASS list has been used for nearly a decade in both seminars and workshops: the fact that the issues are still readily recognized and

Table 16.1 Assessment issues in higher education

Issue identified by PASS issues paper	Issues identified by Rust (2017)
Failure to ensure the assessment of the espoused programme outcomes	Y
Atomisation of assessment	
Students and staff failing to see the links/coherence of the programme	Y
Modules are too short to focus and provide feedback on slowly learnt literacies and/or complex learning	Y
Students and staff adopting a 'tick-box' mentality, focused on marks, engendering a surface approach to learning that can 'encourage' plagiarism and 'game-playing'	Y
Inappropriate 'one-size-fits-all'	N
Over-standardisation in regulations	N
Too much summative assessment, leading to overworked staff, not enough formative assessment and inability to 'see the wood for the trees' in the accumulated results	Y

---

[7]On the UKPSF see https://www.heacademy.ac.uk/ukpsf (date accessed 18.7.19).

[8]See further https://www.seda.ac.uk/pdf (date accessed 18.7.19).

[9]For a useful short article on some of the recent changes and issues, see: https://www.universitiesuk.ac.uk/blog/Pages/Managing-grade-inflation-and-demonstrating-student-improvement.aspx (date accessed 31.10.18); The Office for Students (OfS) is also developing its own responses: https://www.officeforstudents.org.uk/news-blog-and-events/press-and-media/ofs-response-to-reform-grade-inflation-report/ (date accessed 31.10.18).

agreed by participants in current sessions is rather depressing. If these issues are commonplace, it may well be because HE has adopted broadly similar structures across its institutions and disciplines.

UK HE 'converted' from a largely course-based system to one based on modules and 'semesterisation' in the 1990s, to reflect a growing commitment to the system known as CATS (i.e. the Credit Accumulation and Transfer Scheme). It was believed that the accumulation of credits through modules (as defined by specific credit points and at specific levels) would provide the flexibility to best enable students to build the courses they needed for their future careers (e.g. by transfer between institutions and/or courses). The CATS scheme offered a standard approach 'based on the achievement of learning outcomes and a notional ten hours of learning per credit' with surveys in 2009 and 2012 respectively suggesting that 'over 90% of higher education institutions recognise and award credits.' (Souto-Otero, 2013: 22). Whilst the majority of UK HE providers have moved to awarding credit based on CATS, it is questionable whether many students have taken full advantage of this flexibility. Issues such as lack of perceived coherence and atomized assessment seem to be particularly associated with very defined modular systems.

The adoption of modular systems has enabled more complex course and programme structures, with the terminology being used rather differently within different institutions. For simplicity's sake the term 'programmes' will be used for the rest of this chapter, to include both courses and programmes. The key point is that all assessment should be considered from the perspective of determining just how any given assessment contributes to the whole student experience rather than just the specific component of that course where it has appeared. Of course, these issues are all unintended consequences of the way in which we have organised our HE assessment systems: we may be able to gain some insights into unintended consequences in other relevant contexts. Having reviewed studies of performance management systems in organisations, there appear to be 'five salient dysfunctional unintended consequences.' These include 'game-playing', information manipulation, selective attention (where managers become 'fixated' on formal/quantified performance measures), negative changes in social relationships, and an 'illusion of control' whereby managers come to believe that the performance management systems 'accurately and validly reflect 'actual' performance' (Franco-Santos & Otley, 2018). This model suggests further that management tend to design their performance management systems based on 'two key assumptions' about their employees and the organisational context: goal-alignment and goal-uncertainty. We suggest that this model can also be usefully applied to the adoption and implementation of specific assessment frameworks in higher education. Whilst the focus here is on approaches to assessment which very deliberately adopt a programme focus, there are a number of other issues, frameworks, and methods which are also worth considering first, not least the following unresolved issues.

16.3   Unresolved Issues?

16.3.1   Assessment Traditions

It is worth asking where our assessment traditions have come from, and indeed how (and when) they first originated. There may be practices which are so longstanding that we simply fail to ask whether they are they still fit for purpose. Some aspects of current practice seem to be both 'taken for granted' and poorly understood in terms of their origins and rationale. The standard system of undergraduate degree awards (First class honours, Second class honours, higher and lower division, Third class honours, etc.) dates from 1918 in terms of its common usage (Winter, 1994).[10] Can we still rely on a system which is over 100 years old to reflect current social needs and demands? This is not just a problem of historical uncertainty or lack of knowledge, as suggested by Wilbrink (1995) and in his later article (1997):

> The university is one of the oldest institutions in western society. The same mechanisms behind this longevity of the university might have resulted in our copying old and even medieval forms of instruction and assessment unwittingly. ... (we may) have inherited from the past more than we knew, and more than we wish.

16.3.2   Averaging and Grading

Todd Rose makes a compelling argument that 'two ideas serve as the organising principles behind our current system of education,' namely, that 'the average is a reliable index of normality' and that 'an individual's rank on narrow metrics of achievement can be used to judge their talent' (Rose, 2015: 35). He argues against both these ideas, proposing that 'talent is always jagged.' He uses a range of examples—from physical size to psychological traits—to demonstrate that virtually every important characteristic we may wish to measure will have multiple dimensions. To arrive at meaningful measures, we need to take account of these different dimensions: 'if our goal is to identify and nurture individual excellence ... we will only succeed if we pay attention to the distinct jaggedness of every individual' (Rose, 2015: 91).

16.3.3   The Meaning of Marks

There are longstanding criticisms of marking systems, for example, the percentage scale (Dalziel, 1998; Rust, 2011). Rust suggests three fundamental problems: we often apply statistical processes to marks in ways that are 'simply bad practice';

---

[10]An online copy of this report is available at http://files.eric.ed.gov/fulltext/ED394412.pdf (date accessed 18.7.19).

that 'these grading practices actually block teachers from evaluating their students' learning' and that 'the use of numbers in assessment can skew learning in negative ways' (2011: 1). These issues can be further compounded by the differences between HE institutions, for example in the way that they process marks to reach a final decision on students' overall performance. In other words, not all marks are necessarily counted in the final aggregate, while different years or levels of the programme may be weighted differently. There may also be specific rules which determine the overall grade, such as the weighting or importance of the final project or dissertation.

16.3.4 Other Emergent Issues

If assessment of students is designed to prepare them for the demands of their future professional lives then it is necessary to consider the likely impact of broader social, political, and technological changes. For example, a recent survey suggests that 'only 41% of students feel prepared for the digital workplace' (Jisc, 2018) whereas others suggest that the workplace of the future will be transformed by developments in artificial intelligence (AI) and robotics and that education needs to respond to this (Aoun, 2017). Such developments strengthen the case for PFA: students clearly need to demonstrate more sophisticated levels of self-awareness and autonomy, which will in turn equip them for an increasingly uncertain future.

16.4 Introducing Programme-Focused Assessments

Every HE programme confronts the issue of designing an effective, efficient, inclusive and sustainable assessment strategy, which can both deliver key programme outcomes and minimise problems relating to academic integrity and plagiarism.[11] However, it is argued that broad strategic perspectives can easily be neglected in programme planning especially given the ever-increasing pressures on academic staff and programme teams. This can result in rather 'weak' or limited assessment strategies in programme documents. To improve student learning and achieve substantial learning gain, programmes need more substantial and evidence-based assessment strategies. A number of frameworks are now available which can help us to develop and implement more programmatic approaches to assessment.

---

[11] http://www.bradford.ac.uk/pass/ (date accessed 30.11.18).

16.4.1 Sustainable Assessment

Boud's (2000) notion of 'sustainable assessment' was revisited in 2015, using the following definition:

> …an assessment that meets the needs of the present in terms of the demands of formative and summative assessment, but which also prepares students to meet their own future learning needs. (Boud & Soler, 2015: 400)

Clearly, 'informed judgement' is fundamental to this approach (Boud & Falchikov, 2007). 'Key elements' of informed judgement from the student's perspective include 'identifying oneself as an active learner' and 'practising testing and judging' (Boud & Soler, 2015: 402).[12] This approach and more recent work on 'evaluative judgement' (Boud et al., 2018) is fully compatible with the notions of programme assessment discussed below.

16.4.2 Learning-Orientated Assessment

Carless (2015) suggests a learning-oriented assessment framework which proposes 'the interplay of … three elements which impacts significantly on the kind of learning which students derive from assessment processes.' The three elements are 'learning oriented assessment tasks', 'developing evaluative expertise', and 'student engagement with feedback'. (2015: 6) Again this framework can sit very comfortably within a programme assessment approach (Carless et al., 2017).

16.4.3 Assessment Literacy

There is now a significant body of work on the concept of 'assessment literacy.' Especially influential in the UK was the work of Price et al. (2012) which proposed that 'being assessment literate equips one with an appreciation of the purpose and processes of assessment, which enables one to engage deeply with assessment standards' (2012: 10) not least in terms of choosing and using appropriate skills. They conclude that 'assessment only at the module level is far from ideal' and recommend moving towards a 'programme-level assessment strategy' (2012: 48). They suggest that this involves detailed consideration of three main 'decision points,' namely: deciding whether the strategy is best achieved through integrative assessments or by detailed mapping of outcomes, or by some combination of these; deciding on resource allocation; and deciding on the appropriate balance between formative and summative assessment.

---

[12]See further https://www.uts.edu.au/research-and-teaching/learning-and-teaching/assessment-futures/overview (date accessed 18.7.19).

16.5 Frameworks and Concepts Aimed Specifically at Programme Level Assessments

16.5.1 HEA/AdvanceHE Assessment Frameworks

In 'A Marked Improvement: Transforming Assessment in Higher Education' (2012)[13] (termed a 'manifesto for change,' and a 'review tool') the Higher Education Academy (HEA) encouraged HEIs to review and revise their assessment policies and practices. This manifesto was organised into 6 fundamental tenets, including 'Assessment for Learning', and 'Integrating assessment literacy into course design.' The most recent update of this framework includes a new diagram based on three areas of focus: innovative assessment, feedback practices, and self and peer assessment. These are underpinned by the six interconnected tenets to 'provide a stimulus for dialogue to build a shared understanding of how assessment can be transformed.'[14]

16.5.2 EAT Framework

Evans (2016) has conducted a substantial review of the literature relating to assessment and feedback to draft a framework focusing upon three dimensions of practice: assessment literacy, assessment feedback, and assessment design. For the latter, she asserts that 'a programme level assessment approach is useful to fully consider the learning journey of the student and to critically review what we need to assess and how.'

16.5.3 The PASS Project

The PASS project was an NTFS Group Project led by the University of Bradford in partnership with colleagues from other universities similarly interested in assessment strategies, and two Centres for Excellence in Teaching and Learning (CETLs) which focused on assessment.[15] The project aimed firstly to define programme-focused assessment (PFA) and then provide examples and guidance to help other institutions moving in this direction. We defined PFA as:

---

[13] See https://www.heacademy.ac.uk/system/files/a_marked_improvement.pdf (accessed 18.7.19).

[14] https://www.heacademy.ac.uk/individuals/strategic-priorities/assessment#section-3 (accessed 18.7.19).

[15] Both are now sadly defunct: ASKe (Assessment Standards Knowledge Exchange, at Oxford Brookes University) and AfL (Assessment for Learning, based at Northumbria University).

...assessment (which) is specifically designed to address major programme outcomes rather than very specific or isolated components of the course. It follows then that such assessment is integrative in nature, trying to bring together understanding and skills in ways which represent key programme aims. As a result, the assessment is likely to be more authentic and meaningful to students, staff and external stakeholders.[16]

In sum, there are different degrees of PFA, and these PFAs can be implemented in very different ways. We propose two major dimensions which characterise the differing forms of programme assessment (see Fig. 16.1):

- the extent to which the assessment covers all the specified programme outcomes; and
- the weighting of the assessment in the final qualification.

In a conventional modular structure, an individual module will typically be low on both of these dimensions. As this diagram suggests however, there at least four key types of programme-focused assessment, each with its own variants (as set out in Fig. 16.2).

These four variants represent major increases in the integration and weighting of assessment, culminating in the submission of evidence against outcomes. Significantly, this final top quadrant has recently been identified as an aspiration for the 'Connected Curriculum' at University College London (Fung, 2017).

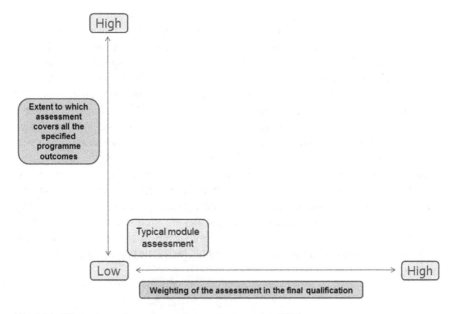

Fig. 16.1 Dimensions of programme-focussed assessment (PFA)

---

[16]www.pass.brad.ac.uk/position-paper.pdf (accessed 18.7.19).

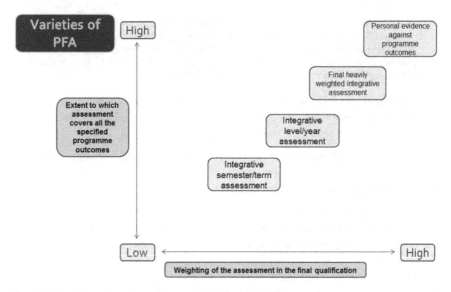

Fig. 16.2 Varieties of programme-focused Assessment (PFA)

16.5.4 Testa

The TESTA project was another NTFS Group Project which ran in parallel with PASS and involved a partnership of 4 English universities, led by the University of Winchester. The project started from a very different perspective, researching eight programmes across the partner universities to define and map their 'assessment environments.' This research was then used to design and evaluate interventions to improve students' assessment experiences. As well as a range of valuable research reports, one very important output of the project was a methodology which has been used (and adapted in some cases) in over 40 UK Universities and in several international contexts (Jessop, 2018; Tomas & Jessop, 2018).[17] As Gibbs and Dunbar-Goddet (2009) have demonstrated previously, there are significant differences between courses in terms of the characteristics which comprise the assessment environment. These characteristics include the volume of formative and summative assessment, the variety of assessment methods, and the volume and types of feedback provided to students. There are still considerable differences between courses and institutions in relation to these characteristics but clearly the balance is also changing (Jessop, 2016).

---

[17]The TESTA website offers a range of resources, including Case Studies and Best Practice Guides, Introduction to main ideas, and methodology. See further: https://www.testa.ac.uk/ (date accessed 18.7.19).

16.6 Key Features of PFA

While there are different varieties of PFA, there are some general characteristics which they share. The most important of these are as follows:

16.6.1 Focus on High-Level Capabilities

Given the integrative nature of PFA, programmes will almost inevitably build assessments which reflect the broader higher-level capabilities needed by students in their future careers. This usually means that the course team has to agree on a relatively small number of essential attributes which will then provide a focus for assessment across the programme. For example, the Peninsula Medical School[18] focussed upon the following three main attributes:

- Applied knowledge of life and human sciences
- Clinical skills
- Personal and professional development.

There is a useful comparison to be made here with some recent developments in the United States, for example the Measuring College Learning project (MCL) (Arum et al., 2016: 15). This work arose from an earlier study which asserted that college learning was having limited impact on student development: the earlier research fuelled public debate and influenced policy-makers who had 'subjected higher education to increasing levels of scrutiny and calls for accountability' (Arum & Roksa, 2011: 2) which is a pattern of behaviour which we in the United Kingdom are only too familiar with. The MCL project aimed to 'put forth disciplinary principles for learning outcomes assessment' emerging from faculty panels in six academic disciplines within a framework of 'core principles' such as '...any single measure of student learning should be a part of a larger holistic assessment plan' (Arum et al., 2016: 8). Each discipline defined 'essential concepts' and 'essential competences': some examples are given in Table 16.2. This approach would be an appropriate starting point for any programme moving towards PFA as noted above.

16.6.2 Innovation in Other Areas of Curriculum and/or Pedagogy

An example of programme assessment which does not involve other significant changes, has yet to be found. Movement towards programmatic assessment inevitably has implications for other aspects of the curriculum and usually means that course

---

[18]https://www.brad.ac.uk/media-v8/site/pass/documents/wp4medschoolcasestudy.pdf (accessed 01.11.18).

Table 16.2 Examples of essential concepts and competencies as defined by MCL (Arum et al., 2016: 21)

Discipline	Essential concepts include	Essential competencies include
Biology	Evolution	Model
	Information Flow	Apply quantitative reasoning
Economics	Individual decision making	Apply the scientific process to economic phenomena
	Markets and other Interactions	Analyse and evaluate behaviours and outcomes using economic concepts and models
History	History as an interpretive account	Evaluate historical accounts
	The relationship of past and present	Interpret primary sources

teams will revise other aspects of their course design. For example, the Peninsula Medical School revised the balance between clinical skills and theoretical study across all years of their programme. The Pharmacy course team at Bradford introduced Team-Based Learning which is now a distinctive feature of their programme.

16.7   PASS and TESTA Revisited—Impact and Influence

Both projects demonstrated the value of programme-focussed approaches and have had a lasting impact on a number of institutions across the UK (Jessop et al., 2014; Whitfield & Hartley, 2017). Arguably, the fundamental ideas behind PFA have become more important whilst some barriers to implementation have clearly increased, e.g. the 'disappearance' of course teams, and the restriction of modular systems (Whitfield & Hartley, 2018). From a follow-up survey in 2016, the authors found evidence of PFA being demonstrated through:

- Stage-based assessments (synoptic exams).
- Integrated assessments at each level of study.
- Cross-modular integrated programme level assessment.

Respondents reported that the impact of PFA on the student experience had 'encouraged students to think 'beyond the module' to how things inter-relate in real practice' and encouraged 'students to bring together different elements of their learning' (Whitfield & Hartley, 2017).

16.7.1   Lasting Impact of Programme Focussed Approaches

The sustained impact of programme-focussed approaches is best demonstrated by two programmes featured in original PASS case studies that have gone on to receive national Collaborative Awards for Teaching Excellence (CATE).[19] The Integrated Programme Assessment team in Biomedical sciences at Brunel University (CATE winners in 2016) reduced student assessment workload by 60% and realised significant increases in their NSS scores, and in student attainment, and graduate level employment rates.[20] The Pharmacy Curriculum Development team at University of Bradford (CATE winners 2017) use team-based learning (TBL) for assessment and learning, and stage-based, self-selected synoptic assignments. Using the PFA principles, they have also developed a 'long-loop' assessment using TBL to ensure that essential learning from stage 1 of the programme is carried over into stage 2.

16.7.2 Advantages of PFA

PFA provides evidence that programme outcomes are being met: students appear to be taking a deeper approach to their learning rather than simply 'learning to the test' and are becoming better equipped to self-assess. "Some skills, literacies, conceptual understandings are 'slowly learnt' and need rehearsal throughout a programme" (Yorke, 2001); the integrative nature of PFA also presents a greater opportunity to develop these aspects.

A further big plus is the potential to reduce and/or provide a more manageable spread of assessment workload for both students and staff. Focusing on the programme helps to also ensure that the variety of assessment does not detract from learning and is 'scaffolded' appropriately throughout the programme. For example, programmes with large written assessment tasks in the final year (such as dissertations for example) should scaffold assessments to develop extended writing skills in earlier years. Whilst variety of choice supports inclusive assessment, too much variety may lead students to focus upon the rules of engagement rather than engage with the learning. Setting those rules of engagement in the first year so that students are able to respond fully to feedback (and refine their skills in subsequent years) will enable greater mastery of that form of assessment by the time they enter their critical final year(s), as Fig. 16.3 sets out.

16.7.3 Barriers?

Five main implications have emerged consistently from PASS and other projects such as TESTA:

---

[19] https://www.heacademy.ac.uk/individuals/national-teaching-fellowship-scheme/CATE (accessed 10.11.18).

[20] See further their Guide to Integrated Programme Assessment, available https://www.brunel.ac.uk/about/awards/integrated-programme-assessment/documents/pdf/IPA-Practical-Guide-0918.pdf (accessed 18.7.19).

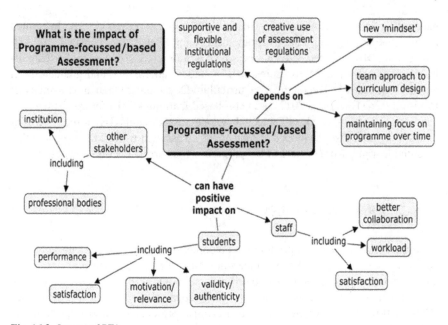

Fig. 16.3 Impact of PFA

1. PFA is not a single-track approach: a holistic approach can be enacted in several different ways.
2. Institutional regulations are critical: the inflexibility of institutional regulations was the most commonly cited barrier to realization. Limitations from professional bodies were also cited. However, certain professional bodies have not only welcomed but commended innovative approaches, for example in the case of University of Bradford's Pharmacy programme. That said, some other professional bodies may not be quite so welcoming.
3. The importance of the programme team cannot be overlooked: in every instance where PFA has been effective, there was evidence of a strong and cohesive team.
4. PFA is not a 'quick fix.' It is a long-term strategy which needs careful planning and should be given the necessary incubation time and space.
5. PFA always has implications for other systems. For example, the implementation of PFA, however modest, is likely to have impact upon and implications for the following:

   - Student induction—particularly for those with previous experience of 'traditional' modular systems.
   - Staff development—some staff may have never taught within anything other than a modular system where module leaders are often autonomous.
   - Timetabling—moving away from a modular approach will often affect a programme's scheduling.

16.8   Conclusion: Looking to the Future

The last few years have seen a significant growth of interest in PFA, with an increasing number of requests for keynote talks and workshops, with new examples of case studies emerging constantly. Some universities have clearly identified PFA as a direction for future development, with others highlighting PASS as a key methodology[21]: '[a] programme level view potentially opens up more possibilities for innovative teaching approaches to enhance the student learning experience.' Such a growth of interest and new initiatives will hopefully be accompanied by further (and more systematic) research and evaluation. Another issue which these developments should help resolve is the question of whether PFA is better suited to courses and programmes which offer a route towards a specific vocational or professional career (such as Pharmacy or Biomedical Sciences). The authors have often been questioned in workshops about the value of PFA to less specifically targeted programmes (e.g. in Social Sciences or Humanities). In response to this it might be argued that the process of revising an assessment strategy based on a specification of high-level programme outcomes should be applicable to any subject area. In fairness, the current evidence in its favour tends to be limited to more scientific areas.

Whatever the final outcome of a PFA initiative, the process will almost inevitably lead to increased dialogues across programme teams and between staff and students. Given what we know about the value of dialogue in other areas of assessment (such as in the development of enhanced assessment literacies), it seems likely that the quality of such dialogue may be the most important factor in delivering improvements to assessment strategies and consequent student performance.

References

Aoun, R. E. (2017). *Robot-proof: Higher education in the age of artificial intelligence.* MIT Press.

Arum, R., & Roksa, J. (2011). *Academically adrift: limited learning on college campuses.* Chicago: University of Chicago Press.

Arum, R., Roksa, J., & Cook, A. (2016). *Improving quality in American higher education.* Jossey-Bass.

Boud, D. (2000). Sustainable assessment: Rethinking assessment for the learning society. *Studies in Continuing Education, 22*(2), 151–167.

Boud, D., Ajjawi, R., Dawson, P., & Tai, J. (Eds.). (2018). *Developing evaluative judgement in higher education: Assessment for knowing and producing quality work.* London: Routledge.

Boud, D., & Falchikov, N. (2007). Developing assessment for informing judgement. In D. Boud & N. Falchikov (Eds.), *Rethinking assessment for higher education: Learning for the longer term, 181–197.* London: Routledge.

---

[21] See information from University of Sheffield at https://www.sheffield.ac.uk/apse/conference/archive/2018/intro (accessed 18.7.19).

Boud, D., & Soler, R. (2015). Sustainable assessment revisited. *Assessment and Evaluation in Higher Education, 41*(3), 400–413.

Carless, D. (2015). *Excellence in university assessment: Learning from award-winning practice.* London: Routledge.

Carless, D., et al. (Eds.). (2017). *Scaling up assessment for learning in higher education.* New York: Springer.

Dalziel, J. (1998). Using marks to assess student performance: Some problems and alternatives. *Assessment and Evaluation in Higher Education, 23*(4), 351–366.

Evans, C. (2016). *Enhancing assessment feedback practice in higher education: The EAT framework.* Available at: https://www.srhe.ac.uk/downloads/events/280_EAT_Guide_CE.pdf (accessed 18.7.19).

Franco-Santos, M., & Otley, D. (2018). Reviewing and theorizing the unintended consequences of performance management systems. *International Journal of Management Reviews, 20*, 696–730. Available at: https://onlinelibrary.wiley.com/doi/epdf/10.1111/ijmr.12183 (accessed 18.7.19).

Fung, D. (2017). *A connected curriculum for higher education.* UCL Press. Available at: http://www.ucl.ac.uk/ucl-press/browse-books/a-connected-curriculum-for-higher-education (accessed 18.7.19).

Gibbs, G., & Dunbar-Godde, H. (2009). Characterising programme-level assessment environments that support learning. *Assessment & Evaluation in Higher Education, 34*(4), 481–489.

Jessop, T. (2016). Changing the culture of assessment and feedback through TESTA. In *Keynote to SEDA Spring Conference.* Available at: https://www.slideshare.net/Tansy1962/testa-seda-keynote-spring-2016.

Jessop, T., El Hakim, Y., & Gibbs, G. (2014). TESTA: A way of thinking about assessment and feedback. *Educational Developments, 14,* 3.

Jessop, T., Hughes, G. (2018). Beyond winners and losers in assessment. In *Teaching in higher education: Perspectives from UCL.* London: UCL Press.

Jisc. (2018). Digital experience insights survey 2018: Findings from students in UK further and higher education. Available online at http://repository.jisc.ac.uk/6967/1/Digital_experience_insights_survey_2018.pdf.

Price, M., Rust, C., O'Donovan, B., Handley, K., & Bryant, R. (2012). *Assessment literacy, the foundation for improving student learning.* Oxford: OCLSD.

Rose, T. (2015). *The end of average: How to succeed in a world that values sameness.* Harmondsworth: Penguin.

Rust, C. (2011). The unscholarly use of numbers in our assessment practices; what will make us change? *International Journal for the Scholarship of Teaching and Learning, 5*(1), January 2011.

Rust, C. (2017). Re-thinking assessment—a programme leader's guide. In E. Leinenon & R. Lawson (Eds.), *Advance copy of chapter to be published in designing undergraduate curriculum* (Available http://ocsld.brookesblogs.net/2017/12/22/re-thinking-assessment-a-programme-leaders-guide/) (accessed 18.7.19).

Souto-Otero, M. (2013). *Review of credit accumulation and transfer policy and practice in UK Higher Education.* Higher Education Academy.

Tomas, C., & Jessop, T. (2018). Struggling and juggling; a comparison of assessment loads in research and teaching-intensive universities. *Assessment and Evaluation in Higher Education.*

Whitfield, R., & Hartley, P. (2017). Whatever happened to programme assessment strategies? *SEDA Educational Developments, 18,* 1.

Wilbrink, B. (1995). *What its historical roots tell us about assessment in higher education today.* Paper to 6th European Conference for Research on Learning and Instruction, Nijmegen.

Wilbrink, B. (1997). Assessment in historical perspective. *Studies in Educational Evaluation, 23,* 31–48.

Winter, R. (Ed.). (1994). *The future of the classified honours degree* Chelmsford, London: Anglia Polytechnic University & the Society for Research into Higher Education.

Yorke, M. (2001). Formative assessment and its relevance to retention. *Higher Education Research and Development, 20*(2), 115–126.

Ruth Whitfield is Senior Educational Developer at the University of Bradford, leading the team responsible for institutional implementation and operation of key educational enhancement initiatives, including technology enhanced learning. She has received institutional recognition for her teaching experience and outstanding contributions to teaching excellence (the University's Baroness Lockwood Award and Vice-Chancellor's Award for Outstanding Achievement) and has developed a national reputation for her management of educational projects e.g. exploration of student transitions in, through and out of HE (DevelopMe and Outduction) and development of programme-focussed assessment through the PASS project which is continuing to influence institutional strategies and practice across the UK. She has recently focused on enhancing the student learning experience by supporting programme leaders in designing and implementing programme-focused assessment. Her most recent publication (with Peter Hartley) is '*Assessment challenges for programme leaders—making the move to programme-focussed assessment*' in Lawrence and Ellis (eds) Supporting programme leaders and programme leadership (2018).

Peter Hartley (NTF) is a HE Consultant, and Visiting Professor at Edge Hill University, following previous roles as Professor of Education Development at Bradford University and Professor of Communication at Sheffield Hallam University, England. A National Teaching Fellow since 2000, he has promoted new technology in education, including the development of award-winning software, led influential development projects for HEA and Jisc and was involved in national initiatives (e.g. CETLs) on a wide range of themes, including institutional online and assessment strategies. His consultancy work includes coaching/CPD initiatives, and institutional strategies for learning spaces and assessment, usually on concepts and approaches tied to the PASS project. Current interests include concept-mapping and visual thinking, and developments in human communication and online interactions. Recent publications include two co-authored chapters in *Advancing Practice in Educational Development* (in Baume and Popovic, 2016).

Chapter 17
Authentic Assessment as a Tool to Bridge the Transition Between Learning and Work

Robyn Davidson, Catherine Snelling, Sophie Karanicolas, Tania Crotti and Braden Phillips

17.1 Introduction

Work Integrated Learning has become a fundamental feature of university courses responding to contemporary workforce demands for flexible and adaptable graduates. It also fulfils the requirements of a Higher Education environment that is becoming increasingly regulated with regards to monitoring and measurement of standards and outcomes (Bosco & Ferns, 2014). For this reason, most university graduate attributes facilitate the link between the workplace and the learning environment (Hill & Walkington, 2016), as well as being a means to evaluate the success and outcomes of each program of study. Graduate attributes commonly include generic skills such as metacognition, critical thinking, self-reflection and self-regulation. Graduates must also have attained discipline specific content that is transferable to a wide range of contexts, with the resilience and adaptability that is critical for survival in these new workplace cultures. Traditionally, assessment focused on discipline-specific content but how this is aligned with the generic skills universities and employers wish graduates to have attained is not always addressed.

R. Davidson (✉) · C. Snelling · S. Karanicolas · T. Crotti · B. Phillips
University of Adelaide, Adelaide, Australia
e-mail: robyn.davidson@adelaide.edu.au

C. Snelling
e-mail: catherine.snelling@adelaide.edu.au

S. Karanicolas
e-mail: sophie.karanicolas@adelaide.edu.au

T. Crotti
e-mail: tania.crotti@adelaide.edu.au

B. Phillips
e-mail: braden.phillips@adelaide.edu.au

© Springer Nature Switzerland AG 2019
A. Diver (ed.), *Employability via Higher Education: Sustainability as Scholarship*,
https://doi.org/10.1007/978-3-030-26342-3_17

Authentic assessment plays a critical role in ensuring that graduates can easily transition from the learning environment to the workplace, whilst learning in a nurturing environment. However, assessment has been traditionally used as the definitive measurement of student learning, rather than being an integral part of the learning process. *Authentic* assessment enables students to develop skills beyond the mere acquisition of discipline knowledge as they 'perform real-world tasks that demonstrate a meaningful application of essential knowledge and skills' (Mueller, 2017). This process should be considered as key to developing graduates who can assimilate into professional practice with relative ease. Authentic assessment must constructively align to mindfully scaffold course design that integrates real-world applications into all aspects of the learning process. This approach to learning provides students with a training ground where they can explore real world tasks in a collaborative and reflective manner, produce creative solutions, and practice the application of knowledge in a low-stakes environment. Because of this learning approach, students steadily develop the confidence to undertake more high-stakes assessment tasks. Authentic assessment has explicit and clear performance criteria that are aligned to explicit learning outcomes that can be easily understood by students. Good practice exemplars are provided to help students determine the level of performance that is expected. To be considered a truly authentic learning environment, teachers must build students' capacity to self-assess by embedding strategic feedback loops that help students become highly self-aware through reflection and critical analysis.

Australian Education researchers Ashford-Rowe, Herrington, & Brown, (2014) have identified eight elements that they consider critical in determining the authenticity of assessment tasks within Higher Education. Using these elements to benchmark assessment design has the 'knock on' effect of influencing the quality of the learning activities. In this chapter, Ashford-Rowe et al.'s (2014) critical elements for designing authentic learning and assessment are used as a framework for course design and the application of this is demonstrated across multiple disciplines: this approach may help other educators redefine their own assessment practices and enhance the links between university and the workplace.

17.2 The Framework Explained

Our Framework is based on Ashford-Rowe et al.'s (2014) eight critical elements that determine authentic assessment. They state that assessment should be challenging, lend itself to the production of a product or performance, and provide a means by which students can transfer knowledge, and in a way that will enhance the skills of metacognition and self-reflection. Consideration also needs to be given to the client or stakeholder view, to ensure fidelity, encourage discussion and feedback, and enable collaboration. Our Framework is illustrated in Fig. 17.1.

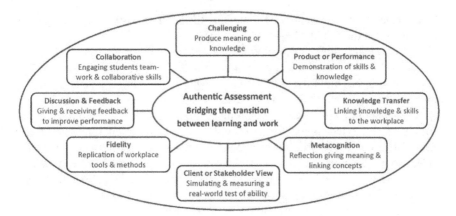

Fig. 17.1 Authentic assessment framework based on Ashford-Rowe, Herrington & Brown's (2014) Critical elements that determine authentic assessment

The Framework firstly encourages educational designers to reflect on the quality of the learning and assessment activity with regards to the level of *challenge* that the activity is posing for the learner. Ideas should be connected to real-work experiences and reflect real-world situations and tasks. A key question that educators need to reflect upon is: '*to what degree does this assessment activity ask the student to utilise knowledge, skills and attitudes that require analysis, synthesis and creation of knowledge across contexts?*' Assessment in this case is not centred around the mere recall and recognition of knowledge, but the ability to solve complex problems in real world applications. Educators are encouraged to provide multiple means whereby students can demonstrate their integrated knowledge and skills through a *product or performance production*, to reflect professional or graduate work contexts. Providing multiple means whereby students can express their skills and knowledge development through assessment activities addresses students' multiple and diverse learning needs and can for example include oral presentations, visual performances, learning logs, reflective portfolios, case study and field visit reports, laboratory reports, models of construction in architecture and clinical and/or work placements.

The Framework also emphasises the needs for the *transferability of knowledge and skills* learnt in one area, to be seamlessly relocated to a different context. In this way educators are developing employability skills in their graduates rather than merely generic skills which could secure employment in a narrow context. Educators need to provide a learning and assessment environment which allows skills learnt in one context to be applied to a range of diverse situations. For example, a graduate oral health therapist needs to be able to confidently provide individualised oral health education to meet the needs of one client in a private practice setting, and at the same time be able to readily analyse the holistic oral health needs of a diverse population in a community care setting. This requires the educator to provide oral health students opportunities to work one-on-one with a diverse range of patients in their urban clinical placements, as well as opportunities for them to work with marginalised communities in rural public health care settings.

For all students within any discipline to be able to work across differing contexts and skills, the Framework asks educators to mindfully design learning and assessment activities that build the skills of *metacognition*. Building students' metacognitive abilities is a skill that needs to be deliberately embedded within the learning and assessment process (Schraw & Moshman, 1995). Students need to reflect upon learning strategies and approaches and devise ways that best support their needs and those of their peers. Peer interaction and reflection, and self-reflection, help to build students' understanding of not just the final assessment outcome but the entire process of learning and self-improvement. When students learn about how they learn, they increase their ability to self-reflect critically, to make links between content areas and see the relevance of their learning to real world contexts. This is one of the most crucial aspects of student engagement. Self-efficacy is built when students learn to readily identify their strengths and areas for improvement, and then are able to address these through self-determined strategies. Students become effective lifelong learners, when they have been prepared to undertake critical and reflective self-assessment tasks throughout their undergraduate experiences (Boud, 2009; Boud & Soler, 2016) that can easily be transferred into future workplace contexts.

Thus, any real-world application should include the *client or stakeholders'* view. This ensures that the assessment item provides an authentic real-world view of the task, adding value and validity to help students articulate the connections between study and work. Client or stakeholder input can take on various approaches, from formal course advisory panels and employment of industry/professional casual staff, to more informal fieldwork experiences and or work placement discussions. Providing authentic case studies (that have occurred in the 'real world,' taken from experts in the workplace, in any given field) will also provide client and stakeholder input. Students themselves, being the primary stakeholders in any learning context, should also have input into the assessment design, adding relevance to the assessment item and consequently generating high stakes investment from their students. The demands that industry/professional bodies exert on universities to offer more relevant courses and deliver enhanced graduate employability, has made universities rethink the development of their students' transferable skills outlined above.[1]

The next criteria that the Framework refers to, is the *fidelity* of an assessment task to the real-work environment. Mowbray et al. (2003) identify fidelity as the extent to which the delivery of an assessment task or intervention adheres to a real-world authentic situation. For this to occur, the learning and assessment item needs to either be conducted in the workplace or in a simulated situation that closely mirrors the real-world situation. Educators and learning designers must create items that include culturally appropriate workplace language, graphics, symbols etc., enabling

---

[1] Deakin University (nd), Authentic Assessment, (available www.deakin.edu.au/__data/assets/pdf_file/0005/268511/AUTHENTIC-ASSESSMENT.pdf accessed 21.11.18.

the task to be as authentic as possible. If a 'real' workplace is not readily available then replication of tools and methods used in the real-world environment (such as simulation or role plays), can contribute to making students feel more familiar with the task and more workplace-ready. If the task that students are asked to complete closely resembles activities in the real world, then educators can feel comfortable that they have embedded fidelity within their assessment task.

Furthermore, the ability to *discuss*, give, and receive *feedback* is critical to workplace performance and builds on all the above-mentioned criteria. Learning to receive and give feedback prepares students for the real world where ones performance is usually quite carefully scrutinised. This provides students with guidance for improvement, and improves their interpersonal, logic, and rhetoric skills. Feedback is also a critical element of constructive alignment of learning outcomes to assessment. It provides a clear roadmap for students, on how they will reach their goals through a scaffolded feedback and learning approach. Educators need to ensure that feedback opportunities are embedded in the learning design process at each stage of learning and assessment preparation. Peer feedback is also another crucial dimension of feedback provision. It encourages students to not only reflect and make judgements on their own performance but on that of another. This is a particular skill that is very useful in the workplace as students need to develop the skill of objectivity, integrity and honesty.

Finally, all criteria for authentic assessment activities culminate in the ability to be able to work in teams and *collaborate*. There is absolutely no doubt that teamwork is an essential part of any modern workplace. Students must learn and be able to communicate effectively, whilst developing collaborative and inclusive team-based work skills. Collaborative tasks create learning environments where students are responsible for contributing to each other's learning. Through sharing ideas and working together students will often see the value of doing the task. There are a range of group-based collaborative approaches that can be employed to create authentic learning tasks from the more structured approaches such as TBL (Team-Based Learning) (TBLC, 2018) and POGIL (Process Orientated Guided Inquiry Learning) (POGIL, 2017) to case studies, concept-mapping and laboratory reports. A learning environment that is presenting real world tasks to be completed supports lively discussion and discourse which consequently nurtures the sense of team and learning community.

17.3 Case Study 1—Accounting

17.3.1 Accounting Concepts and Methods (Introductory Level Accounting Course)

Accounting Concepts and Methods is an introductory level accounting course which has been recently redesigned based on Ashford-Rowe et al.'s (2014) authentic learning and assessment principles. Much consideration was given to important questions such as: *What is relevant in the workplace? How do students learn? What will engage students? How can we keep students attending lectures and being prepared for, and participating in, tutorials?* The assessment pieces were designed to enhance continued learning and understanding, not necessarily always testing knowledge. Learning activities were created that took a scaffolded approach to guide students through the learning process and provide the support needed to enable them to become independent learners over time (Renninger & List, 2012). Apart from the final exam, the major assessment task was the research project. The instructions for this project provided extensive guidance on what to do, in addition to relating the importance of what they are doing to the workplace. Hence, students see relevance rather than it being 'yet another assignment.' Diligent completion of the project should greatly enhance the students' understanding of the course material and provides an opportunity for them to demonstrate this.

17.3.2   To What Extent Does the Assessment Activity Challenge the Assessed Student?

Students are required to examine financial statements, identify components and find linkages, as well as investigate and research the main elements and consider how they relate to the business and industry assigned to them. This requires them to apply theoretical content in practice and can be very challenging as there are many items in the actual reports which are not covered in our more simplified class examples.

17.3.3   Is a Performance, or Product, Required as a Final Assessment Outcome?

Assessment requires students to produce a lengthy report of a professional standard. This requires using multiple software tools that would be used in the workplace and a consideration of whom the intended audience might be, the appropriate language to use and format of the document in addition to providing the required information.

17.3.4   Does the Assessment Activity Require that Transfer of Learning Has Occurred, by Means of Demonstration of Skill?

Students demonstrate the transfer of knowledge and workplace skills by displaying their knowledge of the structure, linkages and individual elements in the annual reports. They also make comparisons between companies and across industries, thereby transferring knowledge and skills learnt in one field and applying them to another.

17.3.5 Does the Assessment Activity Require that Metacognition is Demonstrated, by Means of Critical Reflection, Self-assessment or Evaluation?

Students are required to reflect critically and self-assess their own final report. They do this by framing their work against the detailed marking rubric. Part of the assessment is how well they assessed their own work, based on whether they were overly critical, overconfident, or made a reasonable judgement. Through this self-assessment students identify gaps in their work and have an opportunity to improve their product before it is submitted for grading.

17.3.6 Does the Assessment Require a Product or Performance that Could Be Recognised as Authentic by a Client or Stakeholder?

'Work insights' are inserted throughout the assessment instructions. This is designed to impress upon students the relevance (of what they are doing now) to their future careers in the workplace. They prepare the final report as if it was being presented to their employer rather than the educator.

17.3.7 Is Fidelity Required in the Assessment Environment and Assessment Tools (Actual or Simulated)?

Assessment requires working in teams which is the norm in accounting practices. Additionally, they need to use the multiple workplace tools used in practice: Word documents, spreadsheets, drawing tools, collaborative workspaces etc. The language used and how it is presented is also considered in terms of whether these are appropriate for the workplace.

17.3.8   Does the Assessment Activity Require Discussion and Feedback?

To complete the task successfully, students need to discuss their companies and the industry which they have been assigned, and their research findings. They must combine their findings to successfully move on to each later segment of the task. The task is made up of nine distinct activities all of which build upon the previous task. Students also have ample opportunity and are encouraged to discuss their projects with their educators. As in the workplace, if they were not sure of requirements they would be expected to ask for guidance. Our philosophy, based on Coates' (2007) findings, is that students will be more engaged in their university studies if they see tutors as approachable, and the learning environment is responsive, supportive and challenging.

17.3.9   Does the Assessment Activity Require that Students Collaborate?

This task is conducted in teams of four students. Extensive guidance is given on how to work in teams and the importance of teamworking out in the workplace. Effective collaboration is integral to the successful assessment performance.

17.4   Case Study 2—Investigative Cell Biology

17.4.1   Investigative Cell Biology (3rd Year Research Intensive Pathology Course)

Investigative Cell Biology has been designed to extend student knowledge relating to biology and pathology, whilst providing students with a contemporary understanding of the application and limitations of current research techniques. Today's educator should aim not simply to produce more scientists, but rather to get all students to learn to think about science, like a scientist. Similarly, the goal of education in general is to gets students to think like experts more broadly (Wieman, 2007). To support this, course content is delivered by research-active lecturers and affiliate titleholders from the Adelaide Medical School. Investigative Cell Biology is delivered in a series of 'seminar style' lectures and highlights current research and cutting-edge research methodologies used by research leaders, making it a constantly evolving course. This exposure to current research not only ensures that undergraduate students are abreast of the latest findings but aims to stimulate and motivate them further. As Healy et al. (2010) argued, students felt benefits to their learning when content was delivered by staff that were active in research, including: being taught by enthusiastic staff, enhanced staff credibility, and the reflected glory of being taught by well-known researchers. Investigative Cell Biology involves formative and summative assessments that are designed to promote critical analysis and continuous learning. The course provides affiliates with the unique opportunity to interact with undergraduate students and provides students with the opportunity to interact with potential employers or higher degree supervisors and engage in valuable research-based discussions.

17.4.2 To What Extent Does the Assessment Activity Challenge the Assessed Student?

Investigative Cell Biology assessment involves a review/proposal of a field that aligns with one of the lecture themes. The writing is done in groups of 3 or 4 students and is designed to develop persuasive writing skills and critical interpretation of data. Weekly workshops involve active discussion and live web searching to establish knowledge of research techniques and applications. Students are able to gauge their knowledge and ability to source information in three open-book online, multiple-choice quizzes. Knowledge acquisition and integration from content in lectures and workshops is assessed in a final exam. This course prepares them for employment, higher degree research or postgraduate coursework.

17.4.3 Is a Performance, or Product, Required as a Final Assessment Outcome?

The assessments outcomes are a semester long review/proposal task which is completed in a group in addition to sitting an individual final exam.

17.4.4 Does the Assessment Activity Require that Transfer of Learning Has Occurred, by Means of Demonstration of Skill?

Workshops are run throughout the semester to complement the lecture topics. They are designed to extend knowledge about the basic research techniques available and encourage the students to understand the applications and limitations of each within a research setting. The content taught and discussed in workshops is integrated into the final exam via research scenarios and project design.

17.4.5 Does the Assessment Activity Require that Metacognition is Demonstrated, by Means of Critical Reflection, Self-assessment or Evaluation?

By providing the opportunity for students to submit a dot plan, students are given feedback on interpretation of their research topic early on. The feedback/guidance provided encourages students to reflect critically upon their initial interpretations and amend their content plan accordingly. Students are also provided with a detailed rubric to align their assessment against. Anonymous examples of highly- graded assessments submitted in previous years are provided to enable students to self-evaluate their assessments alongside other sources. In order to break down the learning of discipline specific knowledge, three online multiple-choice question (MCQ) tests are spaced throughout the semester. To further develop their research skills in seeking information from relevant sources, the online MCQ tests are run as open book exams where they have access to their lecture notes as well as web-based searches.

17.4.6 Does the Assessment Require a Product or Performance that Could Be Recognised as Authentic by a Client or Stakeholder?

The review/proposal assessment transitions from traditional review-writing to a grant proposal. Students are asked to critically discuss an area of research with reference to recent original research articles, identify gaps in knowledge or contention, and propose aims to address these. They are essentially providing a business plan to prove why their area is important to research further and thus be funded, which is the underlying premise to any grant. An extension of this would be the teaching of budget inclusion which is now included as a component of the honours year.

17.4.7 Is Fidelity Required in the Assessment Environment and Assessment Tools (Actual or Simulated)?

The review assessment tasks require working in teams which is the norm in the medical research setting. In addition, students need to use multiple medical literature search tools to review current research, critically assess and identify gaps or contention. The assessment extends beyond a standard review by encouraging students to identify the research needed as if they were writing a grant proposal. The language used and how it is presented is also considered as to whether it is appropriate for the workplace as justification of research and writing proposals is critical in research. Assessment tasks run in class as online multiple-choice question tests throughout the semester are in an open book/google access format to encourage students to review material and practise fact finding.

17.4.8 Does the Assessment Activity Require Discussion and Feedback?

To complete the task successfully students are given the opportunity to submit a dot plan within two weeks of the course starting. This encourages the groups to meet as soon as possible to not only discuss the interpretation of their topic and draft a plan of their assignment but to assign tasks and agree on the mode of group communication. The dot plan is provided to the course coordinator and assessor of the topic. Feedback is provided within a week, to guide or clarify structure and interpretation of the topic. This enables students to move forward with more direction. Each topic is set by research active affiliates who are also delivering the material, so students are encouraged to attend lectures for further opportunity to discuss their assignment with academic staff.

17.4.9 Does the Assessment Activity Require that Students Collaborate?

The research review task is conducted in teams of three to four students and assessed as a group piece. During the course, guidance is given at the induction and through email delivered announcements. These encourage regular meetings, matching and agreeing on group expectations, working collaboratively and respectfully in teams and stresses the importance of teamwork in the workplace. The course strives to reinforce that effective collaboration is integral not only to a successful assessment piece but to future workplace funding applications and projects.

17.5 Case Study 3—Clinical Simulation for Oral Health Practice

17.5.1 Clinical Simulation for Oral Health Practice (Level 2 Oral Health Course)

This is a level two course in the Bachelor of Oral Health Program at the Adelaide Dental School. The use of simulation in dental education is well established. Since the first dental school opened in Baltimore in 1840, simulated laboratory practice has been central to undergraduate teaching (Perry et al., 2015) particularly pre-clinical operative skills training. The evolution of rudimentary mannequins into more sophisticated simulator technologies has greatly assisted dental and oral health students to develop manual dexterity skills which are critical for safe and effective clinical practice. Whilst the learning technologies have changed, what has become the educational challenge for this course was to design a contemporary and authentic learning and assessment approach to 'close the gap' between pre-clinical simulation and the real world of the clinic. Beyond the traditional psychomotor components of manual dexterity and operative procedures, cognitive and affective aspects of clinical practice must be included to fully and genuinely prepare the oral health students for future practice. To achieve this pedagogical end a revised methodology, based on Ashford-Rowe et al.'s (2014) Authentic Assessment Framework, has been implemented to nurture a more holistic context within the pre-clinical learning program.

17.5.2   To What Extent Does the Assessment Activity Challenge the Assessed Student?

Students are assessed initially on the basic concepts of the clinical skills being learnt but, as they develop competence, the skills become the basis of a more holistic patient scenario. Rather than simply drilling and filling' plastic teeth which was the traditional model of 'teaching and testing', students must develop a simulated patient course of care. This is a far greater challenge as it requires them to bring together all facets of managing a patient rather than just filling their teeth. This includes creating an electronic case note with a name, date of birth and contact details, entering medical, dental and social data for the patient, creating an appointment schedule and writing up details of each patient 'visit' which is how simulation sessions are subsequently considered. Students work in groups of 4 in a 'practice' to reproduce the nature of the future workplace.

17.5.3   Is a Performance, or Product, Required as a Final Assessment Outcome?

Students manage three simulated patient courses of care over a six-week period. Each patient 'appointment' is formatively assessed by students and tutors and represents 60% of their summative grade for the course. The learning that has been derived from the simulated clinical part of the course underpins the remaining 40% of the final assessment, based on participation in online fora, and the end of semester summative examination.

17.5.4   Does the Assessment Activity Require that Transfer of Learning Has Occurred, by Means of Demonstration of Skill?

As part of the revised learning approach to this course, a suite of online demonstration videos was developed and delivered in a 'flipped classroom' approach. This area of clinical teaching has always included skill demonstration, but often 'on the spot' and with only students at the front able to see. Now the short demonstration clips, co-produced by staff and students, are available ahead of the initial formative assessment activities. Students must compile a procedural checklist for each procedure, which is peer and tutor-reviewed at the start of the subsequent simulation clinic session.

17.5.5   Does the Assessment Activity Require that Metacognition is Demonstrated, by Means of Critical Reflection, Self-assessment or Evaluation?

This is an area of the revised learning and assessment approach for this course that has been critical to the concept of work-readiness for the oral health students. As a profession, dentistry requires continuous self-assessment and evaluation of work quality, patient outcomes and treatment decisions. It has arguably been the most significant challenge for graduate practitioners in their transitioning towards the work environment. Students undertake self-assessment for every simulated appointment, receive peer and tutor feedback throughout the course, and ultimately contribute to their final grade for this component of the course through a critical self-analysis of their overall performance. The rubric the students use is identical to the teacher framework and encompasses all aspects of professional practice including underpinning knowledge, rationale for their decision-making, ergonomics, infection control, hand skills, professional behaviour and time management. Consequently, this requires student performance and capabilities in all aspects of the clinical environment to be holistically assessed, rather than the more piecemeal approach that has been traditionally taken in this area of pre-clinical education.

17.5.6   Does the Assessment Require a Product or Performance that Could Be Recognised as Authentic by a Client or Stakeholder?

The transformation of the previous 'stand-alone' assessment tasks into a series of patient-centred appointments makes this a distinctly authentic clinical performance that any client or stakeholder would recognise. This process includes creating an electronic case-note, devising a realistic treatment plan that is implemented within a clinically accurate time frame, and then recording the details of each procedure to the required dento-legal standard. This is an exact replica of the tasks necessary for future clinical practice. Building this into the simulation program and embedding it in the assessment criteria promotes the integration of the cognitive, affective and psychomotor aspects of graduate practice well before the students commence clinical placement. The simulated practice groups are also typical of how oral health graduates work, rather than in single operator contexts.

17.5.7   Is Fidelity Required in the Assessment Environment and the Assessment Tools (Actual or Simulated)?

To truly enhance the transition from the learning environment (and its related assessment tasks) to the graduate practice context, it is imperative that an elevated level of fidelity is present in the pre-clinical simulation course. This is achieved through close attention to the course design including the simulation manikin becoming a patient with name, date of birth, social, medical and contact data. Just as these factors play a role in treatment planning and sequencing in the real world, students are required to link them to the needs of their simulated patient. Accuracy of professional nomenclature, dento-legal compliance, nationally regulated scope of practice and evidence-based research are all built into the assessment criteria. Indeed, the electronic case note program used in the simulation clinic has been adapted to match the item codes and dental charting format used in clinical placement locations. This has led to a marked improvement in student induction to treating real patients in latter stages of the overall program—many of the traditional challenges with 'putting it all together' have already been achieved in the more authentic learning and assessment now in this course.

17.5.8   Does the Assessment Activity Require Discussion and Feedback?

The defining hallmark of the new learning and assessment approach is the rich discussion and feedback that underpins the overall assessment activity. Each session ends with a student-centred feedback approach, based on the 'Ask-Tell-Ask' model (French et al., 2015). This approach emphasises that students must take the lead in the feedback discussion which promotes reflection and self-assessment. The teacher responds to the learning issues raised by the student and provides guidance for improvement and progress. This also simulates a typical workplace situation where practitioners confer about the progress or outcomes of patient care in the dental setting.

17.5.9 Does the Assessment Activity Require that the Students Collaborate?

Like many professionals, graduate oral health practice practitioners frequently collaborate with colleagues, dental specialists and interdisciplinary health practitioners. This is mirrored in the Clinical Simulation for Oral Health Practice course where students are grouped into 'practices'; this is where they peer-review each other's procedural checklists developed from watching online demonstrations, assist with clinical procedures during simulation sessions and work together on formulating their treatment plans for their simulated patients. These collaborations provide the opportunity for positive outcomes for all students. Nicol et al. (2014) found that 'through reviewing the work of peers, students can learn to take control over their own learning, to generate their own feedback and to be more critical about their own work'.

17.6 Case Study 4—Digital Systems

17.6.1 Digital Systems (2nd Year Electronic Engineering Course)

Digital Systems, a core subject for electrical and electronic engineering undergraduates, is delivered using a flipped classroom to a cohort of around 120 students. The flipped format has been used since 2013 to provide more authentic engineering design experience, including open-ended design problems of moderate complexity. Students prepare for classes with recorded presentations, textbook reading and preliminary theory exercises. In class they apply theory to practice using professional engineering tools, including rapid prototyping hardware that allows designs to be implemented, tested and refined during the class. Low-stakes assessment is used to help students prioritise preparation, maintain engagement with the course, and to provide meaningful continuous feedback. Every workshop, each student spends time one-on-one with a teacher. The student demonstrates the outcomes from their previous workshop as well as their preparation for the current session. The marks available for this assessment keep the process moving, but the opportunities it provides to explain, discuss, reflect and seek clarification are the most important things.

17.6.2   To What Extent Does the Assessment Activity Challenge the Assessed Student?

The workshops require creative application of the theory covered, in preparation for real-world design problems. Students who take the course are typically strong at mathematics and abstract problem solving, however the nature of the discipline is changing and professional attributes such as interpersonal communication and teamwork, and an ability to work on complex open-ended design problems, are now as important as being able to solve isolated circuit analysis problems. The assessed workshops bring these challenges to the fore.

17.6.3   Is a Performance, or Product, Required as a Final Assessment Outcome?

All of the workshops lead to a demonstrable outcome, typically simulation results or a functioning, useful digital circuit. During the weekly one-on-one assessments, students are guided towards explaining their design, justifying their decisions, and reflecting upon the methods used and their broader implications.

17.6.4   Does the Assessment Activity Require that Transfer of Learning Has Occurred, by Means of Demonstration of Skill?

The workshop activities are carefully aligned with the theory covered in preparation sessions and scaffolded so that ideas and techniques are revisited through the semester as class capacity to manage more complex and integrative problems grows. At the outset of the course, students have much more experience with the design of software than with hardware. The relationship between these activities is deliberately used to leverage prior learning via analogies and explicit discussions of similarities and differences.

17.6.5   Does the Assessment Activity Require that Metacognition is Demonstrated, by Means of Critical Reflection, Self-assessment or Evaluation?

Theory preparation exercises are self-assessed against fully worked solutions. Students are encouraged to identify sticky points to raise, either as part of their one-on-one discussion, or during the guided discussions that punctuate the workshop sessions. Every workshop concludes with questions that require reflection upon the week's learning and these often spark interesting conversations in the next week's one-on-one sessions.

17.6.6 Does the Assessment Require a Product or Performance that Could Be Recognised as Authentic by a Client or Stakeholder?

Students build working circuits including an electronic lock, a digital timer and subsystems for a microprocessor. Although these are of modest complexity, the methodologies employed are the same as those used by teams designing contemporary complex digital products. Techniques to manage complexity are treated explicitly and are a recurring theme through the course.

17.6.7 Is Fidelity Required in the Assessment Environment and the Assessment Tools (Actual or Simulated)?

A variety of industry-standard software tools are used to design, simulate, verify and implement the students' designs. Some tasks are completed individually, others in small teams. All of this mirrors professional practice.

17.6.8 Does the Assessment Activity Require Discussion and Feedback?

Exercises that require discussions between students, or instructor-guided class discussions, are interspersed throughout the workshops. These add variety, give students new perspectives and opportunities to reinforce their understanding. Feedback is provided in the one-on-one discussions.

17.6.9 Does the Assessment Activity Require that Students Collaborate?

Most of the substantial design tasks are undertaken in self-selected groups of two or three students. Occasionally discussion exercises require groups to mix, or to collaborate between groups. At this point in the engineering curriculum, the class is already very familiar with group work and few problems arise with the fundamentals of working together. This allows the course to focus on collaborative techniques for complex projects.

17.7 Conclusion

There is no doubt that HE has undergone many changes recently. The most significant one has been the realisation that, for universities to prepare graduates for the ever-changing landscape of the workplace, graduates must develop transferrable skills of employability through a scaffolded, authentic learning and assessment framework. It is no longer sufficient to have mastery of one's own discipline expertise: instead, graduates must have the ability and knowledge to be able to work competently within and across diverse contexts by seeking out ongoing professional development opportunities through self-reflective practices and lifelong learning. The cross disciplinary examples in this chapter have been aligned to Ashford-Rowe et al.'s (2014) framework, covering the eight critical elements of authentic learning and assessment, to hopefully enable other educators to reframe their own course deliveries to better prepare their HE students for the workplace.

References

Ashford-Rowe, K., Herrington, J., & Brown, C. (2014). Establishing the critical elements that determine authentic assessment. *Assessment and Evaluation in Higher Education, 39*(2), 205–222. https://doi.org/10.1080/02602938.2013.819566.

Bosco, A. M., & Ferns S. (2014). Embedding of Authentic Assessment in work-integrated learning curriculum. *Asia-Pacific Journal of Cooperative Education, 15*(4), 281–290. https://www.ijwil.org/files/APJCE_15_4_281_290.pdf.

Boud, D. (2009). How can practice reshape assessment? In G. Joughin (Ed.), *Assessment, learning and judgement in higher education* (pp. 29–43). Dordrecht: Springer.

Boud, D., & Soler, R. (2016). Sustainable assessment revisited. *Assessment and Evaluation in Higher Education, 41*(3), 400–413. https://doi.org/10.1080/02602938.2015.1018133.

Coates, H. (2007). A model of online and general campus-based student engagement. *Assessment and Evaluation in Higher Education, 32*(2), 121–141. https://doi.org/10.1080/02602930600801878.

Deakin University nd, Authentic assessment, Retrieved from www.deakin.edu.au/__data/assets/pdf_file/0005/268511/AUTHENTIC-ASSESSMENT.pdf.

French, J. C., Colbert, C. Y., Pien, L. C., Dannefer, E. F., & Taylor, C. A. (2015). Targeted feedback in the milestones era: utilization of the ask-tell-ask feedback model to promote reflection and self-assessment. *Journal of Surgical Education, 72*(6), e274–e279. https://doi.org/10.1016/j.jsurg.2015.05.016.

Healy, M., Jordan, F., Pell, B., & Short, C. (2010). The research–teaching nexus: A case study of students' awareness, experiences and perceptions of research. *Innovations in Education and Teaching International, 47*(2), 235–246. https://doi.org/10.1080/14703291003718968.

Hill, J., & Walkington, H. (2016). 'Developing graduate attributes through participation in undergraduate research conferences. *Journal of Geography in Higher Education, 40*(2), 222–237. https://doi.org/10.1080/03098265.2016.1140128.

Mowbray, C., Hotler, M. C., Teague, G. B., & Bybee, D. (2003). Fidelity criteria: development, measurement and validation. *American Journal of Evaluation, 24,* 3. https://doi.org/10.1177/109821400302400303.

Mueller, J. (2017). Authentic assessment toolbox, Retrieved from, jfmueller.faculty.noctrl.edu/toolbox/index.htm.

Nicol, D., Thomson, A., & Breslin, C. (2014). Rethinking feedback practices in higher education: A peer review perspective. *Assessment and Evaluation in Higher Education, 39*(1), 102–122. https://doi.org/10.1080/02602938.2013.795518.

Perry, S., Bridges, S. M., & Burrow, M. F. (2015). A review of the use of simulation in dental education. *Simulation in Healthcare: Journal of the Society for Simulation in Healthcare, 10*(1), 31–37. https://doi.org/10.1097/SIH.0000000000000059.

POGIL. 2017, POGIL is a teaching pedagogy that makes students feel engaged, accomplished & empowered. Retrieved from https://www.pogil.org/.

Renninger, K. A. & List, A. (2012). Scaffolding for learning. In: Seel, N. M. (Eds.), *Encyclopedia of the sciences of learning*, Springer, Boston, MA.

Schraw, G., & Moshman, D. (1995). Metacognitive theories. *Educational Psychology Review, 7*(4), 351–371. https://doi.org/10.1007/BF02212307.

TBCL. 2018, Team-based learning collaborative, Retrieved from http://www.teambasedlearning.org/.

Wieman, C. (2007) Why not try a scientific approach to science education?. *Change: The Magazine of Higher Learning, 39*(5), 9–15. https://doi.org/10.3200/chng.39.5.9-15.

Yorke, M. (2010). Employability: Aligning the message, the medium and academic values. *Journal of Teaching and Learning for Graduate Employability, 1*(1), 2–12. https://doi.org/10.21153/jtlge2010vol1no1art545.

Robyn Davidson (Ph.D.) is an Associate Professor, in the Adelaide Business School, University of Adelaide, Australia. She is also Director of Academic Programs and a Senior Fellow in the Higher Education Academy. In 2016, she was admitted into the Adelaide Academy as an Education Specialist and appointed Associate Head of Learning and Teaching of the Business School. Her teaching experience spans various financial accounting and information systems courses in both Adelaide and offshore (in Singapore and China). She specialises in first year transition focussing on course design, and motivating students. Via her Doctoral research, she devised a means of identifying and measuring electronic service quality gaps, testing the method on Australian wineries. Her current research interests are the scholarship of teaching and learning, technology use in teaching, information systems, electronic service quality, Web 2.0 and business models. She has published in education, information systems and business journals.

Catherine Snelling (SFHEA) is an Associate Professor and Education Specialist Academic at the Adelaide Dental School, University of Adelaide, Australia. After undertaking post-graduate studies in on-line education, she has adopted a blended learning approach to her teaching. She has led three UoA-funded Learning and Teaching projects and been an active member on other research teams including two ALTC-funded projects on undergraduate research skill development. She has authored many peer-reviewed articles, and presented at national and international learning and teaching conferences. She is currently joint lead on an Office Learning and Teaching Category 1 Research Grant on building teacher capacity to implement flipped learning within HE. She is a leading dental academic in simulation teaching including the use of virtual reality (haptics) in developing pre-clinical skills in oral health students. As a Director on the governing board of the Australian Dental Council, she led several accreditation teams and was instrumental in developing an examination pathway for overseas qualified dental therapists and dental hygienists, and an Executive member of the College of Oral Health Academics, a special interest group comprising of academics teaching oral health programs across Australasia. She is also a member of the inaugural Adelaide Education Academy Executive group.

Sophie Karanicolas (M.Ed.) is an Associate Professor and Academic Lead for the University of Adelaide's Continuing Professional Development Framework, and an Education Specialist in the Adelaide Education Academy. She is a coordinator in the Bachelor of Oral Health, focussing on human biology and clinical practice. She co-facilitates a Community of Practice within the University on the Flipped Classroom, (recently renamed MALTA -Methods of Engaged Learning Teaching and Assessment), and as a Flipped Global Ambassador (as a part of the Flipped Learning Global Initiative) has jointly led a national Office of Learning and Teaching flipped classroom project, '*Translating Concept to Practice.*' She mentors colleagues on learning innovations and is a member of the University's College of Reviewers, as part of the Teaching Review Program. She is a member of the development team for the first MOOC (Massive Open Online Course), developed by the University of Adelaide: *An Introduction to Essential Human Biology.* She was part of the team which developed, implemented and evaluated a colleague development program: *Becoming an Effective Supervisor and Teacher (BEST).* She is also Chair of the College of Oral Health Academics (COHA), a national body exploring oral health education, and part of the Australian Dental Council Site Evaluation Teams.

Tania Crotti (Ph.D.) is an Associate Professor and Education Specialist Academic in the Adelaide Medical School (AMS), University of Adelaide, Australia. She is the Postgraduate Coordinator Manager for the AMS and a member of the Faculty of Health and Medical Science Higher Degree by Research Comittee. She has worked as a Research Assistant in the Department of Pathology, University of Adelaide. Her Ph.D. (on "*The mechanisms responsible for pathological bone remodeling in inflammatory conditions*") was funded by a Dora Lush, NHMRC Scholarship and her postdoctoral training at the Harvard Affiliated Beth Israel Deaconess Medical Center, Boston, was funded by a CJ Martin, NHMRC Fellowship and an American Arthritis Foundation Fellowship. A/Prof Crotti teaches across 3 year levels to students enrolled in Nursing, Bachelor of Health and Medical Sciences and Medicine, and runs workshops for the AMS Honours programme and PhD students. She is an active scientist in the area of inflammation induced bone loss (Osteoimmunology) and draws themes from this expertise into her teaching activities at both undergraduate and postgraduate levels.

Braden Phillips (Ph.D) is a senior lecturer in the School of Electrical and Electronic Engineering, and Director of Learning and Teaching for the Faculty of Engineering, Computer and Mathematical Sciences at the University of Adelaide, Australia. His research focus is the design of new computing architectures for artificial intelligence. This work draws upon his research interest and experience in digital arithmetic, digital microelectronics, computer architecture, information security, and real-time and embedded systems. Prior to completing his PhD ('*An Optimised Implementation of Public Key Cryptography for Smart Card Processors*') he worked as a process control engineer and was a founding partner in *Current Dynamics*, an electronic hardware design venture. He was a lecturer at Cardiff University in South Wales for 2 years before returning to the University of Adelaide in 2002.

Chapter 18
'Oh, The Places You'll Go': The Importance of Relationships on Postgraduate Research Students' Experiences of Academia

Janine Delahunty and Kathryn Harden-Thew

18.1 Introduction

The profile of the 'postgraduate research student' has undergone enormous change, in part due to global trends toward increasing enrolments, bolstered by university advertising campaigns and government policy (Norton & Cherastidtham, 2014). Postgraduate research students[1] are faced with changing and more stringent requirements focusing on 'higher level development of advanced practitioners' (Fillery-Travis & Robinson, 2018, p. 841). These candidates increasingly have expert knowledge of practice in their field, which can exceed that of their supervisors (Jones, 2018). This progressive shift is reflected in changing demographics, with incoming students characterised by their diversity in age, background, culture, experience, professional standing and desired career outcomes (Becker et al., 2018; Boud et al., 2018; Fillery-Travis & Robinson, 2018; Jones, 2018; Lee, 2018; UA, 2015). However, with the exponential rise in enrolments comes uncertainty around what these research degrees prepare students for, particularly as a future in academia can no longer be guaranteed (Lundsteen, 2014; Marsh & Western, 2016).

Literature surrounding research student experience focuses largely on the outputs or products of student work and the experience of supervision. In these, student voices are often unnoticed, overlooked or unobserved in the very literature that was written in support of them. As if in answer to this silence, there has sprung up a plethora

---

[1] We use the term 'postgraduate research student' to describe a student engaged in a range of programs termed variously, including Ph.D., professional doctoral programs (see Jones, 2018, p. 817), also Masters of Philosophy (M.Phil) or Masters by Research. For brevity, hereafter we refer to them as 'student(s)'.

J. Delahunty (✉) · K. Harden-Thew
University of Wollongong, Wollongong, Australia
e-mail: janined@uow.edu.au

K. Harden-Thew
e-mail: kathrynp@uow.edu.au

© Springer Nature Switzerland AG 2019   275
A. Diver (ed.), *Employability via Higher Education: Sustainability as Scholarship*,
https://doi.org/10.1007/978-3-030-26342-3_18

of social media highlighting research student voices (such as *The Thesis Whisperer*, *PhD talk, #phdchat*). The significance of relationship-development to the research degree process, is often also less or un-acknowledged, as institutionally, the process is flagged by 'measurable' milestones leading to completion. In this chapter, we focus on how relationships impact student experience as they negotiate and position themselves in academic culture during their study period and when considering their futures, thus bringing together academic investigation and students' voices. As early career academics ourselves we have a keen interest (and recent memory) of how the path of employable scholars is trekked. We found much affiliation with the leitmotifs of Dr. Seuss' (1957) *Oh, the places you'll go:* the highs, lows, challenges, uncertainties and unknowns. So, also, did the themes which emerged from the words of our participants, offering insights into a diverse range of experiences of academia and those relationships which sustained them (or not). A review of the literature in the next section focuses on some of the implications of the changing nature of the research degree.

18.2   *Oh, the Places We've Been...* A Literature Review

The research degree process could be described in functional terms as a series of transition periods—flagged by milestones such as course completion, research proposal, data collection, writing up, full draft and so on—which tend to move from more to less structured support. Thus, students are constantly adapting as they navigate from high structural support in the early stages towards becoming an 'expert.' During these times of transition, relationships are often key to how students move into emerging roles, perceptions of self and levels of persistence to succeed in their research degrees (Baker & Pifer, 2011; Whannell & Whannell, 2015). While the outputs of study proposal and thesis are clearly foregrounded, many implicit expectations are rarely discussed and often left for the students themselves to discover and negotiate, often in isolation (Jones, 2018; Lundsteen, 2014). Thus, aside from the research topic, supervisor-student and peer relationships are significant, particularly in the murky area of bridging the unknown to known, and is an important part of the enculturation and identity forming processes.

Although full time research degrees are still the main path chosen 'by those yet to start their working life' (Boud et al., 2018, p. 915), the shift towards practitioner-focused research degrees has ushered in a change in the demographic characteristics of these students, thereby diversifying the cohort (Fillery-Travis & Robinson, 2018; Lee, 2018). This, in part, is reflective of institutions seeking to meet the demands of employers, but also to attract a share of international student market (Jones, 2018). According to Becker et al. (2018) employers are seeking graduates who are able to make connections with the 'deep vertical knowledge' in their particular domain, together with a broad set of soft skills such as 'teamwork, communications, facility with data and technology, an appreciation of diverse cultures, and advanced literacy skills' (p. 18). This demand for employability outside of the academy brings new challenges to supervisors, particularly if their supervision style is more traditional or if they themselves have not worked elsewhere. A student entering a research degree with a high level of expertise in their field requires a different kind of supervisory approach to those who rely on their supervisors for expert input, or to those who have had an uninterrupted progression from school to undergraduate to postgraduate study. Thus, the complexity of diversity at many levels, gives rise to the potential for mismatching expectations, particularly in the supervisory relationship.

Relationships, both within and outside of the academic community seem to become more important during the period of the degree where there is less structured support, and where students may experience a sense of isolation (Baker & Pifer, 2011, p. 9). Baker and Pifer (2011) argue that because these stages are 'unlike any other professional or educational experience' (p. 8) relationships become paramount to helping students navigate basic challenges associated with becoming autonomous, developing a high level of expertise and negotiating identities. During this period, the role of peers is invaluable for modelling socialization as 'agents of community, learning, and development' (Flores-Scott & Nerad, 2012, p. 76). As such, peer relationships can be multi-faceted, encompassing how students 'learn the values, skills, and norms of their discipline or field' as well as provide 'emotional support, general advisement, and specific content knowledge' (p. 76) and how they 'teach each other the practices of research and scholarship' (p. 79).

The changing nature of the research degree also highlights the reality that this qualification is no longer a natural progression into academic employment. While the goal of postgraduate research programs is 'to socialize students into academia [and] prepare students to become researchers and faculty members' through supportive relationships (Rogers-Shaw & Carr-Chellman, 2018, p. 236), the high numbers of students being admitted into degrees precludes any assurance of an academic career path (Jones, 2018; Lundsteen, 2014). As Lundsteen points out, the academic landscape is shifting, and students even though learning to become researchers may have little option but to consider non-academic pathways after completion. This uncertainty however, highlights the crucial role of relationship development throughout the doctoral degree, particularly for future employability. Doing a research degree is often a solitary experience (Jones, 2018), and it may not be made explicit that skills learnt in becoming part of an academic community are transferrable to and desirable for future contexts such as industry employment. Some valuable skills include problem-solving and solutions, working collaboratively, and communicating effectively (Rogers-Shaw & Carr-Chellman, 2018).

We argue that relationships are important shapers of the research experience. To explore the impact of relationships this chapter adopts Lee's (2018) framework of supervisory practices to focus on relational aspects, guided by five themes: functional, enculturation, critical thinking, emancipation and relationship development (explained in the data analysis section). We examine supervisor and peer relationships only but acknowledge that these are not the only relationships that sustain students. The next section outlines the theoretical approach taken.

18.3   Theoretical Approach

To explore how relationships impact students' changing identities and perceptions of belonging, we use the lens of identity theory (Whannell & Whannell, 2015). The voices of students are foregrounded using a narrative approach, addressing the gap between the 'measurable' and student experience. Identity formation as a social construct is dynamic, emergent and dependent on opportunities afforded through ongoing socially-negotiated relationships and interaction (Gee, 2000; Knowles, et al., 2012). We draw on Whannell and Whannell's (2015) University Student Identity Theoretical Model to understand how research students construct a multiplicity of identities, dependent on three factors working together within the social context of academia. These factors are Student Identity, Student Role and Emotional Commitment. Whannell and Whannell (2015) explain that perceptions of 'successful' academic engagement (or otherwise) will influence students' sense of worthiness (identity) and thus their academic behaviours (role), which in turn influences the level of emotional commitment, associated with student identity. Separating the student role (i.e. what they do) from the student identities (who they are) enables a way of understanding the impact of relationships that form during a research degree. The relationships most mentioned in our data are with supervisors, peers and other academics. Sense of worthiness (identity), academic behaviours (role), and emotional commitment are understood within the social context of these relationships.

The focus of qualitative research is to harness theory in order to open up social contexts and relationships to a deeper richer view (Crotty, 1998). Stone and O'Shea (2012) state, 'one of the best ways to understand the actions of individuals is to be allowed to hear their personal stories as they themselves choose to narrate them' (p. 2). Therefore, a narrative approach has been adopted in this research to reveal students' stories, fluid and altering, highlighting themes of belonging, identity formation and role through their stories of every day lived experience, noting conflicts and complexities (Andrews, Squire & Tamboukou, 2008). Such research reveals 'the deep, layered and multifaceted lives of the participants' (Harden-Thew, 2014, p. 71), the 'messiness' of their experience (Spyrou, 2011).

18.4   Methodology

Data was gathered from an anonymous survey of research degree students and recent graduates (N = 425[2]). Following ethics approval from the University of Wollongong, the survey link was sent electronically firstly within Australia and then via various networks and social media between March and July 2018. Respondents were spread across 15 different countries from 98 different institutions studying within a range of disciplines, including humanities and arts, natural sciences (physical, earth, life, medical and health), computer science, mathematics, business and marketing, edu-

---

[2]This total takes into account 5 incomplete surveys which were removed.

cation, engineering, law and theology. The survey gathered demographic information as well as stage of degree, and student status. The qualitative section included questions about milestones, experiences of supervision and peer relationships, hurdles/barriers, goals, support and how well students perceived they were 'finding their place'. These questions were partly informed by the University Student Identity Theoretical Model (Whannell & Whannell, 2015), focusing on relationships and perceptions of successful academic engagement; emotions and perceptions of milestones in terms of 'worthiness' and academic behaviours; and the role of relationships on forming student identity(ies). The narrative approach utilised enables student voices to be foregrounded.

18.4.1 Participants

The diversity within the participants is clear from the demographic information they provided. The majority were female (75%, n = 319), and 23% were male (n = 98) with some preferring not to indicate gender. Almost two-thirds were in the age ranges of 21–29 and 30–39 years (32%, n = 135; 30%, n = 125 respectively). Those who were 40–49 and over 50 years together represented 37% (18%, n = 78; 19%, n = 79 respectively), with twenty being in their 60s and four in their 70s. The youngest was 22 years and the oldest, 74. Of the total, 253 said they had a break in formal study before commencing their research degree, with the length of time varying from 6 months or less (4%, n = 9); 1 to 3 years (46%, n = 116); 4 to 5 years (15%, n = 37) and 6 to 10 years (19%, n = 48). The remainder indicated they had a break of more than 11 years (17%, n = 43), which included four who had a lengthy break of 30–35 years. Most indicated they were domestic students (81%, n = 346), with 74 being international. English is the first language of the majority (82%, n = 348), with 77 indicating first languages other than English (18%) and 36 different first languages named.

All stages of the postgraduate research process were represented—from pre-proposal to recent graduate. Most respondents indicated they were in the data collection/analysis phase and/or writing chapters or publications phase. Table 18.1 summarises this data.

Almost a third said they were part-time, with a small percentage varying between full and part-time at different stages of their candidature. 320 (75%) were enrolled as on-campus students, while 82 (19%) were distance, with some moving between on-campus and distance status over their candidature. Others, although enrolled as on-campus, only attended for supervisory or other meetings, or they were based elsewhere (such as an external research site or satellite campus).

Table 18.1 Stages of the degree represented

Stage of degree	410 responses	% of responses (%)
1 Pre-proposal	59	14
2 Data collection/analysis	58	14
3 Writing chapters/publications	77	19
4 Nearing full draft	39	10
5 About to submit	17	4
6 Awaiting examiners' reports	15	4
7 Completed/graduated	74	18
	339	83
Combination of Stages		
1 & 2 Pre-proposal and data collection/analysis	9	2
1, 2 & 3 Pre-proposal, data collection/analysis, writing	2	0.33
1 & 3 Pre-proposal, writing chapters/publications	2	0.33
2 & 3 Data collection/analysis, writing	52	13
3 & 4 Writing chapters/publications/nearing full draft	4	1
4 & 5 Nearing full draft/about to submit	2	0.33
	71	17

18.5   Data Analysis

Lee's (2018) framework for analysing the impact of supervisory relationships was used to gain a deeper understanding of the conditions under which such relationships developed, either positive or negative. Five themes comprise the framework developed from supervisor perspectives of the 'essence of the modern doctorate' (Lee, 2018, p. 882) (Table 18.2). This framework enabled us to code student perspectives of their supervisor and peer relationships. In preparation, each response was allocated a respondent number with a small sample of the dataset coded first according to Lee's framework and imported into NVivo11 for sentence by sentence coding and then applied to the whole dataset. From this process, a sub-theme emerged, and was added to Relationship development: *co-location*.

18.6   Findings

While there was great diversity amongst the participants, identity formation was surprisingly consistent. Using Lee's five themes as a guide, we analysed the comments from two of the survey questions on supervisor relationships and peer relationships: (1) *What have been your experiences with establishing supervision relationships?*

Table 18.2 Five themes: essence of the modern doctorate framework (adapted from Lee, 2018, p. 882)

	Functional (F[a])	Enculturation (EN)	Critical thinking (CT)	Emancipation (EM)	Relationship development (RD)
	Being proactive to keep in contact with candidates over a longer time frame	Supporting candidates to manage time and career pressures whilst learning how to do academic work	Engaging with the creation of new professional, transdisciplinary knowledge	Enabling candidates to cope with changes in identity from expert to student	Supporting the development of social (as well as intellectual) skills so they can become effective agents of change
Relationship with supervisors	Such as: regular meetings with supervisors, planning, helping to manage, keeping on track	Organizing or facilitating group events/activities, location and proximity, RA work opportunities, collaborative work	Feedback, modelling critical approaches, behaviours, discourse etc.; presentation opportunities, discussions, problem-solving	Guiding (not micro-managing), valuing the research, providing support that enables the development of autonomy	Fostering good relationships, communication, caring for the person (beyond the project), sharing in the journey
Relationships with peers	Such as: relating to peer assistance with performativity to reach milestones, goals	As above but through peer pro-action	As above but with peer pro-action	(No instances found in the data)	As above but with peers plus, additional sub-theme: **Co-location**—relationship development through access to shared space/office (**CoL**)

[a]These abbreviations will be used in the findings

(2) *What kinds of relationships have you developed with your study peers?* In total 316 students provided qualitative comments.

18.6.1 Supervisor Relationships

The qualitative data for the five themes yielded a total of 404 coded instances which provided insight into how students perceived the relationships with their supervisor/s. In order of frequency, relationship development (RD) was most mentioned, coded 142 times; functional (F) 102; emancipation (EM) 69; enculturation (EN) 64; and critical thinking (CT) 27. Some respondents simply evaluated the relationship (e.g. *'my supervisors are great'* R208[3]) which were coded only in terms of polarity. Many students were able to draw from experience of having more than one supervisor. More than half the comments reflected these relationships as positive (53%) but some were negative (21%) and others included a combination of these aspects (23%). The following quotes exemplify typical sentiments, and not surprisingly, many of these quotes[4] integrated more than one of the themes. To foreground the student voice, quotes are presented in their entirety, where practicable.

> *My relationships with my supervisors are excellent. I feel listened to, and my view is valued* (RD). *My supervisors keep an eye out for opportunities (e.g. seminars, conferences, and teaching) that might be appropriate to my development* (EN). *They are very supportive* (RD). *One of my current supervisors was also my honours supervisor, and I have worked (and continue to work) with her as a research assistant. This provides constant contact and opportunities for me to ask any questions related to PhD in an informal setting* (EN) (R249, S1)

> *I was blessed to have great supervisors* (RD). *I believe their attitude towards me has been very important. They are always supportive (emotionally and academically), understanding* (RD), *and have been treating me like a peer rather than a student* (EM). *I believe them being accessible is very important. We meet regularly* (F) (R402, S2)

These quotes highlight how positive relational experiences were fostered by reciprocal communication, attitudes and behaviours towards them as emerging researchers/academics, not merely as students. When supervisors were proactive in connecting students with opportunities to attend events or work, students were being exposed to and learning different ways of being and doing academic work that were discipline or research interest-related. Regular meetings were also mentioned as important for the performative aspect of the degree. However, the perspectives in the following responses provide insight into the effect of supervisor relationships which have been negative:

> *Hard work. Difficult to develop personal relationships from a distance. First primary supervisor leaving three months in highly disruptive and felt disrespectful as not given any indication it was possible when taken on* (RD) (R258, S1)

---

[3] 'R' = respondent identification.

[4] Note: student quotes are followed by respondent number and stage of degree (1–7, see Table 18.1), presented thus: (R233, S2).

> *Supervisors have kept me at a distance throughout this experience* (RD). *Even though I have struggled with the writing they have & continue to give the same advice they have given for the past four years* (EM). *They are also only interested in editing complete chapters which means I can waste up to 3–4 months of work & not realise it* (F). *This relationship has not been helpful or supportive & has turned this experience into the worse academic experience of my life* (RD, EM) (R239, S4)

Many students had multiple supervision experiences and some of these were in stark contrast to each other, as articulated in these responses:

> *My supervisors have been very happy and supportive on both personal and professional levels, which has helped the development of those relationships* (RD). *I have another supervisor that consistently talks down to me, telling me that I'm not good enough to do things on my own* (RD, EM) (R340, S4)

> *My primary supervisor was amazing at reaching out to build a relationship with me. He invited me and my partner to his house for dinner when I first arrived* (RD) *and organised informal meetings over coffee every week* (F). *He consistently invited me and other students to his house for events, to the canteen for lunch or to the pub on campus for drinks after work* (EN)...*My secondary supervisor, however, never got to know me...We hardly spoke outside of supervision meetings and I'm not convinced she even remembered my research topic at times* (RD) (R174, S7)

Students mentioned the role of feedback and frank conversations on their work as beneficial, for example:

> *My supervisors have been wonderful: encouraging and hands-on, perceptive to challenges, frequently giving useful advice and honest feedback* (CT) (R384, S2).

In the next excerpt the effect of non-constructive feedback is evident:

> *I felt that (my supervisor) was attacking me by repeatedly focusing on the things I hadn't done, rather than giving me feedback on the things I had* (CT); *or commenting on the theoretical directions that worked* (rather than honing in on the one that didn't) (EM) (R206, S5)

18.6.2 Peer Relationships

Coding the peer relationship comments yielded a total of 394 instances showing how students perceived these relationships. In order of frequency, relationship development was coded 224 times, enculturation 98, critical thinking 17, functional 6, and emancipation 0. Some respondents simply evaluated the relationship (e.g. *'No study peer relationships formed'* R187), coded for polarity. Interestingly, having access to a (shared) office space was mentioned by 49 respondents mostly as an enabler of peer relationships though sometimes as constraining. These were coded as 'co-location', a sub-theme we added to Relationship Building. Almost half reflected on peer relationships as positive (48%), around a quarter were negative (23%), while another quarter considered positive and negative aspects (25%). Many who considered these relationships in negative terms included that they were distance or part-time students, studying at home or elsewhere, working off-campus full/part-time, lacking time due to family or other commitments. A few stated they were not inclined to invest in peer relationships.

Similar to the findings in the previous section, students often described their experiences with peers in complex ways necessitating multiple coding. The following are some typical insights:

> *I have met a wonderful and supportive group of students* via *my principal supervisor. We are spread out around Australia, however [we meet] via zoom monthly and we get to connect and share our research* (RD, EN). *I've connected on LinkedIn and twitter and regularly engage in sharing ideas, debates and literature* (CT). *We have also met up at a conference, which was great to have some deep conversations* (RD, EN) (R171, S1)

> *My closest study peer is a PhD student from another university...we will often provide emotional support and de-briefs. We know each other's projects quite well and will bounce ideas, share resources, write together and read each other's work* (EN). *If I did not have this peer I would have struggled and felt far more isolated than I have* (RD) (R119, S2)

> *Very close. We met weekly as part of an organized doctoral seminar to give feedback on each other's drafts and ideas* (RD, CT). *That sense of community has been crucial for all of us I think* (EN) (R122, S7)

These students express peer relationships as enhancing the research experience and beyond. Activities organised *by* peers *for* peers also contributed to a sense of belonging through the opportunities that arose for sharing emotionally, socially and academically. However, where peer relationships were under-developed or dysfunctional, the experience was often reflected on negatively. The following provide insight into some mixed experiences in developing peer relations:

> *Because I've largely been working from home I have not had as much contact with my peers as I would have liked* (RD, CoL). *The lack of designated desk space for part-time PhD candidates is a problem* (CoL)...*The most consistent relationships are those with other PhD candidates that are also casual tutors in (professional) Unit - we support each other and try to have lunch at least once over a semester, as well as coffee/lunch* (RD) (R324, S3)

> *Fairly close at the beginning because we shared a common office* (RD, CoL). *Changes to the location of offices disrupted these relationships* (RD, CoL) (R50, S3)

> *Having a large group of peers working in the one room has enabled lifelong relationships to develop* (RD, CoL). *It has also led to disagreements with people with strong and opposing personalities* (RD, CoL) (R346, S2)

A few students spoke of the impact of toxic personalities:

> *Good with some, I have made a few office friends. But some have been quite competitive, gossiping, and negative. Others are very disengaged. The culture is terrible* (RD, EN) (R105, S5)

> *What has hindered is some toxic personalities that makes me anxious about forming connections with others* (RD) (R31, S1)

18.7   Discussion and Conclusions

These findings highlight that the quality of social interaction has significant impact on identity and notions of belonging, with implications for how support through more holistic initiatives may better equip graduates for success during their research degrees and beyond. While each of the themes are intertwined, discussion follows the five themes, together with leitmotifs from Dr. Seuss' *Oh, the places you'll go!* which align playfully with aspects of the student experience.

18.7.1   Functional

> You have brains in your head, you have feet in your shoes, you can steer yourself in any direction you choose

Supervisors were key to the functional aspects of student experience, particularly for keeping on-track as myriad distractions and side-tracks can arise. Developing healthy supervisory relationships helped students with the process of achieving milestones (Fillery-Travis & Robinson, 2018). In particular, regular meetings were deemed valuable, if these established 'shared values, respect for each other and agreeing on expectations' (Lee, 2018, p. 884). Positive peer interactions were also appreciated and added to increasing performativity and milestone achievement. In these relationships, students found positive functional interactions affected all aspects of their study experience.

18.7.2   Enculturation

> You'll be on your way up! You'll be seeing great sights! You'll join the high fliers who soar to high heights.

Becoming part of academic culture is important for these students who frequently work in isolation. Opportunities to feel a sense of belonging—joining 'the high fliers'—provide examples and implicit understandings of the norms and practices of the community. Relationships with supervisors and peers were essential for creating spaces and reasons to interact which enhanced student experiences. These included, but were not limited to, casual coffee catchups, meals shared, seminars, part-time research assistant work or teaching engagements.

Networking opportunities provided by the institution, faculty or supervisor were key to 'helping [students] feel part of the academic community and engaged in the ongoing identity development process' (Baker & Pifer, 2011, p. 9). Flores-Scott and Nerad (2012) acknowledge the role of peers as 'important agents of community, learning, and development' (p. 75). Indeed, development of skills around networking and collaborating contributes to academic identity and confidence, producing greater independence.

18.7.3   Critical Thinking

> And if you go in, should you turn left or right ... or right-and-three-quarters? Or maybe, not quite? Or go around the back and sneak in from behind? Simple it's not, I'm afraid you will find for a mind-maker-upper to make up his mind

The development of academic skills, particularly critical thinking demanded by both the Academy and industry employers, is increasingly impacting the structure of postgraduate research degrees (Jones, 2018). The nature of the feedback provided to students, the opportunities to engage with modelled critical approaches and behaviours, and the openings they are enabled to take up within the Academy all influence student outcomes. This was also significant in the peer relationships students formed which further impacted identity formation (Flores-Scott & Nerad, 2012).

18.7.4   Emancipation

> The waiting place ... that's not for you! Somehow, you'll escape all that waiting and staying. You'll find the bright places where Boom Bands are playing. With banners flip-flapping once more you'll ride high! Ready for anything under the sky.

Student expectations included supervisory practices that ideally aided resilience in the ebb-and-flow of shifting student identities: from knowledgeable outsider to student, toward becoming an independent scholar destined for employment postgraduation. As noted by Rogers-Shaw & Carr-Chellman, when students 'acknowledged feeling respected and recognized by peers and professors in their programs' (2018, p. 246) a greater awareness of their own capabilities resulted. Venturing into the unknown is also a shared responsibility, influenced by 'the identity the learner wishes to maintain' and learning in ways that 'challenge the status quo' (Boud et al., 2018, p. 917). However, where relationships highlighted micro-managing or a perceived lack of respect this led students to doubt their abilities and distrust their supervisors.

18.7.5   Relationship Development

> And when you're alone there's a very good chance you'll meet things that will scare you right out of your pants. There are some, down the road between hither and yon, that can scare you so much you won't want to go on. But on you will go ...

The research degree experience is often likened to an amusement park ride: *'it's like a rollercoaster. Some days are going to be awesome and others are going to be hell. But it's part of the growth process you go through as an academic'* (R305, L2&3). During this 'rollercoaster' ride, the goodwill, friendship and wisdom developed in relationships with supervisors and peers was consistently acknowledged as important to persisting and identity formation. Where positive relationships were developed and sustained, students outlined a greater sense of belonging in the community as well as greater levels of confidence in successful participation. Fillery-Travis and Robinson (2018) emphasize the importance of quality in interpersonal factors which develop 'trust, respect, liking, support, responsiveness, cooperation and openness' (p. 851), contributing to the quality of the student-supervisor relationship. Students also noted that social and intellectual support from supervisors and peers, not only built community but also assisted proactive involvement (Lee, 2018). The converse was also true, where students experienced poor relationships with supervisors or peers, they experienced lower confidence in the academic community, increased frustrations and greater antagonism during the study process.

18.8 Conclusion

Clarity around the significant impact of supervisory and peer relationships on the postgraduate student experience was enabled through Lee's framework (2018). With 425 students contributing to this survey from 15 countries, across all discipline areas, their many voices came together as one. These relationships affected not only their experiences of study from day-to-day, but also their feelings of confidence within the study processes and their determination for future success following their student experience. The leitmotif of Dr. Seuss' children's book harkens to a journey of difficulty, isolation, successes, adventure, hardships and character-building, finishing with this single line…perhaps most relevant to every research student's dream:

> And will you succeed? Yes! You will, indeed! (98 and ¾ percent guaranteed)
> KID YOU'LL MOVE MOUNTAINS!

References

Andrews, M., Squire, C., & Tamboukou, M. (Eds.). (2008). *Doing narrative research*. London: Sage.

Australia, Universities. (2015). *Higher education and research: Facts and figures*. Sydney: Universities Australia.

Baker, V. L., & Pifer, M. J. (2011). The role of relationships in the transition from doctoral student to independent scholar. *Studies in Continuing Education*. https://doi.org/10.1080/0158037X.2010.515569.

Becker, S. A., Brown, M., Dahlstrom, E., Davis, A., DePaul, K., Diaz, V., et al. (2018). *NMC horizon report 2018 higher* (Education ed.). Louisville: CO. EDUCAUSE.

Boud, D., Fillery-Travis, A., Pizzolato, N., & Sutton, B. (2018). The influence of professional doctorates on practice and the workplace. *Studies in Higher Education.* https://doi.org/10.1080/03075079.2018.1438121.

Crotty, M. (1998). *The foundations of social research: Meaning and perspective in the research process.* St Leonards, NSW: Allen and Unwin.

Dr. Seuss. (1957). *Oh, the places you'll go!.* London: Harper Collins Children's Books.

Fillery-Travis, A., & Robinson, L. (2018). Studies in higher education making the familiar strange-a research pedagogy for practice making the familiar strange-a research pedagogy for practice. https://doi.org/10.1080/03075079.2018.1438098org/10.1080/03075079.2018.1438098.

Flores-Scott, E. M., & Nerad, M. (2012). Peers in doctoral education: Unrecognized learning partners. *New Directions for Higher Education, 2012,* 73–83. https://doi.org/10.1002/he.v2012.157.

Gee, J. P. (2000). Identity as an analytic lens for research in education. *Review of Research in Education, 25*(1), 28. https://doi.org/10.3102/0091732X025001099.

Harden-Thew, K. (2014). *Story, restory, negotiation: Emergent bilingual children making the transition to school.* Thesis: University of Wollongong. https://doi.org/10.13140/RG.2.2.12421.55529.

Jones, M. (2018). Contemporary trends in professional doctorates. *Studies in Higher Education.* https://doi.org/10.1080/03075079.2018.1438095.

Knowles, M. S., Holton, E. F., & Swanson, R. A. (2012). *The adult learner: The definitive classic in adult education and human resource development.* Abingdon UK: Routledge.

Lansoght, E. (n.d) *PhDtalk blogspot.* Accessed http://phdtalk.blogspot.com.au/2012/06/ten-great-blogs-for-phd-students.html.

Lee, A. (2018). How can we develop supervisors for the modern doctorate? *Studies in Higher Education.* https://doi.org/10.1080/03075079.2018.1438116.

Lundsteen, N. (2014). Doctoral Career paths and 'Learning to be. In S. Carter & D. Laurs (Eds.), *Generic support for doctoral students: Practice and pedagogy.* New York: Routledge.

Marsh, H., &Western, M. (2016) How to improve research training in Australia— give industry placements to Ph.D. students. *The Conversation, 19 April, 2016.* https://theconversation.com/how-to-improve-research-training-in-australia-give-industry-placements-to-phd-students-57972.

Mewburn, I (n.d.) *The thesis whisperer blog.* Accessed from https://thesiswhisperer.com/.

Norton, A., & Cherastidtham, I., (2014). Mapping Australian higher education, 2014–15, Grattan Institute.

Rogers-Shaw, C., & Carr-Chellman, D. (2018). Developing care and socio-emotional learning in first year doctoral students: Building capacity for success, *13.* https://doi.org/10.28945/4064.

Spyrou, S. (2011). The limits of children's voices: From authenticity to critical, reflexive representation. *Childhood, 18,* 151–165.

Stone, C., & O'Shea, S. (2012). *Transformations and self discovery.* Champaign, Illinois: Common Ground Publishing.

Whannell, R., & Whannell, P. (2015). Identity theory as a theoretical framework to understand attrition for university students in transition. *Student Success, 6*(2), 43–52. https://doi.org/10.5204/ssj.v6i2.286.

Janine Delahunty (Ph.D.) is a Lecturer in Learning, Teaching & Curriculum, at the University of Wollongong, Australia. She works in the Academic Professional Development & Recognition team and is involved in various research projects. Her core interest is how the learning-teaching experience can be enhanced in HE, and how the student experience can be improved through the professional development of staff to foster their teaching and reflective practices. Her research has involved people from diverse backgrounds including first-in-family, regional, and Indigenous students, research degree students, and online educators and learners. Her motivations stem from her own venture into university study as a mature-age student, studying part-time for many years and doing the family-study-work balancing act. She has published across linguistic, HE and academic development journals.

Kathryn Harden-Thew (Ph.D.) came to HE having first taught across school and TAFE sectors. She is now a Lecturer/Academic Developer in the Learning, Teaching and Curriculum Unit at the University of Wollongong, Australia (UOW). She is the Co-ordinator of the Continuing Professional Development Portfolio Review Panel and is an executive member of the WATTLE (Wollongong Academy of Tertiary Teaching & Learning Excellence) committee but her professional passion is equipping sessional teaching staff to develop their teaching practice and better support their students' learning. As an Higher Degree Research (HDR) student and student representative, she became interested in the factors that contribute to and constitute success during this period. Subsequently, her research interests include understanding HDR experience, exploring the role and activity of sessional staff, transitions in HE and barriers to educational success.

Chapter 19
Making Student Internships Work: Navigating Stakeholder Interests and Aspirations at the University-Work Interface

Martha Caddell and Rosemarie McIlwhan

19.1 Introduction

Business and industry collaboration is a focus of engagement across the university landscape, with an emphasis on ensuring students have opportunities to engage in real world opportunities to develop and apply their learning, sitting alongside interests in the broader enhancement of graduate employability and employment (Brooks, Fuller, & Waters, 2012). The interfaces between Higher Education (HE) and graduate careers are often couched in terms of a 'supply chain' with universities seen as playing a key role in providing graduates with high level skills to meet the needs of local and national labour markets (Gunn & Kafmann, 2011; UKCES, 2014; Wilson, 2012). Such interest is given a particular edge within contemporary political and policy discourses, with questions of 'excellence' in university performance and the 'value' of undertaking university study measured and accounted for in relation to post-graduation salary levels. However, there is a risk that 'success' in HE risks being ever more narrowly defined—for individuals and the sector generally—through such a transactional view of impact and gain. Indeed, such a focus raises particular challenges when exploring routes into industries with relatively low salaries, such as the voluntary and charitable sector (i.e. the third sector). Equating graduate 'success' with salary levels risks devaluing the contribution and impact of graduates entering these fields of work.

In addition, the focus on supply chain-type discussions fails to capture the richness of the negotiation of interests and aspirations between stakeholders (students, employers and universities) at the interface between study and work. As they nav-

M. Caddell (✉)
Heriot-Watt University, Edinburgh, Scotland, UK
e-mail: m.caddell@hw.ac.uk

R. McIlwhan
Open University, Milton Keynes, UK
e-mail: rosemarie.mcilwhan@open.ac.uk

igate their way through study, students are continually making critical decisions about career pathways and pragmatic decisions about what work experience and development opportunities they can—and can afford to—explore. The diversity of employer interests and needs means that they too may need to build confidence and skills to support new recruits' transitioning into the workplace. Small and micro-organisations in particular need support to make the most of the university collaborations on offer. (As defined by the European Commission (n.d.) small organisations are those with less than fifty employees, and micro employers are those with less than 10 employees). How stakeholders approach and navigate these diverse interests has a significant bearing on how skills and development challenges will be negotiated, the collaborations that emerge, and the fairness and equality of access to such opportunities.

This chapter offers a critical reflection on the university-work interface through the lens of student internships. Over the past decade considerable focus has been directed to the role of internships as mechanisms for gaining work experience and securing routes to permanent jobs. Internships are increasingly common across a range of sectors, from those with a long history of such positions (creative industries for example) to those, including the third sector, where the term has been less commonplace. Yet internships have also increased in their notoriety for being unpaid, leading to accusations of a 'new elitism' where only those who can afford to work for free can gain the experience necessary to access certain professions. In such a context, the role of universities in developing and supporting opportunities that are meaningful, fair and pedagogically informed is under scrutiny.

To unpack this, the discussion here explores the diversity of stakeholder interests, specifically the spectrum of student employability needs, and the interests and practical challenges faced by host employers in their interactions with universities. Framed around the legal, practical and pedagogic challenges of developing meaningful work experience opportunities for students, it draws as its central case study on the Third Sector Internships Scotland programme (Caddell, Boyle, McIlwhan, & Jones, 2015; Pegg & Caddell, 2016). This national initiative sought to offer students across all Scottish universities the opportunity to apply for paid internships, experience work in the third sector, and receive appropriate feedback on their applications to enhance their employability. The chapter will therefore reflect on the multiple layers of impact and visions of 'success' that any effective employability initiative needs to proffer, as well as the challenges of meeting the needs of diverse stakeholders.

19.2 Austerity, Graduate Employability and the Rise of Internships

In the context of the 'austerity era' there has been considerable concern about the rate of graduate unemployment and the capacity of universities to meet the skills-needs of industry (Andrews & Higson, 2010; Universities UK, 2018). While graduate employment rates have picked up in recent years, and in 2018 at 74.3% 6 months after graduation (AGCAS, 2018), there is still concern about the types of work they are able to secure, with many still in insecure positions or in posts not considered 'graduate level' employment. High youth unemployment is, "endemic in the UK when we go into recession" (Gilleard, 2011: 7).[1] In part this is down to market confidence: in a difficult environment those in the graduate recruitment market will not make the same investment in recruiting and developing graduates.[2] Concerns remain that public sector cuts and continued economic uncertainty will further perpetuate this trend.

A second related concern from the perspective both of employers and HE institutions has been the employability of students. There has been widespread recognition that a 'degree is not enough' and work relevant skills and experience are crucial in a highly competitive job market (CBI, 2009; Tomlinson, 2008). Universities in England are being required to prepare 'employability statements' for each course or programme offered, highlighting the employability skills and attributes gained through study. In addition, universities across the UK are being encouraged to offer opportunities for students to gain 'real world' experience as part of their studies through work placements, work-related projects and employer engagement activities (e.g. SFC, 2010). Against this backdrop, interning has become a taken-for-granted career path into some professions, such as law or some of the creative industries such as the media or fashion. While there has been no national monitoring of the diverse range of employment practices covered by the term, it has been estimated that a quarter of a million employers are operating internships (CIPD, 2010).

Cross-cutting both of these debates is popular and political discussion of the potential exploitation of students and graduates who are working unpaid in order to gain the experience necessary to secure more permanent or paid employment. In recent years attention has focused on the potential elitism of (often unpaid) internship and work placement schemes, where access to opportunities are based on who you know or your ability to work without pay rather than on merit. Such issues have been a key component of recent political discussion on social mobility and employment (e.g. Carmody, 2011; Wilson, 2012). The Milburn Panel on Fair Access to the Professions, for example, notes that "opportunities to undertake internships are not fairly distributed" (Milburn, 2009: 101). Its 2012 follow-up report notes that "Unpaid internships clearly disadvantage those from less affluent backgrounds who cannot afford to work for free for any length of time. They are a barrier to fair access and, indeed, to better social mobility." (Milburn, 2012: 5). What is striking is that nearly a decade on, despite much campaigning, progress has been limited and unpaid internships continue (Montacute, 2018; Sutton Trust, 2014).

---

[1] Carl Gilleard is Chief Executive of the Association of Graduate Recruiters.
[2] Ibid.

19.3   Internships: Legal and Ethical Concerns

The term 'intern' is used multifariously, with different terms, conditions and expectations placed on those undertaking internships. This is exacerbated by the lack of clarity over their employment status as internships are not defined in law. This is important not just in terms of whether interns are paid, but also in relation to other employment rights such as time-off. Some organisations argue that internships are volunteering. If this were the case, then interns would not require to be paid, but there could be no obligations put upon the intern, they would act out of free will and there could be no consequences if they did not act. This does not generally describe the experience of interns, who are invariably expected to work set hours and complete the work allocated to them.

If, however, internships constitute employment then more control could be exercised over the intern, and there would be an obligation to pay at least the national minimum wage and to respect basic employment rights. To be employed whether as a worker or an employee, there must be a contract (verbal or written), and the employee is personally required to carry out the work. Case law has developed several tests to identify if someone is an "employee" including whether a mutuality of obligation exists (i.e. do the employee and the organisation have obligations to each other); whether the employer has control over the work of the employee as well as whether a contract of employment exists and whether the individual must personally carry out the work.

Most internships require the intern to maintain set hours, undertake specific activities and put them under the direction of someone within the organisation who can set tasks and take action against them if they do not complete those tasks. In these circumstances it could be argued that the internship constitutes employment, as such the intern would be entitled to be paid at least the national minimum wage and also to basic employment rights. The legal cases to date have decided that where the intern is clearly doing work that benefits the organisation they should be paid (*Hudson v TPG Web Publishing Ltd* [2011]), and in such circumstances working unpaid or for expenses only is unlawful (*Vetta v Dreamworks Motion Pictures Ltd* [2008]). Whilst it would increasingly appear that internships in the private sector should be paid, the situation is slightly less clear in relation to those in the third sector. An exemption in the National Minimum Wage Act 1998 provides that voluntary workers (those working in a charity or voluntary organisation) are not entitled to the national minimum wage. This exemption was created to:

> ...ensure that volunteers could continue to operate in the voluntary and charitable sectors and could continue to receive reasonable expenses, appropriate subsistence and training, without minimum wage liability. At the same time workers in these sectors retained the right to be paid at least minimum wage (Low Pay Commission, 2011: 97).

Whilst some third sector organisations have used this exemption to justify their ongoing use of unpaid internships, the exemption for voluntary workers was not designed to prevent the voluntary sector from paying its workers; but to enable them to continue working with volunteers i.e. those who genuinely wish to donate their time/experience for no reward and who are not subject to any obligation. The requirement to pay national minimum wage to anyone performing "work" for that organisation remains. All staff working for a charity or voluntary organisation are entitled to minimum wage; and therefore, any intern who is performing "work" could also be entitled to this.

The issue of whether internships are paid or unpaid, is important not just in itself, but for social mobility. Whether or not an internship is paid influences students' ability to undertake the work. Bates (2011) found that "40% of those who had thought about applying for an internship said that they changed their mind as they were not in a position to be able to work for free, and 39% of those who were offered an internship had to turn it down for the same reason". This correlates with the Milburn Panel on Fair Access to the Professions, which found that "you are less likely to be able to do an internship if:

- You lack the means to work for free (socio-economic factors)
- You lack the means to travel or live near to the internship (geographic factors)
- You come from a background in which a professional internship is never considered or discussed (information factors)." (Milburn, 2009: 101).

Such barriers mean that access to employment and to better social mobility are unfairly distributed (Milburn, 2012: 5) with a bias towards those who can afford to work for free. Cullinane and Montacute (2018) estimate that the cost of an internship is £1100 a month in London, and £885 a month in Manchester, working unpaid in these circumstances would require substantial financial backing from family or others, or the ability to work multiple jobs. This clearly disadvantages those from less affluent backgrounds or for whom other circumstances mean that they cannot afford to work for free and reinforces the barriers to social mobility. However, this is not only a personal barrier, but also a societal barrier. If access to internships is limited, this inhibits diversity in the workforce and limits employers' access to talent creating barriers to having the right people in the right jobs, building social cohesion and having a workforce which reflects our global society. Whilst the public recognise the inherent unfairness of being asked to work for free (Sutton Trust, 2014: 3), it would appear that many employers, including those in the third sector, have yet to recognise this and to stop offering unpaid internships.

There has been some suggestion that internships of longer than four weeks should be paid (Cullinane & Montacute, 2018: 6), however this contradicts existing employment law which states that people should be paid for the work that they do i.e. there should not be a period when a person is expected to work for free. It is unclear how such a requirement could be considered to be legal under the current law, or why it would be desirable to amend the law to allow this. Requiring a person to work for a month unpaid would continue to create barriers and limit fair access to employment.

For an internship to be fair it must be paid, so as to eliminate barriers to access and opportunity (socio-economic factors). It also needs to be openly advertised so that anyone can access it (information factors) rather than through word-of-mouth or personal contacts. This creates a more equitable playing field for applicants, a wider talent pool for employers and fairer access to the employment market for everyone.

However, internships also need to be meaningful and have purpose so that they add value to the intern and the organisation.

19.4 Third Sector Internships Scotland

Against this backdrop of concern over graduate employability, efforts were made by the Scottish Funding Council (SFC) to encourage universities to explore new ways of working with industry groups (SFC, 2004, 2010). As part of this, Third Sector Internships Scotland (TSIS) was developed to offer all Scottish university students the opportunity to undertake a meaningful, paid, supported internship in a voluntary organisation, charity or social enterprise (see Caddell et al., 2015) This five year programme supported by the Scottish Funding Council's *Learning to Work 2* initiative (SFC, 2010) was a cross-sector partnership between Queen Margaret University, The Open University in Scotland and the Scottish Council for Voluntary Organisations (SCVO), with support from universities across Scotland. It focused on offering work experience and skills development opportunities for students; promoting the third sector as a graduate career option; and enabling students to make a valuable contribution to the work of Scotland's Third Sector. In doing so it aimed to contribute to the development of work-based learning opportunities and enhance the employability of Scotland's university students. Over the course of the programme, TSIS received 8314 applications from across every university in Scotland and provided 1275 interviews and feedback. The project supported 349 internships of which 94% were hosted by small- and medium-sized employers (Caddell et al., 2015).

TSIS was designed to provide students with real world experience, from the application and interview process to the internship itself. TSIS provided comprehensive support to students and to host third sector organisations at every stage. Students were provided with guidance on applications; detailed, personalised feedback from every interview; as well as support and opportunities for reflection and development throughout the internship. Employers were provided with support to develop the internship project; extensive guidance on recruitment and employment good practice, and support for hosting the internship. TSIS also developed strong links with university careers services to further support students and to raise awareness of the third sector as a potential graduate destination of choice. Significantly, for the TSIS programme meaningful work required meaningful remuneration, therefore all TSIS interns were paid the Scottish Living Wage. This was welcomed by interns and organisations. Many organisations promoted this further, hosting additional internships that they funded themselves.

TSIS initially made the decision to use the term 'internship' to differentiate opportunities on offer from those work placements that were linked to specific modules, programmes of study and institutions. The term was also selected to emphasise the development dimension of the role as well as the more direct (paid) employment relationship between intern and host organisation. Shortly after launching the programme, popular and political attention was drawn to the growth of unpaid internships in certain sectors. Newspaper headlines highlighted the unpaid work required of young people seeking to take their first steps into particular industries, the long hours being worked, and the 'who you know' approach to recruitment that surrounded many of these internships.

TSIS therefore sought to provide a counterpoint to the headline-making unpaid internships, demonstrating how to develop opportunities that were open to all who could benefit from them, not just those who can afford to work for free. This was particularly evident in the dual emphasis on supporting the development of the intern whilst recognising and valuing the skills and capacities they bring to the roles, and the importance of their work making a meaningful contribution to the organisation. This recognition was most directly evident in the payment of a Living Wage to interns and reflected in the working relationships established with the host organisation. In taking this approach, the TSIS programme demonstrated the benefits that such open recruitment can bring to employers, opening space for students with diverse skills to contribute to work in organisations and a sector they may not initially have considered as their first choice career destination.

Taking this programme as a case study allows an exploration of internships as a route into graduate employment and offers a lens through which to explore the dynamics of stakeholder relations at the interface of work and study. In particular, it offers insights into what the universities, employers and students see as making internships meaningful, fair and practically implementable. In our discussion we draw on insights from across the five years of the programme, including surveys and discussions with employers and interns, analysis of intern applications and intern and employer feedback questionnaires.

19.5 Making Internships Meaningful and Fair for Interns

Our research suggested that students applying for TSIS internships were seeking experiences that were different to other activities they had undertaken such as volunteering and part-time work, and that would differentiate them from their peers in the labour market. For some, the internships were viewed as an opportunity to try out an area of work to see whether it is a viable career option, while for others it was viewed as a stepping stone to help them move into their field of interest. TSIS had to strike a balance between offering internships that met specific interests, and highlighting that skills are transferable and can be applied to other fields.

19.5.1 The Value of Fair Pay and Fair Recruitment

Many applicants viewed the third sector as a difficult area within which to gain paid employment, while some were unaware that this was a possibility. Many applicants had some volunteering experience, and some had interning experience. While both activities were viewed as potential routes into the third sector, offering relevant experience and networking opportunities, internships are seen as distinctly different from volunteering, particularly in relation to the level of responsibility and anticipated deliverables associated with the work undertaken. A paid internship was seen as a potential stepping stone into employment, offering a way to extend the level of responsibility and engagement gained through volunteering. As one intern noted, "I feel as though I have been trusted with a great responsibility and that I am being treated as someone with the capacity to handle the task" (Caddell et al., 2015: 68).

The question of payment was critical. Interns contrasted the TSIS experience to other, often unpaid, opportunities. One intern notes:

> Paid internships such as this, with real roles and responsibilities for interns, are invaluable for those who otherwise could not afford to invest the time in gaining contacts and experience for their future careers, and for third sector organisations who otherwise could not afford the time and money to take on an extra employee. I have heard too many tales of people sleeping on their mate's floor while they work for organisations for free, spending the majority of their time bonding with the photocopier and the kettle. (Caddell et al., 2015: 75)

Another stresses the financial implications of unpaid work are not just individual, but have impact on families too:

> I try, as much as possible, to support myself so there is less pressure on my parents to provide for me and have been that way since I was young. The experience I have received from my internship has far surpassed my expectations and there was no way I could have known how valuable the internship would be before I applied. If it had been unpaid, I really would have missed out in not applying. (Caddell et al., 2015: 75)

The attraction was not just for interns, organisations also found paid internships attractive. Many organisations moved from working solely with volunteers to the intern being their first employee. Organisations also appreciated the financial support provided by TSIS and reported that they could not have provided a paid internship or have undertaken the work carried out by the intern without the financial support. Having a fiduciary, employment relationship meant that interns felt more accountable and organisations felt more able to hold interns to account for the work undertaken. This was something which organisations felt that they could not do to the same degree with voluntary workers or volunteers.

In addition to attempting to 'level the playing field' through paying Living Wage salaries, TSIS also sought to support students in accessing relevant work through a visible and open, competence-based recruitment process. Importantly in the context of the high volume of applications, even those who did not succeed in being appointed to an internship still had a meaningful experience as they received guidance and comments on their application and individual feedback on their interview. For many this was their first experience of an open recruitment procedure using competency-based applications forms and a formal interview. This gave them meaningful real world experience in applying for work. Some of the students who were initially unsuccessful, applied for further internships and were subsequently successful having acted on the feedback provided. One intern commented: "This is the first job I have secured where I didn't have a contact to get me a job... I now understand what it means to be professional..." (Caddell et al., 2015: 66)

19.5.2 Making Internship Work Meaningful

Valuing work goes far beyond financial reward. As the case of TSIS highlighted, the content and context of the internship projects were critical in ensuring a meaningful impact on host organisation and the intern themselves. A strong theme in the feedback from students and employers was the 'real world' nature of TSIS internships. These were not projects developed for the benefit of a student, but real tasks that the organisation wished to get done to benefit their core operations. The level of responsibility given to interns was high. Indeed, some noted initial surprise at the degree of responsibility (and in some cases autonomy) they were given, and most appreciated the challenge—and ultimately the rewards—that this brought.

Employers noted that this approach also benefitted the organisation. One employer noted in their post-internship feedback that, "We would hire more interns but only if we could find them similar clearly defined tasks to do with meaningful outcomes. It's not fair to interns to hire them as general dogsbodies, and it won't really benefit the organisation either." On the TSIS programme employers had to clearly identify a project which the intern would be responsible for. The project needed to add value to the organisation, contribute to their core operations and be capable of completion within the time available for the internship. Ensuring that the project was clearly defined in this way, ensured that host organisations gained a meaningful project that they might not otherwise have been able to achieve; and provided interns with a project that developed their skills and which they had ownership of, so could talk to future employers about. It also managed expectations so that interns were asked to do something realistic, with appropriate support and resources and clear development opportunities.

The status of internships (as opposed to volunteering) became meaningful both to organisations and to students. There appeared to be a *de facto* recognition of a difference with interns tending to be offered more specific, often project related roles, with a defined time period for engagement, and volunteers tending to be more *ad hoc* activities on an ongoing basis. Interns perceived a qualitative difference between how employers regard internships—and specifically paid internships—more highly than volunteer activity. Similarly, a host organisation commented that "paid interns are infinitely preferable to volunteers as the employment relationship entails full commitment and allows structured management of project resources" (Caddell, 2012, p. 46). This position is reinforced by the findings of the Milburn Panel (2012: 5) which found that "having work experience or an internship on a CV is even more critical to finding employment now than it was three years ago."

19.6 Partnerships and Collaboration at the University: Work Interface

Facilitating meaningful and mutually beneficial employer engagement remains challenging for many staff in universities. Establishing links with organisations, defining areas of common interest, and sustaining connections over time requires considerable resource, energy and enthusiasm from both parties. This is seen as particularly challenging in the case of small and micro-sized employers, who have less people, time and resource to devote to activities that may be seen as 'additional' to core business, such as university collaborations. Much of the existing literature, policy and practical reviews focus on work with larger businesses, most of which has limited resonance in the context of work with small charities and voluntary organisations.

Given the diversity of the third sector, there was a broad spectrum of organisational size and capacity including many small and micro organisations with limited income and small staff numbers. Indeed, 94% of TSIS host employers were small or micro employers. This raised particular issues in relation to establishing and supporting internships. Creating and managing an internship appeared a daunting prospect for many hosts. TSIS provided guidance for employers throughout the internship process, from support in creating a detailed job description and person specification for that role, through to support once the intern was in post. For many organisations this was the first time they had employed someone, or the first time they had used such a structured process. TSIS sought to support and upskill employers in their recruitment and employment practices, promoting good practice. This focus on transparent, fair and accessible processes for selection of internships fits with the recommendations of the Milburn Panel on Fair Access to the Professions (2012). It suggests that "given their centrality to young people's career prospects, internships should no longer be treated as part of the informal economy. They should be subject to similar rules to other parts of the labour market" (Milburn, 2012: 5).

Employers showed extensive goodwill towards the students and were extremely supportive, including being accommodating of academic requirements or deadlines when required. However, they faced substantial challenges, in particularly having the time and resources to supervise and support an intern. Often these resource challenges meant that internships were delivered on a part-time basis to facilitate access to appropriate support or office space. Whilst this did not affect the internships, it does have implications for universities considering internships or work placements in the third sector as these may not always be possible within the timescale of a standard term/semester. It also has implications for third sector organisations hosting interns. Clear thought needs to be given to who will manage and support the intern, their availability to do so, where and how this will happen and where the intern will work.

It is also important in this context to delineate internships from work placements and the differential award/reward for engagement that each approach implies. ASET (2014) define work-based and placement learning opportunities as those that "are a planned and integrated part of a student's programme of study at a Higher Education provider" (p. 4). They identify the pedagogic value of this type of learning as bringing together "academic theory and workplace practice, integrating the working with the learning" (p. 4). For work placements the time commitment is specified by the university rather than the host organisation, and any sanctions e.g. for non-attendance, are academic rather than employment-related. Work placements are unpaid but undertaken as part of the academic course so completed in academic time i.e. they should not impinge on student's time outside of university when they may be working. The distinction is one which also frames the relationship between the employer and the university. In the case of work placements, the assumption is one of facilitating a learning experience for the student. The more mutually-framed benefits associated with internships proffer a somewhat different 'landscape of collaboration' (Wilson, 2012).

If universities wish to support internships or to request work placements (with attached academic requirements) in the third sector, then they may also need to provide support to host employers. This would include being clear on whether it is an internship or a work placement with associated requirements and academic credit, and the requirements and deadlines that need to be met by the student, clarity on the role and responsibilities of the third sector organisation and the university, and support for the third sector organisation beyond what might be provided for larger organisations or businesses e.g. employment guidance.

19.7 Conclusion

The case study of the Third Sector Internships Scotland programme highlights key challenges that require reflection and action when considering the liminal space between study and work occupied by internships. It brings to the fore the need for universities to consider questions of ethics and fairness in relation to accessing work-based learning opportunities, whether they are embedded in or additional to the curriculum. Questions of financial accessibility need to be seen alongside broader issues of the accessibility of opportunities such as fair recruitment practices.

In addition, the complexity of the relationship between employer, student and university interests highlighted in the TSIS case study suggests the need for a more nuanced and multi-directional view of the knowledge exchange that takes place at the work-study interface. More broadly, there is a need to reconsider the relationship between universities and employers and the notion of placements and internships being a uni-directional 'bridge' or supply chain between study and work. Rather, there is a need to recognise the 'landscape of collaboration' as multi-layered (Wilson, 2012). Small and micro-organisations have much to gain from collaborations with universities, but many need support to build both the capacity and confidence to make meaningful connections. In such contexts universities need to work—individually and collectively—to support such organisations to take advantage of the skills and expertise that students and the wider university community can offer. Such recognition also highlights the importance of looking beyond narrowly-framed (primarily economic) indicators of success and impact of employability efforts. In cases such as TSIS, impact and value-added is strongly evident in the social and cultural change that such internships have—within organisations and in the communities served by such third sector groups. Shifting our thinking from 'supplying' employers' skills needs to collaboration for social impact proffers an alternative way of both initiating and framing university-employer collaboration and the opportunities that are opened to students and graduates.

References

Andrews, J., & Higson, H. (2010). Graduate employability, "Soft Skills" Versus "Hard" business knowledge: A European study. *Higher Education in Europe, 33*(4), 411–422. https://doi.org/10.1080/03797720802522627.

ASET. (2014). *Benefits of placements*. Available at: http://www.asetonline.org/wp-content/uploads/2014/11/ASET-Good-Practice-Guide-2014.pdf. Accessed December 10, 2018.

Bates, C. (2011). *Investigating internships*, London, YouGov. Available at: https://yougov.co.uk/topics/lifestyle/articles-reports/2011/03/23/investigating-internships.

Brooks, R., Fuller, A., & Waters, J. (Eds.). (2012). *Changing spaces of education. New perspectives on the nature of learning*. Abingdon: Routledge.

Caddell, M. (2012). *Making internships work for Scotland's students and third sector organisations*. Edinburgh: Third Sector Internships Scotland.

Caddell, M., Boyle, F., McIlwhan, R., & Jones, H. (2015). *Third sector internships Scotland: Final report*. Edinburgh: TSIS. https://www.open.ac.uk/scotland/sites/www.open.ac.uk.scotland/files/files/ecms/web-content/TSIS-Final-Report.PDF. Accessed December 10, 2018.

Carmody, J. (2011). *Graduate opportunities—The current policy context. Graduate employment and internships* (pp. 37–41). London: Westminster Education Forum (WEF).

CBI and Universities UK. (2009). Future fit: Preparing graduates for the world of work, London: CBI. Available at: https://www.cbi.org.uk/pdf/20090326-CBI-FutureFit-Preparing-graduates-for-the-world-of-work.pdf.

Cullinane, C., & Montacute, R. (2018). *Pay as you go: Internship pay, quality and access in the graduate jobs market*. London: Sutton Trust. https://www.suttontrust.com/research-paper/internships-pay-as-you-go/.

European Commission. (n.d.). What is an SME?. Available at: https://ec.europa.eu/growth/smes/business-friendly-environment/sme-definition_en.

Gilleard, C. (2011). *The current state of graduate employment. Graduate employment and internships*. (pp. 7–10). London: Westminster Education Forum (WEF).

Gunn, V., & Kafmann, K. (2011). Employability and the austerity decade. *Graduates for the 21st Century: Integrating the enhancement themes*. Glasgow, QAA Scotland. Available at: https://www.enhancementthemes.ac.uk/docs/ethemes/graduates-for-the-21st-century/employability-and-the-austerity-decade.pdf?sfvrsn=a63df981_8.

Low Pay Commission. (2011). *National minimum wage*. London: The Stationery Office.

Milburn Panel. (2009). *Unleashing aspiration: Fair access to the professions*. https://webarchive.nationalarchives.gov.uk/20121205062846/http://www.bis.gov.uk/assets/biscore/corporate/migratedd/publications/p/panel-fair-access-to-professions-final-report-21july09.pdf.

Milburn Panel. (2012). *Fair access to professional careers*. https://assets.publishing.service.gov.uk/government/uploads/system/uploads/attachment_data/file/61090/IR_FairAccess_acc2.pdf.

Montacute, R. (2018). *Internships—Unpaid, unadvertised, unfair: Research Brief*, Edition 20, January 2018. London: Sutton Trust. https://www.suttontrust.com/research-paper/internships-unpaid-unadvertised-unfair/.

Pegg, A., & Caddell, M. (2016). Workplaces and policy spaces: Insights from third sector internships Scotland. *Higher Education, Skills and Work-Based Learning, 6*(2), 1–19.

Scottish Funding Council. (2004). *Learning to Work: Enhancing employability and enterprise in Scottish further and higher education.* Available at: https://www.webarchive.org.uk/wayback/archive/20090411224926/http:/www.sfc.ac.uk/publications/pubs_other_sfefcarchive/learning_to_work.pdff.

Scottish Funding Council. (2010). *Learning to Work Two – developing the Council's employability strategy: Consultation outcomes, action plan and invitation to develop proposals.* Consultation Circular SFC/41/2009 18/12/2009. Edinburgh: SFC.

Sutton Trust. (2014). *Internship or indenture: Research brief,* 2 November 2014. London: Sutton Trust. https://www.suttontrust.com/research-paper/internships-unpaid-graduates/.

Tomlinson, M. (2008). 'The degree is not enough': students' perceptions of the role of higher education credentials for graduate work and employability. *British Journal of Sociology of Education, 29*(1), 49–61.

UKCES. (2014). *Forging futures: Building higher level skills through university and employer collaboration.* London: UKCES/Universities UK. https://assets.publishing.service.gov.uk/government/uploads/system/uploads/attachment_data/file/356749/FF_FinalReport_Digital_190914.pdf. Accessed April 3, 2018.

Universities UK. (2018). *Britain thinks—Public perceptions of UK universities.* Available at: http://britainthinks.com/pdfs/Britain-Thinks_Public-perceptions-of-UK-universities_Nov18.pdf. Accessed December 11, 2018.

Wilson, T. (2012). *A review of business—University Collaboration, BIS/12/610.* London: BIS.

Martha Caddell (Ph.D.) is Professor of HE Policy and Practice and Director of the Learning and Teaching Academy at Heriot-Watt University, Edinburgh, Scotland. Her current research and scholarship work focuses on academic identities and careers, discourses of excellence and success in HE, supporting student transitions, and developing flexible curriculum in HE. Her academic background is in the sociology and anthropology of education, with a focus on international policy and practice, skills for development, and education in the context of civil war and political conflict. She is a Principal Fellow of the Higher Education Academy. From 2010–2015 she was Co-Director of Third Sector Internships Scotland.

Rosemarie McIlwhan (LLB) is an Associate Lecturer in Law at the Open University, UK. Her academic background is in law, focusing on human rights and equality, and education, with an emphasis on andragogy. From 2010–2015 she was the Research Consultant for Third Sector Internships Scotland.

Chapter 20
Curiosity and Self-connected Learning: Re-centring the 'I' in Technology-Assisted Learning

Sally Goldspink and Hilary Engward

20.1 Introduction

Innovations in technology shape Higher Education (HE). In the UK, technology provides a direct interface between the institution, lecturer and learner, whether the learner is campus-based or remote. The evolution of distance learning from a mechanism to widen access via flexible and remote participation is filtering into campus-based pedagogic practice. As such, educational research about distance learning can inform the broader HE community because the difference between on-campus and off-campus learning is less overt. We are united through the adoption of technology as a solution-focussed means for managing and improving the delivery of learning and assessment for students. Thus, the educational landscape constantly shifts in response to the developments in technology, and technology is redefining how learning is organised, delivered and managed.

Gurgling underneath the abundance of implementation strategies however, are questions that continue to surface about how meaningful learning actually occurs within the technological domain. Indeed, as Moore and Kersey asserted, 'the more one understands the nature of adult learning, the better one can understand the nature of distance learning' (1996, p. 153). From a pedagogic perspective, learning is messy and multidimensional: people do not learn in a bubble behind their computer screens, removed from their past, present and future selves. When designing courses and learning objects, learning can be misrepresented as linear and compartmentalised within our striving for more active forms of delivery. However, things can potentially get prickly when we step back and consider if what occurs for the individual, fits with our own pedagogic assumptions. In respect of compulsory professional online

S. Goldspink (✉) · H. Engward
Anglia Ruskin University, Cambridge, UK
e-mail: Sally.Goldspink@anglia.ac.uk

H. Engward
e-mail: hilary.engward@anglia.ac.uk

© Springer Nature Switzerland AG 2019
A. Diver (ed.), *Employability via Higher Education: Sustainability as Scholarship*,
https://doi.org/10.1007/978-3-030-26342-3_20

courses, content is often designed to be sequentially clicked through, with questions and tasks, and ending with a test. The means of organising the content is evident, and the learning objects have been carefully constructed for the learner to be 'active' to progress through the content, but what did they gain from the experience? The answer of course depends upon several key issues;

- the motivation for undertaking the learning
- the impact of previous learning on this situation
- whether you see the learning as relevant to your past and present understanding
- the opportunities for future application.

The content is developed with the best possible intentions to promote active learning, but there is often little control over what has actually happened. For example, if I intend to complete the compulsory training as quickly as possible, I will click through the content as quickly as possible. I might also achieve the required pass mark, but what is learnt in terms of content is likely to be limited and superficial. There is less likely to be any meaningful or transformational impact that I will be able to apply and use in the real world. Indeed, the experience may confirm unhelpful assumptions, or serve to underscore that I have better things to do with my time. Therefore, the potential negative experience of learning must be thought about alongside the academic intentions. To be useful post-course, the in-course experience must support learners to be active contributors to their own knowledge as opposed to anonymous recipients or uncritical responders to information. Learning tasks, anecdotally referred to as 'academic hoops' may increase short-term participation but when isolated from the individual have limited, long-term pedagogic value.

Fundamentally, learning must begin with the learner: it cannot be 'given,' despite the multitude of techniques and strategies that technology can offer. If I, as the learner do not see the need for learning, I will not see the relevance of the learning, or see why it will be beneficial in the future. Without an individualised connection to the process and content, I will not be curious to find out more. In essence, if I lack curiosity, I am unlikely to connect to, and learn from, the content presented to me. Interest in education is important. Rethinking assumptions about what useful learning is, means we need to rethink what the end-product of that learning is, at the start of our curriculum design. How can we build individual connectedness into this medium of learning? What are its intended results? How can we build these within the design and delivery of that content? Much is written about the technological revolution in HE relating to what the virtual world can look like and offer from a structural perspective, however, deeper philosophical and theoretical debate is harder to find. So, rather than being drawn into the technical aspects of distance learning, this chapter questions the experience of learning itself, in relation to its long-term function and impact.

Using insights derived from interpretive phenomenology, a learner-centric approach to learning can reallocate taken-for-granted notions of knowledge as authored by others, to learners connecting to, and self-authoring their own understanding. Our proposition is important and necessary at this juncture of the technological advancement in our sector. Technology provides a host of pedagogic advantages but to maximise the opportunities available, the individual learners' experience and their trajectory into employment must steer our pedagogic assumptions, actions and aspirations. As a future-facing activity within HE, the development of learning autonomy via self-connection can influence and contribute to the confident dissemination of graduate qualities in the workplace.

20.2 Pedagogic Context—Looking Back to Move Forwards

In this chapter we argue for the re-visioning of learning, assisted by technology, in terms of curiosity and personal connectedness. With more similarities than differences, exploration of off-campus learning, whether it be termed distance learning, online learning, e-learning, or technologically enhanced learning, needs to be investigated at the individual level to uncover transferrable insights for contemporary, post-compulsory learning. We deliberately use 'distance learning' as generic label for off-campus education because we want to further conceptualise what it means, as a learner, to be physically separated from the academy. Our core concern is the individual learning experience, as without this, the 'human' subscript of learning is missing. Our contention is that individual learning is a necessary pre-cursor to the social elements of learning. Whist this may seem obvious, we must not inadvertently confuse our pedagogic intentions with a homogeneous view of the collective student experience. A student may be observed to be active because they are adding comments to a discussion board or clicking through narrated 'hot spots' on an augmented learning object, but that is not enough: we have to move beyond here-and-now appraisals of participation, to question their deep-level learning experiences. The nuances of personal (i.e. intrinsic) learning can get lost in our assumptions about the benefits of technologically advanced techniques and learning design. Doing, does not necessarily mean learning. To maintain and model our own curiosity, as educators we have to engage with the sometimes quite unsettling dialogues about the longer-term impacts of our current pedagogic actions.

Within HE, learning is recognised as a dynamic process for individuals to know more about their subject of interest, and just as importantly, about themselves in relation to the world around them (Palmer & Zajonc, 2010). These notions are not new: they echo the early writings of John Dewey, on 'active, expressive' learning (1915, p. 20). The humanistic function of education was, for Dewey, to enable people to fulfil their own potential, and to inspire others to do the same (Muraro, 2016). The approach reminds us of the subjectivity of learning through choice, creativity, dignity, and self-worth. Similarly to Dewey, Carl Rogers (1959) (as the founding architect of 'student-centred learning') identified learning as something which is beneficial for the individual and for their interactions both with others and with the world around them. Drawing upon the work of Maslow (1943), Rogers' pioneering approach asserted that genuineness, acceptance, and empathy foster personal growth in an atmosphere where learners are comfortably exposed to new ways of thinking. And yet, he also acknowledged the struggle to give up long-held assumptions.

He believed that individuals must learn for themselves and that a student-centred approach cannot be imposed—only encouraged. Education must be experienced, and so student-centred practice is not purely a teaching technique, rather it demands authentic acceptance (and commitment) on the part of academic staff to attend to each learner, regardless of delivery mode. In the context of distance learning, Laurillard (2013) writes:

> The problem is that transformation is more about the human and organizational aspects of teaching and learning than the technology. We have the ambition. We have the technology. What is missing is what connects the two. (2013, p. 16)

The centrality of the individual learner is obvious: arguably, the missing link is the aspect of deep learning and how an individual connects with their own learning. Hence, an alternative understanding of impact is required for this increasingly used mode of delivery, considering factors such as time, experience, and real-life integration. After all, whilst learners may be geographically distant from the University, they are not distant from themselves. In other words, as potentially new learners, they are not 'new people.' A pedagogic narrative is needed to embrace and respond to the integration of a person's past and present experiences with their future aspirations.

The humanistic orientation of Transformational Learning Theory (TLT) (Mezirow, 2000; Taylor & Cranton, 2013) stresses how experiences, fostered by human-human interactions generate opportunities for lasting change, as explained by Mezirow:

> …learning is understood as the process of using a prior interpretation to construe a new or revised interpretation of the meaning of one's experience in order to guide future action. (1996, p. 162)

Following modifications to Mezirow's concept of a single point of transformation, transformational effects are now seen to slowly 'ripen' (Taylor & Snyder, 2012). Personalised meanings are thought to continually refine, clarify, and progress, which may be difficult to articulate in the short-term. Transformational development therefore is an outcome of deep-level learning, because, 'it is irreversible once completed; that is, once our understandings [have] clarified and we have committed ourselves fully to taking the action it suggests' (Mezirow, 1991, p. 152). When a radically dissimilar or incongruent experience collides with our assumptions, the encounter may be discarded or becomes the catalyst for transformational ideas, but only if we are open to change via our curiosity.

There is a resemblance between Mezirow's ambition for adult learning (i.e. 'to help the individual become a more autonomous thinker by learning to negotiate his or her own values, meanings and, purpose rather than uncritically acting on those of others' (1997, p. 11)), the qualities of degree level scholarship (QAA, 2014) and transferrable employment skills (Universities UK, 2016). However, Northcote and Gosselin (2016) suggest that while evident in the pedagogic parlance, the human-orientation of the curricula can dwindle when there are reduced resources, generic course designs and pedagogic misunderstandings. The presence of the learner can, paradoxically, become fogged and their subjective, deep-level learning experience overlooked in the quest to use technology to make learning more accessible and efficient.

On the longer term, personal consequence of learning, a recent doctoral study by Goldspink (2017) asked the alumni of a part-time, undergraduate distance learning course, about their experiences. Using qualitative Interpretive Phenomenological Analysis (Smith, Flowers & Larkin, 2009), technology-assisted learning was found to instil curiosity and connectedness, when 'learning to learn' is conceptualised as an intrinsic experience which encompasses micro-layers of self-noticed change. The layering of experience resonates with Heideggerian thoughts about how phenomena are experienced in a multitude of ways and responds to the accumulation of deeper levels of understanding. In-depth analysis revealed that transformative, self-connected learning is influenced by insight, willingness, and the courage to engage with learning for beneficial outcomes for the self, which can then be shared and used for the benefit of others. Learning is emphasised as being highly personal and integrated with the life story of the individual. Each learner reacts to the learning experience differently and for learning to be meaningful, the 'I' must be at the forefront of how the learning experience is nurtured and understood. To make this point explicit, a pedagogic notion of self-connected learning is proposed (Goldspink, 2017).

Self-connected learning differs both from notions of self-directed learning and from student-centred learning. Knowles (1975) described self-directed learning as 'a process in which individuals take the initiative without the help of others in diagnosing their learning needs, formulating goals, identifying human and material resources, and evaluating learning outcomes' (1975, p. 18). For Nanney (2004), student-centred learning is 'a broad teaching approach that encompasses replacing lectures with active learning, integrating self-paced learning programs and/or cooperative group situations, ultimately holding the student responsible for his own advances in education' (2004, p. 1). However, neither of these definitions identifies what needs to be done to develop a sense of connectedness and curiosity in learners and learning.

20.3   Thinking About the 'I' in Self-connected Learning

The hermeneutic phenomenology of Heidegger (1927[2010]), Gadamer (1960[2013]) and Merleau-Ponty (1945[2013]) guided and inspired the analytic work, together with the humanistic psychology of Rogers (1959). Evidentially, the experiences of distance learning accumulated in the participants' descriptions of change, linking together affective reasoning (perceptions), thinking habits, and actions, and outlining how embodied learning integrates feelings and thoughts with physical activity. The pedagogic notion of self-connected learning emerged because the participants' physical application of thought contributed to their affective experience and vice versa. Here, self-connected learning is the embodied experience of learning for the self, nurtured in a caring environment to empower ongoing self-efficacy, curiosity and choice. Self-connected learning emphasises introspective development as more powerful than externally based, short-term content recall. In Goldspink's (2017) research, connections between the learning and the self, influenced how other connections were interpreted and used, including:

- connection to the academy
- technological connection to access virtual learning
- pedagogic design connection (learning outcomes, content and assessment)
- connection to external resources
- professional connection to the content via previous and current experience
- connection with peers (in and outside of the course)
- connection with tutors.

The common aspect to these 'connections' is action, whether switching on a computer, checking emails, constructing a discussion board message, or talking to colleagues in the workplace. Action involves decisions based on ideas about the self in relation to the context of the learning experience. As a result, 'self-connected' learning becomes apparent when meaningful participation is based on the dynamic use of self, suggesting that learning is part of the person (Dewey, 1938; Rogers & Freiberg, 1994). Without connecting primarily with the self, other connections (i.e. technological, tutorial and informational) are susceptible to a lack of personal meaning. For educators, instilling self-connection serves as a propositional reminder of the centrality of the embodied experience of learning, which is essential for transferable and lasting impact. The connections are developed into a practical model for designing courses and content, as described below.

20.4   Practice-Based Tenets

Active learning is increasingly popular within the conversations of Higher Education, with the aim of increasing participation. Pedagogic techniques to develop interested and motivated students are often cited in institutional teaching and learning strategies. However, the idea that learners need to be nurtured because they are learning to learn is often omitted. We cannot assume the learner will know what to do in an active curriculum, or even what this means for them. In a similar way, the implementation of a set of technology-led techniques is not always enough to ensure future impact and transferability. To provide learning resources, adopt strategies or test knowledge, without asking 'what does this activity mean for the individual?' is to avoid taking into account connections to the learner's past, present, and future experiences. Compartmentalising learning limits the capacity for learners to use themselves as a substantial learning resource and reduces the likelihood of longer term gains resulting from engagement. To explain further, 5 practice-based tenets shed light (Goldspink & Engward, 2018) on the core features of self-connected learning (Fig. 20.1). Each tenet has a set of suppositions that the learner needs to be supported in achieving, in order to self-connect with their own learning.

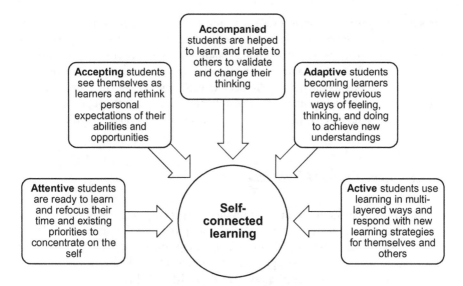

Fig. 20.1 Pedagogical tenets flowing into self-connected learning

Together, the tenets reflect a process of transformation beginning as the learners turn their gaze inwards and embrace new ways of thinking and acting, and the accompaniment of others, especially tutors, who provide stability and excite intellectual risk-taking. This trusted sharing with another is a key component of developing curiosity and self-connected learning. Through sharing the learning content with the experiences of another (e.g. the tutor), togetherness is recognised in separation and/or difference, and is necessary in the development of curiosity. Working as part of a trusted learning relationship provokes enquiry: 'why is this meaningful to me?' and 'why is this seen as different to others'? This may occur irrespective of where the learner is geographically situated: it is the learner establishing a closeness to their learning support, through gaining understanding of the content with another, that develops their own learning autonomy. Integrating a curiosity-based, curricular, content design and assessment therefore shifts the acceptance of knowledge as authored by others (e.g. the tutors), to learners self-authoring their own understanding ('my understanding of it is…'), which in turn is creating a future-facing approach for learning autonomy and sharing ideas.

20.5 Opportunities and Barriers for Self-connected Learning

From an implementation perspective, particular (and sometimes subtle) features of the learning experience offer insights into the opportunities and barriers to self-connected learning. The issues presented in this section, represent the groundwork for building graduate abilities and employability. They are the hidden components for developing the qualities, skills and understanding maturing beyond the acquisition of disciplinary skills or technical knowledge which have traditionally formed the core of most professional courses. We need to look beyond technological solutions to prepare and establish graduates as self-reliant, dynamic agents of social good in an unknown future: indeed, we may need to more closely look at ourselves, as tutors.

20.5.1 Learning and Vulnerability

Learning brings vulnerability, and this might be especially heightened if new learning illuminates a different way of thinking about professional practices. Academic vulnerability is fuelled by novel or stressful learning situations, impeding the transformational process, either by replaying perceptions of previous negative learning experiences or by reinforcing negative views of the self. Learning is not easy: a complex ebb and flow between understanding and not understanding combines with affective comfort and discomfort. Mezirow (1997) argued that transformative change does not occur from experiences pairing easily with existing frames of reference, in what Land and Meyer (2010) refer to as the power of the liminal space. Integrating new knowledge necessitates letting go of previously held ideas and, once done, the consequences are irreversible. Uncertainty is necessary. There are three distinct stages where the individual may feel particularly prone to vulnerability (Goldspink, 2017):

- at the beginning of the course, when learners are in unfamiliar learning territory
- when learners experience time pressures
- when learners feel disconnected from tutors.

Pedagogically, these pressure points present as times where support that is trusted is needed. Despite the abundance of literature about peer learning, the importance of the tutor relationship cannot be understated. In times of difficulty or achievement, the tutor is the anchor point from which learners can explore safely beyond the comfort of the known.

20.5.2 Care and Self-connected Learning

The accompaniment of others, especially tutors, empowers self-connected learning, just as personalised feedback awakens, guides and supports self-discovery (Goldspink, 2017). In this sense, personally-orientated academic interaction is a form of caring. However, the notion of care is complex. Drawing on the work of Heidegger (1927), approaches to care vary depending on the situation we are in. Heidegger recognised care in the form of solicitude, or an attitude to other human beings.

There are therefore three modes of solicitude, firstly, a mode of indifference, where the 'being-there' of others is unnoticed or neglected; secondly, there is 'inauthentic solicitude' which is the type of involvement that 'leaps in' for the other and is characterised as a form of control, albeit well meaning. This method increases unconstructive dependency because others relinquish their struggle and even if they appear to be receiving help, their autonomy is taken from them. Heidegger stressed how caring for others in this way fails to recognise the other person's existential project, with the effect of treating the other as a 'thing' or a 'what.' In contrast to this, authentic solicitude assists others in taking care of - and responsibility for - themselves. Heidegger (2010, p. 123) describes this as a 'leaping ahead' of the other in a way that releases them to face their own 'Being' thereby opening up opportunities to assume and manage the burden of their own existence. Instead of taking over another's task, they are enabled to do it in their own way and deal with the outcome for themselves. In doing so, the unique existential project of the other is both acknowledged and respected. Applying this to education, effective academic care is conveyed through interactions that will inspire learners to autonomously connect to their own learning.

The role of the academic tutor is pivotal to inspire and promote curiosity as a longer-term benefit of learning, as opposed to when tutors 'leap in' with short-term, externally generated solutions or tasks. Heidegger's work exposed hidden insights about the multifaceted and often subtle nature of technology-assisted, tutorial exchanges. When thinking about how language is used in academic tutorials, a forward-facing dialogue to nurture curiosity, whilst still acknowledging academic vulnerability, can include the following questions;

- What does this learning mean to you (past/present/future)?
- How are you going to use this resource/learning activity?
- What have you gained from this resource/learning activity—was it expected?
- In view of your own experience, why do you agree/disagree with this evidence?
- How does this information challenge/validate your previous ways of understanding?
- What strategies are you developing to deal with uncertainty?
- What is different/changing for you—what is that like?
- What will you take forward from this learning/what do you now need to do?
- How will you translate this new knowledge into work/real life?

Formenti (2009) notes that 'Learning does not come out of the blue, as the magic production of an isolated subject; it is an ongoing process, emerging out of a certain kind of interaction' (2009, p. 2). Adaptation from knowledge authored by others, to knowledge authored by oneself (Baxter Magolda, 2010; Baxter Magolda & King, 2012) is guided by the tutor's skills in working with, rather than trying to remove, academic vulnerability in learning. When support is accepted to self-manage emotions, courage is found to challenge previously held assumptions. If learning is disconnected from the self, only surface-level learning that is marginal to the self will occur. Conversely, when new learning is embraced and integrated, alternative perspectives come into view, triggering a change in ways of being and new practices, and motivating the individual to be a dynamic contributor to their world, through embodiment.

20.5.3 Embodiment and Self-connected Learning

Sharan et al., (2008, p. 40) writes that, 'embodied learning involves being attentive to the body and its experiences as a way of knowing.' Merleau-Ponty (1945) similarly proposed that the body holds memories because we are the entirety of our experience. Our bodies, and how we experience within them, are in constant change and flux: they are temporal in their nature. For Heidegger (1927), temporality is non-linear: time does not exist as a removed object, for we ourselves are time. Temporality therefore fuses the dimensions of past, present and future and the temporal frame expands and tapers as attention focuses and then refocuses on subjective, defined experiences. Applied to technology-assisted learning, such 'distance' can refer to the space between the self and one's own learning. Embodied engagement progresses the direction of distance learning toward a holistic, educational approach, empowering learners to become more fully aware of the learning taking place inside the self (Maiese, 2017). Separating ourselves in terms of thinking, feeling, and doing makes little sense, confirming that embodiment in learning involves learners making connections within their temporal existence. To illustrate this point, Goldspink (2017) argues that when learners questioned their previously held assumptions, they became more open to new ways of seeing their world, and to acting in accordance with their newly gained, fresh perspectives.

This intellectual and lived connection is often neglected in the dialogues of technology-assisted learning. Concentrating on the physical body, active learning is visible and evidenced via participation and engagement (Kahu, Stephens, Leach, & Zepke, 2015), often through the requirement of task completion. Embodiment from a phenomenological stance refers however to an embodied presence (not physical presence) within the world. Embodiment through self-connecting in learning facilitates deeper and more transformational outcomes. We forget that it is our body which is the instrument for learning because our bodies tell us about ourselves, our experiences, and our world. As with our body, the role of self-connected learning is often overlooked because 'the self' is largely 'taken-for-granted' (Heidegger, 2010) and less tangible than the technological or structural aspects of learning, which are more easily measurable. The acquisition of self-connected learning encompasses the senses, using the 'whole' of us to interact with our world. Consequently, embodiment has implications for deepening understanding and transferring learning to meaningful:

> Participation is always based on situated negotiation and renegotiation of meaning in the world. This implies that understanding and experience are in constant interaction – indeed are mutually constitutive. The notion of participation thus dissolves dichotomies between cerebral and embodied activity, between contemplation and involvement, between abstrac-

tion and experience: persons, actions, and the world are implicated in all thought, speech, knowing, and learning. (Lave & Wenger, 1991, pp. 51–52)

Ideas of embodiment benefit learners, deepening their exploration and understanding. Facilitation of questions towards the individual themselves, aims to progress them from surface level, short term appraisals towards a critical, longer term inquisitiveness:

- What is your reaction to this resource? Why might that be?
- How do you feel about this information? How might that be useful/not useful?
- What does this content remind you of?
- What is your gut instinct about this? What can you do to confirm/refute your initial appraisal? Why might that be necessary?
- When/where do you study best? Why is that?
- What prevents you from studying?
- What is the dialogue you have with yourself when you get stuck or don't feel motivated?

Such interactions guide learners to recognise how instrumental they are in their own learning and thus develop the confidence to not only effectively question the external world but also themselves as well. The ability to observe the self and evaluate what emerges is a key asset for self-connection, often leading to future learning autonomy.

20.6 Using Self-connected Learning in Practice

When the embodied self is connected with learning, transformational learning is more likely to occur. By reframing the focus away from technology and onto the individual learner, the relationships between learner and tutor is essential: tutors design opportunities for learners to make their own discoveries by linking and evaluating new and existing knowledge within the context of their own experiences. Taking a humanistic approach, the 'inner world' of the learner is respected as tutors offer different levels of support during the learning experience. The tutor starts as a navigational aid, then becomes a critical friend, and finally serves as a sounding box for self-directed ideas. This amounts to a process of 3 sequential facets (Goldspink, 2017):

1. *structured learning*
2. *supported activities*
3. *self-directed participation.*

As shown in Fig. 20.2, through transitional stages in the tutorial relationship, the promotion of individual confidence is crucial for learning progression. Rather than creating dependency based upon the technological presentation of content, academic care creates opportunities for vulnerability in learning, to instigate a self-assured curiosity. Attending to the learner rather than to the technology, similarly increases the potential for transformative educational experiences.

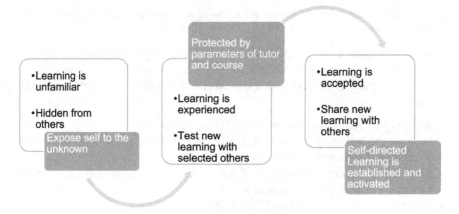

Fig. 20.2 Development of self-directed learning

The key message is that small changes can make a big difference without causing major disruption to current academic processes. In response to the challenges of our times, we may not be able to change how much time we have with our students, but we can think about how we *use* the time that we have with them. Equally, more resources may not be available, but we can re-evaluate how we are using what we do have. This in turn requires the courage to question *what* we are doing and *why* we are doing it. HE plays a commanding role in preparing learners for an unknown future, so our future-facing educational aims must encompass the capability to assertively question, search and critically select knowledge, and to creatively problem solve, resulting in self-directed, producers of knowledge. Table 20.1 indicates how self-connected learning can integrate into existing pedagogic practice.

20.7   Conclusion—New Conversations

In the current economic climate, small changes can make big differences, when part of a nurturing environment. The use of technology must equip graduates with knowledge and skills for today, but also allow them to acquire a self-driven, self-sufficient attitude, which in turn permits them to question and learn, enabling them to succeed in an uncertain and changing world. From a humanistic perspective, the generic student working through online, tutor-set activities (and concealed behind the computer screen) must be restored to the role of active contributor, who can positively use their past to successfully influence their present and future. It is beneficial for learners to recognise themselves as a distinct, important and useful learning resource. To facilitate greater self-connection, further dialogue is needed as to how the mechanisms and practices of educational delivery (including tutorial support) might influence learning autonomy. When the self is connected (or rather, embodied) within the learning,

Table 20.1 Summary of recommendations for educational practice

Recommendation	Application	Examples
Nurturing self-connected learning using a transformational tutorial approach	• Self-connected learning assumes learners have their own unique ways of learning, requiring overt and meaningful pedagogic approaches and practices • Curriculum, content structure, assessment method and tutor actions are explained so learners can take ownership of their curiosity and self-connect to their own learning	• Personalise interactions/feedback with the explicit aim of filtering self-connected learning into everyday life • Use routine verbal and non-verbal dialogue with learners as opportunities to role model effective, humanistic interactions and academic skills • Positively manage the endings of all types of communications; how we leave people is as important as how we engage with them
Simulating curiosity in a nurturing online environment	• Tutors empathetically accept the newness of the distance learning experience and learners are prompted to work proactively with the novelty of their learning situation • Self-connection is advocated for longer term impact	• Direct dependable tutorial support to provide stability at a time of change • Positively reframe academic vulnerability to empower curiosity through safe, psychological engagement with uncertainty in order to preserve and build self-esteem
Promoting ownership of the learning process	• Curriculum design, structure, content and assessment are overtly integrated to encourage learners to refocus their attention toward the self • Redirect learning outcomes toward the experience of learning and the application of new learning • Replace perceptions of faculty as 'knowledge providers' to guiding companions who advocate questioning	• Acknowledging there are no short cuts highlights that the aim is not to make learning easier, but more meaningful • Present learning resources as opportunities to stimulate individualised curiosity • Motivate learners to confidently participate in their own, dynamic learning experience by facilitating and not 'giving' learning

independent and critical reflection is more likely to occur and to be shared with others. Therefore, developing the confidence to be curious is key, given that beyond the academy, learners must be cognitively, affectively and practically equipped and ready to progress by themselves, when tutors and courses are no longer available.

References

Baxter Magolda, M. B., (2010). The interweaving of epistemological, intrapersonal, and interpersonal development in the evolution of self-authorship. In M. B. Baxter Magolda, E. F. Creame, & P. S. Meszaros, (Eds.), *Development and assessment of self-authorship* (pp. 25–43). Sterling, Virginia: Stylus Publishing.

Baxter Magolda, M. B., & King, P. M. (2012). *Assessing meaning making and self-authorship: Theory, research and application.* Hoboken, New Jersey: Wiley.

Dewey, J., (1938). In J. Dewey (Ed.), 1997. *Experience and education.* The Kappa Di Lecturer Series, First Touchstone Edition. New York: Touchstone.

Formenti, L. (2009). *Learning and caring in adult life: How to develop a good theory.* Paper presented at: ESREA Life History and Biography Network Conference, Wisdom and Knowledge in Researching and Learning Lives: Diversity, Differences and Commonalities. Milan, Italy, March 12–15, 2009.

Gadamer, H. -G. (1960 [2013]). *Truth and Method* (J. Weinsheimer and D. G. Marshall, Translation). London: Bloomsbury Revelations.

Goldspink, S. (2017). *A phenomenological exploration of adult, asynchronous distance learning.* Doctoral thesis, Anglia Ruskin University.

Goldspink, S., & Engward, H. (2018). Shedding light on transformational online learning using five practice based tenets: Illuminating the significance of the self. *The Asia Pacific Journal of Contemporary Education and Communication Technology, 5*(2).

Heidegger, M. (1927)[2010]. *Being and time* (J. Stambaugh Translation). Albany, New York: State University of New York Press.

Kahu, E., Stephens, C., Leach, L., & Zepke, N. (2015). Linking academic emotions and student engagement: Mature-Aged distance students' transition to University. *Journal of Further and Higher Education, 39*(4), 481–497.

Knowles, M. S. (1975). *Self-directed learning: A guide for learners and teachers.* New York: Association Press.

Land, R., & Meyer, J. (2010). Threshold concepts and troublesome knowledge: Dynamics of assessment. In J. Meyer, R. Land, & C. Baillie, (Eds.), *Threshold concepts and transformational learning* (pp. 61–80). Rotterdam, Netherlands: Sense Publishers.

Laurillard, D. (2013). In H. Beetham, & R. Shape (2013). *Rethinking pedagogy for a digital age: Designing for 21st century learning.* Abingdon: Routledge.

Lave, J., & Wenger, E. (1991). *Situated learning: Legitimate peripheral participation.* Cambridge: Cambridge University Press.

Maiese, M. (2017). Transformative learning, enactivism, and affectivity. *Studies in Philosophy and Education, 36,* 197–216.

Maslow, A. H. (1943). A theory of human motivation. *Psychological Review 50*(4), 370–396.

Merleau-Ponty, M. (1945)[2013]. *Phenomenology of perception* (D. A. Landes Translation). London: Routledge.

Mezirow, J. (1991). *Transformative dimensions of adult learning.* San Francisco, CA: Jossey-Bass.

Mezirow, J. (1996). Contemporary paradigms of learning. *Adult Education Quarterly, 46*(3), 158–172.

Mezirow, J. (1997). Transformative learning: Theory to practice. *New Directions for Adult and Continuing Education, 74,* 5–12.

Mezirow, J., & Associates. (2000). *Learning as transformation. Critical perspectives on a theory in progress*. San Francisco, CA: Jossey-Bass.

Moore, M. G., & Kearsley, G. (1996). *Distance education: A systems view*. New York: Wadsworth Publishing Company.

Muraro, D. N. (2016). The critical philosophy and the education for John Dewey. *American Journal of Educational Research, 4*(17), 1197–1204.

Nanney, B. (2004). Student-centred learning. In *Proceedings from the 3rd European Conference in E-Learning*. Paris, France, November 25, 2004.

Northcote, M., & Gosselin, K. P. (2016). *Handbook of research on humanizing the distance learning experience*. Hershey, PA: ICI-Global.

Palmer, P. J., & Zajonc, A. (2010). *The heart of higher education*. San Francisco, CA: Jossey-Bass.

Quality Assurance Agency (QAA). (2014). *The frameworks for higher education qualifications of UK Degree-awarding bodies* (Online). Available at: http://www.qaa.ac.uk/publications/information-and-guidance/publication?PubID=2843#.WFp1kv5XXIU.

Rogers, C. (1959). Significant learning: In therapy and in education. *Educational Leadership, 16*, 232–242.

Rogers, C., & Freiberg, H. J. (1994). *Freedom to learn* (3rd ed.). New York: Merrill.

Sharan, B., Merriam, T., & Freiler J. (2008). Learning through the body. *New Directions for Adult and Continuing Education 2008 119*, 37–47.

Smith, J. A., Flowers, P., & Larkin, M. (2009). *Interpretative phenomenological analysis: Theory, method and research*. London: Sage.

Taylor, E., & Cranton, P. (2013). A theory in progress? Issues in transformative learning theory. *European Journal for Research on the Education and Learning of Adults, 4*(1), 33–47.

Taylor, E. W., & Snyder, M. J. (2012). A critical review of research on transformative learning theory 2006–2010. In E. W. Taylor & P. Cranton (Eds.), *Handbook of transformative learning, theory, research, and practice* (pp. 37–54). San Francisco, CA: Jossey-Bass.

Universities UK. (2016). *Higher Education in England: Provision, Skills and Graduates* (Online). Available at: https://www.universitiesuk.ac.uk/policy-and-analysis/reports/Documents/2016/higher-education-in-england-provision-skills-and-graduates.pdf.

Sally Goldspink (EdD.) is a Course Leader in the Faculty of Health, Education, Medicine and Social Care, Anglia Ruskin University, England. Qualifying as an Occupational Therapist in 1994, Sally worked in both clinical and managerial positions in a range of mental health settings. Since joining the academic community in 2003, she has participated in the curriculum development and delivery of pre-registration and continuing professional development courses. Following her M.A. in HE, she achieved her Doctorate using Interpretative Phenomenological Analysis (IPA) to explore the experiences of distance learners. Her publications focus on reflexivity, IPA and self-connected learning. She is interested in the experience of learning and communication in healthcare and education settings.

Hilary Engward (EdD.) is a Senior Research Fellow in the Faculty of Health, Education, Medicine and Social Care, Anglia Ruskin University, England. Her areas of expertise are Ethics and Medical and Healthcare Education. Her work covers aspects of learning, curriculum design, and developing ethics and values as central to the educational process. Her research interests are as follows: Families and veteran health and wellbeing, Health care ethics, Inter-professional ethics, Governance and safety, grounded theory methodology, veterans and families living with limb loss.

Chapter 21
Student Engagement with LinkedIn to Enhance Employability

Emmanuel Mogaji

21.1 Introduction

In a rapidly changing world, the role of social media for building and maintaining networks cannot be overemphasised: millennials are the social media generation, and this is influencing most of their activities, including job searches. Acknowledging that the job-searching strategies of millennials are changing (Smith, 2018), and that social media is being used widely in recruitment processes (El Ouirdi, Segers, El Ouirdi, & Pais, 2015), it has been argued that LinkedIn serves as a channel for recruiting and selecting candidates (Ecleo & Galido, 2017). As universities are both recognised and ranked for their rates of graduate employability (Hall, 2017), it is important to understand the role of LinkedIn in building student networks and improving employability. Noting previous research on LinkedIn in HE (Gerard, 2012; McCorkle & McCorkle, 2012; Peterson & Dover, 2014), this study moves beyond the use of LinkedIn for class assignments, to consider how well students engage with the platform after receiving their grades, to identify the efforts students put into building and maintaining their networks when their tutors are no longer watching. It aims to highlight the challenges of using LinkedIn and offer recommendations for tutors in terms of improving student engagement and employability. It is important to note that LinkedIn is not the only means of improving employability: it is part of a holistic approach towards enhancing opportunities. Students are encouraged to get on LinkedIn to drive up engagement and interactions as they prepare for work. The role of tutors in using LinkedIn to enhance employability cannot be overemphasised however. The focus is on tutors to initiate the process and chart a pathway for students: it is however the student's responsibility to engage.

E. Mogaji (✉)
University of Greenwich, London, UK
e-mail: e.o.mogaji@greenwich.ac.uk

© Springer Nature Switzerland AG 2019
A. Diver (ed.), *Employability via Higher Education: Sustainability as Scholarship*,
https://doi.org/10.1007/978-3-030-26342-3_21

21.2 LinkedIn for Student Engagement

Social networking sites are an increasingly important tool for career development (Baruffaldi, Di Maio, & Landoni, 2017). LinkedIn, as a site for business professionals, focuses on business connections and industry contacts for employers and working professionals (Statista, 2018). With 500 million members worldwide and 250 million active users, it is one of the most popular social networks. There are 40 million students and recent college graduates on LinkedIn, with three million active job listings (Aslam, 2018). Through it, members may create, manage and share their professional profile online, and build and engage with their professional network (LinkedIn, 2018) and it is considered more effective than Facebook in the recruitment process (Nikolaou, 2014). Engaging with the platform builds relationships and is crucial to unlocking opportunities including new jobs or career advice (Shreibati, 2017). UK universities are aware of what LinkedIn can offer and generally encourage students to create a profile. The main concern, however, is how well students engage with this platform *after* they have created their profile. Often it appeared they were not interested, and unwilling to put much effort in. Arguably, many students see social media as a mere platform for entertainment and socialization (Sobaih, Moustafa, Ghandforoush, & Khan, 2016) which may explain to some extent their relative lack of interest in LinkedIn. As Dixon-Todd, Ward, and Coates (2015) further noted, students tend to consider engagement largely in terms of what happened within the classroom. They may, therefore, not necessarily be interested in activities which may be perceived as 'invasion of their privacy' by the university.

21.3 The Personal Tutor's Role

UK Universities have always made efforts to support and enable their students to achieve their potential via personal tutoring (Watts, 2011). Often this involves having a member of the teaching staff support the student throughout their time at university, giving them academic support and pastoral care, to help them develop a rounded and deepened skill set. Research has recognised the importance of personal tutoring as an important tool of student engagement, student retention, progression and achievement. Grant (2006) considered it crucial to providing all-inclusive guidance and support. Por and Barriball (2008) also noted that personal tutors are akin to counsellors and career advisors, deeply interested in their students' progress. It may be argued therefore that personal tutoring is not the same as being a lecturer: it is a distinct and well-defined role that should not be subsumed into other academic tasks or roles. The role of personal tutor goes beyond that of a lecturer and encompasses pastoral, academic and administrative elements. There are specific responsibilities. As Phillips (1994) observed, there are three main areas, namely, teaching, counselling and supporting students. Supporting the students in enhancing their employability skills is however increasingly key. As such, this chapter aims to encourage personal tutors to adopt LinkedIn as an additional tool. Watts (2011) acknowledges that personal tutoring is used throughout UK universities, but may operate differently within them.[1] Often, students remain with the same personal tutor throughout their degree, and may be required to create a LinkedIn profile as part of Personal Development module or portfolio. Some students may then cease to take any interest in maintaining their profile.

21.4   The Challenges of LinkedIn

The benefits of LinkedIn in enhancing employability are well known, however there are challenges that can undermine these benefits. This section highlights the challenges students are facing with regards to using LinkedIn for enhancing employability, building their network to increase their social capital, and creating engaging content to stir up conversation.

21.4.1   Unfamiliarity with LinkedIn

A survey of online population profile in the UK (by BBC and Ipsos MORI) revealed that 75% of 16 to 22-year-olds use Facebook compared to 8% who use LinkedIn. Unlike Instagram, Snapchat or WhatsApp, it seems that LinkedIn is a form of social media that students are not very familiar with. Lack of experience in the use of social media can be a significant limitation for students exposed to a new platform and for tutors trying to incorporate it into their teaching. Unfamiliarity with LinkedIn can inhibit students and tutor interest especially in respect of enhancing employability. Moreover, it can be challenging for those students who are uninterested in social media but made to sign up for it: students and faculty staff can be overloaded with information, finding it distracting and perhaps struggle to use the site as intended.

21.4.2   Building Their Network

For those students who are more familiar with the platform and create a profile (whether to pass an assessment or engage with a professional network) building networks can still be a challenge. It is key for students to build networks to increase their social capital, by connecting with various people on the platform: challenges attach to the quality and quantity of those whom they add, however, given the prevalence

---

[1] At the University of Greenwich, first-year undergraduate students are enrolled on a 15-credit course called Professional and Personal Development (PPD) which runs for 12 weeks. The Personal tutor takes this course in a weekly small group tutorial with about 15 personal tutees.

of 'spam' and 'bot' accounts. Students may simply be connecting randomly for the sake of increasing numbers. Building a network is not however primarily a numbers game. The question of connecting with tutors similarly cannot be ignored. Peterson and Dover discourage this practice, suggesting that tutors might well be swamped with mandated connections, which then might not be well received. And yet the presence of one's tutor on the platform can motivate students to engage more fully, especially where the tutor is treating the platform as a professional platform (with no private matters discussed).

21.4.3 Engagement

Students are expected to stay 'in the loop' to make best use of the platform. They clearly need to know when job vacancies are being advertised, to connect with potential recruiters or a mentor. Often, students are encouraged to post on their profile, to make comments on relevant topics, and to join groups and discussions. They must be strategic however in engaging and in building worthwhile connections. Peterson and Dover give particular credit to those students who start a thread, acknowledging that it is sometimes more difficult for students to post a well- thought-out question than one might think.

21.4.4 Content Creation

Closely linked with engagement is content creation. It is important to create valid content to enable engagement with others, e.g. writing articles, sharing pictures and making comments. The challenges in creating content have been acknowledged: personal tutors might well be expected to put actions in place to help students with content creation. In addition, students need to be made aware of their audiences: who are those who might be interested in their statuses? With whom are they communicating? And what would the audience find most useful on their platform? Often a student's network is made up of other students: if issues discussed in class are posted and shared however, these may become visible to other professionals. It is important therefore to be aware of the potentially very wide reach of social media, not just in terms of immediate contacts but also for larger audiences.

21.4.5 Self-branding

Some students are not in employment: those who are 'in work' may well be employed as, for example, a part-time waitress, bartender or nanny. Putting work experience on LinkedIn to align with their career objectives is important, not least in relation to how they might be describing themselves in their job role. Some tend to describe themselves as students whilst others opt to use their part-time job title. This is also closely related to how they highlight their other accomplishments. Even though they may not yet have any publications or patents as an indication of achievement, students must find a way to showcase something unique about their own personal brand.

21.5 Recommendations for Tutors

These challenges notwithstanding, it is important to remember that every new, meaningful connection could lead potentially to new employment opportunities. This section offers suggestions aimed at debunking negative perceptions about millennials' job attitudes (and at LinkedIn itself) by arguing that tutors must lead the initiative. The role of tutors in enhancing student employability is multi-faceted: they will have to do their best to encourage students to engage more fully with LinkedIn, promoting greater awareness of the long-term benefits of doing so.

21.5.1 Personal Tutors Should Have a Profile

Whoever wants to lead, must lead by example. Personal tutors should have a profile and be conversant with how it works, so that they can encourage their students. If tutors are not engaging on the platform, students may see no reason to join in. Tutors can share their profile in class—a screenshot displaying different sections for example would encourage students to sign up. That said, there are arguments against tutors sharing their profile: if tutors are not actively job-hunting, they may see no need for a LinkedIn profile. Although students use social media for peer interaction, staff might not wish to join in such conversations. There is a need to be mindful of professional boundaries and the tensions which exist between having 'personal' or social connections and maintaining professional responsibility as an academic tutor. Veletsianos and Kimmons (2013) have reported the lived experiences of faculty members within social networking sites, suggesting that there is a tendency for conflicts to arise between their professional identity and social networking. Manca and Ranieri (2016) further highlight a key concern about privacy, which may well discourage some tutors from adopting social media platforms within their teaching. It should be noted however that LinkedIn is not just for active job seekers but allows for the building up of a viable professional network. Students can clearly benefit from such networks, for example gaining potential insights and recommendations for employment, finding visiting lecturers, and meeting industry experts online.

21.5.2 Personal Tutors Should Discuss and Engage

Personal tutors need to do their best to encourage their students to engage with the platform. This means looking beyond the mere getting of grades via completed assessment tasks. Tutors should specifically ask during meetings about the student's LinkedIn profile, and check on progress. Tutors should also access their students' public profile and aim to evaluate it critically: as Por & Barriball (2008) argued, personal tutors are essentially critics and career advisors, who can closely influence and monitor student progress. Who then is better placed to give an honest opinion about a student's public profile than the personal tutor, who wants to see their tutee succeed? They can give advice about the way that they might have branded themselves, on which profile picture they have used, and on how best to enhance a profile. Recruiters are not obliged to provide such feedback, but tutors can share success stories of former students who have successfully used the platform. Similarly, developing greater student confidence in using the platform to its optimum advantage requires time and active participation. Rather than attempting to cover everything in one term or session, the plan should be a longer-term one. Tutors should also engage with their students on the platform, as professionals, liking their comments, or sharing and commenting upon their updates, to build student confidence and promote engagement. Successes can be noted when they meet students in class. For example, if LinkedIn informs you that a student has got a job or an internship, it is good to bring that relationship offline. Lecturers should be able to nurture the engagement process further by monitoring students' online activities and commenting both online and in class.

21.5.3 Tutors Should Nurture

It should also be noted that some students may not really be interested in social media generally. They may not own a smartphone or have sufficient storage space to install another application which could hinder how fully they might engage on the platform. Thus, technical limitations like memory size, battery life, high line costs and a small screen may hinder using mobile technology as a learning tool (Alzaza & Yaakub, 2011). Tutors need to highlight these challenges and find ways of working around them. Insofar as students need to build their networks, it is also important to be mindful of the online connections that they are making. Tutors should bring to the attention of their students the dark side of social media: LinkedIn is no exception. There is an increasing number of internet users who are concerned about negative online experiences (Ofcom, 2018). Unacceptable behaviours include the sending of unsolicited promotional messages, misleading posts and statuses, and anything of a sexual nature. Tutors can also raise awareness of the need for self-branding on LinkedIn. They should not default automatically to '*student at University of ...*' as a headline. Headlines show up in search results and can determine whether or not some someone clicks through to the student's profile. Foss (2019) further considers the headline as the most overlooked LinkedIn profile section, suggesting the need for students to be creative with their headlines and to use important keywords which speak directly to the audience. Avoidance of such terms as "specialize" and "passionate" is to be encouraged given that they are amongst the most overused buzzword by millions of LinkedIn users both within and beyond the UK. (Faraz, 2018).

21.5.4   Tutors Should Share Resources

Tutors can play a key role in curating relevant information and sharing it with their students. This could be industry news that is relevant, or perhaps connecting them with a person of interest that can be a mentor or sharing job openings and vacancies. This is another opportunity to engage more fully with the student tutee: they may find a tutor's content highly relevant to what is being taught in the classroom. Neary (2000) advises personal tutors to encourage reflective practice by students, to better understand the connections between theory and practice. Moreover, this is not just for the students' benefit as it also raises the profile of the tutor, pushing their work to the forefront of people's minds when it comes to finding new opportunities and establishing reputation and expertise. Sharing also keeps tutors informed about the latest trends, ensuring that experience and skill sets are updated.

21.6   Conclusion

This chapter argues the important nature of LinkedIn in terms of professional networking, highlighting one university's efforts to incorporate it into teaching, learning and career advice. Students may not find it engaging (or entertaining enough) to join in with or might consider it as merely another medium for interaction with classmates. In terms of enhancing employability, personal tutors are often best placed to ensure that students fully understand the various benefits of this platform and how they can best utilise, looking beyond its use as an in-class assessment over a few weeks. Understanding the challenges that students face, in terms of self-branding, building up relevant links, and engaging meaningfully with the network, is also key to high quality employability tutoring. Tutors (and careers or employability advisers) should also be seen to be using the medium themselves for example to share their work and stimulate further discussions in class. Higher education administrators will similarly want to ensure that their initiatives for improving graduate's prospects yield significant results. Regular appraisal of student engagement is needed, although the onus clearly remains on the student to make the best use of the opportunities offered.

So far, there is no known alternative to the professional social media site that is LinkedIn. Any championing of LinkedIn must however address its pedagogical stance and ask whether it risks weakening the traditional roles and remits of tutors and students (Manca & Ranieri, 2016). Arguably, it does not. Given that social media is here to stay, its place within learning and teaching cannot be ignored, nor can its significance be overemphasised in our digital age, with 80% of LinkedIn members regarding professional networking as important to career success (Shreibati, 2017). Students need to be made aware of this platform, as a way of developing their digital, interpersonal relationship skills outside of Facebook, Instagram or Snapchat which often do not add much in the way of value to their career prospects after graduation. Facebook and other social media sites can be used for class interactions, but LinkedIn clearly lends itself to improving the employability of students, to developing communication and networking skills that will be useful in getting a job, internship, or graduate role. It allows students to position themselves for prospective job offers, to engage in active networking and join in the conversations happening within their professions or industries.

Even though job search networking is one of the most successful ways to secure employment, it can be perceived as an intimidating activity. This is where tutors (and administrators) can make the process a bit less daunting, for example by highlighting the tangible benefits of building an online network, and by securing mentors who can help students and graduates with their career development. Ultimately however, students have a key part to play in enhancing their own employability. There is a clear need for them to invest significant time and effort in activities developed by their tutors: where tutors have provided opportunities for students to build their network and gain relevant skills, students still need to take responsibility for their own learning. Clearly, a useful platform has been provided, but students must also make sure that they put significant effort into achieving their desired aims.

References

Alzaza, N. S., & Yaakub, A. R. (2011). Students' awareness and requirements of mobile learning services in the higher education environment. *American Journal of Economics and Business Administration, 3*(1), 95–100.

Aslam, S. (2018). *Linkedin by the numbers: stats, demographics & fun facts.* https://www.omnicoreagency.com/linkedin-statistics/. Accessed 2 Feb 2018.

Baruffaldi, S. H., Di Maio, G., & Landoni, P. (2017). Determinants of Ph.D. holders' use of social networking sites: An analysis based on LinkedIn. *Research Policy, 46*(4), 740–750.

Dixon-Todd, Y., Ward, J., & Coates, N. (2015). *Is student engagement the magic wand to create a transformative marketing curriculum?*. Scotland, UK: Academy of Marketing Research Initiative.

Ecleo, J. J., & Galido, A. (2017). Surveying LinkedIn profiles of data scientists: The case of the Philippines. *Procedia Computer Science, 124,* 53–60.

El Ouirdi, M., Segers, J., El Ouirdi, A., & Pais, I. (2015). Predictors of job seekers' self-disclosure on social media. *Computers in Human Behavior, 53*(December), 1–12.

Faraz, D. (2018). *Find the right words to land the right job.* [online] Blog.linkedin.com. Available at: https://blog.linkedin.com/2018/january/25/find-the-right-words-to-land-the-right-job. Accessed 18 July 2019.

Foss, J. (2019). *Does your linkedIn headline suck?.* [online] Themuse.com. Available at: https://www.themuse.com/advice/doesyour-linkedinheadline-suck. Accessed 18 July 2019.

Gerard, J. G. (2012). Linking in with LinkedIn®: Three exercises that enhance professional social networking and career building. *Journal of Management Education, 36*(6), 866–897.

Grant, A. (2006). Personal tutoring: A system in crisis? In L. Thomas & P. Hixenbaugh (Eds.), *Personal tutoring in higher education* (pp. 11–31). Stoke on Trent, UK: Trentham Books.

Hall, R. (2017). *Graduate employability ranking: the best university for getting a job.* https://www.theguardian.com/higher-education-network/2017/sep/11/graduate-employability-ranking-the-best-university-for-getting-a-job. Accessed 2 Feb 2018.

LinkedIn (2018). *About Us.* [Online]. Available at: https://www.linkedin.com/company/linkedin Accessed 3 Mar 2018

Manca, S. & Ranieri, M., 2016. Facebook and the others. Potentials and obstacles of social media for teaching in higher education. *Computers & Education, 95*(April), 216–230.

McCorkle, D. E., & McCorkle, Y. L. (2012). Using LinkedIn in the marketing classroom: Exploratory insights and recommendations for teaching social media/networking. *Marketing Education Review, 22*(2), 157–166.

Mogaji, E. O. (2018). *Are we really engaging with LinkedIn to enhance students' experience.* Stirling, Scotland: Academy of Marketing.

Neary, M. (2000). *Teaching, assessing and evaluation for clinical competence: A practical guide for practitioners and teachers.* Cheltenham, UK: Nelson Thornes.

Nikolaou, I. (2014). Social networking web sites in job search and employee recruitment. *International Journal of Selection and Assessment, 22*(2), 179–189.

Ofcom. (2018). *Adults' media use and attitudes report.* London, UK: Ofcom.

Peterson, R. M., & Dover, H. F. (2014). Building student networks with LinkedIn: The potential for connections, internships, and jobs. *Marketing Education Review, 24*(1), 15–20.

Phillips, R. (1994). Providing student support systems in Project 2000 nurse education programmes—the personal tutor role of nurse teachers. *Nurse Education Today, 14*(3), 216–222.

Por, J., & Barriball, L. (2008). The personal tutor's role in pre-registration nursing education. *The British Journal of Nursing, 17*(2), 99–103.

Shreibati, S., 2017. *Introducing a smarter way to message and build meaningful relationships on LinkedIn.* https://blog.linkedin.com/2017/april/13/introducing-a-smarter-way-to-message-and-build-meaningful-relationships-on-linkedin. Accessed 3 Feb 2018.

Smith, C. (2018). *220 Amazing LinkedIn statistics and facts.* https://expandedramblings.com/index.php/by-the-numbers-a-few-important-linkedin-stats/. Accessed 2 Feb 2018.

Sobaih, A. E., Moustafa, M. A., Ghandforoush, P., & Khan, M. (2016). To use or not to use? Social media in higher education in developing countries. *Computers in Human Behavior, 58*(May), 296–305.

Statista. (2018). *LinkedIn—statistics & facts.* at: https://www.statista.com/topics/951/linkedin/. Accessed 2 Feb 2018.

Veletsianos, G., & Kimmons, R. (2013). Scholars and faculty members' lived experiences in online social networks. *The Internet and Higher Education, 16*, 43–50.

Watts, T. E. (2011). Supporting undergraduate nursing students through structured personal tutoring: Some reflections. *Nurse Education Today, 31*(2), 214–218.

Emmanuel Mogaji (Ph.D.) is a Lecturer in Advertising and Marketing Communications at the University of Greenwich, London. His primary areas of interest are the 'ABCDE' of Marketing Communications (Advertising, Branding, Communications, Digital, Ethics) and technology for enhancing students' teaching and learning experiences. He is a Fellow of the Higher Education Academy, and believes in giving students the opportunity to learn by doing, to think outside the box and challenge norms. He has published several peer-reviewed journal articles and presented his work at many national and international conferences.

Chapter 22
Pre-professional Identity Formation Through Connections with Alumni and the Use of LinkedIn

Julie Fowlie and Clare Forder

22.1 Introduction

The concept of pre-professional identity demands a fresh look at the definition of employability (Jackson, 2016). It requires moving beyond the traditional focus on graduate attributes and experience towards one aimed at helping students visualise themselves in professional roles (Bennett, 2012). Considering only a skills-based approach to employability risks overlooking the complexity of the notion of graduate work-readiness (Hinchliffe & Jolly, 2011), an argument also maintained by Holdsworth (2017), who contends that placing a particular emphasis on experience, may in fact lead to students achieving less. To counter this, Jackson (2016: 926) argues for pre-professional identity development as a means of furthering '…an understanding of and connection with the skills, qualities, conduct, culture and ideology of a student's intended profession. This encourages career exploration, demands career management skills, and provides students with access to new communities of practice' (Wenger, 1998, 2011).

Widely accepted as being difficult to define (Pegg, Waldock, Hendy-Isaac, & Lawton, 2012), the concept of employability is understood in a variety of ways. For employers, it typically translates as 'work-readiness', where universities must produce competent and capable graduates who can make immediately valuable contributions within their new roles (Archer & Davison, 2008; Mason, Williams, & Cranmer, 2009). In the United Kingdom these outcomes are measured by instruments such as the Graduate Outcomes survey (formerly the Destination of Leavers from Higher Education survey) and an annual report on the graduate market produced by *High Fliers*. However, 'employability' can often be viewed quite differently by researchers

J. Fowlie · C. Forder (✉)
University of Brighton, Brighton, UK
e-mail: C.L.Forder@brighton.ac.uk

J. Fowlie
e-mail: j.fowlie@brighton.ac.uk

and students alike, with a number of broader definitions seen in recent literature. To date it has been explained as follows: the set of skills, knowledge, understanding and attributes that make a person more likely to choose occupations in which they can be both satisfied and successful (Dacre Pool & Sewell, 2007); a form of work-specific adaptability (Fugate, Kinicki, & Ashforth, 2004); and the propensity of students to obtain a job (Harvey, 2001). Knight and Yorke (2003: 5) further state that, from a student or graduate perspective, employability is most often seen as the 'set of achievements…that makes [them] more likely to gain employment and be success-ful in their chosen occupations.' Consequently, universities are often positioned right at the crossroads of several competing perspectives: they must respond to employer demands for competent, appropriately-skilled graduates (Pollard et al., 2015) but at the same time they must also provide those opportunities through which students can develop the skills and experience necessary for obtaining work (Helyer & Lee, 2014).

Nonetheless, while there appears to be no 'one size fits all' definition of employ-ability (and although businesses and students might hold different views of the con-cept) one school of thought gaining ground within this debate is that undergraduates must take more responsibility for their own employability (Baker & Henson, 2010; Tymon, 2013). This is thrown into even sharper relief when the current employabil-ity context is viewed through the lens of austerity and economic uncertainty (Gunn & Kafmann, 2011). Drawing upon Harvey's (2005: 3) definition of employability we can see that work-readiness does indeed go well beyond skills, attributes, and experience:

> Employability is more than about developing attributes, techniques or experience just to enable a student to get a job, or to progress with in a current career. It is about learning…In essence, the emphasis is on developing critical, reflective abilities, with a view to empowering and enhancing the learner.

If we are to move into a broader definition and understanding of employability, students' responsibility for their own work-readiness should feature. This chapter will argue that one way of enabling this is to include pre-professional identity development in the way that employability is addressed currently within Higher Education. Our study demonstrates how we have piloted an intervention designed to do so.

22.2   Pre-professional Identity

Jackson (2016) argues that a skills-based approach to employability is too narrow and consequently overlooks the complexity of graduate work-readiness. In a similar vein, Daniels and Brooker (2014) also locate graduate advancement within the context of student identity development, seeing the two notions as part of the same process. They point out that in terms of 'graduate attributes' the role of the student in gaining these skills receives little attention in the literature, and that students are "shaped to fit an institutional concept of work-readiness" (2014: 68). This passive acceptance of graduate (or soon-to-be graduate) identity provides no room for students to explore how such an identity is shaped or to understand their agency within in the process. This ties to our argument that students need to take responsibility both for their own employability and for the creation of their pre-professional identities as they move through their student journey and out into the world of graduate employment.

Closely linked to the notion of pre-professional identity is the idea of community or a landscape of practice (Wenger, 1998, 2011). Defined as 'groups of people who share a concern or passion for something they do and learn how to do it better as they interact regularly' (Wenger, 2011: 1), these will typically share three characteristics, namely, a shared domain of interest; a community in which members help and learn from each other; and shared practice and resources. Within HE, students can engage and interact with a wealth of landscapes of practice, from their own course groups and tutors, through to various societies, careers and employability services, external professional bodies, and employers. Students' participation in these communities supports the formation of their pre-professional identity and contributes to developing useful career management skills (Jackson, 2016). However, this assumes that students will become involved in such landscapes. Taking the community of practice surrounding employability as the most relevant example here, the following review of the literature evidences quite clearly that not all undergraduates will actively engage with the various communities available to them: indeed, some will actively avoid interactions with the people, services, and resources that could help them. As Piazza (2011) argues, career knowledge comes through interactions with a wide variety of people. When those interactions are missing, development of a pre-professional identity is much harder to achieve.

22.3 Promoting Employability

A wealth of employability-related activities is readily available to undergraduates across most disciplines. Firstly, on-campus careers and employability services provide information, advice, and guidance on part-time jobs, placements, graduate schemes, and future careers (Harris, 2001; Rowley & Purcell, 2001; Watts, 1997). They will often negotiate university-employer partnerships and provide direct employer links to students (Lowden, Hall, Elliot, & Lewin, 2011). Secondly, the taught curriculum in some institutions can offer students key opportunities to develop their own employability skills by combining academic and 'practical' intelligence (Yorke & Knight, 2006) either in individual or core modules, throughout a whole curriculum, or as a separate standalone element (Cranmer, 2006). This has sparked some institutional-level tensions however, particularly amongst those who believe that embedding employability may have a detrimental effect on subject curricula (Speight, Lackovic, & Cooker, 2013) and for those who are not convinced that employability *can* be taught (Mason, Williams, Cranmer, & Guile, 2003). However, concerns over skills gaps in the graduate labour market (Jackson, 2013; Mason et al., 2009) have prompted a clear need to focus on employability in terms of pedagogy and curricula as a possible means of closing these gaps and improving graduate outcomes (Jackson, 2014).

Thirdly, extra-curricular activities (ECAs) offer many avenues for students looking to boost their employability. These can be offered by universities or found by students independently. Volunteering (Holdsworth, 2010; Holdsworth, & Brewis, 2014); sport (CBI/NUS, 2011; Thompson et al., 2013); and part-time work (Muldoon, 2009; Gbadamosi, Evans, Richardson, & Ridolfo, 2015) are amongst the more common options. Additionally, although not subject to extensive research, students can take advantage also of a vast array of clubs, societies, networking events, guest lectures, together with developing their own interests (Watson, 2011) to enhance the skills, experience, and competencies needed to be successful both in searching for and securing jobs. In research involving university alumni, Clark, Marsden, Whyatt, Thompson, and Walker (2015) stress that ECAs can have an enduring effect on one's employability. Finally, work-based learning, internships, and industrial placements also provide undergraduates with extensive opportunities to develop their employability (Andrews & Higson, 2008; Hall, Higson, & Bullivant, 2009; Lowden et al., 2011). Engaging in the above-mentioned activities usually improves students' chances of successfully securing a placement, which in turn brings its own benefits, such as fast-tracking into graduate roles (Wilton, 2012) and often a higher starting salary (Brooks & Youngson, 2016).

22.4   Being Responsible for One's Own Employability

It is often presumed that students are aware of these numerous ways of enhancing employability and will want to engage actively with them, and that they are able to make the connection that such participation can lead to improved work-readiness. This is well-explored in the literature which indicates many students are not always sufficiently proactive in their use of university careers and employability services (Archer & Davison, 2008) or that they might simply choose to not draw upon them (Greenbank, 2011). In the case of embedded employability activities, some students may even try to avoid experiencing them at all (Atlay & Harris, 2000): as Stevenson and Clegg (2011) also found, students who do participate in extra-curricular activities often mainly do so not just to enhance their future employability but to make the most of any opportunities that they find themselves facing the time. Similarly, there are often also wide-ranging barriers to undertaking placements and internships. These include (but are not limited to) not wanting to delay graduating by adding a placement year on top of a three-year course (Morgan, 2005), and poor academic performance and/or lack of experience (Balta, Coughlan, & Hobson, 2012). Behavioural factors also contribute, such as lack of confidence (Bullock, Gould, Hejmadi, & Lock, 2009), disinterest or self-doubt (Aggett & Busby, 2011), and not appreciating the longer-term benefits (Brooks & Youngson, 2016). This leads us to question how and whether students are able always to realize that the array of activities described above are clearly designed to enhance their work-readiness (Rae, 2007). As such, it is argued that students should interact as much as possible with the people, activities, and resources that form the landscapes of practice they will need to navigate to begin forming their pre-professional identity. Employability is an active social process which moves away from a basic skills agenda and focuses upon the creation of new identities and contexts (Tomlinson, 2010): it should be supported through the promotion of graduate identity rather than through employability skills per se (Hinchliffe & Jolly, 2011).

22.5 Economic Uncertainty

In uncertain economic times, young people seem to have borne the brunt of austerity measures (Crisp & Powell, 2017). Faced with increased tuition fees (Bolton, 2017; Pennell & West, 2005), being priced out of the housing market (Hoolachan, McKee, Moore, & Soaita, 2017; McKee, Moore, Soaita, & Crawford, 2017) and facing threats to social mobility (Bronk, 2016; Sensier & Devine, 2017) it is not surprising that securing a job is a top priority for many students. However, in some instances, the end goal of gaining employment may often overlook what needs to be done in the first place, to succeed in doing so. This is demonstrated, for example, by students who forgo a placement year in favour of graduating sooner (Morgan, 2005), or by those who choose not to engage in employability-related activity as discussed above. Efforts to change these perceptions are important as it has been shown that young adults who develop strong career navigation skills are typically more satisfied with the jobs they find, and are more likely to stay in their roles for longer (Harrington, Van Deusen, Fraone, & Morelock, 2015).

A further point to consider is the changing nature of the graduate labour market. Reid, Dahlgren, Dahlgren, and Petocz (2011) highlight the necessity of being prepared for volatility and challenge, whilst Tomlinson (2012: 414) outlines how stable employment enjoyed by graduates in the past has now given way to less certain employment futures, including unemployment, and pressures over continual career management. In a climate where job security or a lack thereof affects young people (Miguel Carmo, Cantante, & de Almeida Alves, 2014) and dictates that many are likely to perhaps change jobs up to three times a year (Jerome, Scales, Whithem, & Quain, 2014), the ability to navigate and manage career development is crucial. This again underscores the importance of moving views of employability away from an emphasis on skills-based approaches towards the 'full picture of what is required by the graduate facing the prospect of the labour market' (Bridgstock, 2009). Returning to Jackson's (2016) argument, it is evident that employability needs to encompass a focus on pre-professional identity. Changing external contexts and the need to instil in students the capacity to manage these, means broadening the conceptual understanding of 'employability' by including a new focus on pre-professional identity. However, the literature in this area does not always elucidate the mechanics of how we can broaden students' conceptual understandings of employability and introduce them to the notion of a pre-professional identity and communities of practice. The research we set out in the following pages outlines a specific intervention designed to answer this. We extend Jackson (2016) and Wenger's (1998, 2006, 2010) ideas by introducing and framing alumni as a key community of practice, and using LinkedIn as a tool to facilitate professional identity. In doing so, we reiterate Jackson's (2016: 933) assertion that it is the responsibility of all stakeholders to develop an explicit awareness and connection among students within the identity-formation process.

22.6 Alumni: Role Models and a Community of Practice

Smith, Smith, Taylor-Smith, and Fotheringham (2017) state that part of the social process of identity formation involves role models because they can enable observation of prototypical behaviours, citing academics and family members as the role models identified by the participants in their study. One group, however, which they did not refer to, is alumni. Though a wide body of research on alumni exists, including for example as evidence of successful learning and teaching (Oliver, 2008) or with alumni as financial donors (McDearmon, 2010, 2013), the scarcity of literature linking the influence of alumni on pre-professional identity and employability reveals that they are a potentially untapped resource within these fields. Our study seeks to increase knowledge in this area by demonstrating the positive effect of alumni as role models for undergraduates in terms of identity formation. Our research also echoes Clark, Zukas, and Lent (2011) in finding that alumni do provide another community of practice for students to access.

22.7 Using LinkedIn

LinkedIn is a popular social media platform designed to facilitate online business profiles, professional networks and direct client communication (Ryan & Jones, 2009). Whilst intended for use by the business community, growing numbers of students also use the site. Current statistics (Garcia, 2017) show that approximately 40 million students and recent graduates use LinkedIn, with the UK providing the highest number of student users, after the USA. It is recognised as a valuable tool for career exploration (Gerard, 2012) and a vital platform for showcasing the graduate attributes sought by employers (Peterson and Dover, 2014). It also acts as a job search resource, with thousands of graduate roles and internships advertised each year (Breitbarth, 2016). However, despite LinkedIn boasting high numbers of student users, research has shown that some students often view it as a website intended for those already out in the workplace (Florenthal, 2015), thereby evidencing a clear lack of interest and confidence in its use (Garcia, 2017). This results in a helpful resource being both overlooked and under-used (Bridgstock, 2016; Slone & Gaffney, 2016). With these points in mind, we aimed to find out if our targeted group of students also saw LinkedIn as a barrier rather than a catalyst for career exploration, networking, and identity creation.

22.8   Research Design

Analysis of qualitative data from the 2016 National Student Survey (NSS) revealed that students on our institution's Finance and Investment degree made the highest number of negative comments about a lack of career guidance. Further, quantitative analysis of four years (2012–2016) of data from the Destination of Leavers from Higher Education (DLHE) survey showed that our Finance and Investment graduates experienced higher levels of unemployment (12.7%) compared to the sector average of 9.5%. This prompted a targeted research project designed to address these issues. Prior to conducting the main research phase, we used LinkedIn to connect with those who had recently graduated from the Finance and Investment course in 2015, 2016, and 2017. A total of 102 graduates were contacted and asked to complete a short questionnaire about the course and their career to date. Forty-three graduates (33 male/10 female) connected with us on LinkedIn, with eleven (8 male/3 female) answering the questionnaire. From the eleven responses (and with the respondents' consent) we created profile sheets to share with our student participants. After receiving ethical approval at department level, the whole cohort of final year students (n = 23) on the degree were invited by email to participate. The email explained the study and its background, included participant information sheets and consent forms, and explained that participants' responses would be kept anonymous. It also confirmed that respondents could drop out of the study at any time without repercussions. After a low response rate (n = 4), second year students were also invited to take part, increasing the number of overall participants to ten (nine males, one female, which reflected the demographic of the cohort).

The study was comprised of a series of focus groups (one per month over a four-month period) which were supplemented with tasks set by the researchers for participants to complete and then report back upon before the next focus group began. The initial focus group opened up a discussion on career and employability advice available to students and explored participants' perceptions and experiences of this. We also included questions on participants' career plans and how they intended to achieve them, as well as finding out if any of the group had connections with alumni. The second focus group centred on developing identities, reviewing alumni profiles, and using LinkedIn, while the final two sessions were guided by reflective questions. Reviewing the alumni profiles formed one of the tasks set following the focus groups. Other tasks included creating or updating a LinkedIn profile, making connections with alumni, exploring LinkedIn's alumni tool, and conducting a personal skills audit.

22.9 Findings

22.9.1 Focus Group One—Initial Discussion

From the initial focus group, we established that none of the group had any alumni connections nor had they spoken to any graduates from their course or across the university more widely. Additionally, only two students had attended any employability-related events delivered by alumni or other external professionals (such as guest lectures, networking sessions, or company presentations that had been organised by the department), although a further two reported attending a session on working abroad hosted by the department's employability team. None had made use of the careers service and the majority of the group did not realise that this service was separate from the department's Employability Hub. With regards to LinkedIn, three of the ten participants did not use the platform at all: four had set up a profile but had not since returned to the site. Two stated that they used it occasionally but only one reported that they were a regular user and had maintained an active profile. Four of the ten participants had no plans for after graduation, although two of them would be graduating in only four months' time. Responses on this topic included:

- I'm just going to head up to London to secure any job (final year)
- I'll probably do just anything as I don't have any experience and don't know what to choose (final year)
- I was offered an internship but wasn't really interested so I let it go (final year).

None of the students had definite plans or ideas for how they would set out to achieve their desired careers. All agreed that the roles they were interested in (investment banking, asset management, accounting) were very hard to get into so they would probably 'go for anything to open the door and pay the bills.'

22.9.2 Focus Group Two—Reviewing Alumni Profiles and Discussing LinkedIn

Participants were asked if they used LinkedIn and if they had thought about using social media to help with career prospects. Some of the responses included:

- I do not see the point of LinkedIn (final year)
- I don't understand LinkedIn (final year)
- LinkedIn is of no importance to me at the moment (final year)
- The site is not as professional as it makes out to be (final year)
- Social media is meant to be fun—LinkedIn doesn't sound fun (final year)
- There is no need for me to use LinkedIn (second year)
- LinkedIn has only just come on to my horizon (second year).
- I am not confident enough to connect with others (second year)

22.9.3 Focus Group Three—Reflections on Creating/Updating LinkedIn Profiles and Connecting with Alumni

Participants were asked how participating in the research had changed how they thought about LinkedIn. They were also asked if they had begun to think more about their future careers, and how the alumni profiles had helped with this. Responses included:

- I feel more positive about networking (final year)
- I feel encouraged to be more active and less hesitant (final year)
- I've realised just doing my degree is not enough (final year)
- The alumni profiles were really helpful (second year)
- The alumni profiles have highlighted things I have not considered (second year)
- I have added more things to my profile after looking at others' (second year)

22.9.4 Focus Group Four—Using Professional (Alumni) Networks and Discussing Career Choices

In the final focus group, participants were asked about how developing a professional network had helped them and whether or not LinkedIn had assisted in the exploring of possible career choices. Responses included:

- I no longer ignore notifications about alumni at companies, but I look at their profiles to see the skills and experience they have (final year)
- I feel more confident in using LinkedIn to look for jobs (final year)
- I have contacted everyone in my network to ask for endorsements (final year)
- LinkedIn helped me secure my placement as someone I connected with gave me some detailed advice and he turned out to be my interviewer! (second year)
- I have started to look more closely at company profiles (second year)
- I am starting to add more contacts, but I still don't feel confident connecting with people (second year)

22.10 Discussion

Pre-professional identity creation is inherent in the use of LinkedIn (Bridgstock, 2018). As students are required to create an outward display of their identity in the form of a profile before they can begin networking, this step obliges them to think about how they want to portray themselves in a professional context. However, we discovered amongst our participants an underlying reluctance to make active use of the site, both as individuals (identity formation) and collectively (communities of practice), as reflected in earlier research (Chen & Bryer, 2012; Florenthal, 2015). Initial responses from the first two focus groups also reflected a limited awareness and understanding of how LinkedIn works, as well as a lack of confidence in using it. Participants also believed that it was unnecessary or not important. Despite Cooper and Naatus' (2014: 300) findings that LinkedIn users are happy to link with casual acquaintances or new contacts, our students did not feel the same. While results from a small-scale study cannot be generalised, this may indicate that students do not comprehend the value and effectiveness of LinkedIn at this very early stage of their careers, thereby cutting themselves off from a straightforward means of developing their identity and engaging with various communities of practice. Significantly, today's business world also relies increasingly on social media (Aral, Dellarocas, & Godes, 2013; Kaplan & Haenlein, 2010). Recruiters use LinkedIn and other similar sites to search for and vet potential candidates (Rienties, Tempelaar, Pinckaers, Giesbers, & Lichel, 2012; Zide, Elman, & Shahani-Denning, 2014) whilst job-seekers increasingly rely upon these platforms to perform job searches (Adler, 2016). Companies and employees use them to build connections and develop business (Qualman, 2010). Social networking is recognised therefore as an essential tool, yet often new graduates are entering the world of work unequipped to use it (Benson, Morgan, Filippaios, 2014). Research also tells us that despite the importance of social networking and their positioning in society as 'digital natives' (Wankel, 2016), students can often shy away from connecting with groups that may help them build their networks in meaningful ways (Gerard, 2012: 85). It is therefore imperative that this gap in graduates' skill sets is filled.

Following the change in participants' attitudes towards LinkedIn between the first and second focus groups, and the third and final sessions (i.e. from cautious and disinterested, to motivated and experimental), we argue that involving alumni and providing students with their profiles *before* asking them to engage directly with the website takes a useful step towards closing the gap in graduates' social networking competencies. In this instance alumni provide examples of the professional identities that students can aspire to and comprise a powerful ready-made network for new users of LinkedIn to connect with, perhaps giving them the confidence to make more active use of the platform. More importantly, the new networks which students go on to create by engaging with alumni online can develop into the communities of practice they need to access to further their employability, echoing Wenger's (2010) assertion that communities of practice can capitalise on social media. The findings from the latter part of our study indicate the success of this method, including one participant who secured a work placement via new contacts through LinkedIn. Again, while this cannot be generalised, it hints at the positive effects that combining alumni and LinkedIn in the context of pre-professional identity can have.

22.11   Limitations

The research is limited by its small scale: the findings are not representative of the wider population. Results may have varied if different course cohorts had participated or we had conducted the research with students who held more positive views on LinkedIn. However, as a means of encouraging those with negative perceptions of career guidance, under-developed career plans, and reluctance to develop a professional identity using LinkedIn, our research offers some useful indications.

22.12   Conclusion

Current research on employability and pre-professional identity creation assumes student participation in communities of practice and engagement with people and activities that can instigate a smooth transition from undergraduate to novice professional. However, the assumption that students will actively involve themselves in these situations overlooks the fact that (either through being unaware of what is available to them or by choosing to ignore it) many students do not fully engage in the employability contexts provided for them. Alumni, by acting as role models and demonstrating the '..qualities, conduct, culture and ideology…' (Jackson, 2016:926) of undergraduates' intended professions, are the missing link in the process of developing work-ready graduates. As evidenced in this study, connecting students with recent graduates from their own course broadens their capacity to be 'work-ready' by going beyond the typically narrow focus on employability skills (Hinchliffe & Jolly, 2011). It facilitates pre-professional identity development (in this case through the use of LinkedIn) and, via networking, encourages creation, exploration, and membership of various communities of practice. This contributes to instilling in current students a better sense of responsibility for their own employability, a crucial quality in today's uncertain economic climate.

References

Adler, L. (2016). *New survey reveals 85% of all jobs are filled via networking*. Retrieved from https://www.linkedin.com/pulse/new-survey-reveals-85-all-jobs-filled-via-networking-lou-adler/.

Aggett, M., & Busby, G. (2011). Opting out of internship: Perceptions of hospitality, tourism and events management undergraduates at a British university. *Journal of Hospitality, Leisure, Sports and Tourism Education (Pre-2012), 10*(1), 106.

Andrews, J., & Higson, H. (2008). Graduate employability, 'soft skills' versus 'hard' business knowledge: A European study. *Higher Education in Europe, 33*(4), 411–422.

Aral, S., Dellarocas, C., & Godes, D. (2013). Introduction to the special issue—social media and business transformation: A framework for research. *Information Systems Research, 24*(1), 3–13.

Archer, W., & Davison, J. (2008). *Graduate employability*. The Council for Industry and Higher Education.

Atlay, M., & Harris, R. (2000). An institutional approach to developing students' 'transferable' skills. *Innovations in Education and Training International, 37*(1), 76–84.

Baker, G., & Henson, D. (2010). Promoting employability skills development in a research-intensive university. *Education + Training, 52*(1), 62–75.

Balta, M. E., Coughlan, J. L., & Hobson, P. (2012). Motivations and barriers in undergraduate students' decisions to enrol in placement courses in the UK. *Journal of International Education Research, 8*(4), 399.

Bennett, D. (2012). A creative approach to exploring student identity. *IJCPS-International Journal of Creativity and Problem Solving, 22*(1), 27.

Benson, V., Morgan, S., & Filippaios, F. (2014). Social career management: Social media and employability skills gap. *Computers in Human Behavior, 30,* 519–525.

Bolton, P. (2017). *HE in England from 2012: Funding and Finance.*

Breitbarth, W. (2016). *The power formula for linkedin success (-completely revised): Kick-start your business, brand, and job search.* Greenleaf Book Group.

Bridgstock, R. (2009). The graduate attributes we've overlooked: Enhancing graduate employability through career management skills. *Higher Education Research & Development, 28*(1), 31–44.

Bridgstock, R. (2016). Educating for digital futures: what the learning strategies of digital media professionals can teach higher education. *Innovations in education and teaching international, 53*(3), 306–315.

Bridgstock, R. S. (2018). Educational practices for employability and career development learning through social media: Exploring the potential of LinkedIn. In *Practice Futures for the Common Good.* Sense-Brill Publishers.

Bronk, R. (2016). Let young people move: Why any post-Brexit migration deal must safeguard youth mobility. *LSE Brexit.*

Brooks, R., & Youngson, P. L. (2016). Undergraduate work placements: An analysis of the effects on career progression. *Studies in Higher Education, 41*(9), 1563–1578.

Bullock, K., Gould, V., Hejmadi, M., & Lock, G. (2009). Work placement experience: Should I stay, or should I go? *Higher Education Research & Development, 28*(5), 481–494.

Chen, B., & Bryer, T. (2012). Investigating instructional strategies for using social media in formal and informal learning. *The International Review of Research in Open and Distributed Learning, 13*(1), 87–104.

Clark, G., Marsden, R., Whyatt, J. D., Thompson, L., & Walker, M. (2015). 'It's everything else you do…': Alumni views on extracurricular activities and employability. *Active Learning in Higher Education, 16*(2), 133–147.

Clark, M., Zukas, M., & Lent, N. (2011). Becoming an IT person: Field, habitus and capital in the transition from university to work. *Vocations and Learning, 4*(2), 133–150.

Confederation of British Industry/National Union of Students. (2011). *Working towards your future: Making the most of your time in higher education.* London, UK: CBI.

Cranmer, S. (2006). Enhancing graduate employability: Best intentions and mixed outcomes. *Studies in Higher Education, 31*(2), 169–184.

Crisp, R., & Powell, R. (2017). Young people and UK labour market policy: A critique of 'employability' as a tool for understanding youth unemployment. *Urban Studies, 54*(8), 1784–1807.

Dacre Pool, L., & Sewell, P. (2007). The key to employability: developing a practical model of graduate employability. *Education + Training, 49*(4), 277–289.

Daniels, J., & Brooker, J. (2014). Student identity development in higher education: implications for graduate attributes and work-readiness. *Educational Research, 56*(1), 65–76.

Florenthal, B. (2015). Applying uses and gratifications theory to students' LinkedIn usage. *Young Consumers, 16*(1), 17–35.

Fugate, M., Kinicki, A. J., & Ashforth, B. E. (2004). Employability: A psycho-social construct, its dimensions, and applications. *Journal of Vocational Behavior, 65*(1), 14–38.

Garcia, M. (2017). *How university students can use linkedin to develop career opportunities.* Retrieved from https://topdogsocialmedia.com/university-students-can-use-linkedin-develop-career-opportunities/.

Gbadamosi, G., Evans, C., Richardson, M., & Ridolfo, M. (2015). Employability and students' part-time work in the UK: Does self-efficacy and career aspiration matter? *British Educational Research Journal, 41*(6), 1086–1107.

Gerard, J. G. (2012). Linking in with LinkedIn®: Three exercises that enhance professional social networking and career building. *Journal of Management Education, 36*(6), 866–897.

Greenbank, P. (2011). 'I'd rather talk to someone I know than somebody who knows'—the role of networks in undergraduate career decision-making. *Research in Post-Compulsory Education, 16*(1), 31–45.

Gunn, V., & Kafmann, K. (2011). *Employability and the austerity decade.* Graduates for the 21st Century: Integrating the Enhancement Themes.

Hall, M., Higson, H., & Bullivant, N. (2009). The role of the undergraduate work placement in developing employment competences: Results from a 5-year study of employers. In *DECOWE International Conference* (pp. 24–26).

Harrington, B., Van Deusen, F., Fraone, J. S., & Morelock, J. (2015). *How millennials navigate their careers.* Boston College Center for Work & Family.

Harris, M. (2001). *Developing modern higher education careers services: Report of the review.* DfEE Publications.

Harvey, L. (2001). Defining and measuring employability. *Quality in Higher Education, 7*(2), 97–109.

Harvey, L. (2005). Embedding and integrating employability. *New Directions for Institutional Research, 2005*(128), 13–28.

Helyer, R., & Lee, D. (2014). The role of work experience in the future employability of higher education graduates. *Higher Education Quarterly, 68*(3), 348–372.

Hinchliffe, G. W., & Jolly, A. (2011). Graduate identity and employability. *British Educational Research Journal, 37*(4), 563–584.

Holdsworth, C. (2010). Why volunteer? Understanding motivations for student volunteering. *British Journal of Educational Studies, 58*(4), 421–437.

Holdsworth, C. (2017). The cult of experience: Standing out from the crowd in an era of austerity. *Area, 49*(3), 296–302.

Holdsworth, C., & Brewis, G. (2014). Volunteering, choice and control: A case study of higher education student volunteering. *Journal of Youth Studies, 17*(2), 204–219.

Hoolachan, J., McKee, K., Moore, T., & Soaita, A. M. (2017). 'Generation rent' and the ability to 'settle down': economic and geographical variation in young people's housing transitions. *Journal of Youth Studies, 20*(1), 63–78.

Jackson, D. (2013). Business graduate employability—where are we going wrong? *Higher Education Research & Development, 32*(5), 776–790.

Jackson, D. (2014). Testing a model of undergraduate competence in employability skills and its implications for stakeholders. *Journal of Education and Work, 27*(2), 220–242.

Jackson, D. (2016). Re-conceptualising graduate employability: The importance of pre-professional identity. *Higher Education Research & Development, 35*(5), 925–939.

Jerome, A., Scales, M., Whithem, C., & Quain, B. (2014). Millennials in the workforce: Gen Y workplace strategies for the next century. *E-Journal of Social & Behavioural Research in Business, 5*(1), 1.

Kaplan, A. M., & Haenlein, M. (2010). Users of the world, unite! The challenges and opportunities of Social Media. *Business Horizons, 53*(1), 59–68.

Knight, P. T., & Yorke, M. (2003). Employability and good learning in higher education. *Teaching in Higher education, 8*(1), 3–16.

Lowden, K., Hall, S., Elliot, D., & Lewin, J. (2011). *Employers' perceptions of the employability skills of new graduates.* London, UK: Edge Foundation.

Mason, G., Williams, G., Cranmer, S., & Guile, D. (2003). How much does higher education enhance the employability of graduates?

Mason, G., Williams, G., & Cranmer, S. (2009). Employability skills initiatives in higher education: What effects do they have on graduate labour market outcomes? *Education Economics, 17*(1), 1–30.

McDearmon, J. T. (2010). What's in it for me: A qualitative look into the mindset of young alumni non-donors. *International Journal of Educational Advancement, 10*(1), 33–47.

McDearmon, J. T. (2013). Hail to thee, our alma mater: Alumni role identity and the relationship to institutional support behaviors. *Research in Higher Education, 54*(3), 283–302.

McKee, K., Moore, T., Soaita, A., & Crawford, J. (2017). 'Generation rent 'and the fallacy of choice. *International Journal of Urban and Regional Research, 41*(2), 318–333.

Miguel Carmo, R., Cantante, F., & de Almeida Alves, N. (2014). Time projections: Youth and precarious employment. *Time & Society, 23*(3), 337–357.

Morgan, H. (2005). Why students avoid sandwich placements. In *Presented at Education in a Changing Environment Conference*. University of Salford, 12–13 Jan 2005.

Muldoon, R. (2009). Recognizing the enhancement of graduate attributes and employability through part-time work while at university. *Active Learning in Higher Education, 10*(3), 237–252.

Oliver, B. (2008). Graduate employability as a standard of success in teaching and learning. *Quality & Standards in Higher Education: Making a Difference*, 86.

Pegg, A., Waldock, J., Hendy-Isaac, S., & Lawton, R. (2012). Pedagogy for employability.

Pennell, H., & West, A. (2005). The impact of increased fees on participation in higher education in England. *Higher Education Quarterly, 59*(2), 127–137.

Peterson, R. M., & Dover, H. F. (2014). Building student networks with LinkedIn: The potential for connections, internships, and jobs. *Marketing Education Review, 24*(1), 15–20.

Piazza, R. (2011). The changing role of universities in Italy: Placement services. *Journal for Perspectives of Economic, Political, and Social Integration, 17*(1–2), 173.

Pollard, E., Hirsh, W., Williams, M., Jonathan, B., Marvell, R., Tassinari, A., … & Ball, C. (2015). Understanding employers' graduate recruitment and selection practices. In *BIS Research Paper 231*.

Qualman, E. (2010). *Socialnomics: How social media transforms the way we live and do business.* Wiley.

Rae, D. (2007). Connecting enterprise and graduate employability: challenges to the higher education culture and curriculum? *Education + Training, 49*(8/9), 605–619.

Reid, A., Dahlgren, M. A., Dahlgren, L. O., & Petocz, P. (2011). *From expert student to novice professional* (Vol. 99). Springer.

Rienties, B., Tempelaar, D., Pinckaers, M., Giesbers, B., & Lichel, L. (2010). The diverging effects of social network sites on receiving job information for students and professionals. *International Journal of Sociotechnology and Knowledge Development (IJSKD), 2*(4), 39–53.

Rowley, G., & Purcell, K. (2001). Up to the job? Graduates' perceptions of the UK higher education careers service. *Higher Education Quarterly, 55*(4), 416–435.

Ryan, D., & Jones, C. (2009). Understanding digital marketing, marketing strategies for engaging the digital generation.

Sensier, M., & Devine, F. (2017). Social mobility and brexit: A closer look at England's 'left behind' communities. In *Economics Discussion Paper Series EDP-1709)*. Manchester: University of Manchester, Google Scholar.

Slone, A. R., & Gaffney, A. L. (2016). Assessing students' use of LinkedIn in a business and professional communication course. *Communication Teacher, 30*(4), 206–214.

Smith, S., Smith, C., Taylor-Smith, E., & Fotheringham, J. (2017). Towards graduate employment: exploring student identity through a university-wide employability project. *Journal of Further and Higher Education*, 1–13.

Speight, S., Lackovic, N., & Cooker, L. (2013). The contested curriculum: Academic learning and employability in higher education. *Tertiary Education and Management, 19*(2), 112–126.

Thompson, L. J., Clark, G., Walker, M., & Whyatt, J. D. (2013). 'It's just like an extra string to your bow': Exploring higher education students' perceptions and experiences of extracurricular activity and employability. *Active Learning in Higher Education, 14*(2), 135–147.

Tomlinson, M. (2010). Investing in the self: structure, agency and identity in graduates' employability. *Education, Knowledge & Economy, 4*(2), 73–88.

Tomlinson, M. (2012). Graduate employability: A review of conceptual and empirical themes. *Higher Education Policy, 25*(4), 407–431.

Tymon, A. (2013). The student perspective on employability. *Studies in Higher Education, 38*(6), 841–856.

Wankel, C. (2016). Reframing management education with social media. *Organization Management Journal, 13*(4), 202–213.

Watson, R. (2011). A rationale for the development of an extracurricular employability award at a British university. *Research in Post-compulsory Education, 16*(3), 371–384.

Watts, A. G. (1997). *Strategic directions for careers services in higher education* (NICEC Project Report). AGCAS Administrative Manager, Careers Advisory Service, University of Sheffield.

Wenger, E. (1998). Communities of practice: Learning as a social system. *Systems Thinker, 9*(5), 2–3.

Wenger, E. (2010). Communities of practice and social learning systems: the career of a concept. In *Social Learning Systems and Communities of Practice* (pp. 179–198). London, UK: Springer.

Wenger, E. (2011). *Communities of practice: A brief introduction.*

Wilton, N. (2012). The impact of work placements on skills development and career outcomes for business and management graduates. *Studies in Higher Education, 37*(5), 603–620.

Yorke, M., & Knight, P. (2006). *Embedding employability into the curriculum* (Vol. 3). York, UK: Higher Education Academy.

Zide, J., Elman, B., & Shahani-Denning, C. (2014). LinkedIn and recruitment: How profiles differ across occupations. *Employee Relations, 36*(5), 583–604.

Cooper, B., & Naatus, M.K. (2014). LinkedIn as a learning tool in business education. *American Journal of Business Education, 7*(4), 299–306.

Stevenson, J., & Clegg, S. (2011). Possible selves: students orientating themselves towards the future through extracurricular activity. *British Educational Research Journal, 37*(2), 231–246.

Julie Fowlie (SFHEA) is Deputy Head (Education and Student Experience) at Brighton Business School, University of Brighton, UK. She is interested in improving the student experience, with a focus on helping students develop their employability. She leads on a number of student engagement initiatives and is also responsible for the academic module undertaken by Business School students whilst out on placement. Her research interests include the use of *LinkedIn* and formation of pre-professional identity, alongside success at work and university.

Clare Forder (Ed.D) is Deputy Industrial Placements Officer at Brighton Business School, University of Brighton, UK. She supports students in their search for work placements during their degree and is interested in all aspects of employability. She also assists student engagement activity within the Business School, including leading on the BME Success Project, which supports BME students' career development. Her research interests focus on areas of employability such as pre-professional identity formation, using alumni as role models, and *LinkedIn*.

Part III
Disciplines

Chapter 23
Developing the 'Oven-Ready' Postgraduate: Squeezing a Quart into a Pint Pot to Meet the Employability Agenda

Gillian Forster and Andrew Robson

23.1 Introduction

Increasingly, Universities have been given a clear employability agenda by their various stakeholders, Government, employers, and students alike. The Green and White papers on the Teaching Excellence Framework (TEF) (BIS, 2015, 2016) characterise provision of 'employability' as the means by which Universities will 'evolve,' to provide employers with highly skilled graduates equipped to enter the workforce, with the relevant knowledge and expertise to compete at a global level (Frankham, 2017). The QAA (2015) in its benchmark statements for Masters' Business and Management programmes, also highlights the need for greater focus on employability. Masters programmes should ensure that students develop skills and knowledge within an organisational context, ideally supported by a form of experiential learning, as determined by career entry or career development type programme. Via various reports (CMI, 2014, 2018; The Guardian, 2016) employers repeat the same theme: Universities must do more to meet the real 'on-the-job' needs of business. Employers opine that too many graduates lack appropriate skills, attitudes and dispositions, and that HE could be perceived as "not only [holding] graduates back from gaining satisfactory employment" but having "an inhibiting effect on the performance of employing organizations (ibid), and ultimately the broader economy" (Moore & Morton, 2017, p. 2).

Students, for their part, look to HE to provide them with opportunities to develop transferable skills around team-working and communication, to manage innovation and digital technologies, to network/have work placements within organisations (CMI, 2018) and support in using the "discourse of their experience" to craft

G. Forster (✉) · A. Robson
Northumbria, Newcastle, England, UK
e-mail: Gillian.forster@northumbria.ac.uk

A. Robson
e-mail: Andrew.robson@northumbria.ac.uk

© Springer Nature Switzerland AG 2019
A. Diver (ed.), *Employability via Higher Education: Sustainability as Scholarship*,
https://doi.org/10.1007/978-3-030-26342-3_23

'employer attractive' CVs (Tomlinson, 2008, p. 57). Koris, Ortenblad, and Ojala (2017: p 174) argued that in addition to this employability 'shopping list' business school graduates look to their University experience not just to enable them to replace existing managers on a like-for-like basis but to ensure that they contribute to, or even create, 'humane, ethical and eco-friendly organizations … promoting economic and social welfare and justice.' The gauntlet, it seems, has been well and truly thrown at the feet of HE.

Responses are mixed. Some might argue that a focus on employability is HE's moral duty as students invest time, and increasingly more money, by going into HE, expecting that being a graduate will enhance their ability to perform and progress within the labour market, as opposed to non-graduates (Artess, Hooley, & Mellors-Bourne, 2017). Holmes (2015) and Yorke and Knight (2006) query the centrality of employability within universities' remit, arguing that employability is a more personal, pervasive, and lifelong concern, the responsibility for which cannot be ascribed solely or even mainly to academia. Frankham (2017, p. 631) challenges the notion that Universities offer a 'silver bullet' and frame the employability agenda as 'folly' given how it may contribute to the production of graduates who do not have the dispositions that employers say they want.

Against this turbulent backdrop of internal and external demands from an increasingly wide group of stakeholders and often bludgeoning policy initiatives (together with the mixed responses to them), this chapter argues that a core of experiential learning and skills development, embedded within a postgraduate programme framework can, and indeed does, enhance real student employability. The aim is not to present a model of best practice but to demonstrate how designers of programmes can engineer the best possible intersections between the abilities and aspirations of students and the work-readiness requirements of employers. The chapter describes how, through embedding an employability agenda into the fabric of a programme (as opposed to piecemeal add-ons) (Dacre Pool & Sewell, 2007; Tymon, 2013), curricula have turned ability into aptitude, through high-tech, high-touch facilitation, and intensive professional and personal development, even within resource constraints and despite subject-specific demands. Reflections on the challenges which arose in the initial stages of implementation are offered together with those facing us in the future (CMI, 2018).

23.2   Drivers for Change

As a post-1992 University, the University of Northumbria has historically developed programmes with a vocational leaning. This is particularly true of its business and management arm, Newcastle Business School (NBS). Undergraduate degrees have always incorporated work placements, study-abroad, and a curriculum to encourage personal development and transferable skills. Employability has been embedded into the programmes via a personal development module to prepare for placement, and students also have access to the University's Careers Service and a University-wide initiative entitled 'Passport to Employability' which provides a wide-ranging set of practical opportunities such as networking with organisations to applying for travel funds for activities abroad to build up a better skills profile (Tomlinson, 2008). Unfortunately, postgraduate provision was not as variegated, nor as explicitly driven by an employability agenda. As Wharton and Horrocks (2015) noted, whilst academics might believe there are extensive opportunities for augmenting employability skills within the curriculum, if these opportunities are not explicitly and consistently communicated to students then they will not in fact be perceived, appreciated or acted upon. Whilst there was emphasis on raising self-awareness and personal development via experiential learning interventions, (all of which demonstrated the underpinning philosophy of its design, Kolb's (1984) reflective-practitioner approach to learning), the work placements and opportunities to study abroad were not part of the postgraduate offering. The only explicitly designated employability content and development was a module which ran alongside programme provision, in a distance learning format which resulted in limited student engagement. Feedback from students suggested that whilst a small number of them recognised where they were able to develop and articulate, their employability skills, the majority did not. Our existing employability provision was also perceived by students as very UK-centric, focusing on traditional graduate schemes; it relied heavily on students taking the initiative, and the entirely online provision was seen as inadequate, exacerbated further by providing no formal links with the Careers Service.

In 2015, the University introduced the Programme Framework for Northumbria Awards (PFNA) in response to the national debate advocating Universities' role in the development of employability skills (BIS, 2015, 2016; CMI, 2014; Tholen, 2004; QAA, 2015). Via the four pillars of employability, technology-enhanced learning, research into teaching and enterprise, and assessment for learning, the University put the employability agenda very much at the heart of its programme framework, and all degree programmes have now been rolled out as adhering to these four main principles. The framework provided the opportunity to re-think and enhance postgraduate provision in line with the University's strategic agenda on employability. Our own findings will be touched upon in a later section, after a brief discussion of what 'employability' means, and which skills, attributes and practices it should incorporate, and how, pedagogically, the employability agenda can be successfully delivered. Whilst research into postgraduate students is steadily growing (Coates & Dickinson, 2012; Dickinson, Binns, & Divan, 2015; Kemp, 2009; Matheson & Sutcliffe, 2017; Maxwell, Scott, Macfarlane, & Williamson, 2010; Robson, Forster, & Powell, 2016), most researchers on employability continue to use undergraduate student experiences as the focus of their studies and subsequent recommendations. It was therefore this literature we drew upon during the initial stages of programme design.

23.3   Employability: Form and Content

The working definition for the purposes of programme design was that of Yorke and Knight (2006, p. 8):

> A set of achievements – skills, understandings and personal attributes – that make individuals more likely to gain employment and be successful in their chosen occupations, which benefit themselves, the workforce, the community and the economy.

This does not perhaps explicitly embrace the full spectrum of views on employability, from 'job-getting' (achieved through the acquisition of transferable skills) or the viewing of employability as the student's accumulation of human, social and cultural capital in order to understand and make effective transitions into differing organisational cultures (Clark & Zukas, 2013; Kalfa & Taksa, 2015). Emphasising employability as the development of graduate identity or 'becoming a graduate' (Holmes, 2015) is also relevant, encouraging the understanding of employability as more than just job acquisition per se. Indeed, Yorke and Knight (2006) explicitly state that employability is a work in progress throughout one's life, and implicitly suggest therefore that the development of employability is not vested solely in HE. This view, in particular that of seeing employability as a life-long activity, resonates with the approach to self-development adopted here, which has historically contributed to our underpinning programme philosophy.

In relation to how programmes can focus on employability, the literature identifies various 'employability components,' namely, questions over *which* skills or attributes are key (Andrews & Russell, 2012; Cavanagh, Burston, Southcombe, & Bartram, 2015; CMI, 2014; Jackson, 2014; Kalfa & Taksa, 2015; Kumar, 2015); *who* should be part of the programme design's decision-making process (Cai, 2013; Carey, 2013; Dickinson et al., 2015; McMurray, Dutton, McQuaid, & Richard, 2016; Tymon, 2013); *how* employability should be embedded into programmes (Andrews & Higson, 2008; Dacre Pool & Sewell, 2007; Knight & Yorke, 2003; Wilton, 2012); the importance of internationalising the experience (Young, Sercombe, Sachdev, Naeb & Schartner, 2013); and the pedagogical implications, i.e. providing experiential learning opportunities within an employability focused programme (Karns, 2006; McCarthy & McCarthy, 2006; Piercy, 2013).

23.4   Characteristics of the 'Oven-Ready' Graduate

It is essential to isolate those skills, attributes, characteristics which require development in order to equip graduates as 'employable' or 'oven-ready'. The CMI (2014) provided a clear steer on what these should be, consulting widely with employers, Business Schools and students (National Union of Students (NUS) data) to identify key areas for development, most notably, communication, team-working and problem-solving as the major areas, with motivating others, self- awareness, ethical mind-set and an ability to work across cultures also deemed important, but to a slightly lesser degree. Researchers have focused either on the employers' view (Cai, 2013; McMurray et al., 2016) or that of the students (Bovill, 2014; Carey, 2013; Tomlinson, 2008; Tymon, 2013; Wharton & Horrocks, 2015). As one would expect, there is overlap between these two sets of stakeholders with shared levels of regard for matters such as: communication skills, digital literacy, team-working, work ethic, trustworthiness, motivation, willingness to learn, interpersonal skills, research skills, numeracy, problem-solving skills, independent thinking, initiative and self-direction, self-management. However, Artess et al. (2017) suggest that the skills and attributes identified can differ in terms of relative importance for each respective party. Students, for example, home in on skills and attributes that go beyond employability and, whilst relevant for the workplace, also relate to other contexts such as HE, family life or citizenship. Inevitably, therefore, the literature suggests that the development of these skills and attributes is not solely the responsibility of HE. Frankham (2017) clearly asks how this could be so. However, the more generic definition of employability (which includes the concept of ongoing professional development), especially in the early stages of programme redevelopment, frames many skills and attributes drawn from various frameworks (Andrews & Russell, 2012; Cavanagh et al., 2015; Jackson, 2014; Kalfa & Taksa, 2015; Kumar, 2015) as being of great importance in developing graduate employability. As such, we should attempt to omit nothing. The literature also raised two other issues, however, that were directly applicable to our own experiences and therefore had to be taken into consideration during programme design. Firstly, the skills and attributes included within frameworks could vary across different countries (O'Leary, 2012) which was an especially pertinent factor for us as the majority of our Postgraduate students are EU and International in origin. Secondly, Jackson's (2014) research stressed that employability skills and attributes varied not only by geographical factors but also by more idiosyncratic ones such as gender, work experience, engagement with the employability agenda itself, quality of the skills development on offer, and relationships and activities beyond work.

Rust (2016) takes this last point further, arguing that students only see employability development if they are explicitly aware of the attributes they have, or are currently in the process of developing, understanding how they work together, and thus these can be articulated. In sum, they must transform attributes into valuable personal capital. This finding could go some way towards explaining how other researchers (Wharton & Horrocks, 2015; Tomlinson, 2008) found that students perceive their academic qualifications as having a declining role in shaping their employment outcomes, especially in an increasingly congested, competitive graduate labour market. They instead refer to their "soft credentials" (Tomlinson, 2008, p. 57) such as living away from home, and their life experiences outside their degree as the means by which they will gain employment and develop further employability.

23.5 Stakeholder Involvement

With regards to who should be involved in designing employability into curricula, at the time of development there was consistent agreement that Business Schools must work closely with employers to develop the required skills and attributes (Cai, 2013; CMI, 2014; McMurray et al., 2016) especially for postgraduate students (Dickinson et al., 2015; Kemp, 2009; Maxwell et al., 2010). Various methods designed to integrate employers into the decision-making process have been used, including surveys (Cai, 2013; McMurray et al., 2016), workshops (CMI, 2014) and liaising with Business Advisory Groups and Professional Body Representatives. However, some authors advocate that students should help co-create curricula (Bovill, 2014; Carey, 2013; Tymon, 2013). Student engagement is an expectation of UK quality enhancement processes, but Carey (2013) argues that such engagement has historically co-opted students as a passive voice, evaluating data and thereby acting simply as 'informants.' He advocates that students should be active members of a partnership with academics and thus elevated to the role of 'consultants'. He calls for 'authentic engagement' to represent an overdue shift of focus away 'from condemnation' (which is often a characteristic of conventional consumer-producer relations) towards one of 'recommendation' (Carey, 2013, p. 257). Such active consultation should be an ongoing process where students not only express grievances but are also more creatively involved in identifying solutions. Both Carey (2013) and Bovill (2014) reported that students welcomed such participation, enjoying being involved in decision-making for themselves, but motivated too by a desire to help future students. Tymon (2013) found that directly involving students in the employability agenda—(e.g. defining it, determining what employers want and how these skills could be developed) meant that an earlier lack of engagement with employability-related development was reversed. This was extremely useful in relation to developing our own postgraduate programmes, having hitherto experienced low student engagement i.e. via a virtual learning platform plus centralised careers service. The literature also illuminated the levels of student participation required to facilitate such 'authentic engagement' (Carey, 2013, p. 257). Carey (2013) acknowledged that encouraging students to have a greater say in their learning and teaching experiences can be difficult when confronted with the variance of governance processes in Higher Education Institutions (HEIs), such variance being apparent in, for example, the macro-level nationally determined standards, institutional regulatory frameworks and departmental cultures framing decision-making at the local level. As Bovill (2014) advised, some contexts will demand high levels of participation, whereas in others, participation in only selected components of the curricula would suffice. The key factor that facilitated 'authentic' partnerships and engagement was that when there was active student participation, then student contributions were not only listened to, but acted upon. In short, however, there is no comfy, one-size-fits-all approach to co-creating curricula.

23.6   Implementing an Employability Agenda

Some authors maintain that employability is better and more easily developed outside of the formal curriculum (Andrews & Higson, 2008; Ng & Feldman, 2009), with a particular emphasis on employment-based training and experience. For business undergraduates this is typically via a one-year work placement, between second and final year. Wilton (2012) saw the benefit of this approach, arguing that placements (with the proviso that they are ones of sufficient quality) positively contribute to the development of employability skills and provide students with a head-start. For us, there were two concerns with this approach. Firstly, the Masters' programmes, as at most institutions, were of one-year duration and so it was difficult to see how this model might fit. Secondly, employability provision sitting outside of the formal curriculum was not engaging the students, manifesting in little interaction with the learning portal, very few requests to look at CVs and application forms, and with the central Careers Service reporting only sparse numbers making enquiries or attending employer events.

Knight and Yorke (2003) identified workplace experience and careers advice as two of the four means of enhancing employability, the other two being entrepreneurship modules and portfolios/records of achievement. However, this argument differs from that of others in its insistence that employability training and development will be most effective only if embedded within the formal curriculum. Graduate employability, they argued, is not just measured by employment rates, but by students being able to present convincing evidence that they have the personal qualities and complex achievements that might augur well for workplace performance. Employability is achieved through sustained application over years, not semesters, and it requires complex learning: as a result, its success often depends on how it is promoted right across a programme, not through piecemeal activities. Programmes therefore should be designed in a systemic way with a focus on learning cultures and environments that help students know what they are learning, and why they are learning it, and, most importantly, will provide them with the necessary supports to develop the claims of achievement that make them more employable (Knight & Yorke, 2003, p. 14). To this end, Knight and Yorke (2003) and later Yorke and Knight (2007, p. 158) propose the "USEM account of employability":

(1)   Understanding
(2)   Skills—general and subject-specific, with the ability to apply them
(3)   Efficacy beliefs and other personal qualities
(4)   Metacognition (reflection on practice).

Arguably, a limitation of USEM whilst it provided a systemic way of thinking about employability (i.e. a generic set of principles or interrelated components which must be included in employability focused programmes) it gave little practical detail to the programme designer as to how to actually embed these principles, or what activities to include. The view expressed by Yorke and Knight (2007) themselves is that local variations have to be taken into consideration when applying this framework, but an example of putting theory into practice would perhaps have been useful.

However, building on this work, Dacre Pool and Sewell (2007) do provide practical help, arguing that thinking of employability in such a theoretical way has more to do with selling the employability agenda to academics (both in terms of championing the need for employability teaching, and also providing the research and theory evidence required to convince) than aiding on how to achieve it.

The aim of Dacre Pool and Sewell's work was to inform the planning of programmes and structured employability interventions, and whilst the focus of their 'practical model' was undergraduate provision, their ideas could be easily transferred to postgraduate programmes. Dacre Pool and Sewell (2007) present their "CareerEDGE model" comprising of overlapping and interacting components of:

(1) **De**gree Subject Knowledge, Understanding and Skills
(2) **G**eneric Skills (communication, team-working, managing others etc.)
(3) **E**motional Intelligence (self-awareness, managing emotions, managing relationships, understanding others)
(4) **E**xperience—work and life
(5) **Career** Development Learning—increased self-awareness, career identification and job preparation.

When dovetailed with opportunities for reflection and evaluation of the learning experiences in the different areas, and personal development planning, this provides students with the self-efficacy and self-confidence to develop and enhance their employability. To be successful in producing 'oven-ready' graduates, Dacre Pool and Sewell (2007) argue that not just some of the components but *all* of them must be embedded within programmes. To demonstrate the effectiveness of their model, Dacre Pool, Qualter, and Sewell (2014) more recently undertook empirical research in which 805 graduates were asked about their current employability, considering strengths and areas for improvement, suggesting that the CareerEDGE framework was proving effective both as a developmental and measurement tool in the design, implementation and evaluation of employability and the enhancement of students' self-confidence and perceived employability status. Finally, the HEA's (2013) framework for employability development also provided a useful point of reference in the initial stages of programme design. In addition to the need to embed employability into the curriculum (Dacre Pool & Sewell, 2007; Knight & Yorke, 2003), to support students in pursuit of self-confidence and enhanced levels of reflection (Argyris, 1997; Dacre Pool & Sewell, 2007; Kolb & Kolb, 2005), and (despite some hesitation from others e.g. Knight & Yorke, 2003) to include extra-curricular activities, (especially institutional career guidance services) the HEA framework emphasises the building of links with the labour market and employers. We knew this to be the weakest link in our postgraduate provision, and a problem to be rectified via future programme design.

23.7 Internationalisation

O'Leary (2012) and Jackson (2014) warn that skills and attributes associated with employability could vary from one country to another. This was something to be cognisant of when designing the postgraduate programmes. The CMI report (2014) noted that the ability to work across cultures was one of the core people management skills required by employers, and the literature points to the need for internationalisation of the HE provision (OECD, 2004; Young et al., 2013). By this it does not mean the curricula, but rather the development of skills and attributes which facilitate development of what some call the global mind-set (Lilley, Barker, & Harris, 2015a). Commentators enthuse about the power of an international experience to develop the 'global citizen' a concept best described as an 'ethical and critical thinking disposition' (Lilley et al., 2015a, p. 229) comprising values, capacities and strategic thinking beyond the training for productive careers (Bird & Osland 2006; Lilley, Barker, & Harris, 2015b). Lilley et al. (2015a) see the influence of internationalisation as not just developing a global citizen through the development of specific individual attributes, but enabling four manifestations of change: a broader perspective, accelerated maturity, a cosmopolitan experience brought about by working with different nationalities, and widened horizons.

They are not alone in their thinking. There is no doubt that some students are fully aware of the benefits of engaging with international mobility. Artess et al. (2017) cite a European Commission report (2014) on the Erasmus Programme which found that 85% of Erasmus students were motivated to engage with study abroad to improve their employability, especially to enhance second language skills. Furthermore, these students also reported enhanced personal development, independence and inter-cultural understanding, all of these being skills and attributes previously cited under the label of 'employability'. Indeed, the same report recorded that 75% of employers consulted also considered the international experience was important for recruitment, and over 90% viewed the transferable skills developed through mobility, (such as confidence, tolerance towards others, and curiosity about taking on new challenges) as amongst the skills they sought in graduates. However, UK students' engagement with international mobility was recorded as low at the time of our programme development. Despite the CMI (2014) highlighting working across cultures as a desirable attribute, they also reported only 10% of UK students took up any options to spend time abroad to develop and hone associated skills and attributes. The survey by Mellors-Bourne, Jones, Lawton, and Woodfield (2015) of 3000 students, revealed that students who did engage with short-term mobility programmes perceived all the benefits previously identified by their international peers, namely personal development, independence, enhanced career prospects. However, if the CMI's reported take-up figure is accurate, too few were taking advantage of international opportunities, and therefore, enhanced employability.

This finding had implications for our programme design. For many years, NBS like most Business Schools benefited from large numbers of international students, particularly from Asia, who chose to study abroad in pursuit of developing distinctiveness in their domestic labour markets. However, part of the University's strategy to increase Masters' student numbers, including lowering fees to 'Home' (including EU) students as an incentive, was changing the student profile, principally by increasing substantially the number of UK students. It was therefore important to create an international experience for students who, on paper, were not necessarily attracted to this form of internationalisation in any great numbers, at least not historically. Jones (2013, p. 100) suggests that an alternative but still effective experience could be achieved 'at home' via "experiential learning opportunities in an intercultural context, taking people beyond their standard comfort zones". Such "disorientating dilemmas" lead to the altered perspectives widely perceived to be a significant benefit of the international experience. It is therefore, to these "disorientating dilemmas", or at least the means by which they can be created, that we now turn: namely the benefits of experiential learning.

23.8 Real Play, Not Role Play

Experiential learning is a phrase coined to describe learning that is derived from an opportunity for direct hands-on experience (Baden & Parkes, 2013; Kolb & Kolb, 2005; Kolb, Kolb, Passarelli, & Sharma, 2014). The use of experiential learning in an educational environment has long been considered beneficial to students in the development of employability skills and attributes (Spanjaard, Hall, & Stegemann, 2018), providing, as it does, opportunities to apply their learning in the classroom and previous personal experiences to 'real-world' problem solving (Valenzuela et al., 2017). In addition, experiential learning, it is argued, provides opportunities for self-reflection, challenges existing mindsets, and requires critical evaluation of knowledge, processes and actions in order to generate better understanding and awareness. It also allows students to take ownership of a problem and to experience the consequences of their actions and decisions (Argyris, 1997; Levant, Coulmont, & Sandu, 2016). Essentially experiential learning, via a theory of action perspective (Argyris 1997) comprising planning, thinking, actual experimentation, observation and review, enables learners to develop capabilities (in this case employability capabilities), cognitively, emotionally and physically, that are useful in 'real-world' problem solving. In other words, experiential learning enriches the student's perspective on their self-efficacy (Ardley & Taylor, 2010), a fundamental component of Dacre Pool & Sewell's (2007) key to employability metaphor.

As mentioned above, and consistent with the reflective-practitioner learning philosophy (Schon, 1991) underpinning our provision, elements of experiential learning were longstanding components in these Masters' programmes, particularly through a team-building weekend residential and a team-based business simulation. The residential weekend, located off campus and delivered by external professional facilitators, comprises of various group-based problem-solving activities and opportunities for reflective practice (Argyris, 1997) which enable students to evolve and hone a suite of leadership and team-working skills and attributes as well as helping to build programme identity. Business simulations are extensively lauded for delivering greater learner-orientation (Karns, 2006), underpinned by significant cross-functional and team-based working (Piercy, 2013). These attributes are vital in real world problem solving, increasing self-efficacy, as students make 'real' decisions as opposed to theoretical ones (McCarthy & McCarthy 2006). Other benefits to 'real play not role play' are those associated with how students perceive themselves as a result of the experience. The challenge of engaging in such activities significantly improves the motivation and learning of the student (Karns, 2006), enhancing both self-esteem and individual sense of achievement as well as enabling students to develop a suite of interpersonal skills (Lindquist & Abraham, 1996).

There are some examples of how the effectiveness of the business simulation has been empirically tested (Levant et al., 2016; Piercy, 2013) in assessing student satisfaction and performance. Students enthuse about the value of being put in 'real' situations. More specifically, they attested to their enjoyment of working in diverse groups, engaging in co-operative working and learning from making mistakes, as well as the development of communication skills. Resonating with previously cited views (Karns, 2006; Lindquist & Abraham, 1996), students also believed that their team-working experiences had led to the acquisition of enhanced self-knowledge.

The literature does, however, sound some words of caution with regard to the success of business simulations in their ability to facilitate the development of real world skills and attributes. Levant et al. (2016) reported that Asian students perceived their business simulation, designed to develop soft skills, as less beneficial as compared with their European and African peers. The researchers provide reasons as to why this might be, including language difficulties, different learning techniques, and the fact that it was the first experience of this type of learning for the Asian students included in the study: they acknowledge that further investigation is required. A further consideration for us, particularly because our own business simulation straddles a six-week period of learning, was to take note that the length of the simulation does impact on student commitment to it. Tutor interventions, grounding the resulting experiences in theory, together with suitable time pressures for work completion and the consolidation of student learning via reflective practice are all required to ensure the success of these longer simulations (O'Malley & Ryan 2006).

Whilst the business simulation was a capstone activity within our provision pre-2015, the live-case pedagogies were not (Baden & Parkes, 2013; Kennedy, Lawson, & Walker, 2001; McCarthy & McCarthy, 2006; O'Leary, 2015). In most live-case scenarios, students work with organisations to solve real business problems, although some commentators have introduced job-shadowing (McCarthy & McCarthy, 2006), short placements (Baden & Parkes, 2013) and workshops with practitioners (Baden & Parkes, 2013). In all cases, it is claimed that "live projects" (Ardley & Taylor 2010 p. 849) enable students to develop a variety of skills including interpersonal skills and working with people from diverse backgrounds; the ability to navigate different organisational cultures; and to develop awareness of employer expectations (Kennedy et al., 2001). In short, these capture 'soft' skills as well as the 'harder' skills involved with critical and incisive problem-solving. Baden & Parkes (2013) describe how they taught ethics on two postgraduate programmes by using short placements and live case studies via workshops with practitioners.

Both of these experiential learning interventions gave students the opportunity to work with and learn from 'responsible' business professionals (Bandura, 1997) and also to share business and entrepreneurial challenges and problem-solving with the professionals and their student group. The students themselves reported a growth in self-confidence, together with a sustained belief that business success can be achieved while at the same time remaining ethical. Ardley & Taylor's (2010) research also describes the benefits to their students of working on "live projects", this time with client companies to resolve marketing management problems. Consistent with other research, their students also reported improved knowledge and confidence with regards to team-working and collecting information. Perhaps more interestingly, the students highlighted how a live project, working with real organisations, (and not restricted by theoretical learning only) facilitated the development of their creative skills. The widespread praise reported can be encapsulated by one student, who enthuses that "there is no better education than life" (Ardley & Taylor, 2010, p. 855).

23.9 Squeezing a Quart into a Pint Pot: Postgraduate Programme Development

Three key components needed to be embedded in the design of our postgraduate programmes: an emphasis on real-world experience rather than 'theoretical world' learning (CMI, 2014); the development of transferable skills, e.g. team-working, communication and interpersonal skills, digital competence and project management (Andrews & Russell, 2012; Jackson, 2014; Kalfa & Taksa, 2015); and a global perspective not only to the curriculum, but to the overall learning experience (Jones, 2013; Young et al., 2013). Consistent with best practice (Abraham & Karns, 2009; Dickinson et al., 2015; Maxwell et al., 2010; McMurray et al., 2016; Tymon, 2013) we consulted with our own stakeholders, including current students via focus groups (Carey, 2013) ensuring international representation (O'Leary, 2012), professional bodies and employers on the proposed developments and subsequent programme recalibration. Tymon's (2013) study in which he collected students' views on employability revealed only limited alignment between the views of students and the other stakeholder groups. However, our students sought a curriculum and learning experience that resonated with much of the literature and reports already cited, particularly with respect to the need for soft skills development in relation to team-working, communication and emotional intelligence. How we designed a programme to seamlessly blend the abilities and aspirations of our students with the urgent work-ready requirements of top local, national, and international employers is set out below.

Semester 1	Developing Global Management Competencies I (20 credits)	Specialist Module 1 (programme specific) (20 credits)	Specialist Module 2 (programme specific) (20 credits)	Dissertation Preparation and Research Methods (0 credits)	Academic and Professional Development (0 credits)
Semester 2	Developing Global Management Competencies II (20 credits)	Specialist Module 3 (programme specific) (20 credits)	Specialist Module 4 (programme specific) (20 credits)		
Semester 3	Masters Dissertation or Masters Consultancy Project (60 credits)				

Fig. 23.1 Structure of the one year masters programme

23.10 Programme Design—The Masters Framework, Structure and Content

In designing the suite of Masters programmes, a common framework approach has been adopted, as presented in Figs. 23.1 and 23.2 for the respective 1-year and 2-year programme variants. Taking into consideration the principal findings from the research and our own stakeholders, this framework comprises of:

- A common programme philosophy for teaching and assessment based on experiential learning and reflective practice (Kolb, 2014; Levant et al., 2016; Spanjaard et al., 2018; Valenzuela et al., 2017) yet providing opportunities for real play not role play.
- An internationalised student experience via a set of real world capstone activities, namely the management development residential, the business simulation, and the consultancy project (Artess et al., 2017; Jones, 2013; Young et al., 2013).
- A set of Programme Goals and Objectives around the development and achievement of employability skills and attributes, management and leadership capability, and subject expertise against which students can be measured and assessed. Programme outcomes of this kind are a key requirement of Professional Statutory and Regulatory Body (PSRB) requirements, in particular the Association to Advance Collegiate Schools of Business (AACSB) and its associated Assurance of Learning (AoL). They also enable us to articulate the employability agenda more clearly to students (Knight & Yorke, 2003; Rust, 2016; Wharton & Horrocks, 2015).

The programme design also adheres internally to the previously mentioned PFNA and its protocols, specifically with programme design being centred on semester-based modules of 20-credit value (or multiples thereof). In line with those who seek to embed employability within the curriculum and to provide interventions which run alongside and complement formal provision (Dacre Pool & Sewell, 2007; HEA, 2013; Knight & Yorke, 2003), Fig. 23.1 shows these development inputs which are most conducive to the 'oven ready graduate who is 'employment prepared' and how these inputs are delivered within the framework by Modules I and II of Developing Global Management Competencies.

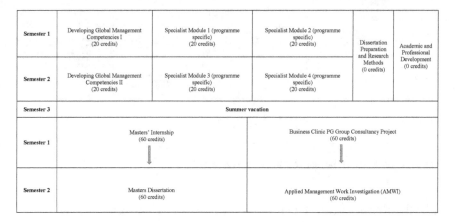

Semester 1	Developing Global Management Competencies I (20 credits)	Specialist Module 1 (programme specific) (20 credits)	Specialist Module 2 (programme specific) (20 credits)	Dissertation Preparation and Research Methods (0 credits)	Academic and Professional Development (0 credits)
Semester 2	Developing Global Management Competencies II (20 credits)	Specialist Module 3 (programme specific) (20 credits)	Specialist Module 4 (programme specific) (20 credits)		
Semester 3	Summer vacation				
Semester 1	Masters' Internship (60 credits) ↓		Business Clinic PG Group Consultancy Project (60 credits) ↓		
Semester 2	Masters Dissertation (60 credits)		Applied Management Work Investigation (AMWI) (60 credits)		

Fig. 23.2 Structure of the two years' masters programme

Developing Global Management Competencies I and II facilitate the necessary 'hard' and 'soft' skills essential for graduate level employability (Andrews & Russell, 2012; Jackson, 2014; Kalfa & Taksa, 2015) via two associated strands running through the pair of modules over the taught duration of the programme. The 'Business Intelligence' strand provides for practical development and application of problem-solving, data modelling, business scorecards, project management and business analytics, developing competencies relating to decision-making and IT application. Complementing this, the 'Emotional and Cultural Intelligence' strand supports the processes of personal and professional development within these areas (CMI, 2014; Dacre Pool & Sewell, 2007; Kurpis & Hunter, 2017) enhancing students' self-awareness and self-efficacy and building their capabilities as independent learners through individual and group learning. Attached to this strand is the well-established experiential learning intervention, the weekend residential event, the aims and content of which have been set out above.

The employability agenda has also been incorporated into the suite of programmes via the zero-credit bearing support modules, Dissertation Preparation, and Research Methods and Academic and Professional Development. The latter introduces the students not only to the development of postgraduate academic skills (e.g. referencing, academic writing, reflective practice) but helps create the vital group identity, required for team-working which in turn paves the way for successful experiential learning interventions (Ardley & Taylor, 2010; Baden & Parkes, 2013). Professional development aspects of employability enhancement are included via University-led initiatives such as one-to-one support from the University Service (Wilton, 2012). Where appropriate, PSRB contributions connect students with professionals in their chosen career (Tymon, 2013). Students' research capabilities are developed through the Dissertation Preparation and Research Methods module, which equips students with necessary skills and ethical training, and provides practical experience of analysing quantitative and qualitative data. In the first instance, the development of these skills and aptitudes enables students to successfully complete their Dissertation or Consultancy Project, but longer term these skills are directly transferable into employment.

Distinctions were made between generalist and specialist masters, by designing specialist masters with stipulated levels of subject content (QAA, 2015) and thereby successfully achieving PSRB accreditation relevant to the particular degree award. Specialist programmes such as Digital Marketing, or Logistics and Supply Chain Management, have 80 credits of discipline-specific taught modules (generalist masters have only 40 credits) and 60 credits of discipline-flavoured Dissertation (discipline relevance being a formal requirement) or Consultancy Project. This level of specialism was awarded accreditation of the Digital Marketing Masters by The Chartered Institute of Marketing (CIM), and for the Logistics and Supply Chain Management Masters, two accreditations from the Chartered Institute of Purchasing and Supply (CIPS) and the Chartered Institute of Logistics and Transport (CILT) were achieved. These accreditations make these programmes highly competitive in the marketplace, serving as endorsements of our employability-focused programmes. With 140 out of 180 credits representing the specialism, the student experience is arguably very discipline-specific. Achieving and demonstrating such a balance addresses certain challenges both internal and external to the School, as discussed below.

Two elements of the programme which are particularly significant in providing real-world learning environments for students (CMI, 2014, 2018) are the Business Simulation and the Consultancy Project. The Business Simulation is a core capstone activity delivered across all the programmes and housed within a strategy-based module (these vary slightly according to the generalist or specialist elements of the respective programmes). Allocated to international teams, students benefit from 'real' experience (strategy setting and integrated decision-making) within a multicultural context (Jones, 2013; Lilley et al., 2015a). However, the Faculty Business Clinic, with its own physical presence and dedicated team, that has facilitated our ability to include 'real-world' experiences within the curriculum, i.e. the management consultancy project. As with 'live-case' study work (Ardley & Taylor, 2010; Baden & Parkes, 2013; McCarthy & McCarthy, 2006; O'Leary, 2015), students are allocated to groups to work on client-based projects. This 'real-world' experience may either relate to a single subject discipline or be multi-functional, where the contribution of an individual can be tailored to their area of specialisation (particularly important for specialist Masters students). The Consultancy Project is an option, not core, but is increasingly popular with students seeking more focus on employability as opposed to academic prowess through the more traditional dissertation.

Bringing the various programme components together in this way helps equip the Masters' graduates with a decision-making and information-handling capabilities, builds capacity for self-working and team-working, and is underpinned by the cultural awareness sought by our stakeholders (CMI, 2014, 2018). Students are provided with research skills, complemented by a body of contemporary functional or specialist knowledge, intertwining theory and practice. Where the one-year Masters' programmes represent a mature offering, the two-year equivalents have emerged from market intelligence pointing to the demand (and indeed for entry into certain job markets, the necessity) for Masters' programmes of longer duration (in particular the sizeable markets of India and China) including elements of work experience or 'real-world' intervention. In addressing this, the two-year programme variants have a first year common in content and delivery with their one-year equivalents, as demonstrated by Fig. 23.2. The second year of these programmes (having Advanced Practice, or Study Abroad) offers more space and time to embed experiential learning opportunities (Ardley & Taylor, 2010; Baden & Parkes, 2013; Spanjaard et al., 2018).

The first of the two-year programme variants is with Advanced Practice: it has been designed to have two pathways. One pathway affords students the opportunity to pursue an Internship with an external organisation for one semester, facilitating 'real-world' experiences of work with all its benefits (Clark & Zukas, 2013; Kalfa & Taksa, 2015). They can choose instead a project aligned to the degree programme pursued, assessed through a reflective portfolio linking experiences and skills to employability. On returning to university the Dissertation is undertaken, potentially informed by the work and experiences captured through the Internship. The alternative pathway involves an academic year spent in the Faculty Business Clinic, on a group-based consultancy project with an external client organisation. The examination of the organisational problem (which may be discipline specific or multidisciplinary, dictating group composition) affords experiential learning through a 'real' problem and requires application of theoretical knowledge to practice (Ardley & Taylor, 2010; Baden & Parkes, 2013). The reality of this application is reinforced for students through the required levels of contact and relationship-building with the client culminating in a presentation of findings and client-focussed reports. This work leads to a substantial group Consultancy Report in second semester and elements of individual input through literature evaluation specific to the selected problem and discipline. Most clients working with the Business Clinic are Public Sector, Not-For-Profit, or SMEs, whose resource base may prohibit high spending (on commercial consultants), but whose 'live' problems are very real and complex. Serving senior client employees provides a challenging work experience, directly transferable into subsequent full-time employment.

The alternative two-year programme variant includes Study Abroad. In the first semester, the student studies outside the UK with a partner University, engaging fully in terms of host classes and assessment, with an additional portfolio of reflective learning, which demonstrates acquisition and development of skills and attributes appropriate for an enhanced personal portfolio of employability. Similar to Internship students, they return to complete the Masters' Dissertation, although certain partnership relationships permit this to be taken with the partner and thus linked to dual awards. This additional travel opportunity, coupled with further cultural assimilation is a 'real' experience that provides insights for those with work aspirations with a multi-national focus (Artess et al., 2017; Mellors-Bourne et al., 2015).

23.11   Responses to the Employability Agenda

Whilst much student feedback has been positive, during the planning and operational phases some academic resistance (Bovill, 2014; Kolb et al., 2014) was encountered. Bovill (2014) notes occasional academic resistance over co-creating curricula with students. Involving students in programme design requires the academic role to evolve beyond the usual position of 'gate-keeper' of curricula, to become facilitators of learning. Discomfort can ensue, not least because of the need to take risks within a different learning environment. The discomfort creates the desire to maintain the status quo, and alternative approaches are resisted. A further challenge centres on how learning is achieved: in this case, given the philosophical positioning of the programmes, it is experiential. Whilst insistence on the highest standards of academic rigour is not diminished, *how* that theory is learned and understood is through its application to 'real world' situations.

The experiential approach to learning requires a different skills set, that moves away from the 'outside-in' style of traditional education in which the 'teacher' is a subject matter expert who transmits what they deem to be the appropriate knowledge and information to students and instead gravitates towards an 'inside-out' approach to learning which requires instead that the tutor taps into internal interest and intrinsic motivations of learners, building on their prior knowledge and experience Kolb et al. (2014, p. 207). Kolb et al. (2014) also suggest that the 'discomfort' of experiential learning is not only experienced by academics, but also by students, unused as they are to this approach, and therefore training for both academic and student is advised. To some extent, pockets of concern were found here amongst academics about the need to play facilitator, a role very different to the more directive one of subject expert. In the initial stages we encouraged staff to self-select onto the experiential learning modules, but as more programmes and opportunities rolled out, we have set up mentoring and work-shadowing for staff development purposes, including the opportunity to study for our PG Certificate in Coaching.

However, what was more apparent in our case was not academics' reluctance to engage with students throughout the consultation process, or to challenge the greater emphasis on experiential learning: instead, resistance was tied to 'subject fiefdom', i.e. the reluctance of some to accept the level of employability embedded into their respective programmes, in particular the two modules of 'hard' and 'soft' skills development. The Internship, Consultancy Project and Study Abroad were unanimously supported, but the presence of the two modules considerably reduced the subject specialist element, and thus severely impacted, apparently, on academic rigour, and the marketability of the programme to potential students. This 'turf war' continues unabated despite positive feedback from students on areas of the programme that academics often resist the most. To some extent, the academics' arguments around 'developmental versus specialism' are strengthened because of the university requirement to adopt a research-rich learning approach to module development and student learning experiences. Given that the majority of academic scholarship within the School is arguably discipline-based, the programmes' critics felt that the subject specific modules represented the greatest opportunity to deliver on this agenda, despite the fact that enquiry-based 'capstones' of Dissertation and Consultancy Project explicitly facilitate student-centred knowledge creation (that is discipline-specific and represents, arguably, the highest level of research-rich learning). Externally, the accrediting PSRBs that are programme specific are particularly keen to ensure a minimum threshold of subject-specific input on the recognised programmes. As such, we have already designed the 'capstone' experiential learning modules covering Masters' Dissertation, Masters' Consultancy Project, Internship and Study Abroad so that they are adequately discipline-focussed. However, some colleagues remain unconvinced, and the debate continues.

From the student perspective, however, there is no doubt that there has been a vocal, enthusiastic response to the initiatives put in place, and what has been especially reassuring is that the students now understand and approve of what we are doing and why (Knight & Yorke, 2003; Rust, 2016; Wharton & Horrocks, 2015). Communication of the employability agenda is crucial to the development of students' confidence and their self-efficacy (Dacre Poole & Sewell, 2007; Karns, 2006; Lindquist & Abraham, 1996), and it would appear for the most part that this has been achieved. For example, students described the employability modules as: "significant to both my career path as well as my personal development".... "I can apply my learned skills in my workplace"... "[the modules] provide excellent tools for use in the real world" and "my confidence has grown and I now feel that I am ready to go into partnership with my brother..." Reassuringly, the more established experiential learning events continue to be perceived by students as providing them with the springboard they need to feel confident in entering the real world, with students reporting: "increased self-knowledge"...enhanced team-working and management skills"... "an opportunity to practice for the real world"... "I now have lots of examples of leading teams that I can add to my CV".

The latest interventions (the Consultancy Project, the Study Abroad and the Internship) despite being in the earliest stages of roll-out, appear to have been received positively by those students who have selected the two year programme, seeing the overall Consultancy Project experience as having "played an undeniable role" in helping them "secure a graduate job" and overall, their experience of this specific intervention has "been a really enjoyable and rewarding experience". Students who selected either Study Abroad or Internship have also reported enjoyment of their experiences, affording them as they have, opportunities to study as far afield as Japan, for example, to graduate with double degrees from our partner institutions, and to be perhaps employed after their internship by their host organisations.

23.12 Ongoing Challenges

It would be naive to suggest that such a radical recalibration of our Masters' provision does not come without associated challenges. Assessment of the competition highlights the growing emphasis on employability, and the need for us to respond accordingly to market demands by providing attractive, fit-for-purpose programmes that will recruit students. In respect of Advanced Practice, Internship or a year-long Consultancy Project, these relatively new variants of Masters provision have garnered considerable interest from potential students. The Consultancy Project especially has proven attractive because of its obvious ability to engage students directly with employers. Understandably, some students are keen to grasp Internship opportunities, perhaps without a full appreciation (in particular within the International study community) of the intensity of (open) competition for such real-world experiences, with University support only able to go so far in helping to realise such ambitions. A further barrier is that most placement-providing organisations are aligned overwhelmingly to one-year work placements aimed at undergraduate students and, thus far, this has proved an obstacle to the introduction of wide-scale internship opportunities for Masters' students over the different timeframe of three months.

The School's Business Clinic offers a supported learning environment in which students can take part in 'real-world' consulting projects but this opportunity is sometimes perceived as less attractive than an Internship. The application of 'real-world' consultancy projects as compared with work placements and Internships is more prevalent across the sector with respect to Masters' programmes, but it would appear that selling the benefits of the opportunity (and its associated academic support), alongside the experiences gained through interaction with senior client staff and providing insights of real value (which may not be the case in all internships, where content and experience are outside the control of the University) represents substantial 'work-in-progress.' Furthermore, many of the consultancy projects are generated from the SME and not-for-profit sectors, which at a superficial level do not appear to be valued as highly by students seeking entry into identifiable, larger organisations. Therefore, although the Business Clinic intervention is a helpful solution where geographic remoteness from larger organisations hinders the real-world openings (which do exist within the sector), some students are still keen to have an internship within a larger, well established and more well-known organisation. A further challenge derives from the students themselves: even such a controlled learning environment as the Business Clinic represents a step too far for some students, perhaps because of language difficulties or cultural expectations (Levant et al., 2016).

In relation to the two-year programme variant with Study Abroad, our experiences thus far resonate with the views of Jones (2013) and the CMI (2014) in that take-up of international opportunities by UK students is limited and has clear room for improvement. To a certain extent this lack of interest from UK students is offset, as might be expected, in the initial stages, by International students with a predisposition for travel and cultural assimilation who seek such Study Abroad opportunities to fulfil their desire to study further in their second language and have additional, different, international experiences. However, it is apparent that more needs to be done to make international opportunities less prohibitive to UK students. There is potential for us to develop further such dual-degree offerings with our mature partner relationships (Business programmes are delivered and assessed in English) as these have proved popular for students moving in either direction between the partners involved. This again, requires more work to be done.

23.13 Conclusion

In their 2014 report, the CMI opined that the process of producing 21st Century leaders and managers was a continuous one, requiring constant innovation on the part of Business Schools, professional bodies, and employers operating in tandem. Four years on, the CMI suggests the most sought-after and prized behaviour in new graduates is a capacity for taking responsibility, closely followed by skills and behaviours in people management, ethical decision-making, problem-solving and critical analysis, collaboration and team-working. Disappointingly however, 61% of organisations still report that graduates lack skills in a number of these areas alongside a deficit in self-awareness (CMI, 2018). As a result, the CMI (2018) have identified the need for universities to increase their efforts to create the 'oven-ready' graduate but with a specific focus on the SME sector. We have already noted that there is relatively less enthusiasm from students to work with SMEs as part of a consultancy project as compared with that for Internships, based on perceptions of differing opportunities afforded by 'higher-profile' employers, so this is a particular focus of improvement for us. However, the latest CMI report (2018) also sets out the requirements of the students themselves. To optimise their employability, students demand a curriculum which provides opportunities for team-working, communication and problem-solving. They want greater engagement with employers, more work experience, and to develop their management and leadership skills. In choosing a programme, students report that they also look for professional accreditations (75%), networking with employers and entrepreneurship opportunities. Whilst our programmes always have room for improvement, it is our view that we go some way to addressing these needs via a menu of internships, study abroad, live-case consultancy projects and an embedded core employability curriculum, underpinned by the philosophy of experiential learning.

We have 'squeezed a quart into a pint pot' to meet the employability agenda. The programme design has not been welcomed by everyone, and there is more work to be done to provide 'oven-ready' graduates (CMI, 2018), but the positive feedback we have received from our own stakeholders would suggest that we are making progress in providing substantive real-world experience in order to apply theoretical world learning.

References

Abraham, S. E., & Karns, L. A. (2009). Do business schools value the competencies that businesses value? *Journal of Education for Business, 84*(6), 350–356.

Andrews, J., & Higson, H. (2008). Graduate employability, 'soft skills' versus 'hard' business knowledge: A European study. *Higher Education in Europe, 33*(4), 413–422.

Andrews, G., & Russell, M. (2012). Employability skills development: strategy, evaluation and impact. *Higher Education, Skills and Work Based Learning, 2*(1), 33–44.

Ardley, B., & Taylor, N. (2010). The student practitioner. Developing skills through the marketing research consultancy project. *Market Intelligence & Planning, 28*(7), 847–861.

Argyris, C. (1997). Learning and teaching: A theory of action perspective. *Journal of Management Education, 21*(1), 9–26.

Artess, J., Hooley, T., & Mellors-Bourne, R. (2017). *Employability: A review of the literature 2012 to 2016*. York: Higher Education Academy. Available at: http://hdl.handle.net/10525/621285. Downloaded June 6, 2018.

Baden, D., & Parkes, C. (2013). Experiential learning: Inspiring the business leaders of tomorrow. *Journal of Management Development, 32*(3), 295–308.

Bandura, A. (1997). *Self-efficacy: The exercise of control*. New York: Freeman.

Bird, A., & Osland, J. S. (2006). Global competencies: An introduction. In H. W. Lane, M. L. Maznevski, M. E. Mendenhall, & J. McNett (Eds.), *Handbook of global management. A guide to managing complexity*. Oxford: Blackwell Publishing.

BIS. (2015). *Fulfilling our potential: Teaching excellence, social mobility and student choice*. London: BIS.

BIS. (2016). *Success as a knowledge economy: Teaching excellence, social mobility and student choice*. London: BIS.

Bovill, C. (2014). An investigation of co-created curricula within higher education in the UK, Ireland and the USA. *Innovations in Education and Teaching International, 51*(1), 15–25.

Cai, Y. (2013). Graduate employability: A conceptual framework for understanding employers' perceptions. *Higher Education, 65,* 457–469.

Carey, P. (2013). Student as co-producer in a marketised higher education system: A case study of students' experience of participation in curriculum design. *Innovations in Education and Teaching International, 50*(3), 250–260.

Cavanagh, J., Burston, M., Southcombe, A., & Bartram, T. (2015). Contributing to a graduate-centred understanding of work readiness: An exploratory study of Australian undergraduate students' perceptions of their employability. *International Journal of Management Education, 13*(3), 278–288.

Chartered Management Institute. (2014). *21st century leaders report*. Available at: http://www.managers.org.uk/~/media/Files/PDF/21st_Century_Leaders_June2014.pdf.

Chartered Management Institute. (2018). *21st century leaders. Building employability through higher education.* Available at: http://www.managers.org.uk/~media/Files/Reports/insights/research/21st_Century_Leaders_CMI_Feb2018.pdf.

Clark, M., & Zukas, M. (2013). A Bourdieusian approach to understanding employability: Becoming a "fish in water". *Journal of Vocational Education and Training, 65*(2), 208–219.

Coates, N., & Dickinson, J. (2012). Meeting international postgraduate student needs: A programme-based model for learning and teaching support. *Innovations in Education and Teaching International, 49*(3), 295–308.

Dacre Pool, L., Qualter, P. J., & Sewell, P. (2014). Exploring the factor structure of the CareerEDGE employability development profile. *Education and Training, 56*(4), 303–313.

Dacre Pool, L., & Sewell, P. (2007). The key to employability: Developing a practical model of graduate employability. *Education and Training, 49*(4), 277–289.

Dickinson, J., Binns, R., & Divan, A. (2015). Embedding employer engagement and employability into masters programmes: Process, implementation and evaluation. *Practice and Evidence of Scholarship of Teaching and Learning in Higher Education, 10*(2), 136–153.

European Commission. (2014). *The Erasmus impact study: Effects of mobility on the skills and employability of students and the internationalisation of higher education institutions*. Luxembourg: European Commission: Education and Culture.

Frankham, J. (2017). Employability and higher education: The follies of the 'Productivity Challenge' in the teaching excellence framework. *Journal of Education Policy, 32*(5), 628–641.

Guardian. (2016). University courses fail to develop basic skills like maths, says OECD. *Guardian,* January 29, 2016.

HEA. (2013). *Framework for embedding employability in higher education*. York: Higher Education Academy.

Holmes, L. (2015). Becoming a graduate: The warranting of an emergent identity. *Education and Training, 57*(2), 219–238.

Jackson, D. (2014). Testing a model of undergraduate competence in employability skills and its implications for stakeholders. *Journal of Education and Work, 27*(2), 220–242.

Jones, E. (2013). Internationalization and employability: The role of intercultural experiences in the development of transferable skills. *Public Money & Management, 33*(2), 95–104. Available at: http://dx.doi.org/10.1080/09540962.2013.763416. Downloaded July 18, 2017.

Kalfa, S., & Taksa, L. (2015). Cultural capital in business higher education: Reconsidering the graduate attributes movement and the focus on employability. *Studies in Higher Education, 40*(4), 580–595.

Karns, G. L. (2006). Learning style differences in the perceived effectiveness of learning activities. *Journal of Marketing Education, 28*(1), 56–63.

Kemp, S. (2009). Embedding employability and employer engagement into postgraduate teaching: A case study from 'environmental management systems'. *Planet, 21*(1), 47–52.

Kennedy, E. J., Lawson, L., & Walker, E. (2001). The case for using live cases: Shifting the paradigm in marketing education. *Journal of Marketing Education, 23*(2), 145–151.

Knight, P. T., & Yorke, M. (2003). Employability and good learning in higher education. *Teaching in Higher Education, 8*(1), 3–16.

Kolb, D. A. (1984). *Experiential learning: Experiences as the source of learning and development.* London: FT Press.

Kolb, D. A. (2014). *Experiential learning: Experience as the source of learning and development.* London: FT Press.

Kolb, A. Y., & Kolb, D. A. (2005). Learning styles and learning spaces: Enhancing experiential learning in higher education. *Academy of Management Learning and Education, 4,* 193–212.

Kolb, A. Y., Kolb, D. A., Passarelli, A., & Sharma, G. (2014). On becoming an experiential educator: The educator role profile. *Simulation & Gaming, 45*(2), 24–234.

Koris, R., Ortenblad, A., & Ojala, T. (2017). From maintaining the status quo to promoting free thinking and inquiry: Business students' perspective on the purpose of business school teaching. *Management Learning, 48*(2), 174–186.

Kumar, A. (2015). *Enabling all learners to SOAR for employability.* York: Higher Education Academy.

Kurpis, L. H., & Hunter, J. (2017). Developing students' cultural intelligence through an experiential learning activity: A cross-cultural consumer behavior (ibid) interview. *Journal of Marketing Education, 39*(1), 30–46.

Levant, Y., Coulmont, M., & Sandu, R. (2016). Business simulation as an active learning activity for developing soft skills. *Accounting Education, 25*(4), 368–395.

Lilley, K., Barker, M., & Harris, N. (2015a). Exploring the process of global citizen learning and the student mind-set. *Journal of Studies in International Education, 19*(3), 225–245.

Lilley, K., Barker, M., & Harris, N. (2015b). Educating global citizens: A good 'idea' or an organisational practice? *Higher Education Research & Development, 34*(5), 957–971.

Lindquist, T. M., & Abraham, R. J. (1996). Whitepeak corporation: A case analysis of a Jigsaw 11 application of cooperative learning. *Accounting Education: A Journal of Theory, Practice and Research, 1,* 113–125.

Matheson, R. & Sutcliffe, M. (2017). Belonging and transition: An exploration of international business students' postgraduate experience. *Innovations in Education and Teaching International.* Available at: https://doi.org/10.1080/14703297.2017.1279558. Downloaded July 18, 2017.

Maxwell, G., Scott, B., Macfarlane, D., & Williamson, E. (2010). Employers as stakeholders in postgraduate employability skills development. *International Journal of Management Education, 8*(2), 13–23.

McCarthy, P. R., & McCarthy, H. M. (2006). When case studies are not enough: Integrating experiential learning into business curricula. *Journal of Education for Business, 81*(4), 201–204.

McMurray, S., Dutton, M., McQuaid, R., & Richard, A. (2016). Employer demands from business graduates. *Education + Training, 58*(1), 112–132.

Mellors-Bourne, R., Jones, E., Lawton, W., & Woodfield, S. (2015). *Student perspectives on going international* [Internet]. Universities UK International Unit. Available from: http://www.go. international.ac.uk/sites/default/files/Student%20Perspectives%20Report.pdf. Accessed July 1, 2018.

Moore, T., & Morton, J. (2017). The myth of job readiness: Written communication, employability and the 'skills gap' in higher education. *Studies in Higher Education, 42*(3), 591–609.

Ng, T. W. H., & Feldman, D. (2009). How broadly does education contribute to job performance? *Personnel Psychology, 62,* 89–134.

O'Leary, S. (2012). Impact of entrepreneurship teaching in higher education on the employability of scientists and engineers. *Industry and Higher Education, 26*(6), 431–442.

O'Leary, S. (2015). Integrating employability into degree programmes using consultancy projects as a form of enterprise. *Industry and Higher Education, 29*(6), 459–468.

O'Malley, L., & Ryan, A. (2006). Pedagogy and relationship marketing. *Journal of Marketing Education, 22,* 195–214.

OECD. (2004). *Career guidance and public policy: Bridging the gap.* Organisation for Economic Co-operation and Development. Paris: OECD.

Piercy, N. (2013). Evaluating experiential learning in the business context: Contributions to group-based and cross-functional working. *Innovations in Education and Teaching, 50*(2), 202–213.

QAA. (2015). Subject benchmark statement master's degrees in business and management. June 2015.http://www.qaa.ac.uk/docs/qaa/subject-benchmark-statements/sbs-business-and-management-15.pdf?sfvrsn=1997f681_14.

Robson, F., Forster, G., & Powell, L. (2016). Participatory learning at residential weekends: Benefit or barrier to learning for the international student? *Innovations in Education and Teaching International, 53*(3), 274–284.

Rust, C. (2016). Shifting the focus from skills to 'graduateness'. *Phoenix, 148,* 8–10.

Schon, D. A. (1991). *The reflective practitioner.* Aldershot: Ashgate.

Spanjaard, D., Hall, T., & Stegemann, N. (2018). Experiential learning: Helping students to become 'career-ready'. *Australasian Marketing Journal, 26,* 163–171. Available at: http://doi.org/10. 1016/j.ausmj.2018.04.003. Downloaded on July 8, 2018.

Tholen, G. (2004). Graduate employability and educational context: A comparison between Great Britain and the Netherlands. *British Educational Research Journal, 40*(1), 1–17.

Tomlinson, M. (2008). 'The degree is not enough': Students' perceptions of the role of higher education credentials for graduate work and employability. *British Journal of Sociology of Education, 29*(1), 49–61.

Tymon, A. (2013). The student perspective on employability. *Studies in Higher Education, 38*(6), 841–856.

Valenzuela, L., Jerez, O. M., Hasbun, B. A., Pizarro, V., Valenzuela, G., & Orsini, C. A. (2017). Closing the gap between business undergraduate education and the organisational environment: A Chilean case study applying experiential learning theory. *Innovations in Education and Teaching International.* Available at: http://dx.doi.org/10.1080/14703297.2017.1295877. Downloaded April 30, 2018.

Wharton, C. Y. & Horrocks, J. (2015). *Students' perceptions of employability within their degree programme: Highlighting the disparity between what academics believe is included and the student experience.* Enhancement and Innovation in Higher Education, June 9–11, 2015. Glasgow, UK. Available at: https://www.researchgate.net/profile/Yvette_Wharton/publication/323628997_ Students%27_perceptions_of_employability_within_their_degree_programme_highlighting_ the_disparity_between_what_academics_believe_is_included_and_the_student_experience/ links/5aa107160f7e9badd9a3c747/Students-perceptions-of-employability-within-their-degree-programme-highlighting-the-disparity-between-what-academics-believe-is-included-and-the-student-experience.pdf. Downloaded July 1, 2017.

Wilton, N. (2012). Employability is in the eye of the beholder: Employer decision-making in the recruitment of work placement students. *Higher Education, Skills and Work-Based Learning, 4*(3), 242–255.

Yorke, M. & Knight, P. (2006). Embedding employability into the curriculum. In *Learning and employability series* (Vol. 1). York: Higher Education Academy.

Yorke, M., & Knight, P. (2007). Evidence-informed pedagogy and the enhancement of student employability. *Teaching in Higher Education, 12*(2), 157–170.

Young, T. J., Sercombe, P. G., Sachdev, I., Naeb, R., & Schartner, A. (2013). Success factors for international postgraduate students' adjustment: Exploring the roles of intercultural competence, language proficiency, social contact and social support. *European Journal of Higher Education, 3*(2), 151–171.

Gillian Forster (Ph.D.) is Principal Lecturer in Organisation and HRM at Newcastle Business School, Northumbria University, UK. Her pedagogical research focuses on enhancing the learning and teaching experience of postgraduate students, the majority of whom are international. Recent research projects have included analysis of the benefits of experiential learning via residential working, embedding employability into the curriculum, and the design of a mentoring programme for female international students. She has extensive experience in the design, development and implementation of Masters Programmes.

Andrew Robson (Ph.D.) is Professor of Learning and Teaching in the Faculty of Business and Law at Northumbria University, UK. His interests in learning and teaching relate to the learning environment, particularly in the context of IT workshops and the delivery of subjects like statistics and data analysis. He also has a significant interest in the deployment of business simulations and working with part-time and International learners on Masters' programmes. Andrew has substantial experience in programme design, development and delivery at Masters' and Undergraduate levels.

Chapter 24
Constructing Careers: Self-awareness, Self-reflection, and Self-efficacy Amongst Undergraduate Business Students

Deborah A. Lock

24.1 Introduction

Over recent years there has been much written about graduate employability (Yorke, 2004). These works range from questions about definition and meaning (Dearing, 1997), what is meant by '*graduateness*' (Glover, Law, & Youngman, 2002), graduate attributes (Osmani et al., 2015) and whose responsibility is it to help students develop the skills required to secure meaningful graduate-level jobs (Tomlinson, & Holmes, 2017). For some, employability is considered as the '*ability to keep the job one has, or to get the job one desires*' (Rothwell & Arnold, 2007, p. 25), whereas for others it is about a '*set of achievements*' that can help an individual gain employment and be successful in their chosen occupations, thereby benefiting themselves and contributing to the socio-economic prosperity of businesses and the wider community (Yorke & Knight, 2006, p. 8). However graduate employability is positioned, the emphasis in UK HE appears, in brief, to be linked to students being able to demonstrate skills and abilities that would be attractive to future employers (Institute for Employment Studies, 2018; Wharton & Horrocks, 2015).

Given the emergence of the Fourth Industrial Revolution, also referred to as Industry 4.0 (Bonekamp & Sure, 2015; PWC, 2014; Xing & Marwala, 2017), and the complexity of the global labour market, it is essential that business schools focus attention on developing graduates who are technically competent, flexible, open to change, and can work across functional boundaries (McMurray, Dutton, McQuaid, & Richard, 2016). Critical to this is that students understand and can work in open innovation environments where collaboration and interdisciplinary learning occurs in the workplace, leading to new products, processes and means of production (Lorenz et al., 2015). This means that students need to understand the nature of employment and discipline fluidity before they graduate so that they are prepared for occupa-

D. A. Lock (✉)
University of Lincoln, Lincoln, England, UK
e-mail: dlock@lincoln.ac.uk

© Springer Nature Switzerland AG 2019
A. Diver (ed.), *Employability via Higher Education: Sustainability as Scholarship*,
https://doi.org/10.1007/978-3-030-26342-3_24

tional complexity (Figueiredo, Biscaia, Rocha, & Teixeira, 2017). In recognition of changeable work environments and the potential for workplace transformation as new models of business emerge, the University of Lincoln has an ambition that on graduation all students will be work-ready with the ability to 'drive and embrace disruption and change' (University of Lincoln, 2016, p. 10).

How and where students get the best opportunity to develop employability skills remains debateable. For example, should employability activities be embedded within the curriculum (Avramenko, 2012; Tymon, 2013) or made available through extracurricular activities (Rae, 2007) or a combination of both? Who should deliver the content? Should it be academic staff, representatives from the professions (Kolmos, Hadgraft, & Holgaard, 2016; Magnell & Kolmos, 2017) or hybrid *'pracademics'* who can draw upon their experiences of working across the boundaries of academia and practice (Posner, 2009). For Pool and Sewell (2007), undergraduate programmes are considered good places to embed employability since students are primarily working towards entering the job market, whereas postgraduate programmes are aimed at students who are seeking to acquire advanced skills and knowledges that can contribute to career *enhancement*. This view of embedding employability into the curriculum is further endorsed by Speight, Lackovic, and Cooker (2013) whose research identified that employers 'disagreed that employability was a separate issue from the subject curriculum' (p. 121), and that the two are part of an holistic approach to developing work-ready graduates. This approach is not without its problems since there is evidence to suggest that traditional teaching and assessment methods (such as exams, lectures, essays and report writing) do not necessarily facilitate the development of employability skills, which means that new and innovative teaching methods may be required, for example, via the 'flipped-classroom' scenario in which students' use of self-assessment auditing tools can be explored, with analysis of real-time case studies to contextualise theory with current situations, and business simulations which provide a risk-free environment for students to experiment in and opportunities for consultancy work (either in partnership with academics or independently). All of these, singularly or in various combinations, offer meaningful learning opportunities which result in the skills that employers are looking for (Archer & Davison, 2008; Clark, Selwood, & Muir, 2011).

Graduate attributes are the skills, competences and behaviours that students develop as a result of engaging in HE. They include visible and invisible attributes, the former being tangible, technical knowledge and know-how (discipline-specific or generalist) which can be applied in the workplace, and the subsequent, more ephemeral and often hard to measure attributes such as social competency, cultural fluency and mind-sets that influence behaviour. Although there is no standard list of graduate attributes which HE institutions adhere to, Osmani et al. (2015) identified eight overarching themes which provide an indicative framework that can be drawn upon to 'future proof' graduates and ensure that they constantly evolve their skills sets. These include:

1. Communication skills,
2. Team work,

3. Motivation and leadership,
4. Critical thinking and problem solving,
5. Flexibility and adaptability,
6. Time and self-management,
7. Meaningful work experience, and
8. Digital literacy.

This list has subsequently been revised to include emotional intelligence and resilience. Although the acquisition of graduate attributes brings no guarantee of employment, identifying the type of attributes that employers appear to expect graduates to possess (in addition to any technical and subject knowledge) provides a structure through which students can develop skills and competences that will differentiate them during a competitive recruitment process. The challenge for educators is how to 'enact an attribute in a classroom situation, and move from describing to applying an attribute in a meaningful way' (Kensington-Miller, Knewstubb, Longley, & Gilbert, 2018, p. 9), and capture invisible behavioural aspects such as social competency, resilience and cultural fluency (Lorenz et al., 2015). It was within the context of these debates that Lincoln International Business School (LIBS) developed an embryonic undergraduate employability infrastructure which seeks to leverage the benefits of both embedded and extracurricular employability activities delivered in collaboration with key stakeholders (academics, professional service staff, placement students and alumni, members of the LIBS advisory board and representatives from the regional and national business communities). The framework is based on the following principles:

P1: *Employability* is *an enabler which is manifested* in the skills, knowledge and attributes that help graduates to be successful in their chosen careers and life choices.

P2: *Graduate attributes* are the behaviours and values that *students develop* during their programme. Although these may be generic attributes such as communication skills, how they are enacted is unique to the individual.

P3: *Employability skills (asset) development* is the triadic responsibility of academic, professional service and business communities, the purpose of which is to help students to maximise their potential through providing access to meaningful learning opportunities that will enhance their employability prospects.

24.2   Lincoln International Business School (LIBS)

Over the last ten years, Lincoln International Business School has undergone a series of incarnations, from a loose amalgamation of Departments, to a School within a College, before finally emerging in April 2016 as a School with a College status. The University originally had three colleges: Art, Social Sciences, and Science. The decision for LIBS to be the fourth stand-alone, autonomous College was two-fold.

Firstly, the rapid growth in student numbers provided sufficiently sustainable income to merit independence, and secondly, the University's ambition to apply for external accreditation through the Association to Advance Collegiate Schools of Business (AACSB) required the business school to be able to demonstrate independence in terms of branding, external market perception, financial management, and academic unit autonomy (AACSB, 2018). This, it was considered, could not be evidenced if the School remained in the existing sibling-parent College relationship.

As part of the preparations for independence, all academic portfolios (undergraduate, postgraduate and work-based distance learning) were reviewed and refreshed in terms of currency, content, and teaching, learning and assessment strategies. The review exercise included:

- Evaluation of student recruitment, progression and retention trends,
- Analysis, horizon-scanning and incorporation of discipline developments,
- Identification of programmes' value-added status along with agreed interventions to address any attainment gaps,
- Realignment of the curricula to reflect business and professional body requirements (hard technical skills and knowledge),
- Five-year trend analysis of the Destination of Leavers from Higher Education (DLHE) by subject area, programme and POLAR status; and
- Reinforcement of graduate attributes through innovative employer-led learning opportunities.

In addition to the above, across the entire portfolio a 'golden thread' was embedded within all of the programmes which reflected the School's underpinning philosophy and commitment to the PRME agenda. In effect, LIBS expects its graduates to understand and apply the three pillars of sustainability (the so-called three P's: people, planet and profit) to their practice as future leaders and managers. As such, all programmes have modules which include lectures and seminars on sustainability, corporate social responsibility and business ethics. It is through these that students are encouraged to develop a strong 'moral compass' (Lock, 2018, p. 5) that will help them meet the challenges of an increasingly complex world with disparate (and in some cases conflicting) cultural and corporate values (Ortenblad, Koris, Farquarson, & Hsu, 2013; Tymon & Mackay, 2016).

24.3   Embedding Employability

Under the auspices of the review, fifteen face-to-face UG programmes were either re-validated or underwent minor modification (see Table 24.1). Where possible, programmes were aligned with relevant professional bodies and exemptions secured so that students could graduate with the opportunity of dual accreditation. This meant that for some programmes (such as accountancy and finance) specific technical skills were embedded from the onset, whilst others (such as business studies) needed these to be added. In addition to technical skills, soft skills development needed to

Table 24.1 2015/2016 revised UG portfolio

Department	Programme
Accountancy, Finance & Economics	B.A. (Hons) Accountancy and Finance B.A. (Hons) Business and Finance B.Sc. (Hons) Banking and Finance B.Sc. (Hons) Business Economics B.Sc. (Hons) Economics B.Sc. (Hons) Finance and Economics
Marketing & Tourism	B.A. (Hons) Advertising and Marketing B.A. (Hons) Business and Marketing B.A. (Hons) Marketing Management B.A. (Hons) Events Management B.A. (Hons) International Tourism Management
People & Organisations	B.A. (Hons) Business and Management
Strategy & Enterprise	B.A. (Hons) Business Studies B.A. (Hons) Business and Enterprise B.A. (Hons) International Business Management

be addressed across the entire portfolio if LIBS was going to strengthen graduate employability prospects and challenge students' pre-conceived notion that subject and technical knowledge are the main attractors for potential employers (Magnell & Kolmos, 2017).

This is a view that appears to be out of line with recent evidence, which suggests that employers are looking for graduates with the right attitudes and behaviours as well as technical knowledge (Thomas, 2017). Skills such as adaptability, resilience, cultural fluency and customer awareness bring 'value-added' benefits to the workplace (CBI & Pearson, 2016; Winstead, Adams, & Sillah, 2011; World Economic Forum, 2018). To provide as many opportunities as possible to gain skills through meaningful work experience, all programmes included a placement option which could be taken between years two and three. LIBS students go to work for a diverse range of companies, including (currently and historically), Price Waterhouse Coopers, Hewlett Packard, L'Oréal, IBM, Marks & Spencer, Panasonic, Toyota, Vauxhall, Warner Bros, British Sky Broadcasting, Boots and Xerox. Some students have headed overseas to China, Australia, Germany, Spain and Hungary, while others have chosen to stay closer to home. Four of the programmes had a part-common foundation year whereby fifty per cent or more of the modules were shared in years one and two: Business and Marketing, Business Studies, Business and Management, and International Business Management. It was within these programmes that various accredited employability interventions were first implemented.

The scaffolding of employability is based on the premise of 'slow and simmering' learning which starts in year one and culminates in year three as students transition from dependent to independent learner, and from student to employee/r (Jackson, 2013a, 2013b). The scaffold comprises of three core elements: extracurricular activities (opt-in, self-selection and in some circumstances competitive such as applying for internships and placements), mandatory accredited modules with outputs that may contribute to the overall degree classification, and an optional accredited module (opt-in, self-selection with a contribution to the degree classification). The overall focus is on raising self-awareness (including student identity construction), fostering self-reflection, encouraging self-development and external engagement through networking, work experience and volunteering (as part of the University's Lincoln Award). In essence, these are activities which position self-efficacy as a mechanism to enhance employability prospects.

To all intents and purposes, the LIBS employability scaffold is reflective of Knight and Yorke's USEM model (2002, p. 264) in that it enables:

– **U**nderstanding (of themselves and the world of work);
– **S**kills acquisition (soft and technical skills);
– **E**fficacy and self-determination (autonomy, action and accountability); and
– **M**etacognition (reflection and self-awareness).

Through this multifaceted approach, LIBS seeks to address some of the issues raised by Yorke and Knight (2006), such as students being unaware of what they have to offer and selling themselves short to prospective employers, and students' limited understanding of the transferability of their degree across different sectors (Ball, 2018).

In year one, modules such as *The Management Professional*, *The Business Professional*, *The Marketing Professional* and *The International Business Professional* have a dual purpose. Firstly, they provide the Programme Leader with an opportunity to 'own' their students. With common (part or otherwise) foundation years, there can be limited opportunity to develop a programme identity, and these modules ring-fence time for this. Secondly, they provide students with the opportunity to reflect upon any pre-existing notions of jobs and sectors that they might have. Explorations into different aspects of professional behaviours and cultures, together with examination of the expectations of employers from different sectors, enables students to develop an embryonic professional identity whilst laying the foundations for employability skills (Daniels & Brooker, 2014; Donovan, 2017). For example, in *The Management Professional* module students consider what it means to be a manager, how teams work, and identify the competencies required of employees in management and leadership positions (Scaratti & Ivaldi, 2015). In addition, they undertake an audit of their own skills, analyse what hard and soft skills and knowledge they already have, identify areas that need further development, and consider how they can demonstrate transferability by linking their skills to the job market. This can be considered as one of the first steps towards step-actualisation, as students develop awareness of themselves and their position in the graduate job market.

In year two, an accredited *Careers and Employability* module builds on notions of job roles, labour market differentiation, and sectoral skills alignment. The module is divided into two sections: theory and practice. The theoretical strand focuses on the economics of employability, the graduate labour market, and social theories of occupational choice. Through this, students gain an understanding of the market in which they will be operating in terms of employment trends, career and skill lifecycles, unbounded careers which straddle traditional job functions, (DeFillippi &

Arthur, 1994) and protean careers which require the ability to future proof employment through assessing, anticipating developments, and gaining the necessary skills and assets to thrive in an ever-changing work-place (William, Baruch, & Ashleigh, 2017; Volmer & Spurk, 2011).

The module's practical elements focus on direct and indirect skills which enhance employment prospects and job satisfaction, such as understanding emotional intelligence, the role of social capital in career progression (Rich, 2015), and the importance of personal, team and organisational resilience (Jackson, Firkto, & Edenboroug, 2007; Seibert, Kraimer, & Heslin, 2016). Formal lectures are supported by workshops which provide students with an opportunity to develop coping strategies such as mindfulness and confidence building (including networking in person and online). A major element of this module is the requirement for all students to attend an external assessment centre and experience psychometric testing at an early stage. The rationale for introducing this at year two is to demystify the professional recruitment process and provide a development opportunity that will build confidence before students are faced with formal assessments when applying for jobs (which quite often happens in their final year). The development of employability skills is formally assessed through reflective logs in which they must demonstrate:

1. Knowledge of the skills sought by graduate employers;
2. Reflection and self-assessment of personal skills and competences mapped to employer needs (Coulson & Harvey, 2013);
3. Engagement with recruitment processes (including receiving, and reflecting on feedback); and
4. Self-directed career management through planning the acquisition of new and updating existing skills and knowledges.

Finally, in year three, the emphasis shifts again, this time away from theories and experiential learning in a 'safe' environment to practical employment support. This includes creative job- searching, preparing for interviews (and all relevant documentation such as CVs and covering letters), and making a good impression (including employer and employee expectation setting and communication skills). Presentations by alumni and prospective employers feature heavily during this period with all students having the opportunity to have a business mentor/coach to support them during the transition from student to employee. These pre-professional identity- construction activities are employability interventions which are aimed at strengthening the connection between the student and the intended professional culture (Jackson, 2013b). To ensure that the full breadth of employability activities that students undertake is captured, the dissertation module has been re-badged as an independent study 'shell' module. Students can therefore either undertake a work-related piece of work or a traditional dissertation. The definition of a work-related assessment is intentionally broad so that it captures: consultancy projects, reflective placement commentaries, and business creation plans. In addition, students can go on study visits that reflect the techniques they are learning in the classroom. For example, visits to Lincolnshire Showground and Lincoln Christmas Market Command Centre demonstrate how the theory of logistics, marketing and events management is applied in practice.

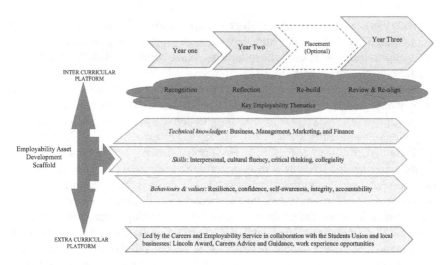

Fig. 24.1 Employability asset development scaffold

The overall scaffold is depicted in Fig. 24.1, which shows the complementary nature of the employability activities delivered by the institutional careers and employability service and student union and how these support LIBS, and how the LIBS curriculum is adapted each year to focus on a specific element of employability. For example, year one concentrates on helping students recognise the key features of employability and year two provides students with a period of self-reflection. The year three curriculum offers activities that encourage students to review the skills they have learnt throughout the course of their studies, and to revisit how these can be further enhanced to improve employability prospects. Although the placement year is optional, those students that do take advantage of this opportunity have the added bonus of testing and rebuilding their skills, as informed by their experiences of the workplace. There has been a 30% increase in students opting for a placement since the new portfolio was launched with its increased emphasis on graduate employability.

24.4   Evaluation to Date

Given that the new portfolio was launched in September 2016, the year one professional identity modules have run twice, and the careers and employability module once. Approximately four hundred and fifty undergraduate students have completed the modules across the two years. Module evaluations to date have been mixed, broadly positive about the breadth of opportunities that have been provided via the accredited modules, and broadly negative about the use of economics as the underpinning theoretical framework. Areas that students identified as best practice included:

1. The management exercises such as creating a LinkedIn profile, chairing a meeting, and running a meeting using video conferencing (Year 1).
2. Access to students returning from placements and an open forum to ask questions about the process of applying for a placement, and the overall experience of being a 'student-employee' (Year 1).
3. The assessment centre (Year 2).

> I really enjoyed Assessment Centre Simulation and I think it is really useful for the real life as it gives a taste of what it is like to get through the application process when applying for a job in the real world.

4. Meet the alumni and employer events which provided an opportunity to demystify the transition from student to employee (Year 2).

Areas identified as in need of further development include:

1. Clearer links between individual programme and *'professional identity'* module learning outcomes (Year 1).
2. Stronger employability skills focus in some practical activities (Year 1).

> At times the activities appeared to more aligned to academic advice and guidance sessions.

3. Review of the economics framework. This had been used to legitimize the inclusion of employability within the curriculum and proved to be unpopular. It was considered *'too economic'* and theoretical by some students, and irrelevant by others (Year 2).
4. Reduce the emphasis on traditional placements and internships and increase the general careers advice and guidance (Year 2).

> I felt that this module was very much geared towards people who wished to take a placement year. Whilst this was my original plan, circumstances changed so I decided not to do one anymore.

5. The marking criteria and feedback from the assessment centre needs greater transparency, and further explanation about how the external systems are aligned with University ones (Year 2).

24.5   Key Challenges

The key academic challenges that emerged during the portfolio review and whilst teaching on the new programmes can be categorised under five themes: discipline dilution, contested curriculum, practice purity, T.E.F. tyranny and student-consumer receptiveness.

24.5.1 Discipline Dilution

With matrixed programmes (which are made up of significant numbers of modules drawn from different departments), there can be tensions between the subjects in terms of visibility in a programme. Finding 'spare' credits required agreement from departments as to which subjects' presence could be 'reduced', and which ones needed to be retained.

24.5.2 Contested Curriculum

The contested nature of the curriculum raised issues about who would be responsible for teaching employability and where it should be placed, that is, in which year. Like the study by Speight et al. (2013), concerns about LIBS academics' lack of experience in the business sector, and limited understanding of employability theories and practices were highlighted as potential barriers to embedding employability. This was addressed by establishing a multidisciplinary teaching team which was comprised of representatives from both academic and staff from the institutional careers service as well as staff who have experience of academia and business—practitioners who also teach. For example, the Director of a mental health NHS service delivers lectures on resilience and coping with uncertainty.

The benefits of this approach were, firstly, that students had the opportunity to apply theory to practice with the support of a practitioner lens, and secondly, that academic and professional service staff were able to work together in an uncontested collaborative 'third space'. As Lock (2017) noted 'Third spaces are collaborative spaces… they mostly occur in areas of practice contestation where stakeholders work together to achieve an agreed goal' (p. 153).' With this in mind, third space theorists such as Bhabha and Rutherford (1990), Whitchurch (2008) and Klein et al. (2013) may well consider LIBS delivery of employability as an example of collegial practices which have emerged through the convergence of separate practice domains.

24.5.3 Practice Purity

It can be argued that for some academics, employability is not necessarily considered a *bona fide* subject. It is not part of a discipline nor is it a subject within a discipline, but instead it is the set of practical skills and competencies that students gain through completion of learning outcomes. In recognition of this, and by means of appeasement, the core year two employability module was framed through an economics lens in that the first six weeks focused on the labour market, the future of work and the global working environment. The supporting seminars and workshops focused on practical activities which focused on 'fitness for employment', and thus, were distinctly different to 'pure' academic work (Knight & Yorke, 2004, p. 226).

24.5.4   TEF and Metrics Tyranny

In spite of the University's aspiration to develop 'a reputation for experimentation and innovation in teaching practice' (University of Lincoln, 2016, p. 8), there was some (justifiable) fear of experimenting with the UG curriculum because of potential student dissatisfaction. If the accredited module was in the final year it would run the risk of adversely affecting the NSS results and by default the subject level TEF-rating for business and management. To mitigate against this, all accredited modules were restricted to years one and two so that any dissatisfaction could be addressed in advance of the annual NSS exercise, and that the module marks would have minimal impact on the overall degree classification.

24.5.5   Student-Consumer Receptiveness

Employability within an accreditation system is not something students necessarily consider when selecting a degree programme. The relevance of various topics covered under the employability umbrella may not be readily apparent to all students, and disengagement due to material that was deemed 'overly abstract and inapplicable to the 'real world' (Nixon et al., 2018, p. 935) was a real risk. As some students pointed out in the module evaluation, employment may not be the primary motivator for embarking on a degree and to assume so would be wrong. To address this, a feed-back/feed-forward process was established with the aim of reinforcing subject and skills relevance for personal as well as career development (see Fig. 24.2).

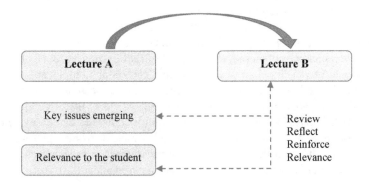

Fig. 24.2   4 × R′ method to reaffirm relevance

There was one further issue which needs to be recognised and that is the cost of the assessment centre. In 2016/17, two hundred and twenty students attended the assessment centre which was approximately 40% of LIBS' entire year two face-to-face undergraduate intake, and it cost £27,500 (£125 per student). This cost was not passed on to the student but incorporated into the general costs incurred by the delivery of the module. This means that when compared to other modules that followed a traditional business school structure (lectures, presentations, workshop, seminars, field trips, simulations), it might be considered an expensive option. It may be unsustainable in the long run given the current economic climate and competitive nature of the market for student numbers, both of which are synonymous with economies of scale and delivering more with less. Having said that, LIBS is like many HE business schools in the UK in that there are growth aspirations and an on-going expectation of significant contributions to the running costs of the University (McKie, 2018). This means that portfolio enhancements like employability development (which contribute to improving student outcomes) could be viewed as a wise investment if it proves to be attractive to prospective students and stakeholders alike.

Given that it is too soon to evaluate the impact of the assessment centre experience, it is likely that a value for money exercise will need to be conducted once the teaching-in of the new portfolio has been completed (*circa* 3–4 years from AY2016/17). Any review would benefit from being done in conjunction with analysis of the employability trends for students who have participated in the accredited modules, alumni feedback on whether the exercise was useful or not and employer feedback as to whether LIBS graduates have the skills and competencies that they are looking for.

24.6   Conclusion

The strength of the LIBS approach to embedding employability within the curriculum is that it is not done in isolation. Rather, it is based on a tri-partite relationship between academia, careers services and employers. These key stakeholders work together to provide students with meaningful employability opportunities which can, and do, enhance employability prospects. There continue to be challenges with articulating generic understandings of employability (Artess, Mellors-Bourne, & Hooley, 2017), and although the development of an accredited careers and employability module provided a theoretical frame through which students could reflect on their career aspirations and understandings of the real world of work, there remains tension about including the development of employability skills and career awareness in the curriculum. Specifically, should employability have a stronger presence within all modules or should it be treated as a separate subject in its own right? Are the learning outcomes something which should be captured under the transferable skills label as the norm for all business and management modules, or is employability asset development something which is distinctly different which merits formal accredited consideration?

If employability is embedded within the curriculum, then the issue of who teaches it needs to be addressed. The 'unconnected' business school academic with little or no experience of working in a business environment or of generally engaging with businesses may not be the most appropriate person. Likewise, careers and employability professionals may not have the necessary technical knowledge that various professions require despite being well versed in the theories and practice of employability and skills development. This is why the 'pracademic' solution that LIBS has loosely adopted appears to be a key route for compromise in that these hybrid individuals can leverage the experiences of both industry and academia and provide students with a broader view of employment, business cultures, functions and roles.

References

AACSB. (2018). *Academic unit accreditation* [Online]. Available at: https://www.aacsb/accreditation/resources/journey/business/academic-unit. Accessed October 26, 2018.

Archer, W., & Davison, J. (2008). *Graduate employability: What do employers think and want?*. London: CBI.

Artess, J., Mellors-Bourne, R., & Hooley, T. (2017). *Employability: A review of the literature 2012–2016*. York: Higher Education Academy.

Avramenko, A. (2012). Enhancing students' employability through business simulation. *Education + Training, 54*(5), 355–367.

Ball, C. (2018). *HECSU salary report [presentation to University of Lincoln]*. Interview, March 26, 2018.

Bhabha, H., & Rutherford, J. (1990). Interview with Homi Bhabha: The third space. In *Identity: Community, Culture, Difference,* pp. 207–221.

Bonekamp, L., & Sure, M. (2015). Consequences of industry 4.0 on human labour and work organisation. *Journal of Business and Media Psychology, 6*(1), 33–40.

CBI & Pearson. (2016). *The right combination: Education and skills survey*. London: CBI and Pearson.

Clark, K., Selwood, A., & Muir, M. (2011). *Mapping employability tool kit* [Online]. Available at: https://www.heacademy.ac.uk/system/files/uwstoolkit.pdf. Accessed October 27, 2018.

Coulson, D., & Harvey, M. (2013). Scaffolfing student reflection for experience-based learning: A framework. *Teaching in Higher Education, 18*(4), 401–413.

Daniels, J., & Brooker, J. (2014). Student identity development in higher education: Implications for graduate attributes and work-readiness. *Educational Research, 56*(1), 65–76.

Dearing, R. (1997). *Higher education in the learning society, report of the national committee of inquiry into higher education*. Norwich: HMSO.

DeFillippi, R. J., & Arthur, M. B. (1994). The boundaryless career: A competency based perspective. *Journal of Organizational Behavior, 15*(4), 307–324.

Donovan, P. (2017). A threshold concept in managing: What students in introductory management courses must know. *Journal of Management Education, 41*(6), 835–851.

Figueiredo, H., Biscaia, R., Rocha, V., & Teixeira, P. (2017). Should we start worrying? Mass higher education, skill demand and the increasingly complex landscape of young graduates' employment. *Studies in Higher Education, 42*(8), 1401–1420.

Glover, D., Law, S., & Youngman, A. (2002). Graduateness and employability: student perceptions of the personal outcomes of university education. *Research in Post Compulsory Education, 7*(3), 293–306.

Guardian. (2018). *Methodology behind the Guardian University guide 2019* [Online]. Available at: https://www.theguardian.com/education/2016/may/23/methodology-behind-the-guardian-university-guide-2017. Accessed May 25, 2018.

IES. (2018). *Institute for employment studies* [Online]. Available at: https://www.employment-studies.co.uk/what-we-know/higher-education-and-graduates. Accessed October 1, 2018.

Jackson, D. (2013a). Business graduate employability—where are we going wrong. *Higher Education Research and Development, 32*(5), 776–790.

Jackson, D. (2013b). Re-conceptualising graduate employability: the importance of pre-professional identity. *Higher Education Research and Development, 35*(5), 925–939.

Jackson, D., Firkto, A., & Edenboroug, M. (2007). Personal resilience as a strategy for surviving and thriving in the face of workplace adversity: A literature review [review paper]. *Journal of Advanced Nursing, 60*(1), 1–9.

Kensington-Miller, B., Knewstubb, B., Longley, A., & Gilbert, A. (2018). From invisible to SEEN: A conceptual framework for identifying, developing and evidencing unassessed graduate attributes. *Higher Education Research and Development, 37*(7), 1439–1453.

Klein, E. J., Taylor, M., Storm, K., & Abrams, L. (2013). Finding a third space in teacher education: Creating an urban teacher residency. *Teaching Education, 24*(1), 27–57.

Knight, P. J., & Yorke, M. (2002). Employability through the curriculum. *Tertiary Education and Management, 8*(4), 261–276.

Knight, P., & Yorke, M. (2004). *Learning, curriculum and employability in higher education.* London: Routledge Falmer.

Kolmos, A., Hadgraft, R. G., & Holgaard, J. E. (2016). Response strategies for curriculum change in engineering. *International Journal of Technology and Design Education, 26,* 391–411.

Lock, D. A. (2017). *Identity construction amongst knowledge transfer staff in English HEIs* (Ph.D. thesis). London: UCL.

Lock, D. A. (2018). *Education Strategy, 2016–21.* Lincoln, UK: Lincoln International Business School.

Lorenz, M., et al. (2015). *Man and machine in industry 4.0,* Boston, USA: The Boston Consulting Group.

Magnell, M., & Kolmos, A. (2017). Employability and work-related learning activities in higher education: How strategies differ across different academic environments. *Tertiiary Education and Management, 23*(2), 103–114.

McKie, A. (2018). *UK universities 'bleeding their business schools dry'* [Online] Available at: https://www.timeshighereducation/news/uk-universities-bleeding-their-business-schools-dry.

McMurray, S., Dutton, M., McQuaid, R. W., & Richard, A. (2016). Employer demands from business graduates. *Education + Training, 58*(1), 112–132.

Nixon, E., Scullion, R., & Hearn, R. (2018). Her majesty the student: Marketised higher education and the narcissistic (dis)satisfactions of the student-consumer. *Studies in Higher Education, 46*(3), 927–943.

Ortenblad, A., Koris, R., Farquarson, M., & Hsu, S. (2013). Business school output: A conceptualisation of business school graduates. *The International Journal of Management Education, 11,* 85–92.

Osmani, M., et al. (2015). Identifying the trends and impact of graduate attributes on employability: A literature review. *Tertiary Education and Management, 21*(4), 367–379.

Pool, L. D., & Sewell, P. (2007). The key to employability: Challenges to the higher education curriculum. *Education + Training, 49*(4), 277–280.

Posner, P. L. (2009). The pracademic: An agenda for re-engating practitioners and academics. *Public Budgeting & Finance, 29*(1), 12–26.

PWC. (2014). *Industry 4.0—Opportunities and challenges of the industrial Internet* [Online]. Available at: https://www.pwc.nl/en/assets/documents/pwc-industrie-4-0.pdf. Accessed November 1, 2018.

Rae, D. (2007). Connecting enterprise and graduate employability: Challenges to the higher education culture and curriculum? *Education + Training, 49*(8/9), 605–619.

Rich, J. (2015). *Employability: Degrees of value (occasional paper 10)*. London: HEPI.

Rothwell, A., & Arnold, J. (2007). Self-percieved employability: Development and validation of a scale. *Personnel Review, 36*(1), 23–41.

Scaratti, G., & Ivaldi, S. (2015). Manager on the ground. *BPA—Applied Psychology Bulletin (Bollettino di Psicologia Applicata), 63*(272).

Seibert, S. E., Kraimer, M. L., & Heslin, P. A. (2016). Developing career resilience and adaptability. *Organizational Dynamics, 45,* 245–257.

Speight, S., Lackovic, N., & Cooker, L. (2013). The contested curriculum: Academic learning and employability in higher education. *Tertiary Education and Management, 19*(2), 112–126.

Thomas, H. (2017). Rethinking and re-evaluating the purpose of the business school. *Rethinking business education: Fit for the future* (pp. 8–9). London: Chartered Association of Business Schools.

Tomlinson, M., & Holmes, L. (Eds.). (2017). *Graduate employability in context: Theory, research and debate*. London: Palgrave MacMillan.

Tymon, A. (2013). The student perspective on employability. *Studies in Higher Education, 38*(6), 841–856.

Tymon, A., & Mackay, M. (2016). Developing business buccaneers: Employer expectations of emergent leaders. *Human Resource Development International, 19*(5), 429–446.

University of Lincoln. (2016). *Thinking ahead: 2016–2021*. Strategic Plan, Lincoln: University of Lincoln.

Volmer, J., & Spurk, D. (2011). Protean and boundaryless career attitudes: Relationships with subjective and objective career success. *Journal for Labour Market Research, 43*(3), 207–218.

Wharton, C. Y., & Horrocks, J. (2015). *Students' perceptions of employability within their degree programme: Highlighting the disparity between what academics believe is included and the student experience.* Glasgow, UK, Enhancement and Innovation in Higher Education, June 9–11, 2015.

Whitchurch, C. (2008). Shifting identities and blurring boundaries: The emergence of third space professionals in UK Higher Education. *Higher Education Quarterly, 62*(4), 377–396.

William, D., Baruch, Y., & Ashleigh, M. (2017). Boundaryless and protean career orientation: A multitude of pathways to graduate employability. In M. Tomlinson & L. Holmes (Eds.), *Graduate employability in context: Theory, research and debate* (pp. 129–150). London: Palgrave MacMillan.

Winstead, A. S., Adams, B. L., & Sillah, M. R. (2011). Teaching the 'soft skills': A professional development curriculum to enhance the employability skills of business graduates. *American Journal of Business Education, 2*(5), 35–44.

World Economic Forum. (2018). *Mapping global transformations: Workforce and employment* [Online]. Available at: https://toplink.weforum.org. Accessed June 10, 2018.

Xing, B., & Marwala, T. (2017). *Implications of the fourth industrial age on higher education* [Online]. Available at: https://arxiv.org/pdf/1703.09643.pdf. Accessed October 29, 2018.

Yorke, M. (2004). *Employability in higher education: What it is—what it is not*. York: Generic Centre, Learning and Teaching Support Network.

Yorke, M., & Knight, P. (2006). Embedding employability into the curriculum. In *Learning and employability series* (Vol. 1). York: Higher Education Academy.

Deborah A. Lock (Ph.D.) is Deputy Head of College & Professor of Inclusivity and Innovation in Teaching, with responsibility for the education portfolio at Lincoln International Business School. This includes programme and curriculum development, flexible employer-led provision (distance learning and a growing degree apprenticeship portfolio), and student employability. Her Ph.D. was on identity construction amongst KT staff in UK universities with a specific focus on career motives, educational practices and relationship management skills. She has led numerous change management programmes including the re-development of UG and PGT academic portfolios, re-branding of a Business School prior to its re-launch, re-alignment of a centralised business development function and the creation of a distributed work-based learning infrastructure. In her research and enterprise roles, she was responsible for the development of a series of executive education and development short course programmes for local and regional business communities under the following themes: leadership, succession planning, and strategies to increase competitiveness.

Chapter 25
Hitting the Ground Running: Group Simulations Within Business School Cohorts

David M. Brown, Ian Charity and Andrew Robson

25.1 Introduction

Academic justifications abound for the use of simulations as a component of learning and assessment strategies within UK business schools. Certain generalisations and preconceptions remain insufficiently challenged, masking widespread barriers to implementation and participation, especially amongst diverse international cohorts. However, the modern debate on simulation use is healthily critical. By linking research on employers' expectations of business graduates (Cronan & Douglas, 2012; Vance, 2007) with analyses of desired pedagogical outcomes, it is possible to assess the extent to which 'Learning Gain' and employability skills are inseparable or might at least be embedded in a conjugated format. The rapidly evolving HE landscape, consumerisation of education and expectations of millennial students all demand that 'pedagogy' and 'employability' discussions of simulations develop in tandem to generate better awareness of their reciprocal effects. By placing business simulations within theoretical contexts i.e. web-based learning applications (Kaplan, Piskin, & Bol, 2009; Newman & Hermans, 2008), collaborative group work and social learning (Hromek & Roffey, 2009), and experiential learning (Chavan, 2011; Hofstede, De Caluwé, & Peters, 2010), the intended links between pedagogy and employability may be critiqued (Bovinet, 2007; Johnson, Johnson, & Smith, 2007; Kozlowski & Ilgen, 2006). By observing learner and educator perceptions of simulations (Chapman, Meuter, Toy, & Wright, 2010; Garber, Hyatt, Boya, & Ausherman, 2012; Vos,

D. M. Brown (✉) · I. Charity · A. Robson
Northumbria, Newcastle, England, UK
e-mail: david.m.brown@northumbria.ac.uk

I. Charity
e-mail: ian.charity@northumbria.ac.uk

A. Robson
e-mail: Andrew.robson@northumbria.ac.uk

© Springer Nature Switzerland AG 2019   389
A. Diver (ed.), *Employability via Higher Education: Sustainability as Scholarship*,
https://doi.org/10.1007/978-3-030-26342-3_25

2015), the first of which are underrepresented in the literature, the theory-practice lacuna may be understood in more detail, by a triangulation of these perspectives.

Much has been written about students' positive affect and behaviour in group business simulations (Kear & Brown, 2015; Neu, 2012), potential covert group dynamics and the effects upon learner experiences and expectations of learner diversity and cohesiveness (Barr, Dixon, & Gassenheimer, Barr et al., 2005; Van Kleef, Van Dijk, Steinel, Harinck, & Van Beest, 2008). Likewise, phenomena such as student cooperation, collaboration and competition are well documented (Fortmüller, 2009; Freeman & Greenacre, 2011; Tuten, 2009), as are the broader, interpersonal issues e.g. social loafing and lone wolf behaviours (Aggarwal & O'Brien, 2008; Dommeyer, 2007). However, there has been scant discussion of their effects upon the embedding of employability skills within simulations. Strategies for maximising the potential of group work and simulations (Kennedy & Dull, 2008; Taylor, Backlund, & Niklasson, 2012; Vos & Brennan, 2010) are analysed here in the context of both pedagogical and employability outcomes, considering also the major cognitive and affective consequences of simulations in terms of student preparedness for employment (Neu, 2012). The level of congruence between simulation objectives and outcomes (Bascoul, Schmitt, Rasolofoarison, Chamberlain, & Lee, 2013; Brennan & Vos, 2013; Vos, 2014) is also gauged, identifying limitations within the current literature, and suggesting avenues for future debate.

25.2   The Adoption of Simulations in Business Schools

Educational games have gained wide acceptance within HE, as universities aim to provide experiences which are less didactic, and more learner-oriented (Karns, 2006; Young, Klemz, & Murphy, 2003). In business schools, simulations constitute an important pedagogical strategy for promoting positive cognitive, affective and behavioural outcomes (Neu, 2012). Within such digital simulations, students must work in teams, assuming the role of managers in fictitious organisations and making decisions based upon their bourgeoning theoretical knowledge and the ever-changing data within the game's virtual landscape. This data may relate to the strengths and capabilities of the simulated organisation, its customer base, its competitors, and the markets in which it and the student teams compete. Simulations provide opportunities for students to gain managerial skills within safe environments where money cannot be lost, and companies cannot be bankrupted. Leading simulation games include *Simbrand*, where student teams build a smartphone brand by assembling product portfolios for penetration of European and Asian markets, and *April*, where teams represent competing European car manufacturers. Business academics often display stronger preferences for Technology Enabled Learning (TEL) than colleagues in other faculties (Buzzard, Crittenden, Crittenden, & McCarty, 2011), or perhaps consider it more congruent to their subject matter. Business schools also place great emphasis on students learning to work collaboratively in groups, anticipating their graduates' working environments. Indeed, these skills are ranked by graduate recruiters more highly than critical thinking and good communication skills (Vance, 2007), and simulation participation has repeatedly been linked with job success and career progression (Cronan & Douglas, 2012; Halfhill & Nielsen, 2007; Steen, 1998). Therefore, whilst academics expect simulations and experiential learning to yield improved learning outcomes (Cheng, Lam, & Chan, 2008), much of the rationale for adopting simulations revolves around the development of students' professional competencies, falling into the categories below.

Simulations encourage open-mindedness amongst participants, as they work in diverse groups, accommodating each other's strengths and limitations, to instil a more consensual managerial ethos that underpins future careers (McCorkle et al., 1999). By making business decisions which are informed by, and impact upon, several different discipline areas, participants gain a more holistic understanding of the interconnected nature of business, rather than developing a silo mentality (Fripp, 1993). This promotes decision-making skills suited to integrated business environments (Mitchell, 2004), which may encourage a more inclusive managerial approach. Many employers note graduates' difficulties in applying theoretically informed knowledge to practice, and active learning strategies such as simulations are partially designed to overcome this (Faria, Hutchinson, Wellington, & Gold, 2009; Hamer, 2000). However, the skill set which employers have found most lacking in business graduates, even more so than group work skills and theory-informed practice competencies, is the ability to interpret and use numerical, particularly financial, data within a quickly evolving, competitive and turbulent commercial marketplace (Ganesh, Sun, & Barat, 2010; Saber & Foster, 2011). Simulation exercises potentially address this (Vos & Brennan, 2010), by placing business students in an environment where they will be held accountable for their decision-making.

Although these considerations centre specifically on developing professional competencies, rather than on more immediate pedagogical gains, the two types of motivation for adoption should not be deemed discrete or mutually exclusive. For instance, the ability of educators to provide instant, synchronous feedback to students, which is facilitated by simulations, may increase learner engagement immediately (Mitchell, 2004; Vos & Brennan, 2010), but also feed a more longitudinal employability agenda by encouraging students to scrutinise their own managerial performances. Likewise, whilst simulations promote competition as a conduit to contextualising knowledge (Bransford, Brown, & Cocking, 1999), the benefit is not purely in terms of short-term understanding, but in vocational gains such as strengthening competitive competencies (Crittenden and Wilson, 2006). Other considerations matter too: levels of congruence between the simulation on the one hand, and the programme/module objectives and institutional mission on the other; instructional style, personal disposition, confidence and technological capabilities of individual educators; levels of acceptance indicated by previous student cohorts (or pilot groups) through evaluation and feedback; and logistical or financial factors such as the costs of software licences, the ease with which simulation usage can be incorporated into the module architecture, access to training (Bobot, 2010), and the competencies and willingness of teaching teams. The decision to adopt simulations may also be driven by levels of intrinsic student motivation, if it is deemed that a cohort requires a simulation to be embedded interdependently within a module to engage them collaboratively (Pinto, Pinto, & Prescott, 1993). Therefore, simulations are adopted for various reasons within both pedagogical and employment agendas and these are largely intertwined. There are, however, several other considerations beyond these, which mediate within, and impact upon, the decision to deploy within a particular curriculum setting.

25.3   Group Work, Simulations and Authentic Learning

A rich tradition of research details how web-based applications have been utilised within learning environments to recreate real-life experiences (Hansen, 2006; Kaplan et al., 2009; Newman & Hermans, 2008; Peltier, Hay, & Drago, 2007; Ryan et al., 2001; Simon, Haghirian, & Schlegelmilch, 2003; Workman, 2004). The most common form is team-based exercises within business curricula (Bolton, 1999), and the most commonly identified benefits include improved communication and employment skills, inspiration towards entrepreneurship, enabling learners to research and analyse financial and numerical data, orienting them towards conflict resolution strategies, acquaintance with forecasting results, problem-solving, and the habituation of interpersonal interaction and leadership (Faria, 2001; Hansen, 2006; Williams, Beard, & Rymer, 1991). An appreciation of cultural diversity, and a willingness to think critically, aids social development within group work (MacGregor et al., 2000). Many students relish the joys and frictions of diverse inter-relationships within collaborative group work (Matthews, 1994), perceiving that it serves a wider range of learning styles (Hendry et al., 2005; O'Sullivan, Rice, Rogerson, & Saunders, 1996). By situating experiential learning in multiple complementary contexts, the use of games facilitates student cognisance of complex concepts (Shaffer, Squire, Halverson, & Gee, 2004). This, in turn, aids attainment of higher cognitive skills (Bloom, 1956; Garris, Ahlers, & Driskell, 2002), enabling participants to learn through close quarters observation of successful team-mate behaviours (Williams et al., 1991). By determining multiple inter-related decision elements, a student's understanding of management can become more integrated (Goosen, Jensen, & Wells, 2001). The meaningfulness, complexity and realism of the tasks are likely to stimulate learners' interest and motivation (Goretsky, 1984; Williams et al., 1991), and their inter-contextualised but repeated presentation is partially intended to increase learners' retention of applied theory (Bacon & Stewart, 2006).

Learning development within group exercises may be considered both social and emotional (Hromek & Roffey, 2009), especially within experiential learning activities, which particularly appeal to business students, who tend to be more kinaesthetic and activity-oriented in their learning styles than the general student population (Karns, 2006). Although passive learning strategies may be suitable for conveying objective information (and economically expedient), most students enjoy longer attention spans and engage higher-order thinking within active learning strategies (Hamer, 2000), which further commends the embedding of such approaches within business courses (Wright, Bitner, & Zeithaml, 1994). A wide variety of learning styles (Kolb & Kolb, 2012) may be accommodated within simulations, which provide learning in each stage (Kolb, 2014; McHaney, White, & Heilman, 2002), and allow students freedom to adopt personalised perspectives in undertaking tasks. This level of learner differentiation not only replicates the diversity that individuals will experience in their subsequent careers, but also boosts metacognition by encouraging them to assess how they can best bridge the theory-practice divide.

Deep learning is a requisite of effective business pedagogy (Bacon & Stewart, 2006). Particularly desirable is the authentic learning achieved by immersing students in business cultures to learn problem-solving skills (Diamond, Koernig, & Iqbal, 2008) and other professional competencies from experienced practitioner-educators (Driscoll, 2000). Digital simulations and other instructional technologies are intended to augment learning by simplifying, expediting or expanding (Peterson, Albaum, Munuera, & Cunningham, 2005), orienting the student towards authentic environments (Karns, 2006). In such processes, learners often recognise the applicability of what they are undertaking to a vocational situation, and this salient demonstration of the exercise's relevance to work is likely to motivate them, multiplying potential benefits.

25.4 Employability as an Outcome

Many of the benefits of business simulations to learners' employability are discussed in academic papers not ostensibly concerned with employability, particularly studies focused primarily on pedagogical issues, seemingly to the exclusion of vocational concerns, but which take it as a de facto end result, an unmentioned, 'once-removed' outcome. Whilst this is largely attributable to the need for narrow research scopes, it could also be considered a limitation of the debate that pedagogical gains in business courses are not always considered within an employability context. However, Johnson et al. (2007) do explicitly explore the links between group work and participants' employability, and the alignment of education with students' future work demands through authentic learning, although not focused specifically on simulations or business schools. The efficacy of group work in preparing students for similar situations within employment is a well-trodden debate (Henke, 1985; Sundstrom, De Meuse, & Futrell, 1990; Pinto et al., 1993). Student needs and expectations have evolved from those of Generation X to the Millennials, driven by the proliferation of digital technology, tuition fees, consumerisation of society, alongside other factors e.g. the evolution of employers' expectations, perhaps more drastic due to the changing nature of work. It is this side of the equation on which the debate on employability via simulations often concentrates.

Many real-life workplace teams perhaps fail due to lack of team development, teamwork skills or experiential learning (Livingstone & Lynch, 2002; Kayes, Kayes, & Kolb, 2005). Likewise, the insurmountable difficulties which many adults encounter in undertaking complex tasks often stem from lack of multiple perspectives and skills, such as problem solving and researching, addressed through business simulations (Bovinet, 2007; Floyd & Gordon, 1998; Katzenbach & Smith, 2005; Kozlowski & Ilgen, 2006). Universities can provide a significant competitive advantage by using pedagogical strategies such as simulations to address these vocational challenges (Bacon & Stewart, 2006). Thus, several functions, activities and competencies are designed into simulations and embedded within learning strategies: teamwork, communication within and across teams, manipulation of theory and data, integrated analysis, cooperation and collaboration, strategy formulation, and problem identification and solution (McCorkle, Alexander, Reardon, & Kling, 2003; Rundle-Thiele, Russell-Bennett, & Dann, 2005; Zantow, Knowlton, & Sharp, 2005).

25.5 Experiential Learning, Professionalism and Business Simulations

The conceptualisation of university education as consumption of educational experiences predates the recent surge in consumerism and marketisation in the UK HE landscape (resulting from tuition fees and other factors) (Watson, 2003), with 'consumer' outcomes taxonomized in terms of cognition, affect and behaviour (Peter & Olson, 2008). This may help explain the migration of business schools from passive to active learning strategies and techniques (Daly, 2001) which endow more meaningful learning experiences (Granitz, 2001) and help orient students towards strategic applications of theory into practical situations (Kneale, 2009). Experiential learning should not be deployed as an antidote to passive methods used elsewhere in a programme of study, but should inform the entire ethos of the learning process, having students reflect longitudinally upon newly acquired knowledge and less recently developed understandings (Armstrong & Mahmud, 2008). In addition to its accommodation of various learning styles (Karns, 2006), experiential learning encourages students to critically analyse their knowledge application, creating meanings (Chavan, 2011) and engaging with emerging information by assimilating it with extant knowledge (Hamer, 2000). This is intended to embed learners socially within practice prior to employment, naturalising them to their intended professional environment in advance, and creating an emotional bond between the learner and business (Hofstede et al., 2010).

Commentators are quick however to extrapolate backwards to the current benefit, from long-term employability to immediate pedagogical gains, perhaps intimating that the latter is prioritised within HEIs, or that educators should be process-driven rather than product-driven in their employability agendas. For instance, the aforementioned employability gains should enthuse and motivate students (Dabbour, 1997; Garcia & Pontrich, 1996) moving then towards higher pedagogical outcomes, performance levels and grades (Drea, Tripp, & Stuenkel, 2005; Perry, Huss, McAuliff, & Galas, 1996), which may be achieved by increasing students' retention of knowledge (Smith & Boyer, 1996) and raising their perceptions of the course efficacy (Karns, 2006). Whilst arguments have been made for greater use of active learning strategies within business schools (Porter & McKibben, 1988), often based upon Kolb's (2014) Learning Cycle or Kolb & Kolb's (2005) Learning Spiral (Vos, 2014), the sparseness and inconclusiveness of the empirical evidence on business simulations (Chin, Dukes, & Gamson, 2009; Gosen & Washbush, 2004) should encourage caution.

25.6 Student and Educator Perceptions of Group Work and Simulations

Whilst business simulations have inclusivity and differentiated learning as their core ethos, many studies have simplified positive comments from student exit-surveys to suggest that student experiences are uniformly positive (Garber et al., 2012), which can be misleading. Most UK students favour at least some utilisation of group work (Chapman, Meuter, Toy, & Wright, 2006), in particular simulations (Bobot, 2010). Many learners find them fun and motivational (Fortmüller, 2009; Hromek & Roffey, 2009) and are encouraged to engage fully with simulations due to their perceived credibility (McHaney et al., 2002), or an entrenched belief that, by doing so, they will attain required learning outcomes and fulfil their potential (McCorkle et al., 2001). However, this positivity is not unanimous. The extent to which a student engages with simulations is at least partially correlated with their previous engagement levels. Similarly, students' broader perceptions of learning exert considerable influence over their perceptions of simulation effectiveness (Washbush & Gosenpud, 1991). This includes attained group marks, especially when compared with levels of academic performance and grade outcome they would have expected to achieve through different assessment strategies (considerations highly influential upon resultant attitudes toward group work). This is also true of the frequency of team exercises, resources allocated to them in class and within modules, learner perceptions of problematic group phenomena such as lone wolf and social loafing behaviours, and the rigour with which educators manage the peer evaluation processes (Pfaff & Huddlestone, 2003).

A less well-explored area is that of educators' equivocal perceptions of simulations and group work. Whilst around two thirds of business academics utilise learning technology, believing that it impacts positively upon delivery of intended learning outcomes, learner engagement and student perceptions, a significant minority are ambivalent towards group work's effectiveness (McCorkle et al., 2001). For some educators, this is due to previous negative experiences or critical incidents, leaving them feeling exposed, or resulting in conflict or negative student feedback. Although these experiences may be infrequent, the 'law of small numbers' or availability heuristic (Tversky & Kahneman, 1973) may prompt educators to recall most readily those memories given their salience or the extent to which they have resulted in personal anxiety. In this way, an isolated forced intervention for a dysfunctional group can overshadow many instances of untroubled, successful group work (Ito, Larsen, Smith, & Cacioppo, 1998). Therefore, when educators misperceive the inherent dynamics, perhaps suffering disproportionately negative perceptions of inclusivity and cohesiveness, this can distort subsequent motivations to adopt business simulations (Chapman et al., 2010), thereby denying both themselves (as educators) and students the benefits of simulation interventions.

25.7 Positive Affect and Behaviour In-Group Business Simulations

By engaging with simulations (and even anticipating engagement), students produce emotional responses to them (Kear & Brown, 2015). These emotions, especially when positive, complement the extrinsic motivations to engage, such as the expected attainment of high marks. Highly motivated students are likely to outperform their peers and achieve those learning outcomes that the simulation intended to produce (Hinck & Ahmed, 2015). Social interdependence theory underpins much of the literature on learning attainment within group work, noting ways in which learning outcomes are predicated not just on individual academic growth, but also on social interdependence and engagement levels (Smith, Sheppard, Johnson, & Johnson, 2005). However, motivation to engage with learning is also driven by students' positive emotions towards simulations (Gee, 2003; Squire, 2003), with resentful or cynical learners faring less well. Many students are fearful or confused at the outset of simulations (Petranek, 2000), especially if it is their first experience of such a learning strategy, or if they feel exposed to the possibility of attaining lower marks. This may be understood as an element of trust in which learners' consent to being partially vulnerable and at the mercy of team mates' actions, if they anticipate that peers will produce a reliable performance throughout the exercise (Neu, 2012). Trust itself arises from trustworthiness, and this relies upon a student's expectations regarding colleagues' abilities, integrity and benevolence, which in turn rest upon prior observations of those team-mates in similar contexts (Mayer, Davis, & Schoorman, 1995). A classmate with a desire to help and support intra-team colleagues is considered benevolent, and expected to adhere to accepted values, namely, being equitable, diligent, honest, timely and reliable, and thus possessing integrity (Neu, 2012). This may suggest that trust is earned over time or denied for non-adherence to these values. However, perceptions of trustworthiness amongst student teams may also be influenced, perhaps unconsciously, by personal prejudices towards someone's race, religion, gender, ethnicity, clothing, appearance or other attributes (Mayer et al., 1995), signposting the acute need for tutor vigilance or intervention, if fairness and equity are to be guaranteed and professional pathways followed.

Often students discuss the strengths and weaknesses of intra-team colleagues, both overtly and covertly, to allocate the most appropriate units of work to each. The attributes most frequently evaluated are benevolence, trustworthiness, integrity and ability, with those students ranked highest usually being allocated the tasks carrying the highest risk. There is danger inherent in this, in that students will approach groupwork as if it were a collection of interrelated yet discrete, autonomous tasks to be collated post hoc (Neu, 2012). This negates several of the key social and collaborative gains intended of simulations and undermines employability skills. By this type of labour division, students may attain proficiency at one task, sacrificing holistic, coherent understanding. Neu (2012) observed four key roles emerging from such piecemeal groups: leaders, who motivate others and coordinate efforts, allocating resources and orienting teams towards intended outcomes; 'hamsters', who diligently follow others, productively but with little desire to dictate the direction of travel; 'creators of inequity', who under-contribute to the task through a combination of laziness, inability, low ambition, poor self-confidence, or even a lack of opportunity to contribute; and 'solvers of inequity', who are active in detecting and tackling under-contribution by a number of means, which may include reactive strategies such as compensating by over-contributing themselves, or proactive ones such as denying task allocations to less motivated or able team-mates. Whilst student team heterogeneity, and its effects upon group performance, has been explored (Bettenhausen, 1991), less is known about the effects of students adopting the above roles, and how those dynamics present themselves between, rather than within, teams. This is potentially deleterious to the professionalising of business students when one considers the way separate teams, (e.g. across departments such as Sales, Marketing, Finance, and Customer Services) must come together successfully in real-work situations.

25.8 Learner Diversity and Heterogeneity, or Cohesiveness and Homogeneity?

Business programmes and modules often serve diverse, multinational cohorts, with students preferring many different learning styles (Frontczak & Rivale, 1991; Karns, 2006) and displaying widely varying skills and attributes, motives, ages and employment statuses (Barr et al., 2005). There is therefore a need for simulations to respect, and cater for, these differences (O'Neil, Wainress, & Baker, 2005). Although many students believe heterogeneity detrimental to simulation team performance, this is unproven and may merely be a smokescreen for the widespread deficiencies which students experience in conflict management (Anderson, 2005). Many students attempt to manage out heterogeneity artificially by clustering with classmates of their own nationality or social group during team formation, perceiving that a cross-cultural team may produce inequitable contributions and abilities (Payne & Monk-Turner, 2006). This is problematic for several reasons: it can unfairly disadvantage overseas students, who may already feel isolated, pre-judged and in need of support; it may prevent universities from honouring their promise of non-segregated, culturally diverse learning and the immersion of overseas students into the local learning culture; it stunts the development of domestic students in terms of cultural awareness; it hinders the internationalisation of the curriculum and student experience from being anything deeper than cosmetic; and it is a barrier to professionalism in an increasingly interconnected, global business environment. There are other advantages that domestic students can enjoy by working with overseas team mates. Whilst neither ethnicity nor age increase a student's numerical aptitudes within simulations, many overseas students are more self-efficacious numerically at the outset of a simulation exercise. Women often gain numerical understanding faster than men within simulations (Brennan & Vos, 2013): student intersectionality, in this case, between being female and having qualified overseas, can bring significant benefits to simulation teams. These benefits are often reciprocal, as the application to practice and the collaboration inherent within simulations produce more positive learning outcomes in women than men (Brew, 2001).

The varying ability levels of learners within many simulation groups allow students to be differentiated from one another and provide distinct contributions. These abilities may centre on writing and communication, harnessing technology, emotional intelligence, mentoring and support, management of processes or people, presentation skills, or the provision of perspectives which complement those of team mates. These abilities are gauged by peers through observing displayed behaviours, the responses which these behaviours elicit from others, and by an unconscious understanding of the nuances of their vocabulary (Neu, 2012). Where all team members are oriented to similarly ambitious goals and there is congruence between their expectations, teams are likely to be cohesive (Bourner et al., 2001; Johnson et al., 2007). Where conflict occurs within groups, this may be incubated, impacting very negatively upon levels of student satisfaction (Van Kleef et al., 2008), invariably undermining the performance of at least one member. Therefore, many students seek to circumvent the random nature of imposed team formation by self-selecting from an existing social network, the exact membership of which may be amended dependent upon the needs of the simulation task to ensure a complementary skill set. This uncertainty avoidance is particularly prevalent where simulation performance is linked to module marks (Neu, 2012). Thus, whilst uncoupling simulations from the marking mechanism, adopting them as a learning strategy and perhaps for formative but summative assessment, may mitigate this effect, the inclusivity of the assessment strategy and its equity across all learner types may be compromised slightly. However, increased student acceptance of intra-group heterogeneity may lead to long-term benefits such as more diverse group composition and more internationalised preparation for the world of work. Trust, low levels of conflict, and especially cohesion within simulation teams increase levels of student enjoyment (Anderson, 2005), and should therefore be monitored and managed by educators to maximise employability gains. Whilst group cohesiveness is often loosely defined and open to interpretation, it should not be conflated with homogeneity. Rather, it results from such factors amongst and between peers as trust, willingness to help, cordiality, mutual personal interests and values, mild or infrequent conflict (if any) and competent handling of conflict, reliability, competence, honesty and integrity, effective listening skills, and a common desire to achieve a good mark and attain higher learning outcomes (Chapman et al., 2010).

25.9 Co-operation, Collaboration and Competition Within Business Simulations

Co-operation and collaboration may be considered equally important to compromise and communications within team work (Katzenbach & Smith, 1994). Co-operative learning is the term given to team-based goal accomplishment achieved interactively (Freeman & Greenacre, 2011). Its constituent tasks may be discrete but, by definition, are interrelated. It is therefore of great benefit to students (Hromek & Roffey, 2009) as it instils attributes such as empathy, motivation, self-esteem, self-control and criticality, helping learners improve their conflict resolution skills and learning outcomes, and building their acceptance of diversity and perceptions of learning (Johnson, Johnson, & Stanne, 2000). Collaborative learning differs slightly from co-operative learning insofar as it entails members working together on one task to accomplish specific outcomes, usually facilitated by the replication of key competitive aspects of real-life business situations (Adobor & Daneshfar, 2006; Wideman et al., 2007). It is particularly effective in enabling learners to utilise theory in practical applications (Tuten, 2009). Despite the spirit of collaboration, students often opt to play competitively if so motivated (Fortmüller, 2009). However, whilst many students become positively oriented towards simulations and more deeply engaged via competition (Kratwohl, Bloom, & Masia, 1964), many others may feel neutral, ambivalent or negatively towards competing against classmates (Meese, Anderman, & Anderman, 2006), and this is likely to be the case more frequently amongst learners from more collectivised cultures.

25.10 Potential Barriers to Success Within Business Simulations

Most students find simulation participation highly beneficial to learning and performance (Wilson et al., 2009), and the benefits are especially conspicuous within assessments having an overtly numerical content (Brennan & Vos, 2013). However, the inconclusive nature of many studies on the efficacy of simulations (Vaidyanathan & Rochford, 1998), and the sparsity of empirical evidence (Gosen & Washbush, 2004), has sparked scepticism over business games (Anderson & Lawton, 1997). Several studies have posed strident challenges to the legitimacy of simulation usage. Chin et al. (2009) reported that only a minimal number of learning simulations had been tested in an academically robust manner. Elsewhere, simulations are dismissed as superficial and lacking an evidenced contribution to learning (Egenfeldt-Nielson, 2007; O'Neil et al., 2005), whilst other research has warned educators not to conflate the undoubted potential of simulations to motivate students, with their more uncertain contributions to learning outcomes (Chin et al., 2009). Furthermore, it has been noted that simulations are not 'a rising tide which lifts all boats', at least not to an equal height, with some students feeling fewer benefits than others (Vaidyanathan

& Rochford, 1998). This directly challenges the idea that simulations foster equity between learners. Perhaps most surprisingly, they have attracted isolated criticism for supposedly supporting lower-level cognitive learning (Anderson & Lawton, 1997) rather than the higher, analytical levels detailed by Bloom (1956), although this accusation is in direct contradiction to conclusions drawn by others (Hsu, 1989).

Many generalised criticisms of experiential learning are indirectly applicable to business simulation use. These include that their effectiveness may be inhibited by poor team dynamics, that largely insurmountable barriers to simulation participation may confront unacculturated students who lack reflexivity, confidence and prepared-ness (Boud et al., 1993) and that disparities in participation levels produce inequity of learning outcomes and attainment levels (Batra, Walvoord, & Krishnan, 1997). Widespread allocation of discrete tasks to individuals within groups counteracts the intended benefits (McCorkle et al., 1999); 'social loafers' under-contribute to tasks, and 'lone wolf' members dominate the direction of tasks or insist on work-ing in isolation, undermining the validity of simulations (Barr et al., 2005; Latane, Williams, & Harkins, 1979). This may see less able learners more likely to be bur-dened by additional pressure and workload, so they benefit less from simulations than high achievers (Hamer, 2000). Many educators experience problems when allo-cating students to teams (Pfaff & Huddlestone, 2003) and teams commonly struggle to delineate expectations and agree goals at project commencement, and to manage inequitable contributions and conflicts professionally (Buckenmyer, 2000). Educa-tors may accidentally erode the authenticity of assessment through an inability to allocate marks accurately and fairly to individuals within teams in a way which reflects their contribution (Tu & Lu, 2005).

All of the above inhibiting factors, whilst damaging if unmanaged, are surmount-able, but only with vigilance, planning and resolve on the part of the educator (Gard-ner & Korth, 1998). However, there is relatively little empirical research into the impact upon students of these negative outcomes (Neu, 2012). Demotivation, dis-tress, confusion and disappointment were recognised in students who had produced unsatisfactory performances within marketing simulations (Kear & Brown, 2015), and their reflections upon the reasons for failure almost invariably focused on col-lective expressions of team underperformance rather than specific decisions which were representative of a real-life situation, thereby diminishing simulation efficacy. Amongst the 16 student group functionality metrics proposed by Chapman et al. (2010), prominent antecedents of success within groups were a lack of arguments, and the fostering of environments in which commitments are honoured, communica-tion is transparent, and participants feel comfortable seeking and giving assistance. Such team mates would make friends, work harmoniously without conflict, trusting each other's abilities, managing group time efficiently, taking an interest in each other, taking pride in their work, collaborating, and dividing work fairly. Additional-ly, the most successful groups would at least implicitly nominate a leader, have fluid, interchangeable roles, and contain members who were all motivated by the achievement of good grades.

25.11   The Prevention of Social Loafing

Social loafing is the deliberate under-contribution to a team task by one or more members, who instead rely on team mates for successful completion of the task (Aggarwal & O'Brien, 2008; Dommeyer, 2007; Payne & Monk-Turner, 2006; Williams, Larkins, & Latané, 1981). Over 40% of students have suffered such behaviours, which are particularly resented (Colbeck et al., 2000). Some loafers may under-contribute marginally in the quantity of their work but more seriously in terms of quality (Strong & Anderson, 1990). As the simulation progresses, a loafer is likely to become emboldened in their delinquency if the educator makes no remedial intervention (Bourner et al., 2001) and thus risks damaging the performances and experiences of team mates (Johnson et al., 2007). Diligent team members are often able to arrest loafing by confronting the offender and agreeing mutually agreed deadlines, standards of conformity and reporting to prevent further 'drift'. However, loafers are frequently excluded completely from tasks (Aggarwal & O'Brien, 2008), and this may undermine task and assessment authenticity, increase others' workloads, and exacerbate (or reward) unacceptable behaviour in increasingly marginalised, alienated members. Preventative and pre-emptive intervention strategies utilised by educators typically involve requesting teams to record meeting minutes or diary entries (Dommeyer, 2007), peer assessment (Aggarwal & O'Brien, 2008), or participation logs which detail individual student participation times and durations (Brandyberry & Bakke, 2006). Such actions are crucial: many students, when they become increasingly annoyed with recidivistic loafing behaviours, resort to deliberately punitive actions such as allocating 'loafers' tasks to which they are ill-suited, omitting them from team meetings and online communications, purposely scheduling meetings at times when they are unable to attend, withholding reasonable support, or setting unattainable deadlines (Payne & Monk-Turner, 2006). All such deliberately destructive actions could produce a snowball effect that exacerbates the problem, deleteriously effecting loafers and contributors alike.

A further complication is the commonality between loafers and strugglers, i.e. those students who unintentionally underperform (McLean, Reid, & Scharf, 1998). Strugglers may suffer due to a linguistic barrier (Rosser, 1998), lack of understanding or low self-esteem. They are, or may perceive themselves to be, lower-ability students, yet perhaps only marginally behind their team mates in terms of understanding and needing relatively little incremental study-time to catch up (Dufour, 2004). Sadly, strugglers are often subjected to the same deleterious team behaviours as social loafers, as contributing students regularly fail to (or choose not to) distinguish between these two types of underperforming group member. These behaviours can continue until the conclusion of the simulation, inhibiting development of those students most in need of and deserving of help, and this often damages the entire group performance (Freeman & Greenacre, 2011). In lacking peer evaluation skills, many students judge strugglers inappropriately and adopt draconian measures (Falchikov & Magin, 1997). Educator vigilance and targeted interventions in which the differ-

ence between the two underachieving learner categories is explained reduce these
misdirected and destructive behaviours (Freeman & Greenacre, 2011).

Peer evaluation mechanisms ensure assessment authenticity, increasing the credibility of group work and boosting student satisfaction (Druskat & Wolff, 1999). They
may also reduce incidences of social loafing by facilitating scrutiny and judgment of
individual performances (Aggarwal & O'Brien, 2008), and this is particularly true
when cohorts are warned at module commencement of forthcoming peer evaluations, and the potential penalties for (corroborated) negative feedback. Whilst some
students refuse to rate peers negatively to avoid conflict or repercussions (Sherrard
et al., 1994), others may simply be more tolerant or forgiving (May & Gueldenzoph,
2006). Some groups 'close ranks' through a pledge of silence, or by equal or collaborative rankings (Neu, 2012). In any case, it is important for educators not to take peer
evaluations at face value, but to seek mitigating evidence from any accused student,
both directly and through their online simulation logs.

25.12   Maximising the Potential of Simulations

As Chapman et al. (2010) suggested, simulations work best when students collaborate, resolve conflict, take pride in their work and goal attainment, and enjoy working
together enough to choose to do so again. To make simulation work as enjoyable
as possible, educators should nurture intra-group communications, trust, conflict-
resolution and cohesion (Huff, Cooper, & Jones, 2002; Williams, Duray, & Reddy,
2006). However, this does not necessarily prepare students for professional careers,
which often entail long periods of pressure and sacrifice with low enjoyment. Creative
problem-solving within simulations may be facilitated by fun and humour, but also by
hypothesis-driven strategies and group opportunism (Anderson, 2005), which may
more closely replicate professional practices. The self-assertion of individuals' social
interdependence within teams can magnify positive outcomes or reduce destructive
behaviours (Freeman & Greenacre, 2011). Course design can assist in this, particularly if students are trained to behave professionally (Prichard, Bizo, & Stratford,
2006), with those trained in meeting management techniques more likely to unify
and stabilise the group (Kennedy & Dull, 2008). Instructor-coaching which continues longitudinally throughout a simulation can improve outcomes (Bolton, 1999;
Taylor et al., 2012), especially where the teaching of reflexive professional skills,
(such as the maintaining of logs and the reviewing of decision making processes)
helps to democratise experiential learning (Moon, 2004; Peltier et al., 2005). This
may be more achievable in teams of three or four students (Wolfe & Chacko, 1983) in
which pedagogical activities correspond closely to the learning styles present (Karns,
2006).

Student attitudes towards group work may be strongly influenced by instructors
(Chapman & Van Auken, 2001), enhancing their ability by engaging them (Deeter-
Schmelz, Kennedy, & Ramsey, 2002). This is achievable partially through 'tutor-
to-student' activities and behaviours, such as encouragement (Kayes et al., 2005),

resolution of social loafing (Dommeyer, 2007), or the provision of increasingly critical, stepped feedback contextualised ever more broadly. It is also assisted by the implementation of 'student-to-tutor' techniques including post-simulation 'executive briefings' and board presentations (Keys & Bell, 1977). The potential of such actions to augment learning is considerable (Crookall, 2010), especially where the perspectives of all participants are explored (Kriz, 2008), and where such activities are undertaken prior to the announcement of final results, to capture students' attention (Bascoul et al., 2013). By promoting reflexivity, conceptualisation and experimental skills, this kind of debrief makes simulation more effective (Rudolph, Simon, Dufresne, & Raemer, 2006; Dieckmann, Molin Friis, Lippert, & Østergaard, 2009), and channels outcomes in a more targeted fashion towards professionalism.

Where collaborative group skills are prepared for through pre-exercise training (Prichard et al., 2006), or where institutions or faculties run separate courses focused on group competencies, student performances in teams may be improved (McCorkle et al., 1999). Educators are advised to clarify the exact modus operandi expected of teams (Wood, 2003), criteria for managing and assessing individuals (Tyagi, 2010), and the functionality and rationale for peer evaluation (May, 2008). In doing so, role ambiguity is reduced, and students feel more surefooted. Wherever possible, best practice dictates that simulation assessment should be longitudinal during and after the simulation, rather than purely at its conclusion, thus ascertaining levels of ongoing student improvement and ensuring engagement (Michael & Chen, 2005; Vos & Brennan, 2010). To elongate the benefits of simulation-based learning further still, post-simulation pedagogical strategies may include reflexive debrief sessions (Kriz, 2008), retrospective performance analysis (Dommeyer, 2007), and a critical discussion of the simulation's relevance to professional practice, which should aim to legitimise its utilisation and motivate learners who are also workers, or who will be in the near future (D'Aloisio, 2006; Knowles, 1984). Verisimilitude, the extent to which students consider the simulation representative of a real business or marketplace, should be monitored carefully to allow any necessary corrective interventions (Chin et al., 2009; Garber et al., 2012), although students with little or no work experience are more likely to find themselves less motivated in this respect.

25.13 Cognitive and Affective Consequences of Group Work and Simulations

Group work consequences may differ from the intended benefits (Neu, 2012). Most instructors are likely to be aware of more conspicuous, behavioural consequences such as the discrete division of labour and group self-selection, but less so of cognitive and affective ones. The main cognitive consequences of simulations are a greater desire for autonomy within a group setting, temptation to coast amongst less committed students who perceive 'grade boost' or a levelling out of marks across teams, and perhaps a sense of injustice. Moreover, perceptions of injustice may stem from witnessing disparities of effort and learning, feeling constrained by a team, resenting lower achievers being marked up and vice versa, or perceiving a reduced likelihood of higher achievers being praised or recognised. Meanwhile, unintended affective group work outcomes for students include anxiety, frustration at team mates, stress from modifying one's behaviours to fit into a team, disappointment at inequitable effort levels, and anger at real or perceived injustices (Neu, 2012). However, certain other affective outcomes may be more positive or constitute relief, when placed in one's preferred social learning network, from team mates' pleasing performances, from being spared the possibility of conspicuous failure associated with individual work, and from successfully completing the tasks. Whilst negative affective consequences require carefully corrective measures, instructors should also understand positive ones (Aggarwal & O'Brien, 2008; Dommeyer, 2007), as they may camouflage the true reasons for the failure or success of a simulation, misinforming their future pedagogical decisions.

25.14 The Extent of Congruence Between Simulation Objectives and Outcomes

Educators adopt business simulations to encourage the development of critical thinking, decision-making and problem-solving skills (Schibrowsky, Peltier, & Boyt, 2002), leadership, public speaking and team-building techniques (Barr & McNeilly, 2002), communication skills, cultural awareness, cross-functional and technological competences, discipline and metacognition (Chonko & Roberts, 1996). Through careful alignment of business game objectives with module or programme content and desired pedagogical outcomes (Cotton, Ahmadi, & Esselborn, 1997), student approaches to business can evolve from the reactive and operational to the more anticipatory and strategic (Vos, 2014). Crittenden & Wilson (2006) divided learning outcomes for Marketing students into material outcomes (ethical awareness, strategic competence, and cross-functional integration) and skill development outcomes (critical thinking, problem-solving and, most importantly, professionalism), which were considered inter-related criteria. Whilst the focus was on addressing the theory-practice divide within university Marketing courses via internships and international exchanges, the outcomes lend themselves well as a framework to assess the effectiveness of business simulation efficacy.

Students who adopt the deepest learning approaches (and who usually perceive that they learn the most) pass through all four stages of Kolb's (1984) experiential learning cycle, thereby experiencing the 'concrete experience' of doing, the 'reflective observation' upon the learning achieved, the 'abstract conceptualisation' of hypothesis-driven strategies, and the 'active experimentation' underpinning their decision-making. Meanwhile, those in relatively shortened learning cycles experience more superficial approaches to learning (Young, Cordill, & Murphy, 2008). The interactivity and 'learning-by-doing' at the centre of simulation exercises is considered conducive to higher-order learning (Fortmüller, 2009; Wideman et al., 2007), and more active engagement (McCorkle et al., 1999). It also supports enhanced communication, technical and support skills, critical reasoning, retention and comprehension (Williams et al., 1991). Despite challenges to the contribution of technology to learning (Peterson et al., 2005), the field is unanimous in proclaiming simulations successful in increasing student enjoyment and self-efficacy (Pollack & Lilly, 2008). Social gains include reductions in bullying, more tolerant attitudes to diverse perspectives (Johnson et al., 2000), focusing learners on sustainability, and raised awareness of the individual learner's place within a broader community of stakeholders (Bascoul et al., 2013).

25.15 Conclusion

Educators can gauge student levels of business comprehension before, during and after simulation participation, but ascertaining the extent of incremental learning gained in respect of problem solving, creative thinking or other qualitatively assessed attributes is less straightforward (Anderson & Lawton, 1997; Vos, 2014). This appears to have hindered research into business simulation usage and, consequently, its efficacy as a conduit to professionalism. Rather than being function-specific, many studies have been top-down and institution-centred in their concerns (Faria et al., 2009), or have relied on student or lecturer perspectives to the neglect of more objective measures (Vos, 2014). As one of the key aims of simulations is to embed employability and professionalism, future research could examine the effects of instructors' prior industrial experiences (or indeed, academic ones) on their perceptions of their student groups (Chapman et al., 2010). Elsewhere, Garber et al. (2012) suggested several avenues for empirical research, e.g. testing simulation models against Kolb's (1984) learning cycle to ascertain suitability for professional training, exploring how group composition and gender-based learning styles affect outcomes, ascertaining the importance of game performance in the assessment of learning and interrogating the effects of group homogeneity and cohesiveness on learning outcomes. Any assessment of simulation effectiveness should consider the dual evaluation of "*hard*" skills attainment relating to knowledge development of business strategisation, functional contribution and integration and holistic decision-making, alongside "*soft*" skills realisation relating to individual learning, teamwork, and heightened self-evaluation, emotional and cultural intelligence.

As more workplace roles are destined to be replaced by Artificial Intelligence and the advance of automation (Korinek & Stiglitz, 2018), it seems increasingly intuitive to use computerised simulations where learners interact with each other and technology synchronously. Moreover, as the marketisation of HE encourages students to focus increasingly on career gains and earning potential resulting from their studies, simulations appear ever more congruent with the landscapes of learning and work, bridging the problematic divide between theory and practice and offering learners assistance on their road to professionalism.

References

Adobor, H., & Daneshfar, A. (2006). Management simulations: determining their effectiveness. *Journal of Management Development, 25*(2), 151–168.

Aggarwal, P., & O'Brien, C. L. (2008). Social loafing on group projects: Structural antecedents and effect on student satisfaction. *Journal of Marketing Education, 30*(3), 255–264.

Anderson, J. R. (2005). The relationship between student perceptions of team dynamics and simulation game outcomes: an individual-level analysis. *Journal of Education for Business, 81*(2), 85–90.

Anderson, P. H., & Lawton, L. (1997). Demonstrating the learning effectiveness of simulation: Where we are and where we need to go. *Developments in Business Simulation and Experiential Learning, 24*, 68–73.

Armstrong, S. J., & Mahmud, A. (2008). Experiential learning and the acquisition of managerial tacit knowledge. *Academy of Management Learning & Education, 7*(2), 189–208.

Bacon, D. R., & Stewart, K. A. (2006). How fast do students forget what they learn in consumer behavior? A longitudinal study. *Journal of Marketing Education, 28*(3), 181–192.

Barr, T. F., Dixon, A. L., & Gassenheimer, J. B. (2005). Exploring the "lone wolf" phenomenon in student teams. *Journal of Marketing Education, 27*(1), 81–90.

Barr, T. F., & McNeilly, K. M. (2002). The value of students' classroom experiences from the eyes of the recruiter: information, implications, and recommendations for marketing educators. *Journal of Marketing Education, 24*(2), 168–173.

Bascoul, G., Schmitt, J., Rasolofoarison, D., Chamberlain, L., & Lee, N. (2013). Using an experiential business game to stimulate sustainable thinking in marketing education. *Journal of Marketing Education, 35*(2), 168–180.

Batra, M. M., Walvoord, B. E., & Krishnan, K. S. (1997). Effective pedagogy for student-team projects. *Journal of Marketing Education, 19*(2), 26–42.

Bettenhausen, K. L. (1991). Five years of groups research: What we have learned and what needs to be addressed. *Journal of Management, 17*(2), 345–381.

Bloom, B. S. (1956). *Taxonomy of educational objectives*. New York: David McKay.

Bobot, L. (2010). Teaching sales and negotiation with combining computer-based simulation and case discussions. *Marketing Education Review, 20*(2), 115–122.

Bolton, M. K. (1999). The role of coaching in student teams: A "just-in-time" approach to learning. *Journal of Management Education, 23*, 233–250.

Boud, D., Cohen, R., & Walker, D. (1993). *Using experience for learning*. Maidenhead: McGraw-Hill.

Bourner, J., Hughes, M., & Bourner, T. (2001). First-year undergraduate experiences of group project work. *Assessment & Evaluation in Higher Education, 26*(1), 19–39.

Bovinet, J. W. (2007). Different skill-set views: A four-year study of marketing students, practitioners and educators. *Journal of Business and Public Affairs, 1*(1), 1–8.

Brandyberry, A. A., & Bakke, S. A. (2006). Mitigating negative behaviors in student project teams: An information technology solution. *Journal of Information Systems Education, 17*(2), 195–203.

Bransford, J. D., Brown, A., & Cocking, R. (1999). *How people learn: Mind, brain, experience, and school*. Washington, DC: National Research Council.

Brennan, R., & Vos, L. (2013). Effects of participation in a simulation game on marketing students' numeracy and financial skills. *Journal of Marketing Education, 35*(3), 259–270.

Brew, A. (2001). Conceptions of research: A phenomenographic study. *Studies in Higher Education, 26*(3), 271–285.

Buckenmyer, J. A. (2000). Using teams for class activities: Making course/classroom teams work. *Journal of Education for Business, 76*(2), 98–107.

Buzzard, C., Crittenden, V. L., Crittenden, W. F., & McCarty, P. (2011). The use of digital technologies in the classroom: A teaching and learning perspective. *Journal of Marketing Education, 20*(10), 1–9.

Chapman, K. J., Meuter, M., Toy, D., & Wright, L. (2006). Can't we pick our own groups? The influence of group selection method on group dynamics and outcomes. *Journal of Management Education, 30*(4), 557–569.

Chapman, K. J., Meuter, M. L., Toy, D., & Wright, L. K. (2010). Are student groups dysfunctional? Perspectives from both sides of the classroom. *Journal of Marketing Education, 32*(1), 39–49.

Chapman, K. J., & Van Auken, S. (2001). Creating positive group project experiences: An examination of the role of the instructor on students' perceptions of group projects. *Journal of Marketing Education, 23*(2), 117–127.

Chavan, M. (2011). Higher education students' attitudes towards experiential learning in international business. *Journal of Teaching in International Business, 22*(2), 126–143.

Cheng, W. Y., Lam, S. F., & Chan, C. Y. (2008). When high achievers and low achievers work in the same group: The roles of group heterogeneity and processes in project-based learning. *British Journal of Educational Psychology, 78*(2), 205–221.

Chin, J., Dukes, R., & Gamson, W. (2009). Assessment in simulation and gaming: A review of the last 40 years. *Simulation & Gaming, 40*(4), 553–568.

Chonko, L. B., & Roberts, J. A. (1996). An innovative introduction to business course: Marketing the skills that marketing majors (and others) as business majors will need for success. *Marketing Education Review, 6*(3), 53–71.

Colbeck, C. L., Campbell, S. E., & Bjorklund, S. A. (2000). Grouping in the dark: What college students learn from group projects. *Journal of Higher Education, 71*(1), 60–83.

Cotton, S., Ahmadi, R., & Esselborn, R. (1997). Assessing simulation games for the classroom. *Assessment Update, 9*(3), 6–7.

Crittenden, V. L., & Wilson, E. J. (2006). Content, pedagogy, and learning outcomes in the international marketing course. *Journal of Teaching in International Business, 17*(1–2), 81–101.

Cronan, T. P., & Douglas, D. E. (2012). A student ERP simulation game: A longitudinal study. *Journal of Computer Information Systems, 53*(1), 3–13.

Crookall, D. (2010). Serious games, debriefing, and simulation/gaming as a discipline. *Simulation & Gaming, 41*(6), 898–920.

Dabbour, K. S. (1997). Applying active learning methods to the design of library instruction for a freshman seminar. *College & Research Libraries, 58*(4), 299–308.

D'Aloisio, A. (2006). Motivating students through awareness of the natural correlation between college learning and corporate work settings. *College Teaching, 54*(2), 225–230.

Daly, S. P. (2001). Student-operated Internet businesses: True experiential learning in entrepreneurship and retail management. *Journal of Marketing Education, 23*(3), 204–215.

Deeter-Schmelz, D. R., Kennedy, K. N., & Ramsey, R. P. (2002). Enriching our understanding of student team effectiveness. *Journal of Marketing Education, 24*(2), 114–124.

Diamond, N., Koernig, S. K., & Iqbal, Z. (2008). Uniting active and deep learning to teach problem-solving skills: Strategic tools and the learning spiral. *Journal of Marketing Education, 30*(10), 116–129.

Dieckmann, P., Molin Friis, S., Lippert, A., & Østergaard, D. (2009). The art and science of debriefing in simulation: ideal and practice. *Medical Teacher, 31*(7), 287–294.

Dommeyer, C. J. (2007). Using the diary method to deal with social loafers on the group project: Its effects on peer evaluations, group behavior, and attitudes. *Journal of Marketing Education, 29*(2), 175–188.

Drea, J. T., Tripp, C., & Stuenkel, K. (2005). An assessment of the effectiveness of an in-class game on marketing students' perceptions and learning outcomes. *Marketing Education Review, 15*(1), 25–33.

Driscoll, M. (2000). *Psychology of learning for instruction.* Needham Heights, MA.: Allyn & Bacon.

Druskat, V. U., & Wolff, S. B. (1999). Effects and timing of developmental peer appraisals in self-managing work groups. *Journal of Applied Psychology, 84*(1), 58.

DuFour, R. (2004). What is a "professional learning community"? *Educational Leadership, 61*(8), 6–11.

Egenfeldt-Nielson, S. (2007). *The educational potential of computer games*. New York, NY: Continuum Press.

Falchikov, N., & Magin, D. (1997). Detecting gender bias in peer marking of students' group process work. *Assessment & Evaluation in Higher Education, 22*(4), 385–396.

Faria, A. J. (2001). The changing nature of business simulation/ gaming research. *Simulation and Gaming, 32*(1), 97–110.

Faria, A. J., Hutchinson, D., Wellington, W. J., & Gold, S. (2009). Developments in business gaming a review of the past 40 years. *Simulation & Gaming, 40*(4), 464–487.

Floyd, C. J., & Gordon, M. E. (1998). What skills are most important? A comparison of employer, student, and staff perceptions. *Journal of Marketing Education, 20*(2), 103–109.

Fortmüller, R. (2009). Learning through business games acquiring competences within virtual realities. *Simulation & Gaming, 40*(1), 68–83.

Freeman, L., & Greenacre, L. (2011). An examination of socially destructive behaviors in group work. *Journal of Marketing Education, 33*(1), 5–17.

Fripp, J. (1993). *Learning through simulations: A guide to the design and use of simulations in business and education*. Maidenhead: McGraw-Hill.

Frontczak, N. & Rivale, G. (1991). An empirical investigation of learning styles in marketing education. In *Proceedings of the Western Marketing Educators' Association* (pp. 93–100).

Ganesh, G., Sun, Q., & Barat, S. (2010). Improving the marketing math skills of marketing undergraduate students through a unique undergraduate marketing math course. *Marketing Education Review, 20*(1), 47–64.

Garber, L. L., Hyatt, E. M., Boya, Ü. Ö., & Ausherman, B. (2012). The association between learning and learning style in instructional marketing Games. *Marketing Education Review, 22*(2), 167–184.

Garcia, T. Y., & Pontrich, P. R. (1996). The effects of autonomy on motivation and performance in the college classroom. *Contemporary Educational Psychology, 21*, 477–486.

Gardner, B. S., & Korth, S. J. (1998). A framework for learning to work in teams. *Journal of Education for Business, 74*(1), 28–33.

Garris, R., Ahlers, R., & Driskell, J. E. (2002). Games, motivation and learning: Simulation and gaming. *An Interdisciplinary Journal of Theory, Practice and Research, 33*(4), 441–467.

Gee, J. P. (2003). What video games have to teach us about learning and literacy. *Computers in Entertainment (CIE), 1*(1), 20.

Goosen, K. R., Jensen, R., & Wells, R. (2001). Purpose and learning benefits of simulations: A design and development perspective. *Simulation & Gaming, 32*(1), 21–39.

Goretsky, M. E. (1984). Class projects as a form of instruction. *Journal of Marketing Education, 6*(3), 33–37.

Gosen, J., & Washbush, J. (2004). A review of scholarship on assessing experiential learning effectiveness. *Simulation & Gaming, 35*(2), 270–293.

Granitz, N. A. (2001). Active learning and morality: Incorporating greater meaning into marketing education. *Marketing Education Review, 11*(2), 25–42.

Halfhill, T. R., & Nielsen, T. M. (2007). Quantifying the "softer side" of management education: An example using teamwork competencies. *Journal of Management Education, 31*(1), 64–80.

Hamer, L. O. (2000). The additive effects of semi structured classroom activities on student learning: An application of classroom-based experiential learning techniques. *Journal of Marketing Education, 22*(1), 25–34.

Hansen, R. S. (2006). Benefits and problems with student teams: Suggestions for improving team projects. *Journal of Education for Business, 82*, 11–19.

Hendry, G. D., Heinrich, P., Lyon, P. M., Barratt, A. L., Simpson, J. M., Hyde, S. J., et al. (2005). Helping students understand their learning styles: Effects on study self-efficacy, preference for group work, and group climate. *Educational Psychology, 25*(4), 395–407.

Henke, J. W. (1985). Bringing reality to the introductory marketing student. *Journal of Marketing Education, 7*(3), 59–71.

Hinck, W., & Ahmed, Z. U. (2015). The effect of anticipatory emotions on students' performance in marketing simulations. *Journal of Research in Marketing and Entrepreneurship, 17*(1), 5–22.

Hofstede, G. J., De Caluwé, L., & Peters, V. (2010). Why simulation games work-in search of the active substance: A synthesis. *Simulation & Gaming, 41*(6), 824–843.

Hromek, R., & Roffey, S. (2009). Promoting social and emotional learning with games:" It's fun and we learn things". *Simulation & Gaming, 40*(5), 626–644.

Hsu, E. (1989). Role-event gaming simulation in management education. *Simulation and Gaming, 20*(4), 409–438.

Huff, L. C., Cooper, J., & Jones, W. (2002). The development and consequences of trust in student project groups. *Journal of Marketing Education, 24*(1), 24–34.

Ito, T. A., Larsen, J. T., Smith, N. K., & Cacioppo, J. T. (1998). Negative information weighs more heavily on the brain: The negativity bias in evaluative categorizations. *Journal of Personality and Social Psychology, 75*(4), 887.

Johnson, D., Johnson, R., & Smith, K. (2007). The state of cooperative learning in post secondary and professional settings. *Educational Psychology Review, 19*, 15–29.

Johnson, D. W., Johnson, R. T., & Stanne, M. B. (2000). *Cooperative learning methods: A meta-analysis*. Minneapolis, MN: University of Minnesota Press.

Kaplan, M. D., Piskin, B., & Bol, B. (2009). Educational blogging: Integrating technology into marketing experience. *Journal of Marketing Education, 32*, 50–63.

Karns, G. L. (2006). Learning style differences in the perceived effectiveness of learning activities. *Journal of Marketing Education, 28*(1), 56–63.

Katzenbach, J. R., & Smith, D. K. (1994). Teams at the top. *The McKinsey Quarterly, 1*, 71.

Katzenbach, J. R., & Smith, D. K. (2005). The discipline of teams. *Harvard Business Review, 83*(7), 162.

Kayes, A. B., Kayes, D. C., & Kolb, D. A. (2005). Experiential learning in teams. *Simulation & Gaming, 36*(3), 330–354.

Kear, A., & Bown, G. R. (2015). Emotional engagement and active learning in a marketing simulation: A review and exploratory study. *International Journal of Advanced Computer Science and Applications, 6*(1), 69–76.

Kennedy, F. A., & Dull, R. B. (2008). Transferable team skills for accounting students. *Accounting Education: An International Journal, 17*(2), 213–224.

Keys, J. B., & Bell, R. R. (1977). A comparative evaluation of the management of learning grid applied to the business policy learning environment. *Journal of Management, 3*(2), 33–39.

Kneale, P. (2009). Teaching and learning for employability: Knowledge is not the only outcome. In H. Fry, S. Ketteridge, & S. Marshall (Eds.), *A handbook for teaching and learning in higher education* (pp. 9–23). Abingdon: Routledge.

Knowles, M. S. (1984). *Andragogy in action: Applying modern principles of adult education*. San Francisco, CA: Jossey-Bass.

Kolb, D. (1984). *Experiential learning as the science of learning and development*. Englewood Cliffs, NJ: Prentice Hall.

Kolb, D. A. (2014). *Experiential learning: Experience as the source of learning and development*. New York City: Pearson Education.

Kolb, A. Y., & Kolb, D. A. (2005). Learning styles and learning spaces: Enhancing experiential learning in higher education. *Academy of Management Learning & Education, 4*(2), 193–212.

Kolb, A. Y., & Kolb, D. A. (2012). Experiential learning theory. *Encyclopedia of the sciences of learning* (pp. 1215–1219). New York City: Springer.

Korinek, A., & Stiglitz, J. E. (2018). Artificial intelligence and its implications for income distribution and unemployment. In A. K. Agarwal (Ed.), *Economics of artificial intelligence*. Chicago: University of Chicago Press.

Kozlowski, S. W., & Ilgen, D. R. (2006). Enhancing the effectiveness of work groups and teams. *Psychological Science in the Public Interest, 7*(3), 77–124.

Kratwohl, D. R., Bloom, B. S., & Masia, B. B. (1964). *Taxonomy of educational objectives. Handbook II: Affective domain*. New York City: David McKay.

Kriz, W. C. (2008). A systemic-constructivist approach to the facilitation and debriefing of simulations and games. *Simulation & Gaming, 41*(5), 663–680.

Latane, B., Williams, K., & Harkins, S. (1979). Many hands make light the work: The causes and consequences of social loafing. *Journal of Personality and Social Psychology, 37*(6), 822.

Livingstone, D., & Lynch, K. (2002). Group project work and student-centred active learning: Two different experiences. *Journal of Geography in Higher Education, 26*(2), 217–237.

MacGregor, J., Cooper, J. L., Smith, K. A. & Robinson, P. (2000). Strategies for energizing large classes: From Small groups to learning communities. The Jossey-Bass higher and adult education series. In *New directions for teaching and learning*.

Matthews, D. B. (1994). An investigation of students' learning styles in various disciplines in colleges and universities. *Journal of Humanistic Education and Development, 33*(2), 65–74.

May, G. L. (2008). The effect of rater training on reducing social style bias in peer evaluation. *Business Communication Quarterly, 71,* 297–313.

May, G. L., & Gueldenzoph, L. E. (2006). The effect of social style on peer evaluation ratings in project teams. *Journal of Business Communication, 43*(1), 4–20.

Mayer, R. C., Davis, J. H., & Schoorman, F. D. (1995). An integrative model of organizational trust. *Academy of Management Review, 20*(3), 709–734.

McCorkle, D. E., Alexander, J. F., & Reardon, J. (2001). Integrating business technology and marketing education: Enhancing the diffusion process through technology champions. *Journal of Marketing Education, 23*(1), 16–24.

McCorkle, D. E., Alexander, J. F., Reardon, J., & Kling, N. D. (2003). Developing self-marketing skills: Are marketing students prepared for the job search? *Journal of Marketing Education, 25*(3), 196–207.

McCorkle, D. E., Reardon, J., Alexander, J. F., Kling, N. D., Harris, R. C., & Iyer, R. V. (1999). Undergraduate marketing students, group projects, and teamwork: The good, the bad, and the ugly? *Journal of Marketing Education, 21*(2), 106–117.

McHaney, R., White, D., & Heilman, G. E. (2002). Simulation project success and failure: Survey findings. *Simulation & Gaming, 33*(1), 49–66.

McLean, C., Reid, C., & Scharf, F. (1998). The development of transferable skills in business studies degrees. *Irish Journal of Management, 19*(1), 47.

Meese, J. L., Anderman, E. M., & Anderman, L. H. (2006). Classroom goal structure, student motivation, and academic achievement. *Annual Review of Psychology, 57,* 487–503.

Michael, D. R., & Chen, S. L. (2005). *Serious games: Games that educate, train, and inform.* London: Muska & Lipman.

Mitchell, R. C. (2004). Combining cases and computer simulations in strategic management courses. *Journal of Education for Business, 79*(4), 198–204.

Moon, J. A. (2004). *A handbook of reflective and experiential learning: Theory and practice.* London: Psychology Press.

Neu, W. A. (2012). Unintended cognitive, affective, and behavioral consequences of group assignments. *Journal of Marketing Education, 34*(1), 67–81.

Newman, A. J., & Hermans, C. M. (2008). Breaking the MBA delivery mould: A multi-group international MBA/practitioner virtual collaborative project. *Marketing Education Review, 18*(1), 9–14.

O'Neil, H. F., Wainress, R., & Baker, E. L. (2005). Classification of earning outcomes: Evidence from the computer games literature. *Curriculum Journal, 16*(4), 455–474.

O'Sullivan, T., Rice, J., Rogerson, S., & Saunders, C. (1996). *Successful group work.* London: Kogan Page.

Payne, B. K., & Monk-Turner, E. (2006). Collaborating with undergraduates: Obstacles and tips. *Journal of Criminal Justice Education, 16*(2), 292–299.

Peltier, J. W., Hay, A., & Drago, W. (2005). The reflective learning continuum: Reflecting on reflection. *Journal of Marketing Education, 27*(3), 250–263.

Peltier, J. W., Schibrowsky, J. A., & Drago, W. (2007). The interdependence of the factors influencing the perceived quality of the online learning experience: A causal model. *Journal of Marketing Education, 29*(2), 140–153.

Perry, N. W., Huss, M. T., McAuliff, B. D., & Galas, J. M. (1996). An active-learning approach to teaching the undergraduate psychology and law course. *Teaching of Psychology, 23*(2), 76–81.

Peter, P. J., & Olson, J. C. (2008). *Consumer behavior and marketing strategy.* Mcgraw-Hill: Maidenhead.

Peterson, R. A., Albaum, G., Munuera, J. L., & Cunningham, W. H. (2005). Reflections on the use of instructional technologies in marketing education. *The Journal of Educators Online, 2*(2), 1–18.

Petranek, C. F. (2000). Written debriefing: the next vital step in learning with simulations. *Simulation & Gaming, 31*(1), 108–118.

Pfaff, E., & Huddlestone, P. (2003). Does it matter if I hate teamwork? What impacts student attitudes toward teamwork. *Journal of Marketing Education, 25*(1), 37–45.

Pinto, M. B., Pinto, J. K., & Prescott, J. E. (1993). Antecedents and consequences of project team cross-functional cooperation. *Management Science, 39*(10), 1281–1297.

Pollack, B. L., & Lilly, B. (2008). Gaining confidence and competence through experiential assignments: An exploration of student self-efficacy and spectrum of inquiry. *Marketing Education Review, 18*(2), 55–66.

Porter, L. W., & McKibben, L. E. (1988). *Management education and development: Drift of thrust into the 21st century.* New York City: McGraw-Hill.

Prichard, J. S., Bizo, L. A., & Stratford, R. J. (2006). The educational impact of team-skills training: Preparing students to work in groups. *British Journal of Educational Psychology, 76*(1), 119–140.

Rosser, S. V. (1998). Group work in science, engineering, and mathematics: Consequences of ignoring gender and race. *College Teaching, 46*(3), 82–88.

Rudolph, J. W., Simon, R., Dufresne, R. L., & Raemer, D. B. (2006). There's no such thing as "nonjudgmental" debriefing: A theory and method for debriefing with good judgment. *Simulation in Healthcare, 1*(1), 49–55.

Rundle-Thiele, S., Russell-Bennett, R., & Dann, S. (2005). The successful preparation and development of future marketing professionals: A recommended methodological framework. *Journal for Advancement of Marketing Education, 7*, 27–35.

Ryan, G., Valverde, M., & Rodríguez-Ardura, I. (2001). Marketing education, distance learning and hypermedia: Teaching "current issues in marketing" in a virtual campus. *Marketing Education Review, 11*(3), 41–53.

Saber, J. L., & Foster, M. K. (2011). The agony and the ecstasy: Teaching marketing metrics to undergraduate business students. *Marketing Education Review, 21*(1), 9–20.

Schibrowsky, J. A., Peltier, J. W., & Boyt, T. E. (2002). A professional school approach to marketing education. *Journal of Marketing Education, 24*(1), 43–55.

Shaffer, D. W., Squire, K. R., Halverson, R., Gee, J. P., & Academic Advanced Distributed Learning Co-Laboratory. (2004). Video games and the future of learning. *Phi Delta Kappan, 87*(2), 105–111.

Sherrard, W. R., Raafat, F., & Weaver, R. R. (1994). An empirical study of peer bias in evaluations: Students rating students. *Journal of Education for Business, 70*(1), 43–47.

Simon, B., Haghirian, P., & Schlegelmilch, B. B. (2003). Enriching global marketing education with virtual classrooms: An effectiveness study. *Marketing Education Review, 13*(3), 27–40.

Smith, E. T., & Boyer, M. A. (1996). Designing in-class simulations. *PS: Political Science & Politics, 29*(04), 690–694.

Smith, K. A., Sheppard, S. D., Johnson, D. W., & Johnson, R. T. (2005). Pedagogies of engagement: Classroom-based practices. *Journal of Engineering Education, 94*(1), 87–101.

Squire, K. (2003). Video games in education. *International Journal of Intelligent Games & Simulation, 2*(1), 49–62.

Steen, M. (1998). Managers seek to balance individual rewards with group goals. *InfoWorld, 20*(37), 91–92.

Strong, J. T., & Anderson, R. E. (1990). Free-riding in group projects: Control mechanisms and preliminary data. *Journal of Marketing Education, 12*(2), 61–67.

Sundstrom, E., De Meuse, K. P., & Futrell, D. (1990). Work teams: Applications and effectiveness. *American Psychologist, 45*(2), 120.

Taylor, A. S. A., Backlund, P., & Niklasson, L. (2012). The coaching cycle a coaching-by-gaming approach in serious games. *Simulation & Gaming, 43*(5), 648–672.

Tu, Y., & Lu, M. (2005). Peer-and-self assessment to reveal the ranking of each individual's contribution to a group project. *Journal of Information Systems Education, 16*(2), 197.

Tuten, T. (2009). Real world experience, virtual world environment: The design and execution of marketing plans in Second Life. *Marketing Education Review, 19*(1), 1–5.

Tversky, A., & Kahneman, D. (1973). Availability: A heuristic for judging frequency and probability. *Cognitive Psychology, 5*(2), 207–232.

Tyagi, P. K. (2010). Expectancy theory and social loafing in marketing research group projects. *The Business Review, 14*(2), 22–27.

Vaidyanathan, R., & Rochford, L. (1998). An exploratory investigation of computer simulations, student preferences, and performance. *Journal of Education for Business, 73*(3), 144–149.

Van Kleef, G. A., Van Dijk, E., Steinel, W., Harinck, F., & Van Beest, I. (2008). Anger in social conflict: Cross-situational comparisons and suggestions for the future. *Group Decision and Negotiation, 17*(1), 13–30.

Vance, E. (2007). College graduates lack key skills, report says. *Chronicle of Higher Education, 53*(22), A30.

Vos, L. (2014). Marketing simulation games: A review of issues in teaching and learning. *The Marketing Review, 14*(1), 67–96.

Vos, L. (2015). Simulation games in business and marketing education: How educators assess student learning from simulations. *The International Journal of Management Education, 13*(1), 57–74.

Vos, L., & Brennan, R. (2010). Marketing simulation games: Student and lecturer perspectives. *Marketing Intelligence and Planning, 28*(7), 882–897.

Washbush, J. B., & Gosenpud, J. J. (1991). Student attitudes about policy course simulations. *Developments in Business Simulation and Experiential Learning, 18,* 105–110.

Watson, S. (2003). Closing the feedback loop: Ensuring effective action from student feedback. *Tertiary Education and Management, 9*(2), 145–157.

Wideman, H. H., Owston, R. D., Brown, C., Kushniruk, A., Ho, F., & Pitts, K. C. (2007). Unpacking the potential of educational gaming: A new tool for gaming research. *Simulation & Gaming, 38*(1), 10–30.

Williams, D. L., Beard, J. D., & Rymer, J. (1991). Team projects: Achieving their full potential. *Journal of Marketing Education, 13*(2), 45–53.

Williams, E. A., Duray, R., & Reddy, V. (2006). Teamwork orientation, group cohesiveness, and student learning: A study of the use of teams in online distance education. *Journal of Management Education, 30*(4), 592–616.

Williams, K., Larkins, S., & Latané, B. (1981). A deterrent to social loafing: Two selecting experiments. *Journal of Personality and Social Psychology, 40,* 303–331.

Wilson, K. A., Bedwell, W. L., Lazzara, E. H., Salas, E., Burke, C. S., Estock, J. L., et al. (2009). Relationships between game attributes and learning outcomes review and research proposals. *Simulation & Gaming, 40*(2), 217–266.

Wolfe, J., & Chacko, T. I. (1983). Education team size effects on business game performance and decision making behaviors. *Decision Sciences, 14*(1), 121–133.

Wood, C. M. (2003). The effects of creating psychological ownership among students in group projects. *Journal of Marketing Education, 25*(3), 240–249.

Workman, M. (2004). Performance and perceived effectiveness in computer-based and computer-aided education: Do cognitive styles make a difference? *Computers in Human Behavior, 20*(4), 517–534.

Wright, L. K., Bitner, M. J., & Zeithaml, V. A. (1994). Paradigm shifts in business education: Using active learning to deliver services marketing content. *Journal of Marketing Education, 16*(3), 5–19.

Young, M. R., Cordill, E. M., & Murphy, J. W. (2008). Evaluating experiential learning activities. *Journal for Advancement of Marketing Education, 13,* 28–40.

Young, M. R., Klemz, B. R., & Murphy, J. W. (2003). Enhancing learning outcomes: The effects of instructional technology, learning styles, instructional methods, and student behavior. *Journal of Marketing Education, 25*(2), 130–142.

Zantow, K., Knowlton, D. S., & Sharp, D. C. (2005). More than fun and games: Reconsidering the virtues of strategic management simulations. *Academy of Management Learning & Education, 4*(4), 451–458.

David M. Brown (Ph.D.) is Senior Lecturer in Marketing at Newcastle Business School, Northumbria University, Newcastle-upon-Tyne, UK. He is Programme Leader for the M.Sc. in Business with Marketing Management/Financial Management/Logistics and Supply Chain Management/Hospitality and Tourism Management/Business Analytics. He is a qualified teacher and Senior Fellow of the Higher Education Academy. He has an 18-year industrial background in major field marketing agencies, client-side branding, B2B capital equipment sales, and motor manufacturer network management. His main research and teaching activities are based around marketing and research methodology. He has been repeatedly nominated for the Northumbria Student Union Student-Led Teaching Awards in the Best Lecturer and Best Supervisor categories, having also taught Masters-level content at the university's London campus and at Accadis Hochschule in Bad Homburg, Germany.

Ian Charity (Ph.D.) is a Senior Lecturer in Research Methods at Newcastle Business School, Northumbria University, Newcastle-upon-Tyne, UK. His background is in quantitative methods, which relates to his teaching (model building, statistical analysis and business research methods). The title of his doctoral research was '*Ph.D. and professional doctorate: higher degrees of separation?*' He teaches on a wide range of programmes, from undergraduate to doctoral level, and supervises dissertation students at both undergraduate and postgraduate levels. He has a strong commitment to pedagogic research: one recent paper on assessment methods and procedures has been accepted as a University Red Guide.

Andrew Robson (Ph.D.) is Professor of Learning and Teaching in the Faculty of Business and Law at Northumbria University, UK. His interests in learning and teaching relate to the learning environment, particularly in the context of IT workshops and the delivery of subjects like statistics and data analysis. He also has a significant interest in the deployment of business simulations and working with part-time and International learners on Masters' programmes. Andrew has substantial experience in programme design, development and delivery at Masters' and Undergraduate levels.

Chapter 26
Pop-up Shops for Increasing Employability and Contributing to Civil Society in Times of Austerity

Inge Hill and Tina Bass

26.1 Introduction: The Impact of Austerity on Higher Education and Society

Universities are increasingly required to generate larger numbers of enterprising, employment-ready graduates (Lord Young, 2014; Preedy & Jones, 2017). This chapter frames austerity from the public-sector perspective, emphasizing reduced public spending, and examining its impact on Higher Education (HE) and charities. Figure 26.1 illustrates impact areas outlining the current socio-economic and political landscape of HE in the UK. Austerity has manifested within HE most significantly through reductions to direct government funding, increased student fees and growing engagement with industry. Simultaneously, increased monitoring of the efficient use of public spending in HE has seen the introduction of the Teaching Excellence Framework (TEF) bringing more focus on employability rates, as measured through the survey on Destinations of Leavers from Higher Education (DLHE), all of which in turn help to determine university rankings (Bolton, 2018; Chalari & Seale, 2017). These rankings put pressure on HE senior management to achieve consistently high rankings, which is then passed down through the management structure to lecturers. These developments constitute processes of change with outcomes that often differ greatly from those of previous decades.

These measures mean also that more creativity, efficiencies and effectiveness are required of lecturers and HE managers, to deliver high quality education. Lecturers need to design and deliver education that will meet the interests of students whilst still also equipping them to meet the employability expectations of future employers. Students are often not (fully) aware of, or indeed aligned with, employers' needs,

I. Hill (✉) · T. Bass
Coventry, Coventry, England, UK
e-mail: aa9964@coventry.ac.uk; inge.hill@pathcreating.com

T. Bass
e-mail: bsx178@coventry.ac.uk

© Springer Nature Switzerland AG 2019   415
A. Diver (ed.), *Employability via Higher Education: Sustainability as Scholarship*,
https://doi.org/10.1007/978-3-030-26342-3_26

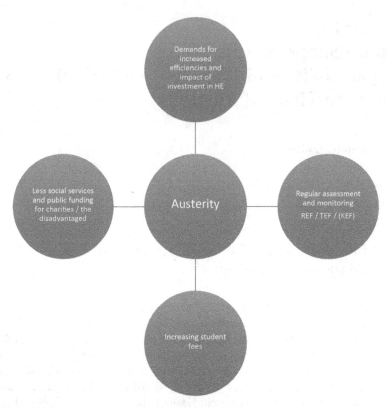

Fig. 26.1 Impacts of austerity measures on society, with a focus on Higher Education

creating a tension between universities' societal roles, i.e. providing education, and meeting employers' expectations, whilst still offering an education that students will hopefully rank highly, even against a backdrop of reduced, finite funding. In the UK, austerity has had wide societal effects, with government funding for the charitable sector also being much-reduced. Less money is available for dealing with social issues at the level of local government, affecting core delivery levels for social services. These changes have increased the pressure on charities: unsurprisingly, this has meant that income from individuals (through donations, legacies and purchases) has become the most important sector income source (NVCO, 2018). Citizens of the future are likely, therefore, to play a significant role in social problem-solving, not just through paying taxes and making donations, but also through genuine engagement with charities e.g. as volunteers or staff.

26.2 Key Concepts

In business, pop-up shops have become a well-known phenomenon. They are defined here as a physical space used for a limited period and offering retail or hospitality services. Pop-up shops may be offered in large retail shopping centres or on the High Street: pop-up restaurants can occur at festivals, or where independent chefs use existing premises but are offering a new style of food as a one-off event or over several days. Pop-up shops are not only used for start-ups to try out the market and gain feedback on a product (Hill, 2015), they are also used by e-businesses who lack a fixed store, which allows them to win over new customers or introduce existing customers to their new products. These varied uses have in common a temporality in terms of location that allows for local-level interactions between the company (through an individual or team) and the public. Despite successful use in the business world, there is little evidence, however, that this business tool has been visibly embedded into HE for pedagogic purposes, nor is it constructively aligned with many learning and teaching strategies (but see Hill 2018a, 2018b).

Within the austerity context, this chapter explains in detail how the real-life scenario pop-up shop was translated into an effective intra-curricular learning activity, offering practice-led learning (Neck & Greene, 2011). The translation was underpinned by the pedagogical concepts of experiential learning and emotional resilience. Experiential learning theory postulates that significant differences in learning success are achieved by engaging with an activity, with new insights transforming learners' ways of looking at the world. These assumptions not only hold for entrepreneurs (Honig & Hopp, 2019; Neck & Corbett, 2018) but also for management learning (Gillespie, 2016). Developing emotional resilience is also significant: it is an important trait of both successful employees and their managers. Organisations need to continuously innovate to remain competitive (Aslan & Araza, 2015), and their staff therefore need to be resilient. Aspects of this include the ability to

- Manage challenging or stressful situations (Gillespie, 2016)
- Bounce back from challenges or lack of success
- React appropriately in the context of risk and recover from "adversity" (Grant & Kinman, 2013)
- Be responsive to external challenges (Homburg, Grozdanovic, & Klarmann, 2007).

Related competencies include emotional intelligence, social skills, an ability to reflect upon one's own actions (Grant & Kinman, 2013; Karakas, 2011), emotional self-awareness (Druskat, Mount, & Sala, 2013) and the need for "attentional control and meaningful goals and values" (Milicevic, Milton, Lekshe, O'Loughlin, 2016, p. 26). Emotional resilience can be developed further through education and training (Aguilar, 2018). In the UK, the competencies that this pop-up shop activity will likely develop are often subsumed under the heading of 'employability' (QAA, 2018) in terms of learned behaviours, expertise, and attributes. One core component of employability is enterprise-related learning; outcomes of becoming employable may include employment and/or starting a new venture. Many academics differentiate, however, between enterprising and entrepreneurial skills (Hannon, 2018; QAA,

2018). The latter are focused on building the competencies for starting up new ventures and developing new products; the former encompass business skills with a focus on considering financial and other impacts of certain actions upon the organization. In sum, enterprise skills are part of entrepreneurial skills.

The development of an entrepreneurial competency framework (Bacigalupo, Kampylis, Punie, & Van den Brande, 2016) was welcomed by the HE sector as a much-needed addition to the work on clarifying related competencies. As Hill (2015) argued, enterprising skills are citizenship skills which everyone should aim to possess, given increasing globalization and digitization, which can lead to accelerated fragmentation of labour markets and result in more 'portfolio' careers, almost certainly with phases of self-employment likely for current and future students. A critical evaluation of how the learning activity of the pop-up shop addresses and builds the competencies that employers expect from graduates follows: exploration of the changing role of the lecturer precedes the discussion of wider implications for how universities can meet the needs of generation Z and the demands of modern labour markets.

26.3   Practice-Led Learning for Employability—The Example of Pop-ups Shops

26.3.1   What Is the Pop-up Shop as a Learning Activity?

One of the most challenging problems lecturers and HE managers face is to develop learning activities that engage students whilst also providing relevant education that equips them for working in a business context, and simultaneously leads to reasonable forms of assessment (Carey & Matlay, 2011). The pop-up shop learning activity (termed 'shop' from this point onwards) meets these requirements (Hill, 2018a, 2018b). The activity is embedded within a social constructivist approach (Lobler, 2006) and employs a practice-led experiential learning strategy (Kolb & Kolb, 2009; Neck & Corbett, 2018). The student learning objectives are as follows (Hill, 2018b):

- Create an 'offer to sell' to the (university) public
- Identify the role of charity donations for citizens and raise money for a self-chosen charity
- Learn to 'bootstrap' for resources
- Develop skills in reflecting upon one's own (enterprising) activities
- Apply business planning and strategic thinking at a micro-level.

These learning objectives address employability (in the sense of being better able to compete for and gain a job) and indeed self-employability, but with a sharp focus on *learning* via *doing* (Neck & Greene, 2011).

26.3.2 Design Features of the Pop-up Shop Learning Activity

The rationale for the design is based on the lead author's own previous experiences:

- Students should ideally have a month in which to prepare for their day, and must agree, in advance on a team structure, sales approach, working hours, and so on. It is best if no more than six students form a team, and the shop should be open ideally for at least four to eight hours.
- Students must carry out a *risk assessment* for the whole process.
- Students are encouraged to *bootstrap* (Hill, 2015), working with the resources they have and can raise. To gain an insight into how easily they can make money based on what they have, what they know, and who they know (to develop a sufficiently attractive offer) is an important learning point. They should *not* be given money.
- Engaging students in *raising money for a charity* of their choice (Hill, 2018a) is a unique feature. Experience shows that a charitable concern should be the beneficiary of any profits generated by the teams. This activity equips students with an understanding of the societal role of individual-giving, as outlined above.
- The "shop" should be set up in a *safe environment* on the university campus, where university security staff can provide protection. This known environment provides safety for more shy team members.
- Staff should agree with students that legitimate *expenses* can be reclaimed via proper receipts, managed by the lecturer.
- The student *debrief* offers an important opportunity for learning support. Across teams, lecturers need to engage students in discussions reflecting on how the activity went and what they learned, and thus linking to Kolb's learning cycle (Kolb, 2014). These lecturer-led reflections are also essential for supporting the meaning-creation process (Higgins & Elliott, 2011).
- Reflective *assessments* are constructively aligned with the above learning outcomes (Biggs, 2011). Assessment forms can vary from reflective essay to video creation. Students at all levels need lecturer guidance on what to reflect upon, guided by questions on skills and knowledge employed and developed, experiences and attributes developed, and learning about themselves. Effective reflection is an essential professional skill which HE needs to develop more fully (Bruno & Dell'Aversana, 2018).

26.3.3 How the Pop-up Shop Develops Employability Skills

A selection of learner activities develops the entrepreneurial competencies suggested by the EntreComp Framework, (Bacigalupo et al., 2016) and the QAA enterprise themes (QAA, 2018) (see Table 26.1). In other words, the shop design addresses all relevant enterprise and entrepreneurial learning outcomes, matching the framework's fifteen competences (in three areas) with selected learner activities, and linking activities to the eight QAA enterprise themes. The shop design goes beyond the

Table 26.1 How pop-up shop student activities develop employability

Student activities (indicative selection)	EntreComp competence areas and competences, (Bagicalupo et al., 2016)	QAA guidance (QAA, 2018)
	(1) "Ideas and opportunities": (A) Spotting opportunities, (B) Creativity, (C) Vision, (D) Valuing ideas, (E) Ethical and sustainable thinking (2) "Resources": (A) Self-awareness and self-efficacy, (B) Motivating and persevering, (C) Mobilizing resources, (D) Financial and economic literacy, (E) Mobilizing others (3) "Into action": (A) Taking initiative, (B) Planning and management, (C) Coping with uncertainty, ambiguity and risk, (D) Working with others and (E) Learning through experience *The selection below focuses on the most important competences*	1. Creativity and Innovation 2. Opportunity recognition, creation and evaluation 3. Decision making supported by critical analysis and judgement 4. Implementation of ideas through leadership and management 5. Reflection and action 6. Interpersonal skills 7. Communication and strategy skill 8. Digital and data skills
Work in teams and make decisions as a team (on product to sell, roles in team etc.)	1 A to D, 3—all	3, 4, 5, 6, 7
Manage and solve conflicts	1 C, 2 A and E, 3 C to E	5, 6
Select charity	(1 E) and more	3, 4, 6
Research what products sell, purchase materials and goods to sell	3 B	2, 6, 7, 8
Develop/create product/services to sell	1 A to D, 2 B,	1, 2, 7
Budget for delivery, decide on pricing	2 D	3, 4, 6, 8
Carry out risk assessment/develop leads and sell to customers	3 C/1 A and B, 3 all	3, 4, 5 3, 4, 5, 7

(continued)

Table 26.1 (continued)

Student activities (indicative selection)	EntreComp competence areas and competences, (Bagicalupo et al., 2016)	QAA guidance (QAA, 2018)
Plan resourcing and delivery on the day	3 B, C, D, E	3, 4
Deliver the pop-up shop in teams	2 D, 3 all	3, 4, 6
Reflect on learning and activities	2 A	5

competencies that the two sector documents discuss, however: it familiarises students with their roles for contributing to income for charities, making connections to wider societal problems. Actively raising funds for a student-selected charity goes beyond a baseline "competenc[y] of ethical and sustainable thinking" (O'Keefe et al., 2018, p. 12), which largely focuses on mindsets. The following examples are indicative of the learning opportunities across the three entrepreneurial areas, namely, "ideas and opportunities", "resources" and "into action" (Bacigalupo et al., 2016) meeting the need for wider employability skills (QAA, 2018) (see Table 26.1):

- *"Ideas and opportunities"*: Students must spot opportunities for selling products to the known target audience on campus. The learning focus across all competencies rests on social learning through team-working, having to make compromises and influencing others. For example, they agree as a team on product selection and on running the stall. In the risk assessment activity students evaluate the potential consequences of running the stall.
- *"Resources"*: Students must combine their skills and resources to run the stall and self-evaluate skills to decide who does what both in preparation and on the day itself. They estimate product costs in advance, based on how many they are likely to sell, developing and applying financial planning skills. For example, if they choose a location with little footfall, they will have to move their tables, and find solutions, such as walking to where the potential customers are with a tray and starting conversations, showing determination in finding potential customers.
- *"Into action"*: Team-working is essential for all decisions that lead to activities for running the shop. Students take the initiative in selecting a charity for which to raise money. They must decide on the products they will sell and plan what resources they need on the day they run their "shop". They must manage payments and keep track of takings; they might have to change how they interact with customers, thinking on their feet as needed. The uncertainty of the number of potential buyers needs to be integrated into the planning and purchasing strategy, as much as the product-pricing strategy.

The "shop" activity allows students to develop *emotional resilience* through having to work in teams and agree on several options. Possibilities for learning include having to accept the selling of a service they might not have chosen individually.

Moreover, they must respond to potential customers perhaps not liking their offer and even refusing to talk to them, developing (customer) responsiveness (Homburg et al., 2007). Similarly, they might learn that their planned activity is too risky. For example, in one iteration, students wanted to offer freshly made sandwiches using a toaster, which the Students' Union (as the space manager) told them was too risky. They immediately reacted and developed a different service using the groups' skills set, which is an example of effective adaptation (Bardoel, Pettit, De Cieri, McMillan, 2014). A mindful tutor can support vulnerable students as a mentor, contextualising the experience of offer-rejection and supporting students to develop appropriate reactions. These experiences link to the entrepreneurial competencies needed to actually start a business, which may also include overcoming fear of failure and acceptance of risk. Reflection also builds evaluative judgement (Boud & Soler, 2016), allowing students to link class-learning to real life situations, which again needs support from the lecturer.

26.4   How the Pop-up Shop Changes the Lecturer's Role

This learning activity successfully employs experiential learning, meeting the call for innovative teaching methods (Carey & Matlay, 2011; Lilischkis, Volkmann & Halbfas, 2015) with the lecturer moving into the role of facilitator and mentor. And yet, this activity requires lecturer behaviours and associated mindsets, which the literature has perhaps given insufficient attention to (Fayolle, 2013; Hannon, 2018). Lecturer input for running the pop-up shop will likely include the following:

- Organization of a location with tables and chairs
- Organizing reflection as part of an assessment strategy
- Managing time slot allocations
- Briefing a class about running a pop-up shop
- Training in organizing a stall
- Facilitating team management
- Answering students' queries
- Mentoring students dealing with challenges
- Collecting the money raised and handing it over to selected charity with students
- Leading debrief and student self-reflection through setting questions
- Marking assessment.

This list illustrates nearly all the lecturer input in terms of staff time and material costs. Key tasks include facilitation and coaching of students for planning and running the activity and careful leadership through reflection and assessment. Comparing lecturer and student activities suggests that this exercise offers effective lecturer resource management whilst also responding to austerity challenges. There are several challenges that lecturers can face, however, from institutional politics and/or bureaucracy, when aiming to be creative in integrating experiential learning into the curriculum (Carey & Matlay, 2011). The proposed activity list above hopefully

Table 26.2 Example of student choices

Decision on what to offer/examples of HOW they can implement this learning	Existing offer examples	Innovations
Service? Decide in teams	Shoe cleaning or decorating; Card making	Game designed for the occasion; bespoke exercise class
Product?	Selling fresh donuts, or stationary, or small gifts	Create gifts for an occasion; baking and selling cupcakes with unique cover and logo
Service and product?	Gift wrapping	Uniquely combine sweets into a flower bunch on request

develops the debate on the value of HE: the lecturers' role shifts to that of facilitator and developer of a learning "framework," offering support in line with student-led learning models (Biggs, 2011; Doyle, 2011). This shop activity considers that learning is more clearly retained when students make choices on what and how to learn, in line with the constructivist approach to learning (Lobler, 2006). The underlying experiential learning approach suggests also that the lecturer supports students in selecting learning activities relevant to their understanding.

An important lecturer task is to support learners in linking their existing knowledge and insights to new, actively-acquired learning. Indeed, students make many decisions on the *content* of their learning and, indeed, *how* they learn it, when participating in the "shop". Table 26.2 presents some of their choices. As such, the suggested assessment design ensures that students learn reflective skills as part of professional practice (Bruno and Dell'Aversana, 2018).

The activity goes beyond traditional approaches and adds relevance to the learning activity by adding the element of selling for a particular purpose, namely, raising funds for a charity. Allowing students to choose which charity they raise money for adds another choice and allows them to own another aspect of the activity. The lecturer role focuses here on setting the framework and ensuring that all students participate in the decisions.

26.5 Discussion

Several challenges arise, and two are discussed here. Firstly, there is an ongoing discussion of the future role of universities, not only for educating 'generation Z', and secondly to meet the changing needs of employers and society. The pop-up shop offers meaningful face-to-face interactions with peers and potential customers, alongside online learning, to meet the challenges of an increasingly digitizing economy (Carretero, Vuorikari, & Punie, 2017). It links the identified needs of generation Z (social interaction and co-creation of experiences, Skinner et al., 2018). Our students have used technology from a very young age: they have developed on the one hand highly sophisticated internet, media and computer skills but admit that their face-to-face communication skills are, for many, a clear weakness (O'Boyle, Atack, & Monahan, 2017; Ricoh Europe, 2015). The pop-up shop activity is an intra-curricular learning activity, aimed at meeting enterprise education demands (Neck & Greene, 2011) to reach out to the largest possible number of students (given that many students simply do not take part in extra- or co-curricular activities, due to lack of time or interest).

The shift in the role of the lecturer to one who supports learning and advises rather than transferring knowledge (Doyle, 2011) is clear: core responsibilities still include provision of the main resources (physical, time-related and social support). The required skills-set is not entirely clear within some of the literature (Biggs, 2011; Doyle, 2011), however. A useful skills' set should include competencies not yet widely offered through postgraduate certificates in the UK, for example, apprecia-tive enquiry, coaching/mentoring, co-operative learning and facilitation. These skills focus on supporting students on their learning journey. Additionally, lecturers need to be supporting learners through emotional challenges to develop their emotional resilience, something for which they will often have had very little training.

Entrepreneurship teaching and learning (Hannon, 2018; Neck & Corbett, 2018) is only one tool on the way to achieving wider employability skills (QAA, 2018).[1] Calls are increasing for universities to radically change their business models: they will need to serve new target customers, including those professionals, who need to update their skills and knowledge in a rapidly changing globalized and digitized economy (Davey, Meerman, & Riedel, 2018). Changing expectations of one's working life (a good work-life balance having the highest priority for generations Y and Z, who seek more opportunities for independent and flexible working, O'Boyle et al., 2017) and the impacts of modern labour markets have led to a further fragmentation of workplaces (Davey et al., 2018; Hill, 2015). The number of full-time jobs available will likely decrease, forcing many into self-employment or perhaps into starting new ventures. The role of universities is increasingly seen as one that must be preparing young people for such portfolio careers (Lord Young, 2014).

26.6   Conclusion

The discussion of the pop-up shop learning activity demonstrates that employability skills can be acquired within the traditional delivery time of a module to maxi-mize learning outcomes for employability and meet the needs of future graduates and their employers. Pop-up shops are an ideal vehicle for encouraging young peo-ple to develop key social and communication skills within a low-risk environment.

---

[1] Currently, Enterprise Educators UK, the main body for Enterprise Education in the UK, is offer-ing exchange workshops to learn from colleagues' experiences across disciplines in these areas (Michels, Beresford, Beresford, & Handley, 2018).

Employability-relevant elements are clearly identifiable (Bacigalupo et al., 2016; QAA, 2018). The actual impact of running this learning activity is outlined elsewhere (Hill, 2018b), but further research is needed to evaluate in more depth the short and long-term impacts on learners' employability. As we have limited knowledge of the impact of lecturer training on student learning (Parsons, Hill, Holland, & Willis, 2012) research on what teaching style has the biggest impact on student learning could reveal further relevant insights for what kind of training is needed. Policy implications are manifold: allocating funding based on university performance measures (primarily generated through student surveys) may often miss the point. Policy-makers need to find better ways to encourage universities to change. Many universities are in the process of re-organizing their core business models and how they deliver societally relevant education. As a learning activity, the "pop-up shop" offers an example of how universities could change the delivery of services to ensure they still have a unique selling point in twenty years' time (Davey et al., 2018). The pop-up shop illustrates also how intra-curricular learning can help meet the needs of future learners, employers, and indeed wider society.[2]

References

Aguilar, E. (2018). *Onward: Cultivating emotional resilience in educators.* Jossey-Bass/Wiley.

Aslan, G., & Araza, A. (2015). Employee innovation resilience: A proposal for multi-dimensional construct. *Business & Management Studies: An International Journal, 3*(3), 290–308.

Bacigalupo, M., Kampylis, P., Punie, Y., & Van den Brande, L. (2016). *Entrecomp: The entrepreneurship competence framework.* Luxembourg: Joint Research Centre of the European Commission. Publications Office of the European Union.

Bardoel, E. A., Pettit, T. M., De Cieri, H., & McMillan, L. (2014). Employee resilience: An emerging challenge for HRM. *Asia Pacific Journal of Human Resources, 52*(3), 279–297.

Biggs, J. (2011). *Aligning teaching for constructing learning.* York, UK: The Higher Education Academy.

Bolton, P. (2018). *Higher education funding in England.* Briefing paper no. 7393, 17 July 2018. London: House of Commons.

Boud, D., & Soler, R. (2016). Sustainable assessment revisited. *Assessment and Evaluation in Higher Education, 41*(3), 400–413.

Bruno, A., & Dell'Aversana, G. (2018). Reflective practicum in higher education: The influence of the learning environment on the quality of learning. *Assessment & Evaluation in Higher Education, 43*(3), 345–358.

Carey, C., & Matlay, H. (2011). Emergent issues in enterprise education: The educator's perspective. *Industry and Higher Education, 25*(6), 441–450.

Carretero, S., Vuorikari, K., & Punie, Y. (2017). *DigComp 2.1. The digital competence framework for citizens.* Luxembourg: Joint Research Centre of the European Commission.

Chalari, A., & Seale, C. (2017). UK students' subjective experiences and responses to higher education austerity: Implications and lessons for the future. *Observatoire de la société britannique, 19,* 229–245.

---

[2]For more detailed teaching instructions see further (Hill, 2018b).

Davey, T., Meerman, A., & Riedel, M. (2018). In a race between education and catastrophe the 4th generation university is winning. In Davey, T., et al. (Eds.), *The future of universities*. Thought-book, University (pp. 168–171). Amsterdam: Industry Innovation Network.

Doyle, T. (2011). *Learner-centered teaching: Putting the research on learning into practice*. Sterling, VA: Stylus Publishing.

Druskat, V. U., Mount, G., & Sala, F. (2013). *Linking emotional intelligence and performance at work: Current research*. New York: Psychology Press.

Fayolle, A. (2013). Personal Views on the Future of Entrepreneurship Education. *Entrepreneurship & Regional Development, 25*(7–8), 692–701.

Gillespie, J. (2016). Can management education create new model leaders? *Management Teaching Review, 1*(1), 52–57.

Grant, L., & Kinman, G. (2013). Emotional resilience in the helping professions and how it can be enhanced. *Health and Social Care Education, 3*(1), 23–34.

Hannon, P. (2018). On becoming and being and entrepreneurship educator: A personal reflection. *Entrepreneurship and Regional Development, 30*(7–8), 698–721.

Higgins, D., & Elliott, C. (2011). Learning to make sense: What works in Entrepreneurial Education? *Journal of European Industrial Training, 35*(4), 345–367.

Hill, I. (2015). *Start up. A practice-based guide to new venture creation*. London: Palgrave MacMillan.

Hill, I. (2018a). Birmingham City University. Using EntreComp to bring credibility to practical entrepreneurial learning activities. In *Joint Research Centre (European Commission), EntreComp into action. Get inspired, make it happen*. Luxembourg: Publications Office of the European Union (last accessed July 27, 2018. https://publications.europa.eu/en/publication-detail/-/publication/4542fd58-20f3-11e8-ac73-01aa75ed71a1/language-en.

Hill, I. (2018b). Pop-up shops. ETC toolkit how-to-guide. In Enterprise Educators UK (Eds.), *ETC toolkit. Enhancing the curriculum*. November 2018. (Last accessed July 17 2019. https://www.etctoolkit.org.uk/all-etc-how-to-guides-case-studies/?toolkitid=3263).

Homburg, C., Grozdanovic, M., & Klarmann, M. (2007). Responsiveness to customers and competitors: The role of affective and cognitive organizational systems. *Journal of Marketing, 71*(3), 18–38.

Honig, B., & Hopp, C. (2019). Learning orientations and learning dynamics: Understanding heterogenous approaches and comparative success in nascent entrepreneurship. *Journal of Business Research, 94*(1), 28–41.

Karakas, F. (2011). Creating creative minds, passionate hearts, and kindred spirits. *Journal of Management Education, 35*(2), 198–226.

Kolb, A., & Kolb, D. A. (2009). Experiential learning theory: A dynamic, holistic approach to management learning, education and development. In S. J. Armstrong & C. V. Fukami (Eds.), *The Sage handbook of management learning, education and development* (pp. 42–68). London: Sage Publishing.

Kolb, D. A. (2014). *Experiential learning: Experience as the source of learning and development* (2nd ed.). New York, NY: Pearson FT Press.

Lilischkis, S., Volkmann, C., Gruenhagen, M., Bischoff, K., & Halbfas, B. (2015). Supporting the entrepreneurial potential of higher education: Final report. European Commission. (Last accessed July 17, 2019, http://www.unios.hr/wp-content/uploads/2016/05/sepHE_Final-Report_2015-06-30_v1-10.pdf).

Lobler, H. (2006). Learning entrepreneurship from a constructivist perspective. *Technology Analysis & Strategic Management, 18*(1), 19–38.

Lord Young, D. (2014). *Enterprise for all: The relevance of enterprise in education*. London: The Crown.

Michels, N., Beresford, R., Beresford, K., & Handley, K. (2018). *From fluctuation and fragility to innovation and sustainability. The role of a member network in UK enterprise education. Industry and Higher Education, 32*(6), 438–450. https://doi.org/10.1177/0950422218805575.

Milicevic, A., Milton, I., Lekshe, V. T., & O'Loughlin, C. (2016). Experiential reflective learning as a foundation for emotional resilience: An evaluation of contemplative emotional training in mental health workers. *International Journal of Educational Research, 80,* 25–36. https://doi. org/10.1016/j.ijer.2016.08.001.

NCVO = The National Council for Voluntary Organisations. (2018). *UK civil society almanac 2018.* https://data.ncvo.org.uk/a/almanac18/income-sources-2015-16/#Types_of_ income. Accessed October 20, 2018.

Neck, H. M., & Corbett, A. C. (2018). The scholarship of teaching and learning entrepreneurship. *Entrepreneurship Education and Pedagogy, 1*(1), 8–41.

Neck, H. M., & Greene, P. G. (2011). Entrepreneurship education: Known worlds and new frontiers. *Journal of Small Business Management, 49*(1), 55–70.

O'Keefe, W., Price, A., Bacigalupo, M., McCallum, E., McMullan, L., Weicht, R. (2018). *EntreComp into action. Get inspired, make it happen. Joint Research Centre (European Commission).* Luxembourg: Publications Office of the European Union (Last accessed July 17 2018. https://publications.europa.eu/en/publication-detail/-/publication/4542fd58-20f3-11e8-ac73-01aa75ed71a1/language-en

O'Boyle, C., Atack, J., & Monahan, K. (2017). *Generation Z enters the workforce.* Last accessed October 27, 2018. https://www2.deloitte.com/insights/us/en/focus/technology-and-the-future-of-work/generation-z-enters-workforce.html.

Parsons, D., Hill, I., Holland, J., & Willis, D. (2012). *Impact of teaching development programmes in higher education.* HEA research series. York: The Higher Education Academy (Last accesssed July 17, 2019. https://www.heacademy.ac.uk/system/files/resources/hea_impact_ teaching_development_prog.pdf).

Preedy, S., & Jones, P. (2017). Student-led enterprise groups and entrepreneurial learning: A UK perspective. *Industry and Higher Education, 31*(2), 101–112.

Quality Assurance Agency. (2012 [2018]). *Enterprise and entrepreneurship education: Guidance for UK higher education providers.* Quality Assurance Agency for Higher Education York.

Ricoh Europe. (2015). *Generation Z is the most challenging, social but insecure group to enter the workplace: Says Ricoh Europe.* https://www.ricoh-europe.com/news-events/news/generation-z-is-the-most-challenging.html. Accessed October 27, 2018.

Skinner, H., Sarpong, D., & White, G. R. T. (2018). Meeting the needs of the Millennials and Generation Z: Gamification in tourism through geocaching. *Journal of Tourism Futures, 4*(1), 93–104.

Inge Hill (Ph.D.) is Senior Lecturer Business Strategy at Coventry University and Senior Fellow of the Higher Education Academy. She is Director of Enterprise Educators UK, the national body for Enterprise Education in the UK, and Chair of the Strategy Special Interest Group with the British Academy of Management. She has over 25 years of teaching and research experience, and is a well-known name in the enterprise education community and sought-after invited speaker on integrating enterprise into the curriculum. She founded two service businesses and won several business awards. In 2015, she founded the JISC online Community of Practice on start-up and new venture creation teaching, and is author of the textbook *Start Up. A practice-based guide to new venture creation* (Hill, 2015, Palgrave MacMillan). She researches small business development applying a practice theory lens.

Tina Bass (Ph.D.) has been teaching in HE for 25 years. She is a Senior Fellow of the UK's Higher Education Academy and has been Deputy Head of School at Coventry University's School of Strategy and Leadership for the last four years. She is currently Co Editor-in Chief of the IHR Journal (*International Higher Education Teaching and Learning*) as well as regularly acting as a reviewer for the *Journal of General Management, Journal of Applied Research in Higher Education,* Sage, Palgrave, and other publishing houses.

Chapter 27
Professional Development Within Second Year Computing Degree Programmes

Janice Whatley

27.1 Introduction

This chapter describes a teaching unit within computing programmes of study at a UK university, that aims to develop a range of employability skills for undergraduate students through careers-based advice and a Live Project. The students involved are mainly from the computing, computer science and software engineering programmes of study, but there also a few games, forensics and animation students. All are following a three-year degree programme, with some taking a year-long placement after their second year of study. This unit of study, called Professional Development, is one of four units that the students take in their second year. Through changes made over the years, the unit can now demonstrate success in preparing students for the workplace. A series of activities have been embedded into the Professional Development unit, to help computing students acquire a range of employability skills. Computing students can be very technically minded, and do not always see the bigger picture of how information systems they produce fit into the workplace and the significance of softer skills in performing well there. The unit has two main components: Professional Development Plan (PDP) skills activities and a Live Project. These will be described below, followed by discussion of the benefits and limitations of the approaches taken.

J. Whatley (✉)
Manchester Metropolitan University, Manchester, England, UK
e-mail: j.whatley@mmu.ac.uk

© Springer Nature Switzerland AG 2019   429
A. Diver (ed.), *Employability via Higher Education: Sustainability as Scholarship*,
https://doi.org/10.1007/978-3-030-26342-3_27

27.2   Rationale for Including PDP Skills in HE and the Live Project

There has been a move towards allowing students to interact more with their environment via a cycle of reviewing and aligning their experiences to previous knowledge. Personal development planning (PDP) literature talks about teamwork skills, but does not specify what sorts of skills, or how they can be acquired (Edwards, 2005). Joy (2005) suggests that only skills such as programming in a particular language or web site design can be assessed as learned skills against given criteria, as the softer skills cannot easily be measured. The literature suggests too that there are issues regarding the "teaching" of such skills and that providing opportunities to acquire them is perhaps a better approach.

One of the strategic aims of the university is to deliver employability as part of the curriculum. To this end a decision was made to include skills regarded as desirable for employers within the teaching activities, to provide students with the opportunity to develop and recognise their skills and improve their self-confidence levels. Burke, Jones and Doherty (2005) identified 4 types of skills: foundation level skills, practical skills, personal attributes and advanced capabilities, also referred to as hard and soft skills. Employers want graduates to be able to apply higher level skills, such as critique, analysis, synthesis and multi-level communication (Harvey, Moon, Geall, & Bower, 1997). These are the advanced capabilities referred to by Burke et al., who concluded that students need opportunities for quality practice to acquire skills. They were not sure if students always recognised that they had gained skills, so some strategies to enable this may be needed. In any event, the desired outcomes from student team projects are: learning about team work processes, project management, problem solving, and communication, together with skills associated with the products of the tasks. Hence, the team project becomes a vehicle for experiential learning. However, it is very difficult to assess the degree of developing these skills, unless students are given an opportunity to reflect on their performance within this team work, and the traditional means of assessing students to provide a "unit grade" does not always work for students in project teams. Within this unit students were thus given a PDP quiz to encourage reflection on skills they recognised as important.

27.3   Why a Project? Why a Group Project? *Why a "Live" Group Project?*

There has been a move towards experiential approaches to gaining skills, through combining knowledge reinforcement with skills practice (Kolb, 1984). A major problem with a lecture-based approach is that the students are usually passive listeners during lectures and often do not get involved or become active in the learning process (Yadav & Xiahou, 2010). Projects provide experiences or situations requiring activity in the learning process, that can enable skills acquisition, known as problem-based learning or activity-oriented teaching. A study conducted by Fonseca and Gómez (2017) at two different universities in Chile, detailed the development of student projects in the area of software development. Through problem-based learning within a project, the skills of autonomous learning, creative product development and teamwork were developed, but the building of communication/presentation skills, technical documentation and sound software engineering practices was found to be limited. The main purpose of a project to promote activity-oriented learning in a software engineering course is to gain some software engineering experience which cannot be obtained through the traditional form of lecturing. Working in a group similarly requires involvement on the part of individuals, and team projects are one form of problem based learning (PBL), where learners are self-directed, assisted by guidance or coaching from tutors, in their pursuit of a solution to a problem (Mergendollar, 2006). Team project-based learning provides greater learning opportunities than problem-based learning on its own, so team projects, particularly in the computing discipline, are a good way to promote constructivist learning, self-directed learning and team work, in an experiential and practical learning environment (Griffiths & Partington, 1992).

There is some debate concerning the extent to which team projects in an educational setting can prepare students for teamwork within the workplace (Dunne & Rawlins, 2000). In the field of health teaching, a study comparing the effectiveness of problem based learning (PBL) and team projects, did cast doubt on whether PBL does indeed help develop transferable skills suitable for project-working in the workplace (Mennin, 2007). Further, it is noted by Hordyk (2007) that there is a need for further understanding of the differences between project team work in the workplace and in the educational setting. Hyland and Johnson (1998) say that any skills learned can apply only to that context, suggesting that there is no such thing as a transferable skill. Other studies carried out in HE do suggest that the results may be transferred to the workplace, e.g. problem solving skills (Banks & Millward, 2007; Lou, 2004; Mennin, 2007; Murthy & Kerr, 2003). In the software engineering context, no two projects are exactly alike, and the processes involved are different for each project (Gary, 2015).

According to the Quality Assurance Agency (QAA) in the UK, there are skills that undergraduate computing students should have an opportunity to develop through experience, as outlined in the latest version of the Computing Subject Benchmark document (QAA, 2016). These are arranged into three types: computing-related cognitive skills, computing-related practical skills and generic skills for employability, some of which are shown in Table 27.1. A statement included in the rationale for the benchmark content says: "Computing graduates apply their understanding, skills, knowledge and experience to create social and economic value by building secure, reliable and usable systems" which is a very wide remit for computing programmes, and the Professional Development unit aims to go some way to cover the essence of this statement.

The range of skills to be gained from higher education hopefully includes management competencies, such as empowerment, development and feedback, interest and ethics, which are cited as important in business, from the perspective of man-

Table 27.1 Relevant statements extracted from the benchmark statements, presented in the 3 levels (QAA, 2016)

Computing-related cognitive skills
The ability to critically evaluate and analyse complex problems, including those with incomplete information, and devise appropriate solutions, within the constraints of a budget
Modelling: use such knowledge and understanding in the modelling and design of computer-based systems for the purposes of comprehension, communication, prediction and the understanding of trade-offs
Professional considerations: recognise the professional, economic, social, environmental, moral and ethical issues involved in the sustainable exploitation of computer technology and be guided by the adoption of appropriate professional, ethical and legal practices
Requirements, practical constraints and computer-based systems (and this includes computer systems, information, security, embedded, and distributed systems) in their context: recognise and analyse criteria and specifications appropriate to specific problems, and plan strategies for their solutions
Critical evaluation and testing: analyse the extent to which a computer-based system meets the criteria defined for its current use and future development
Computing-related practical skills
The ability to plan and manage projects to deliver computing systems within constraints of requirements, timescale and budget
The ability to specify, design and construct reliable, secure and usable computer-based systems
Generic skills for employability
Intellectual skills: critical thinking; making a case; numeracy and literacy; information literacy. The ability to construct well-argued and grammatically correct documents. The ability to locate and retrieve relevant ideas, and ensure these are correctly and accurately referenced and attributed
Self-management: self-awareness and reflection; goal setting and action planning; independence and adaptability; acting on initiative; innovation and creativity. The ability to work unsupervised, plan effectively and meet deadlines, and respond readily to changing situations and priorities
Interaction: reflection and communication: the ability to succinctly present rational and reasoned arguments that address a given problem or opportunity, to a range of audiences (orally, electronically or in writing)
Team working and management: the ability to recognise and make best use of the skills and knowledge of individuals to collaborate. To be able to identify problems and desired outcomes and negotiate to mutually acceptable conclusions. To understand the role of a leader in setting direction and taking responsibility for actions and decisions

aging other people (Cripe & Mansfield, 2002). On the other hand, self-confidence, credibility, and flexibility are included from the perspective of all staff.

In the next section the unit will be described, linking activities to some of the statements in the benchmark to show how the skills have been incorporated.

27.4 History of the Live Project Elements

What started as an experiment six years ago, when the university was able to provide eight teams with a Live Project, grew to 15 projects in the second year, and has since grown to over 55 Live Projects. These are projects from a variety of external organisations, from small start-up businesses run by an individual, to small charitable ventures in need of some low-cost help, and some of the larger companies in the Manchester area. The university has links with local employers through placements and graduate recruitment, and as supporters of the university these employers were asked to contribute a Live Project. A project should be a stand-alone problem, not mission-critical, but one that will occupy a team of six or seven students for about four months. The problems presented to the students range from designing and building a web site, setting up a database system to support customer online searches, to producing an app that visitors can use to find more information in a museum. Each year there have been between 250 and 300 students taking the unit, supported by eight or nine tutors, and the students are divided into teams of six to eight members for the projects.

27.5 Description of the Professional Development Unit

Learning activities of the unit include a Live Project carried out as a team, as well as careers-linked activities to help the students make the most of the experience, so that they can incorporate these in a job application and Curriculum Vitae (CV). The idea is that the students reflect on their experiences through the project, appreciate the skills that they have acquired and are then able to articulate these skills to a potential employer.

In the first few weeks the tutorial sessions were used to provide career-related help, including writing a CV and job application letter, approaching a video interview, Strengths, Weaknesses, Opportunities, Threats (SWOT) analysis, Belbin types, identifying personality types and legal and ethical issues surrounding IT systems, supported by self-learning material. Students were able to use these activities to help with team-building before getting started on the Live Projects. There was also a lecture each week, covering topics related to team-building and managing the project, as well as motivational presentations from representatives of local businesses, who supported the work of the university.

Each tutorial class has between 25 and 30 students, so four projects were selected by the class tutor to offer to their tutorial class. A paragraph outline of the projects was posted on the university learning management system, so that students could self-select into their teams and choose one of the four projects. Contact details for the client were posted for the team, and the first task of the project was to contact their client to arrange an initial meeting. This meeting allowed the client to provide fuller details of the project and for the team to begin the process of negotiating and agreeing what they felt they could achieve in the given time. Thereafter, the teams organised themselves and the project to completion, maintaining regular contact with their client. Each week in the tutorial session the tutor was on hand to offer advice and help. The first task was completion of a project schedule, outlining the deliverables and how these would be produced by means of a project plan. The tutor gave formative feedback on the project schedule, ensuring that the project was manageable for the team and would satisfy the client.

Assessment for the unit comprised summative and formative elements for both the Live Project and skills related activities. The final grade was an individual one, 65% for the project contribution and 35% for skills attainment and legal and ethical issues. Examples of formative feedback are the optional video interviews, team project schedule and team presentation on their project progress. As well as summative feedback for the project and report, at the end of the year a Projects Showcase was held, for teams to present their work in an exhibition style setting, providing experience at presenting in a different format. Live Project clients were invited, together with prospective clients, other university partners, members of staff, and first year computing students.

Each year feedback is elicited from tutors and clients, in the form of their opinions on aspects of the unit. A unit evaluation is given to students for all units they study, and the responses regarding this unit are invaluable for the unit leaders to consider ways in which the unit can be modified the following year. The following section gives feedback from students, clients and tutors, gathered over several years of running the Professional Development unit, highlighting a range of issues and concerns that have arisen. Each year changes were made to delivery methods and activities within the scope of the existing unit specification.

27.6   Experiences from the Unit

This unit is different to others that computing students take, which are technical in nature, have clear outcomes and grading criteria and provide the students with concrete tasks to complete. Here we have a unit that is slightly uncertain, 'woolly' around the edges and requires the students to think differently. They dislike not having clear guidance, and working in teams, and this is often reflected in feedback, such as that given for the National Student Survey (NSS). However, there are many positives to take from much of the feedback we have received, which supports continuing with the unit in this format.

27.6.1 Student Feedback

When asked what they particularly liked about the unit, one aspect that stood out was the experience of working with a real business:

> It allowed me to learn a good amount of detail about each specific role within a business. Talking with someone from a business was great and gave us a lot of information about the current industry and where it looked to be heading.

> Working together with an actual client. The client gave us criteria, feedback, suggestions and

> information on what they required for the project. It gave us some experience in dealing with real clients and also with working within a large group.

> It gave me a good experience of working in the real world, and making decisions myself, instead of them being picked for me.

Amongst the feedback on things the students did not like, the difficulty of sourcing projects of similar scope was noted, together with some deficiencies in tutor support and a perceived 'unfairness' of some grades awarded to individuals:

> The thing that seems unfair to me is the fact that every group has a different client, and this can give an unfair advantage to some groups over others. But this is how the real world works so I guess It's further experience.

> Each team member should be marked individually for their part and another mark for an overall group mark, some members have contributed greatly towards the project….some haven't even bothered. Yet they will still receive roughly the same mark even though their contribution toward the final product is different.

> I think that if the project was started or put into place during the first part of the year when the legal aspects are being discussed, and people then have their groups and some sort of insight to what is going to happen, so they can maybe plan something in their own time.

A need for more information was voiced from students:

> I felt that there was lack of guidance from the start, unless we asked for it. Which can be good. *"How do we start this project?"* was the first question that came to my head. I think you should explain to the groups the starting stages of the project, e.g. talk to your client.

27.6.2 Client Feedback

Clients were asked to rate the performance of their team, considering their understanding of the business context, problem solving ability, performance in meetings, effectiveness of communication, project reporting and team organisation. Comments included the following:

> Considering they had no previous knowledge of our organisation, the group have gained considerable understanding about our processes.

The group were well organised considering the size of group and the amount of ideas from each member pitched in initial meetings. The team became more organised as the project concluded.

The team were effective and professional in meetings, although it was felt that the team could have been better prepared for some meetings.

Communications were professional, timely and effective.

The group were extremely knowledgeable and understood the requirements of the brief. The team also made suggestions for functionality and ideas that might work best aesthetically, based on existing websites which was incredibly helpful.

The group produced a report filled with design decisions which will allow us to see different ways to solve the problem.

The amount of work they have produced is above and beyond what we were expecting.

Some clients did note that their team fell short in several ways:

It seemed like a great idea, excellent opportunity for us to engage with students and to have a fresh approach to a project. I think it needs to be managed much more closely as the group did not seem responsive or engaged and I found it very hard to get in touch with them.

I'm not sure the team knows that IT is about focussing on the customer and that is the most important part of any plan. It may be good to focus more on the customer in future Live Projects so that it reflects what projects are like in companies.

27.6.3   Student Perspectives on Skills

As part of the unit students were asked to say which skills they would like to develop or improve through the unit. An analysis of which skills were most mentioned is given in Table 27.2. It is notable that time management, communication, teamwork, leadership and presentation were the most frequently recognised, all of which are included in the aims of the unit.

27.7   Issues to Be Aware of

In this section different issues experienced with the Professional Development unit are discussed. Some aspects of these issues are difficult to address, but many have influenced alterations to the way in which the unit has been run over the past few years.

27.7.1   Client Issues

The very nature of using a real-life problem and an external client, brings issues, such as a slow response from the client, whether in arranging a first meeting or, more

Table 27.2 Analysis of skills recognised

Skill to develop	Number of times cited
Time management	61
Communication	43
Teamwork	20
Leadership	17
Presentation/public speaking	17
Problem solving	12
Confidence	11
Programming/coding	9
Organisation	5
Decision making/requirements gathering	3
Patience	3
Project planning	2
Report writing	2
Motivation	2
Interface design	1
Interpersonal skills	1
Trust	1

often, later in the project when they need support and feedback. This emphasises the importance of preparing a good project plan at the start, so that the team can continue with the plan in the absence of client contact. The tutor may occasionally have to take over as client, to give feedback on the team's progress in cases when the client becomes unavailable.

In giving feedback to the team there may be considerable variation in quality from the client. Sometimes clients change their minds about the deliverables, or the client may have limited knowledge of software development and is expecting the team to know what the client wants. Some clients are looking for "blue sky" thinking to come up with novel solutions. The client may have a piece of hardware and ask the team to come up with good uses for it, which is a very open-ended project. On the other hand, some clients said in feedback that they could do with more information:

> If there was a bit more information provided by the university to the client, I feel I would have been able to set workloads appropriately to better last the duration of the module.
>
> The group size for future projects of this nature could be considered, and written action plans with timescales for the project distributed to everyone involved.

Students frequently ask why they are not being paid to do something that, within the company, would be addressed by a paid employee. One answer is that the problem posed is often one that is only a "like to have" project, and would be a part of an employee's research, rather than the day to day job. The students need to realise that the Live Project provides opportunities that they otherwise would not have: their research and solutions suggested, benefits the team and individuals just as much as the company, through the learning involved.

27.7.2 Team Member Issues

Students are often reluctant to work in teams for good reasons, which can be difficult for tutors to manage. When team members are absent, without communicating with their team members, this can lead to a lot of bad feeling. To what extent should the tutor intervene? If an individual is absent for several weeks, misses valuable team decision-making, but then turns up and completes much of the work assigned to him/her, to what extent should the individual's team grade be reduced, if at all? There are many variations on this theme, and each should be treated on its merits, though that may reduce the transparency of any grading metrics used.

On one occasion a team sacked their team leader part way through, because he had led the team down a wrong path to develop a solution. This may have been because he gave an impression of confidence: a solution he suggested was accepted by the team without adequate discussion or research. We need to encourage rigorous research into the various alternatives and full discussion of them, so that an informed decision can be made. However, there was real learning from this situation, in the same way that negative research adds to a body of knowledge.

One project was split into two parts: developing the template for a web site design and then populating pages with the required information. This required that two teams communicate with each other, which proved problematic because the teams had different timetables.

27.7.3 Teaching Organisation Issues

The unit feedback indicated some issues that have been considered by the unit leader when modifying the unit delivery. Students felt that lectures were too pedestrian, full of corporate rhetoric and needed much more practical examples of how problems get solved in business. For example, more on management structures, use of agile and scrum methods, negotiation skills, assertiveness, people management and power structures, any of which may arise in individual projects. Students recognised that these were lacking when interacting with clients, because they did not know how to measure their own worth, skill sets, or feel confident to negotiate effectively given an unknown power dynamic.

All students stated that the Coursework Specification needed to reflect reality, as parts of the required content related to things that were not relevant to the specific project they were working on. They did acknowledge that each group was different and that those on different degree pathways may have found the specification easier to follow, although many thought the marking scheme was confusing. Dates given for milestone submissions need to be clear, so that project planning can take these into account.

Team size has generated a lot of discussion over the years, because there is a need to balance the ideal size of a team against the logistics of having enough tutors to support more projects. In a larger team, of about eight students, individuals can 'hide' without impacting the work output, leading to unequal contribution and reward of effort. Smaller teams are suggested, provided there is tutor capacity. One additional feature of the Live Projects is that team structures have been defined from the beginning, so students could elect to take on the role of Team Leader, Deputy Team Leader, Finance Director, Marketing Leader or Sub-Team Leader. Students indicated their preference for a role as they assigned themselves to a group, and some negotiation, between team members and possibly the tutor, was needed to establish satisfactory team roles. Students were also encouraged to evaluate their Belbin types and use these to help choose roles within a team. Some thought needs to be given to whether and how students choose a role at the beginning or adopt a role as the project progresses.

27.8 Conclusion

Live projects have certainly been successful in providing opportunities to practice computing-related cognitive skills and practical skills. Live Projects have also helped students acquire some generic skills for employability and reflection by students encouraged them to think about what they have learned and to be able to articulate their learning to a prospective employer. Working with an external client was particularly good for giving them a chance to see how a real business works, for working with imprecise information, gathering system requirements and problem-solving. Given that these qualities are much sought after in graduates, this Professional Development unit has delivered by helping produce graduates who can show that they are resilient and able to cope with challenging situations. Teams who worked for a charity had the added sense of satisfaction in having helped a worthwhile cause.

In running this sort of team project, the project plan that a team produces is of critical importance for achieving the end-product. Assessment may be a contentious issue and needs to be thought through carefully, in terms of giving a group grade for all or part of the output, and grading the product or the process. Communication between students, clients and tutors needs to be fostered, so that it remains effective throughout the process. Live projects give opportunities for individuals within teams to carry out research, and this needs to be well supported. Learning through the Live Project not only covers team dynamics, but also workplace dynamics and communication within the workplace.

References

Banks, A. P., & Millward, L. J. (2007). Differentiating knowledge in teams: The effect of shared declarative and procedural knowledge on team performance. *Group Dynamics, 11*(2), 95–106.

Burke, V., Jones, I., & Doherty, M. (2005). Analysing student perceptions of transferable skills via undergraduate degree programmes. *Active Learning in Higher Education, 6*(2), 133–144.

Cripe, E. J., & Mansfield, R. S. (2002).*The value-added employee*. Workitect Inc.

Dunne, E., & Rawlins, M. (2000). Bridging the gap between industry and higher education: Training academics to promote student teamwork. *Innovations in Education and Teaching International, 37*(4), 361–371.

Edwards, G. (2005). *Connecting PDP to employer needs and the world of work*. Retrieved September 2007 from http://www.heacademy.ac.uk/resources/detail/id71_connecting_pdp_edwards.

Fonseca, V. M. F., & Gómez, J. (2017). Applying active methodologies for teaching software engineering in computer engineering. *IEEE Revista Iberoamericana de Tecnologias del Aprendizaje, 12*(3), 147–155.

Gary, K. (2015). Project-based learning. *Computer, 48*(9), 98–100.

Griffiths, S., & Partington, P. (1992). *Enabling active learning in small groups*. CVCP Sheffield.

Harvey, L., Moon, J., Geall, V., & Bower, R. (1997). Graduates' work: Organisational change and student's attitudes. Birmingham: CRQ and AGR (sponsored by DfEE and CIHE).

Hordyk, V. (2007). *A convergence of perspectives: Enhancing students' employability*. Paper presented at Education in a Changing Environment, Salford, UK.

Hyland, T., & Johnson, S. (1998). Of cabbages and key skills: Exploding the mythology of core transferable skills in post-school education. *Journal of Further and Higher Education, 22*(2), 163–172.

Joy, M. (2005). Group projects and the computer science curriculum. *Innovations in Education and Teaching International, 42*(1), 15–25.

Kolb, D. (1984). *Experiential learning*. London: Prentice Hall.

Lou, Y. (2004). Learning to solve complex problems through between-group collaboration in project-based online courses. *Distance Education, 25*(1), 49–66.

Mennin, S. (2007). Small-group problem based learning as a complex adaptive system. *Teaching and Teacher Education, 23,* 303–313.

Mergendollar, J. (2006). The effectiveness of problem based instruction: A comparative study of instructional methods and student characteriatics. *The Interdisciplinary Journal of Problem-based Learning, 1*(2), 49–69.

Murthy, U., & Kerr, D. (2003). Decision making performance of interacting groups: An experimental investigation of the effects of task type and communication mode. *Information & Management, 40,* 351–360.

QAA. (2016). http://www.qaa.ac.uk/quality-code/subject-benchmark-statements.

Yadav, S. S., & Xiahou, J. (2010). Integrated project-based learning in software engineering education. In 2010 International Conference on Educational and Network Technology (ICENT) (pp. 34–36). IEEE.

Janice Whatley (Ph.D.) lectures at Manchester Metropolitan University, England, in the School of Computing, Mathematics and Digital Technology. She has a long history of working in the higher education industry, and is skilled in Moodle, Research Design, Lecturing, Educational Technology, and Instructional Design, as well being a former Editor in chief of *The Interdisciplinary Journal of E-Learning and Learning Objects*.

Chapter 28
Using the Living CV to Help Students Take Ownership of Their Learning Gain

Lisa Dibben and Dawn A. Morley

28.1 Introduction

Higher Education policy is creating a culture of expectation that students should have a value-added experience or 'learning gain' (BIS, 2015, 2016) that takes them forward into further study or graduate- level employment, on completing their degree. As academia turns the spotlight on itself and asks what additional measures it can employ to make this happen, there is one important element that cannot be overlooked: students need to take ownership of their learning gain if they are to achieve their potential within and beyond their HE experiences. This chapter's premise is that part of the academic role is to assist students to understand the currency of their learning and constructively build upon, and learn from, their programmes of study as part of their ongoing professional development. The difficulties and challenges of students being able to achieve this are also discussed, via a review of recent literature.

The 'Living CV' (Dibben, 2017) is an initiative that was launched following concerns that third year fashion students failed to show an accurate reflection of their university experience within their CVs when applying for work after graduation. The Living CV encourages students to translate their learning outcomes into CV outputs, so that their hidden learning becomes explicit not only to themselves but to any future employers. It is a concept born from the realisation that students often fail to see how their programmes of learning equip them for a career and it acknowledges that there is often a mismatch between the students' perception of their learning - having to pass units to get through each year - and the currency of that learning in their future workplace.

L. Dibben (✉) · D. A. Morley
Southampton Solent, Southampton, England, UK
e-mail: lisa.dibben@solent.ac.uk

D. A. Morley
e-mail: dawn.morley@solent.ac.uk

© Springer Nature Switzerland AG 2019   441
A. Diver (ed.), *Employability via Higher Education: Sustainability as Scholarship*,
https://doi.org/10.1007/978-3-030-26342-3_28

An exploratory study of 17 final year Fashion Photography undergraduate students was conducted in 2016 and found a link between students' clear understanding of their learning outcomes and an improvement in self-confidence, self-efficacy and satisfaction with their course. Students completed a questionnaire on their levels of work readiness and satisfaction with the course before they were shown how a Living CV could link to their degree and then asked to repeat the questionnaire. Six students demonstrated an immediate improvement in confidence, eight said they could now see how their degree had prepared them for the workplace and nine felt their university education would make employers notice them. This chapter presents the results of a larger, mixed method study completed in August 2018 with 127 students drawn from a range of fashion-related degrees at a university in the south of the UK. Students completed a pre and post questionnaire before and after a presentation on the Living CV and their views were further explored in a focus group and interviews. This study informs debates as to how students' learning can be made more explicit for them and how that knowledge might help them find meaningful employment.

28.2   Literature Review

Much is made of the so-called glut of graduates who flood the workplace, ill equipped for a professional career and unprepared for the demands of industry. The reality is far more nuanced and upbeat. But while statistics consistently show that most graduates are in work three years after completing their degree (HESA, 2016), there is evidence to suggest that a fair proportion of them are in employment that doesn't make the most of the skills earned while completing their degree. In 'Supply and Demand for Higher Level Skills' (2015), Universities UK (UUK) called for better understanding of why certain graduates end up in jobs that do not match their skillset and how that could be remedied. UUK also urged universities and employers to jointly develop a 'skills translation' to pinpoint how and where missing soft skills could be learnt. An earlier CBI/NUS report (2011) acknowledged that a successful transition from HE to the workplace required necessary 'attitudes and aptitudes' being embedded throughout the degree process and for their presence, and value, to be made explicit to students.

It has never been more important to help students understand the purpose behind their course of study and its value. At a time when value for money, and the notion of 'students as consumers' are becoming increasingly common (if contentious) mantras, Tomlinson (2017, p. 464) concludes that, whoever the student, 'there are many shared concerns; particularly around getting a beneficial and equitable 'return' and value from higher education.' Preparation for employability could be the end goal that intrinsically motivates students to engage with their studies from the start. Rothwell, Jewel, & Hardie (2009) see undergraduates' work-readiness as divided into four areas, the first being the student's commitment to the university, the second their perceived external employability, the third their ambition and the fourth their internal employability. The link between students' learning and their future employability is therefore complex. It is built through students' own perceptions of their abilities (Räty, Komulainen, Harvorsén, Nieminen, & Korhonen, 2018) and throughout their period of study, drawing upon the many different elements—such as skills, qualities, conduct, culture, ideology—that help form the whole professional (Jackson, 2016).

One of the roles of the new Office for Students (OfS) in the UK has been to take over the active research project on learning gain originally instigated by HEFCE. This looks at how to measure improvements in knowledge, skills, work-readiness and personal development made by students during their time in HE (OfS, 2018). Over 70 universities and colleges were involved in 13 collaborative projects to pilot and evaluate a range of approaches for measuring learning gain while the National Mixed Methodology Learning Gain Project (NMMLGP) tracked the learning gain of more than 31,000 undergraduate students in 10 HE institutions (OfS, 2018). The acknowledgment of learning gain, and the investment of research into this recently used term within UK HE, has therefore been considerable. The progress report on the HEFCE-funded learning gain programme (HEFCE, 2018) underlies the difficulties of both defining and measuring learning gain. Officially, learning gain

> …is concerned with the distance travelled by students during their course in terms of knowledge, personal growth, acquisition and development of a wide range of skills, and how ready they become for the world of work during the period of their studies. (HEFCE, 2018, p. 2)

Although this is "expected then to have a positive impact beyond higher education" (HEFCE, 2018, p. 4) the pilot interventions were too early to measure longitudinal student progress and the complexities of the interrelated factors of individual student development were accounted for by statistical modelling. The progress report concentrates solely on the many methodologies that can be used to measure learning gain and its future contribution to the increasing web of matrices associated with the Teaching Excellence Framework (HEFCE, 2018). Early analysis of the whole venture has questioned its worth (Kernohan, 2018).

Social learning theorists, such as Etienne Wenger, present an alternative perspective in the learning gain debate whereby individual development is seen as an organic, rather than measurable, phenomenon; "Identity is the vehicle that carries our experiences from context to context" (Wenger, 1998 p. 268). Wenger echoes the work of both Eraut (2000, 2004) and Klein (1998) who emphasise the importance of the process of learning and that students can only effectively use this learning if it is made explicit to them. Cognitive psychologist, Klein (1998), in his research into the work of occupations where one must react quickly under stress, identified structure and strategies for learning expertise so that implicit learning was deliberately identified and used for future learning. These authors refocus the measurement of learning gain onto the ability of students to recognise their development by introducing pedagogy and structure that allows hidden learning to be made explicit. Again, Wenger argues that participation in a social learning situation may not be sufficient to learn (in this case, a university academic programme) but can be augmented by written artefacts, termed 'reification', where learner participation is accelerated by presenting learning in another format. Written programme learning outcomes could be an example of this, if the learning outcomes promote students' understanding, rather than being a managerial step in academic curriculum design (Hussey & Smith, 2003, 2008; Dobbins, Brooks, Jon, Rawlinson, & Norman, 2016).

Brooks, Dobbins, Jon, Rawlinson, and Norman (2014) conducted a study of students' use of learning outcomes across three disciplines at University of Leicester, UK, and found that learning outcomes were useful learning aids and gave focus to students' learning. Barriers to their use included lack of clarity in their wording and a recognition by students that learning outcomes were only a guide, rather than a prescription, to the students' learning potential. Brooks et al. (2014, p.732) concluded that "students want learning outcomes to remain a central part of their learning experience and, indeed, that they would like them to become a more effective part of it". Hussey and Smith (2003) and (Dobbins et al. 2016) support the potential of learning outcomes as both a tool for student-centred learning and heightened accountability. Despite this recognition, no suggestion is made that learning outcomes are taken outside of the academic context to translate students' academic learning into evidence for future employability. Evans et al. (2010) recognised the very real difficulties of 're contextualising' learning across different environments so students' theoretical learning can be used in a practice setting. The ability of students to extract course learning into a format accessible for employers is therefore challenging.

Research for the New College of Humanities (Ali, 2015) found that out of 860 recruiters, 20% discarded CVs before reaching the end and on average only spent 3 min 14 s reading an application. The report concluded that it has "never been more important for jobseekers to impress employers with a really strong CV" (Ali, 2015) and for this reason, students require assistance in connecting their learning, as evidenced through learning outcomes, to their search for jobs.

28.3 Methodology

28.3.1 Phase One

Following ethical approval, a mixed methodological approach was taken whereby 127 students, across all three years from the fashion degrees within the School of Art, Design and Fashion, completed a pre and post questionnaire (Fig. 28.1). In between the two questionnaires, the lead author, familiar to the students as head of the academic programme, conducted a presentation on the Living CV. During the presentation the students were shown an exemplar Living CV of a fictitious student on their course for whom each unit's learning outcomes had been translated into CV outputs. A brief generic personal statement, that referred exclusively to the degree, was also added. There were no extra-curricular activities or part time jobs included. The students were then shown how the exemplar CV had been written and from which units the CV outputs had come. After a brief discussion, the students were asked to complete the same questionnaire again. Students were also able to add qualitative comments about their perceptions of the value of a Living CV.

1. I can see how my degree is preparing me for the workplace
2. I have a CV that clearly records everything I have learnt at University
3. Units on my degree are designed to help me get employment in my chosen field
4. I will be able to use the skills learnt at University to promote myself and get work
5. My university experience makes me feel confident about future employment
6. My university education will make employers notice me
7. My university education has been worthwhile
8. I have an advantage over those people who have not studied for a degree in this subject discipline
9. My degree has helped me become a more confident individual

Fig. 28.1 Questionnaire

28.3.2 Phase Two

The same students were invited to participate in a focus group (n = 8) with the first author where the volunteer students discussed why they decided to study for a degree, their confidence, views on how ready they were for employment and how they thought the Living CV could impact their learning and job prospects. The focus groups were recorded with the students' identities anonymised in the transcript that resulted. Thematic analysis was then conducted to isolate the dominant themes that resulted from the student discussion.

28.3.3 Phase Three

Three individual, semi structured interviews with three new graduates from the school were conducted through recorded telephone interviews by the second author (previously unknown to the students) in July 2018. The anonymised transcript was also subjected to thematic analysis.

28.4 Results

28.4.1 Phase One

Results were on a 1–5 Likert scale with 1 being strongly disagree and 5 being strongly agree (Table 28.1).

Before the Living CV exercise, most students had opted for 4: *I agree that I can see how my degree is preparing me for the workplace'* and this was still the most popular choice after the exercise. However, across the entire group of respondents, 78 students changed their mind after being shown the exemplar CV. Before the exercise,

Table 28.1 I can see how my degree is preparing me for the workplace

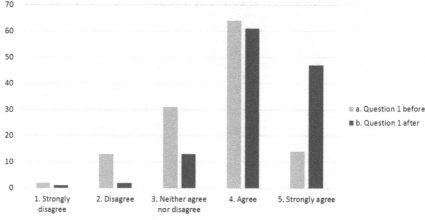

1. I can see how my degree is preparing me for the workplace

a large number of students opted for 3: *Neither agree or disagree.* After the exercise, this reduced significantly and there was a marked increase in those who answered 5: *I strongly agree that I can see how my degree is preparing me for the workplace* (Table 28.2).

By far the majority of students opted for 1 and 2 when considering if they had a CV that clearly recorded everything they had learnt at university, demonstrating that they either strongly disagreed or disagreed. After the exercise, there was a marked shift to answers 4 and 5, however (Table 28.3).

Table 28.2 I have a CV that clearly records everything I have learnt at university

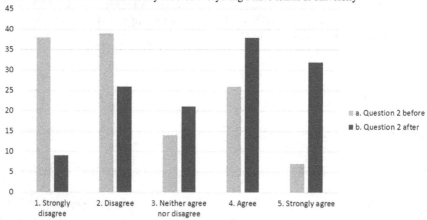

2. I have a CV that clearly records everything I have learnt at University

Table 28.3 Units on my degree are designed to help me gain employment in my chosen field

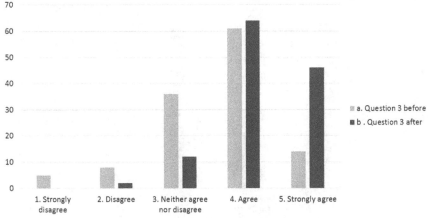

3. Units on my degree are designed to help me get employment in my chosen field

Prior to the exercise, five students had strongly disagreed with the statement *Units on my degree are designed to help me get employment in my chosen field.* After the exemplar CV this reduced to zero. There was a marked increase in the number of students who opted for 5 after the exercise (Table 28.4).

There was little change in the most popular response before and after the exercise; *I agree that I will be able to use the skills learnt at University to promote myself and get work.* However, there was a marked increase in those who strongly agreed after being shown the exemplar Living CV (Table 28.5).

Table 28.4 I will be able to use the skills learnt at University to promote myself and get work

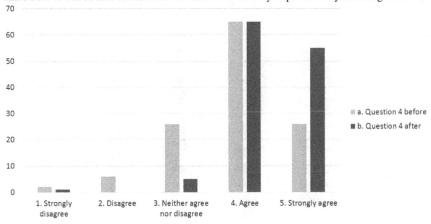

4. I will be able to use the skills learnt at University to promote myself and get work

Table 28.5 My university experience makes me feel confident about future employment

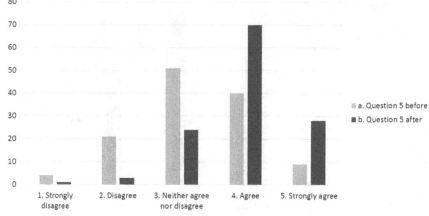

5. My university experience makes me feel confident about future employment

The shift from negative to positive on the statement *My university experience makes me feel more confident about future employment* was pronounced. Prior to the exercise, the majority of students had opted for *Neither agree nor disagree*. After the exercise, the majority either opted for *Agree* or *Strongly agree* (Table 28.6).

A similar pattern to Question 5 emerged with the vast majority of students shifting to *Agree/Strongly Agree* on the statement *My university education will make employers notice me*. No students strongly disagreed after being shown the exemplar Living CV (Table 28.7).

Table 28.6 My university education will make employers notice me

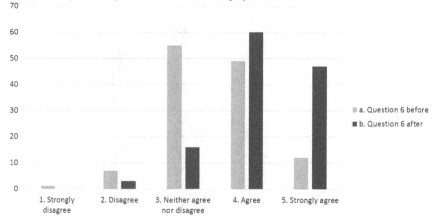

6. My university education will make employers notice me

Table 28.7   My university education has been worthwhile

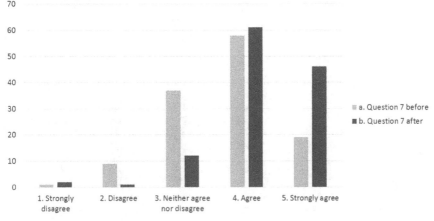

7. My University education has been worthwhile

After being shown the exemplar CV, the large majority of students agreed or strongly agreed that their university education had been worthwhile. Before being shown the exemplar Living CV the majority of students had answered 3 or 4 (Table 28.8).

Like question 7, viewing the exemplar Living CV caused a marked increase in the number of students either agreeing or strongly agreeing to the statement *I have an advantage over those people who have not studied for a degree in this subject discipline* (Table 28.9).

Table 28.8   I have an advantage over those people who have not studied for a degree in this subject discipline

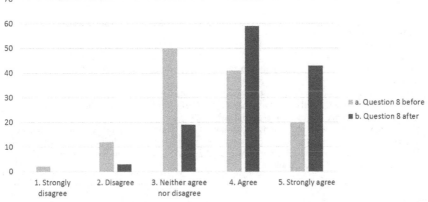

8. I have an advantage over those people who have not studied for a degree in this subject discipline

Table 28.9 My degree has helped me become a more confident individual

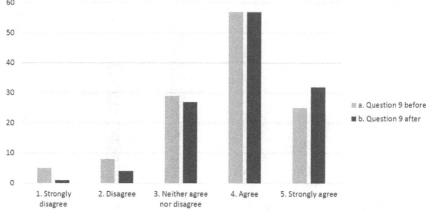

9. My degree has helped me become a more confident individual

While those who agreed with the statement *My degree has helped me become a more confident individual* remained the same before and after the exemplar Living CV was shown, more strongly agreed and fewer strongly disagreed, disagreed or neither agreed or disagreed.

28.5 Students' Written Responses

When students completed the second questionnaire they were given an opportunity to share any thoughts about the Living CV. Some of the comments can be seen in Fig. 28.2.

"It will help me a lot."

"It evolves as I do."

"We can see how we are developing."

"A lot of value. Didn't think of adding in my stuff I've learnt at uni. Yes, I strongly agree with using a Living CV."

"Shows yourself and other employers all the skills developed at Uni."

"Shows employers your skills whilst also having a way of recording all your achievements."

"Shows the experience you can achieve from uni."

"I am really pleased we were introduced to this, it is a fantastic way to really understand how everything we learnt this year can be put in a professional CV format to help get work. Before this lecture I had been quite uncertain about how everything we've been taught can be put into a CV and help us get work in industry. Thank you."

Fig. 28.2 Student responses

28.6   Phase Two and Three

Through thematic analysis, four key themes emerged from the focus group and individual interviews: reasons for going to university, concerns about finding relevant employment, the impact of the Living CV and how the Living CV could be optimised. Students also gave their thoughts on what other measures would help with employment.

28.6.1   Reasons for Going to University

A common response from participants was that they came to university to make contacts, to learn and to develop their professional currency: "*I came to uni because I thought like it was the best way, the only way really, for me to get into the industry, like connections and stuff.*" There was a clear link between the choice of course and their future career goals: "*For me the biggest reason to do a degree is so you can progress up the career ladder, to have a good career set in stone. But it's so competitive out there, a degree is required.*" The idea that a degree "*is the basic minimum*" was reiterated several times. The increase in graduates has changed the job market, "*it's made it so hard to get a job if you don't go to university because it's kind of the done thing now*". Participants recognised that, "*if you don't have a degree you have to have something really pretty special even to just get an interview*".

For some it was also a rite of passage, "*I think you grow as a person*", that signified personal improvement. A wider acknowledgement of success was very much part of this; "*I wanted to be that sibling to have a degree*" and "*I kind of reached my goal just to get to university.*" Although all students expressed concerns about the cost of a degree, they generally felt the experience and learning was worth the investment: "*I think every degree you pay for is crazy, but I think overall the experience is worth it. It's good for building yourself up as well as your education*". One student, however, saw the worth of degree not in the learning but the final outcome: "*You don't know if the course is worth it until the future, until you finish uni and get a job.*"

28.6.2   Concerns About Finding Relevant Employment

Frustration around the difficulty of getting work experience opportunities was a common theme: "*Why should it be so hard? You are being trained in the current things and you can't find work experience. That's like a bit crazy to me.*" and "*people want to kind of see a certain amount of experience – I have two experiences and they want to see three.*" Students across both focus group and individual interviews shared concerns that gaining a degree was no guarantee of future employment in the field in which they had studied, and they found this counter-intuitive: "*No one* comes to uni not to get a job" and "*the point is to get a degree, to get a job*" and "*the most important thing about coming to university is getting a job.*" Participants also expressed concern that they would not stand out from all the other graduates seeking employment: "*One job I went for an interview for they said there were over 2000 applications and all those people had degrees.*" Potential competition was seen as demoralising: "*There's a lot of pressure of failing, the feeling of failing is bad for everyone.*"

28.6.3   The Impact of the Living CV

Students found the Living CV to be an effective record of their learning and one that was easier to understand than the language of traditional learning outcomes: "*I recently looked at a Living CV and it made a lot of sense. It made me think about it a lot more*" and "*I think the learning outcomes language isn't quite understandable, I think it's just so complex you can't really relate to it. But when it's broken down it sort of makes sense.*" The deconstruction of learning outcomes into CV outputs also helped students to view their degree holistically rather than as divided into modules: "*I think I should have taken care a bit more on some of the units as I didn't see the point – but I do now*".

Students also reported that seeing a Living CV made them realise how diverse their skills were and how much they had to offer employers: "*It made me realise that I wasn't just learning about the course – you're actually learning about jobs, you're learning to think creatively and about business too*" and "*I haven't got half of the skills I should have on my CV – I don't know, I haven't got the confidence, it seems like I never even thought of it that way*". Students struggled to recognise the validity of including projects undertaken with industry while at university, as though projects completed within university time did not count as real experience. Those students who had already adapted their CV to become a Living CV reported positive praise and outcomes: "*I had applied for a lot of jobs but they were all declining because I didn't have the experience or work experience, but I used a CV like this and I got the job, instead of using my old CV*".

In addition, students reported increased confidence when seeing their Living CV: "*I think it's professional, I think it looks like someone who knows what they doing. If you read this then you would think they are confident, they are sure they can do all that*". One of the students interviewed admitted that she simply would not have thought about putting all her university experience onto her CV: "*I think it's amazing and it really did open my eyes...like looking back at my units and university, I would never have been confident enough to have put it on there.*"

28.6.4   How the Living CV Could Be Optimised

Students agreed that the Living CV should be two things; compulsory, "*a lot of people on my course …wouldn't do it voluntarily*" *(Student B, interviews)* and delivered in a face-to-face setting rather than online "*if it was online it would get forgotten about because we get so many emails and anything that's not in our brief gets forgotten*" *(Student A, interviews).* It was felt that small group discussion and support were essential to help students fully understand the currency of their learning. The suggested composition of the discussion/support groups varied between fellow students, staff and industry but it was felt that industry would give an independent and informed opinion "*I think they also give more of an honest opinion of work and the CV and what companies are like*" *and* "*They looked through my CV and they looked through my portfolio and just gave me lots of advice that I wouldn't have necessarily known.*"

Additional measures that would help with employability included seeing examples of other students' CVs, the use of a website on up and coming trends, seeing jobs in the context of where you want to live and what you don't want to do "*taking a broader view*" and the need to complete work experience. "*Doing work experience is vital because you find out what the industry is like. I think that needs to be pushed so much – working for a company is a vital part*" *(Student B, interviews)* and "*it prepares you for how you should work professionally, and it gets you used to work life and everything…I tell everyone that work experience is the way forward. The people that don't do work experience are the people that now can't get jobs because they don't have the experience.*" *(Student C, interviews)*

28.7   Analysis

It is a common mistake made by HE institutions that having a suite of vocational degrees with strong industry involvement, bespoke units and a plethora of live briefs, will automatically result in students confidently recording their university education. The research data found that student participants did not appreciate the value of learning outcomes as a tool to translate their learning into evidence for employment. Students found the Living CV helped them to clarify, value and reassess the worth of their university studies in a way that learning outcomes alone failed to do. Participants had often missed making the connection between their learning at university and how they presented their work-readiness to prospective employers. Most students accepted that their degree was designed to help them gain employment within their chosen field and also that the skills they were learning would help them to promote themselves and find work. However, the study found little connection between that knowledge and recording the details on a CV.

The idea of being on employers' radar was further borne out by the question on whether the participants felt their university education would make them noticeable.

At least half of the participants were negative about employers noticing them prior to the Living CV exercise. Qualitative data reinforced the idea that students themselves failed to see a connection between what they were learning and its currency within the job market. Once the Living CV has been introduced, that connection appears to be made. Students' learning was made explicit to them and a means of presenting this to employers was introduced.

One of the most striking findings of this research was the high numbers of students who, before being shown a Living CV, strongly disagreed or disagreed that they had a CV that clearly recorded everything they were learning at university. Once shown an exemplar Living CV the sharp increase in those recording positive responses was notable. The Living CV helped students to develop a more holistic view of their degree and a willingness to explore the value of its different components for future employability. This awareness sometimes developed retrospectively, "*I should have taken care a bit more on some of the units. I didn't see the point before, but I do now*", and underlined the coaching students needed, throughout their programmes, to build on and embed these skills. Information gleaned from interviews favoured the Living CV being compulsory, delivered in groups and with someone – fellow students, an academic or experts from industry – on hand to advise. This would also begin to address participants' lack of confidence in relation to their work readiness. Participants saw a real need for students to complete work experience and add this to their CV, calling it "*vital*" and "*the way forward*" with a clear understanding that university learning alone is not enough to make themselves employable.

28.8   Conclusion and Recommendations

This chapter found that part of the academic role was to assist students in understanding the currency of their learning and constructively build on, and from, their programmes of study, as part of their on-going professional development. Some students simply do not see the currency of their learning unless it is explicitly embedded in the curriculum, nor do they see how or why their programmes of study are constructed in the way that could act as preparation for graduate level employment. This unbalanced equation between learning and employability is clearly articulated by students in the research as they question the commitment to their courses against their ability to find work on graduation.

Students' perceptions of their value-added experience, or learning gain, needs to be disentangled from the context of their modular learning. It is likely that the help towards work readiness would be most beneficial if given over a period of time, and within a supported environment, to address underlying issues such as low self-confidence or self-efficacy. Ensuring the correct level of preparation in accordance with students' stage of study is key, as there is a danger in thinking about undergraduate students as fully-fledged professionals. Daniels & Brooker (2014) argue that there is an inherent problem with the notion of graduate attributes as being concerned with the future identity of the undergraduate rather than with what is current.

The most effective type of 'help' is something that requires further investigation but students, during this study, articulated a preference for personalised and explicit assistance to make them work-ready from the beginning of their academic programmes. Students also highlighted the importance of assistance in securing work experience and mobilising the expertise of people currently involved in the fashion industry. It is evident that these factors could be carefully integrated into a wider ethos of 'work literacy' during the university programme, to include the Living CV but also continuing discussion about (and experience within) the world of work, increased employer engagement and finally, preparation for interview.

Although 127 students were involved in the questionnaire, this study has its limitations. It would be beneficial to follow students' educational journeys and measure their understanding of, and engagement with, units once they clearly understand the purpose (and learning outcomes) of their units of study. The Living CV, which was based on a general overview of the whole course, was conducted in one session and there would be merit in looking at the gradual introduction of the Living CV on a unit-by-unit basis to encourage full buy-in from both students and academics. Although the questionnaires were anonymised, the position of the head of department conducting a focus group with volunteer students from within their own school, may have led to some bias in the responses. Further research could involve introducing the Living CV to students at the start of their degree and revisiting it at regular intervals, discussing the learning outcomes and monitoring its impact on unit engagement. This would also go some way to addressing UUK's call for a clearer skills translation for students to help them find appropriate graduate-level employment upon graduation.

In conclusion, the Living CV can be seen as a positive addition to a suite of employability measures designed to help students take ownership of their learning gain and translate their learning outcomes into CV language. In doing so it allows students to enhance their self-belief and enables them to revisit their own ideas about their work-readiness in a timely and developmental way during, rather than at the end, of their programmes of study. The changing HE landscape requires both academics and students to think of learning 'beyond the curriculum,' looking to lifelong learning and the wider skills, qualities, conduct, culture and ideology (Jackson, 2016) required for identity development in varying work situations.

References

Ali, A. (2015). 'Employers' biggest CV hates revealed in New College of the Humanities research. *The Independent*. Available at https://www.independent.co.uk/student/career-planning/getting-job/employers-biggest-cv-hates-revealed-in-new-college-of-the-humanities-research-10507365.html.

Brooks, S., Dobbins, K., Jon, J. A., Rawlinson, M., & Norman, R. I. (2014). Learning about learning outcomes: The student perspective. *Teaching in Higher Education, 19*(6), 721–733.

CBI/NUS. (2011). *Working towards your future: Making the most of your time in higher education.* Available at http://www.nus.org.uk/Global/CBINUSEmployability%20report_May%.

Daniels, J., & Brooker, J. (2014). Student identity development in higher education: Implications for graduate attributes and work-readiness. *Educational Research, 56*(1), 65–76.

Department of Business, Innovation and Skills. (2015). *Fulfilling our potential: Teaching excellence, social mobility and student choice*, London.

Department of Business, Innovation and Skills. (2016). *Success as a knowledge economy: Teaching excellence, social mobility and student choice*, London.

Dibben, L. (2017). VC conversation: Introduction to the living CV. In G. Baldwin (Ed.).

Dobbins, K., Brooks, S., Jon, J. A., Rawlinson, M., & Norman, R. I. (2016). Understanding and enacting learning outcomes: The academic's perspective. *Studies in Higher Education, 41*(7), 1217–1235.

Eraut, M. (2000). Non-formal learning and tacit knowledge in professional work. *British Journal of Educational Psychology, 70,* 113–136.

Eraut, M. (2004). Informal learning in the workplace. *Studies in Continuing Education, 26*(2), 247–273.

Evans, K., Guile, D., Harris, J., & Allan, H. (2010). Putting knowledge to work: A new approach. *Nurse Education Today, 30*(3), 245–251.

Evans, K., & Guile, D. (2012). Putting different forms of knowledge to work in practice. In J. Higgs, R. Barnett, S. Billett, M. Hutchings, & F. Trede (Eds.), *Practice-based education. Perspectives and strategies* (pp. 113–130). Rotterdam, Boston, Taipei: Sense Publishers.

HEFCE. (2018). *Learning gain in English higher education. Progress report March 2018/03.* Available at http://www.hefce.ac.uk/pubs/year/2018/201803/.

HESA. (2016). *Destination of leavers from higher education longitudinal survey.* Available at https://www.hesa.ac.uk/data-and-analysis/publications/long-destinations-2012-13.

Hussey, T., & Smith, P. (2003). The uses of learning outcomes. *Teaching in Higher Education, 8*(3), 357–368.

Hussey, T., & Smith, P. (2008). Learning outcomes: A conceptual analysis. *Teaching in Higher Education, 13*(1), 107–115.

Jackson, D. (2016). Re-conceptualising graduate employability: The importance of pre-professional identity. *Higher Education Research and Development, 35*(5), 924–939.

Kernohan, D. (2018). *Plenty ventured, but what was gained?* Available at https://wonkhe.com/blogs/plenty-ventured-but-what-was-gained/.

Klein, G. (1998). *Sources of power. How people make decisions.* Cambridge, London: The MIT Press.

Office of Students. (2018). *Learning gain.* Available at https://www.officeforstudents.org.uk/advice-and-guidance/teaching/learning-gain/.

Räty, H., Komulainen, K., Harvorsén, C., Nieminen, A., & Korhonen, M. (2018). University students' perceptions of their 'ability selves' and employability: A pilot study. *Nordic Journal of Studies in Educational Policy, 4*(2), 107–115.

Rothwell, A., Jewell, S., & Hardie, M. (2009). Self-perceived employability: Investigating the responses of post-graduate students. *Journal of Vocational Behaviour, 75*(2), 152–161.

Tomlinson, M. (2017). Student perceptions of themselves as 'consumers' of higher education'. *British Journal of Sociology of Education, 38*(4), 450–467.

Universities UK. (2015). *Supply and demand for higher level skills.* Available at https://www.universitiesuk.ac.uk/policy-and-analysis/reports/Pages/supply-and-demand-for-higher-level-skills.aspx.

Wenger, E. (1998). *Communities of practice. Learning, meaning and identity.* New York: Cambridge University Press.

Lisa Dibben (M.Ed.) is Head of Undergraduate Fashion at Solent University, Southampton, UK. Her first career was as a journalist and her first teaching experience within HE was in teaching, writing, and then managing journalism degrees. Her research interests centre on how and why students learn and providing the right environment, culture and motivation to enable that learning to take place. She is a Senior Fellow of the Higher Education Academy.

Dawn A. Morley (Ph.D.) is a post doctorate research fellow (learning and teaching) at Solent University, Southampton, UK. She has recently edited '*Enhancing employability in HE through work-based learning*' (Palgrave Macmillan, 2018). Her professional doctorate thesis examined how students learn on placement in real world settings and she has a particular interest in to how students add to their university experience to enhance their lifelong learning and work-readiness.

Chapter 29
Using an ePortfolio to Demonstrate Graduate-ness and Employability During Post-graduate Distance Education

C. J. van Staden

29.1 Introduction

Employers want to employ resilient graduates who can work effectively in challenging, ever-changing working environments; therefore, Higher Education (HE) should be responsible for transferring well-rounded, professionally mature graduates into 21st century work places (Devece, Peris-Ortiz, Merogó, & Fuster, 2015). In an attempt to assist HE in this regard, governments globally have identified sets of competencies to be developed to improve the employability of graduates (Australian Curriculum Assessment and Reporting Authority, 2013; Partnership for 21st Century Learning, 2007; Rieckmann, 2010). In the South African context, the South African Qualifications Authority (1997) identified seven Critical Crossfield Outcomes and five Developmental Outcomes that should guide all teaching and learning in HE. All graduates should be able to demonstrate these twelve competencies, namely, the ability to:

1. organise and manage self and activities responsively and effectively
2. use science and technology effectively and critically showing responsibility towards the environment and health of others
3. work effectively with others as members of groups, teams and a community
4. demonstrate an understanding of the world as a set of related systems recognising problem-solving contexts that do not exist in isolation
5. identify and solve problems autonomously; responses display the ability to make responsible decisions using critical and creative thinking
6. collect, analyse, organise, and critically evaluate information
7. communicate effectively using visual, mathematical, and language skills in modes of oral and written presentation
8. reflect on and explore learning strategies

C. J. van Staden (✉)
University of the Free State, Bloemfontein, South Africa
e-mail: christa@christavanstaden.com

© Springer Nature Switzerland AG 2019   459
A. Diver (ed.), *Employability via Higher Education: Sustainability as Scholarship*,
https://doi.org/10.1007/978-3-030-26342-3_29

9. explore educational and career opportunities
10. develop entrepreneurial opportunities
11. be cultural and aesthetically sensitive across social contexts, and
12. participate as a responsible citizen.

Such sets of competencies are known as key, transferable, generic, core, employable, and graduate competencies. To reduce confusion, the term 'key competency' is used within the rest of this chapter to refer to the South African identified employable competencies. The question that I needed to answer in relation to a post-graduate module on Instructional Techniques and Multi Media in Adult Education (INTMAEU) offered by the University of South Africa (Unisa) was: *'How can these key competencies be developed during distance education?'*

29.2   The Context

The University of South Africa is a mega-institution catering primarily for distance education. Most of the modules offered are characterised by large numbers of students. Students do not attend classes; all study materials are provided during registration and students are required to submit assignments to qualify for the final examination. As with global contexts, the success rate of Unisa is lower than those of the four largest contact universities. This is a matter of concern since Unisa enrols annually almost twice as many students (300,000) as the four largest contact universities combined (180,000). Due to the nature of distance education, Unisa relies heavily upon summative assessments in the form of year-end examinations.[1] In respect of the INTMAEU module, it was previously almost impossible to assess the students' ability to use technology and multimedia effectively during their final written examination, therefore, none of their assignments were designed to provide them with opportunities to demonstrate their knowledge, skills, and techniques. Four assignments were designed to assess subject content knowledge, but the students were only required to submit one of these to qualify for the final examination. A high number of students did not submit the three other assignments, avoiding personalised feedback that could have been used to prepare for the examinations. It was also a matter of concern that many students simply dropped out before the final examination. ePortfolios were then piloted within the INTMAEU-curriculum, to replace the final examination.

Globally, many HE institutions are using eportfolios to assess subject-related content knowledge, skills, and techniques (Hager, 2012; Moore, 2016; Penny-Light,

---

[1] Since taking over halfway through the year, I was able to identify problems that needed to be addressed. A month after I was appointed, I was invited to pilot e-portfolios within the INTMAEU-curriculum to replace the final examination. For example, many of the 2104 cohort failed due to a misinterpretation of assignments: the 2015 cohort were required to improve their assignments based on feedback, and to upload both the assessed and improved versions of their learning tasks into their e-portfolios.

2016). Based upon the successful integration of eportfolios into curricula, the Association for American Colleges and Universities (AAC&U) added eportfolios in June 2016 as the eleventh high impact (Watson, Kuh, Rhodes, Penny Light, & Chen, 2016). According to Miller, Rocconi, and Dumford (2018), high impact practices (HIPs) provide students with a career-related advantage through key skill development, engaging learning opportunities and generating 'stories' for potential employers. A learning-oriented approach to assessment has afforded students more opportunities to tell their stories to potential employers.

29.3 A Learning-Oriented Approach to Assessment

The past two centuries have been characterised by a dramatic shift from summative assessment towards competency-based techniques that foster learning and professional growth (Chertoff, 2015). According to Carless (2007), the father of a learning-oriented approach to assessment, this methodology is based upon three principles, namely that:

- learning tasks rather than assessment tasks are designed
- students should be individually and collectively actively involved in assessments, and
- feedback be provided in a timely manner to provide opportunities to improve current as well as future learning.[2]

29.3.1 Learning Tasks Instead of Assessment Tasks

When the focus shifts from assessment tasks to learning tasks, new frameworks need to be developed to enhance lifelong learning and to promote participatory strategies (Rodriguez-Gomez, Quesada-Serra, & Ibarra-Saltz, 2016). According to the Partnership for 21st century skills (2007), it is important to facilitate innovative learning methods that integrate the use of supportive technologies, inquiry and problem-based approaches, and higher order thinking skills. During the design of the 14 learning activities, the development of subject-related content knowledge, skills, and techniques was key, as was that of the twelve key competencies. The competency-statements are broad. Categories identified by the Australian Curriculum Assessment and Reporting Authority's (2013) were used to organize the South African key competencies (van Staden 2016b). Some of the competencies fitted partially within more than one category; therefore, it may seem as if more than twelve competencies have been identified (Table 29.1).

---

[2]See further Van Staden (2016a, b).

Table 29.1 Framework for developing South African key competencies

Life roles	Ways of working	Tools for working	Ways of thinking
• Self-directed learner • Responsible citizen in a global world • Education and career planning skills	• Problem-solving skills • Analytic capabilities • Judgement-making skills • Decision-making skills • Creative expression • Teamworking skills • Ability to respond to the creative work of others	• Use of language, visual and mathematical skills to express self in written or oral communication • Ability to use technology as a learning tool • Ability to use technology as a tool for work • Entrepreneurial skills	• Broad-system thinking skills • Critical thinking skills • Creative thinking skills • Exploration of a variety of learning strategies • Sensitivity across cultural and aesthetical contexts • Metacognitive skills (reflection on the efficiency of learning strategies)

This framework ensured multiple opportunities for the development of key competencies as the students were completing the learning tasks (van Staden, 2016a, b).

29.3.2   Opportunities for Self- and Peer Assessment

The use of eportfolios supported peer-learning through co-operation, communication and the giving and receiving of peer feedback. Students were required to complete an online self-assessment test, but they also had to engage in peer review, via:

- the marked assignments of two peers and provide feedback for improvement
- each page of the e-portfolios and provide feedback for improvement
- the completed e-portfolios and provide feedback for improvement.

29.3.3   Improvement of Feedback

According to Chertoff (2015), eportfolios develop into high impact practices if the assessments are continuous, frequent, criteria-based and developmental. Submission of these assignments allows for frequent, continuous feedback, and students were required to use the feedback to improve their assignments.

29.3.4 Developing Self-regulated Learners

The greatest challenge in HE is to develop self-regulated learners (Mathias, Bruce, & Newton, 2013), therefore, two strategies were used to facilitate the development of self-regulating skills. Firstly, the students had to use a set assessment plan and the planning function of Mahara (the eportfolios system) to plan their learning journeys. These schedules had to be updated as soon as they had completed a learning task. Secondly, a structure was provided for the completion of each assignment to ensure that the students developed their eportfolios over a period of time (see Fig. 29.1).

29.4 Case Study: One Student's ePortfolio

Student X was a top-achiever, a 30 years old, white, married, and female. Although she was a South African citizen, she was regarded as an international candidate as she was teaching abroad. She used the planning function of *Mahara* effectively, demonstrating self-regulating skills during the process, with most assignments submitted

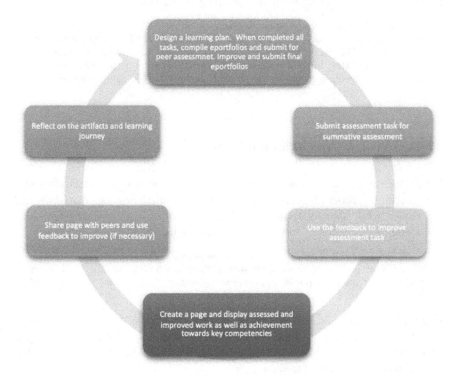

Fig. 29.1 Structure for developing eportfolios (Van Staden, 2016b)

long before the due date, demonstrating (and reflecting upon) all twelve competencies throughout the year.

29.4.1 Science and Technology Skills

The module aimed to equip students with the knowledge, skills, and techniques needed to use technology and multimedia effectively in HE. One assignment required students to develop a lesson plan and present the lesson. As Student X later reflected:

> I was reminded of the fact that preparing a lesson is only half of the work. Reflecting on what works and doesn't work and trying to improve on teaching methods, material, uses of technology, and techniques is a crucial aspect of the education process.

Another assignment required students to use a variety of technologies and multimedia within their classrooms, and they then had to provide feedback on the efficiency thereof. Student X's work demonstrated that she had used colourful presentations, a *WebQuest,* self-designed images, and videos to present subject content and assess her students' knowledge. She also used Adobe Photoshop, Adobe Premier, Microsoft PowerPoint, and Microsoft Word to create images and videos:

> Teaching students of mixed proficiencies is common in my field. It can be challenging to develop, deliver, and assess content, as well as to select methods and techniques to suit such differing levels. Many of the students could barely speak English; some were fluent. As you can imagine, it is almost impossible to meet the needs of such a disparate level. The use of technology and media in education is an absolute necessity that facilitates the process.

29.4.2 Visual, Oral, and Language Skills

For another assignment, students had to implement four teaching methods within their teaching practice. Student X submitted a video demonstrating her skills and techniques, while also displaying her ability to use visual, oral and language skills to communicate effectively in a virtual learning environment:

> … this was a valuable experience for me. This assignment will be extremely beneficial for me since I can use it to demonstrate my skills to future employers. I think it can show my ability to craft and develop lessons, as well as my willingness to try new techniques and methods. In future, I hope to create more e-classes.

In a further assignment, students had to prepare a paper on the use of technology during distance education to be delivered at a conference. The presentation was limited to 5 slides over 5 min; therefore, Student X limited her discussion to audio, video, and computer-based technologies:

> The presentation allowed me to use varied skills together to research and present information. These skills will prove practical for me in the future as I continue to turn my presentations

into videos. I designed all the images in the presentation from scratch using PowerPoint and produced the final video from the PowerPoint presentation. I prefer to create the pictures I need wherever possible because of copyright concerns. It also allows me a creative outlet in my teaching practice.

29.4.3   Problem-Solving Skills

Student X displayed problem-solving skills in most of her reflections, analyzed the learning tasks, identified problems, and provided solutions using critical and creative thinking skills. On designing assessment tasks she noted:

> Too often people focus on assessing students in order to provide them with marks and ignore the broader uses of data. Assessment should be viewed as a way of gathering information to improve the education process. This information comes from various sources: assessments which establish what students know and have to master yet, reflections on teaching practice and methods, and appraisals of material, curricula, and educational institutes.

It was difficult to teach some students whose levels of proficiency in the English Language varied, but again, a solution was provided:

> One way of dealing with varying student levels in the same class is to grade activities. There are assignments that every student has to complete: it might be too easy for some, too difficult for others, and suitable for the average student. The students complete the tasks that are appropriate for their own level. This allows advanced students to attempt more challenging activities and the lower-level students to complete work at their stage of language acquisition. This can be aimed at individuals, or pairs and groups of students of equal proficiency. This process was facilitated and enhanced by the use of technology.

29.4.4   Analytical Skills

Students were also asked to complete an online self-assessment test. Student X's reflections upon this assignment also showcased meta-cognitive skills:

> The self-assessment test enabled me to reflect critically on my learning journey and integrate past, present and potential learning. In addition to this, I was able to connect the different aspects of my learning experience, particularly the inclusion of learning that has taken place outside of the traditional formal learning environment.

She had learned from her mistakes via trial and error:

> I examined how to integrate what I have learned in my daily practice and reflected on what would be useful from my studies into my teaching. It was valuable for me to reflect on how my work experience has enhanced my studies.

Students also had to participate in online fora discussions, and create a wiki. As Student X observed:

...the issue of appropriate netiquette needs to be raised. It is discouraging when people do not acknowledge a person's post, and merely rattle off their own opinion without engaging in real discussion. Students need to be reminded of appropriate behaviours when discussing topics. Just because a discussion is online, does not mean that normal polite conversational conventions should be ignored! A list of do's and don'ts regarding behaviour in the forum would be beneficial, especially for those who are unfamiliar with standard netiquette. Related to the issue of poor netiquette, is the problem of shallow posts that do not demonstrate the application of course content with enough detail or depth. Similar, posts that merely say 'good point' without adding anything further to the discussion should be discouraged.

Students similarly had to co-create an INTMAEU-glossary to displays five of the concepts that they had learned during the year. Although Student X did so, she did not regard this as a collaborative assignment:

Despite the fact that this was meant to be a group project, I did not really feel like I was working with anyone at all. I researched five words, added them under the glossary section on myUnisa, without consulting and discussing it with anyone. It is good to benefit from the work shared by others, but I have a feeling that I might end up referring to published work that has gone through a more rigorous editing and checking process. In concept, this assignment has a lot of potential. In practice, I do not know how useful the information shared will be.[3]

29.4.5   Establishing Co-operative Base Groups

Academic results clearly improve when students establish co-operative base groups (Johnson, Johnson, & Holubec, 2008; Lubbe, 2015; van Staden, 2018). One of the eportfolio assignments required students to use social networking[4] to establish co-operative base groups during the year.[5] Social network analysis was used to investigate the establishment of co-operative base groups during the first six months of the year. Based on Student X's (I3[6]) central position in this social network (Fig. 29.2) she played a leading role within her own base group (van Staden, 2019).

It is interesting to note that the students expanded their relationships across the boundaries of their own base groups. Eight members from other base groups (yellow) used the opportunity to form links with Student X during the first six months of the academic year and she stated: 'background experience working in a variety of countries has enabled *me* to be flexible and adaptive, and open to different ways of completing tasks.'

---

[3] Although this assignment was designed to provide opportunities to co-create a glossary, it could still be done without developing team working skills. Therefore, this assignment needs to be improved upon or regarded as an individual assignment.

[4] Namely, https://arend.co (accessed 09.12.18).

[5] Student X was actively involved in her base group but could not subsequently reflect upon the efficiency or otherwise of this learning strategy, as a new lecturer cancelled the assignment.

[6] The letter refers to the base group, the number given to one of 7 members of the group.

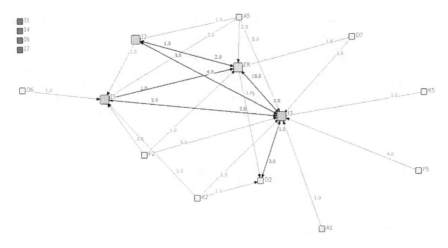

Fig. 29.2 Cooperative base group I (Student X = I3)

29.4.6 Meta-cognitive Skills

Students also had to use the blog-function of *Mahara* to write self-reflective blogs during the course of the year. This was deemed to be the most valuable aspect of the course:

> I have a personal preference for experiential learning, which proposes that learning occurs through experience, specifically learning through reflection on doing. It is not enough to have the learning experience alone, it I also necessary to reflect upon that experience. This is an active process, in which learners incorporate what has been learned. Writing these reflections on my learning experience has enabled me to clearly integrate the learning that I have accomplished with my teaching practice.

Based on her conclusions, she will apply what she has learned in her own teaching practice: 'In future, I will incorporate this kind of reflective practice into my teaching, since adult learners will benefit greatly from assessing their learning.'

29.4.7 Self-directedness

Most of these assignments were designed to provide opportunities to demonstrate self-directedness. Students had to display the assessed and reviewed assignments on their eportfolio pages, but could add videos, images, and other media to describe their learning journeys. Websites such as coggle.it and wordle.it were accessed to create content for the pages. Students had a choice: they could either compare two of the three learning theories described within their prescribed text books, or they could compare one of the described theories with a different theory that had not been outlined or explained within their prescribed text books. Student X directed her own learning by opting to do the latter, comparing Behaviourism with Experiential Learning:

> Examining various learning theories related to adult education is a crucial step in ensuring that I keep up to date, both with well-established and the latest paradigms, in order to improve my teaching process. It is too easy to get into a rut and merely do what is simplest or most familiar. I have the responsibility to improve my teaching practice and contribute to existing educational knowledge bases. Familiarity with learning theories is a necessary foundation.[7]

29.4.8 Broad System-Thinking Skills

Reflections on their own assignments provided further insights into the level of development of this key competency (van Staden, 2016b). As Student X observed:

> 'Completing the Instructional Techniques and Multimedia module was a lot like piecing together a jigsaw puzzle. At first, everything was a jumble of vaguely connected colours and shapes. As I worked through the material, however, I began to recognise the patterns and how the different aspects of the course connected into an integrated whole. This eportfolio showcases my learning journey and is a powerful way to demonstrate my ability to fuse instructional techniques and media.'

29.4.9 Responsible Citizenship

The ability to use intellectual, social and personal resources, to participate as active citizens who contribute to economic development and who flourish as individuals in a diverse and changing world (James & Pollard, 2011) is an important skill. Two online forum posts serve to illustrate the development of this skill:

> I would like to agree with your point, Student Z, about an equilibrium between approaches being needed. As you have noted, sometimes it is necessary to convey information. Students can be self-directed and find out information on their own from a wide variety of sources. However, it can be useful to have someone provide you with guidelines. There is much so with the information available it is difficult to navigate between sources. We cannot ignore the value of the human factor.

> Student Y, I like your illustration of theory and practice. I suppose it is because I already tend to think the wo aspects need to be integrated to be effective. Particularly with adult learners, as Knowles highlights, learner's readiness to learn needs to be considered, and they need to understand how what they are learning will be practical to them. When it comes to your teaching, how do you integrate theory and practice? For example, in my lessons,

---

[7]She added that '...using these two theories in conjunction with each other can create a more holistic learning environment. The Behaviourist learning perspective focuses on external, observable changes, whereas experiential learning emphasises the internalisation of and reflection on the learning journey. Using these two frameworks together can enable integration of objective and subjective aspects of the learning experience.

I usually begin with the theory (usually information and orientation activities) and then provide the students with practice through the application and evaluation activities. What teaching techniques do you employ to integrate theory and practice?

29.4.10   Education and Career Planner

Although none of the assignments focused on the development of this key competency, Student X still demonstrated this key competency in several of her reflections:

> It is important to bring new strategies, theories, methodologies and practices into my teaching repertoire. I function best in situations where I can plan and execute lessons effectively, although flexibility and a recognition of the nature of my students play an essential role in creating frameworks that enhance the learning process.

On the value of her eportfolio for educational and career purposes, she noted that:

> In addition to academic work I have completed for this module, I can demonstrate the skills necessary to integrate technology and media effectively as well as the ability to employ a variety of learning theories, instructional methods, and assessment tools in the planning, implementing and evaluating of my lessons.

29.4.11   Cultural and Aesthetic Sensitivity

Student X's eportfolio together with her interactions in the learning environment demonstrated her sensitivity across various social contexts, for example in respect of those who do not have access to technologies:

> I think technology can revolutionise education, and our access to information, which can transform our lives. It frightens me how far ahead those with access to technology are over those who do not have access to even basic things like a computer in the classroom. The gap is only going to increase. I know technology isn't the only aspect of learning, teaching, and experience, but we are becoming increasingly reliant on all kinds of technology. It is so important that we consider ways to reduce the ever-increasing gap in all societies around the world, and how technology can build bridges which can improve lives.

29.4.12   Entrepreneurial Skills

Although no formal assignment was designed to assess the development of entrepreneurial skills, this competency was also demonstrated by Student X, who started a *WordPress*-blog where she publicly reflected on her learning journeys. Based on the feedback she gets, she shares valuable information. She can also monetize her site as it already hosts advertisements.

29.5 Conclusion

Student X's eportfolio demonstrated clearly that she had gained the knowledge, skills, and techniques to effectively use technology and multimedia to teach at institutions for Higher Education. She was able to use the blog, forum, glossary and wiki very effectively to enhance her own learning. During this experiential learning process, she quickly identified problems that her own students might experience when, for example, she requires them to use these functions: she then provided solutions to improve the learning process for them. Her reflections demonstrated all twelve key competencies that must be developed in South African HE. Her eportfolio can be used to evidence graduate-ness and enhanced employability. She later reflected on her learning journey:

> I hope it does not sound boastful, but I feel proud of my portfolio. Last year I was a bit tired of everything by the end. But after looking at it with fresh eyes, I can see that I came a long way. My first assignments were a lot weaker than the improved versions. I don't think about old essays as much once they're done, but with the eportfolio I reflect, revise, and improve at every step.

Based upon this detailed case study, three recommendations for the improvement of practice can be made. Firstly, it is no longer sufficient to use only prescribed text books: tutors should challenge self-directed students to find extra resources beyond those that are prescribed in course reading lists, and to then evaluate them, and apply the knowledge, skills, and techniques that they have found within their own teaching practices. Secondly, it is no longer sufficient to use a mark or percentage to report on the outcomes of a module: it is now absolutely necessary to report on the development of employability skills as they are acquired during post-secondary education (Hinton, Towell, MacFarlane, & Refling, 2017). Lastly, it is recommended that HE and employers be informed of the rich data created during the development of learning-oriented eportfolios. This data can assist HE providers in understanding which key competencies need to be developed or enhanced further. Employers can also use the eportfolios of job candidates to select the right person for the job vacancy. ePortfolios will underpin and develop into high impact practices if the assessments within them are valid, reliable, practical, and have an impact on teaching, learning and indeed students' motivations for learning (Assessment Reform Group, 2002; Carless, 2007; Knight, 2002). Students should be reminded often that learning is not a race, but a longer term journey. The destination may be predetermined, but they still must pause and reflect upon their own learning to identify any gaps in their skills, techniques, or knowledge: these must be addressed to enable them to complete their journey, as Student X confirms:

> An eportfolio is truly the best way to combine media and instruction. The diploma I have received is valuable, but what is more important is the ability to do something practical. If I had merely regurgitated the textbook in parrot fashion in the exam, I would have a degree, but no skills.

References

Assessment Reform Group. (2002). *The role of teachers in assessment of learning*. London. Retrieved August 21, 2016, from http://www.nuffieldfoundation.org/sites/default/files/files/The-role-of-teachers-in-the-assessment-of-learning.pdf.

Australian Curriculum Assessment and Reporting Authority. (2013). General capabilities in the Australian Curriculum: Personal and social capability, January 27. Retrieved September 3, 2018, from www.acara.edu.au.

Carless, D. (2007). Learning-oriented assessment: Conceptual bases and practical implications. *Innovations in Education and Teaching International, 44*(1), 57–66.

Chertoff, J. (2015). Global differences in electronic portfolio utilization—A review of the literature and research implications. *Journal of Educational Evaluation for Health Professions, 12*, 15.

Devece, C., Peris-Ortiz, M., Merogó, J. M., & Fuster, V. (2015). Linking the development of teamwork and communication skills in higher education. In M. Peris-Ortiz & L. J.M.M. (Eds.), *Sustainable learning in higher education: Developing competencies for the global market place* (pp. 63–171). New York: Springer.

Hager, L. L. (2012). Wading into the technology pool: Learning E-Portfolios in higher education. In *ICICTE 2012 Proceedings* (pp. 444–454). Retrieved from http://search.ebscohost.com/login. aspx?direct=true&db=eue&AN=85747960&site=ehost-live&scope=site.

Hinton, C., Towell, J., MacFarlane, A., & Refling, E. (2017). *Student success EPortfolio: Student, faculty and employer perspectives on the value of EPortfolios in assessing the development of essential employability*. Toronto: The Higher Education Quality Council of Ontario.

James, M., & Pollard, A. (2011). TLRP's ten principles for effective pedagogy: Rationale, development, evidence, argument and impact. *Research Papers in Education, 26*(3), 275–328.

Johnson, D. W., Johnson, R. T., & Holubec, E. J. (2008). *New circles of learning: Cooperation in the classroom and school* (Vol. 4). Interaction Book Company: Edina, MN.

Knight, P. (2002). Summative assessment in higher education: Practices in disarray. *Studies in Higher Education, 27*(3).

Lubbe, A. (2015). *Cooperative base groups in higher Education: The impact on life Sciences students'self-directed learning readiness*. Potchefstroom: North-West University.

Mathias, J., Bruce, M., & Newton, D. P. (2013). Challenging the Western Stereotype: Do Chinese International Foundation Students Learn by Rote? *Research in Post-Compulsay Education, 18*(3), 221–238.

Miller, A. L., Rocconi, L. M., & Dumford, A. D. (2018). Focus on the finish line: Does high-impact practice participation influence career plans and early job attainment? *Higher Education, 75*(3), 489–506.

Moore, J. (2016). *ePortfolios as high-impact practice*. Retrieved August 20, 2016. From http://www.centreforengagedlearning.org/eportfolioashigh-impact-practice.

Partnership for 21st century learning. (2007). *Framework for 21st century learning*. Retrieved November 13, 2018, from http://www.p21.org/our-work/p21-framework.

Penny-Light, T. (2016). ePortfolios: Harnessing the "evidence of experience" for authentic records of achievement. *The AAEEBL EPortfolio Review, 1*(1), 5–12.

Rieckmann, M. (2010). Future-oriented higher education: Which key competencies should be fostered through university teaching and learning? *Futures, 44*(2), 127–135.

Rodriguez-Gomez, G., Quesada-Serra, V., & Ibarra-Saltz, M. (2016). Learning-oriented assessment. *Assessment and Evauation in Higher Education, 41*(1), 35–52.

South African Qualifications Authority. (1997). Proceedings and decisions of SAQA. *SAQA Bulletin, 1*(1), 5–10.

van Staden, C. J. (2016a). 'n Leergeoriënteerde raamwerk vir e-portefeuljeontwikkeling in afstandonderwys. *Suid-Afrikaanse Tydskrif Vir Natuurwetenskap En Tegnologie, 35*(1), 12.

van Staden, C. J. (2016b). A learning-oriented framewok for integrating eportfolios in a postgraduate module in distance education. *AAEEBL EPortfolio Review, 1*(1), 36–55.

van Staden, C. J. (2018). WhatsApp? Die ontwikkeling van'n positief-interafhanklike e-praktyknetwerke tydens die samestelling van e-portefeuljes in afstandhoëronderwys. *LitNet Akademies (Opvoedkunde), 15*(2), 350–396.

van Staden, C. J. (2019). 'n Netwerkperspektief op die gebruik van koöperatiewe basisgroepe as tegniek om samewerking tydens afstandhoëronderwys te bevorder. *Litnet Akademies (Opvoedkunde), 16*(1), 421–472.

Watson, C. E., Kuh, G. D., Rhodes, T., Penny Light, T., & Chen, H. L. (2016). The eleventh high impact practice. *International Journal of EPortfolio, 6*(2), 65–69.

Christa van Staden (Ph.D.) is a research fellow in the Department of South African Sign Language and Deaf Studies of the University of the Free State, South Africa. Previous positions included secondary school teacher, senior lecturer (Education and Instructional Techniques and Multimedia in Adult Education), and post-doctoral fellow. Her research interests include Social Network Analysis, Distance Education, Adult Education and how technology can be used to improve teaching and learning within secondary and HE settings as well as in distance education contexts. Her research papers have been published in various academic journals and presented at several South African and international conferences. She served on the editorial board of the AePR (*AAEEBL ePortfolio Review*) and was managing editor of its fourth issue. She also serves as review editor for several South African and international journals.

Chapter 30
Developing Future Reading and Literacy Specialists in a Fully Online Masters of Reading Education Program

Kelli Bippert⊙, **Bethanie Pletcher and Corinne Valadez**

30.1 Introduction

As online education becomes increasingly common in higher education, university instructors are challenged by the shift from traditional face-to-face instruction to interactions mediated by computer technology. Instructors with an educational philosophy grounded in socio-constructivist theory face tensions between a seemingly impersonal online environment, and the social nature that embodies how learning occurs. The problem addressed here is, *'how do universities develop effective educational professionals through a fully online masters of reading program?'* A socially constructed learning environment includes collaboration and opportunities for social interactions for students to effectively learn (Vygotsky, 1978). Socio-constructivists believe in four basic assumptions of constructivism:

1. Knowledge is not passive, but active
2. Cognition is an adaptive process based on a person's environment
3. Cognition organizes and makes sense of experience
4. Knowing comes from our biology, and social and cultural language-based interactions (Doolittle, 1999, p. 1).

For online instruction to be effective, Doolittle (1999) maintained that certain principles should apply, which include authentic learning experiences, social interactions, students' contributions to their own individual experiences and perspectives, and instructors having a facilitator role in the course (Doolittle, 1999). Even within

K. Bippert (✉) · B. Pletcher · C. Valadez
Texas A&M University-Corpus Christi, Corpus Christi, TX, USA
e-mail: Kelli.Bippert@tamucc.edu

B. Pletcher
e-mail: bethanie.pletcher@tamucc.edu

C. Valadez
e-mail: Corinne.valadez@tamucc.edu

© Springer Nature Switzerland AG 2019
A. Diver (ed.), *Employability via Higher Education: Sustainability as Scholarship*,
https://doi.org/10.1007/978-3-030-26342-3_30

an online learning environment, social interaction between students and instructors require a blending of different teaching techniques to integrate social interactions, as well as adapt to different learning styles (Yoon, 2003). For example, to improve instructor presence, and provide students with authentic application of new learning, additional online tools can be provided to make learning relevant, encourage synchronous student interaction and collaboration, and facilitate discussions of multiple perspectives based on students' individual experiences and contexts. The fully-online Masters of Reading program described here was designed to not only fit a socio-constructivist model of teaching and learning but was also required to meet specific national and state standards. Additionally, these standards demand that the graduate students develop skills that involve experiences and instructor facilitation in four areas, namely, literacy coaching, leadership, literacy advocacy, and practicum.

30.2 Standards for Literacy Professionals

Based on the International Literacy Association 2017 Standards for the Preparation of Literacy Professionals (SLP Standards) (International Literacy Association, 2018), teachers who enter the field as reading or literacy specialists are expected to be provided with instruction and support in professional skill areas before receiving their literacy specialist certification. The standards (summarized in Table 30.1) focus on five professional skills to be developed by a graduate student studying to become a reading or literacy specialist: content mastery, practicum, coaching, leadership, and advocacy. While some of the standards and strands within each of these are easily supported in a fully online program, many of them proved to be a challenge, particularly in the areas of coaching, leadership, advocacy, and practicum. Our Masters of Reading program, therefore, was challenged in a bid to provide this support. The masters programs described in this chapter highlight the instructional strategies that our institution used within online instruction to meet these needs.

30.3 Meeting Reading and Literacy Specialist Standards

In developing the coursework for our university's Masters of Reading program, standards set by two organizations needed consideration: the International Literacy Association's Standards for the Preparation of Literacy Professional (SLP Standards) (2018), and requirements from the Texas State Board of Educator Certification (SBEC). The Standards for the Literacy Professional provided a national and professional standard for the preparation of Reading Specialist, while SBEC provided the requirements necessary for certification in Texas. SBEC, the certification board created in 1995 by the Texas Legislature, "oversees all aspects of the preparation, certification, and standards of conduct of public school educators" (Texas Education Agency, 2018). ILA (2018) identified key shifts in the roles of the Literacy Specialist.

Table 30.1 SLP Standards for the Preparation of Literacy Professionals

Standard 1:

Foundational knowledge

Candidates demonstrate knowledge of major theoretical, conceptual, historical, and evidence-based foundations of literacy and language, the ways in which they interrelate, and the role of the reading/literacy specialist in schools

Standard 2:

Curriculum and instruction

Candidates use foundational knowledge to design literacy curricula to meet needs of learners, especially those who have trouble with literacy; design, implement, and evaluate small-group and individual evidence-based literacy instruction for learners; collaborate with teachers to implement effective literacy practices

Standard 3:

Assessment and evaluation

Candidates understand, select, and use valid, reliable, fair, and appropriate assessment tools to screen, diagnose, and measure student literacy achievement; inform instruction and evaluate interventions; assist teachers in their understanding and use of assessment results; advocate for appropriate literacy practices to relevant stakeholders

Standard 4:

Diversity and equity

Candidates demonstrate knowledge of research, relevant theories, pedagogies, and essential concepts of diversity and equity; demonstrate an understanding of themselves and others as cultural beings; create classrooms and schools that are inclusive and affirming; advocate for equity at school, district, and community levels

Standard 5:

Learners and the literacy environment

Candidates meet the developmental needs of all learners and collaborate with school personnel to use a variety of print and digital materials to engage and motivate all learners; integrate digital technologies in appropriate, safe, and effective ways; foster a positive climate that supports a literacy-rich learning environment

Standard 6:

Professional learning and leadership

Candidates demonstrate the ability to be reflective literacy professionals, who apply their knowledge of adult learning to work collaboratively with colleagues; demonstrate their leadership and facilitation skills; advocate on behalf of teachers, students, families, and communities

Standard 7:

Practicum/clinical experiences

Candidates complete supervised, integrated, extended practical/clinical experiences that include intervention work with students and working with their peers and experienced colleagues; practica include ongoing experiences in school-based setting(s); supervision includes observation and ongoing feedback by qualified supervisors

Adapted from "Standards for the Preparation of Literacy Professionals 2017," by the International Literacy Association, retrieved November 5, 2017, from https://www.literacyworldwide.org/get-resources/standards/standards-2017. Copyright 2018 by International Literacy Association

The roles include Reading/Literacy Specialist, Literacy Coach, and Literacy Coordinators/Supervisors. According to the International Literacy Association (ILA), the primary role of the reading or literacy specialist is to work with "students experiencing difficulties with reading and writing" (p. 3). The literacy coach's primary role is to "work with teachers to improve literacy instruction" (p. 4). SBEC requirements for certification as a Reading Specialist includes a Masters of Reading, or masters degree in a closely related field, 160 practicum hours equally split between elementary and secondary classes, three years teaching experience, and passing the state certification exam. Additionally, these practicum hours require supervision by a certified Reading Specialist.

Whilst some SLP Standards and SBEC requirements are more easily addressed using online instruction, many of the components within the SLP Standards require the use of additional online tools to facility collaboration, peer interactions, and meaningful and explicit feedback on assignments and projects. The SPL standards focus on the development of literacy leaders in four areas: coaching, leadership, advocacy, and practicum. The individual components, summarized in Table 30.2, are addressed below.

30.4 Meeting the Socio-Constructivist Needs of Literacy Professionals: Practicum

One challenge we faced was how to assign the required practicum amongst the courses in the Masters of Reading Program. Practicum hours were defined as 'hours candidates spent observing and actively working with students and teachers.' Once the SLP Standards (ILA, 2018) and SBEC requirements were reviewed, it was determined how 160 practicum hours in a fully online program would look. Faculty reviewed the required courses for the Masters of Reading and assigned required practicum hours to each course, except for Foundations of Research and Advanced Literacy Seminar (see Table 30.3), both of which culminate with a completed action research study. The courses are demanding, and therefore practicum hours are not included.

The required number of practicum hours for each course range between 10 to 40. The Practicum and Supervision course is a six-hour course, and therefore has substantially more practicum hours assigned to it, while several other courses have fewer practicum hours since they are only taught during summer sessions. In this way, the 160 h of practicum required by SBEC were distributed in a logical fashion across many of the required Masters of Reading Program courses.

Table 30.2 Course support for SLP standards

Skill	SLP standard	Online courses
Coach	Standard 2: Curriculum and instruction	READ 5395: Leadership & literacy READ 5697: Reading practicum
	Standard 3: Assessment and evaluation	READ 5395: Leadership & literacy READ 5697: Reading practicum
	Standard 6: Professional learning and leadership	READ 5395: Leadership & literacy READ 5697: Reading practicum
	Standard 7: Practicum/clinical experiences	READ 5395: Leadership & literacy READ 5371: Diagnosis & correction of reading problems READ 5697: Reading practicum
Leader	Standard 3: Assessment and evaluation	READ 5697: Reading practicum READ 5371: Diagnosis & correction of reading problems
	Standard 5: Learners and the literacy environment	READ 5310: Emergent literacy READ 5371: Diagnosis & correction of reading problems READ 5350: Multicultural literacy READ 5381: Advanced children's & adolescent literature READ 5395: Leadership & literacy
	Standard 6: Professional learning and leadership	READ 5395: Leadership & literacy READ 5697: Reading practicum
Advocate	Standard 3: Assessment and evaluation	READ 5371: Diagnosis & correction of reading problems READ 5697: Reading practicum
	Standard 4: Diversity and equity	READ 5350: Multicultural literacy
	Standard 5: Learners and the literacy environment	READ 5395: Leadership & literacy
	Standard 6: Professional learning and leadership	READ 5345: Stages & standards of reading
Practicum	Standard 7: Practicum/clinical experiences	READ 5310: Emergent literacy READ 5392: Psycho-sociolinguistics & reading READ 5371: Diagnosis & correction of reading problems READ 5369: Reading & writing in the content area READ 5396: Literacy research seminar READ 5697: Reading practicum

Table 30.3 Masters of reading courses and practicum hours

Course	Course name	Practicum hours	SPR A	SPR B	SS I	SS II	FALL A	FALL B
READ 5345 READ 6345	Stages and standards	15						X
READ 5369 READ 6369	Content area reading strategies	15[a]						X
READ 5350 READ 6350	Multicultural literacy	10[a]			X			
READ 5371 READ 6371	Diagnosis	15[b]	X					
READ 5372 READ 6372	Assessments	10[b]				X		
READ 5697 READ 6697	Practicum and supervision	40[b]		X				
READ 5392 READ 6392	Psych-soc linguistics	15					X	
READ 5395 READ 6395	Leadership and literacy	20[b]	X					
READ 5396	Advanced literacy seminar (Capstone)	0						X
READ 5310 READ 6310	Emergent literacy	10				X		
READ 5381 READ 6380	Advanced children's and adolescent literature	10[a]			X			
EDFN 5301	Foundations of research	0					X	

[a]Secondary
[b]Split between secondary & elementary

30.5   Coaching Experiences

Crucial to the role of the specialized literacy professional, especially those serving as a Reading Specialist, literacy coach, or other literacy supervisor, is a thorough understanding of not only the foundational knowledge of reading processes (Calo, Sturtevant, & Kopfman, 2015; ILA, 2018; L'Allier, Elish-Piper, & Bean, 2010), but also how to work with other educators to build their capacity in literacy instruction by working as a literacy leader (Allen, 2016; Galloway & Leseaux, 2014; L'Allier et al. 2010; Risko & Vogt, 2016). This section addresses these areas by providing examples of the ways in which instructors might meet relevant SLP Standards. A discussion of how to build candidates' foundational knowledge and literacy leadership skills follows, along with information about accomplishing this in a 100% online degree program.

30.5.1   Foundational Knowledge for Literacy Coaching

In a course entitled *Leadership and Literacy*, students are required to write a paper about a well-known literacy leader. Calo et al. (2015) posited that coaches need to position themselves as learners to effectively lead others. This assignment therefore serves several purposes: (1) candidates are able to devote time to one particular facet of a large area of study in order to build their foundational knowledge; (2) candidates become familiar with one person's work by reading what they have written; (3) candidates immerse themselves in one or two areas of literacy by focusing on what the literacy leader is known for, and (4) candidates are provided with a strong model of one form literacy leadership might take. There are several pieces of literature that we encourage candidates to read as part of their study of the reading process. Alvermann, Unrau, and Ruddell's (2013) Theoretical Models and Processes of Reading is a large collection of seminal works. The SLP Standards (2017) document includes exhaustive lists of sources of important literature on topics related to Standard 1, which requires candidates to "demonstrate knowledge of the major theoretical, conceptual, historical, and evidence-based components of reading" (p. 34).

Students choose from a selection of literacy leaders (provided by the instructor) who are listed in the Reading Hall of Fame or are considered to be a leader in reading and/or other areas of literacy. The list includes those leaders who have made significant contributions to the field of reading instruction by reporting on seminal research studies. This 'limited choice' allows some measure of freedom yet ensures that students are exposed to foundational readings before finishing their degree programmes. Students then use the university's online library services to locate salient pieces (i.e. a minimum of five articles, chapter contributions, or books) of written work by their chosen literacy leader and are advised to begin with the author's work as listed in the 'recommended resources' section of the course syllabus. After reading these sources, they present a survey of the leader's focus area in a paper, along

Table 30.4 Application of practices based on readings by literacy leaders

Literacy leader	Application to current or future teaching practices
Ken Goodman	*Goodman's work in the field psycholinguistics shows that learning to read is an authentic process and that errors made during reading are not things to simply be corrected but can point the teacher in the right direction of…where instruction can be directed to best help the student*
Victoria Risko	*Risko's research on multimedia case methodology and teacher reflection will be useful when designing professional development and coaching teachers during Professional Learning Communities. Including videos of students in my small group intervention classes and allowing time for teachers to analyze the students' difficulties and collaborate to find effective solutions will improve the teachers' ability to problem solve and use alternate perspectives*
Leslie Morrow	*According to Morrow, with careful selection of high-quality literature for the science curriculum, it should be possible to provide students with much more interesting scientific reading. In my classroom, I try diligently to make sure that our environment is rich with literacy resources for all leveled learners. I also spend an equal amount of time ensuring that there is fair representation among the literacy resources provided to my students*
Timothy Shanahan	*Shanahan states that students should have access to a wide range of reading experiences. I can honestly state that for my students who were struggling I may not have allowed as wide a breadth of reading opportunities as needed, or the amount of easier leveled texts may have far outnumbered the more challenging ones*
Richard Allington	*By adopting Allington's advice, I will be able to assist teachers in creating an effective reading instructional block that focuses on the needs of their students. Rather than taking a testing only approach, if students spend time strengthening their reading skills through authentic texts and critical discussions with their peers, they will likely gain the skills needed to pass state assessments*

with supporting evidence from their readings. They are then asked to reflect upon the ways in which their chosen literacy leader's work is, or can be, integrated into both their current work as a practitioner and their future work as a literacy professional. Table 30.4 lists samples of the thoughtful application ideas that students have presented in their papers, as well as several of the literacy leaders included in the list that students may investigate.

30.5.2   Literacy Coaching

Coaching and peer collaboration are two themes running predominantly throughout each SLP Standard. Literacy coaching is an activity that supports student reading achievement (Biancarosa, Bryk, & Dexter, 2010; Heineke, 2013; L'Allier & Elish-Piper, 2006; Sailors & Price, 2010; Toll, 2014). L'Allier et al. (2010) emphasize how imperative it is that the coaches devote large amounts of time working with teachers in individual and group settings. One way we meet this dimension of the standards is by requiring our candidates to engage colleagues at their school campuses in professional development, which many of our students have not yet had the opportunity to do. One particular assignment is embedded in the Leadership and Literacy course and is entitled, "Instructional Leadership and Professional Development Presentation." In the first part of this assignment, students implement an instructional approach, activity, philosophy, or program that is new to their school. They must audit their current instructional practices and evaluate where changes might be needed. After researching the instructional approach, they can attack this assignment in two ways: (1) implement the instruction within their own classrooms and report the results to colleagues, or (2) provide professional development for teachers, encouraging them to implement the method(s) and monitor the implementation, following up as necessary. For those candidates for whom leading professional development is new, there is encouragement to work with one teacher or with a small group of teachers (i.e., one grade level). For those candidates who have more experience, there is encouragement to work with either a small group of teachers, or all teachers at their campuses. As a literacy leader, they will be expected also to disseminate information to critical stakeholders. One way of sharing that information is through professional learning experiences (Risko & Vogt, 2016). They are also to talk with their administrators about the best way to deliver professional development, as keeping administrators involved is also included in the SLP Standards.

For the second part of the assignment, students create a presentation to share with other course members about what they did during the first part of the assignment. They describe the research, implementation plan, professional development session(s), and preliminary results. They also include photos, data, videos, interviews with teachers, or anything which they feel helps demonstrate the impact their leadership has had on their school. Activities such as these provide candidates with authentic practice in "meet[ing] the professional development needs of individual teachers and encourage[ing] professional growth" (Stover, Kissel, Haag, & Shoniker, 2011, p. 498), and building capacity and agency in teachers. The goal, of course, is that teachers will change and enhance their literacy instruction after working with a coach (Vanderburg & Stephens, 2010). These projects are evaluated on the amount of research candidates collect prior to following through with the professional development, the description of how they carried out the professional development, and the description of the how the professional development was received on their campus (see Table 30.5 for examples of implementation).

The SLP Standards (ILA, 2018) document contains a new standard, Standard 7: Practicum and Clinical Experiences, which was added specifically to prepare those serving in Reading Specialist and literacy coach roles (Kern et al., 2018). Furthermore, Lacina and Block (2011) found that the most successful teacher education programs provided students with "consistent, carefully selected, and relevant field experiences" (p. 336). These experiences also emulate those 'professional responsibilities and activities [that] Reading Specialists carry out' (Galloway & Leseaux, 2014). Students are encouraged to spend ten hours observing classroom teaching and ten hours coaching individual teachers or providing professional development

Table 30.5 Instructional leadership project examples

Topic for professional development	Audience
Using mentor sentences to teach grammar as part of the writing workshop	Fourth-grade teachers at several campuses
Reading motivation	Second-grade teachers at one campus
Modeling small group reading instruction	Kindergarten teachers at one campus
Teaching reading strategies through music	Kindergarten through fifth grade teachers at one campus
Using national writing project mini-units to facilitate self-efficacy in a secondary English classroom	High school English teachers at one campus
State comprehension standards	Fourth-grade teachers at one campus
Phonics instruction using the six syllable types	Fourth-grade teachers at one campus

to small groups of teachers (see instructional leadership assignment above). The textbook used for the course, Bean's (2015) *The Reading Specialist*, provides many practical ideas for what candidates might do to fulfill the requirements for these hours.[1]

There exists a great variety of activities due to the contexts in which students work, their interests, and the areas on which their particular schools are focusing (see Table 30.6 for examples). Because of the 100% online format of our master's program (and due to time, travel, and cost constraints) (Schmidt, MacSuga Gage, Gage, Cox, & McLeskey, 2015), we are unable to observe all our students in the field while they provide professional learning experiences in the form of workshops and coaching sessions. To meet this challenge, our students submit the actual training materials and information related to the number of participants present during professional learning experiences. They also submit videos, audio recordings, and/or transcripts of coaching sessions with teachers. Rock et al. (2012) noted how teacher interns

Table 30.6 Examples of observation and practicum activities related to literacy leadership

Examples of observation activities	Examples of practicum activities
Observed a teacher working with a small group on phonemic awareness	Conducted one-hour PD on the use of a specific scope and sequence/resource for phonological awareness
Observed teaching of a whole group lesson followed by stations	Conducted full-day PD on mentor sentences for grammar instruction
Observed small group guided reading lesson	Supported teachers while they administer vocabulary assessments
Observed whole group read-aloud lesson	Led a grade level literacy instruction planning meeting

---

[1] Other ideas for how these roles might be performed in a school can be located in Calo et al. (2015) and Pletcher, Hudson, John, and Scott (2019).

actually favored this procedure because they said it was less intrusive to simply set up a camera than to have someone in the room observing. Specific events are then documented on specific forms that serve as evidence that hours were completed (see Table 30.6).

30.6 Leadership Experiences

The SLP Standards stress the importance of developing campus and district-wide literacy leaders. Literacy professionals require experiences in a variety of leadership roles. While literacy leadership is an invaluable attribute of a campus or district literacy professional, the development of these skills proved to be a challenge for instructors working within a full-online instructional environment. One way that literacy leaders provide support to teachers and staff is through evaluation of literacy curriculum and materials. This leadership role helps to support schools by providing research-based instructional methods and materials focused on students' needs (Bean & Lillenstein, 2012; Moktari, Rosemary, & Edwards, 2007). Graduate students require opportunities to communicate with classmates in an online environment. One way in which this is addressed is in the course Stages and Standards of Reading. Graduate students must create professional presentations that can be either conducted synchronously using an online tele-conferencing application (such as Zoom.us or Webex) or submitted as a recording of their presentations to the instructor. Through these presentations, students share developmentally appropriate instructional methods, along with relevant supporting research. Graduate students are also required to complete this course by creating a strategies notebook, which contains fifteen research-based strategies and activities, each of which include evidence of developmental appropriateness. The target audience addressed in the strategies notebook is any new classroom teacher, with a focus on developing the graduate student's role as literacy leader.

Students are also given opportunities to develop this leadership role via the course Diagnosis and Correction of Reading Problems. Graduate students are required to provide evidence of one-on-one literacy tutoring with an elementary school-aged student throughout the semester. Graduate students assess and evaluate their student's literacy skills, and critically evaluate instructional materials and methods to fit the child's needs. The end-of-course case study thus includes the graduate students' evaluations of the methods used with the young student, along with research-led suggestions for further literacy support. These activities help to develop the literacy professional's ability to not only analyze the child's assessment data, but to effectively communicate the child's needs to and with parents, peers, and other key stakeholders (Bean & Lillenstein, 2012; Moktari, Rosemary, & Edwards, 2007).

Another leadership role required of future literacy professionals is that of providing well-rounded literacy environments for students. Literacy leaders should promote and provide the motivation to read literature in the form of traditional books and electronic sources that reflect the diverse society in which children live (Cunningham &

Stanovich, 1998; Dalton & Protor, 2007; Gambrell, 2011; Guthrie & Wigfield, 2000). Future literacy professionals also need opportunities to consider students' various interests, strengths, needs, and socio-cultural backgrounds (Moll, Amanti, Neff, & Gonzalez, 1992). We develop this leadership role through a course entitled Advanced Children's and Adolescent Literature. Here, graduate students individually analyze and evaluate literature from numerous literacy genres, such as picture books, realistic fiction, and non-fiction forms. Students are also required to choose from a list of books focusing on currently trending texts, some with multicultural or LGBTQ themes, and others with themes that are often challenged by parents and schools. Students submit a report on an evaluation of their chosen texts, but also the online discussion forum to summarize and share their book responses with classmates. This asynchronous way of sharing book summaries and reviews provides the graduate students with a wider range of these more challenging texts, and helps develop the leadership role, by supporting classroom teachers with strategies for using such texts with students.

30.7 Literacy Advocate Experiences

As literacy professionals, the SLP Standards also focus on developing graduate students' role as literacy advocates. As an advocate, the literacy professional need to address classroom teachers, school administrators, parents, and other educational stakeholders on effective instructional methods, curriculum, and educational equity (Bean, 2015; Bean & Ippolito, 2016; Breidenstein, Fahey, Glickman, & Hensley, 2012; Bryk, Gomez, Grunow, & LeMahieu, 2015; Galloway & Lesaux 2014; Walpole & McKenna, 2012). The role of advocate not only requires the literacy professional to be knowledgeable of current literacy trends and issues; it requires the individual to address these topics with teachers, administrators, and the community. In Stages and Standards, for example, students are assigned to identify an issue or trend in literacy education that they find impacts their current teaching environment. These topics vary, from the need to appropriately support English learners' literacy development, to providing instruction that supports critical evaluation of online and digital texts. Graduate students are given choice in how they address the issue or trend; students can either record a presentation (where they discuss the issue or trend while providing evidence-based suggestions) or pen an email addressed to school administration or other educational policy makers. This assignment requires the future literacy leader to not only take a stance on an important, and often controversial, issue but to also demonstrate their ability to support their stance with appropriate and relevant literature. Graduate students not only provide their knowledge of course content but are able to develop important interpersonal and leadership skills focused upon advocacy (Bean, 2015; Bean & Ippolito, 2016; Breidenstein et al., 2012; Bryk, Gomez, Grunow, & LeMahieu, 2015; Galloway & Lesaux, 2014; Walpole & McKennah, 2012).

30.8 Conclusion

Our university uses a variety of online tools and instructional methods to develop literacy professionals who are equipped with the experiences and knowledge required of them at their schools and districts. In our fully-online program, we facilitate the development of students' skills in coaching, leadership, and literacy advocacy despite the distance that exists between students and professors. Providing instruction in a fully-online format offers opportunities for students to gain Higher Education in ways not previously thought possible. While a number of online educational programs remain a popular alternative to face-to-face instruction, providing students with authentic socially constructed learning opportunities remains an ongoing challenge within Higher Education. However, with the increasing number of online tools available to institutions and students, there is now great potential for high quality distance education. By tapping into newly developed online tools, and by promoting collaboration and communication within the online educational programs, we can provide schools and school districts with highly skilled literacy professionals, prepared to support students, teachers, and the community's literacy needs.

References

Allen, J. (2016). *Becoming a literacy leader: Supporting learning and change* (2nd ed.). Portland, ME: Stenhouse.

Alvermann, D. E., Unrau, N. J., & Ruddell, R. B. (2013). *Theoretical models and processes of reading* (6th ed.). Newark, DE: International Reading Association.

Bean, R. M. (2015). *The reading specialist: Leadership and coaching for the classroom, school, and community* (3rd ed.). New York, NY: Guilford Press.

Bean, R. M., & Ippolito, J. (2016). *Cultivating coaching mindsets: An action guide for literacy leaders*. West Palm Beach, FL: Learning Sciences International.

Bean, R. M., & Lillenstein, J. (2012). Response to intervention and the changing roles of schoolwide personnel. *The Reading Teacher, 65*(7), 491–501. https://doi.org/10.1002/TRTR01073.

Biancarosa, G., Bryk, A. S., & Dexter, E. R. (2010). Assessing the value-added effects of literacy collaborative professional development on student learning. *Elementary School Journal, 111*(1), 7–34.

Breidenstein, A., Fahey, K., Glickman, C., & Hensley, F. (2012). *Leading for powerful learning: A guide for instructional leaders*. New York, NY: Teachers College Press.

Bryk, A. S., Gomez, L. M., Grunow, A., & LeMahieu, P. G. (2015). *Learning to improve: How America's schools can get better at getting better*. Cambridge, MA: Harvard University Press.

Calo, K.M., Sturtevant, E.G., & Kopfman, K.M. (2015). Literacy coaches' perspectives of themselves as literacy leaders: Results from a national study of K–12 literacy coaching and leadership. *Literacy Research and Instruction, 54*(1), 1–18. https://doi.org/10.1080/19388071.2014.941050.

Cunningham, A. E., & Stanovich, K. E. (1998). What reading does for the mind. *American Educator, 22*(1–2), 8–15.

Dalton, B., & Protor, C. P. (2007). Reading as thinking: Integrating strategy instruction in a university designed digital literacy environment. In D. S. McNamara (Ed.), *Reading comprehension strategies: Theories, interventions, and technologies* (pp. 421–439). Mahwah, NJ: Lawrence Earlbaum.

Doolittle, P. (1999). *Constructivism and online education.* Retrieved November 16, 2008, from http://edpsychserver.ed.vt.edu/workshops/tohe1999/text/doo2s.doc.

Galloway, E. P., & Lesaux, N. K. (2014). Leader, teacher, diagnostician, colleague, and change agent: A synthesis of the research on the role of the reading specialist in this era of RTI-based literacy reform. *The Reading Teacher, 67*(7), 517–526.

Gambrell, L. B. (2011). Seven rules of engagement: What's most important to know about motivation to read. *The Reading Teacher, 65*(3), 172–178.

Guthrie, J. T., & Wigfield, A. (2000). Engagement and motivation in reading. In M. L. Kamil, P. B. Mosenthal, P. D. Pearson, & R. Barr (Eds.), *Handbook of reading research* (Vol. 3, pp. 403–422). New York, NY: Earlbaum.

Heineke, S. F. (2013). Coaching discourse: Supporting teachers' professional learning. *The Elementary School Journal, 113*(3), 409–433.

International Literacy Association. (2018). *Standards for the preparation of literacy professionals 2017.* DE: Newark.

Kern, D., Bean, R. M., Swan Dagen, A., DeVries, B., Dodge, A., Goatley, V. … Walker-Dalhouse, D. (2018). Preparing reading/literacy specialists to meet changes and challenges: International Literacy Association's Standards 2017. *Literacy Research and Instruction, 57*(3), 209–231.

L'Allier, S., Elish-Piper, L., & Bean, R. M. (2010). What matters for elementary literacy coaching? Guiding principles for instructional improvement and student achievement. *The Reading Teacher, 63*(7), 544–554. https://doi.org/10.1598/RT.63.7.2.

L'Allier, S.K., & Elish-Piper, L. (2006, December). *An initial examination of the effects of literacy coaching on student achievement in reading in grades K–3.* Paper presented at the annual conference of the National Reading Conference, Los Angeles, CA.

Lacina, J., & Block, C.C. (2011). What matters most in distinguished literacy teacher education programs. *Journal of Literacy Research, 43*(4), 319–351.

Moktari, K., Rosemary, C. A., & Edwards, P. A. (2007). Making instructional decisions based on data: What, how and why. *The Reading Teacher, 61*(4), 354–359.

Moll, L., Amanti, C., Neff, D., & Gonzalez, N. (1992). Funds of knowledge for teaching: Using a qualitative approach to connect homes and classrooms. *Theory Into Practice, 31*(2), 132–141.

Pletcher, B. C., Hudson, A., John, L., & Scott, A. (2019). Coaching on borrowed time: Balancing the roles of the Specialized Literacy Professional. *The Reading Teacher, 72*(6), 689–699.

Risko, V. J., & Vogt, M. (2016). *Professional learning in action: An inquiry approach for teachers of literacy.* New York, NY: Teachers College Press.

Rock, M., Gregg, M., Gable, R., Zigmond, N., Blanks, B., Howard, P., & Bullock, L. (2012). Time after time online: An extended study of virtual coaching during distant clinical practice. *Journal of Technology and Teacher Education, 20*(3), 277–304.

Schmidt, M., MacSuga Gage, A., Gage, N., Cox, P., & McLeskey, J. (2015). Bringing the field to the supervisor: Innovation in distance supervision for field-based experiences using mobile technologies. *Rural Special Education Quarterly, 34*(1), 37–43.

Sailors, M., & Price, L. R. (2010). Professional development that supports the teaching of cognitive reading strategy instruction. *Elementary School Journal, 110*(3), 301–322.

Stover, K., Kissel, B., Haag, K., & Shoniker, R. (2011). Differentiated coaching: Fostering reflection with teachers. *The Reading Teacher, 64*(7), 498–509.

Texas Education Agency. (2018). *State board for educator certification.* Retrieved on October 15, 2018 from https://tea.texas.gov/About_TEA/Leadership/State_Board_for_Educator_Certification/.

Toll, C. A. (2014). *The literacy coach's survival guide: Essential questions and practical answers* (2nd ed.). Newark, DE: International Reading Association.

Vanderburg, M., & Stephens, D. (2010). The impact of literacy coaches: What teachers value and how teachers change. *The Elementary School Journal, 111*(1), 141–163.

Vygotsky, L. S. (1978). *Mind in society.* Cambridge, MA: Harvard University Press.

Walpole, S., & McKennah, M. C. (2012). *The literacy coach's handbook: A guide to research-based practice* (2nd ed.). New York, NY: Guilford.

Yoon, S. (2003). In search of meaningful online learning experiences. In S. R. Aragon (Ed.), *Facilitating learning in online environments. New directions for adult and continuing education* (p. 100). San Francisco: Jossey-Bass.

Kelli Bippert (Ph.D.) is Assistant Professor of Literacy Education at Texas A&M University-Corpus Christi. Dr. Bippert's research and scholarship center on adolescent literacy, cultural perceptions of adolescent readers, technology-based reading intervention programs, and the integration of popular culture/media texts to support in-school literacies. She has fifteen years of public school teaching experience with early adolescents.

Bethanie Pletcher (Ed.D) is an Assistant Professor in the Curriculum, Instruction, and Learning Sciences department at Texas A&M University, Corpus Christi, U.S. Her research interests include literacy coaching, reading clinics, and supporting striving early readers. She has published in *The Reading Teacher*, the *Association of Literacy Educators and Researchers Yearbook, Reading Horizons*, and *The Reading Professor*. Prior to her current faculty position, Dr. Pletcher was a Reading Recovery© Teacher, Reading Specialist, and classroom teacher.

Corinne Valadez (Ph.D.) is an Associate Professor and the Silverman Endowed Professor in the Department of Curriculum, Instruction, and Learning Sciences in the College of Education and Human Development at Texas A&M University—Corpus Christi, U.S. She serves as coordinator for the Masters of Reading program. She received her Ph.D. from Texas A & M University in Curriculum and Instruction, and is also a certified Reading Specialist. Prior to teaching at TAMUCC, she taught in public schools for nine years.

Chapter 31
Building Career Readiness for Criminal Law Practice: The Adelaide Law School Experience

Kellie Toole

31.1 Introduction

The fascinating and challenging law of crime enlivens the imagination of many students and inspires them to pursue a career in criminal law. However, a lack of recognised pathways can stymie entry into criminal practice, especially in the competitive global employment market confronting legal graduates. The limited opportunities for gaining experience in criminal practice encourages the embedding of career readiness skills into criminal law curricula. Practical motivation is bolstered because research indicates that embedding career readiness promotes 'deeper and more meaningful understanding of doctrine and principle by allowing students to experience the law in its practical context' (Castles & Hewitt, 2011, p. 91). In this chapter, the example of the compulsory Criminal Law course offered by the Adelaide Law School in South Australia is used to demonstrate a method for integrating career readiness skills into a core curriculum. The chapter champions criminal law as a vehicle for building career readiness, explains the integration of career readiness into this course through simulated client case files, and discusses the benefits and challenges this presents. Whilst criminal procedure varies internationally, the fundamentals of prosecuting and defending criminal defendants transcend regional differences, making the model used in Adelaide relevant across jurisdictions.

K. Toole (✉)
University of Adelaide, Adelaide, Australia
e-mail: kellie.toole@adelaide.edu.au

© Springer Nature Switzerland AG 2019
A. Diver (ed.), *Employability via Higher Education: Sustainability as Scholarship*,
https://doi.org/10.1007/978-3-030-26342-3_31

31.2   Criminal Law and Career Readiness

Criminal law courses are especially appropriate vehicles for strategies designed to develop 'career ready' law graduates and enhance understanding of the substantive law by 'grounding a student's legal education in experience' (Thomson, 2014, p. 415).

31.2.1   The Nature of the Course of Study

Criminal law involves relatively autonomous content that does require prior knowledge of other areas, so career readiness skills can be introduced earlier in a degree program than via clinical education courses. Criminal law cannot be separated from social and psychological conditions, so career readiness skills are inherently connected to critical thinking and to broader educational goals.

31.2.2   The Nature of Criminal Practice

Criminal practice translates well into a simulated client case file because it involves standard documents that can readily be replicated for educational purposes. Criminal matters progress according to standardised procedures that can be incorporated into scenarios tailored to any teaching period. Junior criminal lawyers have a relatively high degree of autonomy, and exercise individual judgments on case strategy that can be imitated in an educational setting.

31.2.3   Lack of Opportunities for Career Development

Criminal firms and chambers are often small, have unpredictable work flow, and lack the resources to provide the placements, clerkships or internships that commercial firms and government departments offer. Criminal lawyers may take instructions from clients and appear in court from their first day of work, and much professional learning happens in courts or holding cells where opportunities for training are limited. Criminal law's unique educational and professional characteristics mean that individual graduates and the profession itself benefit from career readiness skills being embedded within university courses.

31.3   Career Readiness Skills

The concept of career readiness within the University of Adelaide Criminal Law course ('Criminal Law') is interpreted broadly to cover the technical and professional responsibilities of an ethical practitioner. The course assists students in developing 'professional orientation' (Thomson, 1978, p. 84) and establishing a foundation to 'begin to form their professional identities as lawyers' (Thomson, 2014, p. 419) through knowledge and experience of case management; exercising problem solving skills and judgment; facing ethical challenges and professional obligations; and considering issues of well-being and work life balance. However, given the limited time available in a semester, the main priority of the course is to produce 'practice ready' graduates (Borden, 2013, p. 118) with some simulated client case file management experience. The career readiness skills were primarily delivered through, firstly, client files (used in seminars) and, secondly, via sessions from legal drafters, defence lawyers and prosecutors supplementing the lectures delivered by academic staff.

31.4   Curriculum

The Criminal Law course is offered in a 12-week semester in the first year of the Bachelor of Laws (LLB) degree. It covers the substantive law of homicide, dishonesty, assault, and sexual offences; the defences of self defence and mental impairment; and introductory criminal procedure. It utilises a range of teaching methodologies, including a weekly two-hour lecture for the whole cohort, and weekly one-hour seminars for groups of 30 students to apply the law to factual scenarios. Law seminars generally address a different problem-based question on a particular area of law each week. The benefit of this approach is that the factual scenarios can be tailored to a particular area of law, and the students can address multiple scenarios across the semester. However, different weekly scenarios do not necessarily explore the interaction of various areas of law, nor do they allow time for consideration of evidential issues to enable students to feel 'invested' through ongoing engagement with a particular case. For 2018, Criminal Law seminars were structured around two simulated client case files with issues that unfolded as they would in a real-world criminal case. The adoption of the situational learning experience forges a link between substantive law and legal practice, because '[l]earning does not take place in abstract, but through the engagement with "real and lived experiences"' (Brandon & Stodulka, 2007, p. 248).

Students need to make strategic decisions on the progress of the cases, such as whether to plead guilty, proceed to trial and argue a relevant defence, or negotiate for the withdrawal or reduction of charges. Students argue, alternately, from the position of the prosecution or the defence to ensure they will consider issues from different angles. For client case studies to be effective, 'the narrative of the story needs to include a comprehensive history' (Brandon & Stodulka, 2007, p. 247), and so the files include evidence of domestic violence, substance abuse, and mental health issues. These 'back stories' are not only relevant to criminal liability and pleas in mitigation, they also provide the context to criminal offending that an empathetic practitioner needs to understand.

Studies have found that '[l]earning through case study is open-ended. As a result, participants will clarify their insights, and internalise them so they are later able to transfer such learning into their own practice' (Brandon & Stodulka, 2007, p. 246). The evidence on both client files includes multiple perspectives to demonstrate that conflicting views and a high level of uncertainty are inherent to the criminal process, and lawyers need to assess the strength of evidence to determine the likelihood of conviction and/or the success of defences. In the final seminar of the semester, each class reviews the prosecution evidence and defence arguments on each case, and argues for appropriate outcomes. There are no formal resolutions, to demonstrate that different advocates and courts may take differing views on matters of fact and law, the weight attached to various pieces of evidence, the strength of the inferences that can be drawn from the evidence, the cogency of the prosecution and defence case theories, and the persuasiveness of opposing advocates. Overall, Criminal Law students need to develop practical skills in client-focused problem-solving using knowledge of the law, procedural options, and their implications. This process stretches students beyond the confines of learning the substantive law and engaging in traditional legal reasoning.

31.5   Simulated Client Case Files

In the first week of semester, students were given two client files based on the following scenarios. They had to assess the liability of their two 'clients' each week, using case file materials, and their evolving knowledge of the substantive law of offences, defences, criminal procedure, strategy, and social and psychological evidence.

R v Ackerman

Peter Ackerman does not arrive at work and fails to answer his telephone. His concerned colleague notifies police who attend at his residence. They find Peter deceased on the floor of the hallway. He is covered in blood, and apparently has been hit in the head with the bloodied iron that is beside his body. His wife, Alison, is lying beside him. She is crying, and talking incoherently about being frightened, angry, sorry, confused, and shocked. Alison is charged with murder.

In the R v Ackerman case file, students were provided with the charging instrument; the police apprehension report; Alison's offender history which showed no prior convictions; a witness statement from a neighbour who suspected that Peter was abusive and who heard a woman say 'I'm going to kill you' just before Peter's estimated time of death; a witness statement of a police officer that the door was locked when they arrived and there was no evidence of forced entry or the presence of any third person; a record of interview that shows Alison had limited memory of what happened but recalls feeling scared because Peter was drunk; an autopsy report that is consistent with Peter being killed with an iron by a person the size of Alison; a statement from Alison to her lawyer that is consistent with her record of interview; a psychological report that shows Alison has low self-esteem, and reported persistent physical and emotional abuse from Peter; and medical reports that show Alison had injuries consistent with domestic violence which she blamed on a bicycle accident.

The body of evidence is deliberately inconclusive and conflicting, and viable legal outcomes include Alison being:

- Convicted of murder
- Convicted of manslaughter by unlawful and dangerous act
- Convicted of manslaughter due to the partial defence of provocation
- Acquitted by reason of mental impairment
- Acquitted because she was acting in self defence
- Acquitted because she was in a dissociative state.

R v Mann

Danica Melany was at a local hotel. After being harassed by the barman, she was grateful that another patron, Oliver Mann, punched him to defend her. She did not begrudge that Oliver took $200 from the cash register to cover the cost of his sunglasses that were damaged in the altercation. She was happy to have a drink with him, but when she tried to leave she was shocked and traumatised that he tried to force her to have sexual intercourse with him. Oliver is charged with assault causing harm, robbery, and attempted rape.

In the *R v Mann* case file, students were provided with the charging instrument; an offender history that showed Oliver had prior convictions for dishonesty and violence offences; bail papers; a witness statement from the man Oliver punched; a witness statement from the woman who said Oliver put his hand in her pants and tried to rape her; Oliver's record of interview where he says the sexual contact with Danica was consensual and that the barman shoved him first; a medical report indicating the barman suffered serious injuries; a statement of Oliver to his lawyer that contradicts his record of interview; and a certificate of blood alcohol reading indicating Oliver was highly intoxicated at the relevant time.

The body of evidence is deliberately inconclusive and conflicting, and viable legal outcomes include Oliver being:

- Convicted of assault causing harm
- Acquitted of assault causing harm because he was acting in self defence
- Convicted of rape because digital penetration occurred
- Convicted of attempted rape because digital penetration was attempted
- Convicted of indecent assault because no sexual penetration occurred or was attempted but he did put his hand in her underpants
- Acquitted of all of the sexual offences due to lack of evidence to prove them beyond reasonable doubt

- Convicted of robbery because he assaulted the barman in order to steal the money
- Convicted of theft because he stole the money in an incident separate to the assault
- Acquitted of theft and robbery because he genuinely believed he was entitled to the money to replace his sunglasses.

The viability of each option changes on a weekly basis as students learn more about the facts, the evidence, the offences, the defences, and the interaction between them.

31.6 Method of Evaluation

The three following methods of evaluation were employed to determine students' perceptions of the value of embedding career readiness skills within their curriculum, and of the efficacy of the particular career readiness strategy employed in Criminal Law:

i. End of semester University-wide survey of Student Experience of Learning and Teaching ('SELT')—At the University of Adelaide, every course is reviewed every time it is offered, through a voluntary online survey comprising of standard set and open questions on teaching quality, course design, learning activities, and assessments (Planning and Analytics). The survey is anonymous.

ii. End of semester course-based survey ('survey') of career readiness component—A voluntary hard-copy survey was administered in class. Students responded to a series of questions on a five point Likert Scale ranging from 'strongly agree' to 'strongly disagree', and to open questions on the effectiveness of the career readiness strategies. The survey is anonymous.

iii. During semester email feedback ('email')—Students were regularly invited to provide email or in-person feedback to the co-ordinator on any aspect of the course any time throughout the semester. (The in-person feedback has been excluded from this analysis. The email feedback was not anonymous.)

From the 493 students enrolled in Criminal Law in 2018, 96 responses to the survey, 140 SELTs and 13 email feedback messages were received.

31.7 Value of Career Readiness Skills

Students demonstrated an appetite for developing career readiness skills as part of an embedded curriculum within their law degree. 65 of the 96 respondents to the survey strongly agreed that they 'value the opportunity to develop career readiness skills in law' and a further 17 students agreed with the proposition. Only 14 students indicated that they were neutral, strongly disagreed, or disagreed with the proposition. The question of 'How could the course be improved to assist students to develop career readiness skills?' elicited suggestions for more guest speakers; more client files; more detail in existing client files; visual resources such as client interviews; court visits; more information about pathways to criminal law; placements in criminal firms or sessions with practitioners; and assistance with preparing job applications and resumes. The incorporation of career readiness did not have universal support: one student

> …did not enjoy the nature of the career readiness aspect of the course [because] [n]ot everyone wants to practice in criminal law, so I find that this shift from regular courses is too great compared to a standard problem question-based course. (SELT)

However, the weight of student opinion was strongly in its favour. As one student summarised:

> I have really loved the direction this course has taken, particularly focusing on the practical skills and the guest speakers. I have always felt this is something lacking from previous law courses. We learn the law and apply it to a problem question, but do not look at the bigger picture - how it all operates in practice. It has been really excellent exploring the law within the bigger political/policy and ethical context. … I really believe that the course you have developed is the future of law studies. (via email)

31.8 Efficacy of the Approach to Career Readiness

Having established that students welcomed the opportunity to develop career readiness skills, the evaluation proceeded to consider student perceptions on the way that the career readiness skills were embedded in Criminal Law.

31.8.1 Simulated Reality

Research shows that with legal simulations, the 'learning comes from the sense of reality that is created' (Brandon & Stodulka, 2007, p. 247). The documents in the simulated case file were prepared by a practising criminal lawyer,[1] and are indistinguishable from real legal documents: the materials reflect the level of legal complexity appropriate to undergraduate students, and raise issues that balance prosecution and defence perspectives. The students experienced a sense of reality with the case files. The surveys were peppered with praise for their 'practicality,' approximation to 'real life', and 'real world examples.' Students appreciated the exposure to the case files' 'real formatting and facts in a context where they would be found in practice not just in text block,' and preferred 'using case files as opposed to regular problem questions. The detail was phenomenal.' They found that 'the case files with hypothetical

---

[1]Christian Haebich, Principal, Haebich Law, www.haebichlaw.com.au. (The lawyer has 10 years' experience as a sessional teacher in the law school and has been involved in curriculum development in other law courses.)

Table 31.1 Criminal law career readiness survey

Element	Number of respondents
Guest practitioners	43
Case files	41
Lecturers with practical experience	1
Criminal practice strategy	2
Informal catch up with lecturers after class	1

clients and evidence made the content of the course easier to picture being used in real life.' Overwhelmingly, they reported that they had benefitted from 'really considering how the law would apply to real life scenarios', and 'approaching problem questions realistically and strategically instead of mere theoretical application.' The evaluation explored whether students perceived that the simulated reality of the client files assisted the development of their substantive knowledge and/or career readiness.

31.8.2 Achieving Career Readiness

The inclusion of the client case files responded to research findings that the traditional focus on doctrinal analysis and legal reasoning within legal education has 'sublimated the importance of practical, ethical and moral training within university legal education' (Batagol & Hyams, 2012, p. 183). The responses to the open survey question: 'What aspects of the course assisted the development of career readiness skills?' identified the following aspects of the course as assisting preparation for practice (Table 31.1).

The following section explores the connection between the guest practitioners and case files, and the development of career readiness.

31.8.3 Confidence and Awareness

The current competitive employment market generates negative commentary about prospects for law graduates. Criminal Law built awareness of career possibilities, and confidence about entering the profession, as the first stage of career readiness. One student wrote that 'you've managed to make me quite a fan of criminal law, to such an extent that … I would now seriously consider pursuing [it] after uni' (student email). Survey responses also indicated that '…guests helped reassure us there is work in the field and you don't need a HD GPA'. Another student reflected that

…having the DPP [Director of Public Prosecutions] in to talk about all different paths to that position put me at ease. In law school I find that we are constantly told how hard it is to get a job (you *must* get a clerkship, you *must* be top of your class) and it was refreshing to have a *real* person who has been successful talk about their experience.

Another student noted: 'I am really enjoying criminal law and am leaning towards pursuing it in practise. The course helped me relax about finding a job'. One student converted their new-found confidence into work experience before the end of the semester. They reported that 'I really enjoyed this course and I have started a volunteer position because it gave me the confidence to put myself out there and apply'.

31.8.4 Advice on Practical Steps

The course also provided concrete advice to students on how to transition into the profession. Survey respondents valued practitioners explaining 'what steps they took to be where they are' and found that 'having people from different backgrounds talk to us about their career pathway and journey … made me realise the importance of doing work experience early in the degree'. One student noted that the course alleviated stress about employment and 'gave us the tools … to help' secure a graduate position.

31.8.5 Achieving Understanding of Substantive Law

Preparing students for professional practice was only part of the rationale for the introduction of career readiness skills. The initiative also responded to the research that found that often in legal education, 'learning materials or environments are stripped of contextual relevance' (Gutman, McCormack, & Riddle, 2014, p. 103), even though situational learning helps students gain deep knowledge of their subject area. In particular, case files clarify thinking by requiring students to apply content to practical situations with a client in mind (Hewitt & Toole, 2013). The student feedback confirmed that the 'use of the case studies was incredibly effective at building knowledge' (SELT). Of the survey respondents, 52 strongly agreed that the client files helped them understand the substantive law of crime. Only 1 student strongly disagreed with the proposition, and two students disagreed with the proposition. Two students expanded in the SELTS on the academic benefit of the focus on career readiness. One did not

…believe universities are degree factories for a job, that has never been my expectation. University has always been about learning and academia for me. That being said, practical applications to anything have always helped me learn and the case file structure made the theory instantly associated with those facts.

Another student found that the course

...achieved the perfect blend of teaching about theory and practice from both prosecution and defence perspectives. I think this is the only law course that I have done to this date where I feel like I have an idea about the actual legal process in the real world. I loved the use of case studies and how the focus of the course was looking at how the theoretical cases would pan out in real life from the prosecution's charging decisions to the defence's case theories.

However, the integration of career readiness skills with doctrinal study 'can be difficult if the students are not reasonably sure of the substantive material' (Field, 2012, 46). SELT responses indicated that for some students the practical component detracted from the acquisition of content knowledge. One concluded that 'the focus on "career readiness" obviously has its appeal, but I just don't think it translates well to academia'. Another found that skills are 'fundamentally irrelevant if we do not know the law.' The latter survey responses demonstrate the need to reinforce with students that the use of career readiness strategies has more potential to enhance understanding of substantive law than to detract from it.

The following section explores the specific relationship between the client focused approach and the development of substantive knowledge. It is divided into the categories of enjoyment and motivation; fewer fact situations; use of evidence; problem-solving; strategy; and connections between charges.

31.9   Enjoyment and Motivation

Students being motivated to study the course material is a foundation for the engagement and commitment necessary for the development of deep substantive knowledge. Fifty-one respondents to the survey strongly agreed that the career readiness focus increased their enjoyment of studying criminal law. Only 1 student strongly disagreed with the proposition, and two students disagreed with the proposition (the same students who disagreed and strongly disagreed that it enhanced their understanding of the substantive material). One SELT response noted that the course 'has a great real life application, which is easy to wrap your head around in conjunction with what we hear on the news etc. The case file approach capitalised on this and made it feel like a real career-type situation which made it motivating and interesting to work on'. Other SELTs reflected that 'learning the practical components of the law are so important and ... ma[d]e many students engage more with the content', and that a 'practical approach like this was really refreshing and motivating.'

31.9.1   Fewer Fact Situations

Eliminating unproductive preparation time frees students to concentrate on meaningful engagement with the course material. Students built a familiarity with the facts of the client files over the semester, which a number of them cited as assisting in developing their knowledge. The use of just two files reduced the time students spent learning new facts, and allowed them to 'focus on learning the law' (email), and 'consolidate my knowledge on the actual concepts', which made it easier 'to apply and understand the law', and 'prepare and contribute to classes when you didn't have to get your head around a whole new set of facts each week' (surveys and SELTs). The alternative view was also evident, with one student finding the case files 'interesting but I think we need practice dealing with a range of simple fact situations, rather than only applying the law to 2 situations the entire semester' (SELT).

31.9.2 Use of Evidence

Skills in the assessment of evidence, and the inferences that can be drawn from it, are critical to prosecuting or defending a criminal case. Some of the most insightful comments in the survey related to how the client files required students to grapple with issues of evidence and proof in new and challenging ways. For example, rather than being given a weekly fact scenario that states 'Alison hit Peter in the head with an iron because she feared violence from him', students had the much more difficult task of scrutinising the case materials for evidence capable of proving beyond reasonable doubt that Peter was hit with an iron, that Alison was the person who hit him with it, whether she had the requisite subjective fault for murder or the objective fault for manslaughter, or if there was evidence of mental impairment, temporary dissociation, or that met the evidential burden to raise self-defence. One student articulated that

> …the case files gave me a better understanding of the role evidence plays. Looking back on past exams it's a lot harder to see how intention/recklessness would play out in real life. For example, the past exams explicitly tell you what the offender is thinking when it is usually inferred from circumstances and actions in a real case. (SELT)

Another reflected that 'the case files helped me understand the discrepancies with witness statements, therefore giving me a more in-depth understanding of the purpose of the jury and the process of criminal law' (survey).

31.9.3 Problem Solving

The adoption of the client file approach acknowledged that much clinical education, like popular representations of criminal law, was 'grounded in the imagery of litigation and courtroom representation', despite critical work like client interviewing, legal research, and negotiations between defence and prosecution being undertaken outside the courtroom (Maranville et al., 2011–12, p. 522). The case files excluded a trial component, to highlight that collaboration and client-focused problem-solving is as important as the more widely understood adversarial contest. The SELT responses indicate that some students absorbed this approach. One stated that the '[c]ase file approach makes it like a real-life scenario, this course allows you to picture what would actually happen in the workforce as a criminal lawyer. Rather than just learning the principles and laws, it is very practical and helps you understand how to problem solve.'

31.9.4   Strategy

The students adapted well to working from case files but were very challenged by having strategic oversight of a whole case file. Some students relished the strategic aspects of the case file management, and the learning it offered. They appreciated gaining a greater understanding of '[w]orking through charges from P and D point of view,' and '[t]alking about the practical side i.e. prosecution, defence, charge sheets' (surveys). Another elaborated that:

> the course really challenged me to think outside the box - particularly in terms of public policy and using the law in practice e.g. using evidence in a case or thinking about negotiation with the prosecution before even going to court. I had not been challenged like this before. (SELT)

However, other students requested more assistance with adjusting to this aspect of the course. One response suggested that the course could 'start with a clearer expectation of strategic thinking. Emphasise thinking of stakeholders and their conflicting perspectives' (survey). This was valuable feedback and a timely reminder that considering weekly fact scenarios, and then moving on to a completely new fact scenario, is very different to managing a single case over a whole semester. As just one example, on the Ackerman file, students had to take a defence perspective and decide whether to go to trial and risk prosecution proving the elements of murder and/or disproving self-defence, or whether to argue mental impairment to avoid the risk of a conviction for murder, but expose Alison to potential stigma and lengthy detention and supervision; or plead guilty to manslaughter and hope the court would accept the limited evidence of domestic violence and impose a lenient sentence. These decisions require a knowledge of the substantive law and entail sophisticated reasoning about procedural options and their implications, and empathy as to the interests and preferences of the client. Students require support to make strategic assessments confidently and effectively.

31.9.5   Connections Between Charges

Finally, students needed to recognise the complexity and importance of the key intersections across and within charges against a defendant. For example, they had to consider from a prosecution perspective whether there was a connection between Oliver's assault of the barman and the theft of money from the bar. If they were satisfied of a connection, then the conduct was theft with force and the appropriate charge was the major indictable offence of robbery. If there was no such connection, they had to pursue, separately, the lesser offences of theft and assault. With the alleged sexual offending, they had to consider alternative verdicts and timely guilty pleas from the defence perspective. Knowing the difficulties in proving sexual offences that have a subjective mental state, they had to determine whether to go to trial and risk a conviction for rape or attempted rape in the hope of a complete acquittal; or plead to the lesser offence of indecent assault, and sacrifice the chance of an acquittal of a more serious offence in order to avoid the possibility of a conviction for rape or attempted rape. This level of analysis of charge selection practices across two case files in 12 weeks was very challenging. Some students appreciated that by following a client through a simulated case, they could see not only how a single charge could be approached in different ways, but also how different counts on the same charging instrument could interact. One student noted that the '[c]ase studies were great for a sense of consistency and deep analysis to cement understanding. Was a lot easier to make connections between different charges in order to see how the learning can be applied in practice' (SELT). Another student found the case files

made it easier to apply different aspects from the course to one person and it made it easier to gather a holistic understanding of the way different offences work together in a practical sense (e.g. analysing Oliver's liability in regards to a robbery, but then finding out that he may not be guilty of robbery but he may be charged with assault and theft as the violence wasn't linked to the theft). [N]ormally in a law subject we would analyse different topics in the same course as if the topics existed in a vacuum and separate from the other topics. (SELT)

31.10 Conclusion

Law students appreciate the opportunity to develop career readiness skills, but can be taken aback by the reality of just how complex, dynamic and unpredictable the practice of criminal law can be. Despite the challenges, the pilot Criminal Law course indicates that incorporating career readiness skills can be worthwhile from the perspective of both preparing students for legal practice and developing deeper understanding of course material. The approach does not provide a panacea to the challenges of entering the competitive legal job market (Yackee, 2015, p. 620). However, it does stimulate interest in an area of law that is not widely promoted to students, and enables students and graduates seeking employment to show employers that they are familiar with legal case materials; able to identify legal issues from case files; can formulate case strategies from either a prosecution or defence perspective; can discuss issues and options with clients; and negotiate and advocate on behalf of clients. These skills may permit graduates to distinguish themselves in the application process, improve their prospects in securing work, and help them adjust to (and indeed thrive) in legal practice. This approach has the potential to offer significant academic and professional advantage to students, but the experience within this Criminal Law module demonstrates that they do need guidance through the unfamiliar aspects of simulated legal practice to ensure that the stresses of the case file approach does not overwhelm the many benefits that it also offers.

References

Batagol, B., & Hyams, R. (2012). Non-adversarial justice and the three apprenticeships of law. *Australasian Dispute Resolution Journal, 23,* 179–188.
Borden, B. T. (2013). Using the client-file method to teach transactional law. *Chapman Law Review, 17,* 101–118.
Brandon, M., & Stodulka, T. (2007). Effective conflict resolution training through case studies. *Australasian Dispute Resolution Journal, 18,* 245–251.
Castles, M., & Hewitt, A. (2011). Can a law school help develop skilled legal professionals? Situational learning to the rescue! *Alternative Law Journal, 36*(2), 90–95.
Field, H. M. (2012). Experiential learning in a lecture class: Exposing students to the skill of giving useful tax advice. *Pittsburgh Tax Review, 9,* 1–53.
Gutman, J., McCormack, S., & Riddle, M. (2014). ADR in legal education: Evaluating a teaching and learning innovation'. *Australasian Dispute Resolution Journal, 25,* 100–108.
Hewitt, A., & Toole, K. (2013). The practical knowledge conundrum: What practical knowledge should be included in a law school curriculum and how can it be taught? *New Zealand Universities Law Review, 25*(5), 980–1022.
Maranville, D., et al. (2011–12). Re-vision quest: A law school guide to designing experiential courses involving real lawyering. *New York Law School Law Review, 56,* 517–558.
Thomson, C. J. H. (1978). Objectives of legal education—An alternative approach. *The Australian Law Journal, 52,* 83–94.
Thomson, D. I. C. (2014). Defining experiential legal education. *Journal of Experiential Learning, 1,* 401–426.
University of Adelaide, Planning and Analytics. *Student Experience of Learning & Teaching (SELT),* https://www.adelaide.edu.au/planning/selt/.
Yackee, J. W. (2015). Does experiential learning improve JD employment outcomes? *Wisconsin Law Review,* 601–625.

Kellie Toole has a background as a criminal defence lawyer, and has been a law lecturer at the University of Adelaide since 2012. She teaches criminal law and procedure, sentencing and criminal justice, aboriginal people and the law, and military disciplinary law. Her research interests are at the intersection of criminal law and human rights law, including the decision to prosecute by Australian Directors of Public Prosecutions. She is committed to working with students to build a sense of community both within the Law School and also between it and the legal profession. She has acted also as a Well-Being Officer and as part of the Career Readiness team for the Adelaide Law School.

Chapter 32
Leading the Way: A Case Study of Establishing an Employability Scheme at Coventry Law School

Harriet Lodge and Susie Elliott

32.1 Introduction

There is no such thing as the average law student. The number of students accepted to first degree law courses in 2017/18 was 23,605 which is 3.7% higher than in 2016, with BAME students making up two fifths of those accepted (The Law Society, 2017). As such, the national law student body (England and Wales) is now more diverse then it ever has been with students from a wide range of backgrounds and cultures. This increased diversity has meant that the career aspirations of these students are also becoming broader. The declining legal employment market combined with the broad skill set gained by studying law, has meant that many students finish their degree without planning on a career practising law. Coupled with a changing legal sector, HE providers can no longer limit their employability provision to the 'barrister v. solicitor' debate as their service users demand more value for their tuition fees. To demonstrate these changes, this chapter will consider a case study of establishing a law employability scheme at Coventry Law School. It considers the challenges facing the delivery of employability for law students and suggest ways in which these challenges might be overcome.

In order to gain a graduate insight into the scheme, a small survey of Coventry Law School graduates was initiated: they'd had the opportunity to take part in the employability scheme (CLS Grad Survey, 2018). The participants were all recruited via social media and had graduated within the previous three years: they were all

This chapter represents our experience of establishing an employability scheme at Coventry University. At the time, we had not anticipated that we would one day be writing about our experiences and as such, most of our data collection was informal, but with appropriate consents obtained.

H. Lodge (✉) · S. Elliott
Coventry University, Coventry, England, UK
e-mail: ab4472@coventry.ac.uk

S. Elliott
e-mail: Susie.elliott@coventry.ac.uk

© Springer Nature Switzerland AG 2019   503
A. Diver (ed.), *Employability via Higher Education: Sustainability as Scholarship*,
https://doi.org/10.1007/978-3-030-26342-3_32

employed in graduate level roles within both legal and non-legal practice areas.[1] Participants were asked to provide feedback about their engagement with the Law Employability, Diversity and Enrichment Scheme (LEDE) scheme and the benefit they derived from it at the time, as compared with how they valued it now. Participants were also asked to indicate whether their career aspirations had changed between starting their undergraduate programmes and completing them.

32.2   Traditional Routes to Qualification

Students complete a three-year qualifying law degree (QLD) before signing up to a one-year, specialised vocational course which differs depending upon whether they want to be a solicitor or a barrister. Upon successful completion of a vocational course, would-be solicitors must undertake a two-year apprenticeship (known as a training contract) whilst would-be barristers undertake a one-year pupillage and after which, the student should have qualified to practice law. In reality, there is much more to the process as training contracts and pupilages are becoming harder to come by due to the increasing numbers of law graduates (The Law Society, 2017). For those graduates who are not able to gain a training contract or pupillage, there are alternative routes to qualification available such as qualifying through equivalent means (Solicitors Regulation Authority, 2016) or becoming a chartered legal executive (Chartered Institute of Legal Executives, 2017). For many students, however, the cost of the vocational courses and the lack of guaranteed employment afterwards has forced them to consider alternatives to legal practice.[2]

32.3   Why Introduce an Employability Scheme?

Employability in Higher Education (HE) can be defined as

> a set of achievements, skills, understandings and personal attributes - that make individuals more likely to gain employment and be successful in their chosen occupations, which benefits themselves, the workforce, the community and the economy. (Knight & Yorke, 2004)

Employability is one of the key HE buzzwords and representative of the increasing pressures Higher Education Institutions (HEIs) are under to deliver employment ready graduates (Docherty, 2014). Unfortunately, academic excellence is no longer enough for students (CBI, 2009) to enter graduate level legal employment. Students needing to be able to demonstrate attributes that show they are already equipped for the work place. These attributes range from communication skills to creative

---

[1] The fact that the participants are in graduate level employment was not by design.

[2] On the changes proposed by the new Solicitors' Qualifying Examination see https://www.lawsociety.org.uk/law-careers/becoming-a-solicitor/sqe-overview/.

thinking, commercial awareness to personal effectiveness; all of which a student is expected to have obtained during their degree programme (The Law Society, 2018). To meet the demand for employable graduates, HEIs have introduced a range of different employability models including improving their career service provisions and introducing dedicated subject careers advisors. Others have embedded employability into their course curriculums either with a dedicated employability module or more subtly weaving it into course learning outcomes (Scott, Connell, Thomson, & Willison, 2017). In 2014, at Coventry Law School, there was very limited employment support available for the Law students. This was mainly due to staffing issues in what was, at the time, a very small department. There was, however, university-wide careers provision and a new subject-specific careers advisor had just begun working within the Law School.

32.4 LEDE: The Law Employability, Diversity and Enrichment Scheme

The Employability, Diversity and Enrichment Scheme (LEDE) was introduced in September 2014 after it became apparent that the students often lacked an understanding of the realities that would face them upon graduation. The aim of the LEDE Scheme was to bring together the available resources to present law students with a way of enhancing their professionalism and maximising their chances of success once they had left university. Initially, the team responsible for realising this was comprised of an Employment Personal Tutor and a Law School Lecturer. The team reviewed the employability skills of the current cohort, their career aspirations and general feedback from the academic colleagues to shape the first series of LEDE sessions.

  All of the events were advertised on the university VLE/LMS (Moodle), via social media and directly emailed to students who had indicated an interest in a particular topic. The events were all publicised at the start of the semester and then advertised again one or two weeks in advance. A 'booking' system was created for the sessions whereby if students failed to attend three sessions without giving prior notice, they were no longer allowed to attend. The reasoning behind this was to replicate the experience that students would one day have in the workplace. The three strikes rule worked well and seemed to motivate the students to attend. In the scheme's inaugural year, it focussed on providing professional events for the students such as networking with local legal and business professionals, guest lectures and volunteering opportunities. It also ran several skills-based sessions designed to support the students at these professional events and in their future applications. The scheme organisers worked closely with local legal practitioners and other relevant professionals to provide an insightful and applicable programme of events (See Fig. 32.1).

  The first year of the scheme was highly successful, and awarded an excellence prize by the University for its contribution to the development of the University and

2014/2015	2015/2016
Barrister or Solicitor?	Mentoring Scheme Launch
Law Volunteering Fair	Your Legal Career
The Power of Words: Writing Clinic	The big, wide (legal) world!
Using Social Media	What else can I do with my law degree?
Legal Awareness Week	How to network
International Opportunities	Networking
How to Network	Legal Skillz
Law Networking Event	Selling Yourself
Legal Technical Skills	
What else can I do with my law degree?	
Application Speed Dating	
Interview skills	
Mock Interviews	

Fig. 32.1 2014/15 and 2015/2016 LEDE and employment workshops

to its reputation. The scheme received particularly good feedback regarding the networking events with local professionals with students commenting on how beneficial the opportunity was (CLS Grad Survey, 2018). Year one was highly successful in terms of good attendance and student feedback: the model of delivery was incredibly resource-intensive however as sessions were being delivered on a weekly basis which left limited time for preparation and review. In order to make the delivery model more sustainable, it was decided that LEDE sessions would only take place every other week. (Resourcing implications will be discussed in more detail below.)

Year two was also very successful. To supplement the scheme, a mentoring project with the Warwickshire Junior Lawyers Division was introduced so that the students would have access to legal professionals throughout the academic year. The students engaged strongly with the mentoring scheme and with the different workshops (See Fig. 32.1) that had been arranged. The only sessions that were not well attended were duplicate sessions that had already run (and proven popular) the previous year. In addition to core sessions, LEDE was supplemented each year by further workshops and one-to-one appointments with the Law School Employment Tutor. In 2014/15, there were 21 additional workshops and 2015/16 offered 30 workshops. These grew in number to ensure further focus on placements and work experience and to bridge the gap from moving to fortnightly LEDE sessions. These workshops covered the more practical aspects of employability such as how to apply for the industry vocational courses and postgraduate study, and how to write good CVs, cover letters and application forms.

In 2016/17, there were staffing issues which led to a revision in the number of scheduled events that were organised per semester. Instead, 'employability weeks' were organised which provided a focused, intensive number of sessions on a particular topic. For example, in November 2016, the scheme held a pro bono week at the same time as the national campaign, which included sessions on volunteering opportunities, access to justice within the UK and abroad, and social responsibility. This approach proved popular with the students with regards to attendance, however, when 'one-off sessions' were held at a later date there was a lack of engagement from the students and attendance fell significantly. As the scheme matured in its fourth and fifth years, employability provision at Coventry Law School had become multi-faceted. Employability was now embedded in the course learning outcomes; employability modules were compulsory for each undergraduate degree level and LEDE was still going strong. As many of the basic employability skills were now covered within the curriculum, LEDE was able to deliver targeted ad hoc sessions. Certain workshops are still run regularly throughout the academic year, such as guidance on routes to qualification and on alternative legal careers. Last year, the scheme hosted a conference entitled 'Your Future and the Law' which focussed on the needs of the students to be adaptive to the changing legal market and to enhance their own employability by looking to future trends.[3] This new model of delivery allows for a more proactive programme that can respond to changes in the legal market and the student body.

32.5 Challenges

In establishing the LEDE scheme, several challenges became apparent which, it is suggested, are common to employability across the HE sector. The first issue concerned the impact that the changing legal sector was having on the career aspirations, or in some cases the lack of aspirations, that the law students possessed. When the scheme began, it was focussed on traditional legal careers with some odd 'alternative legal careers' sessions thrown into the mix. However, it soon became apparent that this was not reflective of the sector and was, in fact, alienating a proportion of the student body who were still unsure, or simply not planning on going into practice. Feedback from graduates suggested that as students approached their final year of study a number of factors (such as lack of money or reluctance to commit to further training) were causing them uncertainty as to their future (CLS Grad Survey, 2018). This in turn leads to the second challenge which concerns maintaining student engagement with the scheme. Once the novelty factor of the scheme wore off, student sign-ups for the events dropped significantly. The final challenge was one of sustainability. The initial format of the scheme, whilst successful at first, was not

---

[3] See further https://spark.adobe.com/page/VsyKKyMc5n23r/ (accessed 01.11.18).

sustainable over a long period of time, and new methods of delivering employability support were required to alleviate this pressure and to maintain student engagement.

32.5.1   The First Challenge: A Changing Legal Sector

The legal sector has changed significantly over the past twenty years, particularly in light of the global financial crisis in the early 2000s. Legal services have become a commodity as the need for competitive fee structuring has driven the market. The impact of this can be seen in the legal employment market where the number of graduate level vacancies has fallen significantly. In 2016, there was a 3.2% drop in the number of graduates who were employed in the legal industry by the December after they had graduated in comparison with the previous year (High Fliers, 2018). Despite the fall in vacancies, the number of applications to study law at undergraduate and vocational levels has continued to rise. The Bar Standards Board reports that 1424 students enrolled on the Bar Professional Training Course (BPTC) in 2016 despite there being only 474 pupillage vacancies for the same period.[4] This is reiterated by statistics from the Law Society (The Law Society, 2017). The consequences of having high numbers of qualified law graduates has meant that there is now an over-saturation of the legal employment market. This is not a situation confined to the legal sector. Across the graduate employment market generally, the combined effect of greater numbers accessing HE and a highly competitive, overpopulated and crowded job market is that it is highly likely that having a degree is no longer enough to secure graduate level employment (CBI, 2009).

Furthermore, the routes to qualification are now transforming as both vocational courses are set to change in the next few years. The idea behind these changes is to make the professions more accessible to students by allowing for different methods of study which should be less expensive. It is not yet apparent what effect this will have on the legal employment market, but the likelihood is that it will cause further saturation as now becoming a solicitor will be open to students who lack a law degree.

In response to the changes in the legal sector, the LEDE scheme regularly invited industry speakers to deliver employability content to the students. Firstly, this was done to stay in touch with the legal sector and ensure that students were receiving up-to-date information. Secondly, in delivering content this way, students responded more positively to what was being said. This view is supported by Riebe et al., whose study emphasised the impacts of industry/professional guest speakers upon student employability (Riebe, Sibson, Roepen, & Meakins, 2013). The scheme found this was the best way to increase awareness of the industry and for the students to gain a true picture of the legal and graduate job markets: alumni talks had similar impacts. (Students also seemed to buy into these guest talks more quickly than those given by a member of staff that they were perhaps familiar with.) The need for input from the legal industry is particularly important at present with the upcoming changes to

---

[4] '1st six' pupillages in 2016/17: Pupillage is split into six-month blocks totalling at least a year.

the qualification route for would-be solicitors. Interestingly, despite the number of guest speakers (12 in 2014/15) that were available to the students, many graduates commented that they would have liked to have had even more of them, so that they could form a wider understanding of the industry (CLS Grad Survey, 2018).

32.5.2   The Second Challenge: Changing Students

Students themselves have changed in recent years, firstly, in terms of their mentality as 'university customers,' and secondly, with regards to their career aspirations. These two issues together mean that it is often difficult for legal employability schemes to fully satisfy the demands of a student body. Since the introduction of student tuition fees in 1997, much emphasis has been placed on students being 'customers' (Dearing, 1997) which in turn has contributed to the culture of commercialisation in HE (Molesworth, Nixon, & Scullion, 2011). This shift in the HE landscape has led to discussions on whether students now see themselves as consumers or service-users (Bunce, Baird, & Jones, 2017; Tomlinson, 2017). A recent survey by research consultancy COMRES similarly found that 47% of students surveyed did regard themselves as customers of their university (COMRES, 2017). This shift in mentality has led to concerns that students who self-identify as consumers '... may have little interest in what is actually being taught and show reduced responsibility for producing their own knowledge.' (Bunce et al., 2017). This could offer one explanation as to why student engagement with the LEDE scheme was not as consistent or as high as was expected. A simpler explanation may be that the sessions offered by the scheme were not entirely reflective of the fluctuating needs of our students in the light of a changing legal sector.

The second aspect of this challenge relates to student's career aspirations. The majority of students choose to study law with the intention of going into practice, although a small proportion do choose to study law for the broader skills base that it can provide (Chowdrey, 2014). When surveyed, 96% of Coventry Law School graduates stated that at the start of their degree they had planned on going into legal practice (CLS Grad Survey, 2018). However, upon completing their degree, 36% no longer saw themselves as wanting to be practising lawyers. Of this 36%, the majority identified competitiveness within the legal market and the high costs of vocational training as key reasons for why they now no longer wanted to practise. Other participants commented that they had found other professions that better suited their skill sets and career aspirations.

The LEDE scheme responded to the demand for alternative employability through the use of sessions which highlighted just how transferable legal skills are. This included guest speakers from other industries, with (where possible) the guest speaker having studied law. A particular session on legal recruitment for example led one law graduate to comment that 'I found a career that I love and enjoy and that was from an inspirational guest who told the class about recruitment careers.' (CLS Grad Survey 2018). When asked what type of additional events that they wished the

LEDE scheme had offered, participants identified sessions that the scheme had in fact already run. From a coordinator's perspective, this was significant: graduates that had participated in the survey were all regulars of the LEDE Scheme, having attended at least one session during their degree, and as such should have been aware of the usual advertising methods (i.e. e-mail, Moodle and social media). And yet, they had somehow missed several announcements of the very events that they claimed to be seeking out. This could be for a variety of reasons: further research is clearly needed on why such a disconnect might occur.

32.5.3   The Third Challenge: Sustainability

Delivery of an intensive stand-alone employability scheme is difficult to sustain in terms of organisation and resourcing. Feedback from graduates indicated that it was 'key' events such as networking and mock interviews that they found most beneficial. Naturally, these are the events that were the most time-intensive. Aside from organising and delivering sessions, time was needed to develop a network of resources. The LEDE scheme was fortunate to have access to the Law School's alumni list as well as having long-established connections with the local legal profession. However, it still took a year to develop the resource network so that the students were able to benefit from it fully. Even at this stage, five years on, network development is a continuous process and places a further time constraint on the LEDE team.

Linked to the sustainability of staffing is the negative impact that a lack of student engagement has on the LEDE team's morale. Often, limited numbers of students show up to the events, even if they have already committed to attend these. This lack of engagement in employability and career provisions is consistent across the sector however (The Quality Assurance Agency for Higher Education, 2016). Finding the right delivery model for the scheme is therefore very important. HEIs have incorporated employability into their student provision in a variety of ways including stand-alone delivery and embedding it into curricula. Embedding employability via the law curriculum can be done quite subtly through the use of activities such as group exercises (teamwork), problem scenarios (critical thinking) and class discussions (communication). A more direct approach can also be taken by having a specific employability module.[5] The benefits of this model of delivery is that it maintains student engagement and reduces the need for additional resources which would otherwise be required for stand-alone provision. Conversely, the problem with using an embedded model alone is that it cannot cater for the diversity of students and the wide range of career aspirations which can currently be found within most cohorts of law students.

At Coventry Law School, there is currently a hybrid form of delivery. Employability is embedded within the course learning outcomes, there are dedicated employ-

---

[5]For a comparison of these different methods with regards to law students, see Dickinson and Griffiths (2015).

ability modules for each level of all the undergraduate law programmes, and there is a Law Employment Personal Tutor to whom the students have access throughout their time at university. There is also a Central Careers service available for students to get support and careers advice. The fact that employability at Coventry Law School is now embedded within the curriculum has relieved pressure on the scheme to deliver a constant service. This multifaceted approach means that core employability topics are dealt with in the embedded modules which leaves the scheme free to respond to changes in the sector and in relation to student demand.

32.6 Conclusion

Change will be a constant feature of legal education and the legal sector for many years to come. The changes to the professional vocational courses will have a knock-on effect on how and indeed whether students continue to choose to study law. If current trends continue, it is highly likely that the legal employment market will remain saturated and looking towards other career sectors will become a necessary activity for law graduates. In light of this, it is increasingly important that law employability is adaptive to the diverse needs of the law student body. At present, the multi-faceted approach adopted by the Coventry LEDE scheme appears to be the one of the best methods for doing so. The pilot survey of graduates, though only a small sample, confirmed that the core aims of the LEDE scheme were in line with the needs and expectations of students and graduates. Further research needs to be undertaken in order to understand more fully the law student's perspectives on employability and to gauge how their needs can be best met.

References

Bunce, L., Baird, A., & Jones, S. E. (2017). The student-as-consumer approach in higher education and its effects on academic performance. *Studies in Higher Education, 42*(11), 1958–1978.

CBI. (2009). *Future fit: Preparing graduates for the world of work*. CBI Higher Education Task Force.

Chartered Institute of Legal Executives. (2017). *Get into law & qualify with CILEx!* Retrieved from Chartered Institute of Legal Executives, https://www.cilex.org.uk/study.

Chowdrey, N. (2014). *I'm studying law but I don't want to be a lawyer*. Retrieved May 30, 2014 from The Guardian, https://www.theguardian.com/law/2014/may/30/students-alternative-careers-law-degree.

COMRES. (2017). *Universities UK undergraduates survey: A survey of UK university undergraduate students on their relationship with their university*. London: COMRES.

Coventry Law School Graduate Survey 2018.

Dearing, R. (1997). *Higher education in learning society: Report of the national committee of inquiry into higher education*. London: Her Majesty's Stationary Office.

Dickinson, J., & Griffiths, T.-L. (2015). Embedding employability and encouraging engagement with PDP/careers: A case study focussing on law students. *Student Engagement and Experience Journal, 4*(1) (Online).

Docherty, D. (2014). *Universities must produce graduates who are ready for any workplace.* Retrieved May 22, 2014 from The Guardian, https://www.theguardian.com/higher-education-network/2014/may/22/universities-must-produce-graduates-who-are-ready-for-workplace.

High Fliers. (2018). *The graduate market in 2018.* London: High Fliers Ltd.

Knight, P., & Yorke, M. (2004). *Learning, curriculum and employability in higher education.* London: Routledge Falmer.

Molesworth, M., Nixon, E., & Scullion, R. (2011). *The marketisation of higher education and the student as consumer.* Abingdon: Routledge.

Riebe, L., Sibson, R., Roepen, D., & Meakins, K. (2013). Impact of industry guest speakers on business students' perceptions of employability skills development. *Industry and Higher Education, 27*(1), 55–66.

Scott, F. J., Connell, P., Thomson, L. A., & Willison, D. (2017). Empowering students by enhancing their employability skills. *Journal of Further and Higher Education, 43*(5), 692–707.

Solicitors Regulation Authority. (2016, December). *Solicitors regulation authority.* Retrieved from Qualifying through equivalent means, https://www.sra.org.uk/students/resources/equivalent-means-information-pack.page.

The Law Society. (2017). *The law society's annual statistics report 2017.* London: The Law Society.

The Law Society. (2018). *Becoming a solicitor.* Retrieved from The Law Society, https://www.lawsociety.org.uk/law-careers/becoming-a-solicitor/.

The Quality Assurance Agency for Higher Education. (2016). *Evaluating the impact of higher education providers employability measures.* Gloucester: The Quality Assurance Agency for Higher Education.

Tomlinson, M. (2017). Student perceptions of themselves as 'consumers' of higher education. *British Journal of Sociology of Education, 38*(4), 450–467. https://doi.org/10.1080/01425692.2015.1113856.

Harriet Lodge (LLB, LLM) is a lecturer in Law at Coventry University and a former Associate Head (International) with a focus on access to justice, mediation and practical legal training. She is an RICS accredited mediator hoping to commence a Ph.D. on international mediation and access to justice. An LLB graduate of the University of Hull, she was called to the Bar by the Honourable Society of Lincoln's Inn in 2012 and continues to be actively involved with the legal profession. Prior to entering academia, she worked in the voluntary sector as a campaigns officer and legal adviser. Her LLM dissertation focussed upon the discretion of international criminal prosecutors and the effect that such public discretion may have on wider public perceptions of international criminal courts.

Susie Elliott (AFHEA) is an Employment Personal Tutor, and has been based at Coventry University since 2013. She uses her experience in recruitment to guide students and to help them to achieve their career goals. Together with Harriet Lodge she founded Coventry Law School's employability scheme in 2014, which aimed to improve and enrich students employment prospects. In 2015, they were awarded the Cecil Angel Cup for the employability scheme's contribution to enhancing the reputation of the University.

Chapter 33
Increasing Employability Beyond Getting a Job: Engaging Criminal Justice Students in Their Own Professional Development

Ester Ragonese and Steven Altham

33.1 Introduction

The UK's Higher Education (HE) sector has long recognised its changing landscape and the increasing importance placed on developing student's employability beyond the university experience (QAA, 2012). This has however become even more important with the link to the Teaching Excellence Framework (TEF) and a renewed focus on student outcomes and lifelong graduate potential. Employability is not an easily understood concept: there is much debate in relation to not only its meaning but to its effective implementation within the HE sector. This chapter aims to develop a broader understanding of employability and of how the HE sector should engage staff and students in understanding its significance. It offers definitions and examples of how one programme and institution (LJMU) responded to the various challenges via a module delivered to second year undergraduate criminal justice (CJ) students. Briefly, the team worked in partnership with careers staff, employers and students to ensure that its curricular design would embed the skills, knowledge and experiences that students will need in gaining graduate level roles. The barriers and issues faced are discussed, in terms of how these have been overcome: a 'how to do it' framework with 'hints and tips' is also presented here. These can be transplanted into any discipline or programme of study that aims to engage students in building their own self-efficacy and professional development.

E. Ragonese (✉) · S. Altham
Liverpool John Moores University, Liverpool, England, UK
e-mail: e.l.ragonese@ljmu.ac.uk

S. Altham
e-mail: s.altham@ljmu.ac.uk

33.2   Definitions of Employability

This section asks the following questions:

1. What is it that makes us employable?
2. Why are we employable?
3. What makes us unemployable?

These questions lie at the very heart of what is commonly (mis)understood about notions of employability. Hogan, Chamorro-Premuzic, and Kaiser (2013) argue that employability is defined as a dynamic, changing trait that allows an individual to obtain and maintain a formal job. Clark and Zukas (2013) note that, at its simplest, employability is the ability to find a graduate level position in a company after university. Acer [1] however states that employability is about much more than obtaining employment but, rather, is concerned with a person's

> ...long-term capacity to build a career and to prosper in a dynamic labour market. Employability implies qualities of resourcefulness, adaptability and flexibility, whereas employment-related suggests an orientation to the current state of the labour market. As such, employability has more potential as a term to signal the qualities needed for success not only in paid employment but also in other domains of life.

Employability is therefore much more than just about getting a job: it is concerned with developing skills and attributes that will scaffold and allow for future professional growth and development, in other words, transferable skills. Indeed, defining the concept is perhaps less important than the way in which the sector responds to the need for it, in developing successful graduates of the future. Indeed, as Harvey (2003) states, within HE there must be a focus within employability skills on learning, ability, and developing criticality.

33.3   Employability Skills

It is important to reflect upon the meaning of 'skills' means from both a professional and personal perspective:

1. What are employability skills?
2. What employability skills do *we* have?
3. What skills do employers say they want?
4. How do we articulate this to students?
5. How do students articulate the skills that they have?
6. Do we provide them with the necessary tools to do this?
7. How do we translate these to students?

Yorke and Knight (2004:7) described employability as

---

[1] ACCI/ BCA (2002:4).

…a set of achievements – skills, understandings and personal attributes – that make graduates more likely to gain employment and be successful in their chosen occupations, which benefits themselves, the workforce, the community and the economy.

Within this definition, skills are clearly at the core of successful employability, but what are the skills that make graduates successful and what do employers say that they want most? The Confederation of British Industry (CBI) have identified seven key employability skills, namely: team working, business and customer awareness, problem solving, self-management, communication, literacy, numeracy, and data management. Employability skills may be viewed in generic terms as transferrable, focussed on the individual, and allowing for transitions into or towards multiple career paths. Regardless of discipline these skills will 'underpin your success' (Trought, 2012: 5). And yet, specific skills are still required by certain sectors. The CJ field for example requires graduates to be able to demonstrate the following: resilience, respect for others, effective listening, caring, decision-making, organisational aptitude, embracing of change and developing self and others.

Arguably, there are therefore two distinct sides to employability: social skills and cognitive skills, or 'hard' and 'soft' skills (Ragonese, Rees, Ives, & Dray, 2015) with attributes such as cognitive ability and personality serving as key indicators for future job performance (Hogan et al., 2013). Das and Subudhi (2015) suggest that employability is not just a trait that allows people to get a job, rather it is also the ability to sustain high levels of employment throughout one's working career. For McIntye and Buffardi (1999), employability is the understanding of normative behaviours within a professional working context. This includes having a positive attitude towards performance feedback and extroverted social behaviours to promote workplace cohesion among workers. Career success should not therefore necessarily be viewed as a criterion for employability (Olson and Shultz 2013). As Hogan et al. (2013) state, individuals are often predisposed to positively evaluate their careers, resulting in employability bias, especially if they have acquired the skills to do so. Olson and Shultz (2013) similarly argue that to maintain a high level of employability, individuals need to be able to respond to constant and often rapid change. Companies are looking to hire candidates based upon such 'knowledge work.'

Knowledge workers possess the key skills and traits that will make them good investments, willing to stay and perform to high standards within their area of expertise (Noe, Hollenbeck, Gerhart, & Wright, 2011). With the globalised transitioning towards knowledge work, it is imperative that individuals possess the will to adapt to new situations and develop new skills and abilities to contribute to a company's success (Olson & Shultz, 2013). However, it has been noted also that individuals may well thrive in one profession but fail in others. This suggests that employability skills might not only differ over time but also vary in definition across different occupations (Das & Subudhi, 2015). It is therefore important that HE ensures students understand these definitions and articulate the skills within them. A further set of questions arises:

1. Do activities in the curriculum link to the exploration of skills?
2. How do we recognise and celebrate these skills?

3. Are skills implicit or explicit?
4. How do we develop a skills 'toolkit' for the unknown?
5. How do we engage students in authentic discussions about employability?
6. What role does workplace learning have?

33.4   Module History

The second year undergraduate CJ employability module is a core module, included within the CJ degree for over 10 years. Historically it followed a typical structure based around student career management and job recruitment processes. Initially it was a year-long module but was recently reduced to one-semester delivery. This cut in teaching time had a significant effect on the content and focus of the module: drawing on yearly analysis and student feedback, it made ask at this whether it gave our students what they needed to succeed in their professional careers, and then perhaps look to develop it for the future.

Austerity in the sector (brought on by recent large-scale restructuring and a general reduction in government funding) means that the system will demand something different in terms of preparation for graduate employment. Our modular and sector analysis involved input from the academic teaching team, employability staff and the university careers service. It also, crucially, involved local employers, who have real time insight into what students will face once they leave university. Such analysis crucial to curricular and modular design: one of the main findings from our module analysis was the realisation that we had been focussing on the traditional career management topics of *figuring out what you want*, and then learning *how to get* it via application techniques. This knowledge (whilst highly important, and useful throughout a student's future career) was missing out content on what can help students succeed when actually working in professional roles. They were learning to find and then get the job, but not necessarily learning the professional skills needed to *do* the job successfully as indicated by the definitions discussed earlier.

The institution has a wide variety of student support services not least the services focussed on careers and employability. The careers service offered workshops/drop-in support, one to one support for students and additional resources as required. In moving away from more basic careers application content, classroom sessions have become more specifically aimed at developing professional identity and behaviours, work-ready skills and reflective practice, with more connectivity to the services already available. Being 'professional' is no longer linked to certain occupations (i.e. Doctors/Lawyers); many workers from other occupations now consider themselves to be professionals (Evetts, 2013).

By professional behaviours, we mean the way that our students (as developing professionals) should act in the workplace, around colleagues and clients. To have a professional demeanour (calm, reliable, trustworthy), to analyse risk, have expert judgement and high levels of expertise, whilst regularly evaluating themselves and their services. Alongside these behaviours, professional work skills will help our future graduates succeed in their day to day occupational roles. These are skills that the student will actually need to *do* the job, not apply for or gain one, namely, effective teamworking, strong verbal and written communication, the ability to deal successfully with clients in demanding situations. This also involves basic workplace skills that are prevalent in most office-based roles: how to use work phones, be successful in meetings, and networking effectively. Many of these are transferrable in nature, valid across many sectors and roles, and linked into but not necessarily defining the student as a professional (Trede, 2012).

33.5 Module Design

The module is delivered over one semester with twelve teaching weeks and begins by encouraging students to take control of their own professional development. Personal branding matters: when they look at themselves as a future professional, who do they want to be? How are they going to get there? This plan is *individually,* not generic. Social media is covered, teaching the student about the importance of managing their online brand and using career relevant sites such as LinkedIn. Local employability and careers staff give support for the development of this content. The aim then is to increase students' understanding of the sector and the organisations that they may end up working for, focussing upon the skills required to do the job, and the values and aims of these organisations, and encouraging students to match their personal brands to the world after graduation, and find *their* place within it all.

Students must start using professional skills now, taking what they have been taught in the module when engaging with university staff, who are professionals themselves. A simple example is the professional use of email: we set expectations clearly linked to professional behaviours aiming to develop professionalism whilst still studying. This focus on skills is an essential part of the module: the best way to teach students professional skills was to be practical. Telling them 'how to' is not enough: allowing them to then practice the skills together provides a firmer understanding of what being successful means, installing a sense of self-confidence obtained from both 'doing' and 'reflecting.' As Student A later observed, '…giving students the chance to experience interviews and assessment centres beforehand is a great opportunity.'

Employers are crucial to the design and delivery of the module, not only because they 'understand the labour market better than anyone' (Griggs, Scandone, & Battherham, 2018:3) but also because they give students opportunity to engage with those in the roles that they see themselves doing in the future, encouraging and motivating them to take ownership of their employability post-graduation and beyond. Successful engagement with employers led to opportunities for work shadowing/work experience, enhancing knowledge of the sector and further development of their professional skills, within a real-world setting. One form of employer engagement used was the questions and answer session, which allowed students to ask individual questions of employers, again putting the focus firmly upon the student and their owning of their professional development. These sessions are often very 'real' with employers giving up to date examples of what they must deal with in their daily roles, with the highs, lows, and everyday issues they face, and recommendations they would give to students to succeed. Students clearly appreciate these sessions as evidenced by their subsequent feedback.

33.6 Assessment

For learning to be evidenced, assessment methods are embedded into the curriculum design and are authentic to the employability process. Two assessments each carry a 50% weighting, and are aligned with the curriculum, with a focus on transferable skill development and professional behaviours.

33.6.1 Assessment 1: Mock Recruitment

This is an individual assessment, marked by the module leader and an employer. The student is required to deliver a 10-min action plan presentation, followed by four graduate level interview questions, two of which were competency-based, one on the sector and one on diversity.

33.6.2 Assessment 2: Reflective Portfolio

This assessment requires the student to collect and evidence (to a set of co-created criteria) a body of work that demonstrates their learning. This focuses on 'who I am': a CV and personal statement, an elevator pitch, the world of CJ, skills/competencies and experience, description of the field or sector, and reflection on learning.

33.7 Challenges

When introducing an employability module into an academic programme of teaching there are numerous challenges. This section offers analysis of these and several solutions.

33.7.1 Student Engagement

There is always a risk that such a module is seen as 'bolt-on,' not linking to the rest of the programme, perhaps with less academic rigour. Students can struggle to see how the module fits into their overall programme of learning, and this can affect levels of attendance and engagement. In order to make the module fit into expected programme progression in the eyes of our students, the scenarios and examples used were linked directly into academic content taught elsewhere. The module leader teaches the students in other modules and has excellent knowledge of the rest of the programme's contents. This allows the students to make links back to their previous learning, and to look towards upcoming topics, fitting the module's content into the larger programme context. We also tried to move away from generic non-subject-specific career development content (which our students might not link to themselves personally) and tried to make links to more individually-focused learning. The focus on the academic subject and future roles associated with it, the individual student's professional brand and their career journey, encourages students to take greater ownership of the module's contents, increasing their interest and overall engagement. As one alumnus noted:

> Walking into the first lecture of Professional Development I had preconceived ideas of what the module would entail, however I could not have been more pleasantly surprised. I attained skills which I didn't realise I had until I stepped out of the university environment and into a career environment.

33.7.2 Employer Engagement

Integral to the module is the involvement of employers to inspire and motivate students. This can however engender concerns: What if they do not turn up? What if their 'message' does not link positively to what we have taught? Will our students give the right impression to employers who are valued highly by the university? Some of these issues are out of our hands: employers sometimes have emergencies/illnesses where must be cancelled, and we cannot control everything our guest speakers say, nor indeed should we. All we can do is to make sure we have engaging seminars/workshops where there are enough employers that if one is missing, the activities can still go ahead, albeit it with slightly pre-planned amendments. Making sure to link employer content with the rest of the module means working with employers on initial module design and using the same employers regularly and fostering relationships so that they understand what is needed of them. A written brief, highlighting what has come before their session and what will come afterwards can also help.

With regards to student behaviour, prepping them on the importance of professional behaviour around other professionals is key, as well as the need to make a good impression early in the module's content, then reinforcing this on the day of the employer visit. We also make explicit the potential opportunities for the student that can come out of employer networking: as one employer observed: 'Transferable skills like reflective practice and interviewing are crucial in working with offenders and it is excellent to see these skills being developed as part of the curriculum.'

33.7.3   The 'Numbers Game'

As with any practical module, the larger the number of students, the bigger the resource implications. Our answer to this was to use other resources available within the school and university outside of the academic teaching team. Both our local Student Development Coordinator and our dedicated school Careers Advisor became part of the teaching support team, offering employability and professional development support both in timetabled sessions and via extracurricular activities. Relevant lectures were timetabled to coincide with pre-existing careers provision with students encouraged to engage with these alongside individual careers/professional development meetings in their own time.

33.7.4   Internal/External Pressures

Externally, there have been major changes in the CJ sector, such as funding cuts and a large part of what used to be the public sector increasingly privatised, with new companies creating specific objectives and targets. Potential future CJ-related roles and their objectives have changed rapidly. Clearly, we need to keep up to date with these changes, via linked sector research and, for example, by having employers affected by the changes come in for Q and A workshops to discuss the realities of the changes on a day-to-day and career development basis.

Internally the university implemented a new university-wide employability initiative that embedded generic careers content into relevant modules. To effect the most positive integration, we made sure that we understood the main purpose of (and the processes involved in) the initiative, working closely with those who had created it to make the content work for us, rather than against us. Content was considered from the start, working it into the modules design and learning outcomes, making it seamless rather than stand-alone.

33.8   Some Useful 'Hints and Tips'

- Analyse module content annually, making sure that it is relevant, current and linked clearly to the rest of the degree's content and taught in a hands-on way that engages many types of learners.

- Involve employers from your chosen sector, both within the module's delivery to inform and motivate students, but also in terms of initial design, review and future development.
- Do not simply focus on traditional careers content such as 'getting the job.' Focus instead on helping students progress professionally, in terms of when they will be in their chosen role, or other potential future roles, as much as possible. For professional behaviours, transferrable work skills development in a practical context, practical activities work best, placed within the context of the roles/sectors students want to work in.
- Aim to develop individual students as professionals, affecting 'the student culture' to make the transition from student to employee smoother. Students should see their degree as a professional stepping-stone into lifelong career development.
- Actively use appropriate resources outside of the module for support.
- Academic engagement is key, by teaching the students elsewhere on the course, or at least by having a good understanding of the rest of the programme. This allows for greater link up between the Professional Development module and the rest of the student's degree course. If students see how it fits in with the rest of their studies, and its importance, they are more likely to engage with the module.
- Students often do not realise the value of these types of modules straight away, so flexibility is needed from management around initial module feedback: employability modules need time to develop. Where appropriate, course teams can also make links to your module within their own, creating further links across the programme.[2]

33.9 Conclusion

Positive student and employer feedback, alongside continued local support, clearly demonstrates the module's success in various ways. It continues to develop however and as such there are still areas that could be enhanced. Employer involvement in its design and delivery remains key. With so much employer involvement however, one could ask whether all employers are actually qualified to engage with an academic curriculum? Should employers perhaps be trained to better understand HE content development, the role, nature and meaning of learning outcomes, assessments and various teaching methods? As one employer observed: '…it was a really valuable

---

[2] As the programme leader observed: "I have always seen the development of students' employability skills as a priority, but also recognise that students do not always recognise how crucial employability skills are until they are nearing the end of their final year of undergraduate study. That is why I am fully in support of the presence of the module. The module provides content and skills, which other modules on the programme simply do not provide, because it allows students the space to think critically about how ready they are for a career in the CJ sector, while at the same time giving them the tools they need to be successful in employability terms. I can only predict that the importance of the module to the programme as a whole will increase over the coming years.'

experience for me individually as well, specifically as the students identified issues that we as an organisation may want to look at.'

Internally, our CJ programme is currently the only one within the Law School that has a core professional development/employability module. We could consider trying to embed similar modules within our other school-based programmes but must ask how we would justify this to our fellow programme teams. Further, given the many variables that feed into post-HE destinations statistics, trying to link student quantitative data indicating successes back to module-level is not always easy. Real-world work experience remains key to having students gain insights into their potential career paths. It can confirm or end a student's chosen career pathway, help develop skills and offer valuable networking opportunities. A work experience element could be integrated into the module: alternatively, there could be clearer links between this module and a placement module in final year, perhaps with the module being lengthened from one semester to a year-long one. These are just some of the questions that can arise, and require review, in respect of such a module. In sum, the Higher Education and Criminal Justice sectors are ever-changing, often quite rapidly: we must continue to do our best to prepare our students for their future careers. As one alumnus observed:

> Whilst completing the Professional Development module, I failed to recognise just how much the module would assist me when applying for jobs. Through completing the module, I developed my ability to apply for jobs via the competency framework along with presentation skills and interview skills, all of which are crucial in the initial application process and throughout career progression. Furthermore, the module gave me the opportunity to explore the skills I possess, the relevant experience I can provide to employers and factors that motivate me and play a fundamental part in who I am as a person and a potential employee. Subsequently this allowed me to demonstrate my competencies and sell myself to future employers successfully.

References

ACCI/BCA. (2002). *Employability Skills for the Future, Canberra: Department of Education, Science and Training, Commonwealth of Australia.*

CBI. http://www.cbi.org.uk/. Accessed December 1, 2018.

Clark, M., & Zukas, M. (2013). A Bourdieusian approach to understanding employability: Becoming a 'fish in water'. *Journal of Vocational Education & Training, 65*(2), 1–12.

Das, B., & Subudhi, R. (2015). Professional education for employability: A critical review. *Parikalpana: KIIT Journal of Management, 11*(1), 32–45.

Evetts, J. (2013). Professionalism: Value and ideology. *Current Sociology Review 61*(5–6), 778–796. https://journals.sagepub.com/doi/pdf/10.1177/0011392113479316.

Griggs, J., Scandone, B., & Battherham, J. (2018). *How employable is the UK? Meeting the future skills challenge.* https://home.barclays/content/dam/home-barclays/documents/news/2018/Barclays%20Lifeskills%20report_v10.pdf.

Harvey, L. (2003). Transitions from higher education to work: A briefing paper prepared by Lee Harvey. In *Centre for Research and Evaluation, Sheffield Hallam University.* www.qualityreserachinternational.com.

Hogan, R., Chamorro-Premuzic, T., & Kaiser, R. B. (2013). Employability and career success: Bridging the gap between theory and reality. *Industrial and Organizational Psychology: Perspectives on Science and Practice, 6,* 3–16.

McIntye, C., & Buffardi, L. (1999). Employment self-efficacy: A conceptual framework for understanding employability and employment success. *ProQuest Dissertations and Theses.*

Noe, R. A., Hollenbeck, J. R., Gerhart, B., & Wright, P. M. (2011). *Fundamentals of human resource management.* New York, NY: McGraw-Hill Irwin.

Olson, D., & Shultz, K. (2013). Employability and career success: The need for comprehensive definitions of career success. *Industrial and Organizational Psychology, 6*(1), 17–20.

Ragonese, E., Rees, A., Ives, J., & Dray, T. (2015). *The Routledge guide to working in criminal justice: Employability skills and careers in the criminal justice sector.* Oxon/New York: Routledge.

The Quality Assurance Agency. (2012). *The code of practice for the assurance of academic quality and standards in education Section B4: Enabling Student Development and Achievement.* www.qaa.ac.uk/assuring-standards-and-quality/the-quality-code.

Trede, F. (2012). Role of work-integrated learning in developing professionalism and professional identity. *Asia-Pacific Journal of Cooperative Education, 13*(3), 159–167. http://citeseerx.ist.psu.edu/viewdoc/download?doi=10.1.1.688.4390&rep=rep1&type=pdf.

Trought, F. (2012). *Brilliant employability skills: How to stand out from the crowd in the graduate job market.* Edinburgh: Pearson.

Yorke, M., & Knight, P. T. (2004). *Embedding employability into the curriculum.* York: HEA.

Ester Ragonese (NTF) is Associate Dean (Education) for the Faculty of Arts and Professional Social Sciences at Liverpool John Moores University, UK. She is a member of the Criminal Justice Programme Team within The School of Law. She has experience of working in the criminal justice system as a probation officer and has a wide range of research interests e.g. the resettlement of offenders. She works closely with local prisons and community organisations to develop 'best practice' in this area. Improving the student experience and understanding the processes of HE for the development of policy and practice is also a key research interest. She is a National Teaching Fellow and teaches on the PGCert at LJMU, working with staff to encourage them to focus on their teaching practice.

Steven Altham (FHEA, M.A.) is Student Development Coordinator for the School of Law at Liverpool John Moores University, Liverpool, UK. His main focus is on the enhancement of student employability and professional development within and aligned to the academic curriculum. He works as a school-based coordinator between students, academic staff, the university Careers department and external employers, and is a Fellow of the HEA and an LJMU AUA advocate.

Chapter 34
Quiet Silencing: Restricting the Criminological Imagination in the Neoliberal University

Alana Barton, Howard Davis and David Scott

34.1 Introduction: The Critical Imagination and the Neoliberal University

One of the most influential perspectives for critical criminology, and critical social science more generally, is C. Wright Mills' conceptualisation of the 'sociological imagination'. Mills argued that the inability of individuals to recognise and understand the relations of power that connect individual biographies to history, contributes to a disaffecting social order characterised by social alienation, moral insensibility, disproportionate power of a small group of elites, threats to liberty and freedom, and conflict between bureaucratic rationality and human reason. Understanding social structure and, in turn, recognising the intersection between individual lives and social and historical contexts, provides a means to make sense of the world and resist the historical repetition of alienation and oppression. This, for Mills, is 'the promise' of the sociological imagination (Mills, 1959–2000: 3–24). Taking this thesis and applying it to criminology is important for two reasons. Firstly, in disciplinary terms, the project is necessary in order that we may reject narrow, administrative notions of 'crime' which focus too heavily on (often individualised) causes and, in turn, marginalise consideration of structural contexts (Reiner, 2012). Secondly, and important in terms of teaching, a sociological imagination generates 'emancipatory knowledge' which, as Mills perceived, contributes to a transformative politics, the aim of which is to actively challenge injustice and inequality.

A. Barton (✉) · H. Davis
Edge Hill University, Ormskirk, England, UK
e-mail: bartona@edgehill.ac.uk

H. Davis
e-mail: davish@edgehill.ac.uk

D. Scott
Open University, Milton Keynes, England, UK
e-mail: david.scott@open.ac.uk

© Springer Nature Switzerland AG 2019
A. Diver (ed.), *Employability via Higher Education: Sustainability as Scholarship*,
https://doi.org/10.1007/978-3-030-26342-3_34

There are clear overlaps between the fundamental principles of critical criminology and critical pedagogy (Barton, Corteen, Davies, & Hobson, 2010). For critical criminologists, the discipline should be concerned with fostering comradeship, collegiality and solidarity. It should promote intellectual integrity and craftsmanship, whilst emphasising strong political commitment and engagement. Its goal should be the facilitation of emancipatory knowledge through scholarship, activism and, most importantly, education.[1] Similarly, critical pedagogy involves opposing learning relationships that are oppressive, and transforming learners from *objects* of education to *subjects* of their own autonomy. Through this process, it is argued, learners gain not only a critical *understanding* of the world, but are also empowered to *act* (Freire, 2007). This form of 'liberating' education fosters both the '*emergence* of consciousness and *critical intervention* in reality,'[2] so that students become equipped with the critical tools to effect personal and social change.

For Giroux (1988), critical pedagogy is a form of 'cultural politics' which can challenge oppression and make a difference to the quality of human life. It is within this context that a critical pedagogical approach is embedded in the critical social sciences. By problematising the role and power of the state, its agents and practices—often by listening to, and reporting on, the lived realities of those on the receiving end of harms, injustices and abuses of human rights and civil liberties—a central principle of critical criminology is to locate "the 'everyday' routine world within structural and institutional relations," and be inspired to confront injustices and seek change (Chadwick & Scraton, 2006: 98). Giroux (2000) argued also that education should be envisaged as political action by "teaching students to take risks [and] challenge those with power…" (p. 139). The university, therefore, should be "a critical institution infused with the promise of cultivating intellectual insight, the imagination, inquisitiveness, risk-taking, social responsibility, and the struggle for justice" (Giroux, 2015). Thus, these critical values and skills are intended to extend beyond academia and become important capacities for life and, given that many criminology/social science graduates go on to work with some of the most marginalised groups and individuals in society, for future employment.

A reflection on these fundamental principles, their important sociological influences and their utility for teaching and learning in HE, is now more important than ever. We are living in very cold times. Political and popular discourse increasingly 'others' and vilifies the poor and vulnerable as much as the 'criminal.' As Wacquant argues, the decrees of neo-liberalism, involving the withdrawal of welfare and the simultaneous expansion of the punitive/penal state, ensure "the punitive containment and disciplinary supervision of the problem populations dwelling at the margins of the class and cultural order" (2009: xx). History tells us that there are real danger signs here for individuals, specific groups and for social relations generally (Adorno,

---

[1] These priorities are as recommended by the European Group for the Study of Deviance and Social Control, an international network for academics, practitioners, and activists working towards social justice, state accountability and de-carceration. It is the largest critical criminology forum in the world: (See further www.europeangroup.org accessed 31.10.18.

[2] Freire, 2007: 81, (original emphasis).

1967; Gellately & Stoltzfuz, 2001) and criminology (along with its related social science sister-subjects) has a responsibility to respond to these most serious of concerns. Seldom has it been more urgent for those who teach in these disciplines to recognise, emphasise *and disseminate* the political and empathic priorities of their craft or to know, as Becker (1967) might have put it, whose side they are on. For Adorno (1967), the development of empathy and the nurturing of critical political consciousness is the fundamental role of *all* education, with all other gains—practical or theoretical—being merely incidental. Only through these priorities can we hope to challenge the "coldness of the societal monad" and a grievous "indifference to the fate of others" (1967: 9). But how achievable is this in the current political and educational landscape?

In the neoliberal university, which has been reshaped in accordance with aggressive market priorities and business ethos, the logic of academic capitalism has commodified learning and valorised competition. The production of academic knowledge has become prized for its productiveness and capacity to be traded rather than for its integral educational value or its potential to personally, socially and politically reward, enlighten and empower (Barton et al., 2010; Walters, 2007). The neoliberalization of labour markets, particularly in times of austerity, has meant that gaining employment after graduation has become (understandably) a primary objective of most students. Responding to 'consumer preferences', university businesses have, in turn, begun to prioritise 'employability' *above all else*. Employability has become 'fetishized', in that institutions have developed an excessive and irrational commitment to the notion. This is despite it being vaguely defined, contradictory to other educational values and, in terms of effectiveness, poorly evidenced.

Universities have a long history of producing useful and productive citizens (although, of course, they have also been responsible for producing many graduates who have gone on to inflict extensive social and environmental harms). In the present context however, the 'employability' agenda can have serious and negative consequences for staff, students and the academic content of degrees (Boden & Nedeva, 2010). The concept of 'employability' emerged from the 1980s as a response to the demands of a mismanaged and unstable economic environment which required employees to be 'flexible.' As Chertkovskaya (2013) puts it, "[c]ompanies…could no longer offer job security to employees and introduced 'employability' instead, as the new psychological contract". Despite objections from educators it was embraced as a valuable model of labour supply. Neoliberal rhetoric, even at a time of structural, financial and economic crisis, constructed individuals as responsible for their 'employability' and, by default, for their 'unemployability'.

This developed into the 'responsibilisation' of educators for success or failure of graduates in job markets. The significance of employer demands on the substantive educational process was made clear in 2015 when the Universities Minister, Jo Johnson, stated that the motivation behind the Teaching Excellence Framework[3] (TEF) was to create "incentives for universities to devote as much attention to the

---

[3]The Teaching Excellence and Student Outcomes Framework (TEF) is a device, introduced by the government in England, to assess "excellence in teaching at universities and colleges, and how well

quality of teaching as fee-paying students and *prospective employers have a right to expect.*" (Morgan, 2015. Emphasis added). As Collini (2016) notes the phrase 'what employers want' is used 35 times in the Green Paper.[4] Recent changes to TEF (since re-titled Teaching Excellence *and Student Outcome* Framework: emphasis added) mean that individual subject areas, rather than whole institutions, will be measured and compared on 'teaching quality'. However, metric weightings have been altered so that actual *teaching related* measurements (i.e. teaching on the course, assessment and feedback and academic support—all measured through National Student Survey data) are now only worth half as much as metrics around post-graduation employment data as measured by the Destination of Leavers from HEs Survey (DLHE)) Moreover, it is suggested that the employment metrics used in TEF/TESOF will be related to salaries earned and tax paid, which would automatically and unfairly skew the 'competition' against universities in less affluent regions, and those courses that generally produce graduates who enter public services or third sector work. Understandably then, concern is growing over the impact that neoliberal discourse and policy around 'teaching quality' and 'employability' will have on subjects that prioritise *critical* rather than 'neoliberal-friendly' disciplinary content and pedagogical practice.

These concerns are not new. In 2004, Thomas Mathiesen argued that the university had increasingly become a site, not of resistance and contestation, but of acquiescence to powerful discourses and, indeed, of 'silencing'. Mathiesen was not referring to the physical or explicit forms of silencing that we might expect to see in coercive situations, but rather forms that are unobtrusive and 'everyday'. This 'quiet' silencing—the prescribed subordination to imposed ideological (in this case, neoliberal) standpoints—is achieved through a range of processes that are embedded in organisational structures. For Mathiesen, 'quiet' silencing is more difficult to resist and challenge than physical coercion because the former can subvert and corrupt *moral ideals* in ways the latter, often, cannot. This form of silencing is dynamic—its processes develop, intensify and, importantly, become *normalised* over time. The normalisation and routineness of silencing processes render them largely invisible and, often, inevitable. The moral corruption occurs because quiet silencing relies, to some degree, on (often unwitting) *participation* from those who are being silenced. So, depending on the position held within the organisation, individuals might remain silent about policies or practices they find problematic, as a means of self-protection. They may become 'grudgingly tolerant' (but tolerant nonetheless) of the imposition of new philosophies, ventures or systems. Such tolerance can progress to, (often unnoticed) acceptance and sometimes to the willing endorsement of attitudes and actions that may once have been considered problematic.

---

they ensure excellent outcomes for their students in terms of graduate-level employment or further study" (Office for Students, 2018).

[4]J Johnson (MP), Green Paper '*Fulfilling our Potential: Teaching Excellence, Social Mobility and Student Choice*' (2015) Department of Business, Innovation and Skills.

In recent years, organisational and state mechanisms have been used to silence. Competitive neo-liberal league tables (REF,[5] NSS,[6] TEF etc.), which epitomise the antithesis of the collective, empathic politics and values of critical education, provide examples. Opposition to these forms of measurement is strong amongst academics but can be easily silenced when failure to participate and 'succeed' over others is constructed as having negative impacts on colleagues (loss of jobs, loss of research funding) or institutions (reduction in place in league tables; reduction in student numbers and so on). The rhetoric of 'collegiality' and loyalty is cleverly employed so staff become responsibilised for institutional 'success'. Through this process the neoliberal discourse becomes internalised and opposition becomes 'absorbed'.

In the following section of the chapter we draw upon a small scale piece of research conducted with critical criminologists working in Universities in England, Wales and the North of Ireland.[7] Twenty-four academics from 20 different Universities engaged in the study, completing an extensive questionnaire, from which both quantitative and qualitative data were derived.[8] Whilst the study focused on the impacts of the neoliberal education agenda upon both teaching and research, here we reflect upon academics' experiences of the former. Specifically, by utilizing Mathiesen's concept of quiet, or 'silent' silencing, we examine the bearing of 'employability' rhetoric on the university, the discipline of (specifically *critical*) criminology, and staff and student experiences.

34.2   Quiet Silencing in the Neoliberal University?

Responses to the research could be mapped roughly onto the broad themes suggested by Mathiesen. Firstly, many respondents argued that as a consequence of neoliberal policies, there has been a major shift in the nature of the university in terms of its ideals, both in relation to its purposes and in the ways that it is run, or managed. These changes are, many respondents believed, contributing to an erosion of other academic and educational values and placing critical approaches at risk. Second, this involved a process in which the 'business' model and its focus on market derived 'products' is fast becoming normalised. Management drives towards 'impactful' research and 'employability' focussed teaching have become familiar and unrelenting features of academic life. New products, like degree programmes, are required to meet on the one hand, 'consumer' perceptions and preferences in which the degree is increasingly required to be a 'ticket' to a career and lifestyle, and on the other, demands of

---

[5]Research Excellence Framework.

[6]National Student Survey.

[7]The primary research was conducted by David Scott. See Scott (2014) for full data.

[8]The respondents included colleagues from a range of academic positions (Lecturer, Senior Lecturer, Principal Lecturer, Reader, Professor, Research Fellow). Of these, 7 had worked for 5 years or less in academia; 5 had worked between 6 and 10 years; 5 had worked between 10 and 20 years; and 7 had worked for over 20 years. They are anonymised and so referred to in this discussion as R1, R2 etc., followed by their title.

employers for universities to train their prospective job applicants (at the expense of the latter). Third, there were different views among respondents as to the degree to which they were required to acquiesce or participate in these drives and the extent to which critical criminology as a discipline, is at risk of incorporation within a changed set of relationships between universities and a criminal justice system that the former increasingly seeks to serve. This raises major questions for staff as educators and for students as current 'consumers' and future producers, with respondents taking various positions on what grounds there might be for optimism or pessimism and on the possibilities for response and resistance.

34.2.1 The Changing University: Values, Purposes and Management

For many respondents, especially those who had worked in academia for some time, neoliberal forces have morphed the University into an institution that is the antithesis of, not only their own values, but also the University's own traditional principles and purpose. As one noted, the University currently exists "for a different purpose than that of education—it runs as a market driven enterprise [which perceives] other universities as competitors whereas we see them as colleagues" (R7, Senior lecturer).

> A neoliberal university is characterised by internal cost-centred markets, which…desperate for funding of almost any kind, [and] seeking new [national and international] markets relentlessly, [produces] highly commodified relationships between staff, students and administrators. (R6, Professor).

One Senior Lecturer (R7) stated that students have become primarily 'income generators' and, knowing this, "feel a very different connection to the university as a result". In a commodified relationship, students are consumers who purchase a product. In an era of 'employability' promises, that product is increasingly understood to be employment post-graduation. Students expect a tangible return (a job) for their money and thus have particular (and often unrealistic) expectations of what their 'service providers' (individual tutors and universities) should, and are able to, provide. Of particular concern was the two-fold requirement that Universities compete to (a) recruit students by 'selling' them courses at recruitment events and (b) produce 'employment ready' graduates by promoting (sometimes misleading) vocational imperatives. For staff:

> The logic of 'academic capitalism' commodifies knowledge and transforms universities and educational praxis into spaces and modes of service-delivery. Power relations have shifted from professionals to management and in this context managerial 'information' and strategic-competitive rationalities come to supersede critical and reflexive forms of understanding. (R12, Senior Lecturer).

Respondents noted their increasing concern and even discomfort about promoting programmes that take a critical standpoint about state or, for criminology programmes, criminal justice policies and agencies, for fear of deterring applicants and/or facing negative consequences from management.

> It relates to trends towards corporatisation in the University, increasing emphasis on auditing and 'measuring performance' (of staff) and of seeing students as consumers, high tuition charges for students, pressure to enter into research relationships with industry, and an increasingly insecure, part-time workforce. (R1, Senior Lecturer)

In terms of University management, "…it is a hierarchical, macho, managerial style based on a business model of organisation … it is not only pedagogically philistine but lacks any sense of democratic accountability" (R14, Professor). For many colleagues, the neoliberal, anti-democratic and authoritarian tendencies in University management, and the resultant micro-management techniques and reduced autonomy for academic staff, posed a serious threat to the cherished values of education.

> I see it as part of a system that reproduces and does little to contest the current situation of 'worker insecurity'. Students come to university knowing jobs are limited and they know they have to be competitive. Part of being competitive is being quiet and not asking for higher wages, not asking for better conditions, not striking and so on. The university is now taking on this corporate business model and producing and reproducing these structures. (R21, Lecturer)

34.2.2 Normalising the Business and the 'Product'

Participants voiced real concern that the increasing vocational/employability emphasis in universities and erosion of fundamental values within university education was becoming normalised. This happens within detailed and closely monitored processes for creating and selling the business's main product—the academic qualification, especially the bachelor's degree. Attention to 'employability' as one of a range of priorities, officially prescribed and regulated through audit, 'good practice' and intensifying league table competition, might strike some older hands as a familiar turning of the wheel. Initiatives in HE come and go—often with the same wine in relabelled bottles. But academic staff here identified a fundamental re-shaping of education towards schooling underlaid by an assumed coincidence of interest shared by employer and employee. The 'product', marketed, designed, validated and delivered has become the primary site upon which HE's refashioned purpose is brought to bear. Outside speakers from the criminal justice industry, placements, internships, sandwich years, work experience, work related experience and work-related content are increasingly required (in place of non-vocational disciplinary content). 'Good practice' in designing degrees often prioritises the 'input' of employers and the identification of unique selling points for consumers above more old-fashioned concerns such as academic integrity and coherence. New programmes arise from the identification of lucrative markets by management rather than academic expertise and development. Sometimes this might lead to the closure of programmes and departments that are not in vocational 'fashion:' at other times it can subtly, or not so subtly, re-orientate the priorities and content of programmes that do survive and generate new programmes, which, while lacking disciplinary or pedagogic rigour, are sold (and perhaps mis-sold) to students as pathways to specific jobs. For employers of course meanwhile, this scenario presents excellent opportunities for off-loading training costs and raising the perceived 'professionalism' of their workforce.

This pressure to provide 'employable' graduates when there is a dearth of real graduate employment available has a sort of absurdity to it. As Frankham (2017) argues, HE is increasingly constructed as the panacea for a host of economic and social challenges and the university has become an important part of the process of providing workers for an increasingly precarious employment situation. As one respondent put it, "employability is at the heart of the problem. Criminology will soon be criminal justice studies ... the university is now a place to train students for future employment, rather than a place of education" (R23, Principal Lecturer). One participant suggested that "Criminology may be taught by police officers and prison governors in the near future" (R3, Professor) and another felt that focusing on "writing CVs and lots of talks from people in uniforms" (R5, Senior Lecturer) would undoubtedly mean that the academic integrity of courses will be affected.

These concerns are given force by recent developments in policing for example, which is moving very clearly towards not only degree-only recruitment, but to a system in which the overwhelming majority of police officers will have *policing* degrees specifically. In this case the employability agenda becomes self-fulfilling: vocational policing degrees will have more graduates employed by the police than criminology degrees because that is the way that employers will have rigged the game.

More broadly, for many respondents in the study, the prioritisation of 'employability' has led to the increasing marginalisation of the imaginative and theoretically developed 'sociology of deviance' form of criminology, in favour of a shift towards 'state-friendly' vocational and applied forms—for example, crime 'science', forensics, policing studies and offender management. One participant was forthright:

> 'Employability', which is nothing but a blatant intrusion of employer demands on the substantive educational processes, directly affects theoretical work and the familiarisation of students with the process of working with more abstract concepts. (R11, Reader)

"Do not even start" said another participant "...this is killing off any imagination, it forces people far too early to make life-changing choices and often only serves as a 'get a job' service instead of really finding out people's potential" (R12, Senior Lecturer). Many respondents also acknowledged a lack of recognition for activism and activities that reflect priorities of critical pedagogy, even if they would enhance student learning. Of course, activism and campaigning around social and political issues, and specifically organisational harms and criminality may be precisely what employers do *not* want.

Notwithstanding these rather obvious concerns, pressure is increasingly placed on staff to 'vocationalise' existing degree routes. In some universities criminology module leaders are told that they must demonstrate that they include criminal justice practitioners as guest lecturers or employability related 'scenarios' even at the expense of academic content and regardless of the aims of the module. Where the developing criminological 'product' may be heading was a concern of one academic who left little room for doubt about their pessimism.

> Metaphorically speaking, [in ten years' time critical criminologists] will probably be stacking shelves in Tesco whilst mumbling something about structural inequality and social harm. (R21, Lecturer)

The strong indication from these accounts is that academic silences are allowing major changes to be made in line with the employability agenda, especially around the product that is sold and delivered to students and that this is well on the way to being normalised. The extent to which participants saw such changes as posing more fundamental dangers to critical criminology as a discipline are outlined and discussed in the next section.

34.3 Incorporation: Optimism or Pessimism?

Mathiesen's third theme extends concerns around normalisation within organisational silencing by signalling the dangers of incorporation of potential opposition within organisations. The experiences and opinions voiced above indicate that, to a greater or lesser degree, academics find themselves having to acquiesce or actively participate in the changed purposes and specific products of their particular institutions. There were varied opinions however on the extent to which this is happening and the dangers it poses. Many did indeed feel uncomfortably drawn towards the priorities of institutions of the criminal law, criminal justice system and government security and control agendas, and away from the critical theoretical and political foundations of the discipline and critiques of state institutions and agencies.

> By nature, critical criminology depends on a theoretical critique of existing social structures and also on different modes of thinking about society. If this element is being marginalised or sacrificed in the name of labour markets, desirable skills and employability, then critical criminology will also be marginalised. (R11, Reader)

Whilst the potential marginalisation of critical content is problematic enough, as one respondent noted, a deeper danger lies in official appropriation of formerly critical disciplines which results in "...a criminological discipline fixed on 'problem solving' as opposed to [a] 'problem raising' approach" (R22, Research Student). As another participant stated:

> Criminology, unfortunately, [has become] a training school for the police [and] probation [service]. This I believe is an inherent problem with criminology, *further evidencing [...] that criminology in its existence legitimises the state's criminal justice system.* (R17, Lecturer. Emphasis added)

In other words, "the discipline of criminology, within an income led era, has become embedded within the very structures that it ought to be critiquing" (R22, Research Student).

What seems to be a prevailing attitude among university management—that time is infinitely elastic—is a major problem for staff trying to deliver critical teaching and, moreover, is a potential means of securing acquiescence. To take one obvious example, inviting speakers from the criminal justice system might be an increasingly attractive option for time-pressured lecturers. Conversely, the scholarly work required to underpin in-depth critical teaching is time consuming—and the time to deliver such teaching to the student is limited.

It is also important to note that a threat to critical curricula may come from students as well as management. Students arrive at university with their critical imaginations already jeopardized by neoliberal schooling methods built around endless tests, measurements, competition and targets. They have been inculcated with the rhetoric that the primary (or even the only) reason to go to university is for the job at the end. Once at university students become "incentivised through debt" (Ransome, 2011: 212) to follow this neoliberal logic and hence "...the[ir] educational horizons...narrow towards vocational instrumentalism" (Barton & Davis, 2015: 209). So, whilst some respondents may be correct in that there is no direct managerial opposition to critical curricula at some institutions, the challenge may come in how students interpret and evaluate them. Thus, it may remain possible to disseminate critical knowledge, but what becomes silently constrained is the promotion of *understanding* amongst students for whom degrees are viewed (with the support of the university itself) primarily as 'career tickets.'

For some respondents however, there was a more optimistic case to be made. Indeed, one of the most interesting issues from the data was that whilst all respondents talked about a range of problems and constraints, when asked if they had encountered *direct* institutional opposition to implementing a critical criminological teaching curriculum, 20 out of 22 said no. These respondents indicated that much of the critical criminological curriculum has remained unchanged and that critical criminology in the UK is still in a considerable position of strength in terms of numbers of full time academics, post-graduate students and the content of criminological programmes. As one Professor noted:

> In terms of what we teach, there is virtually no interference; we are left to get on with what we want to do. It is interesting as we might have thought that, given the neoliberal propensity to dominate and subjugate, as well as successive government changes to the education system, that the curriculum in HE would have been affected. So far that has not happened although there are signs, for example the endless demand that students learn and pursue work-based programmes is a possible sign of things to come. (R14)

This seems to be good news. However, as Mathiesen argues, 'silent structures' are silent in that they can obscure or mask constraints. He explains for silent silencing to be successful, the impression has to be created that no silencing is actually occurring. In the university context it is important that silencing processes remain hidden from all participants and spectators (that is, academics and students). For example, academic staff may be explicitly asked for comment or criticism (through staff surveys and other feedback mechanisms). The organisation can then (sometimes, but not always) respond, by amending, altering, tinkering with practices or procedures rather than fundamentally changing direction or focus, so things can appear to change. Through this strategy opposition can be 'diverted' away from struggles concerning politics or principles into questions of process, practice and detail.

Ideally, the silencing of opposition is achieved through creation of the belief that "[t]o all appearances, on the surface, your position is entirely 'free'" (Mathiesen, 2004: 23). The account of one participant provided an interesting example of this.

> Apart from the emphasis on work-based learning, and the micro-management of our working lives, I don't think it is that different except we had more time in the past, especially during the summer period. The vanishing act around time has been a crucial impact. (R14, Professor)

It should be noted here that whilst things may not be 'that different' for senior academics or even for those on full time contracts, things have changed considerably for early career academics. In fact, the problem of deteriorating conditions especially in relation to time—with its inevitable implications for critical work—are far deeper than this participant acknowledges (see for example research carried out for the UCU[9] in 2016). We might conclude from this respondent's statement that the silencing of dissent has undoubtedly been successful when one knows, and can articulate, that things have changed drastically yet, at the same time, believe that everything is much the same.

A different argument made by some was that although change is impacting on critical criminology, there are ways and means of resisting and limiting it. Whilst acknowledging that we work within considerable constraints, it was argued we can still devise strategies within our own workplace that can re-articulate policies to reflect the interests of critical analysis. Critical criminology is often perceived as a struggle for hearts as well as minds and so there always exists a prevailing sense of optimism and capacity for resistance amongst critical criminology colleagues. For example, one respondent stated, "I think we will resist—it is the one subject I have hope and faith in, so I see us carrying on, but with significant struggle" (R13, Senior Lecturer). Another believed that "critical criminology will grow in strength in the next 10 years. A number of centres are being set up across the country and there is cooperation between some of the academics involved" (R2, Professor). Another colleague was hopeful that "we have [already] educated a new generation of critical scholars—given the critical discourses coming from students over the last few years there is space for optimism" (R7, Senior Lecturer). At the centre of these arguments on the potential for resistance was the idea of exploiting the contradictions and subverting the logic of the corporate university.

> Crucial is recognising that history is not closed off: it is one of the most important things that Stuart Hall emphasized, it is full of possibilities, so it is easy to become melancholic and pessimistic but the academic workplace like everywhere else has its own problems around legitimacy, like the state more generally. So challenging, contesting and being involved at all sorts of levels was and remains the key to struggle. (R14, Professor)

Direct engagement with students was highlighted as fundamental to the role of the teacher in HE. Relations with students and student engagement with the theoretical and political priorities of critical criminology were remarked on extensively in the

---

[9]University and Colleges Union.

survey as a means of resistance. To some, making alliances with students and presenting a united front against the realities of neoliberal policies in universities may seem naïve. It is almost taken for granted for students to be dismissed as disengaged, conservative (particularly in regard to race, class and inequality) and politically apathetic (Harris, 2013). But are they less radical than in the past and if so, can they be re-engaged? The survey responses indicated that things are perhaps not as clear cut as they first seem.

> Over the last three years, students have appeared to be much more engaged with critical discourses – that is not surprising given the context in which they have grown up and the problems they are currently subjected to. (R7, Senior Lecturer)

> ...Some of the most profound challenges to what has been happening in the last few years have come from student protests, the fall-out and collateral damage from these protests have been shamefully ignored by academics... including critical criminologists. (R14, Professor)

Another possibility for resistance that was voiced by some participants may be loosely termed 'playing the game—but better'. At one level this might simply require linguistic cleverness.

> In some respects, I think that critical pedagogy can be preserved within this context, provided those who are writing the modules and programmes remain committed to a critical edge. Sometimes the demands of the 'bean counters' and those who are interested in marketing within universities can be pacified with careful language and branding. (R1, Senior Lecturer)

At another level however, it was suggested that critical excellence should be shared to ensure 'success' within the wider competitive environment. One academic explained this idea in relation to resisting threats to critical research presented by REF, but the principle of the argument would relate equally to resisting the employability oriented TEF.

> ...we need to share wisdom – for example, critical colleagues who have built 4* impact case studies need to share their success and explain how it can be done. In short, solidarity rather than competition is a wonderful glue, how can we be strategic and employ this solidarity to play the REF game. Not just so we can 'win' the REF game, but so critical researchers obtain the space to do emancipatory scholarship and become highly rated individuals within their own institutions. (R10, Lecturer)

These comments are particularly interesting in that they demonstrate how easily even those who are otherwise condemnatory of the damage caused to critical education by neoliberalism, can still be seduced into its logic. Whilst well intentioned, this respondent's argument clearly misses the point about why the whole REF and TEF agendas (underpinned by the neoliberal valorisation of competition) are problematic. Not everyone can have a 4* case study, or be awarded Gold standards for their teaching. Indeed, the whole point of league tables is that there are winners and there are losers—this is built into the exercise. We cannot resist by playing the game with 'solidarity' because the rules of the game do not allow this—competition is the fundamental element of the process. Thus, we cannot play the game on our own terms because the rules and terms are already drawn up and the game is already rigged. This is to put to one side that the conceptions of 4* REF case studies and 'gold rated' TEF commendations (no matter how critical the curriculum content) are each flawed and we should not be trying to 'all get one'. Indeed, if we do this we are not resisting, we are complying. Motivations for critical scholarly work should not simply be to get 'the best' scores.

Maybe we cannot really 'resist,' at least not in any way that will effect major change. Perhaps we just keep on doing what we can but in the knowledge that it won't change the world, or even the lives or minds of the majority of students. But there is, of course, still a value to resistance even in the knowledge that it will have limited, or perhaps no, impact. Taking an ideological stance—rejecting the commodification of education, upholding the values of collegiality and social justice and refusing to see our colleagues in other universities as 'competitors'—is a choice made because it is believed to be *right*, not because it will necessarily pose any substantial challenge to the ethos of neoliberalism.

34.4 Conclusion: Contexts and Consequences of the Employability Agenda

Critical pedagogy seeks to transform learners from *objects* of education, or perhaps more accurately, objects of schooling and training, to autonomous *subjects*, with a critical understanding of the world and their places within it. The very significant recent shift towards employers' agendas in universities raises considerable concern for critical academics, and particularly as evidenced above, for critical criminologists. Notwithstanding the seductive matrices of employability 'champions', employers' training needs do not 'map' straightforwardly onto the aims and purposes even of academic disciplines traditional in HE, let alone in critical HE. It is naïve to suppose that developing students' consciousness so that they become equipped to effect personal and social change is, or will be, a major priority for private corporations and public agencies whose interests will very often be quite the opposite. Engagement of imagination, inquisitiveness and risk-taking in the service of social justice, as envisaged by Giroux (2015), are at least as likely to be threats to many organisational aims as to complement them. This is indeed one of the key understandings that critical criminology seeks to communicate: that the most extensive and extreme forms of harms, both acute and chronic—from poisoning and pollution to crimes against humanity and genocide—are usually incubated, produced and reproduced within large scale, respectable and legal organisations. There is a fundamental contradiction between an agenda that prioritises training for workplaces and the deep critique *of* those workplaces.

This is not to say that graduates in critical criminology or other subjects critically conceived and delivered cannot or should not work in problematic organisations. It could be argued that many such organisations (and the people they adversely impact) might benefit from employees with developed critical intellectual and empathetic imaginations. But it is to say, that this is a far from simple matter and that managerial imposition of a simplistic employability agenda for the purposes of inter-university competition will almost inevitably be damaging. If the organisations and agencies we critique become our primary customers (directly or indirectly) they will inevitably shape what criminology, and more broadly social science *are,* replacing the academic with the technical and depth with superficiality. The data from respondents discussed above suggests that the level of concern varies among academics, but that there are clearly many who see developments in the neoliberalisation of HE as alarming. Moreover, Mathiesen's work signposts the danger that unless critical academics speak out and act, their relative silence in the face of current developments is likely to lead beyond current forms of adaptation and towards the partial and perhaps complete incorporation of disciplines within the new 'employability' paradigm.

These are dangers that are faced across the humanities and social sciences, but they apply particularly sharply in the case of criminology. History tells us, as Adorno noted above, of the dangers of 'coldness', and of the 'societal monad', indifferent to the fate of others. Just such conditions and characters have originated, facilitated and excused organisational harms (they are rarely classed as 'crimes') from tobacco to asbestos, from fossil fuels to pharmaceuticals. They are, moreover, at the heart of the worst state crimes where conformity and obedience have regularly been shown to be far greater dangers to humanity than non-conformity and disobedience. When the answer to Becker's question 'whose side are you on?' is simply, the side of whoever pays the most, or offers the best prospects to advancement, we have failed. And at a time when those working within various branches of state security across Europe and North America are engaged in mass incarceration, mass surveillance, detaining refugees, arranging for them to drown or turning them back towards torture or death, Gouldner's warning rings loudly:

> If we today concern ourselves exclusively with the technical proficiency of our students and reject all responsibility for their moral sense, or lack of it, we may someday be compelled to accept responsibility for having trained a generation willing to serve in another Auschwitz. (1973: 25).

References

Adorno, T. (1967) *Education after Auschwitz.* Accessed August 15, 2018. http://josswinn.org/wp-content/uploads/2014/12/AdornoEducation.pdf.

Barton, A., Corteen, K., Davies, J., & Hobson, A. (2010). Reading the word and reading the world: The impact of a critical pedagogical approach to the teaching of criminology in HE. *Journal of Criminal Justice Education, 21*(1), 24–41.

Barton, A., & Davis, H. (2015). Neoliberalism, HE and anti-politics: The assault on the criminological imagination. In J. Frauley (Ed.). *C. W. Mills and the criminological imagination* (pp. 201–218). London: Routledge.

Becker, H. S. (1967). Whose side are we on? *Social Problems, 14*(3), 239–247.

Boden, R., & Nedeva, M. (2010). Employing discourse: universities and graduate 'employability. *Journal of Education Policy, 25*(1), 37–54.

Chadwick, K., & Scraton, P. (2006). Critical criminology. In E. McLaughlin & J. Muncie (Eds.), *The Sage dictionary of criminology* (pp. 97–100). London: Sage.

Chertkovskaya, E. (2013) Employability: Is it time we get critical? *The Guardian*, Feb 12th. Accessed August 15, 2018. https://www.theguardian.com/higher-educationnetwork/blog/2013/feb/12/employability-agenda-media-public-debate.

Collini, S. (2016). Who are the spongers now? *London Review of Books, 38*(2), 33–37.

Frankham, J. (2017). Employability and HE: The follies of the 'productivity challenge' in the teaching excellence framework. *Journal of Education Policy, 32*(5), 628–641.

Freire, P. (2007). *Pedagogy of the oppressed*. London: Continuum.

Gellately, R., & Stoltzfuz, N. (2001). Social outsiders and the construction of the community of the people. In N. Gellately & N. Stoltzfus (Eds.), *Social outsiders in Nazi Germany* (pp. 3–19). Oxfordshire: Princeton University Press.

Giroux, H. (1988). *Teachers as intellectuals: Towards a critical pedagogy of learning*. Westport, CT: Greenwood.

Giroux, H. (2000). *Impure acts: The practical politics of cultural studies*. London: Routledge.

Giroux, H. (2015). HE and the politics of disruption. *Truthdig*. Accessed August 15, 2018. https://www.truthdig.com/articles/higher-education-and-the-politics-of-disruption/.

Gouldner, A. (1973). *For sociology: Renewal and critique in sociology today*. Harmondsworth: Penguin.

Harris, J. (2013). Generation Y: Why young voters are backing the conservatives. *The Guardian*. 26 June. Accessed August 16, 2018. https://www.theguardian.com/politics/2013/jun/26/generation-y-young-voters-backing-conservatives.

Mathiesen, T. (2004). *Silently silenced: Essays on the creation of acquiescence in modern society*. Winchester: Waterside Press.

Mills, C. W. (1959–2000). *The sociological imagination*. Oxford: Oxford University Press.

Morgan, J. (2015). Jo Johnson unveils teaching REF plans. *Times HE*, 1 July. Accessed August 15, 2018. https://www.timeshighereducation.com/news/jo-johnson-unveils-teaching-ref-plans.

Ransome, P. (2011). Qualitative pedagogy versus instrumentalism: The antimonies of HE learning and teaching in the United Kingdom. *HE Quarterly, 64*(2), 206–223.

Reiner, R. (2012). Political economy and criminology: The return of the repressed. In S. Hall & S. Winlow (Eds.), *New directions in criminological theory* (pp. 30–51). Abingdon: Routledge.

Scott, D. (2014). Critical criminology and the corporate university. *European Group Newsletter*, May.

UCU. (2016). *Workload is an Education Issue: UCU Workload Survey report*. Accessed August 15, 2018. https://www.ucu.org.uk/media/8195/Workload-is-an-education-issue-UCU-workload-survey-report-2016/pdf/ucu_workloadsurvey_fullreport_jun16.pdf.

Wacquat, L. (2009). *Punishing the poor: The neoliberal government of social insecurity*. Durham, NC: Duke University Press.

Walters, R. (2007) 'Critical Criminology and the Intensification of the Authoritarian State'. *Expanding the Criminological Imagination: Critical Readings in Criminology*, Edited by: Barton, A., Corteen, K., Scott, D. and Whyte, D. 15–37. Devon: Willan.

Alana Barton (Ph.D.) is a Reader in Criminology at Edge Hill University, England, UK. Her research interests and publications focus around prisons and 'prison tourism', austerity and 'war on the poor', the concept of the criminological imagination, and the study of 'agnosis'. She is the author of *Fragile Moralities and Dangerous Sexualities* (2005) and co-editor of *Expanding the Criminological Imagination* (2007) and *Ignorance, Power and Harm* (2018). Her work has been published in a range of books and journals. She is currently involved with the *Learning Together* project, which is concerned with establishing educational pathways between prisons and universities.

Howard Davis (Ph.D.) is Senior Lecturer in Criminology at Edge Hill University, England, UK. He had a previous career as a Social Worker, practising in the fields of child protection, trauma and bereavement. His research and teaching interests include state-corporate harms, criminological and victimological aspects of acute and chronic disasters, media and state legitimisation of 'austerity' and the effects of neoliberalism on Higher Education. His work has been published in a wide range of peer-reviewed academic journals including the *British Journal of Criminology, British Journal of Social Work* and *Disasters.* He is also the co-editor of *Ignorance, Power and Harm* (2018).

David Scott (Ph.D.) works at The Open University, UK, and is a Visiting Professor at The University of Toronto. He has published more than 100 book chapters or articles and 15 books. He is the co-founder of the Journal '*Justice, Power and Resistance*' and a founding director of the independent publisher EG Press. He is a former coordinator of the European Group for the Study of Deviance and Social Control and a member of the Academic Advisory Board for INQUEST.

Chapter 35
Conclusion

Alice Diver and Gerard Diver

35.1 Introduction

> Students play a central role in the achievements of the Sustainable Development Goals (SDGs) for the 2030 Agenda.[1] (Borges et al., 2017: 173)

It remains to be seen whether '…an academic revolution has taken place in higher education in the past half century marked by transformations unprecedented in scope and diversity.' (Altbach, Reisberg, & Rumbley, 2009) It seems fair to state however that,

> …the developments of the recent past are at least as dramatic as those in the 19th century when the research university evolved…and fundamentally redesigned the nature of the university worldwide. The academic changes of the late 20th and early 21st centuries are more extensive due to their global nature and the number of institutions and people they affect. (Altbach et al., 2009)[2]

Economic austerities and political uncertainties seem set to continue for the foreseeable future, both within and beyond the borders of the UK. The wider mission of Higher Education (HE) must therefore surely be to keep engaging as fully as possible with those who are in need, providing or preserving a safe haven for all who wish to push themselves in the pursuit of learning, the embracing of ethical ideals and

---

[1] Borges et al. (2017), on how the Sustainable Development Agenda was created in 2007, via the UN Principles for Responsible Management Education (PRME) under the UN Global Compact.

[2] Altbach et al. (2009) (accessed 12.01.19) adding that 'comprehending this ongoing and dynamic process while being in the midst of it is not an easy task.'

A. Diver · G. Diver (✉)
Liverpool John Moores University, Liverpool, England, UK
e-mail: g.m.diver@ljmu.ac.uk

A. Diver
e-mail: a.r.diver@ljmu.ac.uk

541

A. Diver (ed.), *Employability via Higher Education: Sustainability as Scholarship*,
https://doi.org/10.1007/978-3-030-26342-3_35

work practices, and the furthering of social justice. HE must offer where possible a meaningful 'career springboard' for those seeking socio-economic advancement and/or personal development via the challenges of learning. As such, this collection has sought to analyse the nature, purposes, and remits of HE, particularly in respect of its capacity to affect positively the future employability or 'work-readiness' of our graduates. It has tried to define employability not simply as the achievement of a useful state of industrial preparedness, or narrowly-drawn professionalism. Rather, it argues for a wider, more holistic concept of well-rounded, 'graduate-ness,' underpinned by such key 'whole person' learning (Hoover et al., 2010) factors as e.g. emotional maturity, self-efficacy, resilience, and ethical awareness.[3]

Arguably, a post-graduation desire to engage in lifelong learning, contribute meaningfully to society, and further the wider aims of social justice, can follow on from the achievement of such competencies (Steur, Jansen, & Hoffman, 2012).[4] Whether or not the innovations and ideas presented in this text will aid the creation of what Hall (1976) termed 'protean workers,'[5] or perhaps simply serve to bolster in some way a nervous student's nascent sense of identity and academic 'belongingness' (Yorke, 2016) is a matter for its readers. What is clear however, is that there is an increasingly acute need for university graduates to possess ever more diverse skills (Cohen and Mallon, 1999),[6] so that they might be able to 'self-manage' (Brown and Hesketh, 2004) their future career pathways. They should depart university equipped with the abilities (both academic and practical) needed to engage in critical thinking, and navigate challenging, fluid labour markets which are so often affected by such issues as political crises, deepening austerities, 'fake news,' and an ever-widening range of socio-cultural tensions and divisions.

The first and final substantive chapters of this collection (Evans et al., Chap. 2; Barton et al., Chap. 34) particularly underscore one of the chief aims of this book project, which was to offer (alongside a selection of workable learning and teaching strategies) a usefully critical analysis of the nature and purpose of employability 'training' within HE. Given the wider backdrop of highly challenging structural contexts (Reiner, 2012) on an increasingly global scale,[7] universities are likely to continue to be asked to produce holistically capable (and in many senses, *gifted*) graduate-scholars who can contribute to wider society. As Barton et al argue, tutors must generate the sort of 'emancipatory knowledge' that can further the 'sociological imagination'[8] (Mills, 1959) to challenge injustice and inequality, and highlight the need for equitable, rights-grounded socio-cultural frameworks for learning (Putnam,

---

[3] See further Hoover et al. (2010) on 'desirable executive skills' such as communication, teamworking, interpersonal skills, and problem-solving.

[4] Steur et al. (2012), outlining also how 'intellectual cultivation' amongst learners arises, and arguing that reflective thinking offers the best scope for lifelong learning. See also however the seminal work of Knight and Yorke (2013).

[5] Hall (1976).

[6] Cohen and Mallon (1999) on 'portfolio workers' [as cited by Nicholas (2018)].

[7] Borges et al. (2017) further argue that 'SDGs need concerted global efforts and good governance at all levels, including local, national, regional, and global...' (citing Sachs 2012).

[8] Mills (1959) (as cited by Barton et al., Chap. 33).

1996, 2000).[9] A wider human rights agenda,[10] grounded in principles of equality and human dignity, reminds us further that a juridical right to education does not simply exist within a socio-cultural vacuum, as a sort of stand-alone concept. Rather it is integral to the realisation of many other fundamental human rights goals and targets, such as freedom from poverty,[11] social inclusion (of vulnerable groups and persons),[12] health and well-being, child safeguarding, community development, peace-building,[13] and a meaningful furthering of social justice norms and principles.[14]

And yet, old divisions clearly linger. As Bellino et al. (2017) have observed in respect of the role played by education generally in times of political transition and conflict,

> ...despite the practical and conceptual overlaps between education and transitional justice...scholarship about how both might contribute towards peacebuilding, reconciliation, and recovery from conflict have largely developed in isolation from one another.'[15]

King (2017) has similarly noted that, '...a good deal of the SDG aspirations for expanded rights to, and breadth of, education appears to get lost in their translation to the indicators.'[16] Unterhalter (2017: 2) perhaps adds the most stringent note of caution, however, stating that:

> Unmeasurable processes in education are routinely addressed through appeals to measurement or indicators. The Millennium Development Goals (MDGs) of 2000–2015, the Sustainable Development Goals (SDGs)...and university rankings are some of the most well-known projects that attempt to measure aspects of education, linking the precision of measurement, with imprecisely formulated values.

---

[9]Putnam (2000) [describing social life as 'networks, norms and trust'; see also Putnam (1996) (accessed 01.02.19); see also Arrow (2000)].

[10]See further Borges et al. (2017) on Article 26 of the UNDHR (1948) and the various other rights milestones that have flowed from it, including the UN Millennium Development Goals (MDGs) (2000), and the Sustainable Development Goals (SDGs) (2015), adding however that the SDGs need 'unprecedented mobilization of global knowledge operating across many sectors and regions' and citing King (2016) on how the principal focus is still on 'developing countries' and the 'least developed countries' (King 2016); See also King (2017).

[11]On illiteracy levels and poverty in the least developed countries (LDCs) see Regmi (2015).

[12]On gendered poverty, see further Bradshaw, Chant, and Linneker (2017).

[13]Bellino, Paulson, and Worden (2017).

[14]See however McArthur and Zhang (2018) on how the various disciplines have embraced—or perhaps avoided—the issue. For example, *The Lancet* had the highest number of MDG references amongst 12 academic journals examined ('...it is probably not a coincidence that global health saw the most significant MDG breakthroughs...at least some portion of the health research community considered itself as MDG protagonist—an outlook seemingly not shared across all academic disciplines. The leading economics journals, for instance, rank among the lowest in terms of MDG references)' (available at https://www.brookings.edu/blog/future-development/2018/06/14/who-is-talking-about-the-un-sustainable-development-goals/ accessed 28.02.19).

[15]Bellino et al. (2017).

[16]King (2017) adding that 'the complexity of the global governance architecture for the SDGs and their implementation' is relevant, as is the 'critical lens of the *Global Education Monitoring Report* (2016)'.

Similar warnings are sounded throughout this collection, for example on the dangers of eroding the foundations of a 'democratic education' (Dewey, 1956). As the third and fourth chapters of Section One argue, notions of Quality (Lawton, Chap. 4) and Learning Gain (Gossman and Powell, Chap. 3) within HE may be subject to a worrying degree of 'price-tagging' in respect of their definition, conflation with other concepts, and measurement by both internal and external gauges. What is being taught in HE may differ significantly from what is actually being *learned* by our students, especially where harsh external factors (such as economic austerity and political uncertainty) might well be serving to influence how students and stakeholders view HE's overall purpose and remit. It is important therefore to question what *types* of learning might be most valued and by whom (not forgetting the need for an accurate means of measurement and the reasons *why* measurement is needed, at any given time). As Zelenev (2017: 1654) further stressed,

> … decision-making that is based on public evidence-based and data-driven has a better chance to succeed even if it calls into question some existing conventional approaches…the existing evidence proves that citizens' engagement always make a difference.

If the sole or primary perceived purpose of undertaking a degree is simply to secure the highest-paying job as soon as possible after graduation however, this seems likely to significantly colour the expectations, experiences and aims of learners and teachers alike.[17] At worst, the notions of teaching quality and learning gain may be subsumed within certain learning outcomes that—perhaps through no fault of their own—focus almost entirely upon a fairly narrow range of neatly prescribed assessment activities and the speedy acquisition of industry-relevant skills, much to the exclusion of other innate or learned personal qualities. Little room may be left for independent undertakings, extra-mural or otherwise, that might well align more closely with purely altruistic or creative endeavours, or indeed the pursuit of knowledge for wisdom's sake. If all of this occurs largely in a bid to boost university rankings on 'league tables,' then it can be argued that the purpose of HE has indeed changed quite significantly over the past few decades.

The competitive nature of HE in the wake of its widened-access 'massification' has also clearly altered, perhaps irrevocably:

> …competition has always been a force in academe and can help produce excellence, it can also contribute to a decline in a sense of academic community, mission and traditional values. (Altbach et al., 2009)

It is difficult to see how such an approach sits comfortably with the more expansive, ethical aims of the Sustainable Development Goals ['SDGs'] as outlined in *Agenda*

---

[17]On the Longitudinal Education Outcomes (LEO) data (on graduate earnings), see: https://www.officeforstudents.org.uk/data-and-analysis/graduate-earnings-data-on-unistats/(accessed 28.03.19). See further Kushner's (2011: 311) observations on how evaluations offer 'a unique ethic based on citizen rights to information,' with 'every evaluation [is] itself a case study of society.' He argues however the dangers associated with having 'productivity and economic benefit …outweigh other criteria for measuring program quality…We know that good programs often miss their predicted outcomes—and that weak or even unethical programs can generate desired outcomes.' Kushner (2011).

2030.[18] Put bluntly, graduates who might opt to do voluntary—or low-paid—work in a bid to build a fairer society, will do little to improve their university's employability rankings if the concept of graduate success (or indeed, academic 'teaching excellence') is measured in terms of wages earned, job title held, or taxes paid. Similarly, where there is an over-arching obligation to provide visibly high 'value for money' returns for consumer-modelled, investor-students demanding a clearly evidenced 'graduate premium' (and an increasingly sceptical media and tax-paying public) it is unsurprising that the awarding of higher grades by HEIs might be attributed to some manner of 'inflation.'[19] Staff too may fear that disappointed cohorts might seek some form of recompense or 'retribution' via poor modular or NSS feedback surveys, complaints, or indeed litigation,[20] which could potentially result in public censure, course closures, or staff redundancies. A 'progressively consumerist approach' to the purpose of HE can also easily impact upon wider perceptions of what the 'student journey' might, or should, involve (Dacre Pool et al., Chap. 6). The notion of having a fixed 'calling' towards a particular career for example might lead to the creation of a 'double-edged sword' for employability strategies, where students or graduates are unable or perhaps unwilling to consider alternative pathways or professions (Lysova et al., 2018).[21]

Clearly, numerous 'tensions between global and national approaches to target-setting' do exist also, particularly in relation to issues of 'ownership of the global target discourse' (King, 2016).[22] The traditionally symbiotic nature of HE must be acknowledged: fee-paying students do not simply purchase a product, goods, or services with an instant or presumed, near-automatic return on their initial 'investment.' They must also actively invest *their* time and effort in the pursuit of their studies. (Clements, Chap. 5). Positive job searching behaviours by students, using highly proactive, ethical efforts, from an early stage of the studies, are generally tied to better career outcomes post-graduation. Such a basic truism might at times be overlooked however, in the rush to meet ever-changing goals on generating or maintaining faculty income, improving pass-rates, raising course fees, or meeting retention targets. Student involvement in extra-mural events has also been an important aspect of HE: as Borges et al. (2017) have argued, those who do take part in extra-curricular,

---

[18] See further https://sustainabledevelopment.un.org/post2015/transformingourworld (accessed 12.03.19).

[19] See further https://www.officeforstudents.org.uk/news-blog-and-events/press-and-media/universities-must-get-to-grips-with-spiralling-grade-inflation/ (accessed 02.03.19).

[20] A small but telling body of case law—examined briefly later on in this chapter—has grown up around student disappointment: the role of academics (involved in course administration and in the design and delivery of assessment) is also discussed. See further Palfreyman (2010) on how academic judgement 'immunity' is threatened by ECHR/Judicial Review cases, the Consumer Rights Act 2015, Equality & Discrimination laws, and a growing over-precision in the drafting of 'learning outcomes;' See also Kamvounias and Varnham (2006).

[21] Lysova et al. (2018).

[22] See also Pavlin and Svetlik (2014, p. 420), on how '…the core area for the competitive advantage of European countries seems to be the development of professional human resources via a well-considered higher education system.'

practical activities often tend to gain enhanced levels of maturity (Eklund-Leen and Young, 1997) and a 'greater sense of capacity...competence...increase[d] general knowledge, academic performance and freedom of expression.'[23] They are perhaps more likely to cope with the various challenges of a modern, much more 'flexible, globalised market' (Nicholas, 2018).[24]

Pinto and Ramalheira (2017: 167) similarly note that, often, 'academic credentials are not enough to find a suitable job.'[25] There is a pressing need now for graduates—and their degrees—to be seen as 'distinctive' (Brown and Hesketh, 2004) so as to better enable some measure of 'security on the job market as a whole' (Bernstrøm et al., 2019: 234) rather than simply planning on an extended career within a single firm, discipline or sector. That said, if character-building activities, assessments and course content are perhaps not seen as directly relevant to formal, summative assessments, and tied to a student's presumed career pathway, or necessary in terms of CV-building, then it seems likely that these will struggle to be included in curricula—or indeed much engaged with by learners. They do however have clear value as part of a holistically-wider, 'whole person,' experiential learning experience, not least in relation to making an 'emotional commitment'[26] to one's education. The notion of the relatively untouched, 'gold-plated horse trough' (O'Brien and Walker-Martin, Chap. 8) and the exasperation that students' non-engagement causes HE tutors and support staff, cannot be easily ignored. As with many other aspects of the university journey, the onus must ultimately be upon students (and graduates) to engage meaningfully with their studies, tutors and peers, in both accepting and offering support. They should do so by reflecting clearly upon their own academic performances and commitment levels, viewing these as signifiers of a useful contribution to those communities of learning and practice which they signed up to upon entering HE (whether these are within or beyond their own university, discipline, or geographical region).

If, as Freire (1985) suggested, education can tend often towards the merely or predominantly decorative,[27] then it is important to frame our students from an early stage as having the clear potential to be 'natural stakeholders, leaders in training, and immediate agents of change for the achievement of the 2030 Agenda' (Borges et al., 2017).[28] Requiring them to take active (even if not quite fully proactive) ownership

---

[23] Borges et al. (2017), citing Baker (2008); and also citing Peltier et al. (2008) on how student organizations can contribute to future career preparation by offering 'a professional development environment...and practical learning experiences' (Peltier et al., 2008).

[24] Arguing also that factors such as technology and corporate downsizing 'have increased job mobility and brought attention to the art of self-managing careers' and the need for 'diverse competencies' and 'dynamic fluidity' grounded in 'transferable critical thinking skills'.

[25] See further Tomlinson (2008) (as cited by Pinto and Ramalheira, 2017).

[26] See further Hoover et al. (2010) on the emotional components underpinning behavioural skills, namely, emotional control and emotional management (p. 193).

[27] Freire (1983); see also Freire (1985).

[28] See also Moon (2019), who argues that '...the moral imperative of universities is to tackle societal and global issues and problems...the UN Sustainable Development Goals provide a framework which universities can use to guide teaching, research and practice to address problems of poverty

of their own learning, by expending effort and achieving time-management, and by moderating or honing professional behaviours, is an essential aspect of university success, and most, if not all, career pathways. Such thinking represents a move away from the concept of students being subsumed gently into the 'banking concept' of education, whereby teachers will simply 'feed' knowledge into a passive audience of learners: 'Words should be laden with the meaning of the people's existential experience, and not of the teacher's words ...' (Freire & Slover, 1983).[29]

Personal, past learning histories can easily impact however upon present and future performances (Irving-Bell, Chap. 7). A strong, accurate sense of learner identity clearly matters, especially where the lack of one (or the presence of one steeped in adversity, or failed attempts at earlier learning) may lead students to negatively self-construct a variety of barriers to academic success. Coping with disappointing results, accepting and learning from less than positive peer or tutor feedback, and perhaps being able to engage in goal revision where necessary, are all 'skills' or competencies associated with navigating the modern job market: as Hu et al. (2019: 90) argue 'learning experiences are important sources of self-beliefs for realizing goals' or, conversely, for spotting any degree of

> ...misfit between the current goal and the young person's interests, values and talents, while feedback on goal progress implies that the career goal might not be attainable due to lack of effort, engagement and/or skills/abilities.

35.2 On Self-belief, Self-efficacy, and Holistic, Whole-Person Learning

As Turner (2014: 592) notes, 'without the belief that one can apply one's understanding and skills, one cannot demonstrate nor meaningfully utilise one's understanding and skills.'[30] Resilience, stamina and emotional maturity are integral to career and HE success and to the lowering of HE attrition rates, regardless of academic discipline or jurisdiction (Cusciano et al., Chap. 9). If, as Benson (2006: 173) observed however, having good employability also offers up a revised form of traditional job 'security' then it seems only fair to conclude that 'a new kind of psychological contract' (Bernstrøm et al., 2019) now exists between students, universities, and the

---

and the effects of climate change.' (available at https://www.heacademy.ac.uk/knowledge-hub/95-theses-reforming-higher-education-are-heis-catalysts-sustainable-society, accessed 01.03.19).

[29] See further Freire and Slover (1983) on how '...the student is the subject of the process of learning [to read and write] as an act of knowing and a creative act. The fact that he or she needs the teacher's help, as in any pedagogical situation, does not mean that the teacher's help annuls the student's creativity...' See also Freire (2008).

[30] Turner (2014), stressing that 'while critics of the skills agenda in employability have argued for a shift in focus from skills to action..the two are in fact inextricably linked. Self-belief underpins action and needs to be developed alongside and through the development of skills within the context of the disciplinary curriculum.'

modern job market. Learners in HE must quickly expect to become as prepared as possible for a very wide variety of challenges both in class and in the workplace. Self-perceived or preconceived identities, assumed latent weaknesses, and indeed certain resiliencies and competencies (often borne out of pre-enrolment experiences and/or socio-economic backgrounds) should not be discounted when we are planning (or trying to be supportive during) the student journey (O'Shea and Delahunty, Chap. 11). Learners do, and should, come from a varied range of backgrounds: they will bring with them diverse skill sets that have much to offer in terms of enriching their academic community.[31]

As Zelenev (2017) observes however (in relation to implementing *Agenda 2030* at national levels), 'identifying the bottle-necks and removing the obstacles' is central to achieving success. There will likely always be significantly stressful 'points of transition' for HE students, which must be addressed when learning programmes and assessments are being designed and delivered (Ryan et al. Chap. 10). The critical first year of university (Mullen et al. Chap. 12, Sect. 2) often reveals a number of external or internal impediments to gaining a degree (i.e. mental, physical, emotional, gendered, or financial). These can serve to remind us of the struggles faced elsewhere in society, where even a basic education is, sadly, still a luxury for many people. Similarly, where 'ideals, objectives and actions contained in the national plans linking SDGs and social protection' demand realization, then 'all sectors of society must play a role in the implementation efforts and be involved in all phases of policy action' (McKenzie, 2015).

Having found their own voices, it is to be hoped that HE graduates will in turn use this to benefit those who often lack *any* advocates or platforms, by raising awareness of ethical causes and challenging social injustice in its many forms. As Audenaert et al. (2019) recently stressed, worker-vulnerability (whether through long-term unemployment or 'limited educational attainment and multiple interdependent psychosocial issues') often leads to 'a vicious cycle of lowered human capital, mental health, wellbeing and poverty.'[32] Likewise, there may be several reasons why certain students cannot or will not engage fully with lesson activities, contact hours, pastoral care, peer support programmes or extracurricular activities designed to enhance their academic and employability skills. If we must embed or augment generic or career-specific forms of work-ready 'graduateness,' grounded in desirable personal qualities (i.e. psychological resilience, emotional maturity, ethical diligence, honesty) then we should surely examine and address where possible those barriers to success that exist within our various communities of learning, practice and pedagogy. There is sharp irony in the fact that some HE students cannot always afford to access the internet, or attend classes, whether through increasingly high costs of e.g. travel, accommodation, subsistence, or childcare. Not all students are able to

---

[31] See further the excellent work of McKenzie (2015), on how the increasingly urgent 'need' for widespread, upward social mobility further stigmatises poverty, as 'evidence' of an apparent unwillingness or inability to learn, which may easily mask the presence of 'strong, resourceful, ambitious people who are 'getting by', often with humour and despite facing brutal austerity.'

[32] Audenaert et al. (2019).

take part in highly beneficial yet financially demanding activities, such as unpaid internships (Caddell and McIlwhan, Chap. 19). Further research into pastoral care issues, including an examination of the reasons that students tend to offer as extenuating circumstances for failing to attend classes, meet submission deadlines, or pass (or indeed, perhaps, attend for) assessments, might well reveal that years of acute austerity measures have much to answer for in this regard (Lin, 2006).

The task of 'shaping' ethical, professional, and reliably employable HE graduates must also inculcate an enhanced awareness of the more difficult issues of ethics and social justice, at both domestic and international levels. Graduates should be able to offer evidence to the wider community that their hard-earned scholarship will ultimately make a difference. This is not just in relation to the securing of 'a good job' as soon as possible after graduation, but also in the sense that they, in reading for their degree and successfully completing HE, have achieved something of merit and of which they should be rightly proud. As Steur et al. (2012) noted, 'scholarship and moral citizenship' are 'important elements' of embedding a desire for lifelong learning. This multi-faceted approach to the concept of 'graduateness' fits well with the wider pursuit of student success strategies, that aim to have tutors, students, support workers, university management teams and, in particular, HE policy- makers (not least those overseeing cuts to student support funding) working in unison to evolve practicable solutions to issues such as non-attendance, poor engagement, plagiarism, or too-high attrition rates.

Lack of self-efficacy is clearly often a significant factor in terms of absent or weak student motivation, especially on those pathways where students must engage in successful job-searching activities from an early stage of their degree studies. Certain fundamental, generic traits, innate or learned, do encourage and enable the sort of self-beliefs that are highly valued by most employers, regardless of professional or industrial affiliation: 'self-belief enables action and, therefore, is essential for agency, underpinning the readiness to take part and contribute and the drive to make new ideas happen' (Turner, 2014). Where learners are encouraged to articulate clearly their own employability skills (Bostock, Chap. 13), they will often be much more able to accurately ascertain what their future role(s) might be within wider, multi-disciplinary contexts. They can in turn gain a sense of belonging to wider communities of practice and academic scholarship, even against difficult backdrops of very uncertain economic and political landscapes (Thomson, Chap. 15). Similarly, where a sort of 'wickedness' attaches to modern workplace problems, HE graduates must aim for a high level of inter-disciplinarity and an enhanced sense of global connectedness, allowing them to engage in skilled, strategic networking and demonstrate transferable core skills (Gurbutt, Chap. 14). The ability to forge and maintain collegiate, meaningful relationships is essential for navigating and surviving the many uncertainties of both academia and the modern workplace, post-graduation (Delahunty and Harden-Thew, Chap. 18). Opportunities do exist however, especially in relation to some of the 'pedagogic advantages' afforded by technology via, for example, via intensive online networking, wider alumni groups, and modern distance learning (Mogaji, Chap. 21; Fowlie and Forder, Chap. 22).

In sum, gauging what prospective employers will actually want—and indeed expect—from the university graduates that they might seek to recruit, is particularly important in times of uncertainty and austerity. The dynamic nature of 'the self' might easily remain overlooked or unrecognised: some course designs and content lists may also result in learning being misrepresented as strictly linear, modular, and compartmentalised (Goldspink and Engward, Chap. 20) with instrumental evaluations often tending to be grounded in monitoring only the most superficial aspects of the student learning experience. A programmatic focus on assessments (Whitfield and Hartley, Chap. 16) could offer a means of overcoming or at least addressing this issue. Authenticity within assessments is similarly needed (Davidson et al., Chap. 17) given how practical approaches to HE learning frequently tend to offer the best means of helping students make a successful transition from university into the workplace.

35.3 Authenticity of Approach?

As Morin (2003) highlighted, an authentic education must involve contextualization, implementation, and globalization, in the sense that there often are differing levels of reality between learned theories and lived experiences.[33] In terms of offering innovative learning and teaching suggestions, Delors et al's *Five Pillars of Education* (2006) are clearly acknowledged within the third, more subject-specific section of this collection.[34] *Learning to know* (serving also as a model for lifelong learning) and *Learning to do* (tied to professional education and market pressures, technical and professional competence, team working, and self-efficacy) sit comfortably alongside each other: the modalities of *Learning to live together*, perhaps offer one of the main challenges for modern HEIs given the apparent direction of certain global political trends however (de Paula Arruda Filho (2017). *Learning to be*, is the key pillar that particularly

> …expands the understanding of formal education in conjunction with non-formal and informal education. It indicates that every human being should be prepared to have intellectual autonomy and a critical view of life, in order to be able to formulate their own value judgments, develop the capacity of discernment and of acting in various circumstances. *Education must provide everyone with intellectual forces and references that allow them to understand the surrounding world and perform as responsible and fair actors.* (de Paula Arruda Filho, 2017: 186) [35]

Experiential, 'whole person' models of learning (including e.g. workplace simulations, a programme-embedded employability focus, and charity-driven 'pop-up

---

[33] Morin (2003), [as cited by de Paula Arruda Filho (2017)].

[34] Delors et al. (2006).

[35] (Emphasis added) adding that the 5th pillar (*Learning to transform oneself and society*) also 'recognizes that each one of us can change the world by acting individually and together, and that quality education provides the tools to change society' (p. 186).

shops') can clearly be used to enhance graduate employability.[36] As Forster and Robson (Chap. 23, Sect. 3) argue, experiential learning can sometimes seek to 'squeeze a quart into a pint pot,' with academic, subject expertise perching closely alongside the 'softer' skills ('organisational deftness') so needed and valued within the workplace. Embedding employability widely across undergraduate curricula (as fundamental core skills) can also work however, rather than having certain activities appear as course-extraneous events or aims (Lock, Chap. 24). Such an approach potentially provides opportunities for learners and graduates to 'boundary hop' across the borders and divisions of academic disciplines, professions, industries, and perhaps cross geographic lines also. Brown et al.'s (Chap. 25) substantial review of the literature on simulations, allows for further discussion of their pedagogical benefits and possible limitations, given the 'ever more marketised' HE landscape, where students are looking gimlet-eyed at the promise of a high-earning, 'Graduate Premium'[37] to stave off the likelihood of being unemployed post-graduation.

A constructivist approach to HE learning (Hill et al., Chap. 26) can similarly acknowledge the consequences of austerity, e.g. via an activity ('pop-up shops') aimed at raising much-needed funds for a student-selected charity, whilst at the same time promoting greater student resilience and self-efficacy within practice-relevant, stressful situations. Student placements, career advice provision, and live projects also afford opportunities to bring professional development skills into an ever-evolving arena of undergraduate learning, providing further scope for enhancing or engendering work-readiness (Whatley, Chap. 27). Innovations such as a 'Living CV' (Dibben and Morley, Chap. 28) can tie academic learning outcomes firmly to students' CV outputs. Raising awareness of the relevance of such learning outcomes (through personalised, explicit coaching on 'work literacy') could be more widely integrated into university programmes at all levels, to enable valuable, fuller discussions of lived experiences within the world of work. Increasing employer engagement, and aiding interview preparation, are likely benefits of such an approach. The use of e-portfolios for distance learning (Van Staden, Chap. 29, on South African Education students) similarly allows for the design and inclusion of key *learning* tasks as opposed to more narrowly-focussed assessment tasks.

The gaining of knowledge is *not* simply a passive process but a highly active one, grounded firmly in cognition, adaptive in nature, and tied closely to contextual factors. (Bippert et al, Chap. 30). Online learning clearly requires certain things: authenticity of learning experience, social interaction, and students who are willing and able to make valid contributions in terms of their own experiences and

---

[36] See further Hoover et al. (2010) for a useful discussion of a whole-person learning and experiential/behavioural skill pedagogy, developed for an executive skills course (an MBA), aimed at addressing criticisms over program 'irrelevancy' and graduate skill sets.

[37] See further Kemp-King (2016) arguing that 'No matter what unquantifiable, subjective quality controls—such as the Teaching Excellence Framework (TEF)—are put in place, the planned deregulation of the sector ...could well result in an evolution of English universities echoing America's experience. The new "for-profit" colleges could end up as little more than debt-generating engines with lower and lower entry standards and huge dropout rates blighting the financial future of a generation of graduates—and ultimately the entire economy' (p. 38).

unique perspectives. The role of the tutor here is to be facilitative: flexible teaching techniques matter, as does the provision of opportunities for synchronous communication between learner and tutor. Similarly, adapting learning and teaching methods to meet the increasingly diverse needs of students entering certain professions (K Toole, Chap. 31; Lodge and Elliott, Chap. 32) is not always an easy feat. Linking legal employability for example, to skills-diversity and enrichment, to prepare law students for the rigours of practice and unforeseen career changes, poses certain challenges, but can be achieved. Criminal Justice similarly requires strong working partnerships with interested stakeholders, to form a triadic framework comprising of university careers staff, employers, and the students themselves, who can work together to enhance work-readiness and forge a meaningfully wide community of (academic and professional) practice (Altham and Ragonese, Chap. 33).

35.4   A Note of Caution: Hearing and Heeding 'Student Voices'?

HE has clearly 'been issued with several new challenges' in recent decades, not least in respect of its rapid and unprecedented massification, and the fact that many new entrants to HE will tend to 'need special attention to develop their capacities to the expected level' (Pavlin and Svetlik, 2014: 420).[38] Arguably, HE, and the increasingly juridical right to an education, seems often to be about trying to 'bring the sea to the landlocked' (Casal and Salamé, 2015) [39] through the sharing of scarce or finite resources, on a visibly equitable basis. This image perhaps to some extent also sums up what the authors involved in this project are attempting to do; in sharing our ideas, critiques and experiences, we are trying to alert policymakers to the issues that are hindering the aims of HE, while also finding new ways of helping our learners survive within and beyond university, as employable scholars. As Suleman (2018: 263) has recently observed of the notion of generic employability skills,

> ...the identification of those skills is an impossible endeavour. Agreement is only found on some cognitive, technical, and relational skills...the supply-side approach overlooks economic and social processes that might affect employability. The problem of graduates' employability transcends higher education institutions' provision of useful and matched skills.[40]

Where students tend to focus almost solely on outcomes, they may internalize the importance of future employment pathways; this may in turn yield graduates who lack

---

[38] Arguing further that 'on the other hand, there is a need to support investments' in research and development ... 'whereby these investments shorten technological cycles and rapidly change job requirements which tend to increase...[raising] the problem of the fit between the knowledge and competencies that are acquired and actually required.'

[39] On the challenges associated with this in the literal sense (and the harsh consequences of failing to offer any possible solutions) see Casal and Selamé (2015).

[40] See also Brennan et al. (2013).

the dispositions desired by certain employers. Such a 'highly performative culture' within HE, is perhaps further compounded by being tied to TEF and LEO metrics, and often does little to prepare students for the realities and challenges of the modern workplace (Frankham, 2016) and the demands of achieving a hoped-for, upward-facing 'social mobility.'[41] In respect of the significant role played by universities in tackling social problems such as poverty, injustice, or ignorance of one's rights, it is worth recalling here how the once plain and quite 'pact-like' (Gornitzka et al., 2007) relationship between HE and wider society has clearly altered over recent decades:

> ...initial doubts developed into major debates concerning the foundation of the university as a social institution. Ultimately, the massification of higher education undermined the pact and not only because of the growing costs of higher education... It led to a plurality of belief systems attached to the university, while it also affected the university's role in selecting socioeconomic and political elites. (Maasen & Stensaker, 2011: 759).[42]

Palmer's recent observation (on the UN's SDGs) could perhaps equally be applied to the various questions that hang over the future directions—and potential remit and role—of HEIs:

> Public consultation and public discourse – carried out in regular, visible forums that allow the space for collective and individual voices to discuss the ends and means of sustainable development – will be vital to making the process over the coming 15 years one of genuine development, rather than a political push. (Palmer, 2015: 262)

It can be argued that we are letting our students down if they are exiting university completely unequipped for the many challenges that they will face post-graduation, outside of academia's cushioning environment. A small but significant body of case law deals with this very idea, and is quite telling insofar as it serves to identify and challenge some of the HE systems and policies that have not perhaps worked as well as they could have. Arguably, one section of the 'student voice' is represented here amongst such litigation, albeit as a highly aggrieved expression of disappointment or dissatisfaction with certain aspects of the HE system (e.g. teaching, assessment, inclusion, pastoral care, and administration). Recent court hearings have tended to focus upon the complaints of students who either did not ultimately gain the qual-ification they were expecting to, or who were perhaps removed from their degree course altogether for failing to achieve the grades required to progress. Broadly and briefly summarised, the jurisprudence suggests that 'matters that fall within the remit of general education decisions, may [still] be seen by the courts as beyond their juris-diction.' In other words, certain aspects of learning and teaching still 'enjoy' some measure of academic judgement 'immunity'[43] from judicial oversight and are essen-tially non-juridical. Procedural issues might however more easily 'fall within the

---

[41]For a disheartening view of 'social mobility' see further The 2019 Report of the Social Mobility Commission 'State of the Nation 2018–19: Social Mobility in Great Britain' avail-able at https://assets.publishing.service.gov.uk/government/uploads/system/uploads/attachment_data/file/798404/SMC_State_of_the_Nation_Report_2018-19.pdf (accessed 30.04.19).

[42]Adding that 'research has been decoupled more and more from (mass) higher education and linked to the needs of the national economy'.

[43]Clark v University of Lincolnshire and Humberside [2000] EWCA Civ 129.

concept of natural justice' (Cummings, 2017) and can therefore find themselves sitting directly under the court's gaze, via the process of Judicial Review. Cases involving breaches of contract or the tort of negligence for example—in connection with teaching delivery and marking of assessments—have also featured, as has the issue of the human right to education, under the European Convention.[44]

Decisions likely to affect a student's employment opportunities or their future capacity to earn may be particularly problematic. The recent case of *Siddiqui* [2018][45] is quite significant, given how much time had elapsed since the claimant's under-graduate days. Here, a law graduate was disappointed with having gained a 2.1 rather than the first class law degree that he had set his sights on many years previously. He claimed that the resultant stress, depression, and insomnia had impacted adversely upon his legal career, over two subsequent decades. He argued that the teaching he had received as an undergraduate had been deficient and that the university had therefore been negligent. One module in particular had, he felt, been very harshly marked: in addition to this, an unusually large number of lecturers had been off on sabbaticals at the same time, which had left the department 'understaffed.' The uni-versity conceded that it had indeed encountered some problems, not least in terms of providing cover for a certain module, and admitted that this was directly due to staff shortages. The claimant alleged further that the 'negligently inadequate' teaching had also breached the contractual standard of care required of the university. Similarly, he argued that there had been a failure on the part of his personal tutor to convey information concerning his various illnesses to the relevant authorities responsible for making reasonable adjustments, and for moderating results.

It was suggested by the university that the claimant had himself been lacking in certain 'historian skills' and had failed to undertake the high level of indepen-dent study needed to achieve academic success in this field. Lectures were meant to 'address the inherent structural problems in this particular subject' which repre-sented 'a problematic course.'[46] The fact that some of the students had bought their professors champagne at the end of the year was noted[47]: the court looked in detail too at such matters as class sizes and accepted that extra hours of work had been put in by the tutor who had been delivering the teaching. A letter of complaint received from another former student at the time (sent, apparently, in the spirit of improving things for future cohorts, and in conjunction with a concerned course tutor) was of central importance to the proceedings, in terms of evidencing teaching quality—or the alleged lack of it. The professor's reply to this concerned third party however, was relevant both in relation to the formal complaint and subsequent litigation:

> The logic would be that, in order to be prepared properly for the gobbets paper, it would have been necessary for anything that appeared in the examination paper to have been covered

---

[44] *Croskery's application* [2010] NIQB 129.

[45] *Siddiqui v The Chancellor, Masters & Scholars of the University of Oxford* EWHC 184 (QB).

[46] Ibid., at para 29: the student accepted that it was a difficult course with certain '*issues peculiar to it*'.

[47] Ibid., at para 59.

specifically in class. The expression 'spoon-feeding' comes to mind which is hardly to be expected for an Oxford undergraduate degree course.[48]

The court proceedings were based upon the idea that significant, long-term 'employability harms' had flowed directly from the plaintiff having had a 'serious, adverse reaction to his degree results.' At this point his 'entire identity and personal psyche' had been 'shattered by these poor results.' On the issue of pastoral care, the tutor had no recollection of the student having raised any issues of depression, anxiety or insomnia at any stage, but had apparently advised the student that no documentation would be required from him to evidence his claims of extenuating circumstances. Email exchanges retrieved from the time related to the student having had hay fever. With hindsight, it was argued that factors such as depression, insomnia, and anxiety had played a key part in his poor academic performance. He claimed further that his personal tutor had been fully aware of all of his conditions but had failed to refer this information on to the Proctors (which would have been best practice, rather than a strictly formal requirement, at that time). It is significant that the court examined in detail matters such as the teaching hours and administration surrounding the course, and looked closely at much of the correspondence that had been exchanged between other academics and students. Though eventually dismissed, the claim does raise some difficult questions as to the pastoral care remit of tutors (and the avoidance of tortious or contractual liability) especially in terms of accommodating inherent or unseen conditions or weaknesses, and indeed when spotting and addressing the various challenging circumstances that can hinder students on their journey throughout—and beyond—HE.[49]

In *Re Croskery* (2010),[50] the right to education under Article 2, Protocol 1 of the European Convention (A2P1) was discussed in connection with a student's complaints over dissertation supervision and his final grade award. The court stressed that A2P1 was clearly concerned with preventing the *denial* of *any* right to education, rather than relating to a failure to remove obstacles or barriers to learning from the student pathway. They stated that 'plainly the applicant ...had access to and ha[d] exercised his right to third level education'[51] in spite of his dissatisfaction with his dissertation supervisor. It was further noted that A2P1 said nothing about a human right to be conferred with a degree or indeed any other academic qualification, 'much

---

[48] Adding that, '...last year I was simply (and physically) unable to devote the same amount of time to each student—which, I accept, an exceptionally demanding student, such as [SB], may have taken as an affront to her 'rights'...'.

[49] Other urgent issues –which are beyond the scope of this book but can undoubtedly impact significantly upon students' opportunities for success—include the need to better safeguard students who are vulnerable on the basis of e.g. undeclared or undiagnosed disabilities, mental health issues, financial hardship, gender or sexual orientation. Austerity measures clearly compound the strains on support mechanisms within HE. Greater funding for pastoral care and peer support systems could perhaps be framed as a key component of employability-enhancing measures.

[50] *Croskery's application* [2010] NIQB 129.

[51] Ibid., [per Treacy J, at para 18. Article 6 of the European Convention (on the right to fair hearing) was also discussed].

less ...academic assessment' [and as such]...it [was] not engaged in this case.'[52] A further example can be found in the case of *Re Humzy Hancock* (2007),[53] where an Australian law student was found to have committed three instances of plagiarism during his time as an undergraduate. References for post-graduate practice courses required a formal attestation to his 'good character' by a former tutor and, lacking this, he was denied admission. Significantly, the court held that plagiarism *had* occurred, but, oddly, it had not been defined as such under the University's own Regulations. The court suggested that universities should consider very carefully the wording of their policies on plagiarism, to avoid any such ambiguities in future.

Cases such as these offer useful guidance as to the direction that student litigation might potentially take in future, if the notion of 'employability-harm' takes root. The court's language seems also to focus almost entirely on the *quality* of the academic work being assessed, rather than on the more relevant issue of whether *procedural fairness* had been achieved. This could suggest that there are circumstances where the courts might well intervene and make judgments of an essentially academic nature i.e. on educational decisions, where the '...determination of facts [becomes] a judgment of academic quality and behaviour, not of an expected standard of behaviour' (Cummings, 2017). The earlier case law that the court had referred to in *Humzy Hancock* centred upon the issue of students admitting to plagiarism but then pleading external, mitigating pressures in their 'defence.'[54] Illness, stress and anxiety featured repeatedly, often in respect of—or exacerbated by—financial problems or familial issues. The courts have also considered in detail how questions of 'procedural unfairness' are best interpreted and dealt with by decision-makers and—to a lesser extent—academics carrying out pastoral care duties.[55] In respect of the various processes of academia, it can be argued that the drafting of University Regulations, their application, and the use of academic or administrative discretion (e.g. in determining what exactly constitutes extenuating or mitigating circumstances, cheating,

---

[52] Para 21.

[53] *Re Humzy Hancock* [2007] QSC 034 His reasons for plagiarising are noteworthy: in addition to having collaborated on an essay with a fellow student, he also cited family issues which caused him to run short of time and fail to reference his sources correctly. A third incident involved a 'take-home' paper assessment, which had contained only minimal citation of sources.

[54] The court looked, for example, at *Liveri, Re* [2006] QCA 152, and *AJG, Re* [2004] QCA 88, *Law Society of Tasmania v Richardson* [2003] TASSC 9.

[55] See also *Gopikrishna, R v The Office of the Independent Adjudicator* [2015] EWHC 207, where the issue was one of the student being withdrawn, having failed her second-year medical exams, on the presumption that she had little chance of successfully completing the course. This was deemed 'an act of academic judgement' by the OIA (on which Offices, see further https://www.oiahe.org.uk, accessed 21.03.19). The student argued that the decision-making *process* was unfair, because the university panel had looked only at her first year's performance. Her mitigating circumstances had not been considered, nor had her personal tutor been consulted with (a requirement under the university's own Regulations). Given that these factors equated to clear 'failings of reason and procedure,' the usual norms of academic judgement immunity did not apply.

malpractice, or plagiarism and their levels of seriousness) may well come in for increasing external scrutiny, via formal student complaints or litigation.[56]

35.5 Conclusion

This book project has sought to adopt an inter-disciplinary approach, across a variety of institutions and jurisdictions, to offer a wide range of observations, reflections, and possible suggestions for improving practices and policies within HE.[57] The authors are united in their concerns over the future direction[s] of university learning and teaching, especially in terms of identifying rapidly changing roles and remits, and in aiming to honour both the traditions and spirit of academia, whilst still highlighting the need for ethical, sustainable learning systems and pedagogies. As Haertle, Parkes, Murray, and Hayes (2017) have argued,

> …the academic sector can play a strategic role as change agents, educating the managers of today and tomorrow, incorporating the values of responsible corporate citizenship into their education activities.[58]

More research is needed into a number of issues, for example, the increasingly acute, challenging pastoral care needs of some of our students. More training and support for staff—and for student peer groups—involved in delivering or oversee-ing this type of care, would perhaps go some way towards addressing some of the inequalities and barriers to accessing learning that still exist within HE. The reasons underpinning the rise in the use of essay mills by some students,[59] not to mention the charges of 'grade inflation'[60] laid against some HEIs, also merit further investiga-tion and discussion. The UK's 'attainment gap' affecting Black, Asian and Minority Ethnic students (BAME) is at least now being investigated and addressed, and other

---

[56]See for example *R (Mustafa) v OIA* [2013] EWHC 1379 (Admin) on plagiarism, where the student gained a mark of zero, citing a number of mitigating factors. Having been assigned group work, for example, he claimed that he was unable to either find or join a group, so as to complete his assignment. An extension to the deadline had led to exhaustion and depression, which in turn impacted upon his exam performance. The court looked in detail at the University's definition of plagiarism, noting that it differed to that of other HEIs. The OIA made it clear that questions of plagiarism (and the extent to which these might adversely affect a student's mark) fell under the protective umbrella-immunity of academic judgement. See also *R (Cardao-Pito) v OIA* [2012], EWHC 203 (Admin) where a student complained that 'harassment' by a lecturer had adversely affected his mark.

[57]On the need for an interdisciplinary approach to education (for sustainable development, and to acknowledge differing perspectives on sustainability and corporate social responsibility) see Annan-Diab and Molinari (2017).

[58]Haertle et al. (2017).

[59]See further https://www.qaa.ac.uk/news-events/news/contract-cheating-and-academic-integrity-qaa-responds-to-essay-mill-revelations# (accessed 12.04.19).

[60]See further https://www.qaa.ac.uk/news-events/news/degree-classification-system-consultation (accessed 10.04.19).

campus-level initiatives involving gender and sexual orientation issues are becoming normative.[61] That said, there are no easy, 'quick-fix' answers to the various questions that continue to arise within HE, on the issues of inclusion. Student engagement seems likely to become increasingly triadic in nature, requiring emotional, cognitive, and behavioural elements of input. And yet, much of the learning within HE still occurs largely via prolonged periods of social cognition (i.e. through observation, positive reinforcement, and conversely, at times, via meaningful 'penalty' (Bandura, 1989),[62] mirroring most, if not all, workplaces, and indeed many of the problems of modern society.

The current 'lack of social mobility and the widening gap of inequality' (McKenzie, 2015) for example, cannot be ignored. Academic staff must be increasingly mindful of the obstacles and challenges facing students and graduates, especially in this age of ongoing austerity and increasingly divisive political uncertainties. As McKenzie (2015) has stressed,

> …within communities across the UK, where the poorest people live, are hardships caused by the consequences of structural inequality, a political system that does not engage those who have the least power, disenfranchisement relating to the notion of fairness regarding their families and communities.[63]

Decision-makers must be careful too, to avoid the sort of rhetoric or thinking that places a 'classifying' blame for exclusion upon those who have already been actively or subtly excluded from e.g. education, certain types of employment, and societal approval:

> …known and named, stigmatised because of where they lived, and their practices and behaviours became scrutinised as problems within themselves, rather than methods for managing the difficult situations they encountered. (McKenzie, 2015)

Focusing instead upon human resourcefulness, resilience, community spirit, and a willingness to embrace—and survive—change, offers an alternative approach. By widening access, clearly,

> …the university environment provides a stage for social transformation through education, research and extension. Students…search for fulfilment, personal growth and active participation in the social changes of their time. (Borges et al., 2017)

Students and graduates must be regarded as potential stakeholders within wider communities of academic and professional practice, especially given how HE fits within the contextual frameworks of the UN's PRME principles and the 2030

---

[61] https://www.universitiesuk.ac.uk/policy-and-analysis/reports/Documents/2019/bame-student-attainment-uk-universities-closing-the-gap.pdf (accessed 03.05.19); See also https://www.universitiesuk.ac.uk/news/Pages/Universities-acting-to-close-BAME-student-attainment-gap.aspx (accessed 05.05.19). See also https://www.ljmu.ac.uk/about-us/news/articles/2019/4/30/ljmu-leads-the-way-with-first-campus-wide-free-period-products-in-england; https://www.erasmusmagazine.nl/en/2018/11/02/why-we-need-gender-neutral-toilets/.

[62] Bandura (1989); See also Bandura (2005).

[63] McKenzie (2015) at Loc. 3452, kindle ed).

Agenda for the SDGs.[64] The dangers associated with a lack of 'moral responsibility' (Ghoshal, 2005)[65] are becoming increasingly apparent, on a global scale. Making 'a science' out of Business Studies, for example, runs the risk of ignoring the wider consequences of unsustainability, in terms of adverse environmental impacts and deepening levels of social injustice (Borges et al., 2017). Arguably, having students engage more fully in socially-relevant learning activities such as voluntary sector work placements or internships with NGOs or charitable organisations as part of their degree course, could go some way towards bridging some of the gaps that exist between academia and wider society, perhaps not least by convincing a sometimes quite sceptical public—and suspicious press—of the deeper value of education and lifelong learning.

There are various, fundamental skills needed for 'work-readiness' post-graduation: this is so whether the concept of employability is defined as speedy job-finding, as longer-term career success, or framed as part of a wider notion of opening up opportunities, and making 'greater good' contributions to a sustainably just and fair society. Key aims for HE students and staff should include intellectual improvement, and the promotion of those principled behaviours that will be required from our graduates as employees, and perhaps as future employers themselves. The concept of a basic, underpinning 'work ethic,' though perhaps somewhat unfashionable, could include such qualities as 'good interpersonal skills, initiative, and dependability' (Hill and Petty, 1995).[66] Certain 'boot-camp' qualities are clearly required to succeed (or indeed survive) within both the 'real world' of the workplace, and the more sheltered halls of academia. Personal attributes such as integrity, honesty, and diligence, whether learned or inherent, can be quite easily evidenced via the traditional challenges of HE already present within most academic curricula e.g. meeting tight assessment deadlines, and engaging in self-led reading and independent research. Taking part in more *viva voce*-style activities perhaps to reinforce the learning achieved in written assignments (and prepare students for job interviews), and requiring respectful team-working with others who might not share their point of view or attitude, could also prove useful. Moreover, as the litigation referred to above suggests, if a more formal, contractual relationship now exists between student and university (together with a symbiotic duty of care to avoid negligent or inappropriate behaviours and promote an atmosphere of mutual respect) then we, as staff, are duty bound ourselves to act as community of practice 'exemplars.'[67] We must promote greater awareness too, of how, often,

---

[64]Ibid., arguing further that universities 'are not fully capable of managing CoPs, but they can provide the right environment for the CoPs to succeed'.

[65]Outlining how a scientific-model approach to business studies can easily exclude 'human intentionality or choice' and 'the use of sharp assumptions and deductive reasoning.' On 'the pretence of knowledge' which can also occur in such scenarios, see further von Hayek (1989).

[66]Hill and Petty (1995); see also Park and Hill (2016).

[67]Arguably, we are their 'trustees' too in the sense that we must act equitably and fairly in overseeing their efforts to gain a university education.

...environment affects an individual, and the individual also affects the environment. An individual's emotion and knowledge influence behaviors and societal reactions to behavior serve as feedback. Individuals shape and change their emotions and future actions based on the feedback...self-efficacy and self-regulatory capabilities are important characteristics. (Park and Hill, 2016: 175)

Practitioners and policy-makers in HE should be especially prepared to engage in the sort of sharply reflective practice that we have long encouraged our students to effect in the wake of assessments, by listening to and acting upon feedback, so as to achieve or maintain improvements where possible. Vassilis and Race's (2007) prescient observation merits having the last word:

...the increased benefit of a group of people being involved in shared reflection is even more significant in many situations where collaborative and team activity is to be encouraged. *In short, there has been no better time to get our act together regarding evidencing reflection – both our own reflection, and that of our students.*[68]

References

Altbach, P. G., Reisberg, L., & Rumbley, L. E. (2009) *Trends in global higher education: Tracking an academic revolution—A report prepared for the UNESCO 2009 world conference on higher education.* UN: Educational, Scientific and Cultural Organisation. Available at http://www.cep.edu.rs/public/Altbach,_Reisberg,_Rumbley_Tracking_an_Academic_Revolution,_UNESCO_2009.pdf.

Annan-Diab, F., & Molinari, C. (2017). Interdisciplinarity: Practical approach to advancing education for sustainability and for the sustainable development goals. *The International Journal of Management Education, 15*(2), 73–83.

Arrow, K. J. (2000). Observations on social capital. In P. Dasgupta & I. Serageldin (Eds.), *Social capital: A multifaceted perspective.* Washington DC: The World Bank.

Audenaert, M., et al. (2019). Vulnerable workers' employability competences: The role of establishing clear expectations, developmental inducements, and social organizational goals. *Journal of Business Ethics.* Available at http://hdl.handle.net/1854/LU-8608525. Accessed April 11, 2019.

Baker, C. N. (2008). Under-represented college students and extracurricular involvement: The effects of various student organizations on academic performance. *Social Psychology of Education, 11*(3), 273–298.

Bandura, A. (1989). Social cognitive theory. In R. Vasta (Ed.), *Annals of child development: Six theories of child development* (pp. 1–60). Greenwich: CT; JAI Press.

Bandura, A. (2005). The evolution of social cognitive theory. In K. G. Smith & M. A. Hitt (Eds.), *Great minds in management. Employability skills assessment* (pp. 9–35). Oxford: Oxford University Press.

Bellino, J., Paulson, J., & Worden, E. A. (2017). Working through difficult pasts: Toward thick democracy and transitional justice in education. *Comparative Education, 53*(3), 313–332.

Benson, G. (2006). Employee development, commitment and intention to turnover: A test of 'employability' policies in action. *Human Resource Management Journal, 16*(2), 173–192.

Bernstrøm, V. H., et al. (2019). Employability as an alternative to job security. *Personnel Review, 48*(1), 234–248.

---

[68] Vassilis and Race (2007, p. 76) (emphasis added).

Borges, J. C., et al. (2017). Student organizations and communities of practice: Actions for the 2030 Agenda for sustainable development. *International Journal of Management Education, 15,* 172–182.

Bradshaw, S., Chant, S., & Linneker, B. (2017). Gender and poverty: What we know, don't know, and need to know for Agenda 2030. *Gender, Place & Culture, 24*(12), 1667–1688.

Brennan, J., et al. (2013). *Things we know and don't know about the wider benefits of higher education: A review of the recent literature.* London, UK: LSE.

Brown, P., & Hesketh, A. (2004). *The mismanagement of talent: Employability and jobs in the knowledge economy.* New York: OUP.

Casal, P., & Selamé, N. (2015). Sea for the landlocked: A sustainable development goal? *Journal of Global Ethics, 11*(3), 270–279.

Cohen, L., & Mallon, M. (1999). The transition from organisational employment to portfolio working: Perceptions of boundarylessness. *Work, Employment and Society, 13*(2), 329–352.

Cummings, J. J. (2017). Where courts and academe converge: Findings of fact or academic judgment? *Australia & New Zealand Journal of Law & Education, 12*(1), 97–108.

de Paula Arruda Filho, N. (2017). The Agenda 2030 for responsible management education: An applied methodology. *The International Journal of Management Education, 15*(2), 183–191.

Delors, J., et al. (2006). *Education: A treasure to discover.* São Paulo, Cortez: UNESCO.

Dewey, J. (1956). *Philosophy of education.* Ames, Iowa: Littlefield Adams.

Eklund-Leen, S. J., & Young, R. B. (1997). Attitudes of student organization members and non-members about campus and community involvement. *Community College Review, 24*(4), 71–81.

Frankham, J. (2016). Employability and higher education: The follies of the 'productivity challenge' in the teaching excellence framework. *Journal of Education Policy, 32*(5), 628–641.

Freire, P. (1983). *Pedagogy of the oppressed.* Rio de Janeiro: Peace and Earth.

Freire, P. (1985). *The politics of education: Culture, power, and liberation.* South Hadley, MA: Bergin & Garvey.

Freire, P. (2008). The "banking" concept of education. In D. Bartholomae, A. Petrosky, & S. Waite (Eds.), *Ways of reading.* Boston: Bedford-St. Martin's.

Freire, P., & Slover, L. (1983). The importance of the act of reading. *The Journal of Education, 165*(1), 5–11.

Ghoshal, S. (2005). Bad management theories are destroying good management practices. *Academy of Management Learning & Education, 4*(1), 75–91.

Gornitzka, A., et al. (2007). Europe of knowledge: Search for a new pact. In P. Maassen & J. P. Olsen (Eds.), *University dynamics and European integration* (pp. 181–214). Dordrecht: Springer.

Haertle, J., Parkes, C., Murray, A., & Hayes, R. (2017). PRME: Building a global movement on responsible management education. *The International Journal of Management Education, 15*(2), 66–72.

Hall, D. T. (1976). *Careers in organizations.* Goodyear, CA: Pacific Palisades.

Hill, R. B., & Petty, G. C. (1995). A new look at selected employability skills: A factor analysis of the occupational work ethic. *Journal of Vocational Education Research, 20*(4), 59–73.

Hoover, J. D., et al. (2010). Assessing the effectiveness of whole person learning pedagogy in skill acquisition. *Academy of Management Learning & Education, 9*(2), 192–203.

Hu, S., et al. (2019). Does socioeconomic status shape young people's goal revision processes in the face of negative career feedback? *Journal of Vocational Behaviour, 110,* 89–101.

Kamvounias, P., & Varnham, S. (2006). In-house or in court? Legal challenges to university decisions. *Education & The Law, 18*(1), 1–17.

Kemp-King, S. (2016). *The graduate premium: Manna, myth or plain mis-selling?* The Intergenerational Foundation. Available at http://www.if.org.uk/wp-content/uploads/2016/09/Graduate_Premium_final.compressed.pdf. Accessed February 21, 2019.

King, K. (2016). The global targeting of education and skill: Policy history and comparative perspectives. *Compare: A Journal of Comparative and International Education, 46*(6), 952–975.

King, K. (2017). Lost in translation? The challenge of translating the global education goal and targets into global indicators. *Compare: A Journal of Comparative and International Education, 47* (Issue 6: *Different understandings of quality education across the globe: A special issue on the guiding theme of the BAICE 2016*).

Knight, T., & Yorke, M. (2013). *Embedding employability into the curriculum.* London: HEA.

Kushner, S. (2011). A return to quality. *Evaluation, 17*(3), 309–312.

Lin, C. (2006). Culture shock and social support: An investigation of a Chinese student organization on a US campus. *Journal of Intercultural Communication Research, 35*(2), 117–137.

Lysova, E. I., et al. (2018). Examining calling as a double-edge sword for employability. *Journal of Vocational Behaviour, 104,* 261–272.

Maassen, P., & Stensaker, B. (2011). The knowledge triangle, European higher education policy logics and policy implications. *Higher Education, 61,* 757–769.

McArthur, J., Zhang, C. (2018). *Who is talking about the UN sustainable development goals? Future Development.* https://www.brookings.edu/blog/future-development/2018/06/14/who-is-talking-about-the-un-sustainable-development-goals/.

McKenzie, L. (2015). *Getting by: Estates, class and culture in austerity Britain.* Bristol: Policy Press.

Mills, C. W. (1959). *The sociological imagination.* New York: OUP.

Moon, C. J. (2019). *95 theses for reforming higher education. Are HEIs catalysts for a sustainable society?* Advance HE/HEA. https://www.heacademy.ac.uk/knowledge-hub/95-theses-reforming-higher-education-are-heis-catalysts-sustainable-society. Accessed March 01, 2019.

Morin, E. (2003). *The seven knowledges needed to educate the future.* São Paulo, Cortez, Brasília: UNESCO.

Nicholas, J. M. (2018). Marketable selves: Making sense of employability as a liberal arts undergraduate. *Journal of Vocational Behaviour, 109,* 1–13.

Palfreyman, D. (2010). HE's 'get-out-of-jail-free card. *Perspectives, 14*(4), 114–119.

Palmer, E. (2015). Introduction: The 2030 Agenda. *Journal of Global Ethics, 11*(3), 262–269.

Park, H., & Hill, R. B. (2016). Employability skills assessment: Measuring work ethic for research and learning. *Career and Technical Education Research, 41*(3), 175–194.

Pavlin, S., & Svetlik, I. (2014). Employability of higher education graduates in Europe. *International Journal of Manpower, 35*(4), 418–424.

Peltier, J. W., Scovotti, C., & Pointer, L. (2008). The role the collegiate american marketing association plays in professional and entrepreneurial skill development. *Journal of Marketing Education, 30*(1), 47–56.

Pinto, L. H., & Ramalheira, D. C. (2017). Perceived employability of business graduates: The effect of academic performance and extracurricular activities. *Journal of Vocational Behaviour, 99,* 165–178.

Putnam, R. D. (1996) *Who killed civic America?* https://www.prospectmagazine.co.uk/magazine/whokilledcivicamerica.

Putnam, R. D. (2000). *Bowling alone: The collapse and revival of american community.* New York: Simon and Schuster.

Reiner, R. (2012). Political economy and criminology: The return of the repressed. In S. Hall & S. Winlow (Eds.), *New directions in criminological theory* (pp. 30–51). Abingdon: Routledge.

Regmi, K. (2015). Lifelong learning and post-2015 educational goals: Challenges for the least developed countries. *Compare: A Journal of Comparative and International Education, 45*(2), 317–322.

Sachs, J. D. (2012). From millennium development goals to sustainable development goals. *The Lancet, 379,* 2206–2211.

Steur, J. M., Jansen, E. P. W. A., & Hoffman, W. H. A. (2012). Graduateness: An empirical examination of the formative function of university education. *Higher Education, 64,* 861–874.

Suleman, F. (2018). The employability skills of higher education graduates: Insights into conceptual frameworks and methodological options. *Higher Education, 76*(2), 263–278.

Tomlinson, M. (2008). The degree is not enough: Students' perceptions of the role of higher education credentials for graduate work and employability. *British Journal of Sociology of Education, 29*(1), 49–61.

Turner, N. K. (2014). Development of self-belief for employability in higher education: Ability, efficacy and control in context. *Teaching in Higher Education, 19*(6), 592–602.

Unterhalter, E. (2017). Negative capability? Measuring the unmeasurable in education. *Comparative Education, 53*(1), 1–16.

Vassilis, A., & Race, P. (2007). Enhancing knowledge management in design education through systematic reflection practice. *Concurrent Engineering, 15*(1), 63–76.

Von Hayek, F. A. (1989). The pretence of knowledge. *American Economic Review, 79*(6), 3–7.

Yorke, M. (2016). The development and initial use of a survey of student 'belongingness', engagement and self-confidence in UK higher education. *Assessment & Evaluation in Higher Education, 41*(1), 154–166.

Zelenev, S. (2017). Translating the 2030 Agenda for Sustainable Development into local circumstances: Principles and trade-offs. *International Social Work, 60*(6), 1652–1655.

Case Law

AJG, Re [2004] QCA 88, *Law Society of Tasmania v Richardson* [2003] TASSC 9.
Croskery's Application [2010] NIQB 129.
Gopikrishna, R v The Office of the Independent Adjudicator [2015] EWHC 207.
Liveri, Re [2006] QCA 152.
R (Cardao-Pito) v OIA [2012] EWHC 203 (Admin).
R (Mustafa) v OIA [2013] EWHC 1379 (Admin).
Re Humzy Hancock [2007] QSC 034.
Siddiqui v The Chancellor, Masters & Scholars of the University of Oxford EWHC 184 (QB).

Alice Diver (Ph.D.) is a Senior Lecturer in Law at Liverpool John Moores University, Liverpool, UK having previously worked at Edge Hill University and Ulster University in Northern Ireland. She spent several years as a solicitor in private practice before joining academia in 1993. Her teaching experience includes property law, child & family law, and human rights law. Her research interests focus mainly on adoption, law in literature, and human rights. She is the author of a monograph on closed birth records in law and policy called '*A Law of Blood-ties: The 'right' to access genetic ancestry*' (Springer, 2013) and co-editor of an essay collection entitled '*Justiciability of Human Rights Law in Domestic Jurisdictions*' (Springer, 2015). She has published in a wide variety of peer-reviewed academic journals. She is a long-serving board member of Apex Housing NI, and a trustee of Kinship Care NI.

Gerard Diver (MRes) is a Project Officer at LJMU, Liverpool. He has been involved in a number of Training & Employability initiatives across the UK and Ireland (e.g. *Strive 2 Work)* and has worked as an Employability consultant and part-time tutor with several HEIs in Ireland and the UK. His MRes (2017) involved a multi-disciplinary, longitudinal study of under-graduate degree work placements, and their role in enhancing graduate employability in Ireland. He has published several chapters from it in a number of academic journals. As a former elected representative (2001–2016) in N Ireland, he focused on social and political issues (e.g. urban regeneration, poverty-alleviation, community relations) and established a homelessness forum, in Derry, N Ireland, during his year as mayor of the city (2008–2009). He has participated in international peace-building work in Iraq, Kosovo, Nigeria and South Africa via his involvement with the *Cities in*

Transition Project. His current post involves working with the Liverpool Health Commission, an initiative aimed at reforming health policy across the UK, providing a platform for marginalised, vulnerable groups, affected by issues of injustice and inequality.

CPSIA information can be obtained
at www.ICGtesting.com
Printed in the USA
LVHW080344201020
669178LV00004B/123